The
Black Abolitionist
Papers

Board of Editorial Advisors

The Black Abolitionist Papers

VOLUME III
The United States, 1830–1846

C. Peter Ripley, *Editor*
Roy E. Finkenbine, *Associate Editor*
Michael F. Hembree, *Assistant Editor*
Donald Yacovone, *Assistant Editor*

The University of North Carolina Press
Chapel Hill and London

The paper used in this book meets the guidelines for
permanence and durability of the Committee on Production
Guidelines for Book Longevity of the Council on Library
Resources.

Printed in the United States of America

95 94 93 92 91   5 4 3 2 1

Library of Congress Cataloging-in-Publication Data
(Revised for vol. 3)

The Black abolitionist papers.

  Includes bibliographical references and indexes.
  Contents: v. 1. The British Isles, 1830–1865—
v. 2. Canada, 1830–1865—v. 3. The United States,
1830–1846.
  1. Slavery—United States—Anti-slavery movements—
Sources. 2. Abolitionists—United States—History—19th
century—Sources. 3. Abolitionists—History—19th cen-
tury—Sources. 4. Afro-Americans—History—To 1863—
Sources. I. Ripley, C. Peter, 1941–   .
E449.B624 1985   973'.0496   84-13131
ISBN 0-8078-1625-6 (v. 1)
ISBN 0-8078-1698-1 (v. 2)
ISBN 0-8078-1926-3 (v. 3)

The preparation and publication of this volume were made possible in part by grants from the Program for Editions and the Division of Research Programs of the National Endowment for the Humanities, an independent federal agency, and by grants from the National Historical Publications and Records Commission, The Florida State University, the Ford Foundation, and the Rockefeller Foundation.

For John W. Blassingame,
friend and colleague

Contents

Documents

Illustrations

Maps

Acknowledgments

The Black Abolitionist Papers Project is a cooperative undertaking made possible through the substantial contributions of the project staff, university administrators, librarians and curators of research facilities, colleagues in the profession, and supporters at funding agencies and foundations.

The project editors—Roy E. Finkenbine, Michael F. Hembree, and Donald Yacovone—shared the pleasures of preparing this volume. They read and evaluated hundreds of documents during the selection process, and they wrote notes, headnotes, and sections of the introduction. Roy, Mike, and Don regularly reviewed the documents "one final time" and revised portions of the introduction in what must have seemed like an endless process. Their dedication to a faithful rendering of the black abolitionist past is manifest throughout the volume. This volume is a genuine collaborative effort, and I thank them for their considerable and persistent efforts.

Support from The Florida State University, the National Endowment for the Humanities, the National Historical Publications and Records Commission, the Ford Foundation, and the Rockefeller Foundation made possible the preparation of this volume. Vice-President Augustus Turnbull and William R. Jones at Florida State; Kathy Fuller and David Nichols at NEH; Roger Bruns, Mary Giunta, Sarah Jackson, and Richard Sheldon at NHPRC; Sheila Biddle at the Ford Foundation; and Alberta Arthurs, James O. Gibson, and Lynn Szwaja at the Rockefeller Foundation always made me feel welcome.

We wish to acknowledge the scholars, manuscript curators, repository directors, and librarians who responded to our inquiries for elusive information and allowed us to publish documents from their collections: Clifton Johnson of the Amistad Research Center, Karl Kabelac of the Department of Rare Books and Special Collections at the University of Rochester, Randall K. Burkett of the W. E. B. Du Bois Institute, Theresa Vann of New York City, Esme Bahm of the Moorland-Spingarn Research Center, Roland M. Baumann of the Oberlin College Archives, Barbara Gallucci of the Rochester Public Library, Jonathan Stayer of the Pennsylvania State Archives, Mariam Touba of the New-York Historical Society, and Laura V. Monti of the Boston Public Library. The interlibrary loan staff of The Florida State University Library was enormously helpful. The Florida Resources and Environmental Analysis Center at the Florida State University prepared the maps that appear in the volume.

At Florida State, Vice-President and Provost Gus Turnbull, Associate Vice-President Thomas S. McCaleb, and Director of the Black Studies

Program William R. Jones have been steadfast supporters of the project, even during the tough times. The professional style of Dean Charles F. Cnudde's office has made that association a delight.

Sherry Phillips and Kay Sauers of the dean's office and Shamuna Malik of the Black Studies Program supervised our budgets and administrative paperwork with a cooperative spirit. Cory Burke Yacovone performed those tasks for several years with great efficiency and good cheer. Daniel Disch indexed research materials and performed a variety of project tasks while he was a history graduate student. Pamela Ball transcribed documents and edited notes, headnotes, and the introduction. Her grace with the written word and concern for precise language improved the volume, particularly the introduction. John L. Parker, Jr., kept us current in the world of word processing technology, and Christopher Meyer demonstrated once again the benefits of technology as he watched over our style sheet and prepared the manuscript for publication with a skilled hand.

Joe M. Richardson, Philip Morgan, Jerome Stern, and Lawrence J. Friedman critiqued the series introduction, providing the useful mix of encouragement and criticism we have come to expect from them. David Brion Davis's generous and detailed comments on the manuscript helped us to reassess the introduction and to be more precise and thorough throughout the volume. The volume is improved for their efforts, and we wish to acknowledge their contributions.

Martha, John P., Mary Ann, Jerry, Joe, Phil, and Hal helped make it happen.

Tallahassee, Florida   C. P. R.
May, 1989

Abbreviations

Newspapers, Journals, Directories, and Reference Works

AAM	*Anglo-African Magazine* (New York, New York).
AANYLH	*Afro-Americans in New York Life and History.*
AASR	*American Anti-Slavery Reporter* (New York, New York).
ACAB	James Grant Wilson and John Fiske, eds., *Appletons' Cyclopaedia of American Biography*, 6 vols. (New York, New York, 1888–89).
AF	*Advocate of Freedom* (Augusta, Maine; Brunswick, Maine; Hallowell, Maine).
AHQ	*Arkansas Historical Quarterly.*
AHR	*American Historical Review.*
AHS	*African Historical Studies.*
AM	*American Missionary* (New York, New York).
AP	*Albany Patriot* (Albany, New York).
AQ	*American Quarterly.*
AR	*African Repository* (Washington, D.C.).
ASA	*Anti-Slavery Advocate* (London, England).
ASB	*Anti-Slavery Bugle* (Salem, Ohio; New Lisbon, Ohio).
ASR	*Anti-Slavery Record* (New York, New York).
BDAC	*Biographical Directory of the American Congress, 1774–1971* (Washington, D.C., 1971).
BDGUS	Robert Sobel and John W. Raimo, eds., *Biographical Directory of the Governors of the United States* (Westport, Connecticut, 1978).
BFHA	*Bulletin of the Friends Historical Association.*
BHM	*Bulletin of the History of Medicine.*
BMC	*Morning Chronicle* (Boston, Massachusetts).
BR	*Black Republican* (New Orleans, Louisiana).
BT	*Boston Evening Transcript* (Boston, Massachusetts).
CA	*Colored American* (New York, New York).
CE	*Christian Examiner* (Boston, Massachusetts).
CF	*Christian Freeman* (New York, New York).
CH	*Church History.*
CJH	*Canadian Journal of History.*
CKSHS	*Collections of the Kansas State Historical Society.*
CN	*Christian News* (Glasgow, Scotland).
CR	*Christian Recorder* (Philadelphia, Pennsylvania).
CWH	*Civil War History.*
DAAS	Randall M. Miller and John David Smith, eds., *Dictionary*

	of Afro-American Slavery (Westport, Connecticut, 1988).
DAB	Allen Johnson and Dumas Malone, eds., *Dictionary of American Biography*, 20 vols. (New York, New York, 1928–36).
DANB	Rayford W. Logan and Michael R. Winston, eds., *Dictionary of American Negro Biography* (New York, New York, 1982).
DM	*Douglass' Monthly* (Rochester, New York).
DNB	Sir Leslie Stephen and Sir Sidney Lee, eds., *Dictionary of National Biography*, 22 vols. (London, England, 1885–1901; reprint, 1921–22).
E	*Emancipator* (Boston, Massachusetts; New York, New York).
EIHC	*Essex Institute Historical Collections.*
ESF	*Elevator* (San Francisco, California).
FDP	*Frederick Douglass' Paper* (Rochester, New York).
FJ	*Freedom's Journal* (New York, New York).
FM	*Friend of Man* (Utica, New York).
GUE	*Genius of Universal Emancipation* (Mt. Pleasant, Ohio; Greenville, Tennessee; Baltimore, Maryland; Washington, D.C.; Hennepin, Illinois).
H	*Historian.*
HF	*Herald of Freedom* (Concord, New Hampshire).
HMPEC	*Historical Magazine of the Protestant Episcopal Church.*
IC	*Impartial Citizen* (Syracuse, New York; Boston, Massachusetts).
JAS	*Journal of American Studies.*
JER	*Journal of the Early Republic.*
JITC	*Journal of the Interdenominational Theological Center.*
JNE	*Journal of Negro Education.*
JNH	*Journal of Negro History.*
JPH	*Journal of Presbyterian History.*
JSH	*Journal of Southern History.*
Lib	*Liberator* (Boston, Massachusetts).
LP	*Liberty Press* (Utica, New York).
LS	*Liberty Standard* (Hallowell, Maine).
MA	*Mid-America.*
MAb	*Massachusetts Abolitionist* (Boston, Massachusetts).
MCJ	*Maryland Colonization Journal* (New York, New York).
MH	*Michigan History.*
MHM	*Maryland Historical Magazine.*
ML	*Mirror of Liberty* (New York, New York).

MT	*Mirror of the Times* (San Francisco, California).
MVHR	*Mississippi Valley Historical Review.*
NASS	*National Anti-Slavery Standard* (New York, New York).
NAW	Edward T. James, ed., *Notable American Women, 1607–1950: A Biographical Dictionary,* 3 vols. (Cambridge, Massachusetts, 1971).
NCAB	*National Cyclopaedia of American Biography,* 61 vols. to date (New York, New York, 1898–).
NECAUL	*National Enquirer and Constitutional Advocate of Universal Liberty* (Philadelphia, Pennsylvania).
NEQ	*New England Quarterly.*
NEW	*National Era* (Washington, D.C.).
NHB	*Negro History Bulletin.*
NR	*National Reformer* (Philadelphia, Pennsylvania).
NRB	*Non-Resistant* (Boston, Massachusetts).
NSFA	*Northern Star and Freeman's Advocate* (Albany, New York).
NSt	*North Star* (Rochester, New York).
NYE	*New York Evangelist* (New York, New York).
NYH	*New York Herald* (New York, New York).
NYO	*Observer* (New York, New York).
NYSu	*Sun* (New York, New York).
NYT	*New York Tribune* (New York, New York).
OntH	*Ontario History.*
OR	*Oberlin Review* (Oberlin, Ohio).
P	*Philanthropist* (Mt. Pleasant, Ohio; New Richmond, Ohio; Cincinnati, Ohio).
PA	*Pacific Appeal* (San Francisco, California).
PEB	*Evening Bulletin* (Philadelphia, Pennsylvania).
PF	*Pennsylvania Freeman* (Philadelphia, Pennsylvania).
PFW	*Provincial Freeman* (Windsor, Ontario, Canada; Toronto, Ontario, Canada; Chatham, Ontario, Canada).
PH	*Pennsylvania History.*
Phy	*Phylon.*
PL	*Palladium of Liberty* (Columbus, Ohio).
PMHB	*Pennsylvania Magazine of History and Biography.*
PP	*Pine and Palm* (Boston, Massachusetts; New York, New York).
PPL	*Public Ledger and Daily Transcript* (Philadelphia, Pennsylvania).
PPr	*Press* (Philadelphia, Pennsylvania).
PSQ	*Political Science Quarterly.*
QASM	*Quarterly Anti-Slavery Magazine* (New York, New York).

RA   *Rights of All* (New York, New York).
RCHS   *Records of the Columbia Historical Society*, 53 vols. to
            date (Washington, D.C., 1897–).
RDA   *Rochester Daily Advertiser* (Rochester, New York).
RDC   *Democrat and Chronicle* (Rochester, New York).
RDD   *Rochester Daily Democrat* (Rochester, New York).
RH   *Rochester History.*
RHN   *Ram's Horn* (New York, New York).
RIF   *Rhode Island Freeman* (Providence, Rhode Island).
RIH   *Rhode Island History.*
RPE   *Post Express* (Rochester, New York).
SDS   *Syracuse Daily Standard* (Syracuse, New York).
SJ   *Syracuse Daily Journal* (Syracuse, New York).
SL   *Signal of Liberty* (Ann Arbor, Michigan).
SS   *Southern Studies.*
VF   *Voice of the Fugitive* (Sandwich, Ontario, Canada;
            Windsor, Ontario, Canada).
WA   *Weekly Advocate* (New York, New York).
WAA   *Weekly Anglo-African* (New York, New York).
WMH   *Wisconsin Magazine of History.*
WPHM   *Western Pennsylvania Historical Magazine.*
ZW   *Zion's Watchman* (New York, New York).

Manuscript Repositories

AHMS-ARC   American Home Missionary Society Papers, Amistad
           Research Center, Tulane University, New Orleans,
           Louisiana.
AMA-ARC   American Missionary Association Archives, Amistad
           Research Center, Tulane University, New Orleans,
           Louisiana.
CaOLU   University of Western Ontario, London, Ontario, Canada.
CaOTAr   Ontario Provincial Archives, Toronto, Ontario, Canada.
CaOTCi   City of Toronto Archives, Toronto, Ontario, Canada.
CaOTP   Metropolitan Toronto Central Library, Toronto, Ontario,
           Canada.
DHU   Moorland-Spingarn Research Center, Howard University,
           Washington, D.C.
DLC   Library of Congress, Washington, D.C.
DNA   National Archives, Washington, D.C.
MB   Boston Public Library and Eastern Massachusetts
           Regional Public Library System, Boston, Massachusetts.

MH	Houghton Library, Harvard University, Cambridge, Massachusetts.
MHi	Massachusetts Historical Society, Boston, Massachusetts.
MiD-B	Burton Historical Collection, Detroit Public Library, Detroit, Michigan.
MiU	William L. Clements Library, University of Michigan, Ann Arbor, Michigan.
NjR	Archibald Stevens Alexander Library, Rutgers University, New Brunswick, New Jersey.
NNC	Butler Library, Columbia University, New York, New York.
NN-Sc	Schomburg Center for Research in Black Culture, New York Public Library, New York, New York.
NRU	Rush-Rhees Library, University of Rochester, Rochester, New York.
NSyU	George Arents Research Library, Syracuse University, Syracuse, New York.
OO	Seeley G. Mudd Center, Oberlin College, Oberlin, Ohio.
PHi	Historical Society of Pennsylvania, Philadelphia, Pennsylvania.
PU	Van Pelt Library, University of Pennsylvania, Philadelphia, Pennsylvania.
UkOxU-Rh	Rhodes House Library, Oxford University, Oxford, England.

Editorial Statement

The Black Abolitionist Papers Project began in 1976 with the mission to collect and publish the documentary record of black Americans involved in the movement to end slavery in the United States from 1830 to 1865. The project was conceived from an understanding that broad spans of Afro-American history have eluded scholarly attention because the necessary research materials are not readily available. Many personal papers, business records, newspapers, and other documentary sources simply have not survived. Materials that have endured are often inaccessible because they have not been systematically identified and collected. Except for several small manuscript collections of better-known black figures (usually those that continued to be public figures after emancipation),[1] the letters, speeches, essays, writings, and personal papers of black abolitionists have escaped professional attention. The same is true of antebellum black newspapers.

But the publications of individual historians demonstrated that black abolitionist documents could be unearthed.[2] The black documents that

1. See Mary Ann Shadd Cary Papers, Public Archives of Canada (Ottawa, Ontario), DHU, and CaOTAr; Shadd Family Papers, CaOLU; Rapier Family Papers, DHU; Daniel A. Payne Papers, Wilberforce University (Wilberforce, Ohio); Anderson R. Abbott Papers, CaOTP; John M. Langston Papers, Fisk University (Nashville, Tennessee); Ruffin Family Papers, DHU; Amos G. Beman Papers, Yale University (New Haven, Connecticut); Charles Lenox Remond Papers, Essex Institute (Salem, Massachusetts) and MB; William Still Papers, Rutgers University (New Brunswick, New Jersey); Jacob C. White, Jr., Papers, PHi; Frederick Douglass Papers, DLC, NN-Sc, and DHU; Alexander Crummell Papers, NN-Sc; James T. Holly Papers, General Theological Seminary (New York, New York); J. W. Loguen File, NSyU; Paul Cuffe Papers, New Bedford Free Public Library (New Bedford, Massachusetts). Of these, only the Cary, Cuffe, Remond, Douglass, and Beman collections have significant antebellum documents.

2. A number of black abolitionist documents were reprinted before this project began its work in 1976: Carter G. Woodson, ed., *Negro Orators and Their Orations* (Washington, D.C., 1925), and *The Mind of the Negro as Reflected in Letters Written during the Crisis, 1800–1860* (Washington, D.C., 1926); Dorothy B. Porter, ed., "Early Manuscript Letters Written by Negroes," *JNH* 24:199–210 (April 1939); Benjamin Quarles, ed., "Letters from Negro Leaders to Gerrit Smith," *JNH* 27:432–53 (October 1942); Philip S. Foner, ed., *The Life and Writings of Frederick Douglass*, 5 vols. (New York, N.Y., 1950–75); Howard H. Bell, ed., *Minutes of the Proceedings of the National Negro Conventions, 1830–1864* (New York, N.Y., 1969); Dorothy Sterling, ed., *Speak Out in Thunder Tones: Letters and Other Writings by Black Northerners, 1787–1865* (New York, N.Y., 1973). Pioneer scholarship on the subject that further suggested the availability of documents includes a number of articles on antebellum black Canadian fugitive communities by Fred Landon that appeared in the *Journal of Negro History* and *Ontario History* during the 1920s and 1930s; Dorothy B. Porter, "Sarah Parker Remond, Abolitionist and Physician," *JNH* 20:287–93 (July 1935), and "David M. Ruggles, an Apostle of Human Rights," *JNH* 28:23–50 (January 1943); Herbert Aptheker, *The Negro in the Abolitionist Movement* (New York, N.Y.,

enriched those books and articles were not located in a single collection, repository, or newspaper in any quantity. They were found scattered in the manuscript collections of others (usually whites involved in nineteenth-century reform movements) and in newspapers of the day (usually reform papers but also in the traditional press). Clearly, a significant body of black abolitionist documents survived, but it seemed equally certain that locating the documents would require a thorough search of large numbers of newspapers and a systematic review of a wide range of historical materials, particularly the papers of white individuals and institutions involved in the antislavery movement.

An international search for documents was the first phase of the Black Abolitionist Papers Project. A four-year collection process took the project to thousands of manuscript collections and countless newspapers in England, Scotland, Ireland, and Canada as well as in the United States. This work netted nearly 14,000 letters, speeches, essays, pamphlets, and newspaper editorials from over 200 libraries and 110 newspapers. What resulted is the documentary record of some 300 black men and women and their efforts to end American slavery.[3]

The Black Abolitionist Papers were microfilmed during the second phase of the project. The microfilmed edition contains all the primary documents gathered during the collection phase. The seventeen reels of film are a pristine presentation of the black abolitionist record.[4] The microfilmed edition offers materials that previously were uncollected, unidentified, and frequently unavailable to scholars.

1941); Benjamin Quarles, *Frederick Douglass* (Washington, D.C., 1948); Philip S. Foner, *Frederick Douglass* (New York, N.Y., 1950); Benjamin Quarles, "Ministers without Portfolio," *JNH* 39:27–43 (January 1954); Leon F. Litwack, *North of Slavery: The Negro in the Free States, 1790–1860* (Chicago, Ill., 1961); William H. Pease and Jane H. Pease, *Black Utopia: Negro Communal Experiments in America* (Madison, Wis., 1963); Benjamin Quarles, *Black Abolitionists* (London, 1969); William Edward Farrison, *William Wells Brown: Author and Reformer* (Chicago, Ill., 1969); Robin W. Winks, *The Blacks in Canada: A History* (New Haven, Conn., 1971); Jane H. Pease and William H. Pease, *They Who Would Be Free: Blacks' Search for Freedom, 1830–1861* (New York, N.Y., 1974); Floyd J. Miller, *The Search for a Black Nationality: Black Emigration and Colonization, 1787–1863* (Urbana, Ill., 1975); Richard Blackett, "In Search of International Support for African Colonization: Martin R. Delany's Visit to England, 1860," *CJH* 10:307–24 (December 1975). Several examples of early research on black abolitionists were reprinted in John H. Bracey, Jr., August Meier, and Elliott Rudwick, eds., *Blacks in the Abolitionist Movement* (Belmont, Calif., 1971).
3. This project has not collected or published documents by Frederick Douglass. Douglass's papers are being edited and published by John W. Blassingame and the staff of the Frederick Douglass Papers Project at Yale University.
4. The Black Abolitionist Papers are on seventeen reels of film with a published guide and index (New York, N.Y.: Microfilming Corporation of America, 1981–83; Ann Arbor, Mich.: University Microfilms International, 1984–). The guide contains a description of the collection procedures.

Now in its third phase, the project is publishing a five-volume series of edited and annotated representative documents. Black abolitionist activities in the British Isles and in Canada are treated in separate volumes; three volumes will be devoted to black abolitionists in the United States. The volume organization was suggested by a systematic review of the documents. The documents made clear that black abolitionists had a set of broadly defined goals and objectives wherever they were. But the documents also demonstrated that black abolitionists had a set of specific goals and actions in England, another set in Canada, and a third in the United States.

The U.S. volumes are treated as a series. A single introduction, which appears in volume III, introduces the series. Notes to the documents are not repeated within the U.S. volumes.

The microfilmed and published editions are two discrete historical instruments. The 14,000 microfilmed documents are a rich Afro-American expression of black life in the nineteenth century. Those black voices stand free of intrusion by either editor or historian. The microfilmed edition presents the collected documents. The published volumes are documentary history. Substantial differences separate the two.

The five volumes will accommodate less than 10 percent of the total collection, yet the volumes must tell the ambitious history of a generation of black Americans and their involvement in an international reform movement that spanned thirty-five years in the United States, the British Isles, and Canada. We reconstructed that story by combining documents with written history. A thorough reading of the documents led us to the major themes and elements of black abolitionist activity—the events, ideas, individuals, concepts, and organizations that made up the movement. Then we sought documents that best represented those elements. But given their limited number, the documents alone could only hint at the full dimensions of this complex story. The written history—the volume introduction, the headnotes that precede each document, and the document notes—helps provide a more complete rendition by highlighting the documents' key elements and themes.

The documents led us to yet another principle that governs the volumes. Antislavery was a critical and persistent aspect of antebellum black life, but it cannot correctly be separated from the remainder of black life and culture. Antislavery was part of a broad matrix of black concerns that at times seemed indistinguishable from race relations in the free states, black churches and schools in northern cities, black family life, West Indian immigration, African missionary work, fugitive slave settlements in Canada, and a host of other personal, public, and national matters. Ending slavery was but the most urgent item on the crowded agenda of the black Americans represented in these volumes.

A number of considerations influenced the selection of specific documents published in the volumes. The most important was the responsibility to publish documents that fairly represent the antislavery goals, attitudes, and actions of black abolitionists and, to a lesser extent, that reveal their more personal concerns. There were other considerations as well. We wanted to present documents by as many black abolitionists as possible. We avoided the temptation to rely on the eloquent statements of just a few polished professionals. We sought to document immediate antislavery objectives (often dictated by local needs and issues) as well as broad goals. A mix of document types—letters (both public and private), essays, scientific pieces, short autobiographical narratives, impromptu remarks, formal speeches, circulars, resolutions, and debates—were selected for publication.

We resisted selecting documents that had been published before our work began. But occasionally when a previously published document surfaced as a resonant black expression on an issue, topic, or incident, it was selected for publication. And, with the release of the Black Abolitionist Papers on microfilm, all the documents are more available than in the past. We often found different versions of the same document (usually a speech that appeared in several newspapers). When that happened, we selected the earliest published version of the most complete text. The cluster of documents around particular time periods and topics mirrors black abolitionist activities and concerns. The documents are arranged chronologically within each volume.

A headnote introduces each document. The headnote provides a historical context for the document and offers information designed to enhance the reader's understanding of the document and black abolitionist activities.

Notes identify a variety of items that appear within the documents, such as people, places, events, organizations, institutions, laws, and legal decisions. The notes enrich and clarify the documents. People and events that are covered in standard biographical directories, reference books, or textbooks are treated in brief notes. We have given more space to subjects on which there is little or no readily available information, particularly black individuals and significant events and institutions in the black community. A full note on each item is presented at the first appropriate point in the volume. Notes are not repeated within the volume. Information that appears in a headnote is not repeated in an endnote. The index includes references to all notes.

We have listed sources at the end of footnotes and headnotes. When appropriate, source citations contain references to materials in the microfilmed edition; they appear in brackets as reel and frame numbers (3:0070 reads reel 3, frame 70). The titles of some sources are abbreviated (particularly newspapers, journals, and manuscript repositories); a list of abbreviations appears at the front of the volume.

The axiom that "less is better" governed the project's transcription of documents. Our goal was to publish the documents in a form as close to the original as possible while presenting them in a fashion that enabled the reader to use them easily.

In the letters, the following items are uniformly and silently located regardless of where they appear in the original: place and date, recipient's name and address, salutation, closing, signature, marginal notes, and postscripts. In manuscript documents, idiosyncratic spelling, underlining, and quotation marks are retained. Words that were crossed through in the original are also retained.

The project adopted the following principles for documents found in published sources (newspapers, pamphlets, annual reports, and other nineteenth-century printed material): redundant punctuation is eliminated; quotation marks are converted to modern usage; obvious misspellings and printer's errors are corrected; printer's brackets are converted to parentheses; audience reaction within a speech is treated as a separate sentence with parentheses, for example, (Hear, hear.). We have let stand certain nineteenth-century printing conventions such as setting names or addresses in capital or italic letters in order to maintain the visual character of the document. A line of asterisks signals that material is deleted from a printed document. In no instance is black abolitionist material edited or deleted; but if, for example, a speech was interrupted with material extraneous to the document, the irrelevant material is not published.

The intrusive *sic* is rarely used. Brackets are used in their traditional fashion: to enclose information that we added and to indicate our inability to transcribe words or phrases with certainty. Some examples: we bracketed information added to the salutation and return address of letters; we bracketed material that we believe will aid the reader to comprehend the document, such as [illegible], [rest of page missing]; and we bracketed words and phrases that we believe appeared in the original but are uncertain about because of the quality of the surviving text. We have used brackets in the body of documents sparingly and only when necessary to avoid reader confusion. We have not completed words, added words, corrected spelling, or otherwise provided material in the text of manuscript documents except as noted above.

Our transcription guidelines for manuscript documents differ slightly from those we used for printed sources. We took greater editorial liberties with documents from printed sources because they seldom came to us directly from a black abolitionist's hand. Speeches in particular often had a long editorial trail. Usually reporters wrote them down as they listened from the audience; in some cases this appeared to be done with precision. For example, William Farmer, a British abolitionist and newspaper reporter, was an accomplished stenographer who traveled with

William Wells Brown and took down his speeches verbatim, then made them available to the local press. More often, a local reporter recorded speeches in a less thorough fashion. Speeches and letters that black abolitionists sent to newspapers were apt to pass through the hands of an editor, a publisher, and a typesetter, all of whom might make errors in transcription. Because documents that were reprinted in newspapers often had sections changed or deleted, we have attempted to find the original publication of printed documents.

Our transcription guidelines were influenced by the availability of all the documents in the microfilmed edition. Microfilmed copies of the original documents give the reader ready access to unedited versions of the documents that appear in the published volumes.

The
Black Abolitionist
Papers

Introduction to the American Series
Black Abolitionists in the United States, 1830–1865

Colonization, Immediatism, and Moral Reform

On the Fourth of July in 1830, Rev. Peter Williams, Jr., pastor of the black St. Philip's Episcopal Church in New York City, preached a sermon on American independence. His message that day lacked the patriotic oratory that usually characterized such celebrations. Instead Williams spoke to his parishioners about the hypocrisy of slavery being tolerated in a nation committed to human equality:

> The festivities of this day serve but to impress upon the minds of reflecting men of color, a deeper sense of the cruelty, the injustice, and oppression, of which they have been the victims. While others rejoice in their deliverance from a foreign yoke, they mourn that a yoke a thousand fold more grievous, is fastened upon them. Alas! they are slaves in the midst of freemen; they are slaves to those who boast that freedom is the inalienable right of all; while the clanking of their fetters, and the voice of their wrongs, make a horrid dis-cord in the songs of freedom which resound through the land.[1]

Williams identified three obstacles that prevented blacks from cele-brating American independence. Slavery was first among them—90 per-cent of all black Americans lived in bondage. Second, white Americans used skin color to determine the rights of men—a process that left free blacks in a state of "quasi-freedom," stereotyped in the popular press, denied legal and political rights, victimized by racial violence, and ex-cluded from church, school, and marketplace. Third, supporters of the white-led colonization movement wished to "rid the country of the free colored population" by resettling them in West Africa. Williams re-minded his parishioners that large numbers of blacks, including his own slave father, had fought for the Revolutionary cause, and he asked why the descendants of those heroes were not "treated as well as those who fought against it."[2] Williams's censure of American racial practices—slavery, prejudice, and colonization—reflected the thinking of black abolitionists.

By the late 1820s, blacks considered colonization to be as threatening as slavery and prejudice. The colonization movement was a mix of di-verse interests. Many elements came together behind a common goal—to rid the United States of its free black population, to "drain off" free

1. *E*, 22 April 1834 [1:0413].
2. Ibid.; *DANB*, 660; *AR*, August 1834 [1:0496].

1. Peter Williams, Jr.
Courtesy of John H. Hewitt

blacks and newly emancipated slaves to Africa. Most colonizationists were convinced that the growing number of free blacks threatened the new Republic, arguing that blacks would corrupt American society with their alleged immorality and their reputed inability to cope with freedom. Whites who considered slavery to be a moral evil and hoped that it would end gradually also feared that blacks could never fully adjust to freedom in a white man's country and maintained that their continued presence and growing numbers hardened proslavery sentiments. These gradualist abolitionists reasoned that sending blacks to a colony in Africa would ease white fears, encourage manumission, and, at the same time, provide free blacks with a refuge from American oppression. Some southern slaveholders shared these antislavery sentiments, but most supported colonization for very different reasons. They argued that the presence of emancipated slaves in the South challenged slavery; they insisted that it was dangerous for slaves to see other blacks who were not in bondage and relatively free to come and go and live as they pleased. They thought it best to protect slavery by purging the nation of free blacks before they took the opportunity to "whisper liberty in the ears of the oppressed."[3]

The movement emerged after the American Colonization Society (ACS) —the leading proponent of free black repatriation to the African continent—was established in 1816. Before long the ACS boasted of endorsements from several Protestant denominations, reform clergy, gradualist antislavery societies, fourteen state legislatures, and a host of prominent political figures, including James Madison, James Monroe, Henry Clay, and Daniel Webster. Within six years, the ACS was recruiting black settlers for its newly created Liberian colony on the West African coast.[4]

Most white abolitionists and antislavery organizations at the time supported the ACS. They believed that emancipation would be achieved, peacefully and gradually, through the courts, individual manumissions, and the political process. White abolitionism in the 1820s was dominated by the evangelical movement. Its leaders, often drawn from the ranks of the New England clergy, were dedicated to spreading the Gospel and ameliorating society's problems, including slavery. By linking emancipation with resettlement, the ACS united the evangelicals' desire to end slavery with white fears about the growing number of free blacks in

3. Lawrence J. Friedman, *Inventors of the Promised Land* (New York, N.Y., 1975), 184–92; William Lloyd Garrison, *Thoughts on African Colonization* (Boston, Mass., 1832; reprint, New York, N.Y., 1969), part 2, 20.
4. P. J. Staudenraus, *The African Colonization Movement, 1816–1865* (New York, N.Y., 1961), 12–187; Alice Dana Adams, *The Neglected Period of Anti-Slavery in America* (1908; reprint, Gloucester, Mass., 1964), 106.

society. The ACS claim that colonized blacks would Christianize Africa also appealed to evangelicals.[5]

Most free blacks—particularly in the northern states—rejected colonization. They saw clearly that colonization threatened their future on the American continent. "Here we were born, and here we will die," promised New York City blacks. Philadelphia blacks took the lead, holding four mass meetings between 1817 and 1819 to condemn colonization. Their angry protests set the tone for the struggle that followed. By the late 1820s, the colonization question preoccupied northern black leaders. *Freedom's Journal*, the nation's first black newspaper, became a vocal critic of the colonizationists. David Walker—the Boston black abolitionist whose militant call for slave resistance shocked northern antislavery moderates and southern slaveholders alike—proclaimed that "Our Wretchedness [is] in Consequence of the Colonizing Plan." During the early 1830s, several black national conventions refuted ACS assertions and denounced the organization with the claim that blacks were "aggrieved by its very existence." William Watkins, an educator whose persuasive arguments against colonization had a major influence on the development of immediatist abolitionism, led Baltimore blacks in serving notice that they considered the United States their "only *true and appropriate home.*" Watkins and his followers published anticolonization essays, confronted colonizationist speakers, and intimidated potential emigrants so successfully that the Maryland State Colonization Society abandoned the western shore of the Chesapeake as a field of labor.[6]

From Baltimore to Boston, free black communities rallied against what William C. Nell described as "the hydra-headed monster." Time after time, angry blacks stated their case against Liberian resettlement, affirming their identity as Americans and dismissing the idea of an African return. They reminded whites that blacks had helped build the nation by pushing back the wilderness and fighting for the Revolutionary cause. Brooklyn blacks insisted "we are *countrymen* and *fellow-citizens* . . . we are not strangers." But despite bold and patriotic statements and a vigorous public campaign against colonization, many blacks feared that they might be forced to emigrate. One elderly black woman com-

5. James Brewer Stewart, *Holy Warriors: The Abolitionists and American Slavery* (New York, N.Y., 1976), 29–31; David Brion Davis, *The Problem of Slavery in the Age of Revolution, 1770–1823* (Ithaca, N.Y., 1975).
6. Julie Winch, *Philadelphia's Black Elite: Activism, Accommodation, and the Struggle for Autonomy, 1787–1848* (Philadelphia, Pa., 1988), 35–38; Benjamin Quarles, *Black Abolitionists* (London, 1969), 7; *FJ*, 30 March, 18 May, 8 June, 6 July, 14 September 1827; David Walker, *David Walker's Appeal, in Four Articles; together with a Preamble to the Coloured Citizens of the World*, ed. Charles Wiltse (New York, N.Y., 1965), 45–78; *Minutes and Proceedings of the Third Annual Convention for the Improvement of the People of Colour* . . . (New York, N.Y., 1833), 26 [1:0306]; Penelope Campbell, *Maryland in Africa: The Maryland State Colonization Society, 1831–1857* (Urbana, Ill., 1971), 39–42.

plained that "it was a very wicked thing for them to bring us here in the way they did, but it would be more wicked to send us back." Watching the federal government remove southern Indians to new lands in the West, they feared the worst for themselves.[7]

In their initial critique of the colonization movement, black leaders stripped away the facade of philanthropy, revealing that the movement had no antislavery goals, no sincere concern for the condition of free blacks, and no serious commitment to Christian missions in Africa. As the movement intensified in the late 1820s, blacks began to focus on colonization's role in sustaining slavery and intensifying racial prejudice. For them, the colonizationists' incessant references to black inferiority tended "immediately to justify the slaveholder in his crime, and increase already existing oppression." They argued that restrictive state black laws worked with the colonization appeal to cause free blacks to seek sanctuary in Africa. Black leaders concluded that colonization was a "direct road to perpetuate slavery" and that to leave the country was tantamount to abandoning the slave. They understood the antislavery value of remaining at home and refuting claims of racial inferiority by demonstrating the capacity of blacks for moral and economic improvement.[8] For free blacks, asserting their citizenship, opposing colonization, and creating a place for themselves in American society were acts that threatened slavery.

An organized black abolitionist movement grew out of the battle against colonization. Anticolonization efforts showed blacks what they could accomplish with careful organization and continued protest. During the mid-1820s, the individuals who had led the struggle against the ACS banded together in local abolitionist groups. They organized in behalf of immediate emancipation and racial equality in Boston, New Haven, Philadelphia, Baltimore, and other free black communities. A sense of unity and a shared purpose emerged. David Walker's Massachusetts General Colored Association (MGCA), established in Boston in 1826, initiated a continuing correspondence among northern black leaders. The New York–based *Freedom's Journal* helped linked black abolitionists from Washington, D.C., to Maine by speaking out on colonization, slavery, and racism, by encouraging antislavery activism, and by using local subscription agents who helped spread the message.[9]

By the 1830s, black abolitionists were ready to take their message to

7. Garrison, *Thoughts on African Colonization*, part 2, 17–51; CA, 10 June 1837 [2:0071].
8. *Resolutions and Remonstrances of the People of Colour Against Colonization on the Coast of Africa* (Philadelphia, Pa., 1818), 3–4 [17:0244]; *Lib*, 26 February 1831; *FJ*, 18 May 1827 [2:0058]; *Minutes and Proceedings of the First Annual Convention of the People of Colour* . . . (Philadelphia, Pa., 1831), 15 [1:0083].
9. James Oliver Horton and Louis E. Horton, *Black Bostonians: Family Life and Community Struggle in the Antebellum North* (New York, N.Y., 1979), 81; Adams, *Neglected*

the white antislavery movement. They set out to convince white abolitionists that blacks were not inferior and that colonization did not serve black Americans, free or slave. By persuading key white abolitionists that colonization was wrong, black leaders hoped to weaken an important tenet of gradualist thought and destroy the ACS's reputation as an antislavery organization.

Black abolitionist protests against colonization and calls for the immediate end of slavery came at an opportune time. During the 1820s, the American antislavery movement came under the influence of a complex set of intellectual, social, and economic forces. A growing number of reformers and social leaders in Britain and the United States asserted that slavery impeded economic and social development. They also fostered a sense of collective national accountability for ending slavery. These impulses were complemented by the Second Great Awakening's emphasis upon personal responsibility for eliminating sin, of which slavery was judged the most heinous. Together, these forces shaped the immediatist antislavery movement. Immediatist antislavery thought demanded direct action, called for the immediate end of slavery, and rejected any transitional stage or period of apprenticeship for slaves. Although immediate emancipation became an increasingly ambiguous term that assumed broad connotations, it signaled a break with the gradualist antislavery traditions of the past. The compelling mix of slavery, sin, personal salvation, and economic reform created by the immediatist movement convinced many abolitionists that their own fate and the country's future were inextricably linked to the abolition of slavery. By 1830 black abolitionism joined with the Second Great Awakening, British abolitionism, and other forces to prepare the ground for the transformation of the abolitionist movement.[10]

The conversion of William Lloyd Garrison proved to be of enormous importance in the shift from gradualist to immediatist abolitionism. Garrison began his career as a committed colonizationist and gradualist. He helped Benjamin Lundy publish the *Genius of Universal Emancipation* in Baltimore during 1829–30, where he also worked closely with local free blacks, including William Watkins, Jacob Greener, and

Period of Anti-Slavery, 116n; *GUE*, January, February, May 1831; *Lib*, 28 May 1831; Leroy Graham, *Baltimore: The Nineteenth-Century Black Capital* (Lanham, Md., 1982), 97–111.

10. David Brion Davis, "The Emergence of Immediatism in British and American Antislavery Thought," *MVHR* 49:209–30 (September 1962); Anne C. Loveland, "Evangelicalism and Immediate Emancipation in American Antislavery Thought," *JSH* 32:172–88 (May 1966); David Brion Davis, *Slavery and Human Progress* (New York, N.Y., 1984), 107–258; Duncan Macleod, "From Gradualism to Immediatism: Another Look," *Slavery and Abolition* 3:140–52 (September 1982); see Quarles, *Black Abolitionists*, for the first study to recognize the importance of blacks in the rise of the antislavery movement.

their circle. Their opposition to colonization caused him to rethink the issue. Time spent with James E. Forten and other black leaders in Philadelphia further convinced Garrison of the inadequacy of the ACS position. The humanity and intelligence of the blacks he worked with in those two cities led him to embrace racial equality. The influence of black abolitionists, combined with his work at the *Genius* and his evangelical perspective, pushed Garrison into the immediatist camp. He later told Samuel J. May that "the radical doctrine of *immediate, unconditional* emancipation was revealed to him" during his time in Baltimore. Garrison and black abolitionists soon took the American antislavery movement in a new direction.[11]

Blacks enthusiastically embraced Garrison. Grateful for the new ally, they were eager to see him succeed. When he announced plans in late 1830 to establish an antislavery journal called the *Liberator*, black leaders recruited enough subscribers to pay the initial printing costs. Within five months, Garrison had a subscription list of five hundred readers, nearly all of them black. By 1832 the *Liberator* had more than a dozen black agents scattered from Baltimore to Boston and New York City to Cincinnati. Through their efforts, blacks comprised nearly three-quarters of the paper's twenty-three hundred subscribers by 1834. Blacks provided financial stability for the *Liberator* during these crucial early years by enlisting subscribers, purchasing the bulk of its advertising, and organizing the Colored Liberator Aiding Association to coordinate the paper's fund-raising efforts. Viewing the *Liberator* as their voice, blacks also contributed hundreds of essays and letters to its columns. Garrison acknowledged in 1834 that "the paper . . . belongs especially to the people of color—it is their organ."[12]

Garrison symbolized black hopes for racial change. He adopted the black abolitionist agenda—anticolonization, immediate emancipation, racial equality. Looking back from the vantage point of 1846, Boston blacks pointed out: "We had good enough doctrine before Garrison, but

---

11. Wendell Phillips Garrison and Francis Jackson Garrison, *William Lloyd Garrison, 1805–1879: The Story of His Life*, 4 vols. (New York, N.Y., 1885–89), 1:145, 147–48; Graham, *Baltimore*, 97–111; *GUE*, 27 November 1829; Archibald H. Grimké, *William Lloyd Garrison: The Abolitionist* (New York, N.Y., 1891), 144; Ray Allen Billington, "James Forten: Forgotten Abolitionist," in *Blacks in the Abolitionist Movement*, ed. John H. Bracey, Jr., August Meier, and Elliott Rudwick (Belmont, Calif., 1971), 5, 10, 15n; Samuel J. May, *Some Recollections of Our Antislavery Conflict* (Boston, Mass., 1869), 15; Walter M. Merrill, *Against Wind and Tide: A Biography of William Lloyd Garrison* (Cambridge, Mass., 1963), 31–41.
12. Quarles, *Black Abolitionists*, 19–20; Walter M. Merrill and Louis Ruchames, eds., *The Letters of William Lloyd Garrison*, 6 vols. (Cambridge, Mass., 1971–82), 1:115, 119; Donald M. Jacobs, "William Lloyd Garrison's *Liberator* and Boston's Blacks, 1830–1865," *NEQ* 44:260–62 (June 1971); *Lib*, 12 March 1831 [1:0037]; William Lloyd Garrison and Isaac Knapp, "Shall the *Liberator* Die?" (1834), Anti-Slavery Collection, MB.

we wanted a good example" to show whites. If Garrison could take the black message to white abolitionists, black ideas combined with white influence and resources could then shape a new antislavery movement capable of confronting the racial evils in American society. Black antislavery gatherings regularly invoked his name in reverential tones; black literary and benevolent societies bore his name. But the relationship between blacks and Garrison also had a deeper, more personal quality. Boston and Philadelphia blacks entertained him in their homes. Several black abolitionists followed him from his office to his Roxbury residence each night to protect him from physical attacks. Two prominent Boston blacks—James G. Barbadoes and David Walker—had sons named after him.[13]

Initially, Garrison appealed primarily to blacks. But black leaders and Garrison recognized the need to take their message to a broader audience. Garrison complained that whites did not subscribe to the *Liberator* because they were "indifferent to its object" of ending slavery. He believed that his small following among whites was "partly owing to colonization influence." Something else needed to be done to win public opinion. Black abolitionists including William Watkins recommended that Garrison publish a pamphlet outlining their objections to colonization.[14] The result, *Thoughts on African Colonization*, was published in 1832.

Garrison's book-length critique of the ACS and its Liberian settlement scheme sought to destroy the antislavery reputation of the ACS and to capture the white audience for the immediatist message. In the book's first half, Garrison chided colonizationists for strengthening slavery, removing free blacks, and blocking black advancement in the United States. The second half was devoted to publishing black abolitionist resolutions and addresses opposing colonization. Taken from mass meetings in twenty free black communities, these documents revealed the black rejection of the ACS.

Thoughts had an immediate impact. It sold 2,750 copies in the first nine months, an unprecedented number by antislavery standards. The volume helped turn a large number of white gradualist leaders away from the ACS and toward immediatism. Beriah Green, Elizur Wright, Jr., Amos A. Phelps, J. Miller McKim, Theodore Dwight Weld, Nathaniel P. Rogers, and many others who would soon become leaders in the movement, renounced their support of colonization and joined the immediat-

13. *Proceedings of a Crowded Meeting of the Colored People of Boston Assembled July 15, 1846* (Dublin, Ireland, 1846), 11; Quarles, *Black Abolitionists*, 19–22; Jane H. Pease and William H. Pease, *They Who Would Be Free: Blacks' Search for Freedom, 1830–1861* (New York, N.Y., 1974), 31–32; NECAUL, 31 August 1836 [1:0699].
14. Merrill and Ruchames, *Letters of William Lloyd Garrison*, 1:119; *Lib*, 2 April 1831 [1:0063].

ist American Anti-Slavery Society (AASS). Copies of *Thoughts* were placed in the libraries at Lane Seminary and Western Reserve College to encourage conversions there. Garrison wrote that "conversions from colonization to abolition principles are rapidly multiplying in every quarter." By 1833 many former white gradualists were gathered under Garrison's banner, diminishing the ACS in the process.[15]

Black abolitionists played a major part in taking the anticolonizationist and immediatist message to white gradualists. They encouraged Garrison, provided the essential message for *Thoughts*, and bought hundreds of copies of the pamphlet and distributed them to whites. In Pittsburgh, John B. Vashon distributed dozens of copies to white acquaintances, many of whom left the ACS as a result. Newspaper editor and Presbyterian minister Samuel E. Cornish helped reason Gerrit Smith away from the gradualist fold. James McCune Smith, the Scottish-trained physician whose sharp insights helped direct black abolitionists for three decades, boasted that white enthusiasm for immediatist ideas had been "nurtured into warmth, clothed with lustre and shot up into mid air by the hot sympathies of colored men's bosoms."[16]

Encouraged by Garrison's example, and informed about colonization by blacks, growing numbers of white abolitionists adopted immediatist beliefs, rejecting what Garrison now called the "pernicious doctrine of *gradual* emancipation." They demanded a quick and uncompensated end to slavery, supported black equality, and rejected colonization. These newly minted immediatists, stirred by evangelical beliefs in the sinfulness of slavery, gathered their moral energy to work for its demise. For white abolitionists, the change from gradualism to immediatism had the force of a conversion experience. Immediatism became the religion of the faithful.[17]

The immediatist doctrine found quick converts in New England, New York, Pennsylvania, and Ohio. Hundreds of organizations were formed, beginning with the New England Anti-Slavery Society (NEASS) in 1832. One year later, delegates from several states gathered in Philadelphia to create the AASS, the organization that dominated the movement through

15. John L. Thomas, *The Liberator: William Lloyd Garrison* (Boston, Mass., 1963), 154; Staudenraus, *African Colonization Movement*, 211, 228–31; *AAM*, October 1859; Merrill, *Against Wind and Tide*, 62; Bruce Rosen, "Abolition and Colonization: The Years of Conflict, 1829–1834," *Phy* 33:180, 188 (Summer 1972).

16. William Lloyd Garrison to John B. Vashon, 8 December 1832, Villard Papers, MH [1:0227]; *Lib*, 16 February 1833 [1:0244]; William Lloyd Garrison to Robert Purvis, 30 May, 22 June, 10 December 1832, James Forten to William Lloyd Garrison, 6 May 1832, Sarah M. Douglass to William Lloyd Garrison and Isaac Knapp, 6 December 1832, Anti-Slavery Collection, MB [1:0159–60, 0166–69, 0196–97, 0226, 0229]; *AAM*, October 1859; *FDP*, 26 January 1855 [9:0406].

17. Ronald G. Walters, *American Reformers, 1815–1860* (New York, N.Y., 1978), 79; Davis, "Emergence of Immediatism," 209–30.

the end of the decade. By 1836 over five hundred immediatist antislavery societies had been established across the North.[18]

Encouraged by the conversion of whites, which brought more people and greater resources, blacks grew optimistic about the future of the antislavery movement. In contrast to earlier gradualist organizations, which excluded blacks from membership, black and white abolitionists worked together to organize immediatist societies. The NEASS was organized in Boston's African Baptist Church, and one-fourth of the signers of its statement of principles were black. The Massachusetts General Colored Association soon joined the NEASS, bringing Boston blacks into the emerging immediatist mainstream. Blacks in other cities quickly followed suit. Leading black abolitionists participated in the creation of the AASS; its Declaration of Sentiments was drafted in the home of James McCrummill, a leader in Philadelphia's black community, and thirteen black men served on the society's board of managers in its early years. By 1837 blacks from Massachusetts to Michigan had created more than a dozen AASS auxiliaries, and they were active and conspicuous in interracial state, regional, and local AASS auxiliaries. Black women played a prominent part in the movement by forming and directing female immediatist societies. Susan Paul, Grace and Sarah M. Douglass, Harriet Purvis, and Sarah and Margaretta Forten were officers in the Anti-Slavery Convention of American Women. Maria W. Stewart became one of the first women in American history to lecture on a political subject before an audience of men and women. During the early 1830s, she lectured, wrote essays for Garrison's *Liberator*, and published a volume of her collected works. She condemned slavery and the colonization movement and championed women's rights.[19]

By the mid-1830s, black abolitionists could look to the future with hope and to the recent past with some satisfaction. They had played a major role in redirecting the course of the American antislavery movement. They had discredited the ACS as an antislavery organization, helped convert Garrison and other key American abolitionists to immediatism, and insured the success of Garrison's *Liberator*. In the process, they were influenced by their association with Garrison and other white antislavery activists.

18. Merton L. Dillon, *The Abolitionists: The Growth of a Dissenting Minority* (New York, N.Y., 1974), 91.
19. Robert L. Allen, *Reluctant Reformers: Racism and Social Reform Movements in the United States* (Garden City, N.Y., 1975), 18; Charles H. Wesley, "The Negro in the Organization of Abolition," in *Blacks in the Abolitionist Movement*, ed. Bracey, Meier, and Rudwick, 55–59; *E*, 27 May 1834, 9 March 1837 [1:0458–59, 0997]; John R. McKivigan, *The War against Proslavery Religion: Abolitionism and the Northern Churches* (Ithaca, N.Y., 1984), 203–20; Quarles, *Black Abolitionists*, 26–29; Marilyn Richardson, ed., *Maria W. Stewart, America's First Black Woman Political Writer: Essays and Speeches* (Bloomington, Ind., 1987).

2. Scene from an antislavery convention
From Harper's Weekly, 28 May 1859

The black abolitionist community spoke with a common voice by the 1830s. That had not always been so. In earlier years, two voices challenging American slavery and racism were heard in the black community, one characterized by militancy, the other by moderation. David Walker and like-minded men and women called for independent, forceful action. Confrontational and aggressive, they believed that slavery and prejudice should be challenged with harsh language and aggressive tactics, including violence. Others were hopeful that racial change would be achieved through more conciliatory methods. Encouraged by the growing number of manumissions of slaves, Congress's prohibition of the African slave trade, and the end of slavery in northern states, they advocated the moral reform philosophy that soon became identified with Garrisonian abolitionism. The 1820s were a time of flexibility, when black leaders rarely advocated one tactic to the exclusion of all others. Yet as blacks became part of the white antislavery movement in the 1830s, they muted the militancy advocated by Walker and emphasized the more conciliatory tone of moral reform.

White moral reform appealed to black leaders. Moral reformers believed that society could be perfected through the progress of the individual. Using the instruments of moral suasion—the pulpit, the press, and the power of persuasion—they sought to convince individuals that their material condition, their souls, and the state of the nation all rested upon their moral development. Black leaders endorsed the moral reform doctrine and the moral suasionist tactics of Garrisonian abolitionism, convinced that they provided a peaceful and effective means of awakening the American public to the evils of prejudice and slavery.[20]

During the 1830s, black leaders directly linked moral reform and racial advancement. Ambitious ideas about perfecting man and society offered blacks a framework for their day-to-day efforts to promote social and economic uplift within the black community. They came to believe that moral, mental, and economic improvement would advance the race, and that those black successes would, in time, persuade white Americans that blacks were worthy of freedom and equality. White abolitionists worked to strengthen the black commitment to moral reform. Garrison, Lewis and Arthur Tappan, Simeon S. Jocelyn, and others spoke at black gatherings during these years, advocating moral and mental improvement. Black and white abolitionists soon shared a vision: as reform progressed, all evils attendant upon the human condition—including slavery and prejudice—would vanish.[21]

20. For overviews of white and black reform thought, see John L. Thomas, "Romantic Reform in America, 1815–1865," *AQ* 17:656–81 (Winter 1965); and Frederick Cooper, "Elevating the Race: The Social Thought of Black Leaders, 1827–1850," *AQ* 24:604–25 (December 1972).
21. Pease and Pease, *They Who Would Be Free*, 124–28; *Minutes of the Fourth Annual*

Like the white middle class, black abolitionists endorsed the social values of self-help, education, the work ethic, sobriety, gentility, and the like. They agreed that many blacks—bound by the restraints of a racist society, denied adequate schooling and economic opportunity—fell short of these standards.[22] Blacks were aware that white America disregarded black successes and concentrated instead on breaches of widely accepted social ideals. Ignoring the racial exploitation that perpetuated second-class citizenship, most whites concluded that blacks were intellectually inferior, immoral, dependent, and childlike. These stereotypes became the basis for rationalizing slavery as a positive good and racial inferiority as an indisputable fact. Black leaders of the 1830s—aware of how those stereotypes shaped white attitudes—concluded that American racism resulted from behavioral, intellectual, and economic differences between the races, not the fact of blackness. William Whipper spoke for most black leaders of the decade when he stated that *"the prejudice which exists against [blacks] arises not from the color of their skin, but from their condition."* He concluded that a change in the condition of blacks must precede a change in American race relations. Charles B. Ray agreed: "We must become . . . equal in education and wealth with our white brethren, before we can be equal in standing and influence."[23]

Black abolitionists assumed that the benefits of moral reform would refute white-held stereotypes and dissipate racial prejudice. Black leaders argued that "industry, sobriety, honesty, combined with intelligence and due self-respect . . . must be *looked up to*—can never be *looked down upon*. In their presence, prejudice is abashed, confused and mortified." The burden of proof, Samuel Cornish informed readers of *Freedom's Journal*, was on free blacks. "It is for us," he argued, "to convince the world by uniform propriety of conduct, industry, and economy, that we are worthy of esteem and patronage."[24]

Black abolitionists understood the antislavery burden borne by free blacks. If slavery and prejudice resulted from their condition, then the moral reform of free blacks would shatter racist myths and dramatically alter American race relations. Creating "an intelligent and respectable community of colour [would] do more in breaking the bonds of

---

Convention for the Improvement of the Free People of Colour . . . (New York, N.Y., 1834), 3–7 [1:0464–66]; Winch, *Philadelphia's Black Elite*, 95–96; Adam Dewey Simmons, "Ideologies and Programs of the Negro Antislavery Movement, 1830–1861" (Ph.D. diss., Northwestern University, 1983), 75, 88–91.

22. For an overview of urban free black conditions in the antebellum period, see Leonard P. Curry, *The Free Black in Urban America, 1800–1850: The Shadow of the Dream* (Chicago, Ill., 1981); and Leon F. Litwack, *North of Slavery: The Negro in the Free States, 1790–1860* (Chicago, Ill., 1961).

23. *CA*, 24 June 1837, 23 February 1839 [2:0091, 3:0012].

24. *NSt*, 14 July 1848; *FJ*, 23 March 1827.

slavery than a thousand colonization schemes," argued one black leader. Cornish saw the importance of free black life for racial change: "On our conduct, in a great measure, [the slave's] salvation depends."[25] Using that reasoning, black abolitionists made moral reform the philosophical underpinning of their struggle during the 1830s.

Black abolitionists promoted mutual aid, hard work, thrift, learning, piety, and sobriety as the keys to racial advancement and emancipation. "All eyes are upon us," the editor of the *Colored American* admonished his readers. Editorials lectured readers on the value of reform principles—education, temperance, religion, and economy—while cautioning against lotteries, dancing, public processions, frequenting court trials, and following soldiers in the streets. They warned blacks to avoid the "gaming table, the cotillion and the theatre . . . needless and expensive journeyings, [and] extravagant dress and living." Delegates to the 1834 black national convention condemned public processions and pompous dress by blacks as "vain expenditures" that provoked white racism. Such moralizing underscored a vexing awareness that, in the United States, the misconduct of a single black reflected poorly on the entire race. Black leaders often despaired that their race alone was judged by stringent standards that many whites failed to meet.[26]

Black abolitionists promoted practical expressions of moral reform. The black national convention movement of the early 1830s, which brought together black leaders to develop strategies for racial advancement, adopted a number of moral reform ventures. Encouraged by white reformers, the 1831 gathering endorsed a proposed manual labor college for New Haven, Connecticut. Two years later, the convention's committee on temperance recommended that a Coloured American Temperance Society be established. Additional calls went out to organize Sabbath schools, literary and benevolent societies, and other institutions dedicated to moral and mental improvement. The 1835 convention created the American Moral Reform Society, believing that a national reform organization was the "means best calculated to reach the wants and improve the condition of our people."[27]

Efforts to support a national reform organization failed, but local

25. *FJ*, 31 August 1827; *CA*, 4 March 1837 [1:0993].
26. *CA*, 22 April 1837 [2:0033]; *FJ*, 13 July 1827, 27 June, 1 August 1828, 14, 21, 28 February, 21 March 1829; *RA*, 17 July, 9 October 1829; *CA*, 4 March, 12 August 1837, 10 February, 12 April, 15 December 1838, 19 January 1839, 28 March 1840, 6 March 1841 [1:0992, 2:0144, 0378, 0455, 0676, 0978, 3:0357–58, 0930]; *Minutes of the Fourth Annual Convention* (1834), 14 [1:0469].
27. Winch, *Philadelphia's Black Elite*, 91–129; *Minutes of the First Annual Convention* (1831), 5–7 [1:0078–79]; *Minutes of the Third Annual Convention* (1833), 15–19 [1:0177–79]; *Minutes of the Fifth Annual Convention for the Improvement of the Free People of Colour* (Philadelphia, Pa., 1835), 26, 31 [1:0598, 0601].

moral reform ventures thrived in the 1830s. Mutual aid and social welfare societies flourished in northern black communities. There were sixty-four such associations in Philadelphia alone. In many cities, black women banded together in African Dorcas Associations to provide food, clothing, and fuel to needy members of the race. Institutions such as orphan asylums and homes for the aged enjoyed broad community involvement. Successful black efforts to care for the sick, the homeless, and the destitute lowered the number of blacks dependent upon almshouses during the decade.[28]

Blacks founded hundreds of organizations and institutions dedicated to racial self-improvement and culture—schools, lyceums, literary societies, library companies, debating clubs, and lecture series. In the late 1830s, Philadelphia blacks supported five lyceums and debating clubs, several day and evening schools, a reading room, a library of six hundred volumes, a literary magazine, and dozens of literary societies. Most of these endeavors shared the dual objectives of building good character and improving the mind. New York City's celebrated Phoenix Society (1833) sponsored moral and literary events and operated an evening school for blacks. Founded by Theodore S. Wright and other black abolitionists, it served as a model for local programs to promote black education. The Philomathean Society (1829) met weekly to hear debates, readings, and lectures on subjects ranging from "Geography" to "Patriots of the American Revolution" and "The Duty of Young Men." Some efforts also made a direct link between self-improvement and economic advancement. They sought to imbue blacks with useful skills and a commitment to hard work.[29]

Temperance was an essential component of moral reform. Advocates argued that sobriety would represent black moral advancement, allow more time for intellectual pursuits, and increase black wealth. Black clergymen led this crusade and established dozens of local abstinence societies, often as auxiliaries to their churches. J. W. C. Pennington helped found the Brooklyn Temperance Association in 1830. Cornish, Ray, and Wright were active in New York City temperance circles, as were African Methodist Episcopal Zion (AMEZ) minister Jehiel C. Beman and his son, Amos G. Beman, in Connecticut. John W. Lewis of Providence created the New England Colored Temperance Society in 1836 and remained its moving force for several years. Black abolitionists

28. Dorothy B. Porter, ed., *Early Negro Writing, 1760–1837* (Boston, Mass., 1971), 212; Philip S. Foner, *History of Black Americans*, 3 vols. to date (Westport, Conn., 1975–), 2:239–43.
29. Porter, *Early Negro Writing*, 212; Carleton Mabee, *Black Education in New York State: From Colonial to Modern Times* (Syracuse, N.Y., 1979), 57–59; Daniel Perlman, "Organizations of the Free Negro in New York City, 1800–1860," *JNH* 56:188–90, 191–95 (July 1971); Pease and Pease, *They Who Would Be Free*, 136–38.

established temperance grocery stores and boardinghouses. The temperance appeal found acceptance across a wide spectrum of the black population, and by the end of the decade, nearly every black community in the free states had at least one temperance society.[30]

The moral reform movement offered blacks one of the few organizational means they had—beyond black churches and lodges—for community control and development. As black abolitionists struggled to create and support mutual aid and benevolent associations, schools, literary societies, and temperance organizations, they established credentials as community leaders. By offering opportunities for leadership experience, moral reform organizations of the 1830s helped train the next, more militant generation of black abolitionists that emerged in the 1840s.

While the black commitment to moral reform brought benefits, it also carried burdens. It placed responsibility for change upon blacks. Central to the success of moral reform was the unstated assumption that whites would allow and accept black uplift, and that they would change their racial attitudes in the process. Moral reform failed, in part, because black success could not convince whites to abandon their racist stereotypes and accept black equality.

Moral reform relied upon sincere arguments and the power of persuasion to win converts and to achieve its goals. Those tactics proved useful in advancing some black objectives, but over time they restricted blacks in the methods they might use to gain freedom and equality. Hopeful that moral reform would help improve conditions in the black community and wary of offending Garrisonian allies, harsher antislavery voices grew hesitant. Guided by moral reformers like William Whipper, the 1835 black national convention endorsed *"moral suasion alone"* as the acceptable path to black advancement. The American Moral Reform Society promoted moral suasionist tactics—lectures, the press, and petition campaigns. Constrained by moral reform, most black abolitionists of the 1830s were timid in their language and programs. Two national conventions recommended "a day of fasting and prayer" to protest slavery and prejudice. Another convention recommended establishing permanent local committees, but only where such activity "may be safely done." Black acceptance of moral reform left militant black abolitionism dormant for nearly a decade.[31]

30. Quarles, *Black Abolitionists*, 93–97; *Minutes of a Convention of People of Color, for the Promotion of Temperance in New England* (Providence, R.I., 1836), 3, 8 [1:0710, 0713]; *Lib*, 20 April 1833.
31. *Minutes and Proceedings of the Second Annual Convention for Improvement of the Free People of Colour* . . . (Philadelphia, Pa., 1832), 14, 35–36 [1:0177, 0187–88]; Howard Bell, "The American Moral Reform Society, 1836–1841," *JNE* 27:35 (Winter 1958); Horton and Horton, *Black Bostonians*, 115; *Minutes of the Fourth Annual Convention* (1834), 18 [1:0471]; Simmons, "Ideologies and Programs," 69–75.

During the late 1830s and early 1840s, black abolitionists examined the results of moral reform and concluded that new strategies and tactics were needed in the battle for emancipation and equality. Slavery continued to thrive. Race relations had not improved. The situation was worsening, and black abolitionists had hard evidence in American political and economic life to support that claim. Blacks were denied a share in the extension of voting rights that took place during the Jacksonian era. They lost the franchise in Connecticut, New Jersey, and Pennsylvania. By 1840 some 93 percent of northern free blacks were completely or practically denied the right to vote. Irish immigrants arrived in northern cities in such numbers after 1830 that they threatened to displace black workers from traditional areas of employment. "Junius" informed the *Colored American* that immigrants were "crowding themselves into every place of business and labor, and driving the poor colored American citizen out."[32]

Black abolitionists pointed to other, more frightening evidence. When Texas independence opened up a new market for slaves, the kidnapping of fugitive slaves, children, and the poor dramatically increased in northern black communities. Escalating racial violence in the 1830s mocked moral reform and underscored its failure. Rioting whites beat and abused blacks and destroyed black-owned property, often seeking out the symbols of black success—churches, businesses, the homes of the elite, and meeting places for moral reform organizations. After the vicious Philadelphia race riot of August 1842, Robert Purvis wrote that the "wantonness, brutality and murderous spirit" of the mob had convinced him of the black community's "utter and complete nothingness in public estimation."[33]

Growing segregation, discrimination, disfranchisement, loss of jobs, kidnapping, and racial violence convinced black leaders that moral reform had failed. Although most continued to see its intrinsic worth, black leaders now doubted its value for ending slavery or improving race relations. "Junius" observed that blacks had pursued "respectability, wealth and usefulness," but their situation remained unchanged. If anything, the standard-bearers of moral reform—the black elite—had become special targets for white hostility and violence. The message was clear. Blacks were urged by moral reformers of both races to do more, to succeed, to accumulate and prosper. Yet that very success invited white violence. Disillusioned blacks grew contemptuous of moral reform. Peter

32. Litwack, *North of Slavery*, 74–88, 162–63; CA, 28 July 1838 [2:0541].
33. *NECAUL*, 14 January 1837; Julie Winch, "Philadelphia and the Other Underground Railroad," *PMHB* 111:3–25 (January 1987); Emma J. Lapsansky, " 'Since They Got Those Separate Churches': Afro-Americans and Racism in Jacksonian Philadelphia," *AQ* 32:75 (Spring 1980); Robert Purvis to Henry C. Wright, 22 August 1842, Anti-Slavery Collection, MB [4:0463–64].

Paul Simons complained that the black pulpit and the black press kept calling for "OUR MORAL ELEVATION." He countered that "no nation under the canopy of heaven are given more to good morals and piety than we are." What, he asked, had moral reform achieved? It had made blacks docile and kept them poor, acting as "a conspicuous scarecrow designed expressly . . . to hinder our people from acting collectively for themselves." Even William Whipper, moral reform's proudest advocate, lost heart by 1839, concluding that it was "not lack of elevation, but complexion that deprived the man of color of equal treatment."[34]

By the early 1840s, there was less talk about hard work, accumulation of wealth, temperance, cultivation of the mind, and proper decorum and more calls for assertiveness. Moral reform's failure to improve the situation of Afro-Americans prompted many black abolitionists to explore different options. "We need more radicalism among us," insisted Charles Lenox Remond. He warned blacks that they were "too indefinite in [their] views and sentiments—too slow in [their] movements," and he urged them to fight for their rights and to challenge institutions that discriminated against the race, even at the cost of imprisonment. More and more, black leaders came to share Simons's view that "physical and political efforts are the only methods left for us to adopt."[35]

Independence

Black abolitionism entered a new phase in the 1840s. Disillusioned by the failure of moral reform and frustrated with white abolitionists, blacks reexamined their relationship to the broader antislavery movement. They became less deferential to white leadership and less tolerant of the methods of the previous decade, and they attacked slavery and racism more aggressively. Increasingly militant and practical-minded, they sought strategies more assertive than moral reform and less dogmatic than Garrisonian abolitionism. As they changed, they redefined black abolitionism and created a more independent role for themselves in the antislavery crusade.

This new phase was ushered in as blacks reviewed a decade of close association with white abolitionists. For many black abolitionists, the goodwill, mutual understanding, and shared goals that characterized the early days of the immediatist struggle were lost by the late 1830s. Black optimism was replaced by a disquieting belief that the antislavery movement was tainted with racism, a loss of mission, and senseless infighting.

While working together during the 1830s, blacks learned that white

34. *CA*, 28 July 1838, 1 June 1839 [2:0541, 3:0075–76]; *NR*, December 1839.
35. *Lib*, 21 May 1841 [4:0024–25]; *CA*, 1 June 1839 [3:0076].

abolitionists lacked an abiding commitment to many black goals, particularly racial equality. When immediatist antislavery societies were organized in the early 1830s, whites resolved to fight prejudice and to improve the condition of free blacks, a pledge that many groups wrote into their constitutions. Yet white interest in the battle against prejudice had declined by the end of the decade. Conservatives in the movement thought it a grave mistake to mix the struggle for racial equality with antislavery work, believing that to raise the issue of northern prejudice would alienate potential antislavery converts in the free states; they preferred "leaving those minor appendages to time." Others, believing that slavery was the cause of prejudice, thought it a drain of energy and resources to combat racism while slavery thrived.[36]

Blacks were angry and disappointed that white allies did not share their sense of urgency about the problem of prejudice. While some white abolitionists fought specific racist practices such as the "Negro pew" and laws prohibiting interracial marriage, they ignored the larger social and economic plight of northern blacks, showing how little they understood the nature of the problem. Blacks charged that "while abolitionists have preached immediate Emancipation for the slave States, they have tolerated gradual Emancipation in the free States." Black abolitionists reminded their white allies that slavery and prejudice were inseparable evils that reinforced each other. But white abolitionists were reluctant to accept that idea. Theodore S. Wright complained that his white colleagues "overlooked the giant sin of prejudice . . . at once the parent and the offspring of slavery."[37]

By the late 1830s, black abolitionists were admonishing white abolitionists for failing to conquer their own prejudices. Theodore S. Wright accused his white colleagues of being unable—or unwilling—to "annihilate in their own bosoms, the cord of caste." Samuel Ringgold Ward chided abolitionists "who love the colored man at a distance." Martin R. Delany saw prejudice in the patronizing attitude of many white allies who "presumed to *think* for, dictate to, and *know* better what suited colored people, than they know for themselves." Benjamin F. Roberts discovered a more malicious form of racism "in the effort on the part of certain professed abolitionists to muzzle, exterminate, and put down" the work of black antislavery activists. Blacks complained that many white abolitionists wanted to keep them "a second-rate set of folks."[38]

36. Foner, *History of Black Americans*, 2:511–23; Carleton Mabee, *Black Freedom: The Nonviolent Abolitionists from 1830 through the Civil War* (London, 1970), 92.

37. *FDP*, 9 February, 18 May 1855 [9:0430, 0644–45]; Mabee, *Black Freedom*, 127–38; Louis Ruchames, "Race, Marriage, and Abolition in Massachusetts," *JNH* 40:250–73 (July 1955); *Lib*, 12 June 1836; *CA*, 4 October 1837 [2:0222].

38. *CA*, 14 October 1837 [2:0222, 3:0264]; *NASS*, 2 July 1840 [3:0478]; Martin R. Delany, *The Condition, Elevation, Emigration and Destiny of the Colored People of the*

Blacks blamed prejudice for their secondary position within the movement. Despite conspicuous black involvement in the AASS and its auxiliaries and black financial contributions approximating one-seventh of the organization's annual budget, the antislavery leadership remained almost exclusively white. When blacks obtained positions within the movement, it was seldom on equal terms. Black antislavery agents usually received about one-half the pay of white agents, and black workers in antislavery offices filled subservient positions. William Still and William C. Nell served for decades in antislavery offices and never rose above the level of clerk, although both were skilled, articulate, and experienced. Nell had a respected career as an abolitionist and historian, and Still directed Philadelphia's extensive and elaborate underground railroad system. There were a few exceptions—Samuel Snowden of Boston served as one of the nine counselors of the NEASS, and Theodore Wright and Peter Williams, Jr., spent time on the twelve-member AASS executive committee—but blacks were rarely in charge. For one reader of the *Colored American*, such evidence showed how white abolitionists stifled the elevation of free blacks. "OUR FRIENDS," he stated ruefully, "HINDER OUR IMPROVEMENT."[39]

Blacks were also concerned about the factional feuding that distracted white abolitionists from the primary objective of freeing the slaves. The antislavery crusade began to splinter in the late 1830s over tactics and goals. Garrisonians advocated equality of the sexes, espoused unconventional religious views, questioned biblical authority, and mistrusted institutions, including the political system. They considered moral suasion the only acceptable tactic. Another antislavery group, based largely in New York, sought more limited goals, while being more flexible about methods. They wanted to concentrate on the slavery issue and regarded politics as the surest route to emancipation. In their view, Garrisonians were too radical; their religious beliefs and enthusiasm for so many reforms threatened "the whole fabric of social relations." By 1840 the two factions were beyond compromise. Lewis Tappan led the dissidents out of the AASS annual convention. They established the American and Foreign Anti-Slavery Society (AFASS) as a rival to the AASS and formed the Liberty party in order to run antislavery candidates for political office.[40]

Blacks wanted a return to unified action, but continued white factionalism forced them to choose sides. Some black leaders, particularly in

United States (Philadelphia, Pa., 1852; reprint, New York, N.Y., 1969), 10; Benjamin F. Roberts to Amos A. Phelps, 19 June 1838, Anti-Slavery Collection, MB [2:0499].

39. Pease and Pease, *They Who Would Be Free*, 69–71, 84–86; *CA*, 6 October 1838, 2 November 1839 [2:0605, 3:0252]; *NSt*, 25 February 1848.

40. For an overview of the ideological differences that brought about the antislavery schism of 1840, see Aileen S. Kraditor, *Means and Ends in American Abolitionism: Garrison and His Critics on Strategy and Tactics, 1834–1850* (New York, N.Y., 1969).

Boston and Philadelphia, rallied behind Garrison and the AASS. The majority, however, abandoned Garrisonianism for political action. Western blacks, such as fugitive slave lecturers Henry Bibb and Samuel R. Ward, became ardent supporters of the Liberty party. The religious orthodoxy of the AFASS attracted many black clergymen, including Jehiel C. Beman, Amos G. Beman, Christopher Rush, Samuel Cornish, Theodore S. Wright, Andrew Harris, Stephen Gloucester, and Henry Highland Garnet.[41]

There was no middle ground. A vague *Colored American* editorial favoring political action drew attacks from both the Boston Garrisonians, who rejected all politics, and Gerrit Smith, who wanted the paper to support a specific antislavery party. Garrisonians condemned temperance organizer Jehiel C. Beman after he opened a black employment agency in Boston under the auspices of the Massachusetts Abolition Society, an AFASS affiliate. When John W. Lewis grew tired of abolitionist sniping and resigned as a lecturing agent for the New Hampshire Anti-Slavery Society, the pro-Garrison *Herald of Freedom* accused him of fraud and of lacking the stamina for antislavery work. Samuel R. Ward was continually attacked by Luther Myrick and James C. Jackson of the *Union Herald* for allegedly abandoning Garrisonian tactics in the fight against slavery.[42]

Black abolitionists were surprised and alarmed by the persistence and viciousness of the attacks. Critical issues separated blacks from their white colleagues. Blacks accused whites of fighting over irrelevant issues, of weakening the movement with their squabbling, and of having "forgotten the poor, down-trodden slave." One black abolitionist bluntly reminded both Garrisonians and political abolitionists that issues such as nonresistance, women's rights, and anti-Sabbatarianism were *"neither part, nor parcel of that great and holy cause."* Blacks demanded that white abolitionists again make slavery "the paramount question."[43]

By 1840 black leaders were convinced that the movement had gone astray. Certain that white abolitionists shared neither their commitment to racial equality nor their concern for the slave, black abolitionists sought more autonomy, believing that they alone had the correct vision of antislavery goals.

Independence became the dominant theme of black abolitionism in the

41. *CA*, 30 May, 4 July, 19 September 1840 [3:0443, 0513, 0625]; Thomas Van Rensellaer to Gerrit Smith, 10 March 1841, Gerrit Smith Papers, NSyU [3:0936]; John A. Collins, *Right and Wrong among the Abolitionists of the United States*, 2d ed. (Glasgow, Scotland, 1841), 50; Pease and Pease, *They Who Would Be Free*, 73–79.
42. Pease and Pease, *They Who Would Be Free*, 74–79; *NASS*, 3, 10, 17 September 1840 [3:0605, 0612–13, 0619].
43. *CA*, 7 October 1837, 11 May 1839, 2 May 1840 [2:0215, 0406]; *Lib*, 15 May 1841 [3:0834].

1840s and 1850s. Black leaders reasoned that they had been too reliant upon white abolitionists in the 1830s, and that dependence had been costly in black identity and racial pride. "To be dependent is to be degraded," Frederick Douglass explained; he argued that independence was an "essential condition of respectability" that white patronage, however sympathetic, could not provide. William J. Watkins had little appetite for "the innutritious husks" of white sympathy; he reminded blacks of the hidden, demeaning price of patronage—the loyalty, obedience, and gratitude that whites tacitly expected. Blacks had served a "faithful apprenticeship," Watkins concluded, but the time had come "to hang out *our own shingle.*" In calling for independence, blacks recognized that the antislavery struggle was their responsibility. "It is emphatically our battle," James McCune Smith declared, "no one else can fight it for us."[44]

Black abolitionists prepared to fight on their own, increasingly aware of the differences that separated them from their white allies. By 1840 two distinct abolitionisms existed. Whites approached slavery and freedom on an abstract, ideological plane; blacks defined slavery and freedom in more concrete, experiential terms. White abolitionism drew largely upon evangelical theology and theories of universal reform; black abolitionism was grounded in political philosophy and shaped by daily experiences in a racist society. Religious values contributed to the rise of black abolitionism, but the black antislavery appeal was founded upon the Declaration of Independence, the Constitution, and black participation in the American Revolution and subsequent wars. White abolitionists insisted that antislavery strategies and tactics conform to abstract moral principles. Black abolitionists sought practical change, usually more concerned with results than tactics. Both wanted to end slavery, but unlike their white colleagues, blacks gave equal importance to the fight for racial equality. Black abolitionism extended, in Smith's words, "from the mere act of riding in public conveyances to the liberation of every slave."[45]

Black abolitionists understood that slaves and free blacks shared a common fight. The new generation of leaders in the 1840s, many of them fugitive slaves, acknowledged the relationship between slavery and racism that brought a stronger sense of racial unity. As one former slave emphasized in 1848, it was "more than a mere figure of speech to say that we, as a people, are chained together." This enhanced perception of racial unity gave a seamless quality to the work of emancipation and the efforts to improve the condition of free blacks. Antislavery fused with

44. *FDP*, 9 February, 18 May 1855 [9:0432, 0644–45]; *Report on the Proceedings of the Colored National Convention, Held at Cleveland, Ohio, on Wednesday, September 6, 1848* (Rochester, N.Y., 1848), 19 [5:0775].
45. *FDP*, 9 February 1855 [9:0430]. For the essential discussion of the "two abolitionisms" concept, see Pease and Pease, *They Who Would Be Free*, 3–16.

other free black concerns, imparting to black abolitionism a practical continuity that few white reformers understood. A black temperance gathering could adjourn and immediately reconvene as an antislavery meeting with no change in tenor or participants. A black lecturer could use an antislavery tour to solicit donations for a fledgling black newspaper, a church building fund, or African missions. A black vigilance committee, while aiding fugitive slaves, could also organize a petition campaign for black voting rights.[46] The range and continuity of these activities redefined black abolitionism to include much of northern black life, institutions, and culture.

Independence did not necessarily imply racial separatism. Charles L. Remond, James McCune Smith, and many others who encouraged autonomous black action remained staunch integrationists. Douglass, ever wary of separatist tendencies, carefully balanced the need for independence with his steadfast commitment to racial integration and cooperation. "We must be our own representatives and advocates," he argued, "not exclusively, but peculiarly—not distinct from, but in connection with our white friends."[47] Most blacks concurred. Moreover, their desire for autonomy had to be tempered by the realities of abolitionism. Whites made up a majority in the antislavery movement, held the recognized positions of authority, provided the organizational leadership, and controlled most of the resources. Black abolitionists acknowleged the necessity of cooperating with whites in several important ventures—publishing abolitionist literature, organizing and financing antislavery lecture tours, and obtaining effective legal and political representation. In their ambitious plans for building community institutions and promoting black uplift, they often relied on the generosity of Gerrit Smith, the Tappans, and other white philanthropists. Black abolitionists looked to the antislavery political parties to give their concerns a national political forum. They might chastise their white allies and proclaim black autonomy at one moment but then solicit white assistance at the next. This alternating criticism and approval, defiance and deference, reflected the constant tension that existed between black aspirations for independence on one hand and the realities of a white-controlled antislavery movement on the other.

Despite the apparent necessity of cooperation in the antislavery movement, experience had shown that some things were best done within the black community, away from whites. Promoting civil rights and debating the range of potential antislavery tactics—including violence—often required separate deliberations. The Colored American applauded independent black endeavors: "Where our object is confined to our own

46. Colored National Convention at Cleveland (1848), 18 [5:0777]; Quarles, Black Abolitionists, 96.
47. Colored National Convention at Cleveland (1848), 19 [5:0778].

purposes and for our own advantage, there 'the clearest necessity demands exclusive action.' " By the 1840s, most black abolitionists accepted the practical and symbolic value of racially separate efforts in the fight against slavery and prejudice. As black abolitionists defined their place in the antislavery movement, they remembered that they had succeeded on their own before 1830. They recalled the extent to which the movement "owe[d] its origin and success to blacks." Black nationalist Martin R. Delany wanted it "borne in mind that Anti-Slavery took its rise among *colored men*." In a speech before the AASS, Charles W. Gardner made it clear to his largely white audience that blacks were doing antislavery work when Garrison "was a schoolboy." More and more, black leaders openly regretted abandoning their early independent efforts, ignoring the counsel of David Walker, and relying so heavily on white abolitionists. After 1840 they spoke in more self-reliant and aggressive tones, recovering the militant voice that had been stilled during the 1830s and viewing the past decade as a detour in their efforts to free the slave and end prejudice.[48]

The black abolitionist movement broadened and deepened during the 1840s and 1850s. With independence came new people, new institutions, and a new voice. As the leadership changed, the number of participants increased; blacks of all classes and backgrounds were drawn to antislavery and civil rights activities. Black abolitionists worked toward their goals through new antislavery societies, vigilance committees, and the black church. They made their voices heard through lectures, slave narratives, and an independent press.

New leadership gave direction to independence. Another generation of black leaders came forward during the 1840s. Frederick Douglass, William Wells Brown, Martin R. Delany, Henry Highland Garnet, Samuel Ringgold Ward, Jermain W. Loguen, James McCune Smith, and others filled the void created by the death or decline of older black abolitionists. Key Garrisonians like William Hamilton, Nathaniel Paul, Peter Williams, Jr., James Barbadoes, and James Forten, Sr., had passed from the scene by the early 1840s. Others such as Cornish, William Watkins, and Stephen Gloucester had lost youthful impatience or simply wearied of the fight.[49]

48. *CA*, 27 June 1840 [3:0473]; *FDP*, 26 January 1855 [9:0406]; Delany, *Condition of the Colored People*, 26; *Fourth Annual Report of the American Anti-Slavery Society* (New York, N.Y., 1837), 14 [2:0050]; Benjamin Quarles, "The Breach between Douglass and Garrison," *JNH* 23:152 (April 1938); J. W. C. Pennington, *The Fugitive Blacksmith; or, Events in the History of James W. C. Pennington*, 3d ed. (London, 1850; reprint, Westport, Conn., 1971), 55.
49. William H. Pease and Jane H. Pease, "The Negro Convention Movement," in *Key*

More than a span of years separated the new generation from the old. Most of the early leaders were freeborn, educated, and well situated in trades or professions. These black elites owned homes, property, and businesses in Boston, Philadelphia, New York City, and other established communities. Many of the younger black abolitionists came to the movement by way of the plantation. Douglass, Brown, Garnet, Ward, Loguen, Pennington, Bibb, Lewis and Milton Clarke, and other well-known antislavery advocates of the 1840s had experienced slavery firsthand.

Antislavery labor became a way of measuring leadership. Black abolitionists of the 1830s were community leaders by virtue of their position as members of the black elite. Later in the decade, local leaders of a different type emerged—men like David Ruggles and Lewis Hayden whose antislavery work earned them a standing in the community. Professional abolitionists came on the scene. Skilled practitioners like Frederick Douglass, William Still, and Charles L. Remond supported themselves through their antislavery activities—lecturing, editing black journals, writing and selling their slave narratives, or working in antislavery offices. A large number of professional abolitionists were former slaves whose slave past gave them a distinctive place and a special influence in the movement.[50] Abolitionism offered expanded roles for black women. Sojourner Truth, Barbara Steward, Sarah Parker Remond, Frances Ellen Watkins Harper, and Mary Ann Shadd Cary became professional abolitionists during the 1850s.

The center of black abolitionism shifted westward. In the emerging black communities of the West, class, status, and leadership experience counted for less than in Boston or Philadelphia. While eastern elites remained important, younger blacks from western towns—Buffalo, Syracuse, Rochester, Pittsburgh, Cincinnati, and Detroit—influenced this new phase of black abolitionism. Homegrown western leaders of national stature soon developed; Pittsburgh's Martin R. Delany edited the first black paper published beyond the Allegheny Mountains and became antebellum America's foremost advocate of black nationalism. Frederick Douglass symbolized this change when he left Massachusetts to establish the *North Star* in western New York.

The geographic change can be charted through the black convention movement, which western blacks revived and led. The convention sites tell the story; Buffalo (1843), Troy (1847), Cleveland (1848), Toronto

---

Issues in the Afro-American Experience, 2 vols., ed. Nathan I. Huggins, Martin Kilson, and Daniel M. Fox (New York, N.Y., 1971), 1:197; *DANB,* 234, 481, 660; *Lib,* 20 August 1841; Graham, *Baltimore,* 124; Winch, *Philadelphia's Black Elite,* 165.

50. The emergence and importance of professional abolitionists is discussed in Larry Gara, "The Professional Fugitive in the Abolition Movement," *WMH* 26:196–204 (Spring 1965).

(1851), and Rochester (1853) hosted national gatherings. Forty-seven of
the fifty-eight delegates to the 1843 convention came from Ohio, Michigan, Illinois, and upstate New York. Not a single easterner attended the
1851 North American Convention in Toronto.[51]

Black voices became an essential weapon in the abolitionist battles of
the 1840s. Antislavery strategists regarded northern public opinion as
the key prize in the struggle against slavery. Convincing the North of the
evils of slavery was the first step in destroying the institution. Abolitionists competed with proslavery apologists for public opinion. Defenders
of slavery justified it as a positive good because of its reputed civilizing
and Christianizing influence on blacks, and they assured northerners that
slaves were contented, well cared for, and best left in bondage. They
discredited their critics by pointing out that most abolitionists were
northern whites and free blacks who had no experience with slavery and
had never witnessed it as it really existed. These arguments gained a
sympathetic audience in the North during the 1830s.[52]

Former slaves refuted proslavery claims with firsthand evidence. They
spoke and wrote with authority, hard-earned through bitter encounters
with slavery and prejudice. Using lecture tours and published autobiographies, black abolitionists, particularly fugitive slaves, validated the
antislavery strategy of the 1840s and 1850s. The abolitionist movement
discovered that free black lecturers were more convincing than whites
and that former slaves were the most convincing of all. John A. Collins,
general agent for the Massachusetts Anti-Slavery Society, informed Garrison in 1842 that "the public have itching ears to hear a colored man
speak, and particularly a *slave*." Nothing moved antislavery audiences
like "true narrative fallen from the lips of a veritable fugitive." Antislavery societies rushed black speakers into the field, preferring "one who
has felt in his own person the evils of Slavery, and with the strong voice
of experience can tell of its horrors." The AASS hired Charles L. Remond
as its first black lecturing agent in 1838, and his "singular eloquence"
quickly impressed white audiences and established a place for black abolitionists at the antislavery podium. By the mid-1840s, Frederick Douglass, William Wells Brown, Samuel R. Ward, Henry Bibb, Lewis and
Milton Clarke, Lunsford Lane, and dozens of other former slaves were
lecturing throughout the North. Bibb, an energetic and spirited lecturer
with a dramatic slave past, was swamped with requests to speak; "If I
had a thousand tongues," he wrote, "I could find useful employment

51. *Minutes of the National Convention of Colored Citizens: Held at Buffalo, on the 15th, 16th, 17th, 18th and 19th of August 1843* (New York, N.Y., 1843), 10 [4:0636]; C. Peter Ripley et al., eds., *The Black Abolitionist Papers*, 2 vols. to date (Chapel Hill, N.C., 1985–), 2:160–61n; Winch, *Philadelphia's Black Elite*, 129.
52. C. Peter Ripley, "The Autobiographical Writings of Frederick Douglass," *SS* 14:7 (Spring 1985); Gara, "The Professional Fugitive," 197.

for them all." Not all blacks spoke with the eloquence of Bibb, Douglass, or Remond, but a fugitive's halting, emotional account of slavery proved just as effective as a polished discourse in rousing northern public opinion.[53]

Black lecturers took their message wherever they could find an audience, from local antislavery gatherings to national reform conventions. When recounting their personal experiences as slaves, blacks used a variety of methods to convince their listeners of the horrors of slavery. They displayed artifacts of slavery, everything from branding irons to bullwhips. They reenacted scenes from their escapes; Henry "Box" Brown toured with the crate he used to ship himself out of slavery. William Wells Brown, Henry "Box" Brown, John Still, and Anthony Burns toured with panoramas illustrating scenes from slave life. Some lecturers linked several mediums, displaying panoramas while reading from their memoirs, then offering copies of their books for sale. Black lecturers educated the public about slavery and won converts to the cause. They promoted antislavery organizations and the Liberty and Free Soil parties. And they did much more. They used their status as antislavery lecturers to benefit the black community; while on tour they raised funds to purchase family and friends out of bondage, to build black schools and churches, to support black newspapers, and to aid and protect fugitive slaves.[54]

In many cases, black abolitionists gave fugitive slaves their first opportunity to address white audiences. Benjamin Roberts managed Henry "Box" Brown's appearances, and William Wells Brown introduced William and Ellen Craft and other black speakers to the lecture circuit. Frederick Douglass first learned of organized abolition through his early contacts with black leaders in New York City and New Bedford, Massachusetts. Months before white Garrisonians first heard him in 1841, Douglass delivered antislavery remarks to an AMEZ congregation in New Bedford.[55]

Black speakers often had their best success when they affiliated with an antislavery society that organized their tours. But affiliation inevitably brought close supervision and a patronizing attitude that offended some blacks. When Douglass developed into a skilled speaker and moved

53. Pease and Pease, *They Who Would Be Free*, 33–40; Quarles, *Black Abolitionists*, 61–62; *Lib*, 21 January 1842; Gilbert H. Barnes and Dwight L. Dumond, eds., *Letters of Theodore Dwight Weld, Angelina Grimké Weld, and Sarah Grimké, 1822–1844*, 2 vols. (Washington, D.C., 1934; reprint, Gloucester, Mass., 1965), 2:811; *NASS*, 11 June 1846; *E*, 21 April 1847 [5:0413].

54. Foner, *History of Black Americans*, 2:460.

55. Pease and Pease, *They Who Would Be Free*, 36; R. J. M. Blackett, *Beating against the Barriers: Biographical Essays in Nineteenth-Century Afro-American History* (Baton Rouge, La., 1986), 89–90; Joseph W. Barnes, ed., "The Autobiography of Rev. Thomas James," *RH* 37:7–8 (October 1975); Michael Meyer, ed., *Frederick Douglass: The Narrative and Selected Writings* (New York, N.Y., 1984), 119–20, 154–56.

beyond simply discussing his life as a slave, his white patrons grew concerned, advising him to retain "a little of the plantation speech" in his lectures and to avoid any analysis of slavery; "Give us the facts," they urged, "we will take care of the philosophy." With time and experience, many black speakers broke with their white sponsors and began independent lecturing in the 1840s. After John W. Lewis resigned as agent for the New Hampshire Anti-Slavery Society in 1840, he served as a traveling agent for three black newspapers while conducting his own lecture tours of northern New England. Samuel R. Ward, who was ebony black, six feet tall, and gifted with a strong voice and energetic gestures, was one of the most active independent black speakers of the 1840s, lecturing for ten years in churches, schoolhouses, and town halls from Massachusetts to Wisconsin.[56]

Slave narratives took the antislavery message beyond the lecture halls. They brought slavery into the private lives of white Americans. Subjects too delicate or complex for public expression could have a full rendering in the narratives. By the 1840s, many antislavery activists hoped that the narratives would be an "infallible means of abolitionizing the free states." By articulating "the *victim's account*" of slavery, the narratives proved, as J. W. C. Pennington said, that even "the mildest form of slavery . . . is comparatively the worst form." The slave's own written story provided a detailed and permanent record of slavery that challenged slavery's defenders.[57]

Early on, white abolitionists edited, published, promoted, and distributed the slave narratives. In the 1830s, innovations in print technology allowed mass production of dozens of these works, making them an inexpensive and effective method of spreading the word. By the mid-1840s, the narratives were so successful that they captured the attention of commercial publishers, who then broadened the market, reached more readers, and provided the authors with much-needed income. The narratives of Charles Ball, Pennington, Douglass, Lane, the Clarke brothers, William Wells Brown, and other former slaves reached thousands of readers in the United States and abroad. Sales of Ball's *Slavery in the United States* ballooned when a New York publisher condensed the narrative, bound it in bright red cloth, and reprinted it as *Fifty Years in Chains*. Solomon Northrup's narrative proved a remarkable success,

56. Pease and Pease, *They Who Would Be Free*, 34; Ripley et al., *Black Abolitionist Papers*, 2:314–15; *DANB*, 44, 170–72, 631–32; Robert C. Dick, *Black Protest: Issues and Tactics* (Westport, Conn., 1974), 209–10, 216–17.
57. William L. Andrews, *To Tell a Free Story: The First Century of Afro-American Autobiography, 1760–1865* (Urbana, Ill., 1986), 66–69, 77–81; Frances Smith Foster, *Witnessing Slavery: The Development of the Ante-Bellum Slave Narratives* (Westport, Conn., 1979), 19–20; Gara, "The Professional Fugitive," 197; *CE*, July 1849; *QASM*, no. 4 (1836); Pennington, *Fugitive Blacksmith*, v.

3. Black kidnapping victim dictating his narrative
From Jesse Torrey, *A Portraiture of Domestic Slavery in the United States*
(Philadelphia, 1817)

selling twenty-seven thousand copies in two years. Douglass's immensely popular *Narrative* (1845) was first published by the Garrisonians, but subsequent editions were printed by commercial houses in the United States and abroad. It eventually sold thirty thousand copies and prompted a second autobiography, *My Bondage and My Freedom* (1855).[58]

Through lecture tours and slave narratives, blacks challenged proslavery myths and convinced many northern whites of the evils of slavery and racism. Their eloquence in print or before an audience undermined popular charges of intellectual inferiority. The passion and anger of fugitives such as Ward or Douglass refuted the myth of the contented slave. Slave speakers and authors disabused white audiences of the myth of the kind master with stories of slavery's brutal conditions and consequences—long hours of toil, physical violence, sexual abuse, and separation of slave families. With an authority earned in slavery, black abolitionists increased their influence and established their own essential role in the antislavery movement.

The black press, along with slave narratives and lecture tours, gave black abolitionists their own voice and served as a touchstone for their independence. Some black leaders realized the need for a separate press as early as the 1820s. "Too long have others spoken for us," wrote John B. Russwurm in March 1827, marking the advent of *Freedom's Journal*. But throughout the 1830s, scant resources and devotion to white antislavery journals like the *Liberator* and *Emancipator* restrained blacks from starting their own papers. The 1834 black national convention urged its constituents to support "the *Liberator* . . . and other papers pledged to our cause," making no mention of a black press. White abolitionists frowned on black publishing ventures, insisting that the antislavery movement could not support additional journals and urging blacks to give their loyalty and financial backing to the established reform press. So long as black abolitionists remained dependent on their white allies and committed to unified antislavery action, blacks hesitated to establish their own papers.[59]

The *Colored American* illustrated how an independent voice could aid independent action within the antislavery movement. When Samuel E. Cornish assumed the editorship of the *Colored American* in late February 1837, the paper proudly advertised its black identity and adopted a spirited, independent editorial stance. With an aggressive tone and combative rhetoric, Cornish sometimes sparked rancorous debate, but he helped shape the character of the black press in the early years. His

58. Foster, *Witnessing Slavery*, 21; Philip S. Foner, *Frederick Douglass* (New York, N.Y., 1969), 59–60; Charles T. Davis and Henry Louis Gates, Jr., eds., *The Slaves's Narrative* (Oxford, England, 1985), xvi; Gilbert Osofsky, ed., *Puttin' On Ole Massa* (New York, N.Y., 1969), 64.
59. *FJ*, 16 March 1827; *Minutes of the Fourth Annual Convention* (1834), 12 [1:0468].

Colored American challenged the authority of Garrisonian leadership, rejected long-held assumptions about the antislavery value of moral reform, and urged blacks to "speak out in THUNDER TONES." The *Colored American* struck a responsive chord in northern black communities.[60]

The *Colored American* helped establish the value of a black press. By addressing subjects often neglected or superficially treated by white antislavery newspapers, it underscored the need for blacks to have their own forum. Black identity, the origins and nature of racial prejudice, the character and goals of black institutions, and free black life and culture were among the topics that distinguished the *Colored American* from its white counterparts. The *Colored American* broached sensitive subjects too controversial for the white reform press—"half-educated" black ministers, racial prejudice among blacks, apathy and disunity in the black community, and the meager support blacks gave to their own institutions.[61] When the *Colored American* addressed black concerns, including the goals of black abolitionists, it brought into focus the community's distinctive needs and concerns and established the pattern for most of the black papers that followed.

By the 1840s, black abolitionists had arrived at a consensus on the need for a black press and its importance for independent action. James McCune Smith explained to the delegates at the 1847 black national convention that blacks needed more than the white antislavery press offered—racial hostility on the one hand and patronizing benevolence on the other. "We must command respect," Smith insisted. "This can only be done," he determined, "through a Press of our own." For Smith and black leaders of the 1840s, a black press was essential to achieving their goals of unity, elevation, independence, emancipation, and equality.[62]

Black abolitionists established nearly twenty journals during the 1840s and 1850s. A few achieved modest successes; most were short-lived; many never went beyond a few issues. Pursuing independence had its difficulties, and the black press suffered its share. Limited subscription lists, scant advertising revenues, editorial controversies, personal rivalries, and competition with white antislavery papers kept black journals on the brink of failure. Their survival often depended on the generosity and goodwill of white abolitionists, which reminded black abolitionists of the difficulties of going it alone. The *Colored American* alienated its white patrons in 1840 when Cornish's position on political action

60. *CA*, 7 January, 4 March, 17 June 1837, 9 June, 25 August 1838, 18 May 1839 [2:0565, 3:0069].
61. Ibid., 12, 19 August 1837 [2:0140–41, 0146, 0153, 0155–56].
62. *Proceedings of the National Convention of Colored People, and Their Friends, Held in Troy, N.Y., on the 6th, 7th, 8th, and 9th October 1847* (Troy, N.Y., 1847), 18–30 [5:0493–99].

piqued leaders of the New York State Anti-Slavery Society. Benjamin Roberts, a black printer, encountered thinly veiled hostility from white Garrisonians when he attempted to establish the *Anti-Slavery Herald* in Boston in 1838; he tried again in 1853 with the *Self Elevator*, but without success. Black loyalty to Garrison's *Liberator* meant there was little possibility of establishing a black newspaper in Boston.[63]

No black editor during this period better demonstrated the skill, initiative, and resolve required for success than Frederick Douglass. Two months after Smith's call for an independent black press, Douglass published the first issue of his *North Star*. It marked an unprecedented achievement in black journalism for its intellectual rigor and sophistication and for its remarkable longevity—thirteen years as a weekly. Douglass recognized the symbolic antislavery value of his work. He initialed his writings in the *North Star* and in 1851 renamed it *Frederick Douglass' Paper* to remove doubts among skeptical whites that a fugitive slave with no formal education could become a skilled writer and editor. Douglass's paper was an antislavery journal, although it featured a multitude of subjects and commentaries by a host of contributors. Following an independent editorial course, Douglass consciously directed his paper beyond a black readership to the broader Anglo-American reform audience. Despite editorial controversies and a long-running battle with the Garrisonians, he earned respect for his acumen and literary skills. Douglass combined an ability to measure his times with the talents of a gifted commentator. His achievements gave Douglass an influential role in shaping the antislavery movement, the type of independence that black leaders of the 1850s sought.[64]

The struggle to establish and sustain a black press mirrored the transition from white patronage to independence in black abolitionism. When the *Colored American* addressed black issues, it convinced the black community of the value of having its own papers. When it urged blacks to "speak out in THUNDER TONES," the community transferred its loyalty from the *Liberator* and other white papers to the *Colored American* and the *North Star*. This shift in loyalty gave blacks what proponents of a black press promised—a voice that spoke for both the black community and the black abolitionist movement. Black papers became sources of racial pride and identity, powerful antislavery instruments, and invaluable records of antebellum black life and culture.

The independent black movement of the 1840s was centered in the

63. Pease and Pease, *They Who Would Be Free*, 116–19; Foner, *Frederick Douglass*, 82–88; *CA*, 19 October, 9, 16, 23 November, 7 December 1839, 4 April 1840 [3:0234, 0265, 0273, 0282, 0380]; Horton and Horton, *Black Bostonians*, 82–83.

64. Benjamin Quarles, *Frederick Douglass* (Washington, D.C., 1948), 83–96; Frederick Douglass, *Life and Times of Frederick Douglass*, rev. ed. (Boston, Mass., 1892; reprint, New York, N.Y., 1962), 257–65; *NSt*, 14 January 1848; *FDP*, 26 June 1851.

black community. It was a time of growing involvement in the antislavery crusade. Black leaders earned national recognition for their antislavery work on the local level. Communities encouraged lecturers and gave them an opportunity to find their public voices before they went on tour. Newspapers proved their worth by reflecting community concerns and goals. Expanded community involvement found expression in a host of organizations and institutions newly energized in their dedication to destroying slavery.

Abolitionism became deeply felt throughout the community. During the 1830s, a small number of working-class blacks had attended occasional antislavery meetings, subscribed to antislavery journals, signed petitions, and donated what money they could afford. Yet few blacks had the time, resources, or enthusiasm for sustained involvement. After 1840 more and more blacks were drawn to antislavery and civil rights efforts. The growing threat to fugitive slaves and the persistence of racial discrimination mobilized northern blacks of all stations. Large numbers of blacks participated in suffrage crusades, vigilance committee work, fugitive slave rescues, and campaigns to integrate schools, railroads, and streetcars—all of which required broad involvement by the black community.

Northern black communities battled slavery and prejudice through racially separate organizations, as they had in the 1820s. New groups began to reappear in the late 1830s that relied upon widening black enthusiasm for abolitionist work. The New York Association for the Political Elevation and Improvement of the People of Color involved a cross section of New York City blacks in the fight for equal suffrage. Philadelphia's Leavitt Anti-Slavery Society sought to organize the city's working-class blacks. Similar societies appeared in other black communities during the 1840s and 1850s, often dedicated to combating institutional racism. New York City blacks created the Legal Rights Association to coordinate the struggle against segregated streetcars. Under John Mercer Langston's direction, the Ohio State Anti-Slavery Society, a black statewide association, fought slavery and legal barriers to black progress. Formed in 1858, the society supported a central office, sponsored black lecturers, circulated petitions, and distributed antislavery tracts.[65]

The black church took on new importance in the antislavery movement during the 1840s. The growing number of fugitive slave clergymen made black churches more outspoken and militant. Pennington, Ward, Loguen, Garnet, and other black ministers took their slave past and their antislavery values into the pulpit with them. When repri-

---

65. Perlman, "Organizations of the Free Negro," 188–90; *NECAUL*, 17, 24 June 1837; *CA*, 16 June 1838; Blackett, *Beating against the Barriers*, 60–62; William F. Cheek, "John Mercer Langston: Black Protest Leader and Abolitionist," *CWH* 16:115–16 (June 1970).

manded by a white church official for preaching against slavery, Ward
replied that he would continue to use his pulpit "to rebuke *all* sins, and
to plead for righteousness everywhere." The number of northern black
churches dramatically increased, expanding opportunities for antislavery
involvement. Black Baptist churches grew from ten in 1830, to thirty-
four in 1844, and to sixty-four in 1857. The African Methodist Episcopal (AME) denomination spread quickly into New England, Ohio, Indiana, and Canada West, increasing from 86 congregations in 1836 to 296
a decade later. Other denominations founded dozens of black congregations during the same time.[66]

Black churches doubled as antislavery meetinghouses and centers for
organizational activity. They became sites for protest gatherings, lectures, and planning sessions and sometimes housed black presses—Frederick Douglass published the *North Star* in the basement of one of
Rochester's black Methodist churches. Many churches, particularly black
Baptist and African Methodist congregations, were regular stops on the
underground railroad and sanctuaries for fleeing fugitives. In Boston
Rev. Leonard A. Grimes and his Twelfth Baptist Church aided escaping
slaves, planned the rescue of fugitives held by federal authorities, and
raised funds to purchase the freedom of individual slaves. Black churches
included this work as part of their gospel mandate.[67]

Black clergymen forged other religious organizations into vehicles for
abolitionist activity. Nearly every notable black minister involved in the
antislavery movement became a member of the Union Missionary Society, a predominantly black association formed in 1841 at Hartford.
Led by J. W. C. Pennington, Amos G. Beman, Theodore S. Wright, and
other clerics, it sponsored a range of activities that addressed the goals of
black abolitionists—refugee work among fugitive slaves in Canada West,
Charles B. Ray's outreach to the black poor in New York City, and
African missions. After the society joined the American Missionary Association (AMA) in 1846, Pennington, Wright, Cornish, Garnet, and
Amos N. Freeman served as officers, giving the AMA an aggressive anti-
slavery stance not found in other missionary bodies.[68]

66. Samuel Ringgold Ward to John A. Murray, 10 November 1843, AHMS-ARC [4:0700–
701, 0832]; Mechal Sobel, *Trabelin' On: The Slave Journey to an Afro-Baptist Faith*
(Westport, Conn., 1979), 250–55; Daniel A. Payne, *History of the African Methodist
Episcopal Church* (Nashville, Tenn., 1891; reprint, New York, N.Y., 1968), 113, 121–32,
201, 414–17.
67. Carol V. R. George, "Widening the Circle: The Black Church and the Abolitionist
Crusade, 1830–1860," in *Antislavery Reconsidered: New Perspectives on the Abolitionists*,
ed. Lewis Perry and Michael Fellman (Baton Rouge, La., 1979), 75–95; Quarles, *Frederick
Douglass*, 81; *Lib*, 28 August 1846; *CN*, 28 November 1857 [10:0957]; Horton and
Horton, *Black Bostonians*, 47–48; Monroe Fordham, *Major Themes in Northern Black
Religious Thought, 1800–1860* (Hicksville, N.Y., 1975), 11–51.
68. Clara Merritt De Boer, "The Role of Afro-Americans in the Origin and Work of the

During the days when moral reform was the watchword, denominational authorities, missionary associations, and even some congregations had cautioned black clergymen against "preaching politics on the Sabbath." This softly worded phrase expressed a genuine fear that antislavery activities would incite retaliation against black churches. These attacks, including mob violence, had occurred before. In addition, many black denominations had been hesitant to speak against slavery for fear of reprisals against sister churches in the South. Denominational leaders felt less constrained after many of their southern churches were closed down by fearful whites in the panic following the Denmark Vesey conspiracy (1822) and the Nat Turner revolt (1831). By the 1850s abolitionism was such an integral part of the work of most black congregations that denominational approval was assured. The AME and AMEZ churches, the American Baptist Missionary Convention, and the Evangelical Association of the Colored Ministers of Congregational and Presbyterian Churches all adopted strong denunciations of slavery.[69] By then the mission of the church and the work of many of its pastors were inseparable from the goals of black abolitionism.

Black vigilance committees and the underground railroad embodied the black community's expanding abolitionist commitment and its growing independence. Individual blacks had sheltered fugitive slaves since the colonial era, but that informal assistance did not evolve into organized efforts until the 1830s. When unprecedented numbers of fugitives settled in northern cities and kidnappings became commonplace, black communities established permanent vigilance committees. The New York Committee of Vigilance, founded in 1835 and led by David Ruggles, was one of the most ambitious and aggressive. Although white abolitionists provided important assistance, blacks directed the committee and raised most of its operating revenue. It disseminated information about kidnappers and slave catchers; dispensed food, clothing, money, and medicine to fugitives; provided legal services and temporary shelter; and resettled fugitives in the North or provided safe passage to Canada. It exposed official connivance with kidnapping rings by compiling a *Slaveholder's Directory*, giving the names and addresses of police, judges, and city officials who aided in the seizure of fugitives. The committee monitored the city's port facilities to suppress the illegal slave trade; Ruggles risked

American Missionary Association, 1839–1877" (Ph.D. diss., Rutgers University, 1973), 26–79.
69. Samuel Ringgold Ward to John A. Murray, 10 November 1843, AHMS-ARC [4:0700]; Lapsansky, " 'Since They Got Those Separate Churches,' " 62–63; Milton C. Sernett, *Black Religion and American Evangelicalism: White Protestants, Plantation Missions, and the Flowering of Negro Christianity, 1787–1865* (Metuchen, N.J., 1975), 157; Quarles, *Black Abolitionists*, 82.

his life by boarding ships suspected of hiding kidnapping victims or transporting slaves from Africa or the West Indies.[70] Blacks in Philadelphia, Boston, Detroit, and other northern cities organized similar vigilance associations.

Vigilance committees expanded black abolitionist ranks. They worked with other institutions in the community and provided essential roles for all blacks. Fugitive slaves and black sailors—those who faced the greatest danger of incarceration and enslavement—regularly assisted vigilance committees. Black leaders depended on those whom Robert Johnson called "men of over-alls—men of the wharf—those who could do heavy work in the hour of difficulty." Black working women increased their efforts, notifying black leaders of suspicious whites they encountered in hotels, in boardinghouses, and on the street as they went about their daily tasks. Sailors, stevedores, teamsters, and other black workers formed the backbone of committee work by sheltering and transporting fugitives and by relaying crucial information to committees in other cities. Vigilance committee work brought working-class blacks into closer contact with more experienced black abolitionists, such as Robert Purvis and William Whipper, who provided financial resources and organizational skills. Black congregations sheltered fugitives and opened their buildings to committee meetings. Church-affiliated auxiliaries formed by black women raised the bulk of committee operating funds. Benevolent societies collected food and clothing. The New York City committee's public meetings drew hundreds of blacks to hear its reports and heart-wrenching stories from fugitive slaves. Over time, involvement with vigilant committees heightened black awareness of other issues, building support for the independent antislavery institutions that were emerging in the black community.[71]

As vigilance committees developed, they addressed the broad goals of black abolitionism. While assisting fugitives, they also organized petition campaigns for black suffrage, opposed Jim Crow restrictions, and fought

---

70. Foner, *History of Black Americans*, 1:261, 502; *ESF*, 18 January, 29 March 1873; Thomas R. Mosely, "A History of the New York Manumission Society, 1785–1849" (Ph.D. diss., New York University, 1963), 280–81, 355; Winch, "Philadelphia and the Other Underground Railroad," 3–25; Rhoda G. Freeman, "The Free Negro in New York City in the Era before the Civil War" (Ph.D. diss., Columbia University, 1966), 68, 75–76; *AASR*, June 1834; Dorothy B. Porter, "David Ruggles: An Apostle of Human Rights," *JNH* 28:35–37 (January 1943); *ML*, January 1839; *E*, 15 September 1836, 2 March 1837, 1 March 1838 [1:0702, 2:0392–93]; *CA*, 9, 16 May 1840 [3:0412–13, 0425–26].

71. *Lib*, 11 October 1850 [6:0611–12]; *CA*, 22 May 1841 [4:0029]; *First Annual Report of the New York Committee of Vigilance* (New York, N.Y., 1837), 30–33 [1:0835–36]; *ESF*, 11 January 1873; *ML*, July 1838 [2:0510–12]; *E*, 15 December 1836, 1 March 1838 [2:0393]; *CA*, 20 January 1838, 21 August 1841 [2:0354, 4:0163]; John T. Raymond et al. to William Jenks, 27 October 1842, Latimer Papers, MHi [4:0485]; Freeman, "Free Negro in New York City," 71; Horton and Horton, *Black Bostonians*, 97–101, 112, 120.

for passage of personal liberty laws. Detroit's Colored Vigilant Committee promoted temperance and established schools, debating clubs, reading rooms, and literary societies. Committed to protecting the slave, fighting prejudice, and fostering black uplift, vigilance committees illustrated the growing militancy, independence, and effectiveness of black abolitionists and the continued recognition that black rights "could only be gained by our own exertions."[72]

Vigilance committees were part of a skillfully orchestrated network that operated across the North and the upper South. This "underground railroad," as it was often called, was a loosely linked web of northern vigilance committees and groups of southern blacks who smuggled fugitives and rescued slaves from the upper South. It operated without much white aid beyond that provided by a few dedicated Quaker abolitionists like Levi Coffin and Thomas Garrett. James G. Birney reported in 1837 that "such matters are almost uniformly managed by the colored people."[73]

The underground railroad's organization and success varied from time to time and place to place. One network operated out of Ohio during the 1820s and 1830s. These Ohio blacks—many of them former slaves—liberated slaves in Kentucky and systematically aided runaways who came their way. Many fugitives took up temporary residence in urban black communities or in all-black settlements like Carthagena, Ohio, while others traveled on to the refugee communities of Canada West. The Washington, D.C., section of the underground network displayed uncommon daring and design. Beginning in the mid-1830s and continuing for over a decade, Washington blacks freed thousands of slaves from plantations in Virginia and Maryland. Working in a variety of trades and professions—porters in the U.S. Supreme Court, assistants to federal marshals, operators of common carriage services, or itinerant ministers—these bold blacks utilized their good standing in white society to visit plantations, provide slaves with escape information, and shelter fugitives, sometimes on the property of their white employers. Thomas Tilly, a coachman for a federal marshal, held religious services for slaves on Virginia and Maryland plantations, using the ceremonies to encourage escapes and direct fugitives to safe rendezvous points. Jacob R.

72. *CA*, 14 November 1840, 24 July 1841 [3:0707, 4:0123]; *SL*, 23 January 1843 [4:0527–28]; Katherine Dupre Lumpkin, "The General Plan Was Freedom: A Negro Secret Order on the Underground Railroad," *Phy* 28:63–76 (Spring 1967).
73. Quoted in August Meier and Elliott Rudwick, "The Role of Blacks in the Abolitionist Movement," in *Blacks in the Abolitionist Movement*, ed. Bracey, Meier, and Rudwick, 119–21. Larry Gara, *The Liberty Line: The Legend of the Underground Railroad* (Lexington, Ky., 1961), explores the myth that white abolitionists created a sophisticated, well-organized underground network. He suggests the vigorous role that blacks played in assisting fugitives.

Gibbs, a Baltimore painter who may have aided as many as two thousand fugitives, maintained a file of free papers from deceased blacks, which he gave to runaways to insure their safe passage. When one group of fugitive slaves was captured, the Washington network rescued them from a slave pen where they were being held.[74]

Blacks maintained escape routes throughout the North and upper South. Aided by the Washington group, eastern fugitives traveled overland and by sea to Philadelphia through a network of blacks and Quakers in Maryland, Delaware, and New Jersey. The Philadelphia Vigilance Committee directed runaways (nine thousand between 1830 and 1860 by Robert Purvis's account) to contacts along well-established routes to Pittsburgh and New York City. This eastern network was briefly crippled during the late 1840s by race riots, the decline of personal liberty laws, and increased southern vigilance that forced key members from Washington to leave the area.[75]

Outrage over the Fugitive Slave Law of 1850 expanded the black underground and swelled its ranks. Whites joined as never before, believing that the law threatened constitutional order and civil liberties. The increased threat from slave catchers compelled vigilance committees to renew and expand their efforts. Greater central organization was required, and William Still took the lead. As director and treasurer of the General Vigilance Committee of Philadelphia, he managed the committee's finances (which funded Harriet Tubman's work), maintained contacts in the upper South, and channeled runaways to associates in Pennsylvania and New York. Still organized antislavery meetings, printed handbills, provided legal information to allies in the underground, and used the telegraph to facilitate cooperation among the distant and diverse elements of the underground.[76]

74. George Lucas interview, 14 August 1892, John T. Ward interview, 15 June 1892, Catherine Cummings interview, 23 December 1893, Jacob Clawa interview, 5 August 1892, Henry H. Young interview, 3 August 1895, Florence T. Ray and H. Cordelia Ray, "Sketch of the Life of Rev. Charles B. Ray," Thomas Clement Oliver interview, 31 July 1895, Siebert Collection, MH; *ESF*, 15, 22, 29 September, 27 October 1865, 6 September 1867 [16:0199, 0225–26, 0241, 0366]; *PA*, 30 May 1863 [14:0878]; *CR*, 13 July 1854 [8:0920]; Jacob C. White, Jr., "Minute Book of the Vigilant Committee of Philadelphia, 1839–1844," Leon F. Gardiner Collection, PHi [3:0086–111].
75. White, "Minute Book of the Vigilant Committee," Leon F. Gardiner Collection, PHi [3:0086–111]; *ESF*, 9, 15, 22, 29 September, 27 October 1865, 6 September 1867 [16:0199, 0225–26, 0241, 0366]; *PA*, 30 May 1863 [14:0878]; Ray and Ray, "Life of Rev. Charles B. Ray," Siebert Collection, MH; *NSt*, 14 December 1849 [6:0243]; James A. McGowan, *Station Master on the Underground Railroad: The Life and Letters of Thomas Garrett* (Moylan, Pa., 1977), 47, 51–69.
76. William Still, "Journal of the Underground Railroad, 1852–57," Pennsylvania Abolition Society Papers, PHi [7:0879–1034, 9:0172–205]; William Still, *The Underground Railroad* (Philadelphia, Pa., 1872; reprint, Chicago, Ill., 1970), 20–25, 40–41, 91, 387, 635–36, 742, 764–67.

4. Samuel D. Burris, a leader of the Washington, D.C.,
underground network
From William Still, *Underground Railroad* (Philadelphia, 1872)

As black abolitionists shaped a bolder and more autonomous movement in the 1840s and 1850s, they developed new measures to combat
racism and forced the issue of slavery to the center of American political life. They challenged discrimination and oppression wherever they
found it, using petition campaigns, legal action, legislative appeals,
and economic pressure; when those tactics failed, more confrontational
methods, including violence, found favor. No longer believing that good
works or moral suasion alone could advance their goals, a majority of
black antislavery leaders turned to political action. The struggle for suffrage and acceptance of politics as a primary antislavery weapon embodied the new spirit of independence. Black leaders asserted that the
franchise—"the life blood of political existence"—would secure all their
social and religious institutions. The vote meant political power, and that
power, the *Colored American* declared in 1839, was "a mighty Anti-
Slavery engine."[77]

With the splintering of the antislavery movement and the rise of anti-
slavery politics in the late 1830s, black abolitionists began to invest their
energies and place their hopes in political action. Just as moral reform
and moral suasion once defined black abolitionism, politics now dominated the thinking of black leaders. Politics and the franchise offered
blacks their best hope for achieving equality and ending slavery. The
promise of politics became so persuasive after the 1830s that even most
black Garrisonians voted where permitted. Blacks formed political organizations, ran for state and local offices, and rallied black voters to force
state governments to recognize their rights and address their grievances.
Enfranchisement was the primary goal of black state conventions of the
1840s and 1850s. From the pulpit, in the press, and at black conventions, most black leaders insisted that blacks had "a right and are bound
in conscience, *to use the ballot box*."[78]

The quest for the franchise that began during the late 1830s drew
blacks into antislavery politics. At first blacks regarded voting rights
primarily as a goal in itself—an affirmation of citizenship and a mark of
racial equality. But by the 1840s, black suffrage had become a means to
achieve a range of antislavery objectives. Although blacks failed to expand the suffrage in New York and gained it only in Rhode Island, their
efforts kept civil rights before the public and forced state legislatures
across the North to consider the issue. The very act of petitioning state
legislatures for the vote asserted black rights. Moreover, blacks gained
leadership and organizational experience, which they employed in the
political party battles of the 1850s and in their struggle for enfranchisement during Reconstruction.[79]

77. *CA*, 17 August 1839, 21 November 1840 [3:0714–15].
78. *CA*, 24 November 1838 [2:0660]; Pease and Pease, *They Who Would Be Free*, 175–90.
79. Foner, *History of Black Americans*, 2:341–46; *Lib*, 23 October 1857 [10:0868]; Ste-

Blacks undertook suffrage campaigns in nearly every northern state. Black leaders petitioned, organized suffrage associations, testified before legislative committees, lobbied legislators, distributed printed appeals, and rallied the black community through the black press. The new direction was unmistakable. Black leaders launched suffrage drives in Michigan, Iowa, Indiana, Ohio, Connecticut, and New York. Blacks won the franchise in Wisconsin through a referendum in 1849, although it was quickly reversed by a state electoral commission. Pennsylvania blacks sent eighty-one separate suffrage petitions to the state legislature between 1839 and 1851. New York blacks developed an extensive suffrage organization at the state, county, and local levels, which included sixty-six black suffrage clubs in New York City and Brooklyn in 1860. Under the direction of Henry Highland Garnet, blacks distributed thousands of pamphlets across the state, some of which were printed in German and French to reach immigrant voters.[80]

Most black leaders recognized the importance of political action at the national level but disagreed over which party—Whig, Liberty, Free Soil, or Republican—could best fight slavery and advance civil rights. Political purists clashed with pragmatists over the relative merits of the Liberty and Whig parties. Purists like Samuel Ringgold Ward argued that no black in good conscience could vote for a party like the Whigs that sustained slavery and opposed racial equality. According to Ward, blacks should place their votes only where slavery and prejudice would be attacked and black goals would be defended. More pragmatic-minded abolitionists like the stalwart journalist Samuel Cornish saw no use "in creating for ourselves a political standard of *imaginary perfection*, and cut off the heads of all, who come not up to it." Ward's position might satisfy an abolitionist's conscience, Cornish declared, but it meant that "loss of influence, disenfranchisement and defeat will, assuredly follow such a course." Black political allegiances shifted along the unstable ground of antebellum politics and varied from state to state, but they

---

phen Myers to Gerrit Smith, 22 March 1856, Gerrit Smith Papers, NSyU [10:0085–86]; Richard H. Sewell, *Ballots for Freedom: Antislavery Politics in the United States, 1837–1860* (New York, N.Y., 1976), 178, 184–86.
80. *CA*, 11 March 1837, 5, 12 December 1840, 13 February, 16 October 1841 [1:1002, 3:0734, 0750, 0883–84, 4:0265]; Joel Schor, *Henry Highland Garnet: A Voice of Black Radicalism in the Nineteenth Century* (Westport, Conn., 1977), 32–76; Philip S. Foner and George E. Walker, eds., *Proceedings of the Black State Conventions, 1840–1865*, 2 vols. (Philadelphia, Pa., 1979–80), 1:5–41, 106–17, 181–95, 2:3–6, 20–34; Ronald P. Formisano, "The Edge of Caste: Colored Suffrage in Michigan, 1827–1861," *MH* 56:24–28 (Spring 1972); Charles H. Wesley, *Neglected History: Essays in Negro History by a College President* (Wilberforce, Ohio, 1965), 58–59, 69; Sewell, *Ballots for Freedom*, 178; James McCune Smith to Stephen Myers, 21 September 1860, James McCune Smith to Gerrit Smith, 20 October 1860, Gerrit Smith Papers, NSyU [12:1017–18, 1044–46].

steadfastly opposed the Democratic party, the political symbol of slavery and racial hatred.[81]

Black abolitionists were optimistic over the prospect that the Whig, Liberty, and Free Soil parties would advance at least some of their goals. The rise of an antislavery political party, the adoption of some antislavery goals by the national parties, and the election of abolitionists like Joshua Giddings and Gerrit Smith to Congress persuaded blacks that profound changes were taking place. During the 1830s, few blacks would have predicted that American political parties would run black men for office, yet in the 1840s and 1850s that occurred. In 1848 the Liberty party selected Samuel Ringgold Ward for a state assembly seat and in 1855 named Frederick Douglass as its candidate for New York secretary of state. The Massachusetts Free Soil party nominated William C. Nell for the state legislature in 1850 and two years later ran Robert Morris for mayor of Boston. In 1855 John Mercer Langston won election as an Ohio town clerk on a third-party ticket. Black office seekers garnered only a few successes, but the symbolism of their candidacies fostered black pride and enthusiasm for the political process. The *New York Tribune*'s speculation that the Whigs might run Frederick Douglass for Congress suggests the extent to which black abolitionism had reached into American political life.[82]

Blacks understood that politics offered them limited possibilities; they had too few votes to affect national policy. Still, they gained some political influence at the state and local level. Rhode Island Whigs made direct appeals for the black vote, claiming that their opposition to the expansion of slavery and their support for black suffrage required that blacks "support the party which supported you; give your votes for the men who gave you the right to vote." Where they could vote in sufficient numbers to effect a swing vote between the Democrats and the Whigs, blacks achieved some political goals, such as striking down discriminatory legislation, attacking institutional racism, and passing personal liberty laws. In New Bedford, Massachusetts, blacks held "the balance of power, and hence exert[ed] a potent influence on election day." Blacks cooperated with radical Whigs and Free Soilers in Ohio to eliminate several of the state's most offensive black laws in 1849. Black New Yorkers were the most successful of all. Their votes helped elect Whig

81. *NSt*, 1 September 1848; *CA*, 17 November 1838 [2:0654]; James McCune Smith to Gerrit Smith, 12 May 1848, Gerrit Smith Papers, NSyU [5:0633–34]; Pease and Pease, *They Who Would Be Free*, 173–76, 183–87, 195; Foner, *History of Black Americans*, 3:211–12, 272–79; Quarles, *Black Abolitionists*, 168–74.
82. J. W. C. Pennington to Gerrit Smith, 6–7 November 1852, Gerrit Smith Papers, NSyU [7:0821–23]; *FDP*, 23 September 1848, 23 June 1854, 20 April 1855 [5:0793–94, 10:0085–86]; *Lib*, 14 July, 25 August 1854; Wesley, *Neglected History*, 74–75; Horton and Horton, *Black Bostonians*, 87.

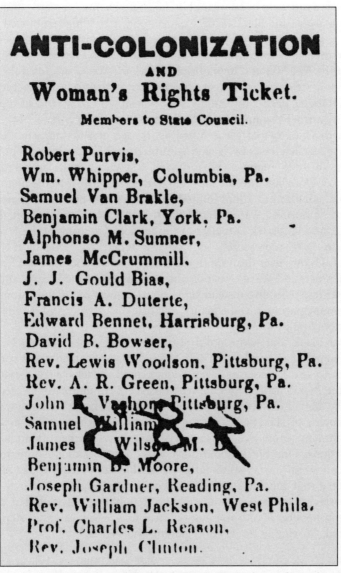

5. Anti-Colonization and Woman's Rights ticket

From Langston Hughes, Milton Meltzer, and C. Eric Lincoln, eds., *A Pictorial History of Blackamericans*, 5th rev. ed. (New York, 1973)

governors and were instrumental in defeating Democrat ward candidates
in New York City. Black leaders understood that Whigs embraced some
black issues because of local, sectional, and constitutional questions
rather than any commitment to racial equality. Nevertheless, until the
rise of the Free Soil and Republican parties, the Whigs attracted the most
black political support and gave blacks most of their political victories.[83]

The Liberty party's unbending abolitionism and commitment to racial
equality attracted numerous black leaders, especially in New York state.
When the Liberty party ran Ward as its vice presidential candidate in
1850, black leaders saw it as a confirmation of their faith in political
action. In 1848 many New York and Massachusetts blacks followed
Frederick Douglass into the Free Soil party, accepting it as the first major
political coalition to adopt limited antislavery principles. The participation of Samuel R. Ward, Henry Bibb, Henry Highland Garnet, Lewis
Clarke, and Frederick Douglass at the founding meeting of the Free Soil
party in 1848 represented, as Douglass remarked, "one of the most
powerful blows ever dealt upon the skull of American prejudice." Douglass, Garnet, and Ward overlooked the weakness of the Liberty and Free
Soil parties, reflecting instead on their usefulness as organizations that
gave emancipation, racial equality, and black leaders a conspicuous place
in national politics.[84]

Most black and white political abolitionists joined the newly organized Republican party in the mid-1850s. They welcomed it as a counter-
weight to the Democrats, even though many blacks were dissatisfied
with the Republican party's limited antislavery commitment—a pledge to
halt the spread of slavery in the territories. For blacks the issue was not
the growth of slavery but its very existence. Furthermore, the party's
commitment to enforce the Fugitive Slave Law mocked its antislavery
pretensions. One black abolitionist wrote in 1860 that Abraham Lincoln's views on slavery were indistinguishable from Henry Clay's, and he
predicted that Lincoln's presidency would simply be another in a series
of proslavery administrations. Yet the Republican party offered blacks
the only possibility of obtaining political power—an essential step, they
believed, for ending slavery and gaining civil rights.[85]

83. *NASS*, 27 March 1851 [6:0864–65]; A. J. Anderson to William C. Nell, 22 February
1860, Anti-Slavery Collection, MB [12:0507–508]; William C. Nell, *The Colored Patriots
of the American Revolution* (Boston, Mass., 1855; reprint, Salem, N.H., 1986), 111–12;
Sewell, *Ballots for Freedom*, 180–81; Wesley, *Neglected History*, 60, 69.
84. *LS*, 14 September 1843 [4:0669]; John J. Zuille et al. to [Gerrit Smith], 13 June 1845,
Gerrit Smith Papers, NSyU [5:0052–53]; *NSt*, 11 August, 1 September 1848; *FDP*, 26
August 1853 [8:0419–20]; *NASS*, 27 March 1851 [6:0864–65]; Quarles, *Black Abolitionists*, 180–86.
85. Quarles, *Black Abolitionists*, 187–90; Foner, *History of Black Americans*, 3:276–79;
FDP, 9 November 1855 [9:0925]; *Lib*, 5 September 1856, 13 July 1860 [10:0285]; *WAA*,
22 December 1860.

For black abolitionists, the realignment of American political parties in the 1840s and 1850s generated optimism and renewed their faith in the self-correcting capacity of a democratic society. Blacks attempted to make the political system an agent of their abolitionism by demanding voting rights and by alternately courting and chastising the political parties. Victories were few. Political power was slow in coming. But the unprecedented opportunities for political involvement open to blacks gave new direction to their abolitionism and new definition to their leadership and helped prepare them for the rigorous political challenges of Reconstruction.

At the same time, black abolitionists called for more militant tactics and aggressive measures to attack the Jim Crow barriers that plagued their daily life. William J. Watkins's command to "agitate, and *agitate*, and AGITATE" was a welcome call for many blacks as they battled prejudice and racist practices in American society. This call to militancy permeated black abolitionism, renewing the movement and opening the way for more assertive action. Nearly every aspect of black life and culture was now included in the definition of black abolitionism, and no tactic was exempt from consideration. Throughout the 1840s and 1850s, blacks challenged American institutions that excluded them—schools, hospitals, hotels and restaurants, voting booths, courts, and militias. They protested with petition campaigns, legal action, legislative appeals, and economic pressure, and when those tactics failed, individual black abolitionists sometimes found confrontation the most practical alternative. Blacks persuaded some northern businesses, state and local governments, and school boards to abandon Jim Crow practices. Although these victories were slow, infrequent, and often personal, they were important. Douglass explained that "as one rises, all must rise."[86]

Blacks challenged Jim Crow practices on railroads and streetcars in nearly every northern state. They organized mass protests, conducted petition campaigns, and testified before state legislative committees. They sat in cars reserved for whites, which sometimes led to violence and bloodshed. Massachusetts blacks, with the cooperation of sympathetic whites like Wendell Phillips, John A. Collins, and Ellis Gray Loring, organized a widespread campaign during the early 1840s to end segregated seating on the state's three major rail lines. Dozens of black abolitionists—including David Ruggles, Frederick Douglass, William C. Nell, Thomas Jinnings, Charles L. Remond, and Mary Newhall Green—forced officials to eject them from white cars. When that failed, blacks and whites boycotted the rail systems. In early 1843, Massachusetts railroads

86. *FDP*, 26 August 1853 [8:0420]; *ASB*, 23 April 1859 [11:0698]; Foner, *History of Black Americans*, 2:346–47; *Lib*, 4 April 1851, 21 November 1856 [6:0875, 10:0382]; Philip S. Foner, ed., *The Life and Writings of Frederick Douglass*, 5 vols. (New York, N.Y., 1950–75), 1:331–35.

abandoned their discriminatory practices. The protests were organized over the objections of Garrisonians who opposed confrontational tactics, but the results, earned at great personal risk, validated the new direction of black abolitionism.[87]

Segregated schools became special targets of black militancy during the 1840s. For many black leaders, separate schools symbolized the institutionalized prejudice that encouraged black acceptance of racism and crushed black aspirations. Individual protests abounded. Possessed with family wealth and an education from Amherst College, Robert Purvis refused to pay property taxes as long as his children were denied equal access to public education on account of their color. William Wells Brown—author, lecturer, and fugitive slave—kept his daughters out of a Jim Crow school rather than give "sanction to the proscriptive prejudice." Organized boycotts met with mixed success in Buffalo, Albany, Rochester, and Kinderhook, New York, and ended Jim Crow education in Massachusetts. Between 1842 and 1845, blacks used boycotts and petition campaigns to integrate schools in Lowell, New Bedford, Salem, Worcester, and Nantucket. In Boston William C. Nell led a decade-long protest movement that gained the support of influential whites like Charles Sumner. Blacks used mass meetings, editorials, picketing, a boycott, and legal action—the unsuccessful *Roberts* v. *Boston* case (1849)— to pressure local officials. The boycott lowered black school attendance by 80 percent as parents organized makeshift classrooms or transported their children to schools in outlying towns. The Massachusetts legislature succumbed to the continued pressure in 1855 and mandated integrated education throughout the state. This victory sparked campaigns against other segregated school systems.[88]

These victories, sometimes small or temporary, had a larger meaning. Each success confirmed the utility of the bolder tactics that black abolitionists favored during the 1840s, demonstrating that direct action could succeed where moral suasion had failed. Looking back at the Massachusetts railroad desegregation campaign, one participant concluded that they had won that battle because blacks had "frequently gone into the cars intended only for white passengers and allowed ourselves to be

87. *FDP*, 5 October 1855 [9:0861]; *E*, 5 July 1848 [5:0697]; *Lib*, 25 February 1842 [4:0370]; Louis Ruchames, "Jim Crow Railroads in Massachusetts," *AQ* 8:62–74 (Spring 1956); Mabee, *Black Freedom*, 115–25; Blackett, *Beating against the Barriers*, 59–62.
88. *PF*, 10 November 1853 [8:0471]; William E. Farrison, *William Wells Brown: Author and Reformer* (Chicago, Ill., 1969), 93–94; Mabee, *Black Education in New York*, 182–88; Arthur O. White, "Salem's Antebellum Black Community: Seedbed of the School Integration Movement," *EIHC* 108:110–14 (April 1972); Stanley K. Schultz, *The Culture Factory: Boston Public Schools, 1789–1860* (New York, N.Y., 1973), 157–206; George T. Downing to William H. Seward, 9 February 1857, Seward Papers, NRU [10:0539].

beaten and dragged out."[89] The growing recognition by black abolitionists was that militant action worked.

As black abolitionists explored an ever-widening range of tactics, they debated the value of violence. For black Americans, the use of force was not simply a philosophical or moral question but a practical matter when facing racist mobs, kidnappers, and slave catchers in growing numbers. Even during the 1830s, when most black abolitionists advocated moral suasion, there were those who justified self-defense, even armed violence, in response to slavery and oppression. The black community rarely hesitated to use force to protect home, family, or friends. During the 1834 riots in New York City, William Hamilton armed himself with "iron missiles" and pledged to die defending his home. Philadelphia blacks took up firearms during the 1835 riots. Three years later, members of the Bethel AME Church tore up the cobblestones in front of the church and piled them inside as weapons to repel attackers. The so-called Boston "Abolition Riot" of 1836 took place when local black women rushed a courtroom, seized two fugitives by force, and whisked them to safety.[90]

Black leaders openly advocated the use of force in self-defense during the 1840s. Their tolerance for physical resistance was the result of thoughtful reflection and hard experience. Many black abolitionists abandoned nonresistance when they began working apart from mainstream white abolitionists and their ideas. The pacificism of the Garrisonians was increasingly irrelevant, and public remarks about violent means became less guarded. The shift away from nonresistance was more than a debate over antislavery ideology or a change in personal style; practical matters were involved. Often abused for their message as well as their race, black abolitionists accepted force as a reasonable way to protect themselves and their property. Nonresistants like Henry C. Wright might counsel abolitionists to return "a kiss for every blow," but fugitive slaves were more inclined to use force when the situation demanded. Black leaders now had little patience with anyone who "recommend[ed] non-resistance to persons who are denied the protection of equitable law." The U.S. Supreme Court left blacks with few alternatives. In *Prigg* v. *Pennsylvania* (1842), the Court struck down state personal liberty laws, removing what little legal protection was available to blacks accused of being fugitive slaves. Reacting to the ruling, Samuel R. Ward —himself a fugitive subject to recapture—concluded that blacks could "do nothing but give physical resistance." By the end of the decade, even

89. *NSt*, 22 June 1849.
90. *AAM*, October 1859, 306; Mifflin W. Gibbs, *Shadow and Light: An Autobiography* (Washington, D.C., 1902), 19–20; Still, *Underground Railroad*, 723–36; Horton and Horton, *Black Bostonians*, 98.

committed black Garrisonians like Charles L. Remond and William Wells Brown tolerated forceful self-defense. Brown admitted he could hardly "counsel non-resistance or act upon its principles."[91]

Black abolitionists were more circumspect on the issue of slave violence. After deferring to the Garrisonian position during the 1830s, black leaders began to sympathize openly with slave revolts in the 1840s. They celebrated slave rebels as cultural heroes and distributed copies of their portraits. Black speakers invoked the names of Denmark Vesey, Nat Turner, Joseph Cinqué of the *Amistad* mutiny (1839), and Madison Washington of the *Creole* uprising (1841), comparing these insurrectionary leaders to America's "Revolutionary fathers." Henry Highland Garnet's "Address to the Slaves," given at the 1843 black national convention, marked a turning point in the black antislavery appeal. It advocated massive civil disobedience and proclaimed that it was the slaves' "SOLEMN AND IMPERATIVE DUTY TO USE EVERY MEANS, BOTH MORAL, INTELLECTUAL, AND PHYSICAL THAT PROMISES SUCCESS." Many black abolitionists distanced themselves from Garnet's endorsement of slave violence, but by the 1850s, few of them denied the slaves' right to fight for their freedom. Events of that decade proved that slavery was too entrenched to be brought down by peaceful means.[92]

The enactment of the Fugitive Slave Law of 1850 provoked a widespread, emotionally charged response. William P. Powell, whose aggressive public statements about slavery and racism matched his antislavery style, charged that the federal government had "declared war" on northern blacks. Disgusted by the Fugitive Slave Law, Powell soon left for England, returning only when civil war appeared certain. Black abolitionists recognized that the law threatened all blacks, not just fugitive slaves, with arbitrary arrest and enslavement. As federal agents, slave catchers, and kidnappers invaded northern black communities, nonresistance no longer seemed morally defensible, let alone practical. Ward argued that blacks had the choice of "dying freemen, or living slaves."[93]

91. Dick, *Black Protest*, 130–33; Pease and Pease, *They Who Would Be Free*, 233–35; Augustus W. Hanson to William Lloyd Garrison, 3 November 1838, Anti-Slavery Collection, MB [2:0629–30]; Schor, *Henry Highland Garnet*, 53; Samuel R. Ward to Gerrit Smith, 18 April 1842, Gerrit Smith Papers, NSyU [4:0424]; *Lib*, 9 July 1847; Farrison, *William Wells Brown*, 124.
92. Henry Highland Garnet, *The Past and Present Condition, and the Destiny, of the Colored Race: A Discourse* (Troy, N.Y., 1848), 16 [5:0585]; Henry Highland Garnet, "An Address to the Slaves of the United States of America," in *Walker's Appeal, with a Brief Sketch of His Life* (New York, N.Y., 1848), 95 [5:0545–48]; *NSt*, 16 June 1848, 18 May 1849 [5:0679, 1092]; *CA*, 27 March, 17 April 1841 [3:0963–64, 0993]; *NASS*, 18 July 1844, 18 March 1847, 3 May 1849 [4:0884, 5:0394, 1076].
93. *Lib*, 11 October 1850.

Blacks reacted with a unity and vigor not seen since the colonization threat of the 1820s, manifesting their anger and defiance in mass meetings throughout the North during the fall of 1850. The protesters adopted a threefold strategy of resistance, rescue, and repeal. The "bowie knife and the revolver," not moral suasion, symbolized the black response. Fifteen hundred people packed a New York City African Methodist Episcopal Zion Church to hear black speakers brush aside Garrisonian pleas for nonresistance and invoke the right of self-defense. At Boston's First Independent Baptist Church, Joshua B. Smith brandished weapons at the podium to demonstrate the proper greeting for slave catchers. Syracuse blacks vowed to resist the law "with daggers in our belts." Numerous black gatherings affirmed the right of collective self-defense and resolved to rescue anyone arrested as a fugitive slave. Vigilance committees were quickly organized in Cleveland, Syracuse, Boston, Springfield (Massachusetts), and other cities. In New York City, the call went out to form a local black militia. Throughout the North, black abolitionists organized petition campaigns to urge the repeal of the "bloodhound bill" and the passage of new personal liberty laws.[94]

The federal government's proslavery actions of the 1850s strengthened black antislavery commitment. Black denominations no longer equivocated. The AME church, previously cautious in its official pronouncements, now charged that "the slave power is bent on its course of systematic oppression and injustice towards our race." Local black congregations mobilized to protect members threatened by the Fugitive Slave Law. Underground railroad operations were revived and expanded. Even in Garrison's hometown, blacks armed themselves, barricaded their homes, and attacked anyone bent on enforcing the Fugitive Slave Law. Black lecturers reported a growing public interest in antislavery. Jermain W. Loguen, fugitive slave and leader of the Syracuse underground railroad, reported that he could meet only half of the requests for his lecture services. "Nothing in the world is so good for the slave as the Kansas-Nebraska bill," insisted the militant Loguen. Blacks perceived a polarization of sentiment, a sharpening of distinctions between slavery and abolitionism. Whites who were once apathetic became convinced that the South was threatening constitutional liberties with the Fugitive Slave Law and increasing sectional tensions by expanding slavery into new territory. As they began to win the battle for northern public opinion, black abolitionists experienced a renewed feeling of optimism. Blacks had long argued that their struggle was one for universal freedom, that

94. *Lib*, 20 September, 4, 11 October 1850, 4 April 1851 [6:0581, 0598, 0611–13, 0875]; *IC*, 28 September, 26 October 1850 [6:0589, 0652]; *SDS*, 24 September 1850 [6:0586]; *SJ*, 19 October 1850 [6:0620]; *PF*, 31 October 1850 [6:0657]; *NASS*, 10, 31 October 1850 [6:0606–11, 0655].

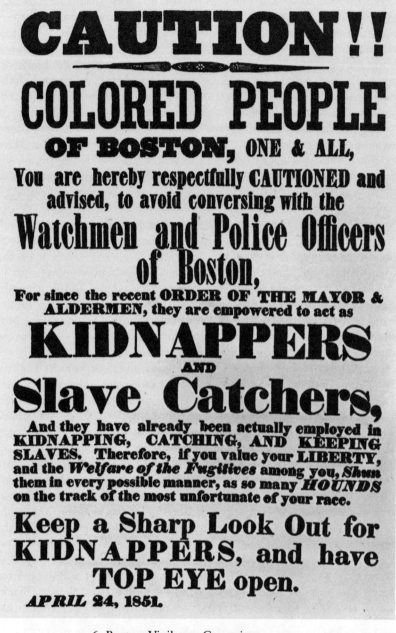

6. Boston Vigilance Committee poster

to restrict the rights of a minority was to jeopardize the rights of all. Now they eagerly awaited a swelling of the abolitionist ranks.[95]

But black abolitionist optimism over the growing interest in the slavery question could not mask the disheartening effects of federal policy. Black Americans had long understood how, in John Mercer Langston's words, slavery reached into "every crevice and cranny of society." Starting in the late 1840s, the Mexican War and the expansion of slavery into new western territories had caused black abolitionists to focus more closely on the relationship between slavery and the federal government. They saw disturbing evidence of the national government's complicity with the slaveholder's interests. Joseph C. Holly denounced the "unhallowed connection and criminality of the North in relation to slavery, and the effects of that institution on the rights and interests of the North." Events of the 1850s—the Fugitive Slave Law, the Kansas-Nebraska Act, attempts to annex Cuba as a slave territory, the campaign to reopen the African slave trade, and the Dred Scott decision—further revealed the domination of proslavery forces over the federal government. Slavery's growing sway over American political life created a crisis in the black community, eventually forcing black leaders to question the progress of the antislavery cause and their place in American society. "We are slaves in the midst of freedom," wrote Martin R. Delany in 1852. The optimism that followed the surge of abolitionist activity after passage of the Fugitive Slave Law faded by the mid-1850s, and each new proslavery victory deepened the alienation felt by many blacks. The westward expansion of slavery, the southern dream of a slaveholding empire in the Caribbean, and efforts to reopen the African slave trade all seemed to indicate a reversal of twenty years of antislavery progress. Delegates at the 1855 black national convention concluded that "there is no foot of American Territory over which slavery is not already triumphant."[96]

The Dred Scott decision all but destroyed black hopes. In *Dred Scott* v. *Sanford* (1857), the Supreme Court affirmed the constitutionality of slavery and denied all blacks any claim to American citizenship. Decades of state and local discrimination now had federal constitutional sanction. William Still concluded that the decision was "more discouraging and more prostrating to the hopes of the colored man than any preceding act

95. Payne, *African Methodist Episcopal Church*, 307; Sobel, *Trabelin' On*, 217; Blackett, *Beating against the Barriers*, 92; FDP, 11 August 1851, 10 June 1852, 3, 24 March, 14 April 1854 [7:0067, 0622, 8:0670, 0694–95, 0734]; VF, 23 April 1851, 18 November 1852 [6:0907, 7:0829].
96. NASS, 19 May 1855 [9:0658]; NSt, 12 May 1848 [5:0635]; David Brion Davis, *The Slave Power Conspiracy and the Paranoid Style* (Baton Rouge, La., 1969), 62–86; Delany, *Condition of the Colored People*, 155; *Proceedings of the Colored National Convention, Held in Philadelphia, October 16th, 17th, and 18th, 1855* (Salem, N.J., 1856), 32 [9:0894].

of tyranny."[97] The bitterness was palpable. In denouncing the decision, black leaders referred time and time again to Chief Justice Roger B. Taney's devastating obiter dictum—blacks "had no rights which the white man was bound to respect."

The federal government's acquiescence to proslavery forces in the 1850s compelled black abolitionists to rethink fundamental questions about identity and race. Working through the crosscurrents of protest and resignation, blacks debated their future as American citizens. They revived well-worn debates over the sources of prejudice. Yet after the experiences of two decades, neither their condition nor their complexion seemed adequate to account for the intractability of American racism. Neither moral reform nor political action seemed a sufficient solution. Charles L. Remond, surveying twenty-five years of antislavery efforts, judged them "complete failures." Blacks who defended the antislavery character of the Constitution found their position increasingly difficult to sustain against H. Ford Douglas, Robert Purvis, and others who repudiated it as a proslavery document. In the wake of the Dred Scott decision, Remond bitterly questioned black devotion to the American nation. "The time has gone by for colored people to talk of patriotism," he declared; "we owe no allegiance to a country which grinds us under its iron heel and treats us like dogs."[98]

The crisis of the 1850s revived black interest in emigration. Although a strong sense of American identity kept most blacks at home, proposals for black settlement beyond the United States had appeared intermittently for decades. Haiti, Jamaica, Trinidad, and other locations had attracted the interest of some black leaders, but they never received widespread support. The specter of colonization made blacks suspicious of an organized exodus. Only Canada, the most accessible sanctuary for fugitive slaves, drew significant numbers of black settlers.[99]

The Fugitive Slave Law clarified the emigration issue for many blacks. Fugitive slaves could either flee the country or live in perpetual fear of the slave catcher. Faced with these alternatives, thousands crossed over the Canadian border, while others left for Britain, Africa, and the Caribbean. This included many fugitives who had been prominent in the abolitionist crusade. Samuel Ringgold Ward, Jermain W. Loguen, and Henry Bibb took refuge in Canada West. William and Ellen Craft, Henry "Box" Brown, and Henry Highland Garnet went to England. Although the

97. *PFW*, 28 March 1857 [10:0596].

98. *NASS*, 23 May 1857 [10:0717]; *FDP*, 3 November 1854, 2 February, 8 June, 31 August 1855 [9:0206, 0420, 0687, 0817]; *Minutes of the State Convention of the Colored Citizens of Ohio* (Columbus, Ohio, 1851), 8–11 [6:0742–43]; *Lib*, 21 May 1858 [11:0227].

99. For a survey of the black emigration movement in the antebellum period, see Floyd J. Miller, *The Search for a Black Nationality: Black Emigration and Colonization, 1787–1863* (Urbana, Ill., 1975).

numbers cannot be precisely determined, reports from underground railroad stations along the Canadian border indicate that this was the largest expatriate movement in American history.[100]

Advocates of emigration placed the departure in a positive light. In *The Condition, Elevation, Emigration and Destiny of the Colored People of the United States* (1852), Martin R. Delany set the tone. He recognized the antislavery value of free black progress but concluded that since racial prejudice made advancement impossible in the United States, blacks should emigrate to Latin America or the Caribbean. Delany, the most important theorist of black nationalism and emigration, called for the creation of an independent black nation. He later became intrigued with the possibilities for West African settlement. After organizing the Niger Valley Exploring Party in 1858, he led an expedition to the region and negotiated with local African rulers for land. Garnet soon followed Delany's proposal by establishing the African Civilization Society, which envisioned black American settlers bringing Christianity, civilization, and commerce to Africa. James T. Holly shared the goal of a black, Christian nationality, but chose Haiti as the location. He believed that the task for black Americans was "raising a Nationality in Haiti—*to prove that in America, there Shall Be No Geography in Liberty! No Distinctions in Race or Nationality.*" The idea of a model black republic in Haiti had a strong appeal for many black Americans. With active recruiters and generous subsidies from the Haitian government, the Haitian immigration movement developed to the point of establishing settlements.[101]

The concept of black nationhood gave emigration an antislavery character. Uriah Boston anticipated that racial prejudice would end when Africa became "a great, powerful, Christian, commercial and industrial nation." James Whitfield believed that slaveholders would fear a black nation in the Caribbean. "The existence of an independent community of negroes upon their southern frontier," he insisted, "is a dangerous example to be held out to their slaves." Both Delany and Garnet hoped to strengthen the antislavery quality of a black nation by introducing the economic weapon of cotton produced by free labor in Africa.[102]

Emigrationists implicitly accepted the moral reformers' argument that condition, not color, caused racial prejudice. Blacks of the 1830s were urged to develop strong moral character and mental skills in order to refute racist arguments. Twenty years later, emigrationists urged blacks to build their own nation for the same reason. By arguing that a power-

100. Ripley et al., *Black Abolitionist Papers*, 2:9–11, 25–28, 193.
101. *WAA*, 27 April 1861 [13:0481]; Miller, *Search for a Black Nationality*, 170–249.
102. *FDP*, 15 November 1853, 27 January 1854, 19 January 1855 [8:0499–501, 0626–27, 9:0393]; Miller, *Search for a Black Nationality*, 219–20.

ful, vibrant black nation would undermine American slavery and racism, emigrationists placed the ideas of moral reform in an international, anti-slavery context.

Black leaders divided over the antislavery value of emigration. For Frederick Douglass, J. W. C. Pennington, George T. Downing, James McCune Smith, and their allies, leaving the country meant forsaking the antislavery struggle, the slave, and any claims to American citizenship. Throughout the North, black communities gathered to oppose emigration programs. New Bedford blacks denounced emigration as "abandoning homes and enslaved brethren, gratifying negro-haters at the North and slavery propagandists at the South." Blacks warned that leaving the country served "only to embolden our oppressors to renew efforts to pass those *hellish black laws*." Calls for a black nationality left most observers unconvinced. Joseph C. Holly disagreed with his brother James's assertion that blacks could only develop a "true type of manhood" under their own sovereignty. Like other antiemigrationists, he argued that the only way to gain respect was to stay and fight for emancipation.[103]

Most black abolitionists resolved to remain in the United States. William Still spoke for the majority when he wrote black friends in Canada West that "the duty to *stay here and fight it out* seems paramount." But like many antiemigrationists of the late 1850s, he stayed with little hope that circumstances would soon improve.[104] Black leaders shared a sense of alienation and despair. A few prominent antiemigrationists even seemed on the verge of accepting the emigration argument: William Whipper prepared to leave for Canada West, William J. Watkins embraced settlement in Haiti, and Frederick Douglass made plans to visit that Caribbean island. But John Brown's raid and the coming of the Civil War interrupted many of these planned departures. After a decade of pessimism and defeat, violence brought new hope.

On 16 October 1859, John Brown led twenty-one men in an unsuccessful attempt to seize the federal arsenal at Harpers Ferry in western Virginia. Five blacks—Shields Green, Osborne P. Anderson, Dangerfield Newby, Lewis S. Leary, and John Copeland, Jr.—fought with him. Brown obtained some funds and other support from black abolitionists and, with better preparation, might have been joined by black militia units from Ohio and Canada West. But most black leaders hesitated to join Brown's campaign. The secrecy and the uncertainty of his plans worried many potential enlistees. Several black abolitionists—Douglass, Delany, William Howard Day, William Lambert, James N. Gloucester, Jermain

103. *FDP*, 22 October 1852, 28 October, 18 November 1853 [7:0797, 8:0463, 0493]; *WAA*, 16 February 1861 [13:0325, 0332].
104. *PFW*, 28 March 1857 [10:0596].

W. Loguen, Harriet Tubman, and others—sympathized with Brown's intentions but feared the retribution whites would unleash upon their
families and upon free blacks. Moreover, they distrusted white authority.
James McCune Smith and George DeBaptiste, who proposed more violent schemes than Brown's, wanted "no help from white men." [105]

Even though Brown failed, the raid riveted the nation's attention on
the issue of slavery. It raised black hopes and refocused abolitionist concern squarely on the "paramount question." In the wake of Brown's trial
and execution, blacks elevated the martyr to the status of an insurrectionary hero. He represented a fusion of militant abolitionism with
America's Revolutionary heritage. J. Sella Martin explained that the only
difference between the Revolution and Brown's act was that "in America,
means have been used for *white* men. . . . John Brown has used his
means for *black* men." The raid sparked a degree of interracial unity not
seen in the antislavery movement since the early days of William Lloyd
Garrison. The commemorative ceremonies that followed Brown's execution brought thousands of whites and blacks together, united in their
veneration of Brown and his actions. [106]

For black abolitionists, the Harpers Ferry raid signaled slavery's imminent demise and renewed black militancy. Buoyed by the raid, black
abolitionists intensified their calls for slave rebellion and armed revolt
against the South. They saw in Brown the "merciless whirlwinds of
God's indignation"—he had died for white sins and had sacrificed himself for black freedom. [107] Most black abolitionists, now convinced that
only violence could end slavery, believed that civil war was inevitable.

Civil War

Three parties with different interests—"the North, the South and the
Negro"—vied for power during the Civil War. From the first clash of
arms, black abolitionists recognized that racial issues were central to the
struggle. Frederick Douglass explained that the "Negro is the key of the
situation—the pivot upon which the whole rebellion turns." It took federal officials much longer to reach that understanding. But as the war
dragged on and Union casualty lists grew, the Lincoln administration

105. Benjamin Quarles, *Allies for Freedom: Blacks and John Brown* (New York, N.Y.,
1974), 39–43, 53, 61–62, 73–74, 76–83, 116; Foner, *History of Black Americans*, 3:251–
63; George Lucas interview, 14 August 1892, Siebert Collection, MH.
106. *Lib*, 9 December 1859, 16 March 1860 [12:0562–63]; *WAA*, 19 November, 3, 10
December 1859, 21 January 1860, 6, 13, 27 April 1861 [12:0230, 0263, 0270–71, 0279,
0285–87, 0494, 13:0465, 0486]; Quarles, *Allies for Freedom*, 160.
107. *WAA*, 29 October, 17 December 1859, 21 April 1860, 6 April 1861 [12:0164, 0299,
0649, 13:0440]; *AAM*, November 1859.

came to realize that it would have to liberate the slave and mobilize free blacks in order to subdue the southern drive for independence.[108]

Blacks and whites approached the war from different perspectives. Most Northern whites fought to preserve the Union. Southern whites pursued independence to defend states' rights, to preserve a way of life, and to make slavery secure. For blacks, the war was more than a conflict between regions or a clash of constitutional interpretations—it was a battle between the forces of freedom and bondage. "The present rebellion," John S. Rock insisted, "is the natural fruit of slavery."[109]

White abolitionists shared the black understanding of the struggle, recognizing that the "war at its foundation is all about the black man," in the words of Elizur Wright, Jr. The conflict focused white abolitionist attention once again directly on slavery. Abolitionists temporarily put aside disputes over roles, responsibilities, and tactics. In a spirit of unity the movement had not seen since the early 1830s, they pressured the Lincoln administration and the nation for emancipation and black military service.[110]

The black community was deeply divided at the start of the war. Most blacks condemned the attack on Fort Sumter. Across the North, they formed independent military units or rushed to enlist in the army, believing that Lincoln's war aims would certainly include emancipation. But their patriotic offer was spurned. The more than 8,500 men who joined black units by the fall of 1861 were rejected for military service. Rebuffed by the national government, blacks became convinced that they would gain nothing by supporting the war effort. Although as much as a third of the black community felt that duty and reason compelled them to stand with the administration, the majority criticized it, arguing that Lincoln would never grant them their rights or emancipate the slaves. The AME church advised blacks not to fight for a country that oppressed them. The black press spread that message under the slogan, "Resistance at home, resistance abroad." The *Weekly Anglo-African* reminded blacks that their primary responsibility was still to the slave. Denounce the government, the paper advised, but organize, drill, and stand ready "as Minute Men, to *respond when the slave calls.*" In the face of official indifference to their patriotism and aspirations, blacks concluded that the government could take care of itself and that they should save their "labors for the slave, and the slave alone."[111]

108. Foner, *Life and Writings of Frederick Douglass*, 3:13.
109. WAA, 14 September 1861, 7 February, 1 August 1863, 23 January 1864 [13:0760]; *Lib*, 18 July 1862 [14:0399].
110. James M. McPherson, *The Struggle for Equality: Abolitionists and the Negro in the Civil War and Reconstruction* (Princeton, N.J., 1964), 61–74; WAA, 12 October 1861, 7 February, 11 April 1863, 9, 23 January 1864 [13:0823].
111. *Lib*, 10 May 1861, 15 August 1862 [13:0525, 14:0439–40]; Alfred M. Green, *Let-*

Not until 1863, when Lincoln emancipated the slaves and called for black troops, did Union war aims and black goals converge. Only then could blacks fight for the Union and pursue abolitionist goals at the same time. Black abolitionists across the North hailed the change as the opportunity they had been seeking. Black military service would help destroy slavery and undermine notions of racial inferiority, the first step in ending prejudice and establishing claims to equal citizenship in the postwar nation. Participation in the war became an abolitionist act, an opportunity to obtain "indemnity for the past, and security for the future."[112]

Black abolitionists believed that a patriotic and courageous call to arms would validate decades of antislavery demands. "The eyes of the whole world are upon you," announced the *Weekly Anglo-African*, "civilized man everywhere waits to see if you will prove yourselves. . . . *Will you vindicate your manhood?*" In that context, black regiments like the Fifty-fourth Massachusetts Regiment—the first regular black army unit organized in the free states—assumed enormous importance. The *Weekly Anglo-African* reported that "every black man and woman feels a special interest in the success of this regiment." Black abolitionists understood that "if, by any means, the 54th should fail, . . . it will be a blow from which we Northern men would never recover." From across the North, blacks flocked to Massachusetts to join up, some of them the sons of black abolitionists. Eventually, more than 186,000 blacks enlisted in the Fifty-fourth and other Union army regiments. The northern black community watched with pride as these units fought bravely at Port Hudson, Milliken's Bend, Fort Wagner, and other battles, proving to skeptics— including the Lincoln administration and the Union military command— that blacks were good soldiers.[113]

Black abolitionists served in many roles crucial to the war effort. H. Ford Douglas and Martin R. Delany eagerly enlisted, and Delany is credited as the first black army officer. Delany, Mary Ann Shadd Cary, William Wells Brown, Henry Highland Garnet, and Jermain W. Loguen were

ters and Discussions on the Formation of Colored Regiments (Philadelphia, Pa., 1862), 3– 4, 7–8, 11 [13:1029]; *WAA*, 20, 27 April, 4, 11 May, 14, 28 September, 5, 12 October 1861, 24 January 1863 [13:0468, 0475, 0490, 0501, 0536, 0755, 0779–80, 0804, 0816– 17]; Clarence E. Walker, *A Rock in a Weary Land: The African Methodist Episcopal Church during the Civil War and Reconstruction* (Baton Rouge, La., 1982), 32–34; *PP*, 25 May 1861 [13:0547].
112. *WAA*, 3, 17 January, 14, 28 February, 14 March, 4, 11, 18 April, 9, 23 May, 4 July, 29 August 1863, 13 February 1864, 18 February 1865.
113. *WAA*, 31 January, 4, 11 April, 30 May, 6, 13 June, 5 December 1863, 23 January, 20 February, 22 October, 5 November, 3 December 1864; John S. Rock to Soldiers of the 5th Regiment, United States Heavy Artillery, 30 May 1864, Ruffin Papers, DHU [15:0379– 80]; *PA*, 16 May 1863 [14:0863]; Benjamin Quarles, *The Negro and the Civil War* (Boston, Mass., 1953), 7, 17, 21.

among the leaders who recruited black troops. They traveled throughout the North addressing mass rallies to convince blacks that the war was now their fight. Trusted and respected by the black community, they quickly filled the Fifty-fourth and Fifty-fifth Massachusetts regiments, then others in Rhode Island, Connecticut, Pennsylvania, and Ohio. They directed enlistees into regiments with sympathetic white officers, protected them from fraudulent enlistment schemes, and served as liaisons between government officials and recruits.[114]

The opportunity for blacks to bear arms generated a wave of optimism among black abolitionists—slavery would end and equal rights would certainly follow. But these feelings were quickly tempered by the Union army's treatment of black recruits. Black soldiers were issued inferior weapons and inadequate rations, paid at less than half the rate of white soldiers, often led by incompetent and racist white officers, relegated to fatigue duty, brutalized for minor breaches of discipline, and executed for infractions of the military code. They lived, said one black spokesman, "under a tyranny inexorable as slavery itself, more absolute and fearful than the inquisition." If whites had received such treatment, one black soldier remarked, "Massachusetts would have inaugurated a rebellion . . . [but] because I am black, they tamper with my rights."[115]

The issue of equal pay became the central concern of black abolitionists, a symbol of the government's mistreatment of black troops. Blacks volunteered with the understanding that they would receive the same pay and treatment as whites. But once in service, the government determined that all blacks, regardless of rank, would receive less pay than a white private. For eighteen months, black soldiers protested by refusing any pay, placing enormous burdens on themselves and their families. Near-mutinous conditions developed in some regiments. Black recruiters resigned their positions and publicly denounced the Lincoln administration. After more than a year of protests, blacks gained the cooperation of prominent Republican politicians, who enacted legislation granting equal pay. Blacks celebrated this victory as an affirmation of their claims to equal treatment as Americans.[116]

---

114. Luis F. Emilio, *History of the Fifty-fourth Regiment of Massachusetts Volunteer Infantry, 1863–1865*, 2d ed. (Boston, Mass., 1894), 12; *WAA*, 11 April, 26 December 1863, 17 September 1864; John S. Rock to Colonel N. C. Russell, 4 April 1864, Ruffin Papers, DHU [15:0299]; Martin R. Delany to Edwin M. Stanton, 15 December 1863, RG 94, Adjutant General's Office, U.S. Colored Troops, DNA [15:0119]; Blackett, *Beating against the Barriers*, 225–40; Ripley et al., *Black Abolitionist Papers*, 2:487–88; McPherson, *Struggle for Equality*, 206–7.

115. *WAA*, 3, 24 October 1863, 30 January, 26 March, 30 April, 16, 30 July, 1 August, 22 October 1864, 15 April 1865; Ira Berlin et al., eds., *Freedom: A Documentary History of Emancipation, 1861–1867*, 2 ser. to date (Cambridge, England, 1982), 2:1, 17–18, 31–32.

116. Berlin et al., *Freedom*, 2:18–22; *WAA*, 11 July 1863, 30 April, 13 July, 12 November 1864.

Despite rampant prejudice, the army created important roles for blacks and produced a large share of the black leadership during Reconstruction. About eighty-seven blacks served as officers and twenty-one more as surgeons and chaplains by the end of the conflict. Many more became noncommissioned officers. Several black officers founded schools and churches for the freedmen. Enlisted men instructed freed slaves in their spare time and later worked for the Freedmen's Bureau or for abolitionist missionary and relief associations in the South. Sixty-four state legislators, three lieutenant governors, four congressmen, and at least forty-one delegates to postwar state constitutional conventions had served in black regiments. P. B. S. Pinchback, Martin R. Delany, John V. De Grasse, Robert Smalls, Henry M. Turner, George E. Stephens, and other Reconstruction leaders had wartime military experience. In New Orleans alone, fifty-nine of the city's Reconstruction leaders had served in the military.[117]

The war changed the relationship between blacks and the federal government. Once feared and hated as the slave catcher's friend, the government became a reluctant "custodian of freedom." It enlisted black troops, ended slavery in the District of Columbia and the territories, and extended diplomatic recognition to Haiti and Liberia. Blacks gained unprecedented access to President Lincoln and acquired a degree of political influence that former generations would have thought impossible. Douglass, Delany, Daniel Payne, and Sojourner Truth were among those invited to the White House. Lincoln discussed matters of national interest with black delegations. Federal troops protected black rallies, and prominent Republicans such as Henry Winter Davis and George S. Boutwell attended black political conventions. Powerful political friends voiced black grievances. Many black abolitionists believed that the nation's leaders were experiencing a revolution in racial attitudes. To Lewis Hayden it seemed that "God in his goodness had placed the right men in the right place at this important crisis."[118]

The "new era of freedom" energized the entire black community. The black underground that had secretly aided the slave during the antebellum years became a partner in the Union war effort. An elaborate black network of churches, freedmen's aid and abolitionist societies, and other

117. Eric Foner, *Reconstruction: America's Unfinished Revolution, 1863–1877* (New York, N.Y., 1988), 9–10; *WAA*, 28 January, 12 July 1865; Berlin et al., *Freedom*, 2:310–11; Howard N. Rabinowitz, ed., *Southern Black Leaders of the Reconstruction Era* (Urbana, Ill., 1982), 168.
118. Foner, *Reconstruction*, 9, 24; Benjamin Quarles, *Lincoln and the Negro* (New York, N.Y., 1962), 115, 204–7; *WAA*, 23 May, 5 September 1863, 23 April, 5 November, 24 December 1864, 7 January 1865; *PA*, 25 October, 28 November, 19 December 1863 [15:0016, 0081, 0129]; George T. Downing to Charles Sumner, 19 February 1863, Sumner Papers, MH [14:0745–46].

benevolent organizations raised funds and collected goods for black soldiers and the freedmen. The American Freedmen's Friend Society (AFFS) of Brooklyn—run by black abolitionists including James N. Gloucester, George T. Downing, William C. Nell, George B. Vashon, and Charles B. Ray—centralized collection efforts and used their contacts with white abolitionists to raise funds. Black churches in Washington served as distribution centers for thousands of dollars worth of food and clothing collected by northern black churches, the AFFS, and similar groups. Blacks also used the network to reunite black families, to resettle freedmen in the North, and to find them employment.[119]

Black women were at the center of these relief efforts. Using experience gained during years of raising funds for the antislavery movement, women's organizations in nearly every northern black community collected funds and supplies to aid black soldiers and the freedmen. The war fostered cooperation among these local associations, North and South, breaking down class, generational, and regional barriers. Washington's Contraband Relief Association (CRA), headed by Elizabeth Keckley, Mary Todd Lincoln's personal servant, distributed a large share of the supplies sent southward by black women's organizations and churches. In its first year, the CRA received almost $900 and countless barrels of supplies. Their successes gave black women unprecedented authority and expanded their public role. Mary Ann Shadd Cary, Frances Ellen Watkins Harper, Sattie Douglas, and other women traveled throughout the North and West promoting black enlistment, lecturing, and raising funds for soldiers, freedmen, and black Canadian settlements.[120]

Dozens of black abolitionists streamed southward to work directly with the freedmen in areas occupied by Union forces. Boston carpenter John Oliver, the first black teacher sent South by the AMA, went to Virginia after hearing an AMA representative speak of "the conditions and educational wants of the slaves who are constantly coming into Fortress Monroe and other places along the line of our army." Once

119. Joe M. Richardson, *Christian Reconstruction: The American Missionary Association and Southern Blacks, 1861–1890* (Athens, Ga., 1986), 97; *CR*, 5 April 1862 [14:0212]; *WAA*, 3, 10, 31 January, 21, 28 March, 26 September 1863, 26 November 1864; *PA*, 10 January 1863 [14:0691]; William Still to Joseph M. Truman, 15 September 1862, Pennsylvania Abolition Society Papers, PHi [14:0498–502]; John Oliver to Simeon S. Jocelyn, 26 September 1863, AMA-ARC [14:1071]; Elizabeth Pleck, *Black Migration and Poverty: Boston, 1865–1900* (New York, N.Y., 1979), 25–28.
120. *WAA*, 8 March 1862, 14 March, 4 April, 12 September, 3, 31 October, 12, 19 December 1863, 9 January, 6, 20 February, 6, 13 August, 5, 26 November 1864, 28 January, 25 February, 4 March, 26 August, 16 September 1865 [16:0118]; *CR*, 11 May 1861, 4 July, 15 August 1863 [13:0526, 14:0949, 1012]; Martin R. Delany, Agent Certification, 24 February 1864, Mary Ann Shadd Cary Papers, DHU [15:0257]; Jim Bearden and Linda Jean Butler, *Shadd: The Life and Times of Mary Shadd Cary* (Toronto, Canada, 1977), 206.

there, he helped direct the flow of food, clothing, and medical supplies from northern relief agencies, while enraging Union army officials with his constant criticism of their treatment of the contraband. Oliver was the first of many black abolitionists who went South during the war. Like Oliver, black teachers, missionaries, and relief workers believed that "the work of Anti-Slavery men is not yet compleat" until the former slaves were ready to assume an equal place in the postwar nation. They understood that their fate was bound up with that of the freedmen.[121]

Black abolitionists carried their antebellum goals into the war years. With new organizations and fresh enthusiasm, they continued to oppose slavery, prejudice, and colonization. Across the nation, blacks defied Jim Crow restrictions on streetcars with organized protests and ride-ins. They lobbied state legislatures to remove the word "white" from state constitutions. The Repeal Association of Chicago sent wealthy black abolitionist John Jones to Springfield as its lobbyist. In Philadelphia, blacks organized the Colored Peoples' Union League to promote their interests. The league held mass rallies to protest discrimination and disfranchisement, to unify the black community, and to gain the cooperation of abolitionists and Union troops. Blacks used wartime conditions to further their claims to full citizenship by defending the nation on the battlefield and paying taxes that helped finance the war. Pennsylvania blacks, who had put more men in uniform than in any other state, were especially outraged that the state's "colored inhabitants receive less justice" than anyone else. Blacks' participation in the war gave their protests more authority.[122]

Black abolitionists' struggles were a continuing process. During peacetime, Civil War, and Reconstruction, the quest for freedom, equality, and justice bound together the Afro-American experience. Secession changed some of the particulars of the debates, but the critical issues of slavery, prejudice, equality, and citizenship remained foremost in black minds. Some black leaders believed in Lincoln's sincerity and hoped he would guide the nation toward antislavery principles, but black hopes faded in the first months of his presidency as he ignored the black agenda, defended the South's right to its slaves, enforced the Fugitive Slave Law, and early in the fighting, overruled his generals who used antislavery

---

121. Richardson, *Christian Reconstruction*, 189–209; John Oliver to William L. Coan, 5 February 1862, Edward Scott to George Whipple, 22 July 1864, AMA-ARC [14:0113, 15:0461–63]; *NASS*, 16 April 1863 [15:0310]; Betty Mansfield, "That Fateful Class: Black Teachers of Virginia's Freedmen, 1861–1882" (Ph.D. diss., Catholic University of America, 1980), 66, 126–33; De Boer, "Afro-Americans in American Missionary Association," 223, 247–53, 297, 304–8; Foner, *History of Black Americans*, 3:412–14; *WAA*, 23 July 1864; Walker, *Rock in a Weary Land*, 48–51, 64.
122. *PA*, 21 March 1863 [14:0767–68]; *WAA*, 13 February, 2 July, 13 August, 3 December 1864, 14, 28 January, 25 February 1865; *Lib*, 6 March 1863 [14:0757].

actions as a way to weaken the South. In nearly every act of the Lincoln administration, blacks saw their interests ignored.

Blacks continued to fight the same abolitionist battles with the Lincoln administration. They had to force emancipation on a president whose first choice was to reunite the nation without reforming the South. Once again they had to combat plans for compensated emancipation; "It is the slave who ought to be compensated," one black abolitionist explained. Blacks were shocked when Lincoln revived the colonization debate by proposing that blacks be removed to Central America or Haiti as solution to the nation's racial problems. With black freedom and the nation's very survival at stake, Lincoln's preoccupation with black expatriation reminded Frances Ellen Watkins Harper "of a man almost dying with a loathsome cancer, and busying himself about having his hair trimmed according to the latest fashion." To most black leaders, Lincoln represented "the godless will of a criminal nation."[123]

Lincoln's Emancipation Proclamation embodied the difficult relationship between black abolitionists and the wartime government and confirmed the black judgment that racial progress was too slow in coming and never granted in full measure. Blacks responded to the Emancipation Proclamation in several ways. For slaves, the proclamation heralded the day of jubilee. Northern blacks understood the measure to be a dramatic change in policy and hailed it as the beginning of black freedom. Not a few idolized Lincoln, setting a precedent for his later canonization as a martyred hero. Baltimore blacks spent almost $600 on a pulpit-sized Bible packed in a silk-lined, black walnut case for the president, to honor his "active participation in furtherance of the cause of the emancipation of our race."[124]

Yet the Emancipation Proclamation left many black abolitionists anxious and disappointed. They understood that the proclamation was a military necessity, not a humanitarian measure; that it was a blow struck at the Confederacy, not on behalf of the slave. Black leaders pointed out that the proclamation came two years after the start of the war, freed only some slaves, and exempted slaves in the border states or those owned by "loyal" masters. By its reservations, the proclamation reinforced slavery in parts of the South. Black abolitionists, well attuned to the halfhearted efforts of professed friends, saw that Lincoln had done the least, rather than the most, against slavery. They accepted Lincoln at his word that emancipation was an unavoidable war measure. "It is *per*

123. *Lib*, 15 August 1862 [14:0441]; *WAA*, 16 March 1861, 16 May, 25 July, 31 October 1863 [13:0064–65, 0412]; *PA*, 14 June, 11 October 1862 [14:0543]; *CR*, 27 September 1862 [14:0511]; Foner, *History of Black Americans*, 3:342–43, 424; Quarles, *Lincoln and the Negro*, 108–20.
124. Quarles, *Lincoln and the Negro*, 206–7.

se," the *Weekly Anglo-African* announced, "no more humanitarian than a hundred pounder rifled cannon."[125]

The proclamation left many black abolitionists with little sense of obligation or thankfulness. The war began as an effort to restore the Union as it was and leave "the black man where he was." For blacks, liberty "has always been a name without meaning, a shadow without substance," as John S. Rock described it. Most black abolitionist leaders believed that the proclamation had been brought forth "by timid and heaven-doubting mid-wives" and would likely "prove an incompetent and abominable abortion."[126]

Lincoln's wartime Reconstruction program offered new evidence of the chasm that separated black abolitionist goals from the national purpose. His December 1863 Proclamation of Amnesty and Reconstruction began the process of bringing the southern states and the defeated rebels back into the Union. It promised a pardon and the return of all rights to Southerners who took an oath of loyalty to the United States and accepted the abolition of slavery. To qualify for readmission, state governments had to write new state constitutions that abolished slavery. But Lincoln only briefly considered enfranchising certain blacks based on their wealth, education, and prewar status, and his plan offered freed slaves few rights and little protection, leaving their futures largely up to white Southerners. James McCune Smith denounced Lincoln for failing to empower blacks, confiscate land, or guarantee Confederate disfranchisement. Lincoln disregarded the black abolitionists' long-held goals of political rights, economic security, and social justice in both North and South. "The President of the United States," William D. Forten declared in 1864, "has, in his reconstruction policy, pronounced a death-knell to our peaceful hopes."[127]

Blacks emerged from the war mindful of the need for continued action. Three months after Appomattox, William Wells Brown told a Fourth of July audience in Framingham, Massachusetts, that "the government has broken faith with the black man," leaving him to "the tyrants of the South." Brown told the cheering crowd that "if there was ever a time when abolitionists should be alert, it is now." The government's reluctant commitment to the freedmen and its apparent unwillingness to control the South convinced black leaders that they must advance bold programs. Blacks understood that they had gained little

125. Foner, *Reconstruction*, 7; *WAA*, 3, 10 January 1863, 16 July 1864.
126. *Lib*, 16 January 1863, 3 June 1864 [14:0697, 15:0387]; *WAA*, 26 September 1863; *PA*, 7 March 1863.
127. Foner, *Reconstruction*, 7; *WAA*, 23 November 1861, 21 March, 5 September 1863, 20 July 1864 [13:0925–26]; Foner, *Life and Writings of Frederick Douglass*, 3:189–90; Philip S. Foner and George E. Walker, eds., *Proceedings of the Black National and State Conventions, 1865–1900*, 1 vol. to date (Philadelphia, Pa., 1986), 58, 60–65.

beyond emancipation and that without political power and social and economic security, their freedom could be easily threatened. They made it their primary responsibility to press public officials for racial equality, civil rights, the vote, and a just Reconstruction of the southern states. Henry Highland Garnet argued that "the battle has just begun in which the fate of the black race in this country is to be decided."[128] After thirty years of antislavery struggle and four years of war, their work was still before them.

War and Reconstruction offered a new opportunity to secure long-sought objectives. Men like Pennington, Brown, Philip Bell, Delany, Garnet, Douglass, and J. Sella Martin saw Reconstruction as part of a continuing struggle dating from the 1820s. They worked hard to impart to the nation the wisdom they had gained through many years of battling prejudice and racism in the North—anything less than full rights and privileges as American citizens would doom all blacks to the second-class status that free blacks in the North had endured since the Revolution. Experience convinced black abolitionists that it was not enough to free the slaves or even give blacks the vote. To enfranchise blacks without providing the means for social and economic equality would leave the job half done. For freedom to have substance, blacks required social and economic security, as well as political power. Blacks fought to secure their rights in the North, to reconstruct southern society, and to prepare the freedmen for the trials ahead.[129]

Decades of abolitionist struggle offered useful lessons for Reconstruction. Black abolitionists counseled aggressive, independent action. "We must exchange the gospel of endurance for the gospel of resistance," the black press urged. Blacks resisted white control, maintaining that only through the "constant assertion of our own manhood" could they "positively obtain and perpetually uphold our equality." Black leaders argued that they, not whites, best understood the freedmen's needs; they fostered racial pride and the belief that only black independence could guarantee black freedom. Robert Hamilton, the editor of the *Anglo-African*, reminded blacks that they could not depend on abolitionist friends or on the federal government to achieve their goals. The American Anti-Slavery Society, the Lincoln administration, and the Radical Republicans all shared some black interests, but those interests fell short of black aspirations for full equality as American citizens. Hamilton urged blacks to take action themselves, or the opportunity for equal rights would slip

128. Farrison, *William Wells Brown*, 397–98; *Lib*, 14 July 1865; *NASS*, 15 July 1865; *WAA*, 26 August 1865.
129. Thomas A. Sanelli, "The Struggle for Black Suffrage in Pennsylvania, 1838–1870" (Ph.D. diss., Temple University, 1978), 149, 164–68, 173, 188–89, 192–94; Roger Lane, *The Roots of Violence in Black Philadelphia, 1860–1900* (Cambridge, Mass., 1986), 49–50, 55; *WAA*, 5, 12 November 1864, 18 February, 6 May 1865.

away. He warned that "a century may elapse before another opportunity shall be afforded for reclaiming and holding our . . . rights."[130]

Throughout the war years and into Reconstruction, black leaders shifted between optimism and despair. They hoped that the Civil War would transform both slaves and free blacks into full citizens and discredit American racial stereotypes, thereby bringing to fruition years of abolitionist efforts. They saw the war as a means for ending slavery, viewed black military service as a way to validate their claim to citizenship, and regarded a just peace as the appropriate time for blacks to be granted equal rights. But black leaders were ambivalent about their future. Wartime experience, especially in the military and in early Reconstruction efforts, confirmed their worst fears. In neither war nor peace did the federal government adopt black abolitionist goals. Black hopes soared when the two parties had shared interests, but black gains came in half measures, grudgingly offered by a government that reluctantly accepted black soldiers because it needed more troops, belatedly freed the slave as a way to weaken the South, and never offered blacks an opportunity to secure equal citizenship.[131]

Black abolitionists understood that their desire for true Reconstruction of the South and for their political, social, and economic enfranchisement rested upon the federal government's willingness to advance their interests. But wartime Reconstruction set the course the government would follow. Black leaders saw firsthand that Washington intended to abandon blacks in order to make peace with the South. The final guarantee of black freedom and independence depended upon Washington's determination to support black rights with a permanent and vigilant occupying force, an unbiased implementation of the law, and the fair opportunity to gain economic security. No such commitment existed.[132]

Black abolitionism transformed antebellum black Americans and left its mark on Afro-American identity, life, and institutions. The devotion

130. *WAA*, 17 January 1863, 13 May, 9 September, 7 October 1865 [16:0181, 0187–88]; *NASS*, 16 April 1864 [15:0309–10]; Martin R. Delany, "Memorandum," 23 July 1865, RG 94, Adjutant General's Office, U.S. Colored Troops, DNA [15:1076–78]; Walker, *Rock in a Weary Land*, 125–32.
131. Walker, *Rock in a Weary Land*, 108; Foner, *Reconstruction*, 41; *WAA*, 18 February, 22 May, 29 July, 26 August 1865 [16:0121]; *BR*, 15 April 1865 [15:0829]; *Lib*, 14 July 1865.
132. *NASS*, 10 June 1865 [15:0946]; *WAA*, 15 April, 1, 8 July, 12 August, 3 September, 16 December 1865 [16:0158–59, 0536]; C. Peter Ripley, *Slaves and Freedmen in Civil War Louisiana* (Baton Rouge, La., 1976), 75; Foner, *Reconstruction*, 183–87; William S. McFeely, *Yankee Stepfather: General O. O. Howard and the Freedmen* (New Haven, Conn., 1968), 320–21; Louis Gerteis, *From Contraband to Freedman: Federal Policy toward Southern Blacks, 1861–1865* (Westport, Conn., 1973), 51–52.

of many white abolitionists to ending slavery is a familiar story of genuine conviction and sacrifice, but in no other country was the free black population so insistently abolitionist and so antagonistic toward slavery and slaveholders. The participation of blacks in the movement gave American abolitionism a unique quality that made their involvement particularly important. Laboring in large and small ways, blacks played a vital role in the rise of the most important reform movement in American history.

Black abolitionists sought to recast the antislavery movement from a battle to end chattel slavery in the South to a broad, national campaign against all forms of racial injustice. From their opposition to colonization in the 1820s to their work against Jim Crow practices during the Civil War, black abolitionists argued that racial prejudice was a fundamental issue inseparable from the question of slavery. By advancing that argument, blacks became the most persistent voice for racial equality in American society and, in the process, defined the central element of black abolitionism.

The broadened definition of black abolitionism governed relations between black and white abolitionists. The unwillingness of most white abolitionists to judge northern prejudice as harshly as southern slaveholding created a tension in antislavery ranks. The enormous amount of time and energy that blacks spent trying to convert fellow abolitionists and the northern public to their larger goals meant that black abolitionism was influenced as much by its struggles with whites in the free states as with slaveholders in the South.

Failing to sway northern whites, black abolitionists turned inward with new direction and energy and helped shape the northern black community. Black abolitionism instilled optimism and confidence among northern free blacks and fugitive slaves. It unified blacks of diverse economic and professional backgrounds, male and female. With a shared sense of purpose, northern blacks created antislavery and reform organizations, established their own press, wrote and published books, and assembled at state and national conventions. Traditional free black institutions—churches, reading rooms, mutual aid societies—were infused with abolitionist sentiment and purpose. While abolitionism gave rise to new black institutions and reshaped existing ones, it also guided blacks into American politics. The growth of antislavery political parties offered blacks an unprecedented opportunity to bring their issues into the center of national life. Their quest for citizenship and an end to discrimination demanded astute and creative political tactics; from the halls of state legislatures to the courts of justice, blacks engaged white institutions—soliciting their support when possible, challenging them when necessary.

Over the three decades before the Civil War, black abolitionism touched an expanding range of black life and left an imposing legacy on Afro-

American society. During the antebellum years, while the black community grew and matured, black abolitionism helped shape its leaders, its institutions, and its citizens. The black antislavery movement engaged ever-increasing numbers from the black community and redefined its leadership. New leaders emerged from antislavery organizations and initiatives; fugitive slaves, lecturers, vigilance committee organizers, and newspaper editors joined the established black elite—the clergy, professionals, and businessmen. Debates over moral reform, colonization, emigration, separate institutions, and reform tactics and goals enriched black intellectual life and helped define the character of Afro-American life and culture in a racist society. Black abolitionism transformed Afro-American society and demanded that the nation reinterpret its first principles of freedom and justice.

1.
The Colonization Controversy

John B. Russwurm to [Edward Jones]
20 March 1830

Joseph R. Dailey to Robert Purvis
12 April 1833

The creation of the American Colonization Society in 1816 and the consequent rise of the colonization movement opened a debate among free blacks. A few black leaders—Lott Cary, John B. Hepburn, John B. Russwurm—supported the ACS. They were drawn to the ACS's plan for a Liberian colony because it promised blacks self-government and the rights and privileges denied them in America. But most black leaders rejected colonization. They claimed America as their home, and they refused to abandon it or the slave. Letters from Liberian emigrants offered conflicting views of life in the colony. Russwurm's 20 March 1830 letter emphasized the opportunities Liberia offered American blacks. It was probably written to Edward Jones, a young Charleston black who was training for missionary work at the ACS-run African Mission School in Hartford, Connecticut; Jones had worked with Russwurm three years earlier on *Freedom's Journal*. A 12 April 1833 letter from Russwurm's business partner, black merchant Joseph R. Dailey, cast the colony in a harsher light. Dailey wrote to Robert Purvis, a member of Philadelphia's black elite, in horrifying detail about the disease, starvation, and death that awaited settlers. One month later, he informed Purvis that Liberia was a "pestiferous Golgotha"—little more than a graveyard for American blacks. Such testimony helped convince most free blacks to reject colonization and to stay in the United States and fight against slavery and racism. Marie Tyler McGraw, "Richmond Free Blacks and African Colonization, 1816–1832," *JAS* 21:214–27 (August 1987); *Lib*, 13 August, 3 September 1831, 28 January 1832 [1:0100, 0112, 0143]; *AR*, September 1844 [4:0910]; Joseph R. Dailey to Robert Purvis, 2 May 1833, Anti-Slavery Collection, MB [1:0278–82]; *DANB*, 364; Randall K. Burkett, "Clergy Profile of Edward Jones," unpublished ms., copy in author's possession.

What my sensations were upon landing I can hardly describe. This town contains double the number of houses I expected, and I am informed that Millsburg and Caldwell each contain nearly as many. The Colonists here (at Monrovia), appear to be thriving—they subsist chiefly by trading with the natives.[1] You here behold coloured men exercising all the duties of offices of which you can scarcely believe, many fulfill the important duties with much dignity.[2] We have here a republic in miniature.

Abduhl Rahhahman[3] has left some writings, which he desired to be transmitted to his relatives. He saw one of his countrymen some short time previous to his death. The same man has visited here since, and appeared to be much affected upon perusing his writings. Mrs. Prince could not inform me of their purport, as the native spoke but little English. He says that Teembo may be reached in eight days, by travelling through the woods, or in ten, by coasting along the shore. He is anxious for Mrs. P. to visit Teembo. It is the current report here that his relatives having received his first letter, immediately forwarded gold dust to the amount of $7,000, which came as near the Colony as King Boatswain's Town, where, learning of his death, from one of our traders, they immediately turned their faces homewards. The native above referred to, says that the British have opened so fine a road, and the distance is so short, that even females travel to Sierra Leone and back in two days.

There is a great field for usefulness here; and, when I look around and behold the Pagan darkness of the land, an aspiration rises to the Heaven that my friend may become a second Brainerd or Elliot.[4] We have two religious societies—a Methodist and Baptist. The German missionary preaches sometimes in the Methodist Church.[5] It is not my desire that you should think that we have not timber or lumber to build our houses; nor *rice* enough to eat. A few hogsheads of tobacco, boxes of pipes, with casks of beads, for the purpose of purchasing fresh provisions from the natives, you will find equally as handy as the sixpences and quarters in the United States. The number of settlers amounts to about 1,500, and the farming establishments of those on the St. Paul's are said to be in fine order. Considerable provisions are also brought into the Cape[6] by the recaptured Africans,[7] who amount to about 400. The natives also bring in some rice, but I have not seen much as yet. The nearest inland trade, of any consequence, is that of King Boatswain, who is the Napoleon of these wilds.[8] His territory is about 150 miles distant. He has always been favourably disposed towards the Colony. He holds a market every day— settles all disputes among his people, and examines into the quality and quantity of all articles brought in for trade. His people appear to be more civilized than the tribes in our own immediate vicinity, upon whom they look down with the greatest contempt. His word is also law to many of them. When they appear among us they wear pantaloons, with a piece of cloth tastefully thrown over their bodies.

I long to see young men, who are now wasting the best of their days in the United States, flocking to this land as the last asylum to the unfortunate. I long for the time when you, my dear friend,[9] shall land on the shores of Africa, a messenger of that Gospel which proclaims liberty to

7. John B. Russwurm
Courtesy of Schomburg Center for Research in Black Culture, The New York Public
Library, Astor, Lenox and Tilden Foundations

the captive, and light to those who sat in great darkness! Oh, my friend, you have a wide career of usefulness before you, and may that Being who has promised his support to his followers ever be nigh to you, and strengthen and make you a second Paul to this Gentile people! Our time is but short in this transitory world, and it therefore becomes us to labour with all our might, lest the darkness overtake us before we are aware of it.

It is the general opinion that the slave trade has nearly expired; but I am informed that nothing is more erroneous, as the trade was never carried on with more vessels nor with greater vigour than it has been for the last two years. Even now, while I am writing, slavers are within forty-four miles of the Colony at Cape Mount.[10]

[John B. Russwurm][11]

African Repository (Washington, D.C.), April 1830.

Liberia
12th April [1833]
[pr] [Jupiter] via N.Yk.

R. Purvis Esq.[12]
My dear Purvis

I had this pleasure on 27th ult. [per Sch.] Dollar via New Yk. since when nothing of importance has transpired worthy of notice; & I wd. not now communicate, were it not that I am likely to be deprived of this solace of my social existence for some time to come, as our "Rainy Season" is fast approaching, & the Coast Traders are not like Shakespeares ghosts[13] [&c.] but from Churchyard [illegible symbol].

You are no doubt expecting to hear something from me relative to the Colony, but yr. anticipations must be suspended a while longer, as the brief interval since my return has only sufficed to enable me to reconnoiter affairs in general, and thro. the aid of an invaluable ally, my suspicions are confirmed that I am considered as a character dangerous to the successful operations of the Society,[14] in consequence of sentiments I had been compelled to express in the Govt. House itself,[15] in opposition to the disgusting [word illegible] & [hireling] arguments pronounced in that place. You must know that this functionary had been extremely hospitable to me since my return; but his hospitality was profusely appreciated. "The [word crossed out] baked [word illegible] did coldly [word illegible]," as while masticating them I was convinced that they were prepared to purchase my independence; and being now convinced that he cannot make a fool of me, he has endeavoured to influence R.[16] to dissolve copartnership with me, assuring him that [he] cd. further his pecuniary concerns & business from the relation in which he stood to the Col. Society & that he was confident that R. could control to his personal

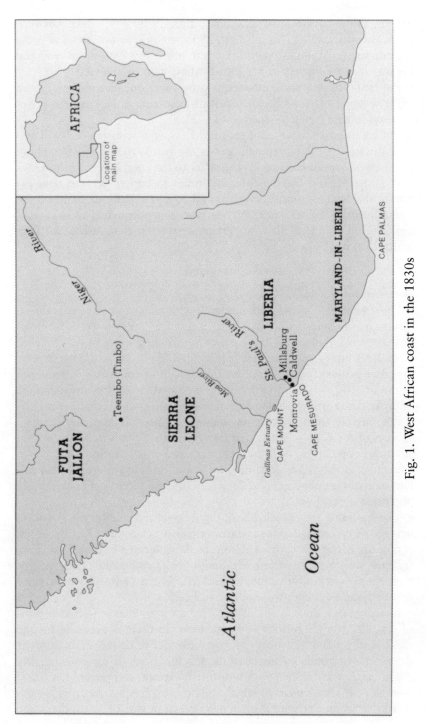

Fig. 1. West African coast in the 1830s

benefit, all the business that have come thro. my influence from America. Is not this laughable? This insidious hypocrite tho. he can boast of being a white man, wd. find it very difficult to effect this himself or even find his way into the Society of my friends of his own complexion.

But he fancies no doubt, that if he can sunder our partnership, he can make a [tool] of R. of his own private emolument, & have me better exposed to his tyrannical operations.

But let this gentleman dare to interfere openly with me & I will employ the innumerable materials within my reach, to unhinge the edifice of his employers & lacerate his character to the core. Is it not murderous that a man should come 3 thousand miles to be free & then have his liberty abridged by another whose moral & intellectual qualifications are insignificant in the extreme; & one whose deportment [word crossed out] should be more of a missionary character, than a fanciful Petit maitre[17] as he is.

> Asperius nihil, est humili,
> Cum surgit in altum [word illegible][18]

In short he is here a complete monarch with as much power guaranteed to him by the Society's Constitution as any [one or two words illegible] Bashaw[19] wd. require for the govt. of his cringing subjects, & or slaves, & to use a fitter expression. He is possessed of no energy of character or inventive genius; & were it not for the mercantile enterprise of a number of the citizens, the Colony wd. present a desolate spectacle; in fact public improvements are suspended & deteriorating, tho. the revenue is considerable, arising from imports on tonnage & merchandise. The local resources of the Colony with regard to agriculture is not in proportion to ¼ of our population; & if the Colonization Society continues to pour in emigrants as they have done the past year,[20] untold sufferings must follow as a certain consequence; & wd. betide the victims of such rash & phrenzied enthusiasm.[21]

The hospitals are crowded with the sick—there is only one physician here, & he is confined to his bed from excessive exertion. The Charleston people are dying daily. Miss Gibbon the daughter of a baptist Clergyman is dead; also the wife of one Mr. Smith a very respectable man; & this moment my clerk informs me that old Mr. Rogers (a wealthy man) is no more!! Insatiate archer will not one suffice?[22]

I hardly think there is any just ground for apprehensions, on my part, of any ultimately injurious consequences; yet there is necessity for the exercise of prudence & [fortitude], forbearance & deliberation, in order the more effectually to frustrate the machinations of my enemies. My blood courses my system with unwanted warmth, & I perambulate that portion of the settlement to which my business is prescribed; with measured thread [line crossed out] an erect cranium when I reflect that since my sojourn in Africa, I have punctiliously observed the golden principle in my dealings with every man, & have made sacrifices before I wd. receive [word crossed out] favors of any one. Tho. I am the youngest merchant, I can without egotism say that I have contributed in a larger proportion to the influence & consequence of the Colony than any other, & yet because I will not consent to join an infamous trio of base & sychopantic [satellites] who are continually poisoning the atmosphere with acclamations in praise of the Society, I am considered the most proper target at which to aim their envenomed hostilities—[two words crossed out] but let them come on, Tray, Snap, Blanch & the whole pack of puppies.[23] You know that I am naturally possessed of a warm imagination, & this excitability is continually kept up from my feelings of disgust, and there by disposing me to intermittent fever. I do reassure you that there are a great many contemptible scoundrels here. Poor Taylor hoisted the Standard of reform & they slunk from it like dastards. I have had my enterprise insulted in America, by many persons, & some that you well know; so that I shall remain here until next spring, & drive my business with all the energy I am possessed of. I shall then leave for Europe, & perhaps come over to my native land to be cheered my dear friend, by light of thy countenance, once more, in great haste adieu,

Jos. R. Dailey[24]

1. Liberia's early settlers developed such an extensive barter trade with native Africans that it inhibited the settler's agricultural development. The settlers exchanged guns, powder, tobacco, rum, beads, and cotton textiles for rice, Indian corn, coffee, peanuts, palm oil, salt, wax, hides, tortoiseshell, ivory, camwood, indigo, wax, and gold dust. Trade relations enmeshed the settlers in West Africa's political economy. They used trade to establish alliances and to protect themselves from warring tribes. Svend E. Holsoe, "A Study of Relations between Settlers and Indigenous Peoples in Western Liberia, 1821–1847," *AHS* 4:331–62 (1971); *AR*, July, November 1831.

2. Although white appointees from the American Colonization Society controlled Liberia until 1841, black settlers held a variety of powerful administrative positions. Lott Cary, a Baptist minister from Richmond, Virginia, governed the colony in the absence of Jehudi Ashmun, the white agent, and expanded its territory along the St. Paul River. Methodist clergyman Anthony D. Williams was vice-agent from 1829 to 1836, when the ACS appointed him acting governor. Blacks in the Maryland-in-Liberia settlement at Cape Palmas enjoyed similar advantages. James Thompson, a Connecticut black, was secretary to the colonial agent. John B. Russwurm served as Monrovia's superintendent of education and as the successful governor of the Cape Palmas colony from 1836 until his death in 1851. Tom W. Shick, *Behold the Promised Land: A History of Afro-American Settler Society in Nineteenth-Century Liberia* (Baltimore, Md., 1980), 41, 64;

C. Abayomi Cassell, *Liberia: History of the First African Republic* (New York, N.Y., 1970), 94; George D. Browne, "History of the Protestant Episcopal Mission in Liberia up to 1838," *HMPEC* 39:21 (March 1970); Archibald Alexander, *A History of Colonization on the West Coast of Africa* (Philadelphia, Pa., 1849), 249–54; Andrew T. Foote, *Africa and the American Flag* (New York, N.Y., 1854), 141–51, 164; *AR*, November 1831.

3. Russwurm refers to Abd al-Rahman Ibrahima (1762–1829), the son of a West African king. Born in Timbo (in contemporary Mali), he was raised as a Muslim and received an extensive education in the Arabic language. While serving in his father's army, he was captured by a rival tribe and sold to English slave traders in 1788. Eventually purchased by Colonel Thomas Foster of Natchez, Mississippi, he remained his slave for forty years. Ibrahima married Isabella, a house servant on the Foster plantation, in 1794; they produced about thirteen children. In the mid-1820s, he met John Coates Cox, a friend of his father, who attempted to win his freedom. Secretary of State Henry Clay, Arthur Tappan, and Thomas H. Gallaudet—all members of the American Colonization Society— soon joined with President John Quincy Adams in taking up Ibrahima's cause. They mistakenly believed that Ibrahima could influence the Moroccan government to open up the West African interior to American trade. They persuaded Foster to free him on the condition that he be removed to Liberia. When the Adams administration realized that Ibrahima was not Moroccan, it turned his case over to the ACS, which agreed to repatriate him and to help raise funds to purchase his wife and children if he would tour on behalf of the organization. Wearing a Moorish costume, he visited Cincinnati, Washington, New York City, Boston, and Philadelphia, astounding northern blacks with his eloquence and knowledge of Arabic. He discussed Liberia with Russwurm in New York City. The tour incensed Ibrahima's former owner who publicly accused Adams of using him to incite slave rebellion and demanded his immediate removal to Liberia. Ibrahima and Isabella arrived at Monrovia during March 1829 and eight of their children followed the next year. Conditions there disillusioned Ibrahima, who quickly advised black Americans that the colony was "not fit for such people as you." In one of his last communications, he warned Russwurm that he would "certainly be a dead man" if he emigrated. Ibrahima himself died less than four months after reaching the colony. *FJ*, 16 May, 29 August 1828; *RA*, 17 July 1829; Terry Alford, *Prince among Slaves* (New York, N.Y., 1977).

4. Russwurm refers to two men well known for their missionary work among the Indians. David Brainerd (1718–1747) was a Presbyterian missionary to Indian tribes in New York, Pennsylvania, and New Jersey from 1743 to 1747. Because of his untimely death, and Jonathan Edwards's famous *Account* (1749), he became a heroic model for nineteenth-century missionaries. John Eliot (1604– 1690), an English-born Puritan minister, did missionary work among the Massachusetts Indians and published an Algonquian translation of the Bible. Joseph Conforti, "Jonathan Edwards's Most Popular Work: 'The Life of David Brainerd' and Nineteenth-Century Evangelical Culture," *CH* 54:188–201 (1985); Alden T. Vaughan, *The New England Frontier: Puritans and Indians, 1620–1675* (Boston, Mass., 1965), 245–52, 276–79, 316–20.

5. The African Baptist Missionary Society of Richmond, founded in 1815 by

black clergymen Lott Cary and Collin Teague, sponsored the first missionary work in Liberia. Cary and Teague settled at Cape Mesurado in 1822 and established the Providence Baptist Church. In 1833, the Baptist Board of Domestic and Foreign Missions was founded in Monrovia to Christianize native Africans. Baptists eventually established about ten other congregations in Liberia. American Methodists began their Liberian labors in 1829 with the arrival of black minister David Payne. The first Methodist church in Monrovia was founded in 1832 and, within four years, the denomination extended its influence to Cape Palmas. Swiss Lutherans established a German mission at Cape Mesurado in 1826 and two years later settled a missionary at Bassa, but by 1831 they had abandoned their Liberian missions. American Episcopalians and Presbyterians also developed Liberian missions during the 1820s and 1830s. Cassell, *Liberia*, 36, 91–103, 264; Penelope Campbell, *Maryland in Africa: The Maryland State Colonization Society, 1831–1857* (Urbana, Ill., 1971), 57–58, 70–82; Browne, "Protestant Episcopal Mission in Liberia," 17–27; *AR*, November 1831; *MCJ*, April 1848; Sylvia M. Jacobs, ed., *Black Americans and the Missionary Movement in Africa* (Westport, Conn., 1982), 8–11, 52–57, 63–68, 201.

6. Russwurm refers to Cape Mesurado on the Liberian coast.

7. Blacks liberated from illegal slave traders were known as recaptured Africans. American naval vessels often took recaptured Africans to Liberia, where many joined Christian churches, attended Sunday schools, and were apprenticed to Liberian colonists. Because of the persistence of the illegal trade, large numbers of recaptured Africans were landed in Liberia. Bell I. Wiley, ed., *Slaves No More: Letters from Liberia, 1833–1869* (Lexington, Ky., 1980), 314.

8. Sao Boso, known to the colonists as King Boatswain, belonged to the Kamara clan of the Mandingo tribe. A skillful leader who dominated the region, his political and military power depended upon the commerce he promoted with Liberia and his involvement with the slave trade. His death in 1836 plunged the area's tribes into turmoil. Shick, *Behold the Promised Land*, 30, 92; Foote, *Africa and the American Flag*, 159.

9. The likely recipient of Russwurm's letter was Edward Jones (ca. 1808–1864), who was in training for African missionary work. Born to members of Charleston's free black elite, he became the first black American college graduate in 1826 when he received a degree from Amherst College. Jones became acquainted with Russwurm while working as an assistant editor for *Freedom's Journal* the following year. He later studied at Andover Theological Seminary and the African Mission School in Hartford, before being ordained an Episcopal priest in 1830. One year later, Jones began a long career as a missionary and educator in Sierra Leone. *DANB*, 364; Burkett, "Clergy Profile of Edward Jones."

10. After Liberia's founding, French slave traders operated five miles from Monrovia, coastal tribes engaged in the lucrative trade, and Sierra Leone refused to suppress its own traders. Slave factories along the West African coast sheltered pirates and traders. Despite British diplomatic negotiations and the presence of British cruisers, the trade continued unabated until 1837 when the trade shifted to the Gallinas. Much to the chagrin of the American Colonization Society, two Liberian settlers were caught trading, and rumors circulated in the United States

concerning Liberian involvement. The trade persisted along the Liberian coast into the 1850s. Holsoe, "Study of Relations between Settlers," 331–62; Wiley, *Slaves No More*, 106–7, 322–23; *AR*, November 1831, March 1832; Foote, *Africa and the American Flag*, 150–55.

11. John B. Russwurm (1799–1851) was born in Jamaica, the son of a slave and an English merchant. He received his early schooling in Quebec and taught for three years at the all-black African School in Boston before entering Bowdoin College in 1824. He graduated in 1826, becoming the second black to earn an American college degree. Russwurm settled in New York City. In 1827 Russwurm and Samuel E. Cornish established *Freedom's Journal*—the first black newspaper in the United States. With Cornish as senior editor, the paper opposed colonization. But shortly after Russwurm became sole proprietor and editor in September 1827, he announced his conversion to colonization, and in early 1829, he accepted an appointment with the Maryland Colonization Society. Northern black leaders were shocked and outraged. Philadelphia blacks burned him in effigy. The *Liberator* later condemned him as "a traitor and a hireling." Critics charged that Russwurm had been bribed by the colonizationists, when in truth he had long nurtured an interest in black emigration. In defending African colonization, Russwurm argued that a separate black nationality was a prerequisite to ending American slavery. After arriving in Monrovia, Russwurm assumed the post of superintendent of education and later served as colonial secretary. He also formed a short-lived business partnership with merchant Joseph R. Dailey. In early 1830, he became editor of the *Liberia Herald*, a position that made him the most prominent black voice of African colonization. He lost his position at the paper in 1835 over an editorial conflict with the colonial governor, John B. Pinney.

Russwurm was appointed governor of the Maryland-in-Liberia settlement at Cape Palmas in 1836. As the first black governor of an African colonial jurisdiction, he carried the additional responsibility of demonstrating black capacity for self-government. His administration was exemplary. He encouraged agricultural development and trade, established a permanent judiciary, and introduced a uniform legal code. His patience, unassuming demeanor, and knowledge of several African languages made him an effective arbiter of disputes between settlers and indigenous tribes. Russwurm's periodic reports, published in the *Maryland Colonization Journal*, offer a revealing black perspective on colonial life in West Africa. He spent his last years working for the annexation of the Maryland-in-Liberia settlement by the newly formed Republic of Liberia. The annexation was completed in 1855, four years after his death. The Maryland Colonization Society commemorated Russwurm by erecting a monument in his honor at Cape Palmas. *DANB*, 538–39; *DAB*, 2:253; *FJ*, 23 January, 25 April 1828, 14, 21 February, 14 March 1829 [17:0534, 0548, 0592–94, 0599]; *Lib*, 16, 30 April, 7 May 1831, 25 February 1832, 9 May 1835 [1:0066–67, 0147, 0584]; *AR*, August 1834 [1:0495–97]; *MCJ*, April 1837, July 1838, January 1850, October 1851 [2:0005, 0517–18, 6:0328]; *CA*, 13 May 1837, 27 January 1838 [2:0057, 0369]; Joseph R. Dailey to Robert Purvis, 15 August 1833, Anti-Slavery Collection, MB [1:0326–30]; William M. Brewer, "John Brown Russwurm," *JNH* 13:413–22 (October 1928); Philip S. Foner, "J. B. Russwurm: A Document,"

JNH 54:393–97 (October 1969); Donald M. Jacobs, "A History of the Boston Negro from the Revolution to the Civil War" (Ph.D. diss., Boston University, 1968), 49–50; Campbell, *Maryland in Africa*, 151, 162, 171, 212.

12. Robert Purvis (1810–1898) was born in Charleston, South Carolina, the son of William Purvis, a cotton broker, and Harriet Judah, the mulatto daughter of a German Jewish merchant and his former slave wife. In 1819 the family moved to Philadelphia. When William Purvis died in 1826, he left a legacy of strong antislavery convictions that particularly influenced Robert, and he left an inheritance that provided for his family. Robert Purvis concluded his formal education after a year at Amherst College then returned to Philadelphia, where he began his abolitionist career by contributing to William Lloyd Garrison's *Liberator* and by helping to organize the American Anti-Slavery Society in 1833. In 1834 Purvis married Harriet Forten, daughter of James Forten, the black abolitionist and wealthy Philadelphia sailmaker. He also traveled to England to blunt colonizationist appeals abroad and to fashion international antislavery cooperation.

Throughout the remainder of the 1830s, Purvis focused his attention on the problems of Pennsylvania blacks and on the creation of a Pennsylvania antislavery network. He joined the Young Men's Anti-Slavery Society of Philadelphia, led the formation of the Pennsylvania Anti-Slavery Society in 1837, and in 1838 chaired the committee of black citizens that drafted the *Appeal of Forty Thousand*—a protest against the Pennsylvania Reform Convention's attempt to take away black suffrage. When the antislavery movement divided in 1840, Purvis remained with the AASS. Although he supported the free produce movement, he vowed to "eschew all means [except] pure morality to end slavery." Passage of the Fugitive Slave Law and ferment among black abolitionists about their role in the movement redirected Purvis's antislavery activities after 1850. Purvis was always a supporter of fugitive slave rescue efforts, and in the 1850s, he became dedicated to that work. He built secret hiding places for fugitive slaves in his Philadelphia home and at his two Byberry farms, and in 1855 he advocated the impeachment of U.S. District Court Judge John K. Kane for his decisions in fugitive slave cases. By 1859 Purvis claimed to be ready "to kill every oppressor" that stood in his or any fugitive's way to freedom.

Purvis's antislavery commitment was reinforced by racial prejudice. The Purvis children were excluded from public schools, and Purvis was refused permission to participate in agricultural competitions and was harassed by antiabolitionists. Purvis cautioned that some abolitionists, thought to be the "only true friends of the colored man, were not consistent in their conduct." During the Civil War, Purvis enlisted blacks in the Union army. After the war, he served as commissioner of the Freedman's Savings Bank, supported passage of the Fourteenth Amendment, and helped found the Pennsylvania Equal Rights Association, an organization dedicated to suffrage for women and blacks. In later life, Purvis continued his work for black equality as well as for municipal reform in Philadelphia. *DANB*, 508–10; William Wells Brown, *The Rising Son; or the Antecedents and the Advancement of the Colored Race* (Boston, Mass., 1874; reprint, New York, N.Y., 1970), 468–69; William Still, *The Underground Railroad* (Philadelphia, Pa., 1872; reprint, Chicago, Ill., 1970), 736–38; Janice Sumler Lewis, "The

Fortens of Philadelphia: An Afro-American Family and Nineteenth-Century Reform" (Ph.D. diss., Georgetown University, 1978), 44–46, 50–52, 65–76, 94–95, 106–8, 184–90, 205–7, 243; *PPr*, 3 August 1890, 16 April 1898; *PEB*, 16 December 1859; *NYH*, 12 May 1854; *PF*, 29 March 1838, 20 December 1848; *Lib*, 17 May, 14 June 1834, 10 August 1836, 10 January 1837, 10 May 1838, 19 August 1842, 1 September 1848, 9 September, 25 November, 6 December 1853, 5 May 1854; *NASS*, 25 October 1849, 20 May 1852, 12 November, 3 December 1853, 13 May 1854, 13 January, 8 September 1855, 7 February 1858, 6 March 1863, 8 April 1865, 22 December 1866, 14 January 1871.

13. Mail leaving Liberia was generally carried by vessels involved in the West African coastal trade. Dailey observes that, unlike Banquo and the ghosts and spirits that frequently appear in William Shakespeare's plays, the vessels visited Liberia infrequently, particularly during the rainy season.

14. The American Colonization Society was founded in 1816 with the primary goal of removing free blacks from the United States, particularly to its colony in Liberia; secondarily, the ACS sought to aid the manumission of slaves and to suppress the slave trade. The society lobbied without success for congressional endorsement of African colonization as national policy. Ralph R. Gurley, longtime ACS secretary and editor of the society's organ, the *African Repository*, forged the ACS into a prominent national association with hundreds of state and local auxiliaries. But during the 1830s and 1840s, the society was weakened by strong opposition from northern free blacks and the growing abolitionist movement, by the conversion of some leading members to abolitionism, by competition from independent and local societies, and by internal division. When Liberians won their independence in 1847, the ACS became merely an advocate of black emigration. Although it was inactive after the Civil War, a skeletal organization remained into the 1960s. During its initial fifty years, the ACS claimed to have collected $2,500,000 for Liberian colonization and to have transported twelve thousand blacks to Africa. P. J. Staudenraus, *The African Colonization Movement, 1816–1865* (New York, N.Y., 1961).

15. Government House was the name given to the Liberia colony's administrative center in Monrovia, which housed the governor. Campbell, *Maryland in Africa*, 28.

16. Dailey refers to his business partner, John B. Russwurm.

17. "Petit maître" is a French idiom meaning "dandy" or "fop."

18. Daily quotes from *In Eutropium* by the fifth-century Roman poet Claudian. Translated from the Latin, this quotation means "nothing is so odious as a clown risen to power."

19. Bashaw, a variant of pasha, was a term used to describe a military commander, a provincial governor, or another man of high rank or office in Morocco or the Ottoman Empire.

20. The American Colonization Society and the Maryland Colonization Society sent 942 colonists to Liberia in 1832 but only 289 the following year. Emigration estimates do not include recaptured Africans or individuals sent by other independent colonization societies. Staudenraus, *African Colonization Movement*, 251; Campbell, *Maryland in Africa*, 44, 57–58.

21. Death and disease plagued the Liberian experiment from its inception.

Black settlers and white agents succumbed to the ravages of malaria, known simply as the "fever." Although 4,571 blacks settled in Liberia during the colony's first twenty-three years, the census of 1843 reported only 2,388 residents. Twenty-two percent of all immigrants died during their first year of residence. Shick, *Behold the Promised Land*, 22–28; Staudenraus, *African Colonization Movement*, 102–3.

22. Dailey quotes from night 1, line 212 of *Night Thoughts* by English poet Edward Young (1683–1765):

> Insatiate archer! could not one suffice?
> Thy shaft flew thrice; and thrice my peace was slain.

Dailey uses these lines to refer to three deaths that had taken place among a group of 145 black settlers who had recently come from Charleston. They landed in Liberia in January 1833, but by May the "withering hand of death" had swept over them, causing many to regret their move. John Givins (1792–?), a free black carpenter and Baptist preacher, left Charleston with his wife Dorothy, two sons, and three daughters. Dorothy Givins, the three daughters, and one son died of malaria shortly after they arrived. Givins soon returned to the United States with his surviving son and became an outspoken critic of colonization. Cloak-maker Catherine Smith (b. 1797), her farmer-husband Carolos Smith (b. 1783), and shoemaker Abraham Rogers (b. 1779) were also among the dozens of free black Charlestonians who died within a few weeks of their coming to the colony. Joseph R. Dailey to Robert Purvis, 2 May, 15 August 1833, Anti-Slavery Collection, MB [1:0280–82, 0326–30]; *AR*, January, February 1833; Tom W. Shick, *Emigrants to Liberia, 1820 to 1843: An Alphabetical Listing* (Newark, Del., 1971), 37, 81, 88; *E*, 20 July 1833 [1:0324].

23. Dailey's playful remark alludes to a line in act 3, scene 6, of William Shakespeare's *King Lear* (1606), in which three imaginary dogs turn against the insane king:

> The little dogs and all,
> Tray, Blanche, and Sweetheart, see
> They bark at me.

Dailey uses this line in reference to attacks he has received from colonizationists.

24. Joseph R. Dailey, a Virginia native, was working as a mariner in Philadelphia by 1820. After sailing to Monrovia, Liberia, in the early 1830s, he joined John B. Russwurm in a short-lived partnership in the West African trade. Dailey remained in Africa well into the 1840s, while maintaining close business and personal ties with prominent Philadelphia blacks. His criticisms of the Liberian colony, particularly its administration and living conditions, attracted widespread attention in the antislavery press. By 1845 Dailey was back in Philadelphia, where he participated in local efforts to support the black press. He returned to Liberia but came back to Philadelphia in 1865, intending "to lay his bones in the soil of his native city." Joseph R. Dailey to Robert Purvis, 12 April, 2 May, 15 August 1833, Anti-Slavery Collection, MB [1:0266–69, 0278–82, 0326–30]; *PF*, 12 November, 24 December 1840, 20 August 1846 [3:0697, 0756, 5:0258]; *CA*, 25 September 1841 [4:0214]; Julie Winch, *Philadelphia's Black Elite: Activ-*

ism, Accommodation, and the Struggle for Autonomy, 1787–1848 (Philadelphia, Pa., 1988), 43–44, 47; James deT. Abajian, *Blacks in Selected Newspapers, Censuses, and Other Sources: An Index to Names and Subjects*, 5 vols. (Boston, Mass., 1976), 1:517; *Philadelphia City Directory*, 1820, 1845; *WAA*, 9 December 1865.

2.
James Forten to William Lloyd Garrison
31 December 1830
6 May 1832

An organized black abolitionist movement evolved from the struggle against colonization. By 1830 black leaders had forged a three-part agenda—fighting colonization, ending slavery, and gaining equal rights —and for the first time, they found white reformers willing to embrace their cause. More than anyone else, William Lloyd Garrison symbolized black hopes for change. Once a supporter of gradual emancipation and black resettlement in Liberia, Garrison, by 1830, had joined blacks in opposing racism, slavery, and colonization. Free blacks welcomed the appearance of the *Liberator*, hailing Garrison's antislavery newspaper as "the faithful representative of our sentiments and interests; the uncompromising advocate of our indefeasible rights." Blacks provided Garrison with indispensable assistance, even guarding him from personal attack. The timely and generous support of black abolitionists such as Philadelphians Joseph R. Cassey and James Forten, Sr., carried the *Liberator* through its first year. Blacks also supported and distributed Garrison's *Thoughts on African Colonization* (1832), certain that it would destroy the American Colonization Society's reputation as an antislavery organization. Two letters by Forten reveal the close relationship between Garrison and black leaders, the importance they placed on his antislavery efforts, and the black role in the rise of an immediatist antislavery movement. *Lib*, 19 February, 12 March, 29 October 1831, 28 January 1848 [1:0032–33, 0037, 0128]; James Forten to William Lloyd Garrison, 20 October 1831, Joseph Cassey to William Lloyd Garrison, 16 October 1832, Anti-Slavery Collection, MB [1:0122–23, 0223–24]; Winch, *Philadelphia's Black Elite*, 81–82.

Philad[elphi]a., [Pennsylvania]
December 31st, 1830

Dear Sir:[1]

I am extremely happy to hear ~~by your letter of the 15 inst.~~ that you are about establishing a Paper in Boston. I hope your efforts may not be in vain; and may the "Liberator" be the means of exposing, more and more, the odious system of Slavery, and of raising up friends to the oppressed and degraded People of Colour, throughout the Union. Whilst so much is doing in the world, to ameliorate the condition of Mankind, and the spirit of Freedom is marching with rapid Strides, and causing Tyrants to tremble; may America awake from the apathy in which she has long slumbered. She must, sooner or later, fall in with the irresistable current. Great efforts are now making in the cause of Liberty: The People are becoming more interested and determined on the subject.

Although the Southern States have enacted severe laws, against the Free People of Colour,[2] they will find it impossible to go in opposition to the Spirit of the Times. We have only to hope, that many such Philanthropists, as Mr. Lundy[3] and yourself, will come forward, to plead our cause; we can never feel sufficiently grateful to ~~that~~ our long tried, faithful and zealous friend Mr. Lundy. He has indeed laboured for us, through evil and good report, and under many disadvantages & hardships; may he hereafter receive his reward.

I learn with the greatest regret, that so much prejudice exists in the Eastern States; but may the "Standard you are about to erect in the Eyes of the Nation" be the means of dispersing those clourds of Error, and of bringing many Advocates to our Cause.

I would have answered your Letter earlier, had it not been owing in the first place, to a multiplicity of business, which prevented me from soliciting Subscribers to your Paper. I herewith enclose you the Money for twenty ~~five~~ seven Subscribers, and their names and places of abode, you will also herewith receive. I would request you to send on a few Extra Papers that I may hand them to my friends.

Wishing you every success, and that the Liberator may have an extensive Patronage. I remain with the greatest Respect. Your's,

James Forten[4]

P.S. I think if Mr. Joseph Cassey[5] will act as your Agent that he will obtain many Subscribers to your Paper.

Philadelphia, [Pennsylvania]
May 6th, 1832

Mr. William Lloyd Garrison
My Dear Sir:

I hasten to reply to your letter, and to comply with the request you make. I sincerely hope your Sanguine expectations may be realized, in regard to the work you are about publishing, and that it may be the means of exposing, in full, the exact views of the colonization society towards the people of color.[6] Such a work is very desirable at present, when the society is making so many converts,[7] and its influence extending like a torrent carrying with it not only a host of avowed enemies, and many declared well wishers, but I am afraid some real friends, who are deceived by its specious pretenses. If sometimes, the weight, numbers, and unbounded influence of the colonizationist, make me almost despair, viewing ourselves as mere pebbles, opposing the course of a mighty torrent over which it rushes unheedingly by; yet, on the other hand, the recollection that <u>ours</u> is the cause of justice—and though feeble, despised, and the victims of a cruel prejudice, we are not overlooked by Him who suffers not a sparrow to fall without his notice[8]—it is then I feel that, although our efforts are hardly visible to those around us, many of whom think our opposition vain and useless, yet we may steadily, though perhaps slowly, raise our barrier against this encroaching torrent of colonization, and before it is to late, check its course. If the popular feeling was not so much in its favour, your work would obtain a much greater circulation, but its advocates in general, will hear nothing on the other side; I think however if you were to send a few coppys to some Bookseller in Philadelphia, they would perhaps sell well, at any rate they would attract public notice, and eventually fall into the hands, of those who, unless they were thus brought before them, might never have right, or impartial views on the subject. Your friends are not inactive in endeavouring to obtain subscribers. Mr. Purvis has already 70, on his list. I must not omit this opportunity of thanking you for the Discourse of the Rev. Mr. May[9] the perusal of which afforded me much pleasure. It would be well if more of his brethern were to follow his example, on our next National Anniversary.[10] An indisposition which has confined me to the house for a week, prevents me expressing my sentiments more fully, my head which is much affected, does not allow me to make much exertion, and warns me to conclude.

My family's[11] best thanks for your kind remembrance of them, we all hope (should nothing occur to prevent) to have the pleasure of seeing you on at the convention. With sincere wishes for your continued success I am, Dear Sir. Yours',

James Forten

1. William Lloyd Garrison (1805–1879) was born in Newburyport, Massachusetts, raised by a local Baptist deacon, and apprenticed to a newspaper editor at age thirteen. After working at Benjamin Lundy's *Genius of Universal Emancipation*, Garrison, in January 1831, founded the *Liberator*, a Boston-based antislavery weekly. With intermittent assistance, he edited the paper for the next thirty-five years. It became the most controversial, best known, and most widely read antislavery newspaper. In addition to advocating immediate abolition of slavery, the paper at various times supported anticolonization, free produce, disunionism, anti-Sabbatarianism, nonresistance (including opposition to political antislavery), and women's rights and generally gave a sympathetic hearing to most other mid-nineteenth-century reform causes. It informed readers about antislavery meetings and activities, published letters from abolitionists and their

critics, reviewed antislavery literature, and reported federal government actions concerning slavery.

From the 1830s on, Garrison was instrumental in organizing the antislavery movement and discrediting the American Colonization Society. He helped found the New England Anti-Slavery Society in 1831 and the American Anti-Slavery Society in 1833. During the 1840s, Garrison consolidated his control of the AASS, rejected political antislavery, promoted international antislavery cooperation (touring England in 1846), and condemned the slave power conspiracy. Although he was disheartened by proslavery government actions in the 1850s, Garrison continued his antislavery efforts until the slaves were emancipated (January 1863) and the Thirteenth Amendment was passed. After the Civil War, Garrison ceased publishing the *Liberator* (December 1865) and left the AASS but pursued various reform interests, including temperance, women's rights, and free trade. *DAB*, 7:168–72.

2. Antebellum southern state legislatures attempted to diminish the difference between free blacks and slaves. Many states passed laws to render free blacks powerless, submissive, and dependent by imposing fines or whippings for those free blacks who associated with slaves, met in large groups, owned firearms or dogs without a license, attended school, or held unauthorized church services. Every southern state barred blacks from testifying in court against whites, and Georgia even denied blacks the right to a jury trial. Georgia, Virginia, and South Carolina also restricted black economic opportunity. Ira Berlin, *Slaves without Masters: The Free Negro in the Antebellum South* (New York, N.Y., 1974), 94–97, 316–17.

3. Benjamin Lundy (1789–1839) was a Quaker abolitionist. In 1821 he founded the *Genius of Universal Emancipation*, an antislavery journal, which he continued to publish intermittently and in various locations until his death. Lundy is best remembered as William Lloyd Garrison's mentor, having recruited the younger abolitionist to help edit the *Genius* in 1829. *DAB*, 11:506–07.

4. James E. Forten (1766–1842), a free black born in Philadelphia, received his education at Anthony Benezet's Quaker school. During the Revolutionary War, he served on an American privateer, which was captured by the British. Forten spent several months on a prison ship and, after his release, resided in England for a year. Upon returning to Philadelphia, he worked as a sailmaker's apprentice for Robert Bridges. He eventually inherited Bridges's firm, the first step in amassing a personal fortune of $100,000, which placed him among the city's wealthiest citizens. His eight children received private tutoring, and he encouraged his daughters as well as his sons to participate in reform organizations and antislavery activities. At their elegant three-story residence on Lombard Street, the Fortens entertained British and American abolitionists, African dignitaries, and other notables. As patriarch of black Philadelphia's most prominent family, Forten's leadership was unsurpassed. He helped establish the Free African Society (1787), the African Masonic Lodge (1797), and St. Thomas's African Episcopal Church (1794), the first black organizations in the city. His philanthropy was extensive. He donated to several of Philadelphia's black churches, helped finance the purchase of Rev. John Gloucester's family from slavery, and covered the legal expenses of fugitive slaves threatened with return to slavery. Forten wrote and spoke on a variety of reform issues—abolition of the slave trade, revision of the

Fugitive Slave Law of 1793, black suffrage, and women's rights. His *Letters From a Man of Color* (1813) was one of the earliest published protests against proscriptive black laws.

In the early nineteenth century, Forten embraced black emigration proposals. He anticipated the development of a strong black nationality and the growth of free trade with Africa. He corresponded with Paul Cuffe and helped finance Cuffe's attempt to establish a black colony in West Africa. He also investigated the prospects for Haitian emigration and gave favorable consideration to the American Colonization Society. The ACS, aware of his social standing, made several attempts to persuade him to settle in Africa. After Cuffe's death in 1817, Forten tempered his enthusiasm for black emigration and gradually strengthened his commitment to racial assimilation.

In the 1820s, he took the lead in opposing colonization and supplied William Lloyd Garrison with the information and funds necessary to compose and publish *Thoughts on African Colonization* (1832). He also collected subscriptions and provided generous financial support for Garrison's *Liberator* in its difficult first years. Forten was a lifelong Garrisonian, helping to found the American Anti-Slavery Society in 1833, supporting the organization financially, and serving on the society's board of managers from 1835 to 1840. He participated in the black national conventions of the 1830s, and despite his age and failing health, the American Moral Reform Society selected him in 1835 as its first president. Forten's military service, business success, and civic reputation made his life a "victory over prejudice," and abolitionists frequently invoked his name as an example of black patriotism and achievement. *DANB*, 234–35; Winch, *Philadelphia's Black Elite*, 8, 11, 18–20, 35–47, 50, 55, 73–74, 81–82, 192n; Lewis, "Fortens of Philadelphia," 21–28, 50–57, 67–68, 72, 78–80.

5. Joseph R. Cassey (1789–1848), a native of the French West Indies, settled in Philadelphia in 1808. A barber, hairdresser, and perfumer by trade, Cassey accumulated considerable wealth by lending money and investing in real estate. He promoted black education, antislavery, and the black press throughout his life. He became involved in moral reform organizations as early as 1818 when he joined the Pennsylvania Augustine Education Society; he later raised funds for a black manual labor college in New Haven and helped organize the Gilbert Lyceum in Philadelphia. Cassey's Caribbean roots and fluency in French contributed to his interest in Haitian emigration proposals in the 1820s. He was active in the black national convention movement, first as a member of the American Society of Free Persons of Colour (1830) and then as treasurer of the American Moral Reform Society. As the first Philadelphia agent for the *Liberator*, Cassey generated early, crucial financial support for the newspaper. William Lloyd Garrison acknowledged that "if not for [Cassey's] zeal, fidelity, and promptness with which he executed his trust, the *Liberator* could not have completed its first [year]." Cassey also distributed the *Abolitionist* and Garrison's *Thoughts on African Colonization* (1832). A member of the American Anti-Slavery Society from its inception, he served on its board of managers from 1834 to 1837. Cassey attended St. Thomas's African Episcopal Church. He married Amy Matilda Williams, the daughter of New York Episcopal clergyman, Peter Williams, Jr., in 1826; she was an active member of the Philadelphia Female Anti-Slavery Society. Cassey suffered from poor health in his later years and died from a heart

ailment in 1848. *Lib*, 24 September 1831, 28 January 1848 [1:0117]; *PF*, 18 November 1847, 13 January 1848 [5:0530]; *NSt*, 9 March 1849 [5:0997]; Joseph R. Cassey to William Lloyd Garrison and Isaac Knapp, 15 February 1834, Anti-Slavery Collection, MB [1:0395–97]; Prince Saunders, *An Address Delivered at the Bethel Church, Philadelphia, on the 30th of September 1818. Before the Pennsylvania Augustine Society for the Education of People of Colour* (Philadelphia, Pa., 1818), 2, 12 [17:0387, 0392]; *Constitution of the American Society of Free Persons of Colour* (Philadelphia, Pa., 1831), 8 [1:0012]; *Minutes and Proceedings of the First Annual Convention of the People of Colour . . .* (Philadelphia, Pa., 1831), 7 [1:0079]; *Minutes and Proceedings of the Second Annual Convention for the Improvement of the Free People of Colour . . .* (Philadelphia, Pa., 1832), 25 [1:0182]; Lewis, "Fortens of Philadelphia," 56, 58, 105; Julie P. Winch, "Leaders of Philadelphia's Black Community, 1787–1848" (Ph.D. diss., Bryn Mawr College, 1982), 40, 59, 83–87, 95, 252, 310–11; Martin R. Delany, *The Condition, Elevation, Emigration and Destiny of the Colored People of the United States* (Philadelphia, Pa., 1852; reprint, New York, N.Y., 1969), 94–95.

6. During the first months of 1832, William Lloyd Garrison researched and wrote *Thoughts on African Colonization*, a 238-page examination of the American movement to return blacks to Africa. Based on extensive analyses of American Colonization Society reports and influenced by black abolitionists, Garrison's volume refuted colonizationist claims that America could solve its racial problems by resettling free blacks and emancipated slaves in an African colony. Garrison argued that ACS members condoned slavery, sought to expel free blacks from America, and denied the possibility of black progress in African freedom. His work also underscored the unanimity of anticolonizationist sentiment among free blacks and demonstrated that blacks regarded themselves not as aliens but as full American citizens. William Lloyd Garrison, *Thoughts on African Colonization* (Boston, Mass., 1832; reprint New York, N.Y., 1969); Walter M. Merrill and Louis Ruchames, eds., *The Letters of William Lloyd Garrison*, 6 vols. (Cambridge, Mass., 1971–82), 4:77, 150–51, 161, 195–96, 255.

7. The American Colonization Society ranked among the nation's most important organizations by the early 1830s. It penetrated every section of the country, establishing seventeen state societies and over two hundred local auxiliaries. Staudenraus, *African Colonization Movement*, 117–49, 207.

8. In Matthew 10:29, the writer discusses divine omniscience by asking: "Are not two sparrows sold for a farthing? and one of them shall not fall on the ground without your Father." Forten paraphrases this verse.

9. Forten refers to Samuel Joseph May's 1832 pamphlet, *A Discourse on Slavery in the United States*. May (1797–1871) fought to integrate the three Unitarian churches he served from 1822 until 1867. A model Garrisonian abolitionist, May also advocated temperance, peace, education, women's rights, and abolition of capital punishment. In 1845 he moved to Syracuse, New York, continuing his reform activities, and in 1851 participated in the rescue of the fugitive slave, "Jerry." *DAB*, 6(2):447–48.

10. Each May, from the 1830s through 1870, American benevolent and reform societies held annual gatherings in New York City known as national anniversaries. The meetings included health reformers, peace and penal reform advo-

cates, education reformers, tract and bible societies, missionary societies, Sunday school unions, the American Anti-Slavery Society, the American and Foreign Anti-Slavery Society, the American Colonization Society, and others. The anniversaries were an opportunity for organizations "to compare notes, hold meetings, and raise money." All utilized a similar format, beginning with religious services on a Sunday, followed by a week of organizational meetings; four to five concurrent meetings were not unusual. Clifford S. Griffin, *Their Brothers' Keepers: Moral Stewardship in the United States, 1800–1865* (New Brunswick, N.J., 1960), 28, 34, 36, 40, 64.

11. In 1832 James Forten's family included his wife Charlotte (1784–1884) and their eight children: James, Jr. (1817–?), Robert Bridges (?–1864), William D., Thomas Francis Willing, Margaretta (1808–1875), Harriet (1810–1875), Sarah Louisa (1814–?), and Mary. Lewis, "Fortens of Philadelphia," 12, 38–51.

3.
William Watkins to William Lloyd Garrison
12 February 1831

Black abolitionists understood the importance of the press in the struggle against slavery, racism, and colonization. Blacks served as subscription agents, solicited funds, and purchased advertising space in antislavery journals, embracing those efforts as part of their responsibilities as abolitionists. Many newspapers benefited from their efforts, but none more than William Lloyd Garrison's *Liberator*. In a 12 February 1831 letter to Garrison, William Watkins, writing under the pseudonym "A Colored Baltimorean," praised the *Liberator*, pledged his support for the recently founded paper, and stated the need for blacks to recognize the value of a reform press. Watkins promised to use his "influence in procuring it a circulation among our people." Through the efforts of black abolitionists like Watkins, blacks made up three-quarters of the *Liberator*'s subscription list by 1834. Benjamin Quarles, *Black Abolitionists* (London, 1969), 19–20, 32–36, 85–89; Jane H. Pease and William H. Pease, *They Who Would Be Free: Blacks' Search for Freedom, 1830–1861* (New York, N.Y., 1974), 31, 113–19.

Baltimore, [Maryland]
Feb. 12, 1831

To the Editor of the Liberator.

DEAR SIR:

I have received and read, with peculiar pleasure, five numbers of your interesting, and to us, invaluable paper. We recognize, in the *Liberator*, the true friend of bleeding humanity; the faithful representative of our sentiments and interests; the uncompromising advocate of our indefeisible rights. Being thus impressed, I shall not only patronize it myself, but shall use my little influence in procuring it a circulation among our people. Were my brethren, in general, sufficiently apprised of the nature of your disinterested and generous undertaking—were they aware of the virulent opposition, the unmerited calumny, the relentless persecution, combined with the numerous privations which the espousal of our unpopular cause has doomed you to encounter—methinks your paper would be richly supported, maugre all the machinations that the ingenuity and malice of evil spirits can devise, or the power of wicked men inflict. But, alas for us! we are, as a body, too blind to our interests. Instead of profiting by the many lessons we have had, on frugality and economy, and diligently pursuing that which contributes to the moral, intellectual, and political elevation of any people, too many of us are grasping at unsubstantial forms; lavishing our hard earnings upon those glittering bubbles which characterize the giddy and the gay in the higher walks of fashionable life. Treading those fascinating paths, in our present condition, is not only imprudent, but as it incapacitates us to pursue objects of far greater utility, must necessarily tend to perpetuate our degradation.

When we say, however, that we are, as a body, blind to our interests, we would not be understood as meaning, we are ignorant of our condition, and unconscious of our rights: this cannot be in America. The *self-evident* principles, "that all men are created *equal*, and endowed by their Creator with certain *unalienable* rights, that among these are life, liberty, and the pursuit of happiness," are as indelibly stamped upon our original faculties, as upon those of the lords of the land. But we would be understood, more particularly, as having reference to our blindness as it regards the influence of the press upon the destinies of any people; especially, when that powerful engine is wielded in behalf of our bleeding cause.

Of the truth of this remark, you have, doubtless, had abundant evidence. Were it otherwise, how comes it that our friend Lundy,[1] that undaunted champion of our rights, has been obliged, for a long series of years, to struggle against wind and tide, to combat, almost singly, the talent, power, and deep-rooted prejudice, that have been arrayed against us, without an efficient support from the people of color? Why is it, that untimely and withering blight was permitted to nip, in the bud, that promising production of your united efforts? Why is it, that our warm and intrepid friend Cornish was not sustained in his laudable efforts to meliorate our condition?[2] Why, I emphatically ask, are all these evils? Are they to be ascribed to a want of gratitude to our benefactors? No people in the world are more grateful to their friends than we, when we know them to be such.

The truth is, these evils, so far as we are concerned, are mainly attributable to the cause I have already assigned: we are, as a body, unacquainted with the salutary influence which an uncorrupted, independent press is calculated to exert upon our future destiny. We hope that the intelligent and influential of our brethren will take this thing into serious consideration, and act accordingly. We know no time more favorable for this, than that of our next general convention.

Before we have done, permit us to express our surprise at the course pursued by some of our religious presses, in regard to the degraded condition and violated rights of the people of color in this country. These papers are edited, we believe, chiefly by ministers of the gospel, many of whom will not, or dare not speak the truth in relation to us, on account of the extreme unpopularity of our cause, or for fear of exciting the ire of their *religious* slaveholding patrons. They can declaim vehemently against intemperance and infidelity in the land; they can thunder across the Atlantic against the shocking barbarities of the slave trade in Africa; they can shout for joy when they hear of the downfall of tyrants, and the progress of liberal principles in the old world; they can commiserate, with extreme sensitiveness, the condition of the unfortunate of other climes; while they can behold, in their own land, the degraded condition of their colored countrymen; while they can see the slave-trader tear asunder the dearest ties of consanguinity—separating, forever, husbands and wives, parents and children, brothers and sisters, without uttering one word in behalf of these unfortunate but innocent sufferers.

But we do not despair; nor will we give place to, or encourage in others, those feelings which such a state of things is naturally calculated to excite. We shall rather cherish those sentiments of forgiveness and those emotions of gratitude, which are inspired by the thought that we have *some* friends—faithful and tried friends, who, in pleading our cause, regard neither the smiles nor the frowns of men. We have been pleased to notice, that some of our religious editors are beginning to act the part of the good Samaritan. The Lord bless them, for their labors of love. They have our prayers and our thanks, and we regret these are all we can bestow. But we are sorry to state, there are others, with whom we are connected, by a double bond of Church membership, who, like the unfeeling priest and Levite, after viewing our condition, "pass by on the other side,"[3] where they now stand, with folded hands, crying, "the subject of slavery involves considerations too weighty for us to decide upon. We are not sufficiently acquainted with local circumstances, and other peculiarities in this case, to enable us to judge for another. *All we can say* is, in the language of the apostle, 'If thou mayest be free, use it rather.' "[4] This language, from such a source, is truly surprising. Nay, when I reflect that ministers of the gospel can indulge in such cowering tergiversation, in relation to one of the greatest evils that ever cursed the globe, or opposed the march of the Redeemer's kingdom, I burn with indignation. I feel that my master's cause is dishonored in the very face of infidelity.

It may be thought, we are rather warm in these strictures: we think otherwise. Extreme frigidity on the one side, should elicit correspondent heat on the other. As these ministers were never called to promulgate such language as they have done, relative to slavery, we shall conclude by reminding them of the language in which their commission runs: "Son of man, I have made thee a watchman unto the house of Israel: therefore hear the words at my mouth, and give them warning from me. When I say unto the wicked, (and are not slaveholders and slave traders preeminently so?) thou shalt surely die; and thou givest him not warning, nor speakest to warn the wicked from his wicked way, to save his life; the same wicked man shall die in his iniquity; but his blood will I require at thy hand. Cry aloud and spare not: lift up thy voice like a trumpet, and show my people their transgressions, and the house of Jacob their sins."[5] These words are of awful import. They impose an obligation on ministers of the gospel, in reference to slaveholders and their abettors, which it would be well for them duly and faithfully to discharge; or, at least, so thinks

A COLORED BALTIMOREAN[6]

Liberator (Boston, Mass.), 19 February 1831.

1. Benjamin Lundy.
2. Samuel E. Cornish (ca. 1796–1858) was born free in Sussex County, Delaware, moved to Philadelphia in 1816, was educated by black minister John Gloucester, and eventually taught at Gloucester's African School. Cornish was licensed to preach in 1819 and ministered two years in Maryland before moving to New York City as pastor of the First Colored Presbyterian Church (later Shiloh Presbyterian Church). He remained there until 1828, when he relinquished the post to his protégé, Theodore S. Wright. Cornish's first years in New York reveal many of the ideas that framed his future reform activity. He opposed colonization, and though he flirted with emigration, he rejected it as a solution to black problems. He believed that education, moral reform, and self-help were the means to improve the condition of free black Americans but never hesitated to censure white prejudice. Cornish's first public forum was as senior editor of *Freedom's Journal*, the first black American newspaper, which was established by Cornish and John Russwurm in 1827. Cornish remained with the paper until its demise in March 1829 and, two months later, established the short-lived *Rights of All*.

Cornish also devoted his energies to black organizations that sponsored practical programs for black improvement. He supported the nascent black convention movement during the early 1830s and worked as an agent for the Phoenix Society of New York (a black protective association that sponsored the Phoenix High School for Colored Youth); he was an organizer of the American Moral Reform Society; and he helped Lewis and Arthur Tappan establish the New York Anti-Slavery Society. In 1835 Cornish became a member of the executive committee of Garrison's American Anti-Slavery Society, a position he held until 1840. In March 1837, he founded the *Colored American*, the most successful of the early black newspapers.

During the late 1830s and early 1840s, Cornish's positions on antislavery and black self-help led him into a series of conflicts and controversies. In June 1839, he was attacked for his opposition to the idea of an antislavery political party, and as a member of the executive committee of the New York State Vigilance Committee, Cornish forced the resignation of David Ruggles as the committee's secretary because of Ruggles's belief in extralegal activities to free fugitive slaves. Cornish was also involved in the schism within the American Anti-Slavery Society, objecting to William Lloyd Garrison's anticlerical tone and his stance on the role of women in the movement. Although he did not support an antislavery political party, he believed in political action as an antislavery instrument and supported the black suffrage movement. For those reasons, as well as his longtime friendship with Lewis Tappan and his anger with the American Anti-Slavery Society for its 1838 decision to drop agents assigned to educate free blacks, Cornish helped organize the American and Foreign Anti-Slavery Society in May 1840 and became a member of its executive committee.

By the mid-1840s, Cornish was estranged from many of his associates in the American and Foreign Anti-Slavery Society over the issue of an antislavery political party. But Cornish did not allow antislavery controversies to interfere with his role in the black church. He helped J. W. C. Pennington organize the Union Missionary Society (1841), assisted Lewis Tappan when he reorganized the society into the American Missionary Association (1845), and served as pastor to Presbyterian churches in New Jersey and the Emmanuel Church of New York City. Cornish continued as an active antislavery reformer well into the 1850s. William H. Pease and Jane H. Pease, *Bound with Them in Chains* (Westport, Conn., 1972), 140–61; David E. Swift, "Black Presbyterian Attacks on Racism: Samuel E. Cornish, Theodore S. Wright, and Their Contemporaries," *JPH* 51: 433–70 (Winter 1973); Quarles, *Black Abolitionists*, 6, 33, 68, 79–80, 109; Howard Bell, "The American Moral Reform Society, 1836–1841," *JNE* 27:34– 40 (Winter 1958); Bella Gross, "Freedom's Journal and the Rights of All," *JNH* 27:241–86 (July 1932); Howard H. Bell, "Free Negroes of the North, 1830– 1835: A Study in National Cooperation," *JNE* 26:447–55 (Fall 1957); Pease and Pease, *They Who Would Be Free*, 12, 24–26, 31, 71, 79–84, 113, 122, 133–34, 136, 175, 194–95, 209–11, 257–58, 291–92; Floyd J. Miller, *The Search for a Black Nationality: Black Emigration and Colonization, 1787–1863* (Urbana, Ill., 1975), 82–84; *DANB*, 134–35.

3. Watkins refers to the parable of the Good Samaritan in Luke 10:29–37, in which a Jew was beaten by robbers and left to die. Jewish religious authorities ignored his condition, but a Samaritan—considered an outcast in Jewish culture—nursed him back to health. Watkins compares many American Christians to the "unfeeling priest and Levite" in their unwillingness to confront racial oppression and slavery.

4. Watkins quotes from 1 Corinthians 7:21, "Art thou called being a servant? care not for it: but if thou mayest be made free, use it rather." St. Paul, who was convinced that the world was about to come to an end, urged Christians not to waste time trying to change their outward condition, but to accept their status, whether slaves or free men.

5. Watkins quotes from Ezekiel 33:7–8.

6. William Watkins (1801–1858) was born to free parents in Baltimore. He received his early education at a school operated by Rev. Daniel Coker, a prominent black Methodist clergyman, at his Sharp Street Church. At age nineteen, Watkins established his own school. The Watkins Academy offered courses in grammar, reading, writing, natural philosophy, music, and mathematics to local black children for twenty-five years. Watkins's oratorical and leadership skills placed him at the forefront of Baltimore's black community from the late 1820s to the early 1840s. Having studied medicine, he frequently prescribed treatments for black patients; he regularly ministered to black parishioners at the city's Sharp Street, John Wesley, Orchard Street, Asbury, and Centennial congregations; and he helped organize a local black literary society. But Watkins is best remembered for his antislavery work. He first attracted attention in late 1826

when he publicly refuted the notion, purported by the American Colonization Society, that free blacks wanted to settle in West Africa. He chastised colonizationists for their patronizing and selfish attitudes, criticized white churches and white clergymen for urging black Christians to settle in a "heathen land," and argued that blacks thought of themselves as Americans, not Africans. Watkins urged blacks to "die in Maryland, under the pressure of unrighteous and cruel laws [rather] than be driven like cattle to the pestilential clime of Liberia." He personally dissuaded many local blacks from emigrating. Watkins penned numerous anticolonization and antislavery essays, which were published in Benjamin Lundy's *Genius of Universal Emancipation* and William Lloyd Garrison's *Liberator* under the pseudonym "A Colored Baltimorean" during the late 1820s and 1830s. He also served as a local subscription agent for the *Liberator* and frequently corresponded with Garrison, thus serving as a conduit linking Baltimore blacks with the broader antislavery movement. After the mid-1830s, Watkins turned his attention from anticolonization to black education, frequently writing on that subject for the *Colored American*. Although never prominent in the black convention movement, he was a charter member of the American Moral Reform Society that emerged from the movement in 1835. He endorsed all of the AMRS's objectives—education, temperance, economy, and universal liberty— but he paid particular attention to the society's educational work. Watkins severed his relationship with the AMRS two years later because he believed that members paid too much attention to semantic questions rather than to antislavery work. Watkins's stature and credibility in the antislavery movement were destroyed when he became attracted to the millennialist ideas of Adventist preacher William Miller in 1844 and was convinced that the world was coming to an end. Baltimore's worsening racial climate prompted Watkins to settle in Toronto, where he opened a grocery in September 1852. He continued to write occasional antislavery essays, publishing them in *Frederick Douglass' Paper* under the pen name "A Colored Canadian." Watkins was the father of William J. Watkins and the uncle of antislavery lecturer Frances Ellen Watkins Harper. Bettye J. Gardner, "William Watkins: Antebellum Black Teacher and Anti-Slavery Writer," *NHB* 39:623–25 (September–October 1976); Leroy Graham, *Baltimore: The Nineteenth-Century Black Capital* (Lanham, Md., 1982), 93–146.

4.
William Watkins to William Lloyd Garrison
May 1831

Black opposition to the American Colonization Society proved crucial
to the rise of an immediatist antislavery movement. Blacks charged that
colonization was a racist and proslavery strategy that widened "the
breach between us and the whites" by strengthening prejudice in the
North and reinforcing slavery in the South. Why else, they asked, would
the ACS describe blacks as inferior if they remained in the United States,
but intelligent and Christian if they chose to emigrate? Black leaders denounced the ACS as a fraud, described its Liberian colony as "a vast
burial ground," and characterized the colonization scheme "as dark as
death and [without] one redeeming virtue in it." By exposing the true
motives of the ACS, blacks destroyed its reputation as a benevolent anti-
slavery organization and convinced many white abolitionists to abandon colonization for immediatist abolitionism. The testimony of black
abolitionists such as William Watkins played an important role in persuading William Lloyd Garrison to oppose colonization and provided
the *Liberator* with evidence to refute ACS claims. One of Watkins's
"Colored Baltimorean" letters, which Garrison printed in the 4 June
1831 issue of the *Liberator*, offered a critique of colonizationist motives. *Lib*, 1 August 1832, 25 January 1834 [1:0210, 0390–92]; Garrison, *Thoughts on African Colonization*, part 2, 13–17 [1:0022–24].

To the Editor of the Liberator.

MR. EDITOR: I have just found time to notice a few very exceptionable features of a communication over the signature of "A Marylander," published, a few days ago, in the *American* of our city.[1] The
writer is unquestionably entitled to the credit of being a thorough-going
colonizationist. He writes in the *true spirit* of the cause. He seems to be
under an excitement produced by the publication of our anti-colonization resolutions. This being the case, it is not to be expected that he
would, throughout his communication, avail himself of the guarded, accommodating, and conciliating language usual with colonization writers
and declaimers. After being convinced that the people of color are not to
be persuaded to leave the land of their birth, and everything vernacular
with them, for "regions" which he tells us are "now dark as the valley of
the shadow of death,"[2] he says, "I would propose then that Maryland
should colonize her own free blacks." He does not add the usual qualification, *"with their own consent:"* he knows this will never be obtained.
He therefore says: "I earnestly *hope* that the time *is now* come when our
state will wake up to all the importance of this subject, and will instantly

commence a *system of measures* imperatively demanded by the *sternest* principles (colonization principles?) of *sound* policy." We would tell this precocious statesman that we are not to be intimidated into colonization *"measures"* by the angry effusions of his illiberal soul; that we [would] rather die in Maryland under the pressure of unrighteous and cruel laws than be driven, like cattle, to the pestilential clime of Liberia, where grievous privation, inevitable disease, and premature death, await us in all their horrors. We are emboldened thus to speak, not from a reliance on the mere arm of flesh; no, it is in the righteousness of our cause, a knowledge of the attributes of Deity, combined with a consciousness of innocence under suffering, that have inspired us with a moral courage which no oppression shall shake, no fulminations overawe. Our limits will not permit us to expatiate, at this time, on the import of the terms, *"a system of measures—the sternest principles,"* &c. We would barely remark that the climax of injustice and cruelty, here suggested, nay, recommended, is the legitimate fruit of the operations of the American colonization societies relative to the free people of color. We have always believed that the *"system of measures"* here recommended, would be the denier resort of these *christian* associations. The unmerited abuse, that has been so unsparingly heaped upon us by colonizationists for expressing our opinions of their project as connected with our happiness, their manifest determination to effectuate their object regardless of our consent, abundantly corroborate the opinion we have long since entertained. We turn, however, from the contemplation of the persecution and oppression, which, it seems, are in reserve for us, to notice, briefly, the moving cause of this virulent and relentless attack upon our rights and happiness. "The *census just taken,*" says "A Marylander," *"admonishes* us in the strongest manner, of the necessity of prompt and efficient measures to drain off this description of our population."[3] Here then is the *patriotic,* the *benevolent,* the *christian,* principle, by which the colonization societies, throughout our land, are actuated. This is the selfish policy of which we complain, and which should be execrated by all *true* patriots, philanthropists, and christians. Our increase is represented as an *"alarming evil—an evil,"* said one of our colonization orators in the pulpit, not long since, "which *threatens* our very *existence.*" Now, if all this be true, how can they, on their own principles, say we can *never* be a people in this country? Surely, they are taking effectual steps to convince us, that the enjoyment of our rights in this, our native land, is not only possible, but highly probable. This we have always believed. And we hope and pray, that it may be accomplished in a way sanctioned by the gospel of peace: "without confused noise, or garments rolled in blood." But this glorious victory over pride and prejudice, by gospel weapons, will never be accomplished by colonization principles. Nor will those ministers of the gospel have any part, or lot, in this matter, who solemnly declare, in the face of heaven and earth, that we can *never enjoy, in this country*, those inalienable rights of man, whose inviolable preservation promotes the welfare of the whole human family. Such ministers virtually declare that they do not believe the doctrines they are bound to preach; that He, from whom they profess to have received their commission, is, indeed, "a hard man, reaping where he has not sown, and gathering where he has not strawed";[4] that He requires of them and their flocks, that which they are morally incapable of performing; that they *cannot* love their neighbor as themselves, or do unto others what they wish done unto themselves, because their Lord, in his wisdom, has given some of their fellow creatures a different color from their own.[5] These temporizing, retrograde reformers are doing a serious injury to the people of color. They heed not the warning of Heaven: "Do my people no harm."[6] They are doing more to strengthen the cruel and unchristian prejudices, already too powerful against us, than all the slaveholders in the Union. They hesitate not to declare, that, in America, we are out of the reach of humanity. They seem to think that the religion of the benevolent Saviour which enjoins, *"honor all men,"* and which explicitly says, "if ye have [no] *respect to persons, ye commit sin*,"[7] is nothing more than a dead letter, or must *for ever* remain powerless, in the United States of America. And have these men the face to contend with the infidels of our land? Why, one infidel, with the bible in his hands, would "chase a thousand, and two put ten thousand to flight."[8] But notwithstanding these discouraging circumstances, our cause will yet triumph. He who is for us, is stronger than all that are against us. "The rulers" of the land may "take counsel together," and some of the professed ministers of Jesus may "come into their secret," but "He that sitteth in the heavens shall laugh: the Lord shall have them in derision."[9] Fear not then, my colored countrymen, but press forward, with a laudable ambition, for all that heaven has intended for you and your children, remembering that the path of duty is the path of safety, and that "righteousness" alone "exalteth a nation."[10]

A COLORED BALTIMOREAN

Liberator (Boston, Mass.), 4 June 1831.

1. The Baltimore *American and Commercial Daily Advertiser*, a leading mercantile journal, was published under various names from 1799 to 1928. It generally published advertisements and business news related to foreign and domestic trade. A letter by "A Marylander" in the 13 May 1831 issue depicted Liberia as a successful experiment and urged Maryland to colonize all *"her own free blacks."* The author insisted that Maryland's increased efforts would prompt other states to act in a similar fashion, leading to a string of settlements along the African coast, the eventual Christianization of Africa, and the elimination of America's

growing free black population. Frank Luther Mott, *American Journalism: A History, 1690–1960* (New York, N.Y., 1962), 188, 557n.

2. "A Marylander" borrows this phrase from Psalms 23:4.

3. According to the federal census, the nation's free black population stood at about 320,000 in 1830, an increase of 20 percent since 1820. Although the northern black population had remained relatively constant, some southern states showed nearly a 25 percent increase in black population during the same decade. Yet in Maryland, despite white fears of a growing black population, blacks actually represented a slightly smaller percentage of the state's total population in 1830 than they had ten years before. While the state's slave population remained constant, the number of free blacks increased from 39,730 to 52,938 during the decade. U.S. Bureau of the Census, *Historical Statistics of the United States, Colonial Times to 1970*, 2 vols. (Washington, D.C., 1975), 1:1–37; U.S. Bureau of the Census, *Negro Population in the United States, 1790–1915* (Washington, D.C., 1918), 51, 57.

4. Watkins quotes from Matthew 25:24.

5. Watkins charges that American clergymen are unable to demonstrate an altruistic concern for their fellow humans (including blacks), which is identified in both the Old and New Testaments as one of the two basic tenets of Jewish religious law: "Thou shalt love thy neighbor as thyself." Lev. 19:18; Matt. 22:39.

6. Watkins probably paraphrases 1 Chronicles 16:22 and Psalms 105:15, "Touch not mine anointed, and do my prophets no harm."

7. Watkins's amalgam of references appears to be drawn from 1 Peter 2:17, Proverbs 28:21, and Acts 10:34, whose basic message is that God does not discriminate against any group and that those who do, oppose divine will.

8. Watkins quotes from Deuteronomy 32:30, "How should one chase a thousand, and two put ten thousand to flight, except their Rock had sold them, and the Lord had shut them up?" He indicates that, with divine approval, antislavery advocates could overcome the forces arrayed against them, including Christian clergymen.

9. Watkins quotes from Psalms 2:2 to indicate that proslavery and other racist politicians "took counsel together against the Lord and his anointed" (abolitionists) by their failure to attack slavery and racial oppression. Using language from Genesis 49:6, he suggests that American clergymen had allied with these politicians. Watkins also quotes Psalms 2:4 to insinuate that these enemies of emancipation were an amusing vexation to God but would ultimately be defeated.

10. Watkins quotes from Proverbs 14:34, "Righteousness exalteth a nation: but sin is a reproach to any people."

5.
Address by Abraham D. Shadd,
Peter Spencer, and William S. Thomas
12 July 1831

Colonization denied black claims to an American identity. James Forten, Sr., remembered watching black soldiers fight at the Battle of Red Bank and seeing black troops from New England pass through Philadelphia on their way to engage the British, but now he worried that "all this appears to be forgotten" amidst the success of American Colonization Society propaganda. Understanding that to concede any issue to the ACS would weaken their claims as Americans, black communities rallied against the society and challenged its program point by point. On 12 July 1831, at a well-attended meeting held in the African Union Methodist Church in Wilmington, Delaware, local blacks affirmed their American heritage, warned that the ACS fostered racism to encourage emigration, and admonished well-intentioned white supporters of the ACS that the organization was "inimical to the best interests of the people of color." Prominent local blacks Abraham D. Shadd, Rev. Peter Spencer, and William S. Thomas were appointed to prepare an address explaining black opposition to colonization to the broader community. *CA*, 2 March 1839 [3:0019]; *Lib*, 12 February 1831 [1:0028]; James Forten to William Lloyd Garrison, 23 February 1831, Anti-Slavery Collection, MB [1:0034–35]; Harold B. Hancock, "Not Quite Men: The Free Negroes of Delaware in the 1830s," *CWH* 17:328–31 (December 1971).

Address of the Free People of Color of
the Borough of Wilmington, Delaware
    We the undersigned, in conformity to the wishes of our brethren, beg leave to present to the public in a calm and unprejudiced manner, our decided and unequivocal disapprobation of the American Colonization Society, and its auxiliaries, in relation to the free people of color in the United States. Convinced as we are, that the operations of this Society have been unchristian and anti-republican in principle, and at variance with our best interests as a people, we had reason to believe that the precepts of religion, the dictates of justice and humanity, would have prevented any considerable portion of the community from lending their aid to a plan which we fear was designed to deprive us of rights that the Declaration of Independence declares are the "unalienable rights" of all men. We were content to remain silent, believing that the justice and patriotism of a magnanimous people would prevent the annals of our native and beloved country from receiving so deep a stain. But observing

the growing strength and influence of that institution, and being well aware that the generality of the public are unacquainted with our views on this important subject, we feel it a duty we owe to ourselves, our children and posterity, to enter our protest against a device so fraught with evil to us. That many sincere friends to our race are engaged in what they conceive to be a philanthropic and benevolent enterprise, we do not hesitate to admit; but that they are deceived, and are acting in a manner calculated most seriously to injure the free people of color, we are equally sensible.

We are natives of the United States; our ancestors were brought to this country by means over which they had no control; we have our attachments to the soil, and we feel that we have rights in common with other Americans; and although deprived through prejudice from entering into the full enjoyment of those rights, we anticipate a period, when in despite of the more than ordinary prejudice which has been the result of this unchristian scheme, "Ethiopia shall stretch forth her hands to God."[1] But that this formidable Society has become a barrier to our improvement, must be apparent to every individual who will but reflect on the course to be pursued by the emissaries of this unhallowed project, many of whom, under the name of ministers of the gospel, use their influence to turn public sentiment to our disadvantage by stigmatizing our morals, misrepresenting our characters, and endeavouring to show what they are pleased to call the sound policy of perpetuating our civil and political disabilities for the avowed purpose of indirectly forcing us to emigrate to the western coast of Africa. That Africa is neither our nation nor home, a due respect to the good sense of the community forbids us to attempt to prove; that our language, habits, manners, morals and religion are all different from those of Africans, is a fact too notorious to admit of controversy. Why then are we called upon to go and settle in a country where we must necessarily be and remain a distinct people, having no common interest with the numerous inhabitants of that vast and extensive country? Experience has proved beyond a doubt, that the climate is such as not to suit the constitutions of the inhabitants of this country; the fevers and various diseases incident to that tropical clime, are such as in most cases to bid defiance to the force of medicine.

The very numerous instances of mortality amongst the emigrants who have been induced to leave this their native, for their adopted country, clearly demonstrate the fallacy of those statements so frequently made by the advocates of colonization in regard to the healthiness of Liberia.

With the deepest regret we have witnessed such an immense sacrifice of life, in advancing a cause which cannot promise the least advantage to the free people of color, who, it was said, were the primary objects to be benefitted by this "heaven-born enterprise." But we beg leave most respectfully to ask the friends of African colonization, whether their christian benevolence cannot in this country be equally as advantageously applied, if they are actuated by that disinterested spirit of love and friendship for us, which they profess? Have not they in the United States a field sufficiently extensive to show it in? There is embosomed within this republic, rising one million free people of color, the greater part of whom are unable to read even the sacred scriptures. Is not their ignorant and degraded situation worthy of the consideration of those enlightened and christian individuals, whose zeal for the cause of the African race has induced them to attempt the establishment of a republican form of government amid the burning sands of Liberia, and the evangelizing of the millions of the Mahometans and pagans that inhabit the interior of that extensive country?[2]

We are constrained to believe that the welfare of the people of color, to say the least, is but a secondary consideration with those engaged in the colonization project. Or why should we be requested to move to Africa, and thus separated from all we hold dear in a moral point of view, before their christian benevolence can be exercised in our behalf? Surely there is no country of which we have any knowledge, that offers greater facilities for the improvement of the unlearned; or where benevolent and philanthropic individuals can find a people, whose situation has greater claims on their christian sympathies, than the people of color. But whilst we behold a settled determination on the part of the American Colonization Society to remove us to Liberia, without using any means to better our condition at home, we are compelled to look with fearful diffidence on every measure of that institution. At a meeting held on the 7th inst. in this borough, the people of color were politely invited to attend, the object of which was to induce the most respectable part of them to emigrate. The meeting was addressed by several reverend gentlemen, and very flattering accounts given on the authority of letters and statements said to have been received from individuals of unquestionable veracity. But we beg leave to say, that those statements differ so widely from letters that we have seen of recent date from the colony, in regard to the condition and circumstances of the colonists, that we are compelled in truth to say that we cannot reconcile such contradictory statements,[3] and are therefore inclined to doubt the former, as they appear to have been prepared to present to the public, for the purpose of enlisting the feelings of our white friends into the measure, and of inducing the enterprising part of the colored community to emigrate at their own expense. That we are in this country a degraded people, we are truly sensible; that our forlorn situation is not attributable to ourselves is admitted by the most ardent friends of colonization; and that our condition cannot be bettered by removing the most exemplary individuals of color from amongst us, we are well convinced, from the consideration that in the same ratio that the industrious part would emigrate, in the same proportion those who would remain would become more degraded, wretched and miserable, and consequently less capable of appreciating the many opportunities which are now offering for the moral and intellectual improvement of our brethren. We, therefore, a portion of those who are the objects of this plan, and amongst those whose happiness, with that of others of our color, it is intended to promote, respectfully but firmly disclaim every connexion with it, and declare our settled determination not to participate in any part of it.

But if this plan is intended to facilitate the emancipation of those who are held in slavery in the South, and the melioration of their condition, by sending them to Liberia; we question very much whether it is calculated to do either. That the emancipation of slaves has been measurably impeded through its influence, except where they have been given up to the Board of Managers,[4] to be colonized in Africa, to us is manifest. And when we contemplate their uneducated and vitiated state, destitute of the arts and unaccustomed to provide even for themselves, we are inevitably led to the conclusion that their situation in that pestilential country will be miserable in the extreme.

The present period is one of deep and increasing interest to the free people of color, relieved from the miseries of slavery and its concomitant evils, with the vast and (to us) unexplored field of literature and science before us, surrounded by many friends whose sympathies and charities need not the Atlantic between us and them, before they can consent to assist in elevating our brethren to the standing of men. We therefore particularly invite their attention to the subject of education and improvement; sensible that it is much better calculated to remove prejudice, and exalt our moral character, than any system of colonization that has been or can be introduced; and in which we believe we shall have the cooperation of the wisest and most philanthropic individuals of which the nation can boast. The utility of learning and its salutary effects on the minds and morals of a people, cannot have escaped the notice of any rational individual situated in a country like this, where in order successfully to prosecute any mechanical or other business, education is indispensible. Our highest moral ambition, at present, should be to acquire for our children a liberal education, give them mechanical trades, and thus fit and prepare them for useful and respectable citizens; and leave the evangelizing of Africa, and the establishing of a republic at Liberia, to those who conceive themselves able to demonstrate the practicability of its accomplishment by means of a people, numbers of whom are more ignorant than even the natives of that country themselves.

In conclusion, we feel it a pleasing duty ever to cherish a grateful respect for those benevolent and truly philanthropic individuals, who have advocated, and still are advocating our rights in our native country. Their indefatigable zeal in the cause of the oppressed will never be forgotten by us, and unborn millions will bless their names in the day when the all-wise Creator, in whom we trust, shall have bidden oppression to cease.

ABRAHAM D. SHADD[5]
PETER SPENCER[6] } Committee to prepare an Address
WM. S. THOMAS[7]

William Lloyd Garrison, *Thoughts on African Colonization* (Boston, Mass., 1832), part 2, 36–40.

1. The authors of the address quote from Psalms 68:31. For antebellum blacks, ancient Ethiopia and Egypt were a source of pride, used to refute white charges of racial inferiority and to promote black nationalism.

2. During the late eighteenth century, Islam spread westward and southward from the western Sudan to present-day Nigeria, gaining numerous converts in the Niger Valley and along the West African coast.

3. American blacks received conflicting reports on conditions among Liberian emigrants. Testimony by returning settlers and letters from West Africa revealed mounting disillusionment. Abolitionists who investigated conditions among the settlers found evidence that challenged official statements by the American Colonization Society. The ACS eventually acknowledged the high incidence of death and disease but blamed the settlers for their own plight, stating that the colonists made foolish mistakes, such as excessive exposure to the sun or eating too many pineapples. Staudenraus, *African Colonization Movement*, 102–3.

4. In 1831 the board of managers of the American Colonization Society consisted of Charles Carroll, president; Ralph Randolph Gurley, secretary; Richard Smith, treasurer; James C. Dunn, publisher of the *African Repository*; and several vice-presidents that included Francis Scott Key, Henry Clay, Thomas S. Grimké, and Theodore Frelinghuysen. *AR*, January, February 1830.

5. Abraham D. Shadd (1801–1882), a Pennsylvania-born free black, operated a shoemaking business in Wilmington, Delaware, before moving to nearby West Chester, Pennsylvania, in the early 1830s. He used both his Wilmington home and his West Chester farm to hide fugitive slaves escaping along the underground railroad. A vigorous opponent of slavery, Shadd was one of five blacks appointed to the board of managers of the American Anti-Slavery Society at its founding meeting in 1833. He acted as a local subscription agent for several antislavery papers—particularly the *Liberator, Emancipator, National Reformer,* and *Colored American*—during the following decade. Shadd was also a prominent figure in the early black convention movement. He attended the first four black national conventions and presided over the third, which was held in Philadelphia in 1833. He was a leading delegate to Pennsylvania's 1841 and 1848 black state conventions. Shadd, a militant advocate of black civil rights, helped lead an extensive protest against Pennsylvania's disfranchisement of black voters in the late 1830s. Although he was an early critic of colonizationist efforts, he later endorsed Canadian immigration, resettled his family in Canada West in 1851, and served on the General Board of Commissioners of the National Emigration Convention, which gave tepid support to Martin R. Delany's Niger Valley Ex-

ploring Party in 1858. But Shadd refused to abandon Canada West. An active participant in local politics, in 1859 he gained a seat on the Raleigh Town Council, becoming the first black to hold elected office in the British North American Provinces. Shadd remained in Ontario after the Civil War. He and his wife Harriet Shadd produced thirteen children, including five—Mary Ann Shadd Cary, Isaac D. Shadd, Alfred S. Shadd, Emaline Shadd, and Abraham W. Shadd—who had distinguished careers in Canada and the United States. Robin W. Winks, *The Blacks in Canada: A History* (New Haven, Conn., 1971), 215; Hancock, "Not Quite Men," 329; Daniel G. Hill, *The Freedom-Seekers: Blacks in Early Canada* (Agincourt, Ontario, 1981), 202–5; Garrison, *Thoughts on African Colonization*, 36–40 [1:0098]; Philip S. Foner and George E. Walker, eds., *Proceedings of the Black State Conventions, 1840–1865*, 2 vols. (Philadelphia, Pa., 1979–80), 110, 118–19; *Minutes and Proceedings of the Third Annual Convention for the Improvement of the Free People of Colour* ... (New York, N.Y., 1833), 5 [1:0294]; *CA*, 25 July, 15, 22 August 1840 [3:0534, 0563, 0578]; *WAA*, 14 December 1861 [13:0976]; Martin R. Delany, *Official Report of The Niger Valley Exploring Party* (Leeds, England, 1861), 12–13 [11:0336]; *NR*, February 1839; *IC*, 5 December 1849 [6:0234].

6. Peter Spencer (1782–1843), founder of the African Union Methodist denomination, was born a slave in Kent County, Maryland. Gaining his freedom upon the death of his master, he settled in Wilmington during the 1790s. Educated at a local private school (probably run by Quakers), he eventually became a teacher and mechanic. Spencer attended the Asbury Methodist Church until segregated seating provoked him to lead a group of about forty black parishioners out of the church and to establish a separate church in 1805. In 1813 he broke with the Methodist denomination and formed the African Union Methodist church—the first black denomination in the United States. Although he attended the organizational meeting of the African Methodist Episcopal church in 1816, he declined to join the new denomination because of differences over matters of church organization and polity. With Spencer as the presiding elder, the African Union Methodist church grew to thirty-one congregations in six states. Because of his dominance, the AUM congregations were frequently referred to as Spencer churches. The AUM church had a democratic structure that relied on lay preachers and permitted women to join the ministry. Although the church never grew as large as the African Methodist Episcopal and African Methodist Episcopal Zion denominations, its less formal and more emotionally expressive religious service attracted slaves as well as free blacks. Spencer participated in the black national convention movement in the 1830s and he made his Wilmington church the center of anticolonization and antislavery activity in Delaware. The Big Quarterly—the denomination's annual gathering in Wilmington—brought free blacks and slaves together and provided an opportunity for Thomas Garrett, Harriet Tubman, and other abolitionists who encouraged and assisted slaves to escape. *CA*, 21 October 1837 [2:0235]; *Minutes of the First Annual Convention* (1831), 8 [1:0080]; *Minutes of the Second Annual Convention* (1832), 15 [1:0177]; Harry V. Richardson, *Dark Salvation: The Story of Methodism as It Developed among Blacks in America* (Garden City, N.Y., 1976), 79, 80, 84; Daniel A. Payne, *History of the African Methodist Episcopal Church* (Nashville, Tenn., 1891; reprint, New York, N.Y., 1968), 13; Lewis W. Baldwin,

"Invisible" Strands of African Methodism (Metuchen, N.J., 1983), 2, 38–39, 52–54, 62, 68, 145, 152, 237–39; Hancock, "Not Quite Men," 328–29.

7. William S. Thomas, a Wilmington free black, taught at a school run by the African School Society. In addition to anticolonization activity, he participated in the black national convention movement in the early 1830s. *Minutes of the First Annual Convention* (1831), 8 [1:0080]; *Minutes of the Second National Convention* (1832), 25 [1:0182]; Hancock, "Not Quite Men," 330.

6.
Address by Abraham D. Shadd,
William Hamilton, and William Whipper
13 June 1832

Between 1830 and 1835, black leaders met in annual national conventions to promote unified action. Four topics—colonization, Canadian immigration, education, and moral reform—overshadowed other concerns. White reformers often attended, addressed, and influenced these early black conventions. The 1832 gathering met from 4–13 June at the First African Presbyterian Church in the heart of Philadelphia's black community. Twenty-nine delegates from eight states participated, and several whites spoke, including William Lloyd Garrison. One of the convention's first actions was to appoint a committee consisting of Abraham D. Shadd, William Hamilton of New York City, and William Whipper of Philadelphia to write an address to free blacks expressing the delegates' views on major issues. Their report, which was read and adopted on the final day of the convention, opposed the American Colonization Society, expressed support for Canadian immigration, called for a black manual labor college, and encouraged temperance. Reflecting Garrison's philosophy, it asked blacks to act as "a body . . . devising plans and measures, for their personal and mental elevation, by *moral suasion alone*." William H. Pease and Jane H. Pease, "The Negro Convention Movement," in *Key Issues in the Afro-American Experience*, 2 vols., ed. Nathan I. Huggins, Martin Kilson, and Daniel M. Fox (New York, N.Y., 1971), 1:191–205; *Minutes of the Second Annual Convention* (1832), 3–5, 29, 32–36 [1:0171–72, 0184, 0186–88].

To the Free Colored Inhabitants of these United States.
FELLOW CITIZENS:
   We have again been permitted to associate in our representative character, from the different sections of this Union, to pour into one common stream, the afflictions, the prayers, and sympathies of our oppressed people; the axis of time has brought around this glorious, annual event. And we are again brought to rejoice that the wisdom of Divine Providence has protected us during a year, whose autumnal harvest, has been a reign of terror and persecution, and whose winter has almost frozen the streams of humanity, by its frigid legislation.[1] It is under the influence of times and feelings like these, that we now address you. Of a people situated as we are, little can be said, except that it becomes our duty, strictly to watch those causes that operate against our interests and privileges; and to guard against whatever measures that will either lower us in

the scale of being, or perpetuate our degradation in the eyes of the civilized world.

The effects of Slavery on the bond, and Colonization on the free. Of the first we shall say but little, but will here repeat the language of a high-minded Virginian in the legislature of that state, on the recent discussion of the slave question before that honorable body, who declared, that man could not hold property in man and that the master held no right to the slave, either by law of nature or a patentee from God, but by the will of society; which we declare to be an unjust usurpation of the rights and privileges of men.[2]

But how beautiful must the prospect be to the philanthropist, to view us, the children of persecution, grown to manhood, associating in our delegated character, to devise plans and means for our moral elevation, and attracting the attention of the wise and good, over the whole country, who are anxiously watching our deliberations.

We have here to inform you, that we have patiently listened to the able and eloquent arguments produced by the Rev. R. R. Gurley, Secretary of the American Colonization Society, in behalf of the doings of said Society, and Wm. Lloyd Garrison, Esq. in opposition to its action.[3]

A more favorable opportunity to arrive at truth seldom has been witnessed, but while we admire the distinguished piety and christian feelings, with which he so solemnly portrayed the doctrines of that institution; we do now *assert*, that the result of the same, has tended more deeply to rivet our solid conviction, that the doctrines of said Society, are at enmity with the principles and precepts of religion, humanity and justice, and should be regarded by every man of color in these United States, as an evil for magnitude, unexcelled, and whose doctrines aim at the entire extinction of the free colored population and the riveting of Slavery.

We might here repeat our protest against that institution, but it is unnecessary, your views and sentiments have long since gone to the world, the wings of the wind have borne your disapprobation to that institution. Time itself cannot erase it. You have dated your opposition from its beginning, and your views are strengthened by time and circumstances, and they hold the uppermost seat in your affections. We have not been unmindful of the compulsory laws which caused our brethren in Ohio, to seek new homes in a distant land, there to share and suffer all the inconveniences of exiles in an uncultivated region, which has led us to admire the benevolent feelings of a rival government in its liberal protection to strangers, which has induced us to recommend to you, to exercise your best endeavors, to collect monies to secure the purchase of lands in the Canadas, for those who may by oppressive legislative enactments, be obliged to move thither.[4]

In contributing to our brethren that aid which will secure them a refuge in a storm, we would not wish to be understood, as to possessing any inclination to remove, nor in the least to impoverish that noble sentiment which we rejoice in exclaiming

> This is *our* own,
> Our native land.[5]

All that we have done, humanity dictated it, neither inclination nor alienated feelings to our country prescribed it, but that power which is above all other considerations, viz: The law of necessity.

We yet anticipate in the moral strength of this nation, a final redemption from those evils that have been illegitimately entailed on us as a people. We yet expect by due exertions on our part, together with the aid of the benevolent philanthropists of our country, to acquire a moral and intellectual strength, that will unshaft the calumnious darts of our adversaries, and present to the world a general character, that they will feel bound to respect and admire.

It will be seen by a reference to our proceedings, that we have again recommended the further prosecution of the contemplated college, proposed by the last Convention, to be established at New Haven, under the rules and regulations then established. A place for its location will be selected in a climate and neighborhood, where its inhabitants are less prejudiced to our rights and privileges. The proceedings of the citizens of New Haven, with regard to the erection of the college, were a disgrace to themselves, and cast a stigma on the reputed fame of New England and the country.[6] We are unwilling that the character of the whole country shall sink by the proceedings of a few. We are determined to present to another portion of the country not far distant, and at no very remote period, the opportunity of gaining for them the character of a truly philanthropic spirit, and of retrieving the character of the country, by the disreputable proceedings of New Haven. We must have colleges and high schools on the manual labor system, where our youth may be instructed in all the arts of civilized life. If we ever expect to see the influence of prejudice decrease, and ourselves respected, it must be by the blessings of an enlightened education. It must be by being in possession of that classical knowledge which promotes genius, and causes man to soar up to those high intellectual enjoyments and acquirements, which places him in a situation, to shed upon a country and a people, that scientific grandeur which is imperishable by time, and drowns in oblivions cup their moral degradation. Those who think that our primary schools are capable of effecting this, are a century behind the age, when to have proved a question in the rule of three, was considered a higher attainment, than solving the most difficult problem in Euclid is now.[7] They might have at that time performed, what some people expect of them now, in the then barren state of science, but they are now no longer capable of reflecting brilliancy on our national character, which will elevate us from our present situation. If we wish to be respected, we must build our moral character, on a base as broad and high as the nation itself—our country and our character require it—we have performed all the duties from the menial to the soldier—our fathers shed their blood in the great struggle for independence. In the late war between Great Britain and the United States, a proclamation was issued to the free colored inhabitants of Louisiana, Sept. 21st, 1814, inviting them to take up arms in defense of their country, by Gen. Andrew Jackson. And in order that you may have an idea of the manner in which they acquitted themselves on that perilous occasion, we will refer you to the proclamation of Thomas Butler, Aid-de-Camp.[8]

You there see that your country expects much from you, and that you have much to call you into action, morally, religiously, and scientifically. Prepare yourselves to occupy the several stations to which the wisdom of your country may promote you. We have been told in this Convention, by the Secretary of the American Colonization Society, that there are causes which forbid our advancement in this country, which no humanity, no legislation and no religion can control. Believe it not. Is not humanity susceptible of all the tender feelings of benevolence? Is not legislation supreme—and is not religion virtuous? Our oppressed situation arises from their opposite causes. There is an awakening spirit in our people to promote their elevation, which speaks volumes in their behalf. We anticipated at the close of the last Convention, a larger representation and an increased number of delegates; we were not deceived, the number has been tenfold.[9] And we have a right to expect that future Conventions will be increased by a geometrical ratio, until we shall present a body, not inferior in numbers to our state legislatures, and the *phenomena* of an *oppressed people*, deprived of the rights of citizenship, in the midst of an enlightened nation, devising plans and measures, for their personal and mental elevation, by *moral suasion alone*.

In recommending you a path to pursue for our present good and future elevation, we have taken into consideration, the circumstances of the free colored population, so far as it was possible to ascertain their views and sentiments, hoping that at a future Convention, you will all come ably represented, and that your wishes and views, may receive that deliberation and attention, for which this body is particularly associated.

Finally, before taking our leave, we would admonish you, by all that you hold dear, beware of that bewitching evil, that bane of society, that curse of the world, that fell destroyer of the best prospects, and the last hope of civilized man, INTEMPERANCE.

Be righteous, be honest, be just, be economical, be prudent, offend not the laws of your country—in a word, live in that purity of life, by both precept and example—live in the constant pursuit of that moral and intellectual strength, which will invigorate your understandings, and render you illustrious in the eyes of civilized nations, when they will assert, that all that illustrious worth, which was once possessed by the Egyptians, and slept for ages, has now arisen in their descendants, the inhabitants of the new world.

Minutes and Proceedings of the Second Annual Convention for the Improvement of the Free People of Colour in these United States, Held by Adjournments in the City of Philadelphia, From the 4th to the 13th of June, inclusive, 1832 (Philadelphia, Pa., 1832), 32–36.

1. The authors refer to the reaction of southern state legislatures to the Nat Turner insurrection (1831). New laws dramatically restricted the activities of slaves and free blacks, prohibited social and economic interchange, curtailed black assemblies, and encouraged colonization.

2. The authors refer to the 1831–32 debate over slavery in the Virginia legislature, which followed Nat Turner's rebellion. Thomas Jefferson Randolph, Charles J. Faulkner, and William Ballard Preston led a fight for gradual emancipation. All three believed that public safety should outweigh the demands of private property. The "high-minded" Virginian to whom the authors refer may be Preston, who declared that the people's "happiness is incompatible with slavery." The legislature rejected all abolitionist measures. Alison Goodyear Freehling, *Drift toward Dissolution: The Virginia Slavery Debate of 1831–1832* (Baton Rouge, La., 1982), 36–81, 122–69.

3. On 5 June 1832, amid objections, Ralph Randolph Gurley defended the American Colonization Society before the 1832 black national convention. Garrison and John B. Vashon rebutted Gurley's arguments. Born in Lebanon, Connecticut, and educated at Yale, Gurley (1797–1872) moved to Washington, D.C., in 1822. Becoming affiliated with the ACS, he served successively as agent, secretary, vice-president, and lifetime director, remaining with the society until his death. He lectured widely on colonization in the United States and Britain. A Presbyterian clergyman, Gurley frequently preached in black churches and worked among the black poor in Washington. *Minutes of the Second Annual Convention* (1832), 6–11 [1:0173–75]; *DAB*, 8:56–57.

4. In 1829 Cincinnati officials determined to enforce Ohio's black laws, a series of state enactments and constitutional provisions that abridged black rights. Blacks could not carry arms, sit on a jury, or serve in the militia and were required to register and post a $500 bond or leave Cincinnati within thirty days. A delegation of black Cincinnatians visited Sir John Colborne, the lieutenant governor of Upper Canada (now Ontario), and were assured that they would be welcome in the province. Using funds provided by concerned Quakers, these leaders purchased eight hundred acres in Upper Canada and organized the Wilberforce community, an all-black agrarian experiment that continued until 1836. When a race riot broke out in Cincinnati in 1830, more than a thousand blacks left the city, many for Wilberforce. Believing that blacks could achieve economic independence and political and social respect as farmers in Upper Canada, black national conventions that met in Philadelphia in 1830 and 1831 enthusiastically

endorsed mass emigration to the province. Richard C. Wade, "The Negro in Cincinnati, 1800–1830," *JNH* 39:48–57 (January 1954); William H. Pease and Jane H. Pease, *Black Utopia: Negro Communal Experiments in America* (Madison, Wisc., 1963), 46–62; Winch, *Philadelphia's Black Elite*, 66–67.

5. The authors of the address borrow from canto 6, stanza 1, of Sir Walter Scott's *The Lay of the Last Minstrel* (1805):

> Breathes there the man, with soul so dead,
> Who never to himself hath said,
> This is my own, my native land!

6. In 1829 Samuel E. Cornish urged blacks to establish a manual labor college that would offer "a thorough classical education." At a black national convention two years later, Simeon S. Jocelyn, William Lloyd Garrison, and Arthur Tappan proposed that such a school be created. The delegates embraced the plan, pledged to raise $20,000, named Cornish to direct the fund-raising, and insisted that a majority of the college's trustees be black. Black leaders envisioned the college as part of a separate educational system that would include primary and secondary schools. They invested their hopes for black uplift in the college, maintaining that its success would refute the racist views of the American Colonization Society. New Haven was the proposed site of the school. But in September 1831, angry white residents from New Haven resolved to prevent establishment of the school, claiming that it would promote abolitionism. The next month rioters harassed the Tappan family and demolished the home of a local black. The 1832 black national convention reaffirmed its commitment to a manual labor college and resolved to find another location. Primus Hall and John T. Hilton led the renewed effort, cooperating with the New England Anti-Slavery Society to collect $50,000 for the college and supporting Garrison's 1833 British fund-raising tour. The 1833 and 1834 conventions reported efforts to found similar schools in Philadelphia, New York, and Boston. Black cooperation with the NEASS led to the founding of the Noyes Academy in Canaan, New Hampshire, but its destruction in 1835 ended black hopes for a manual labor institution. *Minutes of the First Annual Convention* (1831), 5–7, 13–15; *Minutes of the Second Annual Convention* (1832), 22–27, 34; *Minutes of the Third Annual Convention* (1833), 7–14, 29–34; *Minutes of the Fourth Annual Convention for the Improvement of the Free People of Colour* . . . (New York, N.Y., 1834), 11–12; *Minutes of the Fifth Annual Convention for the Improvement of the Free People of Colour* . . . (Philadelphia, Pa., 1835), 17; *Lib*, 24 September, 8, 22, 29 October, 12, 19 November 1831, 29 September 1832, 11 May 1833, 4 July, 5 September, 3 October 1835; *E*, 16 September 1834; Bertram Wyatt-Brown, *Lewis Tappan and the Evangelical War against Slavery* (Cleveland, Ohio, 1969), 87–90; William Louis Lang, "Black Bootstraps: The Abolitionist Educators' Ideology and the Education of the Free Negro, 1828–1860" (Ph.D. diss., University of Delaware, 1974), 82–99.

7. The authors use two mathematical elements—the rule of three and euclidean geometry—to suggest the differences between existing black schools and the ambitious goals of the New Haven Labor College. They contrast a basic algebraic formula with the entire study of points, lines, surfaces, and solids found in the work of Euclid (ca. 300 B.C.), a Greek mathematician.

8. Anticipating a British invasion of New Orleans during the War of 1812, Andrew Jackson recruited black troops to defend the city. In an October 1814 address, "To the Free Coloured Inhabitants of Louisiana," Jackson honored the black volunteers as "brave fellow citizens" and promised them the same pay, bounties, supplies, and 160-acre land grant given to white soldiers. In December Jackson's aide-de-camp, Thomas Butler, reiterated Jackson's sentiments and praise. Black leaders regarded the two documents as concrete evidence of black valor and patriotism and argued that Jackson's reference to "fellow citizens" was proof that they deserved every constitutional right enjoyed by all Americans. Although more than six hundred free blacks fought at the January 1815 battle of New Orleans, the federal government excluded blacks from the army in 1820. Philip S. Foner, *History of Black Americans*, 3 vols. to date (Westport, Conn., 1975–), 1:487–92; William C. Nell, *Services of Colored Americans in the Wars of 1776 and 1812* (Boston, Mass., 1852) [7:0281–83].

9. Fifteen delegates from Pennsylvania, Maryland, New York, Delaware, and Virginia attended the 1831 black national convention. An undetermined number of other individuals, black and white, also participated in the meeting. Twenty-nine blacks attended the 1832 convention, including, for the first time, delegates from New Jersey, Massachusetts, Connecticut, and Rhode Island. *Minutes of the First Annual Convention* (1831), 3 [1:0077]; *Minutes of the Second Annual Convention* (1832), 3–4 [1:0171–72].

7.

Speech by Sarah M. Douglass
Delivered before the Female Literary
Society of Philadelphia
Philadelphia, Pennsylvania
[June 1832]

Black women participated in the immediatist antislavery movement from its beginning. Sarah M. Douglass and Maria W. Stewart conducted public lectures and wrote for the reform press at a time when such activities were generally reserved for men. Philadelphia's black women were especially active abolitionists. Douglass, a member of the city's black elite, increased her antislavery efforts in the early 1830s after the Pennsylvania legislature considered measures to restrict free black rights and to strengthen fugitive slave laws. The uncertain nature of black freedom, the growing threat of kidnapping, and contact with female fugitives increased her identification with the slave. In late June or early July 1832, Douglass addressed the Female Literary Society of Philadelphia, a newly formed black organization that read and discussed essays written by members on a variety of topics. She reviewed the course of her antislavery commitment and urged members to turn their full attention to slavery. Marilyn Richardson, ed., *Maria W. Stewart, America's First Black Woman Political Writer: Essays and Speeches* (Bloomington, Ind., 1987), 3–27; *NAW*, 1:511–12; *GUE*, May, August 1831; *Lib*, 3 December 1831, 30 June, 28 July 1832 [1:0210]; Pease and Pease, *They Who Would Be Free*, 213.

MY FRIENDS—MY SISTERS:

How important is the occasion for which we have assembled ourselves together this evening, to hold a feast, to feed our never-dying minds, to excite each other to deeds of mercy, words of peace; to stir up in the bosom of each, gratitude to God for his increasing goodness, and feeling of deep sympathy for our brethren and sisters, who are in this land of christian light and liberty held in bondage the most cruel and degrading—to make their cause our own!

An English writer has said, "We must feel deeply before we can act rightly; from that absorbing, heart-rendering compassion for ourselves springs a deeper sympathy for others, and from a sense of our weakness and our own upbraidings arises a disposition to be indulgent, to forbear, to forgive." This is my experience. One short year ago, how different were my feelings on the subject of slavery! It is true, the wail of the captive sometimes came to my ear in the midst of my happiness, and caused my heart to bleed for his wrongs; but, alas! the impression was as evanescent as the early cloud and morning dew. I had formed a little world of my own, and cared not to move beyond its precincts. But how was the scene changed when I beheld the oppressor lurking on the border of my own peaceful home![1] I saw his iron hand stretched forth to seize me as his prey, and the cause of the slave became my own. I started up, and with one mighty effort threw from me the lethargy which had covered me as a mantle for years; and determined, by the help of the Almighty, to use every exertion in my power to elevate the character of my wronged and neglected race. One year ago, I detested the slaveholder; now I can pity and pray for him. Has not this been your experience, my sisters? Have you not felt as I have felt upon this thrilling subject? My heart assures me some of you have.

And now, my sisters, I would earnestly and affectionately press upon you the necessity of placing your whole dependence on God; poor, weak, finite creatures as we are, we can do nothing for ourselves. He is all powerful; He is waiting to be gracious to us as a people. Do you feel your inability to do good? Come to Him who giveth liberally and upbraideth not; bring your wrongs and fears to Him, as you would to a tender parent—He will sympathise with you. I know from blessed, heart-cheering experience the excellency of having a God to trust to in seasons of trial and conflict. What but this can support us should the pestilence which has devastated Asia be born to us by the summer breezes?[2] What but this can uphold our fainting footsteps in the swellings of Jordan? It is the only thing worth living for—the only thing that can disarm death of his sting. I am earnestly solicitous that each of us may adopt this language:

"I have no hope in man, but much in God—
Much in the rock of ages."

In conclusion, I would respectfully recommend that our mental feast should commence by reading a portion of the Holy Scriptures. A pause should proceed the reading for supplication. It is my wish that the reading and conversation should be altogether directed to the subject of slavery. The refreshment which may be offered to you for the body, will be of the most simple kind, that you may feel for those who have nothing to refresh body and mind.

Liberator (Boston, Mass.), 21 July 1832.

1. Sarah M. Douglass (1806–1882), the daughter of black abolitionists Robert and Grace Bustill Douglass, became an active abolitionist in her mid-twenties. She received extensive tutoring as a child. After teaching briefly in New York, she opened her own school in Philadelphia, which provided black women with a rare opportunity to receive the equivalent of a high school education. She took a supervisory position in 1853 with the Quaker-sponsored Institute for Colored

Youth, where she remained until 1877. Douglass expanded the restricted women's curriculum by lecturing on physiology and hygiene—subjects she studied at the Female Medical College of Pennsylvania (1852–53) and at Pennsylvania Medical University (1855–58). She also lectured on these subjects in evening classes for adults and at meetings of the Banneker Institute.

While a young girl, Douglass became aware of the social restrictions placed on blacks and women. She attended Quaker meetings with her mother until the racial prejudice and the "Negro pew" became insufferable. She helped organize and sustain several women's reform organizations, including the Female Literary Society of Philadelphia and the Philadelphia Female Anti-Slavery Society. As an officer of the Women's Association, she was involved in fund-raising fairs for the black press. She was also a founding member of the Gilbert Lyceum, wrote for the *Liberator* under the pseudonym "Zillah," and contributed to the *Anglo-African Magazine*. Douglass nurtured a lifelong friendship with Angelina and Sarah Grimké and through her correspondence, provided them with a poignant black perspective on the effects of racial prejudice. In 1855 she married black Episcopal clergyman William Douglass. After the Civil War, she served as vice-president of the women's branch of the Freedmen's Aid Society. *DANB*, 186–87; *NAW*, 1:511–12; Dorothy Sterling, ed., *We Are Your Sisters: Black Women in the Nineteenth Century* (New York, N.Y., 1984), 110–12, 126–32; *Lib*, 7 April, 30 June, 7, 21, 28 July, 18 August, 1 September, 15 December 1832 [1:0157, 0199, 0201, 0204, 0210, 0217, 0220, 0231]; *NSt*, 9 March, 25 June, 20 December 1849 [5:0997, 6:0044, 0137]; *AAM*, May 1859 [11:0718]; *WAA*, 12 March 1860, 1 March, 19 April 1862.

2. Cholera broke out in the Ganges delta of India in 1826, spread to Russia in 1830, and swept across Europe within a year. By the summer of 1832, the disease had infected all major American seaports, including Philadelphia. Charles E. Rosenberg, *The Cholera Years: The United States in 1832, 1849, and 1866* (Chicago, Ill., 1962), 6, 14, 24–39, 60.

8.
Speech by William Whipper
Delivered before the Colored Temperance
Society of Philadelphia
Philadelphia, Pennsylvania
8 January 1834

During the 1830s, leaders such as William Whipper believed that white prejudice against blacks arose *"not from the color of their skin, but from their condition."* Arguing that white racism and discriminatory practices would disappear as free blacks improved their social and economic situation, they advocated mutual aid, hard work, thrift, learning, piety, and sobriety as the keys to racial advancement. Nothing better demonstrated black commitment to moral reform than their involvement in the temperance movement. Black abolitionists established temperance boardinghouses, restaurants, and grocery stores; published temperance newspapers; and organized local and regional temperance societies. Nearly every black community boasted of at least one such society by 1840. The Colored Temperance Society of Philadelphia was probably established in response to recommendations made at the 1832 black national convention. In his 8 January 1834 presidential address, Whipper explained that if free blacks adopted moral reform principles, they would undermine the rationale for slavery and racial prejudice. Donald Yacovone, "The Transformation of the Black Temperance Movement, 1827–1854" *JER* 8:281–97 (Fall 1988); *Minutes of the Third Annual Convention* (1833), 15–16 [1:0300–301].

Fellow Member:

Having been so highly honored by your suffrages, as to be elevated to the distinguished situation of presiding over this institution, the claims of duty require of me[1] the arduous task of explaining the motives and considerations that should actuate us in promoting it objects.

Those who associate themselves for the improvement of their moral condition, are exercising the highest order of legislation. The present is an era for us to notice the evils, and mark the moral depravity, that have afflicted the human family since they have fallen from that holy estate that our first parents enjoyed.

Intemperance, that blighting monster, that extirpator of the human species, has slain mankind with a power that can only be likened unto the *axe*, which in the march of civilization is rapidly clearing our native forests. It is an evil for magnitude unexcelled, and in the history of the world must stand without a parallel. Even negro slavery, horrible as it is, painted in its most ignominious colors, and ferreted out in all its degrading consequences, is but a concomitant. Probably to no people on earth would this language be more objectionable than to the present audience; yet I firmly believe it to be strictly true. To a people like ours, whose whole history is wrapt in the most obsequious degradation, multiplied injuries and tyrannical barbarity, from the effects of domestic slavery, they might be inclined to suppose than no human scourge had ever surpassed it in the enormity of its inflictions. But a still greater tyrant reigns. It fills a more extensive range—it occupies a higher seat; and swells its influence over the dominions of our world. It is found in the palace; it exists in the forum; it mingles with society; its abode is by the fireside; it is felt in the sanctuary; it despises the prejudices of caste; it seeks its victims alike among the learned and ignorant, the poor and the rich; it confines itself neither to the geographical lines of state or territory, of nation or continent; but disdaining all local attachments, it claims for its domain the map of the universe.

It is not my intention, on the present occasion, to delineate its features. You all, probably, have seen the base original revelling in all its loathsomeness, defying alike the imagination of the poet, and the pencil of the artist, to describe its ghastly countenance and destructive mien. The time may come when my limits may allow me to enter into the economy of the subject; but for the present, I must only refer to the able speeches and writings of the temperance reformers, that are now so successfully revolutionizing public opinion on this important question.[2] I could quote from ecclesiastical history, and prove that the voluntary use of "ardent spirits"[3] is inconsistent with the spirit of the gospel and our holy religion. I could refer to medical authority to prove its deleterious effect on the human system. I claim not the high privilege of being a pioneer in this cause. But I hold it to be my duty to pass by all these, and approach the subject on new grounds; and I am proud to say that years have elapsed since I adopted the following sentiments, viz:

That the people of color, in these United States, (above any other class of citizens) are morally, politically and religiously bound to support the cause of temperance, as advocated and supported in our country.

We are indebted to the ingenuity of man for the two greatest evils that ever scourged the human family, viz. Intemperance and Slavery. I mean by the former, that intemperance which has arisen from the use of ardent spirits. By the latter, we are to consider that species of slavery, generally termed negro slavery. I cannot probably better call your attention to the subject, than by presenting for your consideration the comparative evils they inflict, and the forcible claims their very existence has upon the wise and the good, for their total extermination from the face of the earth. If I shall be able to convince those who hear me, that the former is as wicked and heinous as the latter, I feel confident that they will lend their influence to exterminate its roots from the soil of society.

8. William Whipper
Courtesy of New York State Historical Association, Cooperstown

The principle effects of these evils on the character and interests of mankind you are familiar with. I need only present you with a few facts, asking leave to place them in the scales of Justice, regulated by right and reason, and suffer you to form your own conclusions.

We shall begin with negro slavery.
What have been its effects on society and mankind generally?

Why, it has made the master (though of human form, and bound by christian obligations to love and seek the welfare of himself and those around him) a tyrant—a murderer of his species—an earthly demon, pouring out his wrath on the innocent and unoffending, inflicting torments and stripes on the aged and infirm, separating husband and wife, parents and their offspring, like cattle and beasts of burden; and to communicate the same wicked lesson to his children and survivors who visit on unborn generations the same penalties; and society around him copies his example. Although born in the image of his Maker, his life and acts bear the impress of Satan. He dies, and leaves his country taxed with national cruelty—his heirs in the possession of God's creatures, with their multiplied increase.

Now, what are its effects on the slave? Why, the dense fog of slave-holding cruelty, falling like mildew, smites the earliest dawn of his intellect, and destroys it in the bud. His mind, that was formed to soar into infinite space, and there admire and explore the beauties of creation, and the splendor of worlds—scarcely moves beyond the measure of his chains. His body, unlike the animals of the forest, is without the natural covering to shelter his person from the pitiless storm; yet, like them, he seldom receives protection from the burning suns and chilling snows. Though born and reared in the image of man, he walks to and fro with the taciturnity of the brute. His mind not being permitted to expand he remains destitute of that compound that God intended for his creatures, viz. a union of mind and body; but in the stature of the latter he roams over the earth a walking animal.

It is of materials like these, that the ligaments of society in slavehold-ing countries are formed. While the oppressor deserves the condign punishment of an insulted Providence, and the just execration of the wise and good, the prayers of the righteous ought to ascend upwards, in torrents of supplication and appeal to Heaven for their deliverance. Who will charge me with injustice in this description?

But it now becomes our duty to describe the *tyrant* intemperance—a *demon* more ferocious in his character and despotic in the cruelty of his infliction and the destructiveness of his sway. All that I have said, or that can be said against slavery, is truly applicable to intemperance. It is happy for mankind and the glory of humanity, that the wickedness of the former is confined to Africa and her descendants; while the latter abhorring all national distinctions, spreads its "wide wasting calamity" over the great family of nations. It far surpasses the former in the cruelty of its depredations, the number of its victims, and its deathless ignominy. If their afflictions were equal, the ratio of numbers alone would turn the scale. But we shall exhibit some of its destructive feats, that the former, with all its atrocities, is incapable of achieving. The slave is only kept in subjection because his mind remains stupefied; for both the security of the master and contentment of the slave forbid its expansion, because no large number of intelligent beings can remain enslaved—for light and knowledge would dissolve the compact, melt the bands, and burst the chains asunder. The tyrant Elrius makes no such limited pretensions to the perpetuity of his power; but, as if determined to keep mankind in awe, and subject the world to his control, he frequently reaches after the mightiest intellect, makes him bow his haughty head, bend his knee, fall down and worship the god Bacchus, and lay his trophies at his feet.[4] So that in the possession of intelligence and learning, there is no safe retreat from his grasp. If the slave has wealth, he may purchase his freedom. But to the subject of intemperance, wealth only strengthens his chains; for it furnishes him with materials to revel in his guilt, and fans the flames of his destruction. The slave hates his situation, and only remains in it because his bonds are forcible. The other loves it, because having slain his reason and self-respect, it promotes his animal luxury.

The slaveholder dreads rebellion and insurrectionary movements; but the tyrant intemperance fears them not, for those whom he oppresses most, love him best. He is an able ruler, alike skillful in the cabinet and the field; though a murderer and a despot, he reigns in the hearts of his subjects. He is the prince of tacticians, heads a large army, and when he desires the acquisition of numbers to procure new territory, he martials his soldiers, and stretches his magic wand, possessing in himself the power of the magnet. Thousands follow after him, and join the train; few desert his camp; and when arrayed for combat, are seemingly invulnerable; but *all fall in battle.*

The slave may escape from the rule and presence of his master, by flying to a land of freedom; but the subject of intemperance finds that *his* master is almost omnipresent. He may leave his state or country, and become adopted in another realm, but even there he finds that the omniscient eye of his master is upon him, and the same consequences await him. The odiousness of the traffic is far more desperate in its extent and cruelty, owing to the limited value of the subject, and the protection given to the trade. Slaves generally command such a price, that none but capitalists can engage in its guilt, or reap its gains. But the intemperance traffic is so republican in its nature, that every person, who can buy a glass of liquid poison, can purchase a subject—can rob and deprive a family of their protector or slay on the funeral pyre some unguarded young man, or some unfortunate female. The facilities for its perpetuation are superior to that of either the slave trade or domestic slavery: for in connection with the heavy purchases of the one, there is to be added the expense of rearing and supporting the slave—but the other, as the advocate of intemperance would say, "enjoying an uncontrollable liberty," supports himself, and bestows his profits to the cause, and thus perpetuates the misery of millions.

I could extend the chain of comparison much further; but I am willing to submit it to your consideration without further comment, trusting that you will regulate your decision by the weight of the evidence.

But I have said that negro slavery is but a concomitant of intemperance. Do you desire the proof? I refer you to Clarkson, and other historians on the slave trade,[5] and you will discover that I am borne out in the assertion, that one of its earliest achievements (although then in its infant state)—like the tempter in Eden—was to secure the "slave trade" by inducing the native Africans to sell their brethren[6] while under its influence, and by that artifice it was effected. Is there a person of color in these United States, calling into recollection the features of that abominable trade—its murderous effect on our mother country, and our very existence in this country—our paternal relation to Africa, to humanity and religion—and its excruciating effects on upwards of two millions of our brethren in this our native land; is there one who is not equally ready to denounce the tyranny of the one, and the guilt of the other? Shall we, by the flood of our indignation, bear the names of the perpetrators of that trade into the pit of infamy, without accompanying with them the means by which their designs were executed? Is not ardent spirit susceptible of the same power in like hands? If our hostility to slavery arises, as it justly should, from its deleterious and demoralizing effects on the human family; ought not our hatred to intemperance be founded on the same principles? Can we consistently support the vices of the one, while we detest the vices of the other? Are not both obnoxious in the sight of heaven? If the slaveholder merits the indignation of the christian public, for perpetuating his system of crime and oppression, is not the retailer of ardent spirits equally culpable? Are we prepared to send forth our denunciations against American slavery, while we are nurturing and supporting a like system, and one that I have said is pregnant with and inflicts greater evils on the human race?

But having already given you the parallel, I ask you to draw your own conclusions. Have we not reason to fear that they will reflect back our language, and tell us "to remove the mote from our own eyes?"[7] Is not that system of society that justifies each equally base? Are not the supporters of each individually guilty of a gross violation of public morals, nay, even virtue and religion? I propound these questions for your consideration: weigh them.

I will leave you in the possession of these facts, while I pass on the consideration of the following question, viz. this being the present state of things, is not every man of color in these United States morally, politically and religiously bound to support the temperance reform, as advocated in our country?

To assert that we are morally bound to support the cause, is only to say that our obligations to our Maker and society impose upon us the duty of promoting the welfare of our species. Though the doctrine of the immorality of the "traffic in ardent spirits" is of modern origin, yet its legality has been sanctioned by men we readily believe, when they place the same stigma on domestic slavery; and it is still advocated, and has become adopted into the creed of the ablest reformers of the age. That it promises the moral purity of society, all must admit. But what says the objector? Why, its laws are too binding. We want the liberty of drinking when we please, and then letting it alone. We want no control in this matter. We abhor binding force. But what is the amount of these objections? Why, uncontrollable liberty would be the most despotic tyrant that ever existed; it would gratify an absolute and unconditional lust of the human passions; it would dethrone all power, destroy our institutions, and overthrow the foundations of all government; it would leave mankind without protection for either their property or persons. It is a liberty that was never intended for man; it was forbidden by our Creator, when He pointed to the "forbidden fruit" and said, in "the day thou eatest thereof, thou shalt surely die."[8]

Yet I firmly believe that if the three hundred thousand free colored people possessed such a character, the moral force and influence it would send forth would disperse slavery from our land. Yes, it would reverse the present order of things; it would reorganize public opinion, dissolve the calumnies of our enemies, and remove all the prejudices against our complexion; for there is nothing in the ordination of Providence calculated to degrade us in the eyes of the world, or prevent our occupying the highest situation in the order of intellectual beings. And when the nations of the earth can point to our whole people, and find them possessing a character, the christian base of which is as broad and high as that of the individual I have exhibited in miniature, it will be then that they will regard us as virtuous ornaments—that our sable hue will be changed from a badge of degradation to a badge of honor—that the more dark the complexion, the more frizzled the hair, the more illustrious the personage. It will be then, even in this country, that that glorious achievement will be completed, which has been asserted by a distinguished divine to be beyond the powers of humanity, legislation or religion to control. It will be then that when our brethren are visiting our mother country on errands of mercy, to christianize and evangelize that benighted continent, they will carry with them the materials for rearing up free institutions and the blessings of civilization. It will be then that the whole christian world, disdaining to count what they now term a homely visage and black complexion, will rise up and call her blessed. Is there not chivalry enough in us to accomplish this moral enterprise? Let every one answer for himself—not for another. If our enemies should reply in the negative, we should scout the idea. Would it not be equally offensive coming from any other source? Is there any too poor to purchase it, any too rich to enjoy it, any too wise to apply it, or any too ignorant to profit by it? I am positively not aware of any method so well calculated to effect this desirable result as the *temperance reform.* I wish not to be understood to insinuate, that we are more intemperate than the whites, for I do not believe it; but that we must be more pure than they, before we can be duly respected, becomes self-evident from the situation we at present occupy in our country.

Ardent spirit is so fruitful in iniquity, that the reformers of the present day regard it as the forbidden fruit. But the doctrine of the objectors might be pursued still further. The primary object of this institution is to harmonize, bless and elevate mankind.

In all great causes, there must be pioneers, who will breast the storm, and bear the burden. These have gone before, and it now becomes our duty to sustain them. The icy obstacles that have beset their path have been melted in the crucible of truth; and a glorious prospect is before us. Though a chance cloud may interpose itself, and darken our meridian way, it will be our duty *still to preserve.* It is our duty to inform and enlighten public opinion on this subject. Let us aim at a correct public opinion, and cease to regard who frames the laws; for it is on this basis that all laws are founded. Hence that legislation that fixes the morals, must ever be regarded supreme; and thus all "uncontrollable liberty" is checked by governmental power.

But we are now particularly called upon to support the temperance cause, for the single reason that if we neglect it, the very temperance reformation in this country will prove to us the greatest *curse.* If it be left to the whites, we shall be as widely separated in morals as complexion; and then our elevation is scarcely to be hoped for. To succeed and be respected, we must be superior in morals, before the balance of power will allow us to be admitted as their equals.

Show me the man of color in this country who possesses an unquestionable character for piety, morality and probity, and I will point you to a truly noble being. He stands alone on his own merits, clothed, it is true, in the badge of complexional degradation—without the title of citizenship—without the enjoyment of a participation in the affairs of his government—without any share in the administration of its laws—without the hope of earthly reward or future fame; yet, under all these disadvantages, his virtues are seen embellishing his character, and encircling his name. He lives a model for the world—an honor to his country, but a slave to its laws.

But if we believe that there is no present necessity for this reform; that this "uncontrollable liberty," with regard to the voluntary use of ardent spirits, needs no check, let us go on and fill up the measure of our iniquity. Let us ask the monster to extend still further his blessings of human misery on our world—let us solicit him to add to his hundreds of millions of murdered victims, thousands of millions in order that our voracious appetites may be satisfied at the slaughter-house of his vengeance; hoping that the summit of his ambition may be achieved, and the vortex of his misery filled. Let us view the present state of things and survey our peculiar situations; and then let me ask you, if the voice of public opinion was ever needed to sustain a reform; is it not now, and are we not bound, both by precept and example, to hasten the cause?

But the question may be asked, "Can a radical change be achieved?" I answer in the affirmative. We must have our institution placed on a pure moral basis, and we must plead for the natural, moral and political elevation of our whole people. We must respectfully appeal to and beseech our brethren to join heart and hand in the measure. We must earnestly remonstrate against their present course; and then if there be those who are deaf to all the appeals of reason, our *institution* must rise in its power and denounce the traffic. The grog-shops and taverns must be termed nuisances and disturbers of public peace and private enjoyments. If we cannot invoke their reason, we must provoke their passions; and this will bring forth retort; and retort will lead to discussion; and discussion will elicit enquiry; and enquiry will beget truth; and truth will bring conviction; and thus the reform will be completed. It will never do to content ourselves with crying out against the taverns and grog-shops; that will never bring about a reform; their *political action* is too powerful to be overcome. If I wished to rule an intemperate community, powerful as the press is acknowledged to be, I would choose their influence as preferable; for they in part control the latter, and their power is strongly felt in our legislative assemblies; and they more than partially rule our government. They are founded on the faith of public immorality, and are suffered to exist only by the impurity of public opinion; and they flourish in proportion to the liquid cravings of the community. And it would be of little consequence to remove these while that opinion exists; because those whom they accommodate would be left to get the liquid poison elsewhere. They were erected to supply the public wants; and many of them by man, who, when separated from the traffic, are honorable and praiseworthy citizens. These, like other industrious men, have sought that employment which they consider most profitable. Therefore it becomes our duty to undermine the interests of this traffic by moral action; and then these will be induced to relinquish the trade and convert their establishments into merchandise more profitable to themselves and certainly less destructive to their fellow citizens. There must be inns, hotels and boarding houses for the accommodation of travellers and the public; but these should not be suffered to sell "ardent spirits."[9]

The time is already come when we should all stand united as one man in this great moral contest, holding the high and invincible ground, that intemperance is an enemy to our civil and political improvement; and that we must oppose its advocates and supporters without distinction of color.

When the advocates of slavery cry out "How is the evil to be removed?" we tell them to "quit stealing"—"destroy the market, and render the whole system worthless." Can we say otherwise to the advocates of intemperance than to quit "poisoning," and the trade will die of itself? There are probably no two evils so closely allied, that the cure for the one is applicable to the other; and just so in their perpetuation. And the guilt of each is shrouded in the corruption of public opinion.

The slaveholder who says that he desires slavery to be abolished, and will not manumit his slaves; we doubt the sincerity of his assertions. The moderate drinker, who says he wishes drunkenness swept from the land, and still keeps on drinking—shall we believe him? He, like the former, says that "I am strictly in favor of temperance, but I hate your fanatical denunciations, your cold water societies[10] for reform. Let every man be his own guardian. I hate both drunkards and drunkenness. I like moderation in every thing." So says the moderate drinker. But yet, under his very system of self-government, has the evil arisen with all its accumulated power. Will the same evil or the same legislation cure itself? Certainly not. And if this "uncontrollable liberty" is to be the ruling monitor, it will be impossible to fix a moral boundary. The man who drinks his small glass of brandy in a day or a week, will infringe on another's rights, if he reproves him who drinks his quart in a day or an hour—for each, in the exercise of this guaranteed liberty, only satisfied his own thirst. We should despise neither the drunkard nor those engaged in the traffic; we should hate their ways, and our admonitions should flow from a love to their welfare. These moderate men appear to be true *facsimiles* of another class of citizens, called colonizationists. They both cry out against the evil, and propose their remedies; but figures, "which cannot lie," prove the inefficiency of their plans; for their application has only operated like extinguishing fire with oil; for both intemperance and slavery have flourished under their cure. The superiority of associated bodies over isolated individuals, in expressing their disapprobation of any measure, is so self-evident, that I would not insult your senses by adducing proof. Mark the revolution in public opinion produced in the Eastern States, in regard to the use and sale of ardent spirits; and then

mark the consequence. In that same region have risen up our most powerful friends, who wish to elevate our moral and political condition; and
wherever we see what we term a true abolitionist, he is invariably a
friend of the temperance cause. It is their enlightened views of human
good that lead them to advocate the exalted principles of human rights.
And shall we contemn their exertions by our principles and practises?
Can there be any of our people, who advocate our improvement, and
view drunkenness as an evil, who will not lend their aid and influence to
stay it? Can they be so blind to their dearest interests, and those of
posterity? Let their acts answer! We are certainly bound to prepare the
way for the rising generation. No doubt the present race of drunkards
will live out their days in their own way; but let us rescue posterity from
the evils that intemperance inflicts on the present race.

Liberator (Boston, Mass.), 21, 28 June, 5 July 1834.

1. William Whipper (ca. 1804–1876) was born in Lancaster, Pennsylvania, the
son of a white merchant and his black domestic servant. He moved to Philadelphia in the 1820s and later opened a "free labor and temperance grocery store."
Settling in nearby Columbia in 1835, he formed a partnership with black entre-
preneur Stephen Smith and nurtured a small inheritance until it grew into a
successful business. Whipper and Smith ranked among the wealthiest antebellum
black Americans. Their investments included a lumberyard, a merchant ship on
Lake Erie, railroad freight cars, and extensive property holdings in Pennsylvania
and Canada West. Whipper operated a major underground railroad station in
Columbia for more than twenty years. Using his business to aid the fugitive slave,
he provided hundreds of fugitives with shelter and temporary employment and
facilitated their settlement in Canada West.

Whipper gained prominence as a black intellectual and moral reformer in the
1830s. Not an eloquent speaker, he wrote numerous resolutions, reports, and
addresses, several of which were published as pamphlets. Under his guidance, the
black national convention movement of the 1830s affirmed the primacy of moral
reform. His efforts to create a national reform organization came to fruition in
1835 with the founding of the American Moral Reform Society. He served as the
organization's corresponding secretary and edited its monthly journal, the *National Reformer*. He shaped the ideological character of the AMRS, but his
abstract reformism and opposition to racially separate organizations provoked
criticism from those who wanted the society to address specific black issues.

Whipper maintained a lifelong commitment to moral reform but came to
question its antislavery value. By 1839 he had concluded that it was "not lack of
elevation, but complexion that deprived the man of color of equal treatment."
And he held little hope for the growth of abolitionism in the churches, believing
that even churches in black denominations could not escape the proslavery influences pervading American Protestantism. In the wake of the Fugitive Slave Law
of 1850, he grew pessimistic yet continued to counsel against violence.

Whipper tempered his opposition to racial separatism in the 1850s. At the

1853 black national convention, he helped draft the plan for the National Council of Colored People and accepted the necessity for separate black schools. He became more receptive to black emigration proposals, eventually endorsing the African Civilization Society. His plans to settle in Canada West were interrupted by the outbreak of the Civil War. During the war, he sat on a Philadelphia committee that promoted black enlistment in the Union army. He later served as vice-president of the Pennsylvania State Equal Rights League. Whipper ended his distinguished business and abolitionist career in the early 1870s as a cashier for the Philadelphia branch of the Freedman's Savings Bank. His son, William J. Whipper, was an abolitionist, Civil War veteran, and noted Reconstruction politician. *DANB*, 643; Richard P. McCormick, "William Whipper: Moral Reformer," *PH* 43:23–46 (January 1976); Still, *Underground Railroad*, 762–67; *Lib*, 14 April 1832 [1:0157–58]; *NSt*, 1, 29 September, 10 November 1848 [5:0764, 0799, 0824]; *FDP*, 13 May 1852, 17 November, 1 December 1854, 2 February 1855 [7:0580, 9:0234, 0255, 0420].

2. Concern over the harmful effects of alcohol began with the publication of Dr. Benjamin Rush's *Inquiry into the Effects of Spirituous Liquors* (1784). During the Second Great Awakening, both evangelicals and liberals took up the antiliquor cause. The American Temperance Society was formed in 1826, and within eight years, this national organization had established approximately five thousand state and local auxiliaries, particularly in the eastern United States. Although concern over sin motivated some temperance adherents, many others associated alcohol with the social problems that resulted from the industrial revolution. Ian Tyrrell, *Sobering Up: From Temperance to Prohibition in Antebellum America, 1800–1860* (Westport, Conn., 1979).

3. "Ardent spirits" refers to whiskey, gin, and other distilled alcoholic beverages, not to fermented beverages. Only after the late 1830s did total abstinence come to dominate the thinking of temperance advocates.

4. Whipper probably refers to Eleleus, another name for Bacchus, the ancient Roman god of wine and revelry.

5. Thomas Clarkson (1760–1846), a leading English abolitionist, wrote a two-volume history of the African slave trade. Beginning in the 1780s, he toured Britain, collecting information and statistics on the brutality of the nefarious traffic and the mortality rates of the slaves, writing antislavery tracts, presenting evidence to parliamentary committees, holding public meetings, and distributing pamphlets.

6. Due to the collaboration of tribal officials, more than six million West Africans were sold to European slave traders during the period of the Atlantic slave trade.

7. Whipper paraphrases Matthew 7:3–5, which reprimands those who criticize slight faults in others but fail to see greater faults in themselves.

8. Whipper quotes from Genesis 2:17, in which God forbids Adam and Eve to eat the fruit of one tree in the Garden of Eden: "But of the tree of the knowledge of good and evil, thou shalt not eat of it: for in the day that thou eatest thereof thou shalt surely die."

9. Temperance hotels and boardinghouses sprang up throughout the northeastern United States during the antebellum period to provide liquor-free accom-

modations for travelers. They sometimes served as social centers for local temperance supporters as well.

10. Cold water became a powerful symbol for the antebellum temperance movement, signifying a pure, natural beverage. Societies promoted its healthful benefits and celebrated its Christian virtues.

9.
Constitution of the Colored Anti-Slavery Society of Newark
9 May 1834

Excluded from membership in the old gradualist organizations, black abolitionists quickly joined the emerging immediatist movement. Many enlisted in interracial auxiliaries of the American Anti-Slavery Society. Boston blacks merged their six-year-old Massachusetts General Colored Association into the nascent New England Anti-Slavery Society, while other black communities created new antislavery associations. By 1837 more than a dozen black AASS auxiliaries functioned throughout the North. The Colored Anti-Slavery Society of Newark exemplified black enthusiasm for immediatism. Organized on 3 May 1834 by local clergymen and working-class blacks, it endorsed immediatist principles and expressed the close identification that Newark blacks felt with the slave. The gathering authorized Rev. Henry Drayton, Peter Johnson, Elijah Smith, Daniel Haden, and Jacob Wheeler to draft a constitution for the society. Six days later, local blacks reconvened at Drayton's First African Methodist Church and unanimously adopted the document that the committee had prepared. The society came under the control of Samuel Ringgold Ward in 1838 and helped to launch his distinguished antislavery career. Quarles, *Black Abolitionists*, 26–29; James Oliver Horton and Lois E. Horton, *Black Bostonians: Family Life and Community Struggle in the Antebellum North* (New York, N.Y., 1979), 81, 88; *E*, 27 May 1834 [1:0458]; *CA*, 21 July 1838 [2:0533].

PREAMBLE

Whereas, the King eternal, immortal, and invisible, the most high God, hath made of one blood all nations of men, to dwell on all the face of the earth, and hath commanded them to love their neighbors as themselves; and whereas our fathers have been held in bondage in the United States, two hundred years, and kept in ignorance, blindness, and gross darkness, by the lovers of filthy lucre; and whereas the people of the United States assembled in the city of Philadelphia, on the 4th day of July, 1776, in the presence of Almighty God, declared that all mankind are created equal, and that they are endowed by their Creator with certain inalienable rights, among which are life, liberty, and the pursuit of happiness. And whereas after the lapse of nearly sixty years, since the faith and honor of the American people were pledged to this avowal before Almighty God, and the world, upwards of two millions of our colored brethren, are still held in bondage. Whereas it is our opinion, that if all the blood of our colored brethren, shed by the people of the United States, since the Declaration of Independence, was kept in a reservoir, the framers of that instrument, and their successors might swim in it. And whereas a meeting of delegates from Anti-Slavery societies and the friends of emancipation, convened at the Delphi building, in the city of Philadelphia, on the 4th day of December, 1833, for the purpose of forming a national Anti-Slavery Society;[1] and whereas the Anti-Slavery Society, in this declaration are determined to use all godly, holy and lawful means, to undo our heavy burden, and to break every yoke, that the oppressed may go free.[2] We deem it to be our duty to use all holy and lawful means to aid the National Anti-Slavery Society in their great and glorious undertaking. We do hereby agree, with a prayerful reliance on the Divine aid, to form ourselves into a society to be governed by the following

CONSTITUTION

ARTICLE 1st. This society shall be called the Colored Anti-Slavery Society, of the township of Newark, Essex county, N.J. auxiliary to the American Anti-Slavery Society.

ART. 2d. The object of this society shall be, to endeavour by all honest means sanctioned by law, humanity and religion, to collect funds, to aid the American Anti-Slavery Society, to effect the immediate abolition of slavery in the United States, to improve the character of us the free people of color, to inform and correct public opinion in relation to our situation and rights, and to obtain for us, equal civil and religious privileges with the white inhabitants of the land.

ART. 3d. The officers of this society shall be a President, Vice President, Secretary, Treasurer, and three Counsellors. These shall constitute the Board of Managers.

ART. 4th. There shall be an annual meeting of this society on the first Thursday in May, for the choice of officers, and for such other business as shall be deemed expedient.

ART. 5th. The Board of Managers shall have power to call special meetings of the society as they shall think proper.

ART. 6th. Any person by subscribing to the above preamble and constitution, shall become a member of this society.

ART. 7th. This constitution may be altered or amended, by a vote of two thirds of the members present at any annual meeting.

The following gentlemen were elected officers, viz.

Rev. HENRY DRAYTON,
President.[3]
JOHN D. CLOSSON, Vice-
President.
ABRAHAM B. RAY, Secretary.

BENJAMIN B. WOODRUFF,
Treasurer.
Counsellors.—Peter Johnson,
Pompy Prall, and Jacob King[4]

Emancipator (New York, N.Y.), 27 May 1834.

1. The American Anti-Slavery Society—a national organization designed to coordinate and promote local antislavery societies in the free states—was founded at a convention held in Philadelphia during December 1833 by abolitionists from nine states. The society became the most influential and active abolitionist association in the United States and remained in existence until April 1870. The *Emancipator* was its official organ. Between 1837 and 1840, a series of general debates about the nature of antislavery reform, as well as disputes about political antislavery and the role of women in the movement, fragmented the society and culminated in May 1840 with the formation of the rival American and Foreign Anti-Slavery Society. In the wake of the split, the AASS became a thoroughly Garrisonian organization. It sponsored publication of the New York–based *National Anti-Slavery Standard* (1840–70), admitted women into full participation, shunned direct political antislavery action, and championed anticolonization, nonresistance, and disunion. Garrison resigned from the society after the Civil War, but Wendell Phillips and others used the association to press for black suffrage. *Lib*, 4 January 1834; Louis Filler, *The Crusade against Slavery: Friends, Foes, and Reforms, 1820–1860* (Algonac, Mich., 1986), 86–87, 123, 160–71; John L. Thomas, *The Liberator: William Lloyd Garrison* (Boston, Mass., 1963), 171–76, 246–48, 269–70, 362–66, 431–35; Aileen S. Kraditor, *Means and Ends in American Abolitionism: Garrison and His Critics on Strategy and Tactics* (New York, N.Y., 1969), 5, 38.

2. The authors of the constitution borrow from Isaiah 58:6,

> Is not this the fast that I have chosen?
> To loose the bands of wickedness
> To undo the heavy burdens
> And to let the oppressed go free,
> And that ye break every yoke?

3. Henry Drayton (?–1837) was born a slave in South Carolina. He gained his freedom, possibly with the aid of black clergyman Morris Brown. Drayton attended the founding convention of the African Methodist Episcopal church at Philadelphia in 1816, and as an AME deacon, assisted Brown in establishing a church in Charleston. He was forced to leave South Carolina in 1822 in the wake of the Denmark Vesey insurrection. He served as superintendent for the First Colored Wesleyan Methodist Church in New York City in the late 1820s. Drayton withdrew from the AME church in 1830 and joined the African Methodist Episcopal Zion church the following year. He itinerated in Hartford and Middletown, Connecticut, before finally settling in Newark, New Jersey, where he taught school and served a local black congregation. Drayton was the president of the Colored Anti-Slavery Society of Newark, an American Anti-Slavery Society auxiliary, and represented Newark at the 1834 black national conven-

tion. He died in 1837, while attending an AMEZ convention in New York City. Payne, *African Methodist Episcopal Church*, 26, 34; Dorothy Porter, *Early Negro Writing, 1760–1837* (Boston, Mass., 1971), 197; *FJ*, 6 June 1828; *E*, 27 May 1834 [1:0458]; *Lib*, 23 June, 7 July 1832 [1:0198, 0200]; *ZW*, 10 June 1837 [2:0073]; *Minutes of the Fourth Annual Convention* (1834), 8 [1:0466]; Jeremiah Asher, *Incidents in the Life of the Rev. J. Asher* (London, 1850), 39 [6:0479]; Winch, *Philadelphia's Black Elite*, 14, 102–3.

4. Except for Henry Drayton, all of the initial officers of the Colored Anti-Slavery Society of Newark were working-class blacks. Jacob D. King (1806–?) worked as a cooper, Pompy Prall (1771–?) served as sexton of the First African Methodist Church, and Abraham B. Ray (1798–?), Peter Johnson (1790–?), John D. Closson, and Benjamin B. Woodruff were laborers. Most were longtime residents of Newark and were active in local antislavery and civil rights efforts. Closson, a vocal opponent of colonization, was a delegate to the 1834 and 1835 black national conventions, and both Johnson and King signed the call for a black national gathering in 1840. Woodruff and King helped organize local First of August celebrations. Except for Ray, who had moved to Sparta, New Jersey, by 1850, these men remained in Newark, and both Prall and Johnson eventually accumulated $500 worth of real estate. King remained the most active abolitionist, serving during the late 1850s as treasurer of the Relief Association, a local organization that assisted fugitive slaves escaping along the underground railroad. *Newark City Directory*, 1835–61; U.S. Census, 1850; *Lib*, 11 May 1833; *Minutes of the Fourth Annual Convention* (1834), 8 [1:0466]; *Minutes of the Fifth Annual Convention* (1835), 8 [1:0589]; Abajian, *Blacks in Selected Newspapers*, 1:361, 428, 2:138, 729; *CA*, 25 July 1840 [3:0534–35]; *WAA*, 15 October 1859 [12:0133].

10.
James R. Bradley to Lydia Maria Child
3 June 1834

Former slaves were particularly effective antislavery advocates. Having
experienced bondage firsthand, they spoke and wrote about slavery
with irrefutable authority, making them formidable opponents of proslavery propagandists. James R. Bradley's experiences were similar to
those of many former slaves in the antislavery movement. After buying
his freedom from his Arkansas master, he enrolled at Lane Seminary in
Cincinnati, a center of student abolitionism. Students Henry B. Stanton
and Theodore Dwight Weld enlisted Bradley's assistance, recognizing
the role he could play in their local struggle against colonizationists and
antiabolitionists. At one student debate, Bradley spoke for over two
hours, discrediting charges that abolitionism would be "unsafe to the
community" and informing his audience that slaves desired "*liberty and
education.*" Word of Bradley's success eventually reached abolitionists
in Boston. At Lydia Maria Child's request, Bradley sketched an account
of his slave experiences, which he forwarded to her in a 3 June 1834 letter. Child published a heavily edited version of Bradley's narrative in
The Oasis (1834), an abolitionist gift book. It was widely reprinted in
the antislavery press. Lawrence Lesick, *The Lane Rebels: Evangelicalism
and Antislavery in Antebellum America* (Metuchen, N.J., 1980), 80–81;
Robert H. Abzug, *Passionate Liberator: Theodore Dwight Weld and the
Dilemma of Reform* (New York, N.Y., 1980), 90–91; *Lib,* 29 March
1834; *E,* 4 November 1834; *NYE,* 1 November 1834; *HF,* 7 March
1835; Theodore Dwight Weld to Lydia Maria Child, 3 June 1834, Anti-
Slavery Collection, MB.

June 3, 183[4]

Dear Madam:[1]

I am now going to try to write a little account of my life as nearly as I
can remember. It makes me sorrowful to think of my past days. They
have been very dark and full of tears. I always longed and prayed for
liberty. I sometimes hoped I should get it and then I would think and
pray and study out some way to earn money enough to buy myself by
working nights, and then something would fall out and all my hopes
would die and it seemed as though I must live and die a slave without
anyone to pity me. But I will begin as far back as I can remember. When I
was between two and three years old the soul destroyers tore me from my
tender mothe[r's] arms somewhere in Africa far back from the sea. They
carried me along distance to the ships. I looked back and wept all the
way. The ship was full of men and women loaded down with chains. As I

was so small they let me run about on deck. After many long days they brought me to Charlestown SC.[2] Then a slave holder bought me and took me up into Pendleton county. I suppose that I stayed with him about six months. Then he sold me to a man whose name was Bradley. ~~Every~~ Ever since then I have been called by that name. This man was called a wonderfully kind master and he was more kind than most masters. He gave me enough to eat and did not beat me so much as masters g[enera]lly do. But all that was nothing to me. I spent many sleepless nights and bathed my face in tears because I was a slave. I [asked] and groaned for liberty. My master kept me ignorant of every thing that he could. They never told me any thing about my soul, nor that I was a sinner against God. When I got to be fourteen years old I remember that I used to think a great deal about freedom. It was my hearts desire. I could not get it out of my mind. I looked back and thought how much I had passed through and how much my mind had ached to be free and to feel within me the life of liberty and then I looked ahead and all that I could see was hopeless bondage dark and dreary and my heart ached as though it must break. As I have said before I was beter treated than most of the slaves that I knew. I never suffered for food. I never was flogged with a whip but oh my soul my flesh was tormented with kicks and knocks more than I can tell. When I was a boy my master knocked me down number of times. Once when i was nine years old he got angry and knocked me down and I lost my senses and lay some time. When I came to myself he told me that he thought he had killed me. At another time he struck me with curry comb and and sunk the knob into my head. I have said that I had food enough. I wish I could say as much about my cloathes but I must let tat a lone as I cant think of any suitable words to use in telling you just how I fared as to cloathes. They used to work me very hard. I had to be in the field always by sunrise and worked till dark stopping at noon only long enough to eat dinner. When I was abut fifteen years old I took what was called the cold plague by being overworked. I was sick alon[g] time. My master came to me one day while I was lieing and groning with pain and said "he will never be of any more use to me. I would as soon knock him in the head as if he was an opossum," and often his chil would come with axes and knifeves and shake them at me and prick me and make as tho. they would knock me in the head but I have [word illegible] a bout this. The Lord at length raised me up but I lost intirely the use of one of my ancles. About this time my master moved to the Arkansas territory and died. The family the[n] hired me out & after alittle while my mistress sent for me to come back and take care of the plantation and said that she could not get long without me. After my master died I began to contrive how I might buy [word or words missing]. After working all day for my mistress I used to go to bed and ~~sleeping~~ three or four hours and get up and work the rest of the night for myself. I used to make working collars for horses out of husks by plaiting them. I could make one collar in about eight hours. I [usua]lly took time enough from my sleep to make two collars in a week. The collars would sell for fifty cents apiece. One summer I used to take from my sleep from three to four hours every night. But I found after a while that I was growing weak and faint and had to sleep more. The first money I got I laid out for a pig. The next year I saved thirteen and the next about thirty. Ther was a gret deal of wild land there that belonged to Congress.[3] I used to go out and dig up little patches with my hoe and there and plat corn and get up in the night and tend it. With this corn I fatted my hogs and used to sell a number every year. B[esides] this I used to raise little patches of tobbacco and sell it and by more corn for my hogs. In this way I worked five years and found after taking out my [losses] that I had got one hundred and sixty dollars. With this money I hired my time for two years. During these two years I worked almost all the time night and day.[4] The [fire] of liberty burned within me so strong and strung up my nerves and raged up my soul so much that I could do with very little rest and sleep, and could do a gret deal more work in a day than I ever did before. When the two years were worked out I had earned three hundred dollars [besides] feeding and cloathing myself. When the two years were out I went home and hired my time for eighteen months more and went two hundred and fifty miles west nearly to Texas where I could make more money. After working there eighteen months I made enough to buy myself which I did in 1833 just bout one year ago. I paid for myself in all about [three] hundred dollars including what I paid for my time.

As soon as I was free I started for a free state and came to Cincinnati. When I arrived there I heard of Lane Seminary[5] two miles out of the city. I longed to get an education. I had been praying to God for years that my poor dark mind might see the light of knowledge. I asked for admission into the Seminary. They pitied me [and] took [me] in though I knew nothing of the studies which were required for admission. I am so ignorant that I suppose that it will take me two years to get up with the lowest class in the Institution. I am situated as pleasantly and treated just as kindly and as much like a brother by the students as tho. my skin was as white and my education was as good as that of any member of the Seminary. In everything I am treated just like an equal and an [own] brother. Thank the Lord prejudice against color is too mean a thing to live in Lane Seminary. If my life is spared I expect to spend some years here and prepare to preach the Gospel.[6]

I will now mention a few things which I could not bring in very well as I was going along with my story. In the year 1828 I saw some Christians who talked with me about my soul. [Word illegible] showed me that I [words illegible] and that I must [r]epent of my sins and live to do good.

The holy spirit led me to the cross of Christ and there I trust my soul was washed in the blood that cleaneth from all sin[s]. Oh how I longed then to read that I might study the Bible. I made out to get an old spelling book and carried it in my hat all the time for many months until I could spell pretty well and read easy words. When I got up in the night to work I would generally read a few minutes if I could manage to get a light and indeed every chance I could get I worked away at my spelling book. After I had learned to read, I tried to learn to write. I persuaded one of my mistressess young sons to teach me. The second night my mistress came in and bustled about and scolded her son and called him out and I over heard her say to him. "You fool what are you doing. If you teach him to write he will write himself a pass and run away and we shall lose him." So that was the end of my instruction in writing. How[ever] I perservered and made marks of all sorts and shapes that I could think of and ~~copy letters out~~ by turning every way after a long time I got so that I [c]ould write pretty plain. I have said a good deal about my desire for liberty. How strange it is that any body should believe that a human being <u>could</u> be a <u>slave</u> and feel contented. I dont believe there ever was a slave who did not long for liberty. I know very well that slaveholders take a great deal of pain to make the people of free states believe ~~believe~~ that this class are happy and contented—and I kn[o]w too that I never ~~saw~~ knew a slave—no matter how well he was treated—that did not long to be free. There is one thing about this that people of free states dont understand. When they talk with slaves and ask them if they dont want their liberty and if they wouldnt like to be free like white men—they say no—and very likely they will go on and say that they wouldnt leave their master for the world, when at the same time they have [been] along time been laying plans to get free and desire liberty more than anything else in the world. The truth is and every <u>slave</u> knows it—if he should say he wanted to be free and should show any weariness and discontent because he is a slave he is sure to be treated harsher and worked harder for it. So they are always very careful not to show any weariness and particularly when they are asked questions about freedom by white men. When the slaves are together by themselves alone, they are always talking about liberty, <u>liberty</u> is the great thought and feeling that fills the mind full all the time. I could say a gret many things more but as you requested in your letter to my dear friend Mr. Weld that I would write a "short account" of my life I am afraid that I have written too much already and will say but a few words more. My heart is full and flows over when I hear what is doing for the poor broken hearted slave and free man of color. God will help those who take the part of the oppressed. Yes blessed be ~~God~~ his name he will s[u]rely do it. Dear Madam I do not know you personally but I have seen your book on slavery and have read much of you, and I do hope to meet you at the resurrection of the Just. I thank God that he has given to the poor bleeding slave and to all the oppressed colored race such a dear friend. May God graciously preserve you—dear Madam, and bless your labors and make you great in this holy cause until you see all the walls of prejudice broke down and all the chains of slavery broken to pices and all of every color sitting down—together at Jesus feet, a band of brethren speaking kind words and looking upon each others faces in love and as they expect to love each other and live together in heaven, be willing to love each other and live together on earth.

Anti-Slavery Collection, Boston Public Library, Boston Massachusetts. Published by courtesy of the Trustees of the Boston Public Library.

1. Lydia Maria Child (1802–1880), one of the most important female Garrisonian abolitionists, served on the executive committee of the American Anti-Slavery Society and as editor of the *National Anti-Slavery Standard*. Child wrote romance novels, texts on domestic economy, and a history of women. She befriended blacks, editing Harriet Jacobs's *Incidents in the Life of a Slave Girl* (1861). Her *Appeal in Favor of that Class of Americans Called Africans* (1833) remains a sophisticated statement on slavery and equality. She married the mercurial abolitionist, David Lee Child. *NAW*, 1:330–33; Harriet A. Jacobs, *Incidents in the Life of a Slave Girl*, ed. Jean Fagan Yellin (Cambridge, Mass., 1987), 3–4.

2. Charleston was a primary American entrepôt for African slavers. From 1670 to 1808, more than 100,000 slaves entered South Carolina through the port of Charleston. Once in Charleston, slaves were processed and sold by more than a hundred local slave trading firms. Elizabeth Donnan, "The Slave Trade into South Carolina before the Revolution," *AHR* 33:804–28 (July 1928); *DAAS*, 96–98.

3. Bradley probably refers to lands obtained by Congress during the mid-1820s when the Choctaw and Cherokee Indians were expelled from the Arkansas Territory. Ray Allen Billington, *Westward Expansion: A History of the American Frontier*, 3d ed. (New York, N.Y., 1967), 469–71.

4. Some slaves were allowed to "hire their own time," depending on local labor needs, economic conditions, and the attitude of their white owners. Those slaves lived in the twilight between slavery and freedom, bargaining for their labor, paying a portion of their earnings to their owners, while remaining under strict white supervision. Self-hiring provided some slaves with an opportunity to earn sufficient money to purchase their freedom, but by 1860 most states had restricted self-hiring. Robert S. Starobin, *Industrial Slavery in the Old South* (New York, N.Y., 1970), 134–37.

5. Lane Seminary was founded near Cincinnati in 1828 to prepare candidates for the Presbyterian and Congregational ministries. Lane achieved notoriety in 1834, when a debate over immediate abolition and colonization inspired some seventy-five students (led by Theodore Dwight Weld and Henry B. Stanton) to ally with the abolitionists. When the Lane board of trustees prohibited further antislavery activism, most students voluntarily withdrew from the school. Some of these so-called "Lane rebels" later enrolled at Oberlin College. Nearly all

remained active in the antislavery movement, profoundly influencing antebellum American reform. Lesick, *The Lane Rebels*.

6. James R. Bradley was admitted into Lane Seminary's literary department on 28 May 1833 and quickly joined the student rebels in their attack on colonization. He was a manager of the student antislavery society and snubbed a personal invitation by the school's president, Lyman Beecher, to attend a meeting in Beecher's home to diffuse the spreading student rebellion. In October 1834, Bradley joined with twenty-eight other students in withdrawing from Lane. The next year, he enrolled at Oberlin College, becoming the school's first black student. He was admitted into Oberlin's preparatory facility, the Sheffield Manual Labor School, in 1836 but never graduated. *Lib*, 29 March 1834; Lesick, *The Lane Rebels*, 95, 205; Robert S. Fletcher, *A History of Oberlin College: From Its Foundation through the Civil War*, 2 vols. (Oberlin, Ohio, 1943), 1:55–56, 154, 162, 183, 189, 533; Oberlin College Catalog & Record of Colored Students, 1835–62, Cowles Papers, OO [1:0542].

11.
Sarah L. Forten to Elizabeth H. Whittier
23 March 1835

The residences of black leaders often served as gathering places for re-formers and centers for organizing reform activities. In New York City, Thomas Van Rensellaer regularly opened "his heart and his home" to abolitionists. The homes of James Forten, Sr., and Robert Purvis, both located on Lombard Street in the center of Philadelphia's black commu-nity, bustled with antislavery activity. On any given day, a visitor might encounter a white abolitionist, a fugitive slave, the child of an African chief, a committee meeting of the Philadelphia Female Anti-Slavery Society, or a planning session of the Vigilant Committee of Philadel-phia. Sarah L. Forten's 23 March 1835 letter to antislavery acquaint-ance Elizabeth H. Whittier conveys the excitement generated in the Forten and Purvis households by the visit of English abolitionist George Thompson. Wendell Phillips Garrison and Francis Jackson Garrison, *William Lloyd Garrison, 1805–1879: The Story of His Life*, 4 vols. (New York, N.Y., 1885–89), 2:355–56; Lewis, "The Fortens of Phila-delphia," 39–40, 50–53, 108–9.

Philad[elphi]a, [Pennsylvania]
March 23, 1835
Monday 10' P.M.

My Dear Friend:[1]
   I am now hastily penning a few lines to inform you of the visit of our noble friend and advocate George Thompson—he has paid us two visits, and four admirable lectures[2] from him have quite captivated our good citizens, never before have we listened to such surprising power of ora-tory—never has there been such an awakning of consciences—his elo-quence surpasses any thing ever before heard. On Saturday last he ad-dressed the Female Anti-Slavery Society, and spoke to the hearts most feelingly. After the address—fifty six ladies signed their names to our constitution;[3] so you see this was doing a great deal among our plegh-matic people; I have had many opportunities of being in Mr. Thompsons Society—and find him a most delightful and companionable person, he is witty—full of anecdote—and very lively, he staid at my sisters—Mrs. Purvis[4]—and we really loved him—not only for his greatness—but for his goodness. He has had large audiences each night of his lectures—and so crowded was the church the evening on which he commenced his admirable address on St. Domingo that the gallery—from the tremen-dous pressure had nearly given way—the alarm was excessive—and the meeting adjourned in great confusion—this was truly unfortunate, as the

accident occured in the middle part of this most admirable subject. Tomorrow evening he intends to finish his lecture—I anticipate great pleasure and information from it.

You will scarcely be able to read this hasty scrawl. I am now writing with four or five gentlemen (all abolitionists) talking about Thompson. Of course I can't help giving my ears to them, while my eyes only rest upon the paper. I've stoped just now to join in a hearty burst of laughter elicited by the repitition of one of Mr. T———s, delightful anecdotes. Mr. Garrison is also in the city—and his brother in law Mr. Benson[5]— the latter gentleman is staying at Mr. Purvis'.[6] Do you perceive that we are indeed highly favoured in having such three such highly valued friends with us. I send this letter by Mr. Garrison to put in the Post office at Boston—I must really stop, as I have another letter to write tonight to Mrs. Fuller of Boston[7]—do you know her? She is a very fine woman and I have been much gratified by an intimacy with her. Will you have us kindly remembered to your family—my Fathers regards to your Brother[8] —if he should be in Haverhill—Farewell my dear Friend—and believe me always your friend.

Sarah L Forten[9]

PS. I have been looking over this badly written letter and am almost ashamed to send it—if I had time I would really write another[,] yet you will forgive it and attribute its defects to the haste in which it was "thrown off"—rather than to any other cause. I recall with feelings of shame, Hanah More's advice to young Ladies—wherein she recommends them "never to write a letter in a careless or slovenly manner—it is a sign of ill breeding or indifference."[10] &c. &c. My excuse is haste—and one which I hope will, for this time, at least, be accepted.

Yours,

SLF

Whittier Papers, Central Michigan University, Mount Pleasant, Michigan. Published by permission.

1. Elizabeth Hussey Whittier (1815–1864), the sister and literary confidante of poet John Greenleaf Whittier, was an active abolitionist. She penned antislavery verse, helped found the Boston Female Anti-Slavery Society, and assumed a leadership role in female antislavery societies in Haverhill and Amesbury, Massachusetts. In 1839 she helped her brother edit the *Pennsylvania Freeman*. *Lib*, 16 September 1864; Edward Wagenknecht, *John Greenleaf Whittier: A Portrait in Paradox* (New York, N.Y., 1967), 4, 9, 29, 31, 143–48, 162, 249, 437, 477–79; John A. Pollard, *John Greenleaf Whittier: Friend of Man* (Boston, Mass., 1949), 527n.

2. George Thompson (1804–1878), William Lloyd Garrison's most powerful abolitionist ally in Britain, visited Philadelphia twice during his controversial 1834–35 tour of the United States. First in late February, then again in late

March, he delivered a series of well-received antislavery lectures in the city. So many people crammed into the Cherry Street Reformed Presbyterian Church to hear one Thompson lecture that the gallery floor collapsed. He spoke in favor of immediatism and defended his right to address American audiences, a point repeatedly challenged by many who thought him a foreign agitator bent on breaking up the Union. Abolitionists considered Thompson's tour a great success. A powerful orator, he again traveled to the United States in 1851 and during the Civil War. C. Duncan Rice, "The Anti-Slavery Mission of George Thompson to the United States, 1834–35," *JAS* 2:13–31 (April 1968); Merrill and Ruchames, *Letters of William Lloyd Garrison*, 1:467–69.

3. In 1833 Philadelphia antislavery women founded the Philadelphia Female Anti-Slavery Society. Fourteen women, predominantly Quakers, including black abolitionists Margaretta Forten and Sarah McCrummill, drew up a constitution that denounced slavery and racism as "contrary to the laws of God, and to the . . . Declaration of Independence." It called for all "professing Christians" to oppose the sin of slavery and work for black uplift. Any woman, regardless of race, who subscribed to the society's principles and paid the required dues could join. The PFASS, an auxiliary of the AASS, distributed antislavery tracts, sponsored antislavery speakers, supported a school for black children, petitioned Congress, and sent funds to the Pennsylvania Anti-Slavery Society and the *Pennsylvania Freeman*. Between 1833 and 1861, the PFASS raised about $32,000 through its antislavery fairs. It disbanded in 1870. Ira V. Brown, "Cradle of Feminism: The Philadelphia Female Anti-Slavery Society, 1833–1840," *PMHB* 52:143–66 (April 1978).

4. Harriet Forten Purvis (1810–1875) was the daughter of black abolitionists James and Charlotte Forten. She and her sisters received a formal education and learned about antislavery and other reforms while growing up in the Forten household—a center of local abolitionist activity. Her marriage to Robert Purvis in 1832 united two of Philadelphia's most prominent black families. She and her husband traveled to Britain in 1834, helping to spread the anticolonization message among abolitionists there. A founding member of the Philadelphia Female Anti-Slavery Society, she participated in the society's annual antislavery fairs and represented the association at the 1838 and 1839 meetings of the Anti-Slavery Convention of American Women. Purvis made her country home in Byberry, Pennsylvania, an important station on the underground railroad used by many of the estimated nine thousand fugitive slaves that passed through Pennsylvania.

Purvis's reform interests ranged beyond abolitionism—she spoke at public gatherings on women's rights and joined with other Philadelphia blacks in 1841 to organize the Gilbert Lyceum. Active in the struggle for women's rights and universal suffrage after the Civil War, she joined the American Equal Rights Association, attended the association's 1867 convention, and served as the last secretary of the Pennsylvania Anti-Slavery Society. *PF*, 18 November 1847, 20 September 1849, 31 October 1850 [5:0530, 6:0162, 0658]; *NSt*, 10 November 1848 [5:0825]; Winch, "Leaders of Philadelphia's Black Community," 321–22, 339n; Lewis, "The Fortens of Philadelphia," 44, 74, 105–7, 206; *DANB*, 509; Sterling, *We Are Your Sisters*, 119–21.

5. George W. Benson (1808–1879), William Lloyd Garrison's brother-in-law, advocated peace, nonresistance, and anti-Sabbatarianism and helped found a

communitarian settlement in Northampton, Massachusetts, in 1842. A merchant in Providence, Rhode Island, he later moved to New York City, then to Kansas, where he served in the state legislature. Merrill and Ruchames, *Letters of William Lloyd Garrison*, 2:xxiii–xxiv.

6. Robert Purvis lived at 270 Lombard Street, in the heart of Philadelphia's black community, during the 1830s and early 1840s. There he frequently welcomed visiting white abolitionists, hid fugitive slaves, and hosted meetings of the Vigilant Committee of Philadelphia. As a result of these activities, the house twice became a target for antiabolitionist mobs, prompting Purvis to move his family to the nearby town of Byberry. *Philadelphia City Directory*, 1844; Lewis, "The Fortens of Philadelphia," 50–51; Joseph A. Boromé, "The Vigilant Committee of Philadelphia," *PMHB* 92:321, 326, 343–46 (July 1968).

7. Lydia L. Fuller of Boston was the wife of John E. Fuller, a close friend and follower of William Lloyd Garrison during the 1830s, who later broke with the Garrisonians. She helped run a boardinghouse and participated in the Boston Female Anti-Slavery Society and the Anti-Slavery Convention of American Women. Merrill and Ruchames, *Letters of William Lloyd Garrison*, 1:470; *Boston City Directory*, 1839–42; *Lib*, "Extra," [1840]; *Proceedings of the Anti-Slavery Convention of American Women, Held in the City of New York, May 9th, 10th, 11th, and 12th, 1837* (New York, N.Y., 1837), 4.

8. John Greenleaf Whittier (1807–1892), a Quaker author, poet, newspaper editor, and abolitionist, lived in Haverhill, Massachusetts. Whittier was a founding member of the American Anti-Slavery Society. A political abolitionist, he worked with Henry B. Stanton to establish the Liberty party (1839) and supported Frémont (1856) and Lincoln (1860) for the presidency. He is well remembered for his poem, *Snow-Bound*. Pollard, *John Greenleaf Whittier*.

9. Sarah L. Forten (1814–?), the youngest daughter of James and Charlotte Forten, received a formal education and nurtured her literary talents by writing antislavery poetry and essays. Her poetry was read at antislavery meetings, and her work appeared in the *Liberator* under the pseudonyms "A," "Ada," and "Magawisca." A founding member of the Philadelphia Female Anti-Slavery Society, she held several offices in the society, helped organize the society's annual antislavery fairs, and served on a committee to raise funds for Pennsylvania Hall. In 1837 she attended the Anti-Slavery Convention of American Women with her sister, Harriet Forten Purvis. The following year, she married Joseph Purvis, Robert Purvis's younger brother. Like her sister, Harriet, she maintained a lifelong friendship with Angelina and Sarah Grimké, and her correspondence provided the Grimké sisters with personal testimony on the effects of racial prejudice. Sterling, *We Are Your Sisters*, 114, 119, 121–26; Lewis, "The Fortens of Philadelphia," 40–41, 60–63; Winch, "Leaders of Philadelphia's Black Community," 97, 341n, 463, 519; Sarah Forten to Angelina Grimké, 15 April 1837, Weld-Grimké Papers, MiU [2:0020–22].

10. Hannah More (1745–1833), an English author and moralist, devoted herself to the writing of advice manuals, novels, and poetry, and the dissemination of evangelical religion and ethics. Her *Strictures on the Modern System of Female Education* (1799) was reprinted in England and the United States throughout the early nineteenth century and helped define attitudes toward women. Mary G. Jones, *Hannah More* (London, 1952), 3–14, 96–102, 114–21.

12.
Address by William Whipper, Alfred Niger,
and Augustus Price
3 June 1835

Philadelphia blacks dominated the early convention movement. They
sent the greatest number of delegates and hosted five of the first six
black national gatherings. Their interest in moral reform eventually
overshadowed other concerns, particularly at the June 1835 convention,
which assembled in Philadelphia's Wesley African Methodist Church.
Encouraged by William Whipper and cheered by several white abolitionists in attendance, the thirty-five delegates called for the formation
of an American Moral Reform Society devoted to universal reform principles—"Education, Temperance, Economy, and Universal Liberty."
Seven Philadelphia blacks were elected as officers of the new organization. On the third day of the convention, delegates selected Whipper,
Alfred Niger of Providence, and Augustus Price of Washington to draft
a manifesto explaining the purpose and principles of the AMRS to a
broader audience. The ensuing document was largely Whipper's effort.
Entitled "To the American People," it charged that "the depravity of our
morals" provoked racial prejudice and claimed that moral reform offered the best means for improving the condition of black Americans.
Reflecting Whipper's integrationist ideology, it called for the elimination
of "national distinctions, complexional variations, geographical lines,
and sectional bounds" in the society's conduct. Winch, *Philadelphia's
Black Elite*, 102–29; *Minutes of the Fifth Annual Convention* (1835),
4–5, 8 [1:0587–89].

Fellow Citizens—We form a portion of the people of this continent, on
whom an unmeasurable amount of obloquy, and scorn, and contempt
have been poured, on account of the depravity of our morals; and who
have been educated under the influence of a system, that impairs the
mental vigour, blights with its blasting influence the only successful hope
on which the mind can be reared, that keeps from our grasp the fruits of
knowledge, the favor of just and equitable laws, and presents a formidable barrier to the prosecution of arts and sciences of civilized life. The
lucrative avocations, mechanic arts, and civil associations by which men
acquire a knowledge of government, and the nature of human affairs,
have been almost wholly reserved as a dignified reward, suited only to
the interest and use of the fairer complexion. Yet, in despite of all these,
when all the avenues of privileged life have been closed against us, our
hands bound with stationary fetters, our minds left to grope in the prison
cell of impenetrable gloom, and our whole action regulated by constitu-

tional law and a perverse public sentiment, we have been tauntingly required to prove the dignity of our human nature, by disrobing ourselves of inferiority, and exhibiting to the world our profound Scholars, distinguished Philosophers, learned Jurists, and distinguished Statesmen. The very expectation on which such a requisition is founded, to say the least, is unreasonable, for it is only when the seed is sown that we can justly hope to reap. If amidst all the difficulties with which we have been surrounded, and the privations which we have suffered, we presented an equal amount of intelligence with that class of Americans that have been so peculiarly favoured, a *very grave* and *dangerous* question would present itself to the world, on the natural equality of man, and the best rule of logic would place those who have oppressed us, in the scale of inferiority. This we do not desire; we love the appellation that records the natural and universal rights of man (to enjoy all the attributes of human happiness) too well, to deprive a single being on earth of such an heavenly inheritance. We can never consent to degrade the creation of man by even attempting to defend the impartiality of his Author. If there be those who doubt that we are made in the image of God, and are endowed with those attributes which the Deity has given to man, we will exhibit them our "hands and side."

The general assertion that superiority of mind is the natural offspring of a fair complexion, arrays itself against the experience of the past and present age, and both natural and physiological science. The ignorance that exists on this subject we are not accountable for, nor are we willing to admit a theory alike irreconcilable with philosophy and common sense.

It is in view of these mighty evils that exist in our country, which are truly national, that has caused us to meet in annual convention for six successive years to take into consideration the best method of remedying our present situation by contributing to their removal;[1] during which period we have associated the collected wisdom of our people, in their representative character, from half the states of this Union, extending from Maine to Washington, southernly, and from thence westwardly to Cincinnati, Ohio, and have come to the conclusion to form a National Moral Reform Society,[2] as a means best calculated to reach the wants and improve the condition of our people.

We have selected four valuable subjects for rallying points, viz.: Education, Temperance, Economy, and Universal Liberty. We hope to make our people, in theory and practice, thoroughly acquainted with these subjects, as a method of future action. Having placed our institution on the high and indisputable ground of natural laws and human rights, and being guided and actuated by the law of universal love to our fellow men, we have buried in the bosom of Christian benevolence all those national distinctions, complexional variations, geographical lines, and sectional bounds that have hitherto marked the history, character and operations of men; and now boldly plead for the Christian and moral elevation of the human race. To aid us in its completion, we shall endeavour to enlist the sympathies and benevolence of the Christian, moral and political world. Without regard to creeds, we shall only ask for the fulfillment of Christian duty, as the surest method of extending righteousness and justice. We shall aim to procure the abolition of those hateful and unnecessary distinctions by which the human family has hitherto been recognized, and only desire that they may be distinguished by their virtues and vices.

We hope to unite the colored population in those principles of Moral Reform. 1st. As a measure necessary to be practiced by all rational and intelligent beings, for the promotion of peace, harmony and concord in society. 2d. As a measure necessary to aid in effecting the total abolition of slavery. And 3d. As having a tendency to effect the destruction of vice universally.

In order to [do] this, we will appoint agents to disseminate these truths among our people, and establish auxiliaries wherever practicable, that the same leaven of righteousness and justice may animate the body politic. We will establish a press, and through it make known to the world our progress in the arts, science, and civilization. For aid in the prosecution of our undertaking we shall appeal to the benevolence of nations, but more particularly to our own. For, as God has so abundantly blessed her with internal resources as a means of gratifying her spiritual and temporal wants, so we believe she should employ them to his honor and glory, in disseminating the blessings of education, peace, happiness and prosperity to her own fellow citizens. And if America is to be instrumental through the providence of Almighty God in blessing other portions of the peopled earth, by extending to the heathen and Pagan idolater the knowledge of the true God, a pure science, an unadulterated religion, an exalted and benevolent philanthropy, how necessary is it that she should first purify her own dominions, by extending to all her children those divine and precious gifts; so when she shall have joined other nations in rearing the standard for the redemption of the world, every ray of light that may reach those benighted regions will, when falling on the prism of truth, present one pure, unmixed stream of Christian love, and cease to becloud the horizon of everlasting justice. We will first appeal to the Christian churches to take the lead in establishing the principles of supreme love to God, and universal love to man. We will do all in our power to aid her in forming a moral structure against which "the gates of hell cannot prevail."[3]

We plead for the extension of those principles on which our government was formed, that it in turn may become purified from those iniquitous inconsistencies into which she has fallen by her aberration from first principles; that the laws of our country may cease to conflict with the spirit of that sacred instrument, the Declaration of American Independence. We believe in a pure, unmixed republicanism, as a form of government best suited to the condition of man, by its promoting equality, virtue, and happiness to all within its jurisdiction. We love our country, and pray for the perpetuation of its government, that it may yet stand illustrious before the nations of the earth, both for the purity of its precepts, and the mildness and equableness of its laws.

We shall advocate the cause of peace, believing that whatever tends to the destruction of human life, is at variance with the precepts of the Gospel, and at enmity with the well being of individuals as well as of society. We shall endeavour to promote education, with sound morality, not that we shall become "learned and mighty," but "great and good." We shall advocate temperance in all things, and total abstinence from all alcoholic liquors. We shall advocate a system of *economy*, not only because luxury is injurious to individuals, but because its practice exercises an influence on society, which in its very nature is sinful. We shall advocate universal liberty, as the inalienable right of every individual born in the world, and a right which cannot be taken away by government itself, without an unjust exercise of power. We shall exhibit our sympathy, for our suffering brethren, by petitioning congress to procure the immediate abolition of slavery in the District of Columbia, and her territories. We shall endeavour to strengthen public sentiment against slavery, so long as a slave treads the soil of these United States. We shall aim at the extinction of mental thraldom; an evil much more dangerous and exceeding the former, both in extent and power. We shall persuade our brethren from using the products of slave labour, both as a moral and Christian duty, and as a means by which the slave system may be successfully abrogated. We shall appeal to the coloured churches to take decisive measures to rid themselves of the sin of slavery and immorality. We shall endeavour to pledge all the ministers and elders of our churches to the cause of Moral Reform. We hope to train the undisciplined youth in moral pursuits, and we shall anxiously endeavour to impress on our people everywhere, that in moral elevation true happiness consists. We feel bound to pursue the present course as a duty we owe to ourselves, our God, our common country, and the interests of suffering humanity. The free coloured population of the United States now amounts to about 400,000, and are constantly increasing by a double process, and we believe that the philanthropic exertions that are now making in our country for the abolition of slavery, will shortly remove the fetters from thousands annually, and these will be continually adding to our number. We are unable to conceive of any better method by which we can aid the cause of human liberty, than by improving our general character, and embracing within our grasp the liberated slave for moral and mental culture. By pursuing this course we shall certainly remove many of the objections to immediate emancipation. And we further believe, that all who have either thought or felt deeply on this subject will not only sanction such an organization, but will feel bound to aid in promoting its objects. We shall intreat those that are constantly persecuting and calumniating our general character, to cease with their vituperations, and suffer a people already bowed to the dust, to breath out their existence in peace and quietude. We will intreat our brethren to bear with Christian fortitude the scoffs and indignation that may be cast on them on account of their complexion, and pity the source from whence it emanates, knowing it is the offspring of wickedness and ignorance.

In the present state of society, we must expect to endure many difficulties, until the world improves in wisdom, and a polite education, and a more liberal and enlightened philosophy supplants the present system of national education. If we but fully rest ourselves on the dignity of human nature, and maintain a bold, enduring front against all opposition, the monster, prejudice, will fall humbly at our feet. Prejudice, like slavery, cannot stand the omnipotence of Truth. It is as impossible for a bold, clear and discriminating mind that can calmly and dispassionately survey the structure upon which prejudice is founded, and the materials of which it is composed, to be chained within its grasp, as it is for the puny arm of rebellious man to control the operations of the universe.

We will endeavour to establish in our people a correct knowledge of their own immortal worth, their high derivation as rational, moral and intelligent beings. We shall appeal to them to abandon their prejudices against all complexion and bury them in oblivion, and endeavour to live in the same country as children of one common father, and as brethren possessing the same holy, religious faith, and with a zeal determined on the promotion of great and glorious objects. We shall endeavour to impress on them, at all times, to maintain in every station of life that affability of manner, meekness, humility, and gentleness, that ornaments the Christian character; and finally we will appeal to Heaven for the purity of our motives, and at the rectitude of our intentions, and to men for the means of prosecuting them; to Christians, philanthropists and patriots, without regard to creed, profession, or party. In short, we shall aim to whatever seemeth good, consistent with these principles, for the promotion and welfare of our people.

Having now stated the most prominent objects that will command our attention and support, there are others, that from mere *custom* and usage, many might suppose it were our duty to vindicate. From these we must respectfully dissent, viz.: We will not stoop to contend with those who style us inferior beings. And as we know of no earthly tribunal of sufficient competency and impartiality to decide on a question, involving the natural superiority of individuals and nations, we shall not submit so grave a decision to creatures like ourselves, and especially to our ene-mies. In the preamble of our constitution, we claim to be American citizens, and we will not waste our time by holding converse with those who deny us this privilege, unless they first prove that man is not a citizen of that country in which he was born and reared. Those that desire to discuss with us the propriety of remaining in this country, or of the method of our operations, must first admit us as a cardinal point, their equals by nature, possessing like themselves, from God, all those inalienable rights, that are universally admitted to be the property of his creatures. We will not admit that strength of mind lies concealed in the complexion of the body. Having now performed a duty we owed to the people of these United States, in explaining the whole course of action, of an Institution for the improvement of the morals, bearing the broad and illustrious title of American, we view in anticipation, the most happy results to our beloved country, and will most heartily rejoice, if that in an hour of danger, we shall have been fortunate enough to have aided in rescuing her from the evils into which she has fallen; and we do most cordially hope that a moral fabric may be reared, that will promote the cause of righteousness and justice throughout the universe.

WILLIAM WHIPPER
ALFRED NIGER[4]
AUGUSTUS PRICE[5]

Minutes of the Fifth Annual Convention for the Improvement of the Free People of Colour in the United States, Held by Adjournments in the Wesley Church, Philadelphia, from the First to the Fifth of June, Inclusive, 1835 (Philadelphia, Pa., 1835), 25–31.

1. In mid-September 1830, Philadelphia's African Methodist Episcopal bishop, Richard Allen, issued a formal call for a national convention of free blacks to meet in that city during 20–24 September. Twenty-six free men from seven states responded. The convocation began a series of six annual meetings of free blacks (1830–35) and set in motion the first phase of the black convention movement in America. The meetings generally focused on the issues of slavery, colonization, and northern racial prejudice, but some promoted special projects. The black convention movement of the 1830s is best characterized by its commitment to black self-help, moral regeneration, and entrepreneurship as the best means to total assimilation into white society. It also helped spawn the militant black leadership of the 1840s and established a set of priorities to be achieved by concerted black action. Bell, "Free Negroes of the North," 447–55; Pease and Pease, "The Negro Convention Movement," 191–96; Jane H. Pease and William H. Pease, "Negro Conventions and the Problem of Black Leadership," *JAS* 2:29–44 (September 1971).

2. The founding of the American Moral Reform Society marked the culmina-tion of the black national convention movement of the 1830s. The 1835 black national convention, meeting at Philadelphia, organized the AMRS by drafting a

constitution and a "Declaration of Sentiments." The AMRS opened its membership to those who embraced "Education, Temperance, Economy, and Universal
Liberty." Auxiliary societies were organized in Pittsburgh, Baltimore, Providence, Troy, and two New Jersey towns. Local reform organizations—temperance groups, education associations, and religious societies—were invited to send
delegates to AMRS annual meetings. Although constituted as a racially integrated, national reform organization, the AMRS failed to fulfill that promise.
Few whites participated and it never became a truly national organization. Philadelphia blacks dominated the organization—they controlled the board of managers, and Philadelphians James Forten, Joseph Cassey, William Whipper, Robert
Purvis, and James Forten, Jr., held the other key positions. Whipper, the most
influential member, served as corresponding secretary and as editor of the society's monthly organ, the *National Reformer*.

As an abolitionist organization, the AMRS promised to send antislavery petitions to Congress, promote boycotts of slave produce, and oppose proslavery
influences in the American churches. But little evidence exists to suggest that the
society accomplished these objectives. Personal and philosophical rivalries divided the New York and Philadelphia black leadership. Many members—Junius
C. Morel, Frederick Hinton, William Watkins, and Samuel Cornish—criticized
the society for failing to go beyond abstract reform principles or to develop a
concrete program that addressed the problems of black Americans. The AMRS
was never an effective agent of moral reform, although it did help sharpen the
debate on black abolitionist strategies and tactics. The decline of the AMRS in
the early 1840s paralleled the waning appeal of moral reform as an antislavery
strategy. The *National Reformer* suspended publication after one year. The
AMRS held its last annual meeting in 1841. The convention scheduled for the
following year was cancelled, a casualty of the race riots of August 1842. Winch,
Philadelphia's Black Elite, 108–29; Bell, "American Moral Reform Society," 34–
41; *NASS*, 11 August 1842 [4:0461].

3. The authors of the address freely quote from Matthew 16:18 to emphasize
the invincibility of the "moral structure" that the American Moral Reform Society hoped to create.

4. Alfred Niger (1800–?) was born in Rhode Island. He lived and worked as a
barber in Providence from 1824 to 1860. Niger participated in the black national
convention movement in the 1830s, acted as an agent for the *Liberator*, and took
a leading part in local antislavery and anticolonization activities. In the 1840s, he
was a vice-president of the Rhode Island Anti-Slavery Society. Niger became
involved in the voting rights issue in the late 1830s, when the state government
considered taxing black property holders. He sat on a special committee established to appeal directly to the state legislature for black suffrage. When working-class whites began agitating for voting rights in the early 1840s, Niger attended meetings of the white-dominated Suffrage Association, where he became
the object of a divisive conflict over the role of blacks in the movement to expand
the franchise. *Providence City Directory*, 1824–60; *Lib*, 5 November 1831
[1:0132]; *NASS*, 23 December 1841 [4:0325]; *Constitution of the American
Society*, iv [1:0010]; *Minutes of the First Annual Convention* (1831), 8 [1:0080];
Minutes of the Second Annual Convention (1832), 15 [1:0172]; *Minutes of
the Third Annual Convention* (1833), 24 [1:0305]; *Minutes of the Fourth An-*

nual Convention (1834), 35 [1:0480]; *Minutes of the Fifth Annual Convention* (1835), 5, 20 [1:0588, 0595]; Irving H. Bartlett, *From Slave to Citizen: The Story of the Negro in Rhode Island* (Providence, R.I., 1954), 39–40; Robert J. Cottrol, *The Afro-Yankees: Providence's Black Community in the Antebellum Era* (Westport, Conn., 1982), 69–73; Merrill and Ruchames, *Letters of William Lloyd Garrison*, 1:124–25.

5. Augustus Price, a Washington, D.C., free black and "Doorkeeper of the White House," was raised and educated at Andrew Jackson's Hermitage in Tennessee. He was described as being of mixed African, Indian, and white descent, and some evidence suggests that his father may have been a Revolutionary War officer and statesman. Price went with Jackson to Washington in the 1820s. As the president's trusted servant and private secretary, he was present at private White House meetings and cabinet discussions and apparently helped the president draft and transcribe important documents. Price attended the 1835 black national convention and submitted the resolution to establish the American Moral Reform Society. *Minutes of the Fifth Annual Convention* (1835), 4, 10, 18, 21 [1:0587, 0590, 0594, 0596]; *WAA*, 15 December 1860.

13.
Speech by James Forten, Jr.
Delivered before the Philadelphia Female
Anti-Slavery Society
Philadelphia, Pennsylvania
14 April 1836

Black abolitionists understood that their future was inextricably bound
with the fate of the slave. They rejected gradualism and its ally, colonization, for failing to emancipate the slaves and for aggravating racial
antagonism toward free blacks. They embraced immediatism as a moral
imperative, a religious tenet, and a political responsibility. Aware of the
significance of these efforts, black abolitionists appealed to the conscience of the nation, arguing that Americans could not be true to their
Christian faith or their democratic principles and remain silent on such
an egregious injustice as slavery. In a speech before the Philadelphia
Female Anti-Slavery Society on 14 April 1836, James Forten, Jr., praised
the abolitionist work of local black and white women but exhorted
them on to increased activity with a warning that their failure to speak
out would guarantee the perpetuation of slavery and racial prejudice.
"To falter now," he admonished, "would be to surrender your pure and
unsullied principles into the hands of a vicious and perverted portion of
the community." Lewis, "The Fortens of Philadelphia," 42, 92–96.

LADIES—There is nothing that could more forcibly induce me[1] to
express my humble sentiments at all times, than an entire consciousness
that it is the duty of every individual who would wish to see the foul
curse of slavery swept forever from the land—who wishes to become one
amongst the undaunted advocates of the oppressed—who wishes to deal
justly and love mercy. In a word, it is my indispensable duty, in view of
the wretched, the helpless, the friendless condition of my countrymen in
chains, to raise my voice, feeble though it be, in their behalf; to plead for
the restoration of their inalienable rights. As to the character of the
ANTI-SLAVERY SOCIETY,[2] it requires but one glance from an impartial
eye, to discover the purity of its motives—the great strength of its moral
energies; its high and benevolent—its holy and life giving principles.
These are the foundations, the very architecture of Abolition, and prove
its sovereignty. In fact, all associated bodies which have for their great
aim the destruction of tyranny, and the moral and intellectual improvement of mankind, have been, and ever will be, considered as bearing a
decided superiority over all others. And how well may this Association,
before which I now have the honour to appear, be deemed one of that
description; and still more is its superiority increased from a knowledge

of the truth that it is composed entirely of your sex. It stands aloof from the storms of passion and political tumult, exhibiting in its extended and Christian views a disposition to produce an immediate reformation of the heart and soul. Never before has there been a subject brought into the arena of public investigation, so fraught with humanity—so alive to the best interest of our country—so dear to all those for whose benefit it was intended, as the one which now calls you together. How varied and abundant—how eloquent and soul-thrilling have been the arguments advanced in its defence, by the greatest and best of the land; and yet, so boundless is the theme—so inexhaustible the fountain, that even the infant may be heard lisping a prayer for the redemption of the perishing captive.

LADIES—The task you are called upon to perform is certainly of vital importance. Great is the responsibility which this association imposes upon you; however, I need scarcely remind you of it, feeling confident that long before this you have made a practical and familiar acquaintance with all its bearings, and with every sentence contained in your society's sacred declaration; ever remembering that in it is concentrated one of the noblest objects that ever animated the breast of a highly favoured people—*the immediate and unconditional abolition of Slavery*. It is the acknowledgement of a broad principle like this, and recommending it to a prejudiced public, who have been all along accustomed to reason upon the dangerous doctrine of gradualism, viewing it as the only safe and efficient remedy for this monstrous evil which has brought about such an excitement, and convulsed our country from North to South; an excitement which I have every reason to believe will prove a powerful engine towards the furtherance of your noble cause. As to this opposition now arrayed against you, terrible as it appears, it is no more than what you might anticipate; it is a fate which, in this age of iniquity, must inevitably follow such a change as your society proposes to effect. For what else is to be expected for a measure the tendency of which is to check the tide of corruption—to make narrower the limits of tyrannical power—to unite *liberty* and *law*—to save the body of the oppressed from the blood-stained lash of the oppressor—and to secure a greater respect and obedience to Him who wills the happiness of all mankind, and who endowed them with life, and liberty, as conducive to that happiness? What else, I repeat, can be expected but opposition, at a time like this, when brute force reigns supreme; when ministers of the Gospel, commissioned to spread the light of Christianity among all nations are overleaping the pale of the church, forsaking the holy path, and sowing the seeds of discord where they should plant the "olive branch of peace." When liberty has dwindled into a mere shadow, its vitality being lost, shrouded in darkness, swallowed up as it were in the eternal dumbness of the grave. This, my friends, is the present situation of things, and warns you that the desperate struggle has commenced between *freedom* and *despotism*—*light* and *darkness*. This is the hour you are called upon to move with a bold and fearless step; there must be no lukewarmness, no shrinking from the pointed finger of scorn, or the contemptuous vociferation of the enemy; no withholding your aid, or concealing your mighty influence behind the screen of timidity; no receding from the foothold you have already gained. To falter now, would be to surrender your pure and unsullied principles into the hands of a vicious and perverted portion of the community, who are anxiously waiting to see you grow weak and faint-hearted; you would be casting the whole spirit and genius of patriotism into that polluted current just described. To falter now would retard the glorious day of emancipation which is now dawning, for years, perhaps forever. But why should you pause? It is true that public opinion is bitter against you, and exercises a powerful influence over the minds of many; it is also true that you are frustrated in nearly every attempt to procure a place to hold your meetings, and the hue and cry is raised, "Down with the incendiaries—hang all who dare to open their mouths in vindication of equal rights;" still, this would be no excuse for a dereliction of duty; you are not bound to follow public opinion constantly and lose sight of the demands of justice; for it is plain to be seen that public opinion, in its present state, is greatly at fault; it affixes the seal of condemnation upon you without giving you an opportunity to be fairly heard; therefore I think the obligation ought to cease, and you pursue a more natural course by looking to your own thoughts and feelings as a guide, and not to the words of others. Again—in order to promote your antislavery principles you should make it the topic of your conversation amidst your acquaintances, in every family circle, and in the shades of private life. Be assured that by acting thus, hundreds will rise up to your aid.

I will now claim your indulgence for a few moments while I make some remarks on the subject of natural rights. It certainly is one of great magnitude. I will not, however, enter into an extensive discussion of its various branches; but would earnestly suggest it for the future consideration of our friends. Of what incalculable value must these rights be to those who possess them unrestricted? And yet they were intended for all—high and low—rich and poor—of whatever clime or complexion. They were spoken into existence along with the world; and although the establishment of legal authority was unknown to us, and there "subsisted not a vestige of civil government anywhere, still they would belong to man." Or, if we who form this present assembly were, by some sudden and unknown cause, thrown upon a desolate spot in the remotest corner of the Globe, we would, from the very first moment, be entitled to these rights—the right to the produce of our own labour, to our limbs, life, liberty and property—perfect rights, not human institutions, but Divine ordinations. Now, with these facts before you, the question should arise, whether all your fellow creatures are in the full enjoyment of these rights. If you look to the South, you will see how they are violated—how outrage, oppression and wrong has blighted them—how man (corrupted worm of the earth), forgetting his accountability to God, suffering passion and avarice to dethrone reason, has torn them from his fellow man. Yes, the poor slave is deprived of these rights—these great essentials to man's happiness—these bountiful gifts of nature—he does not possess even as much freedom "as the beasts that perish."[3] My friends, reflect for a moment upon what constitutes natural rights; analyze them, search deep into their component parts, and then ask yourselves if slavery recognises any of them? Why, every rational being who has bestowed one thought upon the inhuman traffic must come to the conclusion that it does not. Again, look on the other side of the picture—turn your eyes to your own city, and behold the class of American citizens with whom I am identified; see them borne down by the weight of innumerable persecutions, their situation but little better than the millions of their brethren now suffering under the galling yoke of servitude; they are nearly stripped of their rights. The remorseless hand of prejudice—the despoiler of our rights—our inveterate foe, whose birth place is the nethermost pit—year after year wages an ignoble warfare against us. If we are arrested on suspicion of having stolen our own bodies, and run away with them, so few are the advocates we have at the Bar of Justice, that the pleadings of humanity are silenced, and we too frequently consigned to hopeless bondage. If our property be destroyed by a cowardly and ruffian mob, our persons maltreated and our limbs broken, the hand of charity is scarcely extended to the sufferer; seldom do we find that redress showed to us which would be fully bestowed upon any other class of people similarly situated. The omnipotent Being said, "Let there be light." Is it permitted to shine brightly around our path? No. Where is that all-powerful light of knowledge? Where are the academies thrown open for our reception, that we may come in and quench our parched lips at the fountain of Literature?[4] With but few exceptions there are none; even the doors of the sanctuary, devoted to all that is sacred, are closed against us. And is this fair—is it noble—is it generous—is it patriotic—is it consistent with the professions of our republican principles? Was it ever intended that man should lift his rebel hand against the natural rights of his brother, and try to uproot them from his breast? That he should thus tamper with the works of nature—should thus presumptuously exercise his own will in defiance of the benevolent and comprehensive wisdom of Providence? My friends, ought not the united efforts of every Christian be aimed at the destruction of this persecution, which, like a universal pall, overspreads our prospects? Is not the call imperative? What have we done to merit this abuse? Have we usurped the authorities of the land? No. Are we out-laws—cut-throats? No. Are we not men, in common with other men; fully capable of appreciating the inestimable worth of these rights, which are our own? True, we are told by our enemies that we are inferior to them in intellect—our mental faculties being of the lowest order—that we stand but one degree above the brute creation; these are assertions without a shadow of proof; they tie our feet and seal our mouths, and then exclaim, "see how superior we are to these people!" They have no authority for crushing us to the ground, therefore we will not cease to urge our case, calmly and dispassionately. We are stimulated to act thus by the instinct of our natures. There is nothing that our enemies can bring against us but the colour of our skin; and is this not a mean, pitiful objection to the elevation of anyone? Oh! what a shameful prejudice. If this is to be our judge, if the uncertain and wavering shades of colour are to decide whether we shall be entitled to rights in common with our fellow citizens (which is all we ask), if mercy and compassion is to be disregarded, and beneficence utterly annihilated, no longer to strengthen, guide and ennoble the hearts of men, then has our country's grandeur fallen—then has she sunk into a state which would have disgraced the dark ages, when civilization was unknown, and man had not yet begun to do homage to the potency of mind. We claim our rights, then, not as a mere boon, for that would be doing violence to that honest pride which is always found pervading the breast and flowing through every vein of conscious innocence, but we claim them as rights guaranteed by the living God—natural, indefeasible rights.

There is another point to which I would draw your notice. The recent scenes in Congress are a specimen of the evil times we live in, the corrupted atmosphere we breathe. There, behold the Constitution of the United States—our national compact, the great organ of national sentiment, perjured, immolated upon the alter of expediency there; the right to petition, the right of free discussion, the freedom of speech, the freedom of the press—rights which should be the pride and boast of a republic, are trampled under foot, scoffed at by statesmen and senators, and the gag and Lynch law[5] held up as a model of the glorious march of *Virtue, Liberty,* and *Independence*; as the dearest gift that a noble and dignified people could transfer to posterity; why posterity would spurn such a legacy as coming from heathens, and not from their Christian forefathers. The demands of the South are growing every day more extravagant, insolent and imperative. As an evidence of this, I have only to refer you to the report and resolutions adopted in the Legislature of South Carolina, published in the 9th number of the Liberator. I allude to the report of the Joint Committee of Federal Relations, on so much of Gov. M'Duffie's message as relates to the institution of domestic slavery, and the proceedings of the Abolitionists in the non-slaveholding states. It ought to be extensively read, for I think it would be the means of arousing many to a sense of the danger which threatens their own liberties. I will read a few of the resolutions offered by Mr. Hamilton, chairman of that most grave and reverend committee.

> *Resolved*, That the formation of Abolition Societies, and the acts and doings of certain fanatics calling themselves Abolitionists, in the non-slaveholding states of this confederacy, are in direct violation of the obligations of the compact of Union, dissocial and incendiary in the extreme.

> *Resolved*, That the Legislature of South Carolina, having every confidence in the justice and friendship of the non-slaveholding states, announces to her co-states her confident expectations, and she earnestly requests that the governments of these states will promptly and effectually suppress all those associations within their respective limits, purporting to be Abolition Societies: and that they will make it highly penal to print, publish and distribute newspapers, pamphlets, tracts, and pictorial representations, calculated and having an obvious tendency to excite the slaves of the southern states to insurrection and revolt.

> *Resolved*, In order that a salutary negative may be put on the mischievous and unfounded assumption of some of the Abolitionists—the non-slaveholding states are requested to disclaim, by legislative declaration, all rights, either on the part of themselves or the government of the United States, to interfere in any manner with domestic slavery, either in the states or in the territories where it exists.[6]

Was ever a request so modest? There never was a request more unreasonable, more abominable—evincing in its tone the greatest insult that could be offered to a free and independent people. But what do the majority of the citizens in the North [think] about the matter? Why, I regret to have it in my power to say, that, with few exceptions, they are yielding to this daring presumption of the South; tamely acquiescing without venturing even as much as a word in reply. They ask of them to relinquish the sacred and legitimate right to think and act as they please. Freemen are, in one sense, threatened with slavery; the chains are shaken in their faces, and yet they appear unwilling to resist them as becomes freemen. Such votaries are they at the shrine of mammon that they have not courage enough to join the standard of patriotism which their fathers reared, and with the dignity of a free and unshackled people, repel with scorn, this unheard of infringement upon their dearest rights—this death-blow to their own liberties. My friends, do you ask why I thus speak? It is because I love America; it is my native land; because I feel as one should feel who sees destruction, like a corroding cancer, eating into the very heart of his country, and would make one struggle to save her—because I love the stars and stripes, emblems of our National Flag—and long to see the day when not a slave shall be found resting under its shadow; when it shall play with the winds pure and unstained by the blood of "captive millions."

Again, the South most earnestly and respectfully solicits the North to let the question of slavery alone, and leave it to their bountiful honesty and humanity to settle. Why, honesty, I fear, has fled from the South, long ago; sincerity has fallen asleep there; pity has hidden herself; justice cannot find the way; helper is not at home; charity lies dangerously ill; benevolence is under arrest; faith is nearly extinguished; truth has long since been buried, and conscience is nailed on the wall. Now, do you think it would be better to leave it to the bountiful honesty and humanity of the South to settle? No, no. Only yield to them in this one particular and they will find you vulnerable in every other. I can tell you, my hearers, if the North once sinks into profound silence on this momentous subject, you may then bid farewell to peace, order and reform; then the condition of your fellow creatures in the southern section of our country will never be ameliorated; then may the poor slave look upon his weighty chains, and exclaim, in the agony of his heart,

> To these I am immutably doomed; the glimmering rays of hope are lost to me forever; robbed of all that is dear to man, I stand a monument of my country's ingratitude. A *husband*, yet separated from the dearest tie which binds me to this earth. A *father*, yet compelled to stifle the feelings of a father, and witness a helpless offspring torn by a savage hand from its mother's fond embrace, no longer to call her by that endearing title. A wretched slave, I look upon the departing brightness of the setting sun, and when her glorious light revisits the morn, these clanking irons tell me I am that slave still; still am I to linger out a life of ignominious servitude, till death shall unloose these heavy bars—unfetter my body and soul.

Will not the wrath of offended Heaven visit my guilty brethren? My friends, this is no chimera of the imagination, but it is the reality; and I beseech you to consider it as such. Cease not to do as you are now doing, notwithstanding the invidious frowns that may be cast upon your efforts; regard not these—for bear in mind that the future prosperity of the nation rests upon the successful labours of the Abolitionists; this is as certain as that there is a God above. Recollect you have this distinction—you have brought down upon your heads the anger of many foes for that good which you seek to do your country; you are insulted and sneered at because you feel for the prescribed, the defenceless, the down-trodden; you are despised because you would raise them in the scale of beings; you are charged as coming out to the world with the Bible in one hand and a firebrand in the other. May you never be ashamed of that firebrand. It is a holy fire, kindled from every page of that sacred chronicle.

You are called fanatics. Well, what if you are? Ought you to shrink from this name? God forbid. There is an eloquence in such fanaticism, for it whispers hope to the slave; there is sanctity in it, for it contains the consecrated spirit of religion; it is the fanaticism of a Benezet,[7] a Rush,[8] a Franklin,[9] a Jay;[10] the same that animated and inspired the heart of the writer of the Declaration of Independence.[11] Then flinch not from your high duty; continue to warn the South of the awful volcano they are recklessly sleeping over; and bid them remember, too, that the drops of blood which trickle down the lacerated back of the slave, will not sink into the barren soil. No, they will rise to the common God of nature and humanity, and cry aloud for vengeance on his destroyer's head. Bid them think of this, that they may see from what quarter the terrible tempest will come; not from the breakings out of insurrections, so much dreaded, but for which men are indebted to the imagery of their minds more than to fact; not from the fanatics, or the publication of their papers, calculated to spread desolation and blood, and sever the Union, as is now basely asserted, but it will come from HIM who has declared "Vengeance is mine, and I will repay."[12]

You are not aiming to injure your southern brethren, but to benefit them; to save them from the impending storm. You are not seeking the destruction of the Union; but to render it still stronger; to link it together in one universal chain of *Justice* and *Love*, and *Freedom*. The Faith you have embraced teaches you to live in the bonds of charity with all mankind. It is not by the force of arms that Abolitionists expect to remove one of the greatest curses that ever afflicted or disgraced humanity; but by the majesty of moral power. Oh! how callous, how completely destitute of feeling, must that person be, who can think of the wrongs done to the innocent and unoffending captive, and not drop one tear of pity—who can look upon slavery and not shudder at its inhuman barbarities? It is a withering blight to the country in which it exists—a deadly poison to the soil on which it is suffered to breathe—and to satiate the cravings of its appetite, it feeds, like a vulture, upon the vitals of its victims. But it is in vain that I attempt to draw a proper likeness of its horrors; it is far beyond the reach of my abilities to describe to you the endless atrocities which characterize the system. Well was it said by Thomas Jefferson, that "God has no attribute which can take sides with such oppression."[13] See what gigantic force is concentrated in these few words—God has no attribute which can take sides with such oppression.

Ladies—I feel that I should have confined my remarks more particularly to your society, and not have extended them to the whole field of Abolition. Pardon me for the digression.

I rejoice to see you engaged in this mighty cause; it befits you; it is your province; your aid and influence is greatly to be desired in this hour of peril; it never was, never can be insignificant. Examine the records of history, and you will find that woman has been called upon in the severest trials of public emergency. That your efforts will stimulate the men to renewed exertion I have not the slightest doubt; for, in general, the pride of man's heart is such, that while he is willing to grant unto woman exclusively, many conspicuous and dignified privileges, he at the same time feels an innate disposition to check the modest ardour of her zeal and ambition, and revolts at the idea of her managing the reigns of improvement. Therefore, you have only to be constantly exhibiting some new proof of your interest in the cause of the oppressed, and shame, if not duty, will urge our sex on the march. It has often been said by anti-abolitionists that the females have no right to interfere with the question of slavery, or petition for its overthrow; that they had better be at home attending to their domestic affairs, &c.[14] What a gross error—what an anti-christian spirit this bespeaks. Were not the holy commands, "Remember them that are in bonds, as bound with them,"[15] and "Do unto others as ye would they should do unto you,"[16] intended for women to obey as well as man? Most assuredly they were. But from whom does this attack upon your rights come? Not, I am confident, from the respectable portion of our citizens, but invariably from men alienated by avarice and self-importance from that courtesy and respect which is due to your sex on all occasions; such "men of property and standing" as mingled with the rank breath, and maniac spirit, of the mob at Boston;[17] men (I am sorry to say) like the Representative from Virginia, Mr. Wise,[18] who, lost to all shame, openly declared you to be devils incarnate. And for what? Why, because the ladies in the several states north of the Potomac, in the magnitude of their philanthropy, with hearts filled with mercy, choose to raise their voices in behalf of the suffering and the dumb—because they choose to exercise their legal privileges, and offer their time and talents as a sacrifice, in order that the District of Columbia may be freed, and washed clean from the stains of blood, cruelty and crime. It is for acting thus that you received so refined a compliment. Truly, some of our great men at the South are hand and hand in iniquity: they are men after the heart of the tyrant Nero, who wished that all the Romans had but one neck that he might destroy them all at a single blow. This is just the position in which these Neros of a modern mould would like to place all who dare to utter one syllable against the sin of slavery— that is if they had the power.

But, Ladies, I verily believe that the time is fast approaching when thought, feeling and action, the three principle elements of public opinion, will be so revolutionized as to turn the scale in your favour; when the prejudice and contumely of your foes will be held in the utmost contempt by an enlightened community. You have already been the means of awakening hundreds from the deep slumber into which they have fallen; they have arisen, and put on the armour of righteousness, and gone forth to battle. Yours is the cause of Truth, and must prevail over error; it is the cause of sympathy, and therefore it calls aloud for the aid of woman.

> Sympathy is woman's attribute,
> By that she has reign'd—by that she will reign.

Yours is the cause of Christianity; for it pleads that the mental and physical powers of millions may not be wasted—buried forever in ruins; that virtue may not be sacrificed at the altar of lasciviousness; making the South but one vast gulf of infamy; that the affections of a parent may not be sundered; that hearts may not be broken; that souls, bearing the impress of the Deity—the proof of their celestial origin and eternal duration—may not be lost. It is for all these you plead, and you must be victorious; never was there a contest commenced on more hallowed principles. Yes, my friends, from the height of your holy cause, as from a mountain, I see already rising the new glory and grandeur of regenerated—FREE—America! And on the corner stone of that mighty fabric, posterity shall read your names. But if there be the shadow of a doubt still remaining in the breasts of anyone present as to your success, I would beg them to cast their eyes across the broad bosom of the Atlantic, and call to mind the scenes which transpired a short time since. (There shone the influence of a woman!) Call to mind the 1st of August,[19] a day never to be forgotten by the real philanthropist; when *Justice*, mantled in renovated splendour, with an arm nerved to action—her brow lighted up by a ray from Heaven, mounted on the car of *Freedom*, betook her way to the spot where *Slavery* was stalking over the land, making fearful ravages among human beings. There the "lust of gain, had made the fiercest and fellest exhibition of its hardihood." There, Justice looked, on the one hand, to the "prosperity of the lordly oppressor, wrung from the sufferings of a captive and subjugated people;" and on the other, to the "tears and untold agony of the hundreds beneath him." There, was heard the sighs and stifled groans of the once happy and gay; hopes blighted in the bud. There, cruelty had wrought untimely furrows upon the cheek of youth. She saw all this; but the supplicating cry of mercy did not fall unheeded upon her ear. No. She smote the monster in the height of his power; link after link fell from the massive chain, and *eight hundred thousand human beings sprung into life again.*

It was WOMAN who guided that car! It was woman who prompted Justice to the work. Then commenced the glorious Jubilee; then the eye, once dim, was seen radiant with joy—

Caste and proscription cease,
The Bondsman wakes to Liberty; he sleeps in peace.
Read the great charter on his brow:
"I am a MAN, a BROTHER now."

Ladies, ought not this to be enough to induce you to persevere? I am sure you are just as capable as your sisters of England;[20] let me entreat you, then, to be forever on the watch; let your motto be—*onward*. Oh! forget not the thrilling appeals of that Christian missionary, GEORGE THOMPSON; he whose brilliant talents and matchless eloquence illumined all they touched; he who left his native land, and appeared among you like a guiding star, shedding rays of peace and good will to all mankind; his voice still may be heard, and bids you onward. A voice speaks from the sainted ashes of WILBERFORCE,[21] and bids you onward. A voice from our GARRISON of Liberty is wafted to your ears on every Eastern breeze; it speaks in tones of thunder, and bids you onward—onward. Then, pause not—tremble not—God is with you; you contend for the privilege of "breaking the bonds and letting the oppressed go free."[22] Obey the commands of the Bible—upon this rock hang all your hopes—and in the darkest and most perilous hour of your enterprise, your fortitude will not forsake you; and, remembering under what influences you have reared the Banner of Universal Freedom, will be constrained to admit that no power on earth can ever oppose the ARM OF OMNIPOTENCE.

James Forten, Jr., *An Address Delivered Before the Ladies' Anti-Slavery Society of Philadelphia, On the Evening of the 14th of April, 1836* (Philadelphia, Pa., 1836), 3–16.

1. James Forten, Jr. (1817–?), the eldest son of James and Charlotte Forten, received private tutoring and an antislavery education in the Forten household—a gathering place for abolitionists, African dignitaries, and reformers. Encouraged by his parents to become involved in black community affairs, he joined the Young Men's Library Association and the Young Men's Anti-Slavery Society of Philadelphia. Forten contributed to the *Liberator* under the pseudonym "F" and, during the late 1830s, he served as secretary of the American Moral Reform Society, his most prominent public role. He opposed colonization and supported the struggle for black voting rights in Pennsylvania. A talented musician, Forten belonged to the Philadelphia Union Musical Association and often performed at antislavery meetings. *NECAUL*, 24 August 1836 [1:0694]; *PF*, 22 March 1838 [2:0440]; Lewis, "The Fortens of Philadelphia," 38–39, 41–42, 49–50, 75–76, 92–93; Winch, *Philadelphia's Black Elite*, 85–86, 110, 139, 191–92n, 211n.
2. Forten refers to the American Anti-Slavery Society.
3. Forten borrows from Psalms 49:12, "Nevertheless man being in honour abideth not: he is like the beasts that perish."
4. Before the Civil War, most northern black children were excluded, either by

custom or law, from attending school with their white peers. In 1834 Pennsylvania legislated a general system of public education that technically allowed black children to attend the school of their choice, but segregation continued, particularly in the Philadelphia schools to which Forten refers. An 1881 Pennsylvania law desegregated the common school system, but even after an 1882 court case upheld the intent of the legislation, local school boards continued to evade integration. Leon F. Litwack, *North of Slavery: The Negro in the Free States, 1790–1860* (Chicago, Ill., 1961), 114–16; Harry C. Silcox, "Delay and Neglect: Negro Public Education in Antebellum Philadelphia, 1800–1860," *PMHB* 97:444–64 (October 1973); Edward J. Price, "School Segregation in Nineteenth-Century Pennsylvania," *PH* 43:121–37 (April 1976).

5. Forten refers to two means that southerners used to suppress discussion of slavery. Congress enacted the gag rule in 1836 to suppress abolitionist petitions seeking to prevent the annexation of Texas. In less than a year, 415,000 petitions had reached Congress. To satisfy southern legislators, Congress refused to consider any petitions regarding slavery. John Quincy Adams led the fight against the rule, which remained in force until 1844. The term "Lynch law" was used by antebellum southerners to refer to extralegal action, usually mob violence, that was perpetrated against an individual or individuals suspected of violating accepted community standards. The violence often took the form of whipping, flogging, or tarring and feathering; occasionally it included scourging or burning to death. After 1830, the "Lynch law" was a growing response to antislavery agitation. James Brewer Stewart, *Holy Warriors: The Abolitionists and American Slavery* (New York, N.Y., 1976), 83–85; James Elbert Cutler, *Lynch Law* (New York, N.Y., 1905), 113, 116, 120.

6. Hoping to convince southerners of the sinfulness of slavery, the American Anti-Slavery Society deluged the mails with antislavery literature during 1835–36. Southerners feared that this campaign would incite slave rebellion. On 29 July 1835, a mob broke into a Charleston post office and burned abolitionist papers and tracts. Governor George McDuffie of South Carolina responded by calling for the suppression of abolitionist activities. Answering the governor's call, the South Carolina legislature appointed a Joint Committee on Federal Relations, which recommended a program to defend slavery against this "incendiary" literature. James Hamilton, Jr., a popular politician, presented the committee's report—which was reprinted in the 27 February 1836 issue of the *Liberator*—and it was hastily adopted by the legislature. The report asked northern states to outlaw antislavery societies and to disclaim any intention of interfering with the institution of slavery. It also threatened censorship of the mails. Abolitionists claimed that such actions were violations of civil liberties. W. Sherman Savage, *The Controversy over the Distribution of Abolition Literature, 1830–1860* (Washington, D.C., 1938), 9–18, 44–45; *Lib*, 27 February 1836.

7. Anthony Benezet (1713–1784), a French born Huguenot-turned-Quaker, became one of the earliest American opponents of slavery. He immigrated to the colonies in 1731, settling in Philadelphia. After two decades in business and teaching, he wrote profusely on abolitionism, temperance, Indians, and Quaker history. He is best remembered for *A Caution and Warning to Great Britain and Her Colonies on the Calamitous State of the Enslaved Negroes* (1766). *DAB*, 2:177–78.

8. Benjamin Rush (1745–1813), a pioneer in American medicine, helped found the Pennsylvania Abolition Society and was an early advocate of temperance and penal reform. A signer of the Declaration of Independence, he served in the Continental Congress and was appointed surgeon-general of the army during the Revolution. *DAB*, 16:227–31.

9. Benjamin Franklin (1706–1790), a Philadelphia printer, Enlightenment philosopher, scientist, inventor, Revolutionary War diplomat, politician, and delegate to the 1787 Constitutional Convention, was also the first president of the Pennsylvania Abolition Society. *DAB*, 6:585–98.

10. William Jay (1789–1858) was a judge who wrote widely on reform issues. He favored immediate emancipation over colonization and gradual emancipation, worked for the abolition of the slave trade in the District of Columbia, contributed to the *Emancipator*, and helped organize the New York City Anti-Slavery Society. Jay was a president of the American Peace Society and a founding member of the American Bible Society. *DAB*, 5(2):11–12; *NYT*, 16 October 1858.

11. Forten refers to Thomas Jefferson (1743–1826), who penned the initial draft of the Declaration of Independence. *DAB*, 10:17–35.

12. Forten quotes from Romans 12:19.

13. Writing of American slavery in *Notes on the State of Virginia* (1785), Query 18, Thomas Jefferson states: "The Almighty has no attribute which can take sides with us in such a contest."

14. During the nineteenth century, most middle-class Americans believed in two divinely ordained, sexually segregated social spheres: a private domestic one for women and an aggressive public one for men. Only those activities perceived as extensions of feminine qualities of purity, piety, and submission—including missionary work, philanthropy, and teaching—were acceptable roles for women.

15. Forten quotes from Hebrews 13:3.

16. Forten paraphrases Matthew 7:12, which is frequently called the "Golden Rule": "Therefore all things whatsoever ye would that men should do to you, do ye even so to them: for this is the law and the prophets."

17. Forten refers to the mobbing of William Lloyd Garrison on 21 October 1835. Garrison's association with the English abolitionist, George Thompson, convinced many northern "men of property and standing" that Garrison was an English dupe bent on destroying the Union. Over one hundred rioters, urged on by members of the upper class, broke up a meeting of the Boston Female Anti-Slavery Society. Unable to find Thompson, they seized Garrison and threw a rope around his neck but were foiled in their attempt to lynch him. The incident became a cause célèbre among abolitionists who defended their right to free speech and assembly. Leonard L. Richards, *"Gentlemen of Property and Standing": Anti-Abolition Mobs in Jacksonian America* (New York, N.Y., 1970), 20–27, 63–71.

18. Henry A. Wise (1806–1876), a Virginia lawyer and politician, served in Congress (1833–44) and as minister to Brazil (1844–47). He first denounced antislavery petition campaigns in 1835 and vigorously defended the gag rule. As governor of Virginia (1856–60), Wise suppressed the Harpers Ferry insurrection and carried out John Brown's execution. He became a Confederate general

during the Civil War despite his initial hesitation to support secession. *DAB*, 20:423–25.

19. The first of August was celebrated by abolitionists to commemorate the ending of slavery in the British Empire on 1 August 1834.

20. Beginning in the early 1820s, British women organized separate antislavery societies, wrote and spoke out against slavery in the British Empire, established contacts with American abolitionists, petitioned Parliament to end slavery, and raised funds for antislavery lecturers. But none had greater impact than Elizabeth Heyrick; her pamphlet, *Immediate, Not Gradual Abolition* (1824), discredited gradualist theory and implicated everyone, not just slaveholders, in the sin of slavery. Clare Taylor, ed., *British and American Abolitionists: An Episode in Transatlantic Understanding* (Edinburgh, 1974), 54–56, 61–63; Betty Fladeland, *Men and Brothers: Anglo-American Antislavery Cooperation* (Urbana, Ill., 1972), 177–79, 220; *Lib*, 13 July 1833.

21. William Wilberforce (1759–1833) sat in the House of Commons (1780–1825), where he led the parliamentary campaign against the slave trade. Wilberforce introduced the first bill for the abolition of West Indian slavery and helped organize the Society for the Mitigation and Gradual Abolition of Slavery in 1823. *DNB*, 21:208–17.

22. Forten paraphrases Isaiah 58:6.

14.
Founding the New York Committee of Vigilance

David Ruggles to Editor, New York *Sun*
[July 1836]

Resolutions by Thomas Van Rensellaer,
Jacob Francis, and David Ruggles
Delivered at Phoenix Hall, New York, New York
27 September 1836

Proceedings of a Meeting of the New York
Committee of Vigilance
Convened at 165 Chapel Street, New York, New York
21 November 1836

Many northern black communities created vigilance committees during the late 1830s and early 1840s to protect the growing number of fugitive slaves and to prevent the systematic kidnapping of free blacks into slavery. According to one report, proportionally more blacks were seized in New York City than on the West African coast. Local black leaders founded the New York Committee of Vigilance in 1835 as an organized response to the crisis. Guided by David Ruggles, the committee provided food, shelter, clothing, and legal counsel to fugitive slaves; watched the waterfront for illegal slave ships; obstructed the work of slave catchers; exposed official connivance with kidnapping rings; and distributed information about slave catchers throughout the black community. In its first three years of operation, the Committee of Vigilance was involved with 522 fugitive slave cases. Ruggles and the committee enjoyed widespread community support; black churches and social institutions provided most of the committee's operating funds and its public meetings drew huge audiences. The following three documents reveal the efforts of Ruggles and the committee in 1836 to protect local blacks and to publicize the kidnapping threat through the reform and popular press. *FJ*, 14 November 1828 [17:058]; *PA*, 21 June 1862; *ML*, July 1838 [2:0510–12]; *E*, 15 December 1836; *CA*, 20 January 1838 [2:0354].

KIDNAPPING IN THE CITY OF NEW YORK
It is too bad to be told, much less to be endured! On Saturday, 23d inst., about 12 o'clock, Mr. George Jones, a respectable free colored man, was arrested at 21 Broadway by certain police officers, upon the

pretext of his having "committed assault and battery." Mr. Jones being conscious that no such charge could be sustained against him, refused to go with the officers; his employers, placing high confidence in his integrity, advised him to go and answer to the charge, promising that any assistance should be afforded to satisfy the end of justice. He proceeded with the officers, accompanied with a gentleman who would have stood his bail—he was locked up in Bridewell[1]—his friend was told that "when he was wanted he could be sent for." Between the hours of 1 and 2 o'clock, Mr. Jones was carried before the Hon. Richard Riker, Recorder of the city of New York.[2] In the absence of his friends, and in the presence of several notorious kidnappers, who preferred and by oath sustained that he was a runaway slave, Poor Jones (having no one to utter a word in his behalf, but a boy, in the absence of numerous friends who could have borne testimony to his freedom,) was by the Recorder pronounced to be a SLAVE!

In less than three hours after his arrest, he was bound in chains, dragged through the streets like a brute beast to the shambles! My depressed countrymen, we are all liable; your wives and children are at the mercy of merciless kidnappers. We have no protection in law—because the legislators withhold justice. We must no longer depend on the interposition of the Manumission or Anti-Slavery Societies, in the hope of peaceable and just protection;[3] where such outrages are committed, peace and justice cannot dwell. While we are subject to be thus inhumanly practiced upon, no man is safe; we must look to our own safety and protection from kidnappers! remembering that "self-defence is the first law of nature."[4]

Let a meeting be called—let every man who has sympathy in his heart to feel when bleeding humanity is thus stabbed afresh, attend the meeting; let a remedy be prescribed to protect us from slavery! Whenever necessity requires, let that remedy be applied. Come what will, anything is better than slavery! Yours, &c.

DAVID RUGGLES[5]

Liberator (Boston, Mass.), 6 August 1836.

Whereas, the barbarous practice of kidnapping continually menaces, endangers, and invades the peace, safety and *liberty* of every colored citizen in these United States. And, whereas, Captains of Merchant's vessels, Slaveholders, Slavetraders, and their kidnapping agents have sold into slavery, citizens of the State of New York. And, whereas, the alarming precedent, lately established in this city, has firmly convinced us in the belief, that the people of color can expect no protection from the laws, as at present administered, without the benefit of trial by jury.[6]

9. David Ruggles
Courtesy of Amistad Research Center, New Orleans, Louisiana

And whereas, we view with grief and indignation the conduct of the Hon. Richard Riker, Recorder of the city of New York, in the case of Abraham Goslee,[7] whom he refused the benefit of *three* important witnesses, and pronounced him a *slave*—then denied him the benefit of the writ of *Homino replegiando*,[8] and unjustly granted or issued a writ of *Habeas Corpus* to reduce him to slavery.

Be it therefore, Resolved, That while we the people of color, are deprived of that *bulwark of personal freedom*, a trial by jury, it is in vain to look for justice in the courts of law, especially where every advantage is given to slaveholders and kidnappers by the law and practice of those courts.

Resolved, That humanity and justice dictate, that every colored citizen unite his every effort to procure for every person who may be arrested as a fugitive slave a trial by jury; and the removal of such legal abuses as may at present exist, and continue those efforts in every proper and legal manner, until our rights be established.

> Thomas Van Rensellaer[9]
> Jacob Francis[10]   }Committee
> David Ruggles

Emancipator (New York, N.Y.), 6 October 1836.

At a meeting of the friends of human rights holden in the city of New York, Nov. 21, 1836, for the purpose of adopting measures to ascertain if possible, the extent to which the cruel practice of kidnapping men, women and children, is carried on in this city, and to aid such unfortunate persons as may be in danger of being *reduced* to *slavery*, in maintaining their rights—Robert Brown, Esq. was called to the chair, and David Ruggles appointed secretary.

The meeting being impressed with the alarming *fact* that any colored person within this state is liable to be arrested as a *fugitive from slavery* and put upon his defence to prove his freedom, and that any *such* person thus arrested is denied the *right of trial by jury*, and, therefore, subject to a hurried trial, often without the aid of a friend or a counsellor. We hold ourselves bound by the golden rule of our Saviour to aid them, *to do to others as we would have them do to us*. It is therefore

Resolved, That William Johnston,[11] David Ruggles, Robert Brown, George R. Barker,[12] J. W. Higgins,[13] be appointed a committee to aid the people of color, legally, to obtain their rights.[14]

Resolved, That this committee be authorized to add to their number, and to fill vacancies.

Resolved, That this meeting commend the committee to the confidence of the people of color and to the liberality and support of the friends of human rights.

Robert Brown, Chairman
David Ruggles, Secretary

This committee have since addressed a circular to the friends of human rights for funds to aid them in the accomplishment of the following objects:

1. To protect unoffending, defenseless, and endangered persons of color, by securing their rights as far as practicable.

2. By obtaining for them when arrested, under the pretext of being *fugitive slaves*, such protection as the law will afford.

The chairman next called on the members of the "effective committee," as it is termed, to come forward and pay in their monthly collections.

Mr. Ruggles explained—This committee consists of about 100 persons, male and female. Each member takes a small book, and enters in it the names of ten or twelve of his or her friends, and solicits from each a penny a week. Some pay more than a penny, and some who have no books, pay a given sum, 50 cents or more the month. And it is in this way that the operations of the committee have hitherto been mostly sustained.

After the collections were paid in, the chairman said, that in "securing their rights so far as practicable" to "unoffending, defenseless and endangered persons of color," this committee did not scruple to help *fugitive slaves* to places of safety. This business was almost wholly neglected previous to the organization of this committee. They had, however, an agent in their employ,[15] whose business it was to look up and look after such cases, and render the individuals such assistance as they needed. The operations of the committee had been somewhat limited it was true for want of funds, yet they had done something. They had saved about *THREE HUNDRED* persons, in one way and another, from being carried back into slavery, and the prospect now was that funds would be wanted no longer. The colored people of the city were awake, and he never saw them pay in their money so freely and promptly as to this committee. He supposed the reason was, that this was *practical* abolition. He found too that just in proportion as they felt the influence of this committee and contributed in aid of its objects, they became active and enterprising and virtuous, and ready to contribute to other benevolent objects.

Mr. Johnston said he would call the attention of the meeting first to some of the transactions of the committee within a month or two past.

The relief of fugitives was indeed one branch of their business but it was not the whole, nor indeed was it now even the major part of it. Before stating the facts to which he proposed to call attention, he would add his testimony to that of the worthy chairman, that in proportion as the colored people have enlisted in this enterprise and felt its influence, they have been ready to do other good works. He would also say, that previous to the operations of this committee, the half of the evils to which the people of color are subjected were not known. We knew much before it was true, but since the existence of this committee, we have discovered evils that we have never dreamed of before. We had supposed they labored under evils inflicted only by the baser sort of people, but we have now found that it is not so. Persons of all classes are concerned in the atrocities in question. The committee have acted on Job's principle, "the cause that I knew not I searched out,"[16] and they have found facts of the most astonishing character. They have, for example, found instances in which colored seamen, who have been there taken on shore and actually sold as slaves.[17] They recently had a case of that kind and had endeavoured, though as yet in vain, to bring the guilty wretch to justice. He would mention here the

CASE OF JAMES EMERSON

On the 24th of August, as he was on the East River side, near the water, the captain of a vessel enticed him on board. The vessel was bound to Petersburg, VA., and the captain told the boy he should be gone only nine days, and should then return. He took the boy to Baltimore. The white crew left the vessel there and the boy becoming uneasy, wished to leave also. The Captain said, "You are not in New York now, but in Baltimore—you must remember that you can't do here as you can there," at the same time threatening to sell him. This was overheard by a colored man of the name of Gideon Gross. This man spoke to the boy the first opportunity that occurred, and learning what the facts were, took the boy on shore, concealed him, or had him lodged in some place of safety and started for this city to procure the evidence of his freedom, with what success and by what means, the following certificate will show.

NEW YORK, [New York]
Nov 21, 1836

This is to certify, that from information given by the bearer, Gideon Gross, some weeks since, I went to Baltimore, in order to rescue a boy from slavery, named James Emerson, which I succeeded in doing, and brought the boy back with me to this city. It is my firm belief had it not been for the exertion and information given by the said Gideon, who accompanied me to Baltimore, that the boy would now have been in slavery. Gideon informed me that he was obliged to sell a part of his clothing to pay his passage from Baltimore.

JOHN D. WOODWARD[18]

(Intense interest was here awakened in the meeting, by the introduction of Gideon to the meeting.) Mr. Johnston then proceeded—

Another evil, to which colored people are subjected, is the kidnapping of colored children at the North. There were frequent notices in this city, of children lost. The Committee had learned how they were lost. It was only yesterday (Sabbath) morning, that he was accosted by a person in great distress who had missed a boy 11 years of age. He had been employed in a boarding house in Broadway (304), frequented by southerners, and on Saturday evening was sent with a note to 523 Broadway, which he delivered and has not been heard of since.

Mr. J. mentioned several other cases, commenting on them with great force and interest.

Mr. Ruggles next addressed the meeting. He would not undertake to deliver an address, but would simply state a few facts; and before doing so, as Mr. J. had introduced to the meeting the emancipat*or*, he would beg leave to introduce the emancipat*ed*. James Emerson then came forward, and was introduced by Mr. R. to the meeting, and the leading facts in the case recapitulated. And this, said Mr. R., is one case out of many. Not long ago, Capt. Whitby, of the brig *Enterprise*, N.C. shipped a colored man by the name of A. Freeman, and then, as two of the crew testified, actually sold him. I entered a complaint, and the captain was arrested, but finally acquitted on the mere negative testimony of some of the other hands who said they did not *see* him do it.[19]

Another fact. About four weeks since, a vessel arrived in this port, from Gambia Africa. The owner of the vessel was a black man and the son of a noted slave dealer on the coast of Gambia. The captain was white, but the crew, 12 in number, were black. About a week after their arrival here, three of them went to the South; whether sent or enticed, we do not know.[20]

Another case. It is also known that on Friday evening, November 18, a colored man was arrested as a fugitive by one Nash, under the direction of the notorious Boudinot. There is very little doubt that Boudinot knew the man was a free man and used Nash as a tool. Be this, as it may, the man was arrested, and on Saturday morning when the trial was to come on, Strang, the kidnapper's lawyer, said they would not prosecute the case farther. They had the best of reasons for it. They had found out, in some way, that the man was a freeman and had a British protection in his pocket. The kidnapper was subsequently arrested for a false imprisonment of the alleged fugitive and Nash, who assisted in the arrest of the alleged fugitive stood bail for him. This Nash is one of our city marshals.[21]

Mr. R. mentioned other facts showing that kidnapping—downright kidnapping is carried on upon a large scale in this city and with the connivance and assistance, too, of men in civil authority. Mr. Garrison,[22] at the call of the chairman, then addressed the meeting in a very interesting and impressive manner, and subsequently remarks of great interest were made by several other individuals, and the meeting was closed by an appropriate hymn.

Friend of Man (Utica, N.Y.), 22 December 1836.

1. Bridewell Jail, New York City's second prison, sat between Broadway and the northwest corner of City Hall Park. Construction of the jail began in 1775 and was completed during the Revolutionary War. Elizabeth Dike Lewis, "Old Prisons and Punishments," in *Historic New York*, 2 vols., ed. Maud Wilde Goodwin et al. (New York, N.Y., 1898), 2:83–118.

2. Richard Riker (1773–1842) was a prominent attorney and public official in antebellum New York City. As city recorder from 1815 to 1838, with brief interruptions he became an influential figure in the local Democratic party. Fitz-Greene Halleck memorialized Riker in the poem, "The Recorder." *NCAB*, 3:385.

3. Prior to the formation of the New York Committee of Vigilance in 1835, the New York Manumission Society was the primary local institution responsible for prosecuting kidnappers, disseminating information on the legal rights of blacks, and protecting the city's black children, who were a frequent target for kidnapping. From its founding in 1785 until 1849, the manumission society worked closely with the city's black community, but here Ruggles calls for more aggressive action than manumission and antislavery societies traditionally provided. Rhoda G. Freeman, "The Free Negro in New York City in the Era before the Civil War" (Ph.D. diss., Columbia University, 1966), 64–67, 319–26; Thomas R. Mosely, "A History of the New York Manumission Society, 1785–1849" (Ph.D. diss., New York University, 1963).

4. Ruggles paraphrases a line from part 1 of John Dryden's *Absalom and Achitophel* (1682): "Self-defence is nature's eldest law."

5. David Ruggles (1810–1849) was born to free black parents in Norwich, Connecticut. Settling in New York City, he gained widespread respect as the "uncompromising, and indefatigable friend of the slave and universal freedom." From 1829 to 1833, he operated a temperance grocery, a bookshop and reading room—where he distributed antislavery tracts—and a printing business in New York City. In 1833 he became a traveling agent for the *Emancipator* to raise funds for the American Anti-Slavery Society and to boost the newspaper's circulation. Ruggles, who considered a free press to be the primary bulwark against slavery, devoted his editorial career to promoting abolitionism, racial pride, and black uplift. After assisting Samuel Cornish at the *Colored American* in 1837, he edited and published the *Mirror of Liberty*, an organ for the New York Commit-

tee of Vigilance from 1838 to 1841. Ruggles later attempted to establish the *Genius of Freedom.*

As a leader of the New York Committee of Vigilance from 1835 to 1839, Ruggles discovered slaves illegally retained in the city by their southern masters, searched vessels engaged in the illegal slave trade, fought official connivance in the kidnapping of free blacks, and secured writs of habeas corpus from uncooperative white judges to win the release of fugitives. He personally assisted in the escape of over six hundred fugitives, directing them to the black underground. This success made him a target of the "New York Kidnapping Club." He was repeatedly jailed by justices and constables who wanted to destroy the vigilance committee. One confinement in 1839 endangered his health and his already failing eyesight.

Ruggles denounced slavery and advocated full civil rights and suffrage for all people, regardless of race or sex, by pursuing the "largest liberty," asserting that "women's rights are as sacred as men's rights." He acknowledged the debt blacks owed to white reformers but maintained that black freedom ultimately depended upon black effort. Ruggles's support for the National Reform Convention of Colored Citizens reflected his desire for greater militancy and an autonomous black reform movement. Still, he carried the deep ambivalence of many black leaders who simultaneously advocated black nationalism and integrationism.

Between 1837 and 1840, Ruggles, Samuel Cornish, and some other vigilance committee members became bitter enemies. The committee was eventually destroyed by lawsuits and financial mismanagement. Nearly blind, Ruggles resigned from his duties in 1839. With donations from black allies and Lydia Maria Child, Ruggles joined the Northampton Association of Education and Industry and founded the nation's first hydropathic treatment center. The success of his "water cure" facility and the "cutaneous electricity" treatments he offered brought him renown and financial stability. His untimely death at age thirty-nine silenced a powerful black voice. *Lib*, 5 October 1838, 19 June 1840 [2:0602, 3:0460]; David Ruggles, *An Antidote for a Poisonous Combination* (New York, N.Y., 1838) [2:0403–20]; David Ruggles, *A Plea for "A Man and a Brother"* (New York, N.Y., 1839), 6–15 [2:0702–6]; Samuel May, *Some Recollections of Our Antislavery Conflict* (Boston, Mass., 1869), 285–86; *ML*, July 1838 [2:0516]; *E*, 13 January 1835, 15 December 1836, 23 January 1840 [1:0555, 3:0323]; *CA*, 15 September 1838; *ZW*, 14 January 1837 [1:0905]; *NASS*, 20 August, 1 October 1840 [3:0567, 0640]; *HF*, 25 January 1840; George Walker, "Afro-American in New York City, 1827–1860" (Ph.D. diss., Columbia University, 1975), 121–22, 239; Dorothy Porter, "David Ruggles: An Apostle of Human Rights," *JNH* 28:23–50 (January 1943).

6. The Fugitive Slave Law of 1793 established procedures for the recovery of fugitive slaves but offered little legal protection to blacks. Claimants could recover a slave by presenting oral testimony before a federal judge or local magistrate, who alone decided the status of the accused. Ambiguities in the law allowed some slave catchers to seize blacks without even subjecting their cases to judicial review. Many northern free blacks were enslaved under this law. *DAAS*, 275–76.

7. Abraham Goslee (1810–?) was arrested in New York City on 29 August 1836 and charged with being a fugitive slave. During the court proceedings that

followed, evidence and testimony indicated that he was a free black from Somerset County, Maryland, who had settled in New York City in the early 1830s. John F. Collier, a Maryland slaveowner, claimed that Goslee was actually Jessie Collier, his slave, who had escaped from Somerset County in April 1835. City Recorder Richard Riker ruled in favor of the slaveowner. Despite last-minute legal maneuvers by the defense attorney and the sheriff, Goslee was remanded to Collier and returned to Maryland. *First Annual Report of the New York Committee of Vigilance* (New York, N.Y, 1837), 19–29 [1:0829–35].

8. A writ *de homine replegiando* freed individuals imprisoned or held by a private party by giving security that they would appear in court to answer charges. It has been superseded by the writ of *habeas corpus* in contemporary American law.

9. Thomas Van Rensellaer, a New York City restaurateur and newspaper editor, was born a slave in New York but escaped from his master in early 1819. He settled in New York City in the mid-1830s and opened a cellar restaurant. A literate, articulate businessman, Van Rensellaer was a prominent figure in black community affairs. He supervised a Sabbath school, served on the board of the Phoenix Society, and helped found New York's Society for the Promotion of Education among Colored Children. He spoke at anticolonization meetings, officiated at First of August celebrations, and attended the 1833 and 1847 black national conventions. His most notable roles in the 1830s were as a leader of the New York Committee of Vigilance and as an organizer of the petition campaign for black voting rights.

A Garrisonian, Van Rensellaer served as an agent for the *Liberator*, acted as vice-president of the United Anti-Slavery Society of New York, and sat on the American Anti-Slavery Society's executive committee. William Lloyd Garrison, Frederick Douglass, and other antislavery notables enjoyed his hospitality while in New York. The antislavery schism of 1840 placed Van Rensellaer in an awkward situation. He remained loyal to Garrison yet tried to maintain good relations with James G. Birney, Gerrit Smith, and other political abolitionists in New York. He believed that blacks had an important role as arbitrators in the antislavery split. In order to strengthen the Garrisonian contingent in New York, he founded the Manhattan Anti-Slavery Society in 1840. His ongoing polemic against political antislavery in the columns of the *Colored American* alienated many New York abolitionists. He sparked a debate in 1841 when he urged blacks not to take up arms against Britain in the event of an Anglo-American war. He became even more controversial by allegedly describing his own race as a "proslavery and priest-ridden people." His detractors resorted to a personal attack. Consequently he spent much of his time refuting allegations of racial discrimination at his restaurant, of backsliding on temperance, and of playing billiards on the Sabbath.

In 1847 Van Rensellaer joined Willis Hodges as coeditor of the short-lived *Ram's Horn*. After Hodges left the paper in 1848, Van Rensellaer continued the enterprise (employing Frederick Douglass as nominal coeditor), but with little success. At the same time, he apparently attempted to establish a land company in conjunction with black settlement on Gerrit Smith's property in upstate New York. He participated in the public protest against the Fugitive Slave Law in the 1850s and spoke against disunionism at the American Anti-Slavery Society's annual meetings. After 1855 he was no longer active in public life. *CA*, 15 July, 12 August 1837, 29 March 1838, 2, 30 May, 10, 24, 31 October 1840, 23 January, 13, 27 February, 29 May, 5, 26 June, 10 July 1841 [2:0114, 0295, 0452, 3:0406, 0443, 0651, 0668, 0680, 0859, 0883, 4:0038, 0045]; *Lib*, 5 June 1840, 5 July 1844, 6 September 1850 [4:0875, 6:0574]; *NSt*, 22 April 1849, 5 April 1850 [6:0438–39]; *NASS*, 24 September 1840 [3:0627]; *E*, 4 February 1834, 2 November, 29 December 1836, 25 June 1840 [1:0727, 0761, 3:0469]; *FM*, 22 December 1836 [1:0758]; *ASB*, 23 July 1853, 3 June 1854; *Minutes of the Third Annual Convention* (1833), 4 [1:0295]; *Proceedings of the National Convention of Colored People, and Their Friends, Held in Troy, N.Y., on the 6th, 7th, 8th, and 9th October 1847* (Troy, N.Y., 1847), 3 [5:0486]; Garrison and Garrison, *William Lloyd Garrison*, 2:355–56; Thomas Van Rensellaer to Gerrit Smith, 10 March 1841, 11 February 1847, Gerrit Smith Papers, NSyU [3:0936–37, 5:0370]; Thomas Van Rensellaer to William Lloyd Garrison, 24 March 1839, Anti-Slavery Collection, MB [3:0045]; *New York City Directory*, 1850–55.

10. Jacob Francis was born in England but moved to New York City and participated in local civil rights and temperance efforts during the 1830s and 1840s. He settled in California about 1849 and soon became prominent in the San Francisco black community. Francis served as president of the Young Men's Association—a local civil rights organization—and helped found and direct the San Francisco Athenaeum (1853), a black library company and debate society, which was the first black literary society formed in California. He represented local blacks at the 1855 and 1856 black state conventions and chaired the former session. Francis moved to Victoria in 1858 and opened a saloon. He became an outspoken opponent of local prejudice, battled to keep the city's schools and churches free of caste distinctions, and twice sued local bar owners who refused to serve him. Francis entered local politics and ran for the Victoria legislative assembly in 1861; he won, but was refused his seat on a technicality. He served as Victoria subscription agent for the *Pacific Appeal* in the early 1860s. Francis returned to New York City at the end of the Civil War. James W. Pilton, "Negro Settlement in British Columbia, 1858–1871" (M.A. thesis, University of British Columbia, 1951), 98–100, 185–86, 197, 199; *E*, 6 October 1836, 21 December 1837 [1:0706, 2:0308]; *NASS*, 16 July 1846 [5:0249]; *FDP*, 22 September 1854, 6 April 1855; *MT*, 12 December 1857; *WAA*, 19 November 1859; Foner and Walker, *Proceedings of the Black State Conventions*, 2:112, 132–33, 155; *San Francisco City Directory*, 1858; Crawford Kilian, *Go Do Some Great Thing: The Black Pioneers of British Columbia* (Vancouver, British Columbia, 1978), 66–67, 75–76, 136; *PA*, 19, 26 April 1862, 20 June 1863, 30 July 1864; *ESF*, 30 June 1865; *WAA*, 8 July 1865.

11. William Johnston, an English-born abolitionist, settled in New York City by the mid-1830s. He served as treasurer of the New York Committee of Vigilance from its inception through the early 1840s. When the New York State Vigilance Committee was organized in 1848, he became a member of its executive board. He also sat on the executive committee of the American and Foreign Anti-Slavery Society. He traveled to England in 1843 to address the annual convention of the British and Foreign Anti-Slavery Society. Johnston is sometimes confused with William P. Johnson, a New York City black, who was also involved in vigilance committee work. *First Annual Report of the New York Com-*

mittee of Vigilance, 6; *Lib*, 26 December 1835 [1:0636]; *E*, 16 November 1837, 9 May 1838, 4 December 1844 [2:0270, 0478]; *ML*, July 1838 [2:510–12]; *CA*, 20 February 1841 [3:0902]; *ASR*, 14 June 1843 [4:0587]; *NEW*, 1 July 1848 [5:0698]; *Remonstrance Against the Course Pursued by the Evangelical Alliance Against Slavery* (New York, N.Y., 1847) [5:0453–61]; "Circular of the New York State Vigilance Committee," August 1848, Drayton, Sayers, and English Papers, DLC.

12. George R. Barker, a New York City broker, served on the executive committee of the New York Committee of Vigilance in the late 1830s, participated in the New York Young Men's Anti-Slavery Society, and joined the American Anti-Slavery Society's anticolonization efforts. During the 1840s, he apparently became a political abolitionist. *Lib*, 13 July 1833; *CA*, 15 July 1837, 25 August 1838, 23 November 1839 [2:0113, 0561, 3:0277]; *IC*, 27 March 1850 [6:0426]; Thomas C. Brown, *Examination of Thomas C. Brown* (New York, N.Y., 1834), 18 [1:0442]; *New York City Directory*, 1833–39.

13. James W. Higgins, a New York City grocer, participated in state and local antislavery activities in the 1830s. He signed the 1835 call for the founding convention of the New York State Anti-Slavery Society, chaired the executive committee of the New York Committee of Vigilance, and supported David Ruggles's efforts to publish the *Mirror of Liberty*. Higgins moved to New Jersey in the 1840s but apparently continued to operate a business in New York City. *RDD*, 2 October 1835 [1:0632]; *Lib*, 16 November 1838 [2:0650]; *E*, 23 January 1840 [3:0323]; *New York City Directory*, 1820–45.

14. David Ruggles and other New York black leaders organized the New York Committee of Vigilance in 1835 to protect the burgeoning number of runaways and kidnapping victims. The committee cooperated with prominent white abolitionists like Lewis Tappan and Isaac T. Hopper and retained white lawyers to aid fugitive slaves, foil kidnappings, and bring suit against ship captains who trafficked in slaves. Ruggles battled judicial indifference and repeatedly risked his life for fugitives. The committee disseminated abolitionist ideas through its public meetings and in the *Mirror of Liberty*, its official organ. Ruggles also cooperated with the New York Manumission Society to bring suit in the Dixon case, winning the right to a jury trial for blacks accused of being fugitives. For Ruggles the Dixon case was "a question of liberty or slavery—law or anarchy." After several failed attempts, the state legislature adopted a modified jury trial law in 1840, only to have it weakened by the *Prigg* v. *Pennsylvania* (1842) decision. During its existence, the committee rescued about 1,373 people, earning the reputation as the black community's only effective guardian against kidnappers and slave catchers. Financial burdens, a lawsuit emanating from a letter Ruggles published in the *Colored American*, and ensuing internal dissension led to the committee's demise after 1842. *First Annual Report of the New York Committee of Vigilance*, 32–82 [1:0836–61]; *ML*, July 1838 [2:0511]; *E*, 19 January 1837, 24 May, 26 July 1838 [2:0478, 0539]; *ZW*, 18 November 1837 [2:0272]; *CA*, 20 January, 8 September 1838, 31 August 1839, 4 April 1840, 20 March 1841 [2:0354, 0579, 3:0380–81, 0954]; Thomas D. Morris, *Free Men All: The Personal Liberty Laws of the North, 1780–1861* (Baltimore, Md., 1974), 79–83; Walker, "Afro-American in New York City," 241–42, 276; *NASS*, 15 September 1842 [4:0469].

15. The agent referred to was David Ruggles who received a salary of $400 per year. Ruggles, *A Plea*, 5 [2:0702–3].

16. Johnston quotes from Job 29:16, "I was a father to the poor: and the cause which I knew not I searched out." He uses this verse in reference to the investigative work of the New York Committee of Vigilance.

17. Johnston refers to the black seamen's acts.

18. John D. Woodward was a merchant in New York City in the late 1830s. *New York City Directory*, 1836–39.

19. Anthony Freeman, a New York City free black on the schooner *Enterprise*, was taken to North Carolina and sold into slavery by a Captain Whitney. The committee's annual report apparently contradicts Johnston, stating that no charges were brought against Whitney because of insufficient evidence. *First Annual Report of the New York Committee of Vigilance*, 50 [1:0845].

20. On 4 January 1837, Joseph Gavino informed David Ruggles that John Russell, a black seamen's landlord, had illegally imported three Gambian slaves into New York City on the brig *Governor Temple* the previous August. The Gambians were then transferred to a New Orleans–bound vessel and sold. Ruggles verified Gavino's charges and published them in the *Colored American* without the permission of its editor, Samuel Cornish. Russell sued Ruggles and the *Colored American* for libel and won his suit in October 1838. Cornish denounced Ruggles and blamed him for the incident. The controversy eventually rent the local black community and prompted Ruggles's resignation as agent of the New York Committee of Vigilance. In July 1839, a public meeting was called to raise the funds to pay Russell and to save the *Colored American* from foreclosure. Joseph Gavino to David Ruggles, 4 January 1837, [William Jay] to Samuel Cornish, 5 November 1838, Jay Family Papers, NNC [2:0631–32, 0639]; *E*, 1 March 1838 [2:0393]; *ML*, July 1838 [2:0510]; *CA*, 7, 28 October 1837, 20 October, 3, 10, 17 November 1838, 26 January, 23 February, 11 May, 27 July, 31 August, 7, 14 September, 23 November 1839, 5 September 1840 [2:0214, 0251, 0621–23, 0648, 0657, 0985, 3:0009, 0190, 0196, 0203, 0277, 0610]; Ruggles, *A Plea*, 6–15 [2:0702–6].

21. Ruggles refers to Tobias Boudinot, a former butcher, who became constable of New York's third ward. He exploited his position to operate a kidnapping ring with Daniel D. Nash, John Lyon, and two Virginians—Edward R. Waddy of Northampton County and F. H. Pettis, an Orange County lawyer. Known informally as the "New York Kidnapping Club," they cooperated with city recorder Richard Riker to retrieve runaways and seize free blacks. Ruggles may refer to the seizure of a fugitive named Peter (or Peters) who was enticed to leave his Greenwich, Connecticut, home in December 1836 by a black man hired by Boudinot. *New York City Directory*, 1828–44; *FM*, 22 December 1836; *E*, 15 September 1836, 2 March 1837, 1 March 1838 [1:0702, 2:0392–93]; *CA*, 15 September 1836, 9, 16 May 1840 [1:0702, 3:0412–13, 0425–26]; Freeman, "Free Negro in New York City," 68, 75–76; *AASR*, June 1834; *ML*, January 1839.

22. William Lloyd Garrison.

15.
Theodore S. Wright and Racial Prejudice

Theodore S. Wright to Archibald Alexander
11 October 1836

Speech by Theodore S. Wright
Delivered at the Bleecker Street Church
Utica, New York
20 October 1836

Black abolitionists spoke and wrote about racial prejudice with an authority born of personal experience. Theodore S. Wright of New York City was verbally abused and physically assaulted by a southern student when he visited his alma mater, Princeton Seminary, on 20 September 1836. He described the attack and reflected on its meaning in an 11 October letter to Archibald Alexander, the seminary's chief administrator. Although Alexander sympathized with Wright's plight, he was unable to prevent a similar incident two years later when Princeton students attacked Edward A. Jones, another black seminary graduate. A month after Wright's assault at Princeton, he spoke in favor of a resolution condemning racial prejudice before the annual meeting of the New York State Anti-Slavery Society. Wright's recent encounter with racial violence made his words all the more poignant and persuasive for the nearly 450 delegates gathered at Utica's Bleecker Street Church. Peter M. Bergman, *Chronological History of the Negro in America* (New York, N.Y., 1969), 165; *FM*, 27 October 1836; Alice H. Henderson, "The History of the New York State Anti-Slavery Society" (Ph.D. diss., University of Michigan, 1963), 91–98.

> *New York*
> *October, 11th, 1836*

Rev. Archibald Alexander, D.D.[1]
Rev. and dear Friend:

In addressing you on this occasion, I do not detain you by the formality of an apology for the liberty I have taken, lest I should betray a want of those feelings of confidence and respect towards you, which my former relations to you as pupil, and our existing relation as brethren in the holy ministry ought to inspire.

If any apology were in place, I would advert to my anxiety that there may be before your mind, a detail of the circumstances of that wanton abuse, which I received on the day after the Seminary[2] closed, from a reckless young man, represented to me as belonging to the College, but who, I have just learned, was some time since dismissed from the Institution. A member of the Faculty of the College kindly intimated to me, that my assailant endeavored to find a palliation for his abuse in some alleged imprudence on my part, which in the sequel you will find to be a mere pretext.

In this matter I am blameless. I appeal to all who witnessed the occurrence. If I said or did aught indecorous, either as a man or as a Christian. You, no doubt, sir, recollect that on Tuesday the 20th of last month, the "Literary Society of the Alumni of Nassau Hall"[3] convened at the chapel of the Seminary for the purpose of hearing their annual address. Desirous of partaking of the intellectual repast which was very justly anticipated, I was induced to attend. Accordingly, when the time arrived for the exercises to commence, I repaired to the place of meeting. I found the chapel crowded to overflowing. I was favored to stand inside by the door. After occupying that position some time, benches were passed in and placed in one of the aisles. Like those near me I availed myself of a seat on one of those benches, perhaps ten feet from the door. There I sat until the close of the exercises. The band had played; the President[4] had announced the appointments for the evening, and the audience had arisen to withdraw; when I heard with suprise the ungentlemanly outcry, "Out with the nigger"—"Out with the nigger," but I had not the least idea that I was the victim until seized by the collar by a young man *who kicked me two or three times in the most ruthless manner*—at the same time saying, "What do you do here? What do you do here? Don't let me see you here again." Just at this instant an individual, who I am informed is a member of the Seminary, laid hold of the infatuated young man and prevented his farther abuse. With an air of conscious self-importance, he exclaimed, as if he had effected some noble exploit, "My name, sir, is Ancrum; my name is Ancrum."

Happy I am to say, that at that critical moment I was not left to become recreant to the comforting, but self-denying doctrine of non-resistance, so effective in curbing that vindictive spirit which naturally rises when suddenly assailed. Thankful am I that I was kept from lifting so much as a finger in self-defense, but continued my way out of the house.

I have felt very solicitous since this unhappy occurrence, not merely that I have apprehended evil resulting to myself, but lest the affair should be so construed as to attach blame to some individual connected with the Theological Seminary, which I should most deeply regret. Permit me, sir, in the fullness of my soul to say, that I cherish feelings of profound respect and affection for my "Alma Mater," for the worthy professors and students.[5] During the three years in which it was my privilege to sustain an immediate connection with the Seminary, and the eight subsequent years, throughout the whole of which I have enjoyed the immediate counsel and support of the beloved Professors, and a delightful intercourse with the students, I have been received and treated in accordance with the [fathers] and relations, which we sustained to each other, which we are devoted. Considerations like these induced me to visit the Seminary at the close of your last term, during which my soul was truly refreshed.

In reflecting upon this unfortunate occurrence, it is manifest, that in attempting to degrade me, the rash youth has degraded himself in the eyes of all, whose opinions are worth regarding. I covet not the heart or the head of him who in open day, in such a place, on such an occasion, in the presence of such an audience, and after such an address, could perpetrate an act so glaringly inconsistent, so degrading, so mean.

Dear sir, I am ever mindful of the fact, that with the lives of those who have been connected with our useful Institution, is identified its honor, and the glory of our Divine Master. Without apprehension as to the result, I am entirely willing to submit to the decision of the public, whether or not, throughout my "public life," I have maintained a deportment in consistency with my relation to the church and to society. Comparatively speaking, it is of small moment to me, what I am called to encounter. Let me be persecuted and frowned upon, because of my identity with a class despised and oppressed, or for my feeble efforts to roll away the mountain obstacles which retard their moral and intellectual elevation. Let every epithet which vile and unprincipled men can devise be heaped upon me, let me be assailed by the hand of ruthless and even beardless violence, and I will smile, and be happy, so long as I may stand forth to the view of Infinite Excellence, and of pure minded men, clad in the robes of moral worth; so long as I am enabled to "maintain a conscience void of offence toward God and toward man."[6]

May the Lord bless you and yours, and continue your health and strength and usefulness. Yours in the bonds of the Gospel,

Theodore S. Wright[7]
Pastor of the First Colored
Presbyterian Church, New York[8]

Emancipator (New York, N.Y.), 27 October 1836.

Rev. THEODORE S. WRIGHT of New York, spoke on the following resolution:

Resolved, That the prejudice peculiar to our country, which subjects our colored brethren to a degrading distinction in our worshipping assemblies, and schools, which withholds from them that kind and courteous treatment to which as well as other citizens, they have a right, at public houses, on board steamboats, in stages, and in places of public concourse, is the very spirit of slavery, is nefarious and wicked and should be practically reprobated and discountenanced.

Mr. President,[9] with much feeling do I rise to address the Society[10] on this resolution, and I should hardly have been induced to have done it, had I not been requested. I confess I am personally interested in this resolution. But, were it not for the fact that none can feel the lash but those who have it put upon them; that none know where the chain galls but those who wear it, I would not address you.

This is serious business, sir. The prejudice which exists against the colored man, the freeman, is like the atmosphere everywhere felt by him. It is true that in these United States, and in this state, there are men, like myself, colored with a skin like my own, who are not subjected to the lash; who are not liable to have their wives and infants torn from them; from whose hand the Bible is not taken. It is true that we may walk abroad; we may enjoy our domestic comforts, our families; retire to the closet; visit the sanctuary, and may be permitted to urge on our children and our neighbors in well doing. But, sir, still we are slaves—everywhere we feel the chain galling us. It is by that prejudice which the resolution condemns; the spirit of slavery; the law which has been enacted here, by a corrupt public sentiment, through the influence of slavery which treats moral agents, different from the rule of God, which treats them irrespective of their morals or intellectual cultivation. This spirit is withering all our hopes, and oft times causes the colored parent as he looks upon his child, to wish he had never been born. Often is the heart of the colored mother, as she presses her child to her bosom, filled with sorrow to think that, by reason of this prejudice, it is cut off from all hopes of usefulness in this land. Sir, this prejudice is wicked.

If the nation and church understood this matter, I would not say a word on this question; I would not speak a word about that killing influence that destroys the colored man's reputation. This influence cuts us off from every thing; it follows us up from childhood to manhood; it excludes us from all stations of profit, usefulness and honor; takes away from us all motive for pressing forward in enterprises, useful and important to the world and to ourselves.

In the first place, it cuts us off from the advantages of the mechanic arts, almost entirely. A colored man can hardly learn a trade, and if he does, it is difficult for him to find anyone who will employ him to work at that trade, in any part of the State. In most of our large cities, there are associations of mechanics, who legislate out of their society colored men. And in many cases, where our young men have learned trades, they have had to come down to low employments, for want of encouragement in these trades.

It must be a matter of rejoicing to know that in this place, many colored fathers and mothers have the privileges of education. It must be a matter of rejoicing, that in this vicinity colored parents can have their children trained up in schools. At present, we find the colleges barred against us.

I will say nothing about the inconvenience which I have experienced myself, and which every man of color experiences, though made in the image of God. I will say nothing about the inconvenience we find in traveling; how we are frowned upon and despised. No matter how we may demean ourselves, we find embarrassments everywhere.

But, sir, this prejudice goes farther. It debars men from heaven. While, sir, this slavery cuts off the colored portion of the community from religious privileges, men are made infidels. What, they demand, is your Christianity? How do you regard your brethren? How do you treat them at the Lord's table? Where is your consistency in talking about the heathen; traversing the ocean to circulate the Bible everywhere, while you frown upon them at your door? These things meet us, and weigh down our spirits.

And, sir, the constitution of society, moulded by this prejudice, destroys souls. I have known extensively, that in revivals which have been blest and enjoyed, in this part of the country, the colored population were overlooked. I recollect an instance. The Lord God was pouring out His Spirit. He was entering every house, and sinners were converted. I asked, Where is the colored man? where is my brother? where is my sister? who is feeling for him and her? who is weeping for them? who is endeavouring to pull them out of the fire? No reply was made. I was asked to go around with one of the elders, and visit them. We went, and they humbled themselves. The church commenced efficient efforts, and God blessed them as soon as they began to act for these people, as though they had souls.

And, sir, the manner in which our churches are regulated destroys souls. Whilst the church is thrown open to everybody, and one says, come, come in and share the blessings of the sanctuary, this is the gate to heaven—he says to the colored man, *be careful where you take your stand*. I know an efficient church in this State, where a respectable colored man went to the house of God, and was going to take a seat in the gallery, and one of the officers contended with him, and says—"you can not go there, sir."

In one place the people had come together to the house of the Lord. The Sermon was about to be preached—the emblems were about to be administered—and all at once the persons who managed the church, thought the value of their pews would be diminished, if the colored people sat in them. They objected to their sitting there, and the colored people left and went into the gallery, and that too when they were thinking of soon handling the memorials of the broken body and shed blood of the Savior! And, sir, this prejudice follows the colored man everywhere, and depresses his spirits.

Thanks be to God, there is a buoyant principle that elevates the poor down-trodden colored man above all this: It is that there is society which regards man according to his worth; it is the fact, that when he looks up to Heaven, he knows that God treats him like a man. He knows that there Jesus looks upon him in love, if he only loves him; that God treats him as a moral agent, irrespective of caste, or the circumstances in which he may be placed. Amid the embarrassments which he has to meet, and the scorn and contempt that is heaped upon him, he is cheered by the hope that he will soon be disenthralled, and soon, like a bird let forth from its cage, wing his flight to Jesus, where he can be happy, and may look down with pity upon the man who despises the poor slave for being what God made him, and the man who despises him, because he is identified with the poor slave. Blessed be God for the principles of the Gospel. Were it not for these, and for the fact that a better day is dawning, I would not wish to live. Blessed be God for the anti-slavery movement. Blessed be God that there is a war waging with slavery, that the granite rock is about to be rolled from its base. But as long as the colored man is looked upon as an inferior caste, so long will they disregard his cries, his groans, his shrieks.

I rejoice, sir, in this Society; and I deem the day when I joined this Society, as one of the proudest days of my life. And I know I can die better, in more peace, today, to know that there are men who will plead the cause of my children.

Let me, through you, sir, request this delegation, to take hold of this subject. This will silence the slaveholder, when he says, where is your love for the slave? Where is your love for the colored man who is crushed at your feet? Talking to us about emancipating our slaves when you are enslaving them by your feelings, and doing more violence to them by your prejudice, than we are to the slaves by our treatment! They call on us to evince our love for the slave, by treating man as man, the colored man as a man, according to his worth.

Friend of Man (Utica, N.Y.), 27 October 1836.

1. Archibald Alexander (1772–1851), a prominent Presbyterian divine, led the movement to found Princeton Seminary in 1812, then served as its chief administrator and first professor of theology. Although an avid colonizationist, he sympathized with free black concerns and promoted missionary work among Philadelphia blacks. Alexander wrote *A History of Colonization on the West Coast of Africa* (1846), an authoritative chronicle of the movement. *DAB*, 1:162–63; John F. Hageman, *History of Princeton and Its Institutions*, 2 vols. (Philadelphia, Pa., 1879), 2:341–46, 365–71; Andrew E. Murray, *Presbyterians and the Negro: A History* (Philadelphia, Pa., 1966), 32, 77.

2. Princeton Seminary was founded in 1812 on the campus of Princeton College in New Jersey. By the mid-1830s, it had become the most popular and influential Presbyterian seminary in the United States, graduating sixty to seventy ministerial candidates each year. Hageman, *History of Princeton*, 2:324–74.

3. The Literary Society of the Alumni of Nassau Hall, an auxiliary of the Alumni Association of Nassau Hall, was organized in 1832 and was composed of Princeton College graduates and honorary members. Each year the society selected a distinguished speaker to address the association's annual meeting, which convened the day prior to commencement exercises in September. Hageman, *History of Princeton*, 2:302, 321.

4. James Carnahan (1775–1859), a Presbyterian clergyman and educator, served as the president of Princeton College from 1823 to 1854. *DAB*, 3:498.

5. Wright studied at Princeton Seminary from 1825 through 1828, graduating in the latter year. Edward Howell Roberts, comp., *Biographical Catalogue of the Princeton Theological Seminary* (Princeton, N.J., 1933), 40.

6. Wright quotes from Acts 24:16.

7. Theodore S. Wright (1797–1847) was born in New Jersey, the son of Richard P. G. Wright, an early black abolitionist and opponent of colonization. The younger Wright attended New York City's African Free School, where he was taught by Samuel E. Cornish, who became his lifelong friend and mentor. He continued his studies at Princeton Seminary, earning the enmity of fellow students, faculty, and administrators by serving as an agent for Cornish's fledgling newspaper, *Freedom's Journal*. Wright and Cornish, both staunch anticolonizationists, later collaborated on a well-known tract, *The Colonization Scheme Considered* (1840). In 1828 Wright replaced Cornish as pastor of the First Colored Presbyterian Church in New York City. The congregation prospered under Wright's tutelage, becoming the second largest black congregation in the city. Wright also led local moral reform efforts. He organized the Phoenix Society to encourage black progress in "morals, literature and the mechanical arts" and established a church-affiliated temperance society. During the mid-1830s, he enrolled black youths from the city in Gerrit Smith's manual labor school at Peterboro, New York, and helped establish and guide the Phoenix High School for Colored Youth.

Few blacks could rival Wright's involvement in major antislavery organizations. He was a founding member of the American Anti-Slavery Society, served on its executive committee during the 1830s, and helped organize the New York State Anti-Slavery Society. Wright became the first black to address an integrated antislavery gathering when he spoke at the 1835 New England Anti-Slavery Convention. When the antislavery movement divided in 1840, Wright's objections to Garrisonian radicalism and personal ties to the Tappans drew him into the new American and Foreign Anti-Slavery Society. He later served on the society's executive committee. Wright became a committed political abolitionist and worked for the Liberty party during the 1840s.

Wright's abolitionism encompassed a wide range of black concerns, particularly racial prejudice. He cautioned white abolitionists about their inability to "annihilate in their own bosom the cord of caste." Wright was instrumental in forming the New York Committee of Vigilance in the mid-1830s. He helped lead the struggle for black suffrage in New York state as a founder of the New York

Association for the Political Elevation and Improvement of the People of Color (1838) and as a delegate of the black state convention at Albany in 1840. He was active in other black conventions. At the 1843 national gathering in Buffalo, he supported Henry Highland Garnet's call for slave violence. During his last years, Wright turned his attention to African missions. He helped found the Union Missionary Society in 1841, served as the society's treasurer, and later was a vice-president of the American Missionary Association. By 1845 ill health forced him to curtail his reform activities. *DANB*, 675–76, Swift, "Black Presbyterian Attacks on Racism," 433–70; Foner and Walker, *Proceedings of the Black State Conventions*, 1:5–15, 32; Theodore S. Wright to Gerrit Smith, 4 September 1834, Gerrit Smith Papers, NSyU [1:0524]; *Lib*, 3 October 1835, 2 April 1847; *NYE*, 24 September 1836 [1:0704]; *HF*, 4 November 1837 [2:0255]; *CA*, 5 August 1837, 6 October 1838, 11 May 1839, 18 January 1841 [2:0134, 0607, 3:0056, 0808]; *E*, 27 September 1838, 17 January 1839 [3:0904]; *NASS*, 3 June 1847; *LS*, 5 November 1846 [5:0279]; *LP*, 19 November 1846 [5:0282].

8. The First Colored Presbyterian Church of New York City, commonly known as the Shiloh Church, was founded in 1822 by Samuel E. Cornish. Between 1822 and 1866, it was situated at various locations. Cornish ministered to the congregation until 1828 and was succeeded by noted black abolitionists Theodore S. Wright (1828–47), J. W. C. Pennington (1848–55), and Henry Highland Garnet (1855–64). Arguably the city's most important black church, it was a gathering place for black activists and regularly hosted antislavery meetings. Murray, *Presbyterians and the Negro*, 37, 137; Walker, "Afro-American in New York City," 134–35; *E*, 21 December 1837 [2:0308]; *CA*, 17 August 1839 [3:0175].

9. Wright refers to Gerrit Smith, who had been elected president of the New York State Anti-Slavery Society earlier in the meeting. *FM*, 27 October 1836.

10. The New York State Anti-Slavery Society was founded in dramatic fashion on 21 October 1835 when delegates met in Utica to forge forty-two local groups into a state society. An antiabolitionist mob attacked the convention and delegates were forced to complete their business the following day at Gerrit Smith's Peterboro home. Vigorous and well-financed in its early years, the NYSASS contributed heavily to the American Anti-Slavery Society, supported lecturing agents, and sponsored its own newspaper, the *Friend of Man*, which was edited by William Goodell. During the late 1830s, the society embraced political abolition. When the AASS divided over the issue in 1840, the NYSASS remained independent of both the Garrisonians and the Tappanites, instead organizing the Liberty party. Although the NYSASS soon became indistinguishable from the Liberty party, it maintained some vestiges of independent existence until 1848. Henderson, "New York State Anti-Slavery Society."

16.
Address by William Watkins,
Jacob M. Moore, and Jacob C. White, Sr.
[November 1836]

Although many black congregations were centers of antislavery activity and regular stops on the underground railroad, they were under considerable pressure to avoid the struggle. White denominations warned their black congregations against preaching an antislavery message from the pulpit, causing many to temper their public actions and statements. Black denominations hesitated to speak against slavery for fear of reprisals against sister churches in the South. Yet the American Moral Reform Society regarded black churches as natural allies in the campaign against slavery. The AMRS considered the problem at its August 1836 convention. At the request of the board, William Watkins and Jacob M. Moore of Baltimore and Jacob C. White, Sr., of Philadelphia authored an "Address to the Colored Churches in the Free States," which was published and distributed by the board later that year. The circular asserted that slavery was a sin and that Christian duty required unceasing moral opposition to such an injustice. It called upon black churches and denominations to stop equivocating, to state boldly their opposition to slavery, and to encourage their members to boycott cotton, tobacco, sugar, rice, and other products of slave labor. Milton C. Sernett, *Black Religion and American Evangelicalism: White Protestants, Plantation Missions, and the Flowering of Negro Christianity, 1787–1865* (Metuchen, N.J., 1975), 155–59; *Lib*, 2 July 1836; *NECAUL*, 24 August 1836.

To the Colored Churches In The Free States
FATHERS, BRETHREN AND FRIENDS:

In pursuance of the duty imposed on us by the following resolution, adopted at a special meeting of the American Moral Reform Society, held in the city of Philadelphia, in June last, we proceed to address you.

> *Resolved*, That there be a committee of three appointed, to draft an Address to the Colored Churches, requesting them to take measures to admonish their members against aiding the system of American Slavery, by using the products of slave labor.[1]

The substance on which said resolution is based, may be found in the pledge we have already given, in our address to the American people, "that we shall persuade our brethen against using the products of slave labor, both as a moral and Christian duty and as a means by which the slave system may be successfully abrogated; and that we will appeal to the colored churches, to take decisive measures to rid themselves of the sin of slavery and immorality."[2] The predication on which this duty is founded is, that domestic slavery, as it exists in our country, is opposed to both moral and Christian duty—the well being of man—the moral attributes of Jehovah, and consequently obstructs the progress of the Redeemer's kingdom throughout the universe. And we do aver, that the criminality attendant on the existence of American slavery is national— and that all who aid or abet this "accursed traffic" in the *bodies* and *souls* of men, by purchase, sale or barter, in either their persons, or the products thereof—are guilty of producing all the rapine, blood, murder and cruelties, in which the system itself so much abounds. Therefore, it is both a moral and Christian duty to aid in its overthrow.

We are certainly not indifferent to the fact, that in the present organization of society, the colored people in the free states, are deeply engaged in supporting the unrighteous commerce against the rights and liberties of their brethren at the south—a commerce that shuts out the light of the Gospel and brutalizes their fellow beings—a commerce freighted with such inhumanity, *ought not* to receive the patronage of the *Christian world.*

We are also well aware, that the colored churches are common participants in the crime, and that their ministers', deacons', and elders' voices are bound in deathly silence on a subject, that aims not only at the subjugation of millions of "immortal souls," but at the overthrow of the Christian Church.

How long! we ask you as Christians, will you remain silent and inactive, when the voice of Europe, and thousands of Christians in America, are crying onward! Is it a matter of no serious consideration to you, as individuals, and as members of the Christian Church, that you are supporting, day by day, in your daily repast, a system of piracy and soul-murder, which Jehovah abhors, and over which "humanity weeps?" Can you lay your hands on your hearts, and appeal to the Father of Mercies to bless your basket and your store, while you are rewarding the oppressor for robbing "God's poor?"

Will ye longer continue to ask God, who looks upon sin without the least allowance, to bless such portions of your table necessaries as may have been derived from the production of iniquity? We hope not. Is the giant sin of slavery to be winked at in the face of the command, "be ye not partakers of other man's sins?"[3]

In making this appeal to you, we are not indifferent to the fact, that there are many difficulties to be met with, in attempting the overthrow of a system that had well nigh paralyzed the *virtue of the world*—spread its hideous mantle around the whole organization of society—and consequently become interwoven in all the customs, habits, systems, veins and arteries of the body politic.

But, let not these difficulties, nor the magnitude of the monster Slavery intimidate us. Though he spread himself like a "green bay tree"[4] over the whole forest of nature, and usher forth his effluvia to the clouds—while there is a God in heaven to rebuke, or zealous Christians on earth to confront him with the sword of the truth and justice, we have nothing to fear, for *he* must fall prostrate before the Omnipotence of "Divine Power."

To be successful, we must prosecute our labors with holiness of purpose, and with a willingness of sacrifice, commensurate with the undertaking. We only ask the sacrifice of evil practices. Slavery is chiefly upheld by "avarice and luxury." If these only be suffered to fall, they will carry the monster with them. But it is not our intention at this time to give you a dissertation on the subject of slavery; our duty is of less magnitude; and will be fulfilled, by simply submitting the doctrines contained in the resolution, for your prayerful consideration and strict examination.

We desire that the Christian Church shall take the cognizance of the resolution, and settle the question—not whether slavery is *sinful*, for that is already acknowledged—but whether a voluntary use of the products of slave labor is *sinful*, when tried by Gospel rules. If so, we hope ministers, elders, church and people, will recognize it as such, and exercise their noblest energies to impress its doctrines on their congregations, so that a practical abstinence may be effected. If not, let the resolution fall to the ground. Therefore we leave the resolution with the Christian and his conscience, with the hope that truth and righteousness will triumph.

It may not be inappropriate, before closing the address, to give you a few of the reasons which lead us to believe, that the doctrines contained in the resolution are founded in truth, and are consequently binding on every friend of religion, morality, and human rights.

1. We maintain that slavery is a sin; and that liberty is the inalienable birthright of every man, given him by his Creator, and that he who deprives a human being of this liberty, usurps the "prerogative of Jehovah."

2. Slavery is a transgression of the Divine law, "render unto Caesar the things that are Caesar's",[5] &c. &c.—and being of itself sinful, it is incapable of producing "any good thing." Hence, the labor of the slave having been wrested from him by injustice, we deny the right of the "MASTER," to *transfer the product of that labor*, or anyone to purchase it, except from the slave himself. "The system being wrong in the beginning, cannot of itself change its nature." Hence we maintain that every individual who purchases the products of such labor from the master, becomes accessory to the guilt of robbing the slave of his just right. And it does not alter the case—no matter how many transfers have been made of said products—no more than the right to enjoy liberty becomes alien-

ated by the frequent transfer of the slaves through many generations. Hence we assert, that both the planter and the consumer, are maintaining a piracy on the rights of their fellow men; and *each* are guilty of the sin consequent on his degradation. Awake! awake then to righteousness: pray let this sin no longer be laid to your charge. You have so long stood back in the cause of temperance,[6] that the voice of those that were once ready to perish by the intoxicating draught, are now found ushering forth their anathemas against you. And if you will longer, by your activity, silence, and guilty acquiescence in the sin of American slavery,[7] be found protracting the period of joyful deliverance to the slaves, the prayers of the oppressed will ascend up to Jehovah's throne, and then invoke upon you the wrath of an avenging God! If you would reclaim the abandoned—check the guilty—instruct the ignorant—warn the unwary—give light to the blind—stop the progress of iniquity in all its various channels—encourage the despondent—increase the faith of the doubting—enlarge the views of all who profess to know and love the Lord—and, finally, if you desire to see the people of this world become the people of our Lord and his Christ, you must not only keep pace with all the moral and Christian enterprises of this age—but you must raise your banner as high as God's truth, and as broad as his love.

We are aware that there may be many existing apologies, with regard to the action of colored churches on the subject of slavery; but we deny that they have any rightful being. It may be said that they are for the most part, but subordinate bodies, and should necessarily wait for the action of the great bodies, with whom they are connected, and then follow in the train. This we deny; because it is impossible to find scriptural authority for a moment's delay in "doing good." And besides, while they are guided by the truths of divine revelation, they have as good a right to *lead* as to be *led*. When the voice of God commands us to "remember those that are in bonds, as bound with them,"[8] we should do it *now*, without waiting the approval of Ecclesiastical Conventions, General Assemblies, Presbyteries, Synods, Conferences, or any body of men on earth, no matter how enlightened. Besides, the American Church is so polluted with the spirit of slavery,[9] that the colored churches are already enslaved; and are either denied the rights and privileges of church members, or the social privileges of Christian fellowship. And the sooner some exertions are made to extirpate this evil spirit from the Christian Churches, the sooner we may expect to see those that profess to be born of God, practising the command, "love one another." There may be those that desire to be excused, because they say that colored people can do nothing to bring about an emancipation of the slaves, as they have no voice in government. Well, but slavery is a spiritual, and moral, as well as a political evil. Cannot we pray and preach against oppression? Cannot we join the many thousands of our fellow citizens, who are sending up petitions to Heaven for their deliverance? Can we not aid in overthrowing the immoralities that uphold slavery, without which it would have long since fallen? Surely you have both a moral, and religious influence. Then why not exert it? The poor slave needs all our aid. These *moral* and Christian duties will be required from all; and it will be of little use, when we appear before Jehovah's throne, to plead in palliation of our negligence that we are *Colored*.

Though the church, the world, and the government under which you live, may excuse you, God (who makes no distinction in complexion), bids you "cry aloud and spare not."[10]

What! have the free colored people nothing to do with slavery, while 2,500,000 of their brethren are writhing under its galling chains? Nothing to do with slavery, when there are at this time about 400,000 free people of color in these United States, ninety-nine hundredths of whom are upholding the system every day, by purchasing the products thereof? Of these about 150,000 live in the free states; which, to use the lowest average term, spend ten dollars a year, in the purchase of slave cotton, tobacco, rice, sugar and molasses—which amounts to $1,500,000 annually—and at a rate of ten per cent, would place in the coffers of the slaveholders a net profit of $150,000 annually. And is this doing nothing for the support of slavery? Can the colored churches wink at this? Is it nothing to *us*, that the system of slavery has so corrupted the commerce of the country, that the whole free colored population are made by its operations to contribute near half a million annually to its support. Nothing to do with slavery while there are free colored men that are such "devils incarnate" as to betray and sell their brethren into slavery who have escaped from their cruel oppressors!

There have been many illustrious instances of sacrifices by the advocates of liberty, in past ages, that were altogether unconnected with religious principles, and that have been nobly sustained, although they require much greater deprivations of the comforts of life than any we are called upon to sustain. In support of this remark, we have only to look back to the memorable history of the *tea tax*,[11] that ended in establishing the independence of this country.

We might go on, and multiply facts upon facts, arguments upon arguments, and successfully prove that we all are verily guilty—"that our brother's blood is upon us"[12]—that it is our duty to hasten to a speedy repentance; "live unto righteousness; cease to do evil and learn to do well;" and take immediate measures to abstain, as far as possible, from the use of such products as are purchased with the tears, blood, and sweat of the unrewarded toil of the poor slave, lest the visitation of an Almighty hand bring down upon us the retribution of divine Justice.

Published by the Board of Managers of the American Moral Reform Society.

JOHN P. BURR, *Chairman*[13]
Rev. MORRIS BROWN[14]
JOHN B. ROBERTS[15]
THOMAS BUTLER[16]
F. A. HINTON[17]
JOSHUA BROWN[18]
S. H. GLOUCESTER,
Secretary[19]

N.B. Editors, friendly to the object of this Address, are requested to give it an insertion.

National Enquirer (Philadelphia, Pa.), 12 November 1836.

1. The authors mistakenly refer to a 16 June 1836 meeting of the American Moral Reform Society Board of Managers, which was called to prepare for the society's annual convention. On the second day of the convention (held 8–10 August in Philadelphia), William Whipper presented two resolutions, each calling for a "committee of three" to draft addresses to American churches. The first resolution requested an "Address to the Christian Churches" concerning the "unholy prejudice that exists against complexion." The drafting committee consisted of three Philadelphians—Whipper, Robert Purvis, and John P. Burr. The second resolution called for an "Address to the Colored Churches," urging them to boycott slave produce. This is the address that William Watkins and Jacob M. Moore of Baltimore and Jacob C. White of Philadelphia were asked to draft. The *National Enquirer* published both addresses. *Lib*, 2 July 1836; *NECAUL*, 24 August, 12 November, 3 December 1836.

2. The authors quote from a manifesto entitled "To the American People," drafted by William Whipper, Alfred Niger, and Augustus Price at the 1835 black national convention, at which the American Moral Reform Society was founded. *Minutes of the Fifth Annual Convention* (1835), 25–31 [1:0598–601].

3. The authors borrow from Ephesians 5:7, in which St. Paul, writing about "the children of disobedience," urges the Christian community at Ephesus to "be not ye therefore partakers with them."

4. Quoting Psalms 37:35, the authors compare slavery to the spread of wickedness in the world: "I have seen the wicked in great power, and spreading himself like a green bay tree."

5. The authors quote from Matthew 22:21.

6. The authors overstate the case. Blacks eagerly embraced temperance principles during the antebellum period. An organized black temperance movement began in 1829 with the establishment of temperance societies in New Haven and New York City. By the mid-1830s, national, regional, and local temperance societies had been formed in every northern black community. Hundreds of church-related and independent literary and benevolent societies espoused temperance principles. The black national convention movement advocated abstinence from distilled alcohol as a central element of its moral reform program. By the late

1830s, the message of total abstinence from all alcoholic beverages could be heard regularly from the black pulpit and press. Black abolitionists readily incorporated temperance principles into their antislavery thought. Total abstinence was also intended to prove the moral worth of the black community to whites. It would prevent blacks from wasting their limited financial resources and help direct funds into the construction of schools, churches, and other black institutions. Yacovone, "Transformation of the Black Temperance Movement."

7. Black denominations remained relatively silent on the subject of slavery until the 1850s. Although many northern black congregations were centers of antislavery activity and black clergymen were heavily involved in the movement, ties to southern black churches kept black denominations from assuming an aggressive antislavery role. The experience of the African Methodist Episcopal church illustrates the dilemma that slavery posed. The AME's General Conference dodged the issue until 1856 when revision of the denomination's *Discipline* forced it to the forefront. Despite denouncing slavery as the "sum of all villainies," delegates refused to expel slaveholding members. Purists demanded that the church dissociate itself completely from the institution of slavery. But border-state and southern delegates asserted that such a course would incite white hostility. Also, although black slaveholding was an embarrassing admission, the practice was often used to protect family members and emancipate slaves. Black denominations could not condemn slavery and slaveholders too forcefully without endangering their southern congregations and alienating faithful members. Sernett, *Black Religion and American Evangelicalism*, 149–59; Payne, *African Methodist Episcopal Church*, 307–8, 335–45.

8. The authors quote from Hebrews 13:3.

9. No major denomination denounced slavery during the antebellum period. The reasons for this silence varied by denomination but included the fear of offending slaveholding members, fiercely independent local churches, and proslavery theologians. Powerful denominational hierarchies easily suppressed antislavery debate in general councils and purged the antislavery message from religious publications. Yet the relationship between northern churches and the antislavery movement defies comfortable generalization. Many of the movement's most prominent leaders were clerics, and concerted efforts by abolitionists heightened the sensitivity of northern churches to the issue of slavery by the 1850s. Certain evangelical sects, particularly the Society of Friends and the American Baptist Free Mission Society, were active in the movement. John R. McKivigan, *The War against Proslavery Religion: Abolitionism and the Northern Churches, 1830–1865* (Ithaca, N.Y., 1984).

10. The authors borrow from Isaiah 58:1, "Cry aloud, spare not, lift up thy voice like a trumpet, and shew my people their transgression, and the house of Jacob their sins."

11. The British government granted a monopoly to the East India Company under the Tea Act of 1773, provided they collect a three pence duty in the colonies. American colonists believed that the act violated the constitutional limits of Parliamentary authority. Colonial opposition culminated in the famous Boston Tea Party of 16 December 1773.

12. The authors quote from the story of Cane and Abel in Genesis 4:10–11.

13. John P. Burr (1792–?), a black Philadelphia barber, was a New Jersey

native. Family records and oral testimony suggest that he was the son of Aaron Burr and Burr's Haitian-born governess. Burr ran a barbershop and hairdressing salon at his home, which also served the black community as a gathering place for literary societies and other organizations. He founded the Demosthenian Institute (a literary society), belonged to the Banneker Institute, and attended St. Thomas's African Episcopal Church. His wife, Hetty Burr, was a member of the Philadelphia Female Anti-Slavery Society. Burr flirted briefly with Haitian emigration proposals in the 1820s, but he publicly opposed African colonization and worked closely with William Lloyd Garrison in the early 1830s, serving as an agent for the *Liberator*. He participated in the black national convention movement, first as president of the permanent convention board, and then as chairman of the board of managers of the American Moral Reform Society. When the Pennsylvania Reform Convention threatened black voting rights, he coauthored the *Appeal of Forty Thousand* (1838) in protest. Burr worked diligently with the underground railroad; he sheltered fugitive slaves in hidden rooms at his home and escorted fugitives into the state (posing as a slaveholder in one instance). After passage of the Fugitive Slave Law of 1850, he helped organize the Special Vigilance Committee and the General Vigilance Committee of Philadelphia. During the Civil War, he joined local efforts to promote black enlistment in the Union army. Winch, "Leaders of Philadelphia's Black Community," 34, 252, 279, 485; Allen B. Ballard, *One More Day's Journey: The Story of a Family and a People* (New York, N.Y., 1984), 55–56, 68–69; *Minutes of the Third Annual Convention* (1833), 24 [1:0305]; *Minutes of the Fourth Annual Convention* (1834), 35 [1:0480]; *Minutes of the Fifth Annual Convention* (1835), 3, 14, 32 [1:0587, 0592, 0601]; *PF*, 22 March, 6 September 1838, 24 January 1839 [2:0440, 0575, 0983]; *Lib*, 2 May 1835 [1:0580]; *CA*, 15 September 1838, 24 April 1841 [2:0588, 3:1001]; *NSt*, 10 November 1848, 7 September 1849 [5:0825–26, 6:0134]; *FDP*, 13 November 1851 [7:0177]; *WAA*, 7 July 1860 [12:0856]; *VF*, 15 January 1852 [7:0350]; *PA*, 15 August 1863; Still, *Underground Railroad*, 611–12 [7:0853].

14. Morris Brown (1770–1849), the second bishop of the African Methodist Episcopal church, was born free in Charleston, South Carolina. After receiving a license to preach from the Methodist Episcopal denomination, he ministered to free blacks and slaves alike. Brown spent a year in prison for using income from his bootmaking trade to help slaves purchase their freedom. In 1818 he organized an AME congregation in Charleston. By 1822 his congregation had nearly two thousand members, making it the second largest AME church. In the wake of the Denmark Vesey insurrection, Charleston whites regarded Brown's church as a source of black conspiracy and sedition; state law eventually forced the church to close. Threatened with legal prosecution, Brown left South Carolina for Philadelphia, where he worked as a bootmaker and an itinerant AME minister. In 1828 he was ordained bishop and, three years later, succeeded Richard Allen as superintendent of the AME church. Brown presided over the AME church during a period of dramatic expansion in thirteen states and Canada West. He traveled extensively, often on horseback, to attend church conferences and special religious services. In addition to his church duties, he served on the board of managers of the American Moral Reform Society, helped found the Union Missionary Society, and joined the protest against black disfranchisement

in Pennsylvania. Paralyzed by a stroke, he spent his last five years in poor health, devoting his limited energies to church concerns. *DANB*, 69–70; Alexander W. Wayman, *Cyclopaedia of African Methodism* (Baltimore, Md., 1882), 2–3; Payne, *African Methodist Episcopal Church*, 22, 26, 58, 179, 236, 261–62; Winch, "Leaders of Philadelphia Black Community," 36–37; *CA*, 10 June 1837, 4 September 1841 [2:0069, 4:0184].

15. John B. Roberts, a former slave and Philadelphia merchant, was active in several antislavery and moral reform organizations. In the late 1820s, he chaired the Colored Reading Society and belonged to the Benjamin Lundy Philanthropic Society. At meetings of the Temperance Society of Bethel Church, he pledged to make his business a "temperance store." Roberts served on the board of managers of the American Moral Reform Society and later joined the Philadelphia Young Men's Anti-Slavery Society. Roberts apparently resettled in New York City in the 1850s. He participated in local efforts to promote the black press and joined the black voting rights campaign as general agent for the New York City and State League Association. Porter, *Early Negro Writing*, 105–6; Winch, "Leaders of Philadelphia's Black Community," 65, 67, 97, 339, 384; Walker, "Afro-American in New York City," 184n; *NECAUL*, 24 August 1836 [1:0695]; *FDP*, 19 January 1855 [9:0390]; *New York City Directory*, 1854–60.

16. Thomas Butler, a Philadelphia barber, was active in the black national convention movement of the early 1830s and later served on the board of managers of the American Moral Reform Society. In 1838 he joined the protest against black disfranchisement in Pennsylvania. A successful businessman, Butler accumulated $7,500 in personal wealth. His wife Elizabeth was a member of the Philadelphia Female Anti-Slavery Society. They both attended the First African Presbyterian Church. Winch, "Leaders of Philadelphia's Black Community," 80, 85, 339, 356, 485; *Minutes of the Second Annual Convention* (1832), 2, 21 [1:0171, 0180]; *Minutes of the Third Annual Convention* (1833), 3, 5–6, 23 [1:0294–96, 0304]; *Minutes of the Fourth Annual Convention* (1834), 9, 14, 16, 18 [1:0467, 0469–71].

17. Frederick A. Hinton (1804–1849), a free black from North Carolina, was a barber and the proprietor of a "gentlemen's dressing room" in Philadelphia. In 1828 he married Ada Howell Hinton, who later became a member of the Philadelphia Female Anti-Slavery Society. He attended early black national conventions and assumed a prominent role in several black organizations in the 1830s. Hinton served on the board of managers of the American Moral Reform Society until 1837 when he broke with the integrationist leadership of the AMRS and joined the rival Association for Mental and Moral Improvement. His published criticisms of the AMRS's integrated approach to reform sparked a debate among black leaders on the questions of black identity and the scope of moral reform societies. A committed abolitionist and civil rights advocate, Hinton was a member of the Philadelphia Young Men's Anti-Slavery Society and a delegate to the 1840 convention of the Pennsylvania Anti-Slavery Society. He belonged to a small circle of Philadelphia blacks who were personally acquainted with William Lloyd Garrison and who generated substantial support for the *Liberator*. He participated in local efforts to sustain the black press and to establish a black manual labor college in New Haven. In the late 1830s, Hinton joined the struggle to preserve black voting rights in Pennsylvania and coauthored (with Charles

Gardner) a memorial against black disfranchisement, which was presented to the state constitutional reform convention. About the same time, he turned his attention to Caribbean emigration. British colonial officials gave him a commission in 1840 to recruit black settlers for Trinidad, but he failed to arouse much enthusiasm in the black community.

Hinton was among those Philadelphia blacks who tempered their antislavery activity in the wake of local race riots. The burning of Pennsylvania Hall in 1838 particularly disheartened him because he had served on the business committee responsible for its construction. After the riots, he accused abolitionists of provoking racial violence and attacked Garrison personally for his radical views on women's rights and marriage. A pious member of St. Thomas's African Episcopal Church, Hinton suffered a tragic personal life. His first child, born in 1829, lived only three months. His wife and another daughter contracted scarlet fever and died in 1835. He remarried but lost a third daughter in 1841 and his son in 1847. Hinton himself succumbed to cholera during an 1849 epidemic in Philadelphia. *FJ*, 26 October 1827; *RA*, 7 August, 9 October 1829; *E*, 20 July 1833 [1:0326]; *NECAUL*, 24 August 1836, 2 November 1837, 1 March 1838 [1:0694, 2:0253, 0394–95]; *CA*, 10 June, 19 August, 2, 16 September, 9 December 1837, 1 September 1838 [2:0069, 0153, 0172, 0186, 0296, 0300, 0572]; *Lib*, 12 March, 24 September 1831, 18 April 1845 [1:0037, 0117, 5:0001]; *PF*, 22 March, 6 September 1838, 7 November 1839, 7 July 1840 [2:0440, 0575, 3:0258, 0514]; Frederick A. Hinton to Isaac Knapp, 12 July 1833, Frederick A. Hinton to William Lloyd Garrison and Isaac Knapp, 10 December 1833, Anti-Slavery Collection, MB [1:0319, 0384]; *Constitution of the American Society*, iv [1:0010]; *Minutes of the Second Annual Convention* (1832), 3 [1:0191]; *Minutes of the Third Annual Convention* (1833), 3 [1:0294]; *Minutes of the Fourth Annual Convention* (1834), 9 [1:0867]; *Minutes of the Fifth Annual Convention* (1835), 4 [1:0587]; Winch, "Leaders of Philadelphia's Black Community," 39, 57–59, 77, 216, 262–64, 272, 308, 339n, 387, 489, 506, 555.

18. Joshua Brown (1801–?) settled in Philadelphia in the 1820s. Although originally a slave in Delaware, he was readily accepted as a leader by the city's free black community. He served as treasurer of St. Thomas's African Episcopal Church, established a thriving clothing business, and by 1850 had acquired $4,000 in real estate. Through his participation in the black national convention movement in the 1830s, Brown attained a seat on the board of managers of the American Moral Reform Society. He also joined the all-black Leavitt Anti-Slavery Society. Brown supported the black press, protested against the revival of colonizationist enthusiasm in the 1850s, and remained active in black concerns—including freedmen's aid—during and after the Civil War as recording secretary of the Pennsylvania Civil, Social, and Statistical Association. Winch, "Leaders of Philadelphia's Black Community," 39, 78, 109n, 341n; Abajian, *Blacks in Selected Newspapers*, 271; "Black Organizational Members, Sorted by Name," Philadelphia Social History Project, PU; *Constitution of the American Society*, 3 [1:0012]; *Minutes of the Fourth Annual Convention* (1834), 35 [1:0480]; *Minutes of the Fifth Annual Convention* (1835), 14 [1:0592]; *FDP*, 29 April 1852, 1 December 1854 [7:0546, 9:0253].

19. Stephen H. Gloucester (1802–1850) was born a slave in Tennessee. His father, John Gloucester, became the first ordained black Presbyterian minister in

the United States. Sons John, James, Jeremiah, and Stephen followed him into the ministry. John Gloucester purchased Stephen's freedom for $400 and brought him to Philadelphia in 1814. Upon reaching adulthood, Stephen established himself among the city's free black elite through diligent efforts on behalf of anticolonization, moral reform, education, and the black press. He supervised an academy for black youth in the late 1820s, established a reading room for black adults, and promoted education through the Philadelphia Sunday School Society. He served as secretary of the American Moral Reform Society and as a officer of the Union Missionary Society. In 1838 he joined Philip A. Bell and Charles B. Ray as copublisher and coproprietor of the *Colored American* but never fulfilled his ambitious plans to publish a Philadelphia edition of the paper. Gloucester represented Philadelphia blacks at the 1837 annual meeting of the American Anti-Slavery Society. Initially a Garrisonian, he became dissatisfied with what he perceived as Garrison's anticlericalism and lack of concern for free black issues. Gloucester organized the all-black Leavitt Anti-Slavery Society in 1837 and encouraged black churches to sponsor similar societies in Philadelphia. He was one of eight black ministers who helped establish the American and Foreign Anti-Slavery Society in 1840. He later urged blacks to support the Liberty party.

After marrying Anne Crusoe of Washington, D.C., in 1831, Gloucester struggled to support their large family, selling secondhand clothing and relying on his wife's work as a washerwoman to supplement the family income. Ironically, he successfully raised money for the Second African Presbyterian Church. He organized fund-raising fairs in Philadelphia and New York to cover the church's debts. In 1842 the congregation called him to fill the vacancy left by Rev. Andrew Harris's death, but any satisfaction derived from this promotion quickly ended when a racist mob destroyed his church. The Philadelphia race riots of August 1842 left Gloucester broken and dispirited. He became cautious, defensive, and accommodating. In soliciting funds to build a new church, he publicly disavowed his church's involvement with abolitionism. He later closed his new Central Presbyterian Church to abolitionist meetings. While touring Britain in 1847, he courted conservative opinion with a tepid antislavery message. He addressed a British and Foreign Anti-Slavery Society convention and spoke at meetings of the Free Church of Scotland (a church notorious for fellowshipping with slaveholders), criticizing abolitionists as violent, impolitic, and detrimental to the antislavery cause. Gloucester's conduct in Britain shocked abolitionists on both sides of the Atlantic. Philadelphia blacks held public meetings to repudiate his statements. Frederick Douglass denounced him as "one of the vilest traitors to his race that ever lived." Ostracized from the abolitionist movement, Gloucester spent his last years serving his congregation. He died of pneumonia in 1850. *FJ*, 2 November 1827, 12 September 1828; *IC*, 12 June 1850 [6:0523]; *NECAUL*, 29 October 1836, 17 June, 26 October 1837 [1:0724, 2:0076, 0242]; *Lib*, 14 May, 9 July 1831; *CA*, 30 September, 21 October, 4 November, 9 December 1837, 22 March, 2 June, 18 August, 13 October, 10 November 1838, 30 April, 12 December 1840, 4 September 1841 [2:0206, 0238, 0261, 0300, 0440, 0479, 0558, 0615, 0616, 0664, 3:0443, 0745, 4:0184]; *E*, 1 September 1842 [4:0466]; *NASS*, 15 September 1842, 28 November 1844; *NSt*, 4 February, 3 March, 25 August, 1 September 1848 [5:0571, 0760, 0765]; *PF*, 1 September 1838, 23 September 1847 [2:0575, 5:0471]; *ASR*, 1 June 1847 [5:0429]; Census Facts collected by Benjamin C. Bacon and Charles Gardner, 1838, Pennsylvania Abolition Society Papers, PHi; Winch, "Leaders of Philadelphia's Black Community," 39, 43, 45, 59, 78, 85, 307, 313–14, 323, 425, 512–14, 517, 545; Stephen H. Gloucester to Philadelphia Sunday School Society, 4, 24 February 1836, Leon F. Gardiner Collection, PHi [1:0648].

17.
Sarah L. Forten to Elizabeth H. Whittier
25 December 1836

The collaboration and friendship among black and white abolitionist women, especially in Boston and Philadelphia, challenged social customs and repudiated racial stereotypes. Grace and Sarah Douglass, Sarah McCrummill, and the Forten and Purvis women shared the leadership of the Philadelphia Female Anti-Slavery Society with white women abolitionists. Interracial cooperation was particularly evident in the antislavery fairs that women organized to raise funds to sustain state and national antislavery societies and the antislavery press. Customarily held during the Christmas week, the fairs became major social events where fugitive slaves such as William Wells Brown read from their narratives and antislavery singing groups such as the Hutchinson family entertained abolitionists from across the country. The fairs placed traditional female activities in a reform context. Women sold pastry made from free produce goods, pot holders renamed "anti-slavery holders," needlework carrying antislavery messages, and antislavery gift books. Sarah L. Forten's 25 December 1836 letter to Elizabeth H. Whittier provides a detailed portrait of Philadelphia's first antislavery fair, which raised more than $400 for the PFASS. By 1861 the society's yearly bazaars had raised about $32,000, money that was crucial to the survival of the movement. N. Orwin Rush, "Lucretia Mott and the Philadelphia Antislavery Fairs," *BFHA* 35:69–75 (Autumn 1946); Brown, "Cradle of Feminism," 145–48, 150–58; Winch, *Philadelphia's Black Elite*, 85–87.

Philadelphia, [Pennsylvania]
Dec[ember] 25th, 1836

My Dear Elizabeth:

I have delayed replying to your kind letter untill now because I wished to give you an account of our Anti Slavery <u>Fair</u>—and I knew you would be gratified by a description of it and of the good success [we] had—I presume I may as well dash into the subject ~~the subject~~ at once for a commencement, 'as to wait and place it in the middle part—or at the end of my letter. Our Society have been making preparations for the last four months to get up this Sale—and many very beautiful fancy productions did they manafacture for the occasion. The[y] hired the Fire Mens Hall in North St. below arch—and decorated it with evergreens—and flowers—and had it brilliantly lighted—there was six Tables—including a refreshment Table—on which most of the eatables were presented—three large Pound Cakes—Oranges—and Grapes were given to us—so our expenses were not great—and the proceeds amounted to more than three

FAIR.

The Ladies (of color) of the town of Frankfort propose giving a **FAIR,** at the house of **Mrs. RILLA HARRIS,** (*alias,* Simpson,) on Thursday evening next, for benevolent purposes, under the superintendence of Mrs. Rilla Harris.

All the delicacies of the season will be served up in the most palatable style----such as *Ice Creams, Cakes, Lemonades, Jellies, Fruits, Nuts, &c. &c.*

It is hoped, as the proceeds are to be applied to benevolent purposes, that the citizens generally will turn out and aid in the enterprise.

JULY 6, 1847.

10. Advertisement for a black women's fair

hundred Dollars—we only had the Hall for a day and two evenings—so you may see we done well for so short a time. There was twel[ve] Ladies superintending the Tables. We had a Post Office opened—for letters to be distributed at 12½ cts. apiece. A Young Lady and myself were superintending Post Mistresses—and we delivered upwards of one hundred letters—nearly one half of which we were obliged to pen ourselves. We were as busy as we could be all the time—and much amusement was afforded by the dispatch with which the mails arrived. In t[he] course of the evening a few lines addressed to the Ladies presiding—were handed in by a Young Gentleman—they are good—and I'll copy them for you at the end of my letter. I wish you could have been here—to contribute and receive a share of the general satisfaction.

Lines addressed to the Ladies presiding at the fair—

> The AntiSlavery Fair—are fair indeed,
> Their pretty eyes from every table,
> Deep blue—dark hazel—or bright sable;
> Will many [of] us captive lead,
> Sow tis not fair—that those who say
> That Slaves should be emancipated,
> Should so forget the word today
> (By victory, perhaps elated)
> As to reduce to Slavery,
> Those gentlemen who call to see
> What they can buy with ready cash,
> Yet they are made to feel the lash
> (The eye lash) which it is quite plain,
> Though not perhaps inflicting pain
> Soon catches—then proceedes to bind
> All that are call'd the Batchelor kind.
> Ye fair ones of the Fair today,
> May this be called a fair proceeding?
> Ye fairly take our hearts away;
> Unfairly us to bondage leading
> —————————————
> "All should be free"—"None should be bound"
> This is your boasted theory,
> Whilst in the act—y'r fairly found
> Depriving us of liberty.

There are—as you will percieve several errors in the lines, but as the writer does not aspire to be call'd a Poet—and the effusion was so appropriate to the occasion, I dare say he will not take offence at my transcribing them. They afforded us considerable merriment and if they win a smile from you—he will no doubt be amply repaid. Our excellent friend and advocate Gerrit Smith has been here and we are more than gratified by an acquaintance with him—he has brought his Wife and Daughter, a girl of fourteen years[1]—to spend the Winter in our City—and we are delighted with them both. Miss Smiths health has not been good and her Parents think a change of air will be of service to her. Mrs. S——— is one of the plainest woman in her dress I ever saw. I learn that she devotes nearly all her income to benevolent purposes—this is so praiseworthy I could not forbear to mention it to you. She is also one of these lovely—good natured looking women who take ones heart on the instant. Mr. Smith has gone home.

I have this instant learned with deep regret and suprise of the Death of one of our valuable friends to the Abolition cause—Dr. Edwin P. Atlee[2]—he was only confined to his bed one week—and we were not at all aware that he was dangerously ill—and I have been more than grieved by his sudden demise. He was a ~~active~~ noble member of the Society—and took an active part in many good works. Your Brother—I presume is acquainted with him and will feel regret that one of our useful men has been called away from his good works here—though I doubt not but that he has gone to receive his reward in Heaven. His Parents and Brothers and Sister have gone to Michigan to live—and as he was ill only one week, they will receive a severe shock—one, which they will not soon recover from.

As this is Christmas and two or three of my Relatives have come in to pass the day with us—I am unable to arrange my letter in better order—for a half dozen voices are holding forth on different subjects—making it rather impossible to write in a collected manner. You will therefore receive my excuses for whatever errors you should find. Please accept from myself and family[3] the usual congratulations of the Season with the hope that you may be spared to see many returns of it. I send you one of my Brother Robert Purvis's addresses—on the demise of Thos Shipley.[4] I will no longer intrude upon your time My Dear Friend—but ask you to write me only when you are at leisure. Your Friend

Sarah L Forten

Whittier Papers, Central Michigan University, Mount Pleasant, Michigan. Published by permission.

1. Gerrit Smith (1797–1874), a wealthy landowner, reformer, and philanthropist of Peterboro, New York, was visiting Philadelphia with his wife Ann and daughter Elizabeth. Smith headed a powerful circle of western New York abolitionists by the mid-1830s. He left the American Anti-Slavery Society in 1840 in favor of political antislavery and, after serving briefly in Congress, became disillusioned by federal support for slavery. A friend, patron, and frequent correspondent of many black abolitionists, he attempted to establish a black farming settlement on a large tract of family land, aided runaway slaves (participating in

the famous Jerry rescue), subsidized free-state settlers in Kansas, and conspired with John Brown to incite a slave insurrection at Harpers Ferry. Smith fought for black suffrage after the Civil War. Ralph V. Harlow, *Gerrit Smith, Philanthropist and Reformer* (New York, N.Y., 1939); Lawrence J. Friedman, *Gregarious Saints: Self and Community in American Abolitionism, 1830–1870* (Cambridge, England, 1982), 96–126.

2. Edwin P. Atlee (1799–1836), a Philadelphia physician and Quaker abolitionist, became secretary of the Pennsylvania Abolition Society in the 1820s. He was later a founding member of the American Anti-Slavery Society, chaired the committee that drafted its Declaration of Sentiments, and served on its board of managers until his death. Atlee was highly regarded by Philadelphia blacks, and he addressed the 1835 black national convention. *NECAUL*, 24 December 1836, 28 January 1837; *Lib*, 30 July 1836 [1:0677]; Merrill and Ruchames, *Letters of William Lloyd Garrison*, 1:383–84; *Minutes of the Fifth Annual Convention* (1835), 7 [1:0589].

3. At the time of her letter, Sarah Forten still lived with her parents, James and Charlotte Forten. She had four brothers and three sisters: James, Jr., Robert Bridges, William, Thomas Francis Willing, Margaretta, Harriet, and Mary. Lewis, "The Fortens of Philadelphia," 12, 38–51.

4. Robert Purvis eulogized pioneer abolitionist Thomas Shipley before a 23 November 1836 gathering at St. Thomas's African Episcopal Church in Philadelphia, using the occasion to promote moral reform and immediatist abolitionism. His remarks were published as *A Tribute to the Memory of Thomas Shipley, the Philanthropist* (1836). Shipley (1786–1836), a Philadelphia Quaker lawyer, was a leading figure in the Pennsylvania Abolition Society and a founding member of the American Anti-Slavery Society. He counselled blacks on a variety of legal matters and worked to protect fugitive slaves. During the Philadelphia race riots of 1835, he risked his life to protect black lives and property. His heroic conduct, together with his lifelong commitment to antislavery and civil rights, brought him respect in the black community. An estimated three thousand blacks attended his funeral. Robert Purvis, *A Tribute to the Memory of Thomas Shipley, the Philanthropist* (Philadelphia, Pa., 1836) [1:0733–41]; *Lib*, 24 September, 10, 22 October 1836; *NECAUL*, 15 October 1836; Morris, *Free Men All*, 49–50.

18.
Speech by Charles W. Gardner
Delivered at the Broadway Tabernacle
New York, New York
9 May 1837

Black abolitionists frequently recounted free black accomplishments to support their call for emancipation. Every successful black merchant or skilled artisan, every black church or school, and every eloquent black speaker refuted the racist arguments of proslavery theorists. In a 9 May 1837 speech before the annual meeting of the American Anti-Slavery Society, delivered at the Broadway Tabernacle in New York City, Rev. Charles W. Gardner reviewed black social, religious, intellectual, and economic progress in the face of grinding oppression. He reminded white abolitionists that free blacks were fighting for their rights "when William Lloyd Garrison was a schoolboy." Gardner's presence, his eloquence, and the force of his logic made the black clergyman "a standing monument—a present witness to the truth of his arguments," according to one observer who heard the speech. *Lib*, 19 May, 2 June 1837.

Rev. CHARLES GARDNER,[1] a man of color, and pastor of a Presbyterian church in Philadelphia, presented the following:

> *Resolved*, That sufficient evidence has been given to the world to convince the enlightened public, that the immediate emancipation of the colored people is morally right and politically safe.

Permit me, sir (said Mr. G.), to say, that this day is to me of the highest interest. When I cast my eye over this respectable and enlightened congregation, I see that the doctrines of this resolution will be responded to by every intelligent mind. Let me take a view of what American slavery is. It consists in this: in making men chattels; in brutalizing the image of God, the purchase of the blood of Jesus Christ; impressing its seal on childhood, and wresting from the hand of the rightful owner that exercise of the judgement for which he is accountable only to God. It denies to the slave, and in many parts of the country to the free colored people also, access to that heavenly chart, which is laid down by Jehovah as the only safe rule of faith and practice, the liberty of reading and understanding how he may serve God acceptably.[2] It withholds from him all the proceeds of his labor, except a scanty subsistence, and two suits of clothing in a year, of the coarsest description. Is it morally right and politically safe to abolish such a system immediately?

Let us look at the evidences. They are not drawn from the days of Hannibal,[3] nor from a period a thousand years back, nor even one hundred years since; but from today—from things as they are, and may be seen to be—in our own times—now.

The first evidence I will give, is that of the slaveholders themselves. They are certainly good witnesses. In their daily papers, you will see, at any time, advertisements for the sale of ten, twenty, fifty, or one hundred valuable negroes, recommended and qualified in such terms as these: Jack, a good farmer; Joe, a skilful carpenter; Bob, a first-rate shoemaker; Jim, a capital blacksmith, fully guaranteed; Bets, a good washerwoman; Nell, a faithful nurse; Sall, a seamstress, fully guaranteed. Is not that evidence that they may be safely made free? If, under the oppressions of slavery, they can become skilful mechanics, trusty housekeepers, and safe nurses, would they be less so, if made fully free. I trow not. If they sustain so much moral worth while crowded within the small circle which slavery allows, what would they not exhibit, if placed in circumstances to develop all the powers with which they are endowed by a beneficent Creator?

In the second place, I will call your attention to the evidence from the disposition that has been manifested by those who have already obtained their freedom. It is in evidence, that those who have been slaves, and who have been liberated, by gift or will, or by their own industry, have ever manifested the strongest and tenderest affection for the family of their former masters. I was once honored with a travelling connection in the Methodist Episcopal conference of Philadelphia, and labored in the peninsula between the Delaware and Chesapeake bays, where I had great opportunity of becoming acquainted with the disposition of the people of color. I will say, that I do not know of more ignorant people on earth, than many of the field hands on that peninsula. And I believe the mass of the whites are about as ignorant. For, once I was travelling the Lewistown circuit, I was called to preach a sermon at the execution of two black men, one of whom had murdered his master. A short time before, the Court of Oyer[4] had sentenced a white man to death for murdering his wife and child, and he had been hanged. About three weeks afterwards, the court appointed for the trial of slaves sentenced these two black men to death, and the time was appointed. When we went from the prison to the gallows, only a short distance, we found such a mass of people assembled, with stands for the sale of cider, and cakes, and rum, that the sheriff could with great difficulty force a passage. And this, notwithstanding there had been a white man hanged three weeks before. Is not this evidence of the degradation of the whites? How, then, can you expect to find an enlightened community of colored people among such masters?

But I found many people of color, who had obtained their freedom, and had purchased lots, and built cabins, where they had their pigs and chickens, and seemed to be comfortable and improving. I have seen the children of their former masters come to these people and ask for something to eat, and I have seen every thing of the best in the cabin provided for them. I asked one aged woman, "Sister Judy, who was that young lady I saw here?" "Ah!" said she, "it was my old master's daughter: many a time I have been severely beaten for her sake; but, poor thing, she is very poor now, and has nothing but what her friends give her. I forgive her now, and look to God for my reward. I have no right to take vengeance, and I do the best I can for her, when she comes here, to get something good to eat." Here is the evidence. Shall such benevolence as this, when exhibited by those who have every reason to take vengeance, be passed by? Shall those who have such a spirit be kept in bondage?

A third evidence to be considered, is drawn from the general character of the people of color, including their situation, and their ability to get along in the world. Let it be remembered, that the man of color has to labor against wind and tide, to meet all the prejudices, and contend with all the proscription and opposition of the times. Notwithstanding this, I can show that the colored man is capable of making headway under all his disadvantages. Go with me to Baltimore, and in Howard Street, we will find a man of color who, seven years ago, paid $600 for his own body and soul, and $300 or more for his wife: now he owns nearly a block of ground, with three brick houses, two of which would rent in New York for $300 apiece, and the other for $700, besides several wooden tenements.[5] Come to Philadelphia, and there is a man named Hales, who has twice paid $350 for himself, being cheated out of the first payment by his *humane* master. Now he has on the front of his lot a three-story house, and on the rear, such buildings as rent for more than $600 a year.

In Philadelphia, we have fourteen respectable congregations of colored people. We own several churches that are worth from $25,000 to $50,000 each. The whole amount of our public property, in churches, school houses, and burial grounds, is more than two hundred thousand dollars, the greater part paid for by ourselves. Several pay schools are supported by us. About sixty beneficial societies do much to provide for the sick and the helpless, and for the burial of the dead, paying for these objects from eight to twelve thousand dollars a year. Not a colored person of any respectability, however poor, is buried at the expense of the poor funds in Philadelphia. In New York, there are six or eight churches, with beneficial societies, and schools, and other useful institutions.[6] So in other cities. It is true, we have in Philadelphia, and elsewhere, a low class of colored people, who are both degraded and vicious: but who is to blame? I live near the church in which I have the honor to officiate; and in one square there are fifteen grog-shops located by the authority of the city; and in the immediate neighborhood there are forty-five. When *you* set the trap, is the rabbit to be blamed for being caught?

The weary traveller or laborer is snared in the gins that are set by those in authority, who ought to know better. But amidst all our difficulties, the man of color advances in a surprising degree. And when the people of color are compared with other portions of the laboring class in the community, I venture to declare, that in regard to the number of the vicious and the wretched, they will not overrun the common ratio.

In the fourth place, I will notice the evidence drawn from the power of intellect exhibited by the man of color. I know our heads have been measured, to determine whether we had as much brains as blood.[7] I know that prejudice has blinded the eyes of many who ought to have seen and acknowledged the truth. I know the popular delusion everywhere prevailing, has extended its influence even over ourselves; and that many among us have tacitly consented to admit that we were an inferior race. But I will appeal to facts. I will mention one case, and I am happy to see a reverend gentleman in the house who can attest it. There was a man who used to travel with Bishop Asbury, named Harry Hosier, who was a most extraordinary natural orator, and was admitted by the bishop to be a correct theologian. When he was preaching on the peninsula, he came to Bohemia manor, in the neighborhood of Esquire Bassett's, afterwards Governor of Delaware, but now removed, I trust, to his heavenly rest.[8] One Sabbath day, Esquire Bassett had his church minister to dine with him, and while they were at table, his servant came in, and whispered to Mrs. Bassett. The Esquire asked, "What does Joe want?" Mrs. B. replied, "He wants to go and hear a colored man preach." He turned to the clergyman, and said, "A colored man preach! Did you ever hear of a nigger's preaching? Let us go." So he told the man to bring up the carriage, and they would go and hear Joe's preacher. When they came to the place, which was in the woods a few miles distant, Esquire Bassett rolled a log near to the stump where the preacher stood, and they sat down to hear. The old gentleman stood up, and took his text. Doubtless, he was abashed at seeing all the masters in the neighborhood. But he preached his sermon. After he was through, Esquire Bassett took him by the hand, and asked him, "Where were you educated?" "I have no education, sir." "Can you not read?" "No, sir, I know only one in the book and that letter is O." "Well," said he, "I have been to college and seminaries, and if I were to be hung for it I could not preach such a sermon as that." But this is not the whole. Conviction seized upon his soul, under the preaching of that sermon, and he became a Christian, and lived a faithful member of the Methodist Episcopal church, and died in the full assurance of a glorious immortality. Now, bring me a white man, that don't know a letter in the book but O, who can preach a systematic gospel sermon, and be pronounced by an intelligent congregation a correct theologian.

We have among us a number of men, who know but little about

reading but yet are able preachers of the gospel. Last Sabbath, I had the pleasure of inviting to our pulpit a preacher named Shadrach Green, of Kentucky, a man 26 or 27 years of age—a slave. His humane master had sold his soul and body to himself for a thousand dollars. In preaching, he took for his text the words, "Behold what manner of love the Father hath bestowed upon us, that we should be called the sons of God." He commenced with a description of the excellent gifts of God in prophecy. Secondly, the exact fulfilment of prophecy, in the coming, life, and death of Jesus Christ. Then he laid open the sufferings of Christ, and showed the goodness of God in giving forth the influences of his Spirit on the hearts of sinners. And he crowned the whole with a declaration of the manner in which God had visited his own soul. "Behold," said he "what manner of love the Father hath bestowed upon us, that we should be called the sons of God."[9] Now, that man could scarcely read a chapter in the book. Was there no natural talent here—no moral power—no material to work upon—no foundation for a superstructure of cultivation, that would have shone with brilliancy? And, thanks be to God, he was not a mulatto, either, but a black man. There are some people foolish enough to think a few drops of white blood in our veins will impart more gifts and powers than a black man can exhibit.

These are but a few of the statements of facts which I might make. But, surely, in the mouth of two or three witnesses, every word shall be established. Here let me say, that no small sagacity has been evinced by the people of color, in their course respecting the great contest now going on in this nation. We have always had our own views on this subject. We view slavery to be like the carnal mind, which is not subject to the law of God, neither indeed can be. And therefore it must be abolished, and not ameliorated. There is no such thing as ameliorating slavery. You might as well talk of having the love of God in a carnal mind.

William Lloyd Garrison has been branded as the individual who turned the people of color against the colonization scheme. But I can tell you, sir, that when William Lloyd Garrison was a schoolboy, the people of color in different parts of the country were holding extensive meetings, which always agreed in declaring that they regarded the scheme as visionary in itself, and calculated only to rivet the chains of those who remain in slavery.[10] I had the pleasure of hearing the Hon. Charles Fenton Mercer, of Virginia, declare frankly that the Colonization Society never would be able to accomplish their objects. The Hon. William S. Archer told me the same in conversation.[11] How far it may act beneficially, in abolishing the slave trade, or in planting benevolence and civilization in Africa, I leave for time to disclose. But these facts show, that as to its bearings on ourselves, the people of color were not asleep. Long before William Lloyd Garrison was a man, we had fixed our *veto* on it.

From its very commencement, we had washed our hand of all connection with it.

It is said by the pro-slavery party, that the people of color, so far as they are informed on the subject, are opposed to the principles and measures of the abolitionists. Sir, I deny it. I know I speak the language of every intelligent man of color in the United States, that has had the opportunity of understanding the subject, when I say that we do approve of the benevolent scheme of immediate emancipation. There may be some at the South, who are respectable and intelligent, but who are not allowed to read for themselves the truth of the matter, because it is considered treason for a colored man to read, and treason to receive or give a book or a paper; and some of these may disapprove of the abolition principles, because they do not understand them. But with this exception, we approve of them to a man, and are ready to stand by our friends, and to hold up the hands of our Moseses and our Aarons, and give them our best wishes, our sincere prayers, and all the pecuniary aid our circumstances admit.

I have another evidence to offer, in support of this resolution; and that is from the law of God. When God gave his law to Moses, he said to him, "Come up hither." And the mountains shook, and the lightning flashed, and the thunders rolled, and the clouds appeared, portending that God was about to give law to men. And what is that law? He enjoins this precept, "Lay up these my words in your heart, and in your soul, and bind them for a sign upon your hand, that they may be as frontlets between your eyes. And ye shall teach them [to] your children, speaking of them when thou sittest in thy house, and when thou walkest by the way, when thou liest down, and when thou risest up. And thou shalt write them upon the door-posts of thy house, and upon thy gates."[12] See, then, the wickedness of those laws which go contrary to the law of God, and say to the slave, "You shall not read these Scriptures, nor understand them, nor teach them to your children, nor obey them." Is it not morally right, and politically safe, to abolish such a system?

I say, then, that immediate abolition is both morally right and politically safe. Is it not right and safe to let men go free, who are proved capable of being governed by the laws of God? If all the moral worth and influence that has been lost to the world through American slavery, could be condensed into real matter, and placed in the scale, with the Atlas mountains[13] in the opposite, the mountain scale would kick the beam, as though it were a feather's weight. Such is the withering influence of American slavery on the man of color.

And now, sir, considering the proscription we labor under, would it be a wonder if we were all a debased set of wretches, involved in the greatest vice and misery that can be expressed? We ought to be better than we are—that is clear. But would it be a wonder if we were a thousand times worse?

Seeing, then, that under all our disadvantages and provocations, we have given evidence of a benevolent and a peaceful disposition—that we have never been turbulent citizens—that there have been no simultaneous movements for insurrection—and that we have given the clearest proofs of our loyalty—is it not morally right that we should enjoy the same privileges with other citizens? Is it not politically safe that the people of color should be free?

Fourth Annual Report of the American Anti-Slavery Society (New York, N.Y., 1837), 11–15.

1. Charles W. Gardner (1782–1863) was born near Shoemakertown, New Jersey. About 1809 he began an itinerant ministry to Methodist congregations in Philadelphia, Washington, Maryland, and Delaware. Gardner's experiences in the Chesapeake region convinced him of the evils of slavery and colonization. He used the pulpit to attack slavery and lobbied federal officials to set aside American territory for freed slaves as an alternative to African resettlement. His vocal opposition to slavery and colonization brought rebukes from Methodist officials and harassment and threats from many whites in the border states. Colonization society officials in Baltimore had him arrested and driven from the city, and similar threats forced him to flee to New York.

Gardner resettled in Philadelphia in the early 1830s. In 1836 he began a twelve-year tenure as pastor of the First African Presbyterian Church. His experience, reputation, and "polished eloquence" earned him a position of leadership in the city's black community. He attended the early black national conventions, participated in the American Moral Reform Society, and fought against black disfranchisement. In 1838 Gardner helped the Pennsylvania Abolition Society compile a special census of local free blacks—a valuable historical record of black life in antebellum Philadelphia. He considered the 1838 census a measure of black progress and frequently drew upon this and other statistics to support his arguments against slavery, colonization, and proscriptive black laws. Gardner's abolitionism infused his pastoral work and he criticized the church for its ties to slavery and colonization. He belonged to the American Anti-Slavery Society, and in 1837 he became the first black to address the society's annual meeting. He also attended the founding convention of the Pennsylvania Anti-Slavery Society that same year. Gardner broke with the Garrisonians in the late 1830s over what he perceived as their anticlericalism and social radicalism, and he subsequently joined the American and Foreign Anti-Slavery Society. In the early 1840s, he helped organize the Union Missionary Society and briefly served as president of the Vigilant Committee of Philadelphia. Despite his impressive antislavery credentials, he could not escape the criticism that abolitionists directed at black Presbyterian churches in Philadelphia. Frederick Douglass questioned Gardner's abolitionism and accused him of pastoring two slaveholding congregations in Tennessee.

After leaving Philadelphia in the late 1840s, Gardner served congregations throughout the Northeast, including the Talcott Street Congregational Church in Hartford. Wherever he preached, he continued to speak and work for local black issues. While in Princeton, he helped organize a campaign to protect the voting rights of New Jersey blacks. Later as pastor of the Colored Union Church in Newport, Rhode Island (1852–58), he served on the State Council of the Colored People. Gardner joined the Evangelical Association of the Colored Ministers of Congregational and Presbyterian Churches in the late 1850s. He spent his final years as pastor of the Second Presbyterian Church in Harrisburg, Pennsylvania. *Lib,* 28 July, 18 August 1832, 19 August 1842, 24 April 1863 [1:0208–9, 0215, 4:0046]; *NECAUL,* 24 August 1836 [1:0695–96]; *CA,* 15 September 1838, 10 June 1837, 28 August 1841 [2:0069, 0588, 4:0179]; *PF,* 16 July 1840, 15 March, 31 May 1849 [3:0523–24, 5:1006, 6:0003]; *E,* 22, 29 April 1834 [1:0414, 0415–16]; *FDP,* 28 October 1853 [8:0462–63]; *CR,* 17 August 1854 [9:0003]; *RIF,* 17 March 1854 [8:0686]; *AR,* May 1835 [1:0578]; *WAA,* 24 September 1859 [12:0069]; *Fourth Annual Report of the American Anti-Slavery Society* (New York, N.Y., 1837), 11–15 [2:0049–51]; Benjamin Bacon and Charles W. Gardner, *The Present State and Condition of the Free People of Color of the City of Philadelphia* (Philadelphia, Pa., 1838) [2:0315–38]; J. W. C. Pennington to Horace Greeley and William Harned, 27 November 1852, Jay Papers, NNC [7:0839]; Charles W. Gardner mss., 12 December 1839, Western Anti-Slavery Society Papers, DLC [3:0523–24]; Winch, *Philadelphia's Black Elite,* 64–65, 83–84, 89, 94, 110, 137–38, 161; Robert G. Sherer, Jr., "Negro Churches in Rhode Island before 1860," *RIH* 25:11–12 (January 1966).

2. During the 1830s, most southern state legislatures (except those in Maryland, Kentucky, and Tennessee) outlawed teaching slaves to read and write. A few southern states even denied literacy to free blacks. These laws prevented most slaves from reading the Bible, but many memorized portions of the Bible, and biblical stories became part of the oral tradition of the slaves. Eugene D. Genovese, *Roll, Jordan, Roll: The World the Slaves Made* (New York, N.Y., 1972), 561–66; Berlin, *Slaves without Masters,* 286.

3. Hannibal, a Carthaginian general who invaded the Roman Empire between 218 and 211 B.C., was often reputed by nineteenth-century black historians to be black.

4. A court of Oyer and Terminer is a specially convened court that hears cases of treasons, felonies, and misdemeanors.

5. Gardner probably refers to Samuel Hackett, a carter who lived at 76 South Howard Street in Baltimore during the late 1830s. Howard Street was one of the principal thoroughfares in antebellum Baltimore. *Baltimore City Directory,* 1835–38; Raphael Semmes, ed., *Baltimore as Seen by Visitors, 1783–1860* (Baltimore, Md., 1953), 27, 91.

6. By 1840, 16,358 blacks lived in New York City and 10,507 in Philadelphia. Despite grinding social and economic oppression, these black communities sustained numerous social, benevolent, and religious institutions. New York had nine black churches and the greater Philadelphia area had seventeen. By the late 1830s, blacks had organized thirty mutual aid societies in New York and eighty in Philadelphia, forty-seven of which were supported by black women.

Black New Yorkers founded about a half dozen other benevolent societies including the Colored Orphan Asylum, a temperance society, three masonic lodges, a young men's antislavery society, and the well-known New York Committee of Vigilance. City blacks also operated at least two private instruction societies and a small school in the basement of St. Philip's Episcopal Church. They regularly aided the seven free schools of the New York Manumission Society until 1834, when the schools came under the control of the city. The African Dorcas Association provided clothing to students attending manumission society schools and money to aspiring ministers and teachers. In 1837 the Phoenix Society opened a black school that, at its height, employed thirteen teachers. Two other black literary societies also provided educational services and, through their public lecture series, became a training ground for future abolitionists.

Black Philadelphians operated nine free and ten pay schools; six more were either partially free or under white control. They also owned a public hall and supported five literary societies, two male and three female. The Philadelphia Library Company of Colored Persons and the Demosthenian Institute had substantial libraries, and the latter published its own newspaper, the *Demosthenian Shield*, in the 1840s. Local blacks established two tract, two Bible, and four temperance societies and one moral reform association. Antebellum Philadelphia became a center for black freemasonry, with as many as ten lodges chartered by 1850. Separate labor organizations also existed for black coachmen, porters, and mechanics. Bacon and Gardner, *Present State and Condition*, 5–40 [2:0317–34]; *CA*, 28 March 1840; Dorothy Porter, "The Organized Educational Activities of Negro Literary Societies, 1828–1846," in *The Making of Black America: Essays in Negro Life and History*, 2 vols., ed. August Meier and Elliot Rudwick (New York, N.Y., 1969), 1:276–88; Walker, "Afro-American in New York," 65–156; Leonard P. Curry, *The Free Black in Urban America, 1800–1850: The Shadow of the Dream* (Chicago, Ill., 1981), 196–215, 250.

7. Antebellum phrenologists, anthropologists, and medical researchers equated intelligence with brain size. Many contended that blacks and American Indians possessed smaller brains than whites and were, therefore, inferior races.

8. Harry Hosier (ca. 1750–1806), an illiterate black preacher, accompanied Francis Asbury, Thomas Coke, Richard Whatcoat, and other Methodist evangelists on their travels throughout the eastern United States from 1780 until his death. Although lacking formal training, Hosier's outstanding oratory converted many blacks and whites to the Methodist faith. Bishop Asbury (1745–1816), who organized the Methodist Episcopal church in 1784, admitted that audiences preferred Hosier's preaching to his own. Although Asbury and Hosier frequently preached at Bohemia Manor, Richard Bassett's huge estate in northern Delaware and Maryland, the event discussed by Gardner apparently occurred in the early 1780s. Bassett (1761–1815), a lawyer, legislator, and signer of the Constitution, later served as governor of Delaware (1799–1801). After converting to Methodism, he freed his many slaves, founded the Delaware Society for Promoting the Abolition of Slavery (1788), and worked to end the slave trade. Warren T. Smith, "Harry Hosier: Black Preacher Extraordinary," *JITC* 7:111–28 (Spring 1980); Richardson, *Dark Salvation*, 170–74, 182; L. C. Rudolph, *Francis Asbury* (Nashville, Tenn., 1966), 7; *BDGUS*, 1:212–13; John A. Munroe, *Colonial Delaware: A History* (Millwood, N.Y., 1978), 51, 189–92.

9. Green used 1 John 3:1 as the textual basis for his sermon.

10. Long before the publication of William Lloyd Garrison's *Thoughts on*

African Colonization (1832), northern free blacks denounced the American Colonization Society's program to repatriate blacks to Africa. In January 1817, one month after the founding of the ACS, Philadelphia's blacks overwhelmingly rejected the society. Similar protests continued throughout the decade. During the late 1820s, Samuel E. Cornish challenged colonizationists in his newspapers, *Freedom's Journal* and *Rights of All*. By 1829 black abolitionists James Forten of Philadelphia and William Watkins of Baltimore had converted Garrison from colonization. The Nat Turner rebellion (1831) provoked northern state legislatures to appropriate funds for colonizing their free black populations. Reacting to this hysteria, and encouraged by the *Liberator*, blacks from Washington to Boston staged public demonstrations damning the ACS in 1831 and 1832. Although many blacks supported an emigration site as a refuge from oppression, the protesters held the ACS responsible for inciting racism, degrading blacks, and supporting slavery. Blacks regularly reminded colonizationists of their role in winning American independence and building the nation. Garrison, *Thoughts on African Colonization*, part 2; R. J. M. Blackett, "Anglo-American Opposition to Liberian Colonization, 1831–1833," *H* 41:276–94 (February 1979); Foner, *History of Black Americans*, 1:589–94, 2:295–99.

11. Charles Fenton Mercer (1778–1858) and William S. Archer (1789–1855) were both experienced lawyers and Whig politicians who represented Virginia in the U.S. Congress during the 1820s and 1830s. Mercer helped found the American Colonization Society and remained an enthusiastic advocate of colonization until his death. Archer was a staunch defender of southern interests and later became an ardent advocate of Texas annexation in the Senate. *DAB*, 1:342–43, 12:539; Douglas R. Egerton, " 'Its Origin is Not a Little Curious': A New Look at the American Colonization Society," *JER* 5:463–80 (Winter 1985).

12. Gardner quotes from Deuteronomy 11:18–20, a command that Moses was said to have received from God on Mount Sinai (in modern-day Egypt).

13. The Atlas Mountains are located in North Africa, stretching through Morocco, Algeria, and Tunisia.

19.
Editorial by Samuel E. Cornish
4 March 1837

The emergence of an independent black press gave black abolitionists a public voice. When Samuel E. Cornish assumed the editorship of the *Weekly Advocate* in March 1837, he proudly proclaimed the newspaper's black identity by renaming it the *Colored American* and then proceeded to build it into the most influential black newspaper of the decade. In his 4 March 1837 inaugural issue, Cornish explained the need for a black press. A black journal, he argued, would energize northern blacks, address their specific circumstances, "enlist the sympathy of the nation" by publicizing their grievances, and serve as a striking illustration of black elevation and progress. He hoped that the *Colored American* would encourage the black community to "speak out in THUNDER TONES." Cornish's efforts demonstrated the value of an independent black press and paved the way for more successful and sophisticated black newspapers like *Frederick Douglass' Paper* and the *Weekly Anglo-African* in the 1850s. Pease and Pease, *They Who Would Be Free*, 108–19; Quarles, *Black Abolitionists*, 86.

Why We Should Have A Paper
1. Because the colored people of these United States have to contend with all the multiplied ills of slavery, more cruel in its practice and unlimited in its duration than was ever before inflicted upon any people; and we are proscribed and pressed down by prejudice more wicked and fatal than even slavery itself. These evils not only pervade the length and breadth of the land, but they have their strong hold in the Church of Jesus Christ, where they abide and act themselves out, contrary to all its holy precepts. Colored men must do something, must make some effort to drive these "abominations of desolation" from the church and the world; they must establish and maintain the PRESS, and through it speak out in THUNDER TONES, until the nation repent and render to every man that which is just and equal—and until the church possess herself of the mind which was in Christ Jesus, and cease to oppress her poor brother, because God hath dyed him a darker hue.

2. Because our afflicted population in the free states, are scattered in handfuls over nearly 5000 towns, and can only be reached by the Press— a public journal must therefore be sent down, at least weekly, to rouse them up. To call all their energies into action—and where they have been down trodden, paralyzed and worn out, to create new energies for them, that such dry bones may live.

Such an organ can be furnished at little cost, so as to come within the reach of every man, and carry to him lessons of instruction on religion and morals, lessons on industry and economy—until our entire people are of one heart and of one mind, in all the means of their salvation, both temporal and spiritual.

3. Because without such an organ we never can enlist the sympathy of the nation in our behalf, and in the behalf of the slave; and until this be done, we shall have accomplished nothing nor shall we have proved ourselves worthy to be freemen and to have our grievances redressed. Before the wise and good awake and consecrate themselves to our cause, we ourselves must have proclaimed our oppression and wrongs from the HOUSE-TOP. When did Greece and Poland win the sympathy of the world; after they had published their wrongs, asserted their rights and sued for freedom at the hands of their oppressors.[1] Then, and only, then were they worthy to be freemen, nor should *we* expect the *boon*, until we feel its importance and pray for its possession. With us this is to be a great moral struggle, and let us brethren, be united in our efforts.

4. Because no class of men, however pious and benevolent, can take our place in the great work of redeeming our character and removing our disabilities. They may identify themselves with us, and enter into our sympathies. Still it is ours to will and do—both of which, we trust, are about to be done, and in the doing of which, this journal[2] *as an appropriate engine*, may exert a powerful agency. We propose to make it a journal of facts and of instruction. It will go out freighted with information for all—it will tell tales of woe, both in the church and out of the church; such as are calculated to make the heart to bleed and the ear to burn. It will bring to light many hidden things, which must be revealed and repented of, or this nation must perish.

Colored American (New York, N.Y.), 4 March 1837.

1. Greek and Polish movements for independence sparked widespread popular support across Europe and in the United States. Between 1821 and 1832, the Greeks fought to end centuries of Turkish domination; they succeeded only after the delayed intervention of the major European powers. In 1830–31, Polish nationalists attempted to throw off Russian rule but internal dissension and the failure of western European powers to intervene led to crushing failure.

2. The *Colored American* first appeared in January 1837 as the *Weekly Advocate*. Under the direction of proprietor Philip A. Bell and Robert Sears, a white printer, the New York City journal emphasized general antislavery and moral reform themes. When Samuel Cornish became editor in March, he renamed the paper and made it a forum for black issues. Within a year, he had eighteen hundred subscribers, dozens of subscription agents throughout the Northeast, and the generous financial support of Arthur Tappan, Gerrit Smith, and other white abolitionists. But despite Cornish's initial successes, the *Colored American* struggled through several changes of ownership and editorial staff, ongoing fi-

nancial problems, and frequent editorial disputes after 1838. Proprietorship passed from Bell to a twenty-eight-member Committee of Publication, then to the trio of Bell, Stephen Gloucester, and Charles B. Ray. Gloucester's attempt to publish a Philadelphia edition failed. Ray replaced Cornish and James McCune Smith as editor in mid-1839, but a libel suit devastated the paper's finances, forcing him to halt publication and reorganize the paper early the next year. The journal also alienated many patrons and subscribers by attacking the Garrisonians and the American Moral Reform Society and by printing ambiguous editorials on political antislavery. Even with these difficulties, the *Colored American* continued until December 1841, earning distinction as the longest running, most successful black newspaper of its time. Donald M. Jacobs, ed., *Antebellum Black Newspapers* (Westport, Conn., 1976), 207, 229–30, 451–54; *CA*, 4 March, 11 November 1837, 2, 9, 16 June 1838, 22 June, 23 November 1839, 7 March, 23 May 1840.

20.
Editorial by Samuel E. Cornish
4 March 1837

"Every colored man is an abolitionist, and the slaveholders know it," proclaimed one black clergyman. Black abolitionists were aware that free black life and culture carried an implicit antislavery message—by their daily lives, blacks could dispel the proslavery myths of black dependency and inferiority. Given that understanding, black leaders were particularly concerned with the image that free blacks projected to white society and urged them to live by moral reform principles—temperance, hard work, education, and piety. A 4 March 1837 editorial by Samuel Cornish in the *Colored American* warned readers that their behavior was under close scrutiny by friend and foe alike, and that the general elevation of free blacks would provide an irrefutable argument for emancipation. He reminded free blacks of their obligation to the slaves—"On *our* conduct, in a great measure, *their* salvation depends." Payne, *African Methodist Episcopal Church*, 339; *Minutes of the Second Annual Convention* (1832), 35–36; CA, 24 June 1837 [2:0091].

Responsibility of Colored People in the Free States

Brethren, God hath laid on us great responsibility—we have to act an important part, an fill an important place, in the great cause of humanity and religion—and in the work of emancipation. On *our* conduct and exertions much, very much depends. It is our part, by virtue, prudence and industry, to uphold the hands of our devoted and sacrificing friends—let us not be found wanting. Should we prove unworthy [of] our few privileges, we shall furnish our enemies the strongest arguments, with which to oppose the emancipation of the slave, and to hinder the elevation of the free.

On the other hand, should we establish for ourselves a character—should we as a people, become more religious and moral, more industrious and prudent, than other classes of community, it will be impossible to keep us down. This we should do, we are more oppressed and proscribed than others, therefore we should be more circumspect and more diligent than others.

We live in an age of reform, and if we lay not hold of every means of reformation and improvement, we shall be left in the background, and the contrast between our condition and that of our white brethren will be widened—then let us as a whole people, avail ourselves of every measure calculated to cultivate the mind and elevate the morals. No oppressed COLORED AMERICAN, who wishes to occupy that elevation in society, which God has designed he should occupy, should be intemperate or even touch, as a beverage, intoxicating drinks, none should be idle or extravagant, none profane the Sabbath nor neglect the sanctuary of God, but all, all should be up and doing, should work while it is day. We owe it to ourselves and we owe it to the poor slaves, who are our brethren.

On *our* conduct, in a great measure, *their* salvation depends. Let us show that we are worthy to be freemen; it will be the strongest appeal to the judgement and conscience of the slave-holder and his abettors, that can be furnished; and it will be a sure means of our elevation in society, and to the possession of all our rights, as men and citizens. But brethren we are encouraged in these matters—we rejoice that there is a redeeming spirit abroad in the land: and merely suggest these things, to stir up your pure minds by way of remembrance.

Colored American (New York, N.Y.), 4 March 1837.

21.
Sarah L. Forten to Angelina E. Grimké
15 April 1837

When Quaker activists William Bassett and Angelina and Sarah Grimké sought to improve their understanding of white racism, they solicited personal testimony from black friends Sarah M. Douglass and Sarah L. Forten. Members of Philadelphia's black elite, both Douglass and Forten had suffered from racist behavior. Douglass's reply to Bassett told of the humiliation of enduring segregated seating in Quaker meetinghouses. In a poignant 15 April 1837 letter to Angelina Grimké, Forten described her thoughts on racial prejudice. She admitted to harboring "bitter feelings" toward whites as a result of the mistreatment she had suffered and blamed the colonization movement for exacerbating white racism.
Forten informed the Grimké sisters that even white reformers had failed to rid themselves of this "all-powerful prejudice" against blacks. Gilbert H. Barnes and Dwight L. Dumond, eds., *Letters of Theodore Dwight Weld, Angelina Grimké Weld, and Sarah Grimké, 1822–1844*, 2 vols. (Washington, D.C., 1934; reprint, Gloucester, Mass., 1965), 2:574, 829–32; Sterling, *We Are Your Sisters*, 130–31.

> Philadelphia, [Pennsylvania]
> April 15th, 1837

Esteemed Friend:[1]
I have to thank you for the interest which has led you to address a letter to me on a subject which claims so large a share of your attention—in making a reply to the question proposed by you I might truly advance the excuse of inability—but you well know how to compassionate the weakness of one who has written but little on the subject, and who has untill very lately lived and acted more for herself than for the good of others. I confess that I am wholly indebted to the Abolition cause for arousing me from apathy and indifference, shedding light into a mind which has been too long wrapt in selfish darkness.

In reply to your question—of the "effect of Prejudice" on myself, I must acknowledge that it has often embittered my feelings, particularly when I recollect that we are the innocent ~~cause~~ victims of it—for you are well aware that it originates from dislike to the color of the skin, as much as from the degradation of Slavery—I am peculiarly sensitive on this point, and consequently seek to avoid as much as possible from mingling with those who exist under its influence. I must also own that it has often engendered feelings of discontent and mortification in my breast when I saw that many were preferred before me, who by education—birth—or worldly circumstances were no better than myself—their sole claim to notice depending on the superior advantage of being <u>white</u>—but I am striving to live above such heart burnings—and will learn to "bear and forbear" believing that a spirit of forbearance under such evils is all that we as a people can well exert.

Colonization is—as you well know the offspring of Prejudice—it has doubtless had a baneful influence on our People. I despise the aim of that Institution most heartily—and have never yet met one man or woman of Color who thought better of it than I do. I believe, with all just and good persons—that it originated more immediately from prejudice than from philanthropy—the longing desire of a Separtion—induces this belief—and the Spirit of "This is not your Country" is made manifest by the many obstacles it throws in the way of their advancement—mentally and morally. No doubt but that there has always existed the same amount of prejudice in the minds of Americans towards the descendants of Africa—it wanted only the spirit of Colinization to call it into action. It can be seen in the exclusion of the Colored people from their Churches, or placing them in obscure corners. We see it; in their being debarred from a participation with others in acquiring any useful knowledge—public lectures are not usually free to the colored people—they may not avail themselves of the right to drink at the fountain of learning—or gain an insight into the arts and science of our favored land—all this—and more do they feel accutely—I only marvel that they are in possession of any knowledge at all, circumscribed as they have been by an all pervading—all-powerful prejudice. Even our professed friends have not yet rid themselves of it—to some of them it clings like a dark mantle obscuring their many virtues and choking up the avenues to higher and nobler sentiments. I recollect the words of one of the best and least prejudiced men in the Abolition ranks. Ah said he—"I can recall the time when in walking with a Colored brother, the darker the night, the better Abolitionist was I"—he does not say so now—but my friends how much of this leaven still lingers in the hearts of our white brethern and sisters is oftentimes made manifest to us—but when we recollect what great sacrifices to public sentiment they are called upon to make, we cannot wholly blame them. Many—very many are anxious to take up the cross—but how few are strong enough to bear it!! For our own family—we have to thank a kind Providence for placing us in a situation that has hitherto prevented us from falling under the weight of this evil—we feel it—but in a slight degree compared with many others. We are not much dependant upon the <u>tender mercies</u> of our enemies—always having resources within ourselves to which we can apply. We are not disturbed in our social relations—we never travel far from home and seldom go to public places unless quite sure that admission [is] free to all—therefore, we meet with none of these mortifications which might otherwise ensue.[2] I would recommend to my Colored friends to follow our example and they would be spared some very painful realities.

My Father[3] bids me tell you that White and Colored men have worked with him from his first commencement in business—one man (a White) has been with him nearly thirty seven years—very few of his hired men have been foreigners—nearly all are natives of this Country—the greatest harmony and good feeling exists between them—he has usually 1[6] or twenty journeymen, one half of whom are White—but I am not aware of any White Sailmaker who employs colored men. I think it should be reciprocal—do not you?

Do you know wether the Ladies have fixed on the day for holding their Convention? [Do] you not think it would be best to hold it the day before the mens meeting—for most of us would be desirous to be present at both meetings. Could you not suggest this plan? There will probably be a large delegation from our Society. My sisters purpose going but not as Delegates.[4] I presume there will be a sale of fancy Articles there, as we were requested to send some of our work. We are all quite busy preparing something pretty & useful. Several of our schools will have some specimens of work & penmanship to be sent. My Brother James[5] will mark those Handkerchiefs with pleasure but we hope you do not think there will be anything to pay for them—by no means—he generally marks those we sell for the society when he has leisure, and it is gratifying to him to do so.

Our noble Friend Burleigh[6] is spending his strength Daily in the good cause—he should be more careful of his health for it is yielding fast by reason of his much speaking. Shall I apologize for taking up such a large share of your valuable time as will be requisite to peruse this long letter but in writing to you I forget that I address you for the first time. We all feel deeply sensible of your labors of love for our people—and we trust that you may continue to receive strength from above to sustain you in your trials. My Parents and Sisters unite with me in affection to you and your excellent Sister.[7] Yours Affectionately,

Sarah L. Forten

P.S. I have seen by your letter to S. Douglass[8] that you were kind enough to make application for us to stay at Mr. Greens house.[9] We thank you for this attention to our wants. We expect to be able to avail ourselves of the hospitality of Rev. P. Williams[10]—while in New York.

Weld-Grimké Papers, William L. Clements Library, University of Michigan, Ann Arbor, Michigan. Published by permission.

1. Angelina E. Grimké (1805–1879) and her sister Sarah M. Grimké (1792–1873) were born and reared in a slaveholding family in Charleston. After moving

to Philadelphia in the 1820s, they were attracted to the antislavery cause. Their antislavery pamphlets aroused public interest and Angelina created a sensation in 1837 by speaking before audiences of both sexes. This drew public rebuke and thrust the Grimké sisters into the center of the debate over women's rights. Angelina married abolitionist Theodore Dwight Weld in 1838. Shortly thereafter, both sisters retired from the movement, devoting the remainder of their lives to schoolteaching and domestic duties. *NAW*, 2:97–99.

2. The wealth, intelligence, and social respectability of James Forten, Sr., sheltered the members of the Forten family from some of the effects of racial prejudice. Forten kept his family away from many public events and exhibitions and hired tutors to teach his children. Even so, family members could not escape the wrath of marauding whites or avoid discriminatory treatment in their business relations. Lewis, "The Fortens of Philadelphia," 92–95.

3. James Forten, Sr.

4. The first annual meeting of the Anti-Slavery Convention of American Women convened at the same time as its male counterpart, the American Anti-Slavery Society, in New York City during 9–12 May 1837. Fifteen of the seventy-one delegates, including black abolitionists Grace Douglass and Sarah M. Douglass, were delegates sent by the Philadelphia Female Anti-Slavery Society. The ASCAW was the earliest attempt to create a national organization of abolitionist women and reflected growing concern over the status of women in American society. It continued to meet through 1839, then disbanded because of women's growing role in the AASS. *Anti-Slavery Convention of American Women* (1837), 4; *Lib*, 2 June 1837; Blanche Glassman Hersh, *The Slavery of Sex: Feminist-Abolitionists in America* (Urbana, Ill., 1978), 16–17, 24–25.

5. James Forten, Jr.

6. Charles Calistus Burleigh (1810–1878) was born in Plainfield, Connecticut. An early advocate of Garrisonian abolitionism, he worked closely with Samuel Joseph May to defend Prudence Crandall's right to operate a school for black children. He was an antislavery lecturer and writer and editor of the *Pennsylvania Freeman*. His commitment to racial equality made him popular among blacks. Merrill and Ruchames, *Letters of William Lloyd Garrison*, 2:72.

7. Forten refers to Sarah M. Grimké.

8. Sarah M. Douglass.

9. William Green, Jr. (1796–1881), a prosperous merchant and evangelical reformer, resided at 7 Augustus Street in New York City. A close friend of Arthur and Lewis Tappan, he helped found the New York City Anti-Slavery Society and the American Anti-Slavery Society in 1833. Green served as the first treasurer of the AASS but left the movement in 1838 to devote more of his time to moral reform efforts. Merrill and Ruchames, *Letters of William Lloyd Garrison*, 5:425; Barnes and Dumond, *Letters of Theodore Dwight Weld*, 1:149.

10. Peter Williams, Jr. (ca. 1780–1840), a black Episcopal clergyman, was born in New Brunswick, New Jersey, to a black indentured servant mother and a slave father who had fought in the American Revolution. He grew up in New York City, obtained his early education at the African Free School, and later studied under Episcopal theologian John Henry Hobart. After worshipping with a group of black Episcopalians for seven years, Williams organized them in 1819 into St. Philip's Episcopal Church. He was ordained into the priesthood in 1826.

Under his guidance, St. Philip's congregation grew to more than 220 families by the 1830s.

As the pastor of one of New York City's largest black churches, Williams became a recognized leader of the local black community. His involvement with black civic organizations began in 1810 with the African Society for Mutual Relief. In 1827 he joined the effort to establish *Freedom's Journal*, the first black American newspaper. Williams worked throughout his adult life to improve and assist black education. He founded the African Dorcas Association (1828) and New York's Phoenix Society (1833) to aid black scholars and played a leading role in an unsuccessful attempt to establish a black manual labor college in New Haven. Williams personally extended financial assistance to promising black students, and his church provided space for both day and evening schools.

Williams firmly established his credentials as a leading black abolitionist by the 1830s. His *Oration on the Abolition of the Slave Trade* (1808) was one of the first black antislavery speeches to be published. Although he favored voluntary black settlement in Canada and Haiti and encouraged John B. Russwurm and Joseph R. Dailey to move to Liberia, he became an outspoken critic of the colonization movement by the late 1820s. Williams soon embraced the emerging immediatist movement, served on the board of managers of the nascent American Anti-Slavery Society from 1833 to 1836, and became one of three blacks elected in 1834 to the society's executive committee.

But Williams's ministry and antislavery activism were dealt a severe blow in the summer of 1834. Rumors that he had conducted an interracial marriage provoked a white mob to destroy his church and rectory. In the wake of this violence, Bishop Benjamin Onderdonk—his ecclesiastical superior—admonished him to publicly resign his offices in antislavery organizations. Despite strong feelings of obligation to the slave, Williams's concern for his congregation prompted him to acquiesce to the bishop's request. Yet he remained active in both black community affairs and the antislavery movement. His 1836 voyage to England received widespread attention in the antislavery press because of the discrimination he endured during his passage, and because the passport that he obtained affirmed black claims to American citizenship. One year before his death, Williams attended the AASS annual meeting and voiced support for political action against slavery. *DANB*, 660–61; *Lib*, 19, 26 July 1834; *CA*, 24 October 1840 [3:0675]; *NASS*, 10 April 1858; John Hewitt, "The Sacking of St. Philip's Church, New York," *HMPEC* 49:7–20 (March 1980).

22.
Debating the Causes of Racial Prejudice

"W." to Samuel E. Cornish
[June 1837]

Editorial by Samuel E. Cornish
8 July 1837

Most black abolitionists of the 1830s accepted moral reform as an
effective strategy for combating racial prejudice. They believed that
white bigotry stemmed from the condition of blacks and argued that as
blacks improved their social, intellectual, and economic situation, racism would gradually disappear. This rationale for moral reform appeared in a letter signed "W" in the 24 June 1837 issue of the *Colored
American*. Earlier correspondence by "W" indicates that he was a black
teacher in New York City, probably Ransom F. Wake. One week later,
the New York *Observer*, a Presbyterian journal, reprinted a portion of
the letter with critical remarks. Samuel Cornish, the editor the *Colored
American*, took exception to the *Observer*'s comments, particularly the
paper's suggestion that blacks were wholly responsible for their own circumstances in American society. In an 8 July editorial, Cornish argued
that the condition of black Americans was the result of racial prejudice,
not its cause. *WA*, 18 February 1837 [1:0947]; *CA*, 22 April, 28 October 1837 [2:0031, 0247].

Brother Cornish:

  Since my communication of 22d April, I have scarcely had time to
write, and much less to *think*. I intended, long ere this, to have given you
my views upon the subject of *elevating the colored people*; but better late
than never, if worth any thing.

  I remarked in a former communication, in speaking upon this subject,
that "universal emancipation would not do it—universal suffrage would
not do it—it is the work of one's self."[1] It is true that the *whites* have
much to do to remove obstacles, break down barriers, and raise the voice
of invitation and encouragement. Slavery must be *abolished* before the
colored man *can rise*; that work ought to be done immediately; the
obligation to do it at once is imperative; God has commanded it, and
therefore it *can be done*. But the *elevation* of the colored people, from the
nature of the case, must be gradual.

  Among an enlightened and civilized people, where moral and intellectual worth, instead of physical strength, raises men to stations of respectability and honor, it cannot be supposed that any thing can be done for

the colored people, which will at once raise them to an equality with the whites.

A man who couldn't write his name, and who didn't know even the letter "O" in the Alphabet, might as well attempt to vie with a Daniel Webster in the Halls of Congress,[2] or a George Thompson in London Exeter Hall.[3] They can be elevated no faster than they become intelligent, virtuous, enterprising, and religious.

As many of the colored people as can, and especially the young, must break away from their present degraded and degrading services, they must aspire to something higher than the office of a boot-black, a porter, a street scavenger, a hackman, a cook, and a drudge; these are all honest occupations, and if a man cannot qualify himself for any other service, he is justified in pursuing these; but can he ever expect to rise in society? The young have no excuse for continuing in ignorance—schools are being established, and facilities are being multiplied which puts it within the reach of every young man, *black* or *white*, to get an education.

The young men (I speak particularly to them) should at once set themselves about getting an education suited to the various professions and occupations which they design to pursue in after life. Let them prepare for the ministry, for the law, for teaching, for the editorial chair, for the counting house, for the mechanic's shop, and for the farm: let them be "workmen who shall not be ashamed" in whatever they undertake; and notwithstanding the embarrassments and discouragements with which they may meet in the road to eminence, the time *will come*—yes, our children will see the day, when the color of the skin will be no obstacle to the highest honor in the gift of the people.

The truth is, that the real ground of prejudice is not the *color of the skin*, but the *condition*. We have so long associated *color* with *condition*, that we have forgotten the fact, and have charged the offence to the wrong account.

The colored people should all understand this, that *the prejudice which exists against them arises not from the color of their skin, but from their condition*. Hence they may see that, just in proportion as they elevate their condition, prejudice will wear away. There is a strong prejudice existing against the whites, of a degraded character; it is of course against their condition, and they can never be elevated or respected, until they become sober, industrious, intelligent, and religious. Moral and intellectual attainments will raise *any* man from the gutter to the throne, and a man may attain to almost any degree of eminence, if he makes his mark, and then goes to work intelligently and wisely to accomplish it.

Yours, in the best of bonds,

W.

Colored American (New York, N.Y.), 24 June 1837.

We have more difficulty, in understanding and accounting for the course pursued by the *New York Observer*,[4] in reference to the Slavery and prejudice of our land, than in anything else.

We have always esteemed Mr. Morse as the colored man's friend, and as being opposed to American Slavery. But we have never been able to back this opinion, by any evidence from his writings. The pages of the *New York Observer*, for the last five years, have contained the most *flimsy sophistry, and the wildest ethics*, in palliation of the great moral sin of the nation.

Messrs. Morse and Tracy[5] have done more in the last five years, to allay the first awakenings of guilt, and to smother the first risings of repentance, both in church and state, than all other men in the nation combined. WHEREVER, and WHENEVER, they have seen the instrumentalities of repentance, and righteousness, doing their perfect work, they have stepped in, between conscience and its victim, and interposed their sophisticated opiates, lulling churches and communities to moral sleep—and destroying the most holy compunctions.

Had there not been a moral and metaphysical *threadbareness* in their efforts, and had not God been against them, they long since, would have ruined the cause of righteousness, and humanity.

Great responsibility rests on these two brothers. The eye of all intelligent Colored Americans is upon them. Let them beware, lest, haply, they find themselves fighting against God.

We have been led to these remarks, at the present time, from the *ingenious, unfair and injurious use*, made of the following remarks, in the 25th number of our paper, by the editors of the *Observer*.

We insert the paragraphs that they may speak for themselves.

PREJUDICE AGAINST COLOR

We are glad to see the following just remarks in the *Colored American*, published in this city.

"The truth is, that the real ground of prejudice is not the *color of the skin* but the *condition*. We have so long associated *color* with *condition*, that we have forgotten the fact, and have charged the offence to the wrong account.

The colored people should all understand this, that *the prejudice which exists against them arises not from the color of the skin, but from their condition*. Hence they may see that just in proportion as they elevate their condition, prejudice will wear away. There is a strong prejudice against whites of a degraded character; it is of course against their condition; and they can never be elevated or respected, until they become sober, industrious, intelligent and religious.

The 'condition' of colored people in this country is partly their own fault, in that they have not always made the best possible use of the advantages within their reach, and still more, perhaps, the fault of the whites, who have not done so much for them as they ought. Of late, we think both classes, to a considerable extent, are disposed to do better than formerly. Let the colored people take the work into their own hands, attend to their own moral and intellectual improvement, make it manifest to all men that they desire respect, and they will have it."—*Observer*[6]

REMARKS

The ideas contained in the extract from our paper, may with profit, be impressed on colored men—they are true in the abstract. But it is an OUTRAGE on truth and common sense, if not upon moral principle, to make the use of them which the *Observer* has done.

"The 'condition' of colored people in this country is partly their own fault." HORRIBLE! If the editors mean the *moral "condition"* we have nothing to say, but if they mean the social and political *"condition,"* and these are the subjects of controversy, we deny it in toto.

The colored people of these "United States" are the involuntary subjects of a social and political despotism, alike unrighteous and cruel; the guilt of which lies, WHOLLY at the white man's door. He is responsible for all its fatal consequences, and why should brother Morse and Tracy, preach any other doctrine?

Is the colored man degraded? Who degraded him? The white man—the church of Jesus Christ. Has she not organized all her institutions? does she not perform all her holy services? and arrange all her sanctuaries and seats, in obedience to the spirit of CASTE—PREJUDICE AGAINST COLOR? Does she not take from, and deny the colored man all the means of improvement, respectability, and education? Truly she does.

Where is the church in this city, in Boston, or anywhere else, which makes the same arrangements for her most respectable colored members, that she does for her white ones? or that throws open her institutions of learning to colored, as she does to white youth?

We know instances in which colored members in some of our white churches, are as wealthy, as moral, as intelligent, and as refined as any of the white members—as far removed from what is called the degraded mass, as any white man in the country, except in their complexion; and yet the ministers and people of the said churches, draw the strong cord of caste, and cherish the same paralysing, unholy prejudice against them, which they do against the most degraded. Still the editors of the *Observer* tell us, "The condition of the colored people in this country is partly their own fault!" Shame on these intelligent brethren, to wish, in this way, to lull the consciences of the church and the community, to sleep in their sin against God, and cruel inhumanity to his image.

Let us here tell the editors, that white men, however morally degraded, enjoy all the privileges and immunities of church and state. In the church we speak of them as non-professors. All the institutions of the land are thrown open to them. They are eligible to the highest honors in the gift of the people, all of which are denied colored men. And yet their "condition" PARTLY THEIR OWN FAULT!!!—*Alas.*

Is "judgement turned away backward?" Does "justice stand afar off?" Has "truth fallen in the street?"—and "is equity banished forever?"[7]

Colored American (New York, N.Y.), 8 July 1837.

1. "W." refers to two brief essays that were published in the *Colored American* in 1837. One on the need for racial equality appeared in the 22 April issue. An earlier piece on black elevation, which appeared in the 8 April issue, was the source of the above quote.

2. Daniel Webster (1782–1852) of Massachusetts was antebellum America's greatest orator and one of its most important political figures. An accomplished lawyer, Webster began a career in national politics in 1827 as a congressman, senator, secretary of state, Whig party leader, and frequent presidential hopeful. His 1820 attack on the slave trade and the Webster-Hayne debate marked him as the country's greatest exponent of liberty and union. But his defense of the 1850 Fugitive Slave Law diminished his stature in the North and made him anathema to liberal reformers. Maurice Baxter, *One and Inseparable: Daniel Webster and the Union* (Cambridge, Mass., 1984).

3. Exeter Hall in the Strand, London, opened in 1831. Its seating capacity of three thousand accommodated the annual May meetings of philanthropic and religious societies and made it a frequent site of antislavery rallies. Henry B. Wheatley, *London Past and Present*, 3 vols. (London, 1891), 3:26.

4. The *Observer*, an organ of the Presbyterian church, was founded in 1823 by Sidney E. and Richard C. Morse. It promoted a variety of causes, including colonization, temperance, peace, moral reform, black uplift, and personal liberty laws. Although it condemned slavery and Texas annexation, the conservative *Observer* held radical abolitionists responsible for strengthening support for slavery, which made the journal suspect among northern free blacks. Frank Luther Mott, *A History of American Magazines, 1741–1850* (Cambridge, Mass., 1938), 373; *NYO*, 29 April, 6 May, 1 July, 12 August 1837.

5. Cornish refers to Sidney E. Morse (1794–1871) and Joseph Tracy (1793–1874), Congregational clergymen who edited the New York *Observer* during the late 1830s. Both were opponents of the antislavery movement. Morse's polemical *Letter on American Slavery* (1847) denounced abolitionists as enemies of democracy. Tracy, a prominent figure in the American Colonization Society, rallied opposition to Garrison's anticolonizationist views and in 1834 called for the formation of the moderate American Union for the Relief and Improvement of the Colored Race. He authored several works on Liberian missionary activity and

helped found Liberia College. Merrill and Ruchames, *Letters of William Lloyd Garrison*, 1:577, 2:24–25, 381; Staudenraus, *African Colonization Movement*, 212, 240, 308.

6. These remarks originally appeared in the 1 July 1837 issue of the New York *Observer*.

7. Cornish paraphrases Isaiah 59:14 in a series of four questions.

23.
William Watkins to Samuel E. Cornish
8 June 1837

Black clergymen constituted much of the leadership of free black communities. Many became ministers through a religious conversion or calling experience and lacked formal education or theological training. More sophisticated black leaders such as William Watkins, Samuel Ringgold Ward, Lewis Woodson, Mary Ann Shadd Cary, and Daniel Payne, many of whom were members of the clergy, were troubled by the influence that these ministers wielded. They argued that the anti-intellectualism and emotional preaching style popular among black clergymen fostered racial stereotypes and hindered the development of effective leaders. In William Watkins's 8 June 1837 letter to Samuel Cornish, the first of three published in the *Colored American* on the subject, Watkins, himself a lay pastor, criticized "*the incompetency of the colored ministry*," calling it "a most serious obstacle to the improvement of our people." He acknowledged that slavery and racial prejudice barred blacks from theological training but deplored their lack of knowledge of the scriptures and their animosity toward ministerial education. Although Watkins directed his criticisms at the black clergy, he also addressed the question of how the black community defined leadership. Sernett, *Black Religion and American Evangelicalism*, 139–41; C. Peter Ripley et al. eds., *The Black Abolitionist Papers*, 2 vols. to date (Chapel Hill, N.C., 1985–), 2:228, 235–36n; *NSt*, 23 March 1849 [5:1009]; *CA*, 24 June, 1 July 1837, 13, 27 January 1838 [2:0088, 0095, 0097–98, 0347, 0367].

                                        Baltimore, [Maryland]
                                        June 8th, 1837

DEAR FRIEND:

I rejoice to see you once more in the editorial chair. The enterprise in which you are engaged is of no ordinary magnitude. It involves on your part numerous privations, corroding cares, and weighty responsibilities. If judiciously conducted, it should receive the unqualified approbation of every lover of his country—every philanthropist—and every Christian. Above all, it should receive—as it is doubtless entitled to—efficient patronage from those for whose elevation you anxiously labour; I mean from every colored American who has the means and the privilege to sustain you in your noble undertaking. If you should be so fortunate as to obtain the latter, be content if you have awarded you but a modicum of the former.

That moral reformer who indulges the hope that for his labours of

love in behalf of suffering humanity, he will receive universal and unqualified commendation, will be most grievously disappointed; more especially if he is the man he ought to be: a man of unbending integrity; a
man who suffers no consideration of paltry interest, or the loss of popu-
larity to sway him in the faithful and fearless discharge of his duty to his
God, his fellow creatures, and himself. Such a one is inevitably doomed
to suffer persecution; but if he be careful to know that it is "for righteousness' sake," he has abundant cause to rejoice, for so persecuted they
the prophets that were before him.

Being actuated by these views, I have long since come to the conclusion—that if we discover evils, we should point them out without undue
regard to the praise or censure of our fellow beings. Accordingly, I have
frequently felt it my duty, both in public and private, to bear an humble
testimony against those ministers of the gospel who have scorned to
recognise as brethren those "for whom Christ died"—their prescribed
colored countrymen. And now I feel called upon to come a little nearer
home.

There is, my dear Sir, for the most part, at the fountainhead of our
colored communities, a most serious obstacle to the improvement of our
people; an obstacle which cannot, for many years, be wholly obviated,
but which should, so far as it is practicable, be removed, and such incipi-
ent measures adopted as will check, for the future, the evil to which we
have alluded. But what is this evil? It is in unequivocal terms, *the
incompetency of the colored ministry, in general, to supply the intellectual wants of the colored population of the country.*

This proposition will not be denied by any intelligent observer—it is
far beyond refutation. And we state the fact not as the *fault* of the
colored clergy, but as their *misfortune.* Had many of them been blessed
with the same advantage for mental improvement as others, they would
today know no superiors. But it has been far otherwise with them; born,
for the most part, in slavery, they have been denied the rudiments of a
common English education; emancipated, they have found themselves in
circumstances not very favourable to intellectual culture; and having
unfortunately received erroneous impressions in regard to the true import of certain passages of scripture, as, for instance, "The letter killeth
but the Spirit giveth life"[1]—"Take no thought how or what ye shall
speak; for it shall be given you in that same hour what ye shall speak"[2]—
"For ye see your calling, brethren, how that not many wise men after
the flesh, not many mighty, not many noble, are called; but God hath
chosen the foolish things of the world to confound the things which are
mighty,&c.&c."[3]

Many of them, I say, having separated these passages from their true
and lawful connexion, and given them a construction, favourable to
their circumstances; a construction induced too frequently by a disposi-

tion adverse to study—and, moreover, finding that they have acquired the art of communicating *heat* without *light*—that they can get up a temporary excitement among a portion of their hearers, without bringing forth out of the treasury of the Lord's things new and old, they are not careful to "give attendance to reading," or to study to show themselves approved, workmen that need not be ashamed rightly dividing the word of truth.[4] The consequence is, many are very imperfect readers, and being such, are unable to "search the scriptures" satisfactorily to themselves, and incompetent to expound them to the edification of their intelligent hearers. Hence, being radically deficient in their knowledge of the scriptures, they not only sometimes fail to "preach the word," but too often with the confidence of inspiration, "speak the things which do not become sound doctrine."[5]

The writer knows that some of them are in the habit of publicly denouncing as unworthy of their stations such of their brother ministers as cannot assent to such a singularity of dress, as will identify with the venerable ancients, or with "the old time Christians."

Others publicly decry every thing like learning in the ministry, and by their inuendoes, it would seem, endeavour to inculcate the idea, that learning and piety are inimical to each other. Some publicly condemn those who consult commentators for information, as men who do not rely upon the great head of the church, but trust in an arm of flesh; and if a minister should be known to commit occasionally some of his thoughts to paper, or suffer to be seen in the pulpit, for the assistance of his memory, a small piece of paper, embracing the heads, &c. of his discourse, he is by *some* (for there are honourable exceptions), publicly held up to ridicule as an idolater, or one whose sole dependence is upon what they are pleased to call "a little paper god." The consequences of such public teachings upon both the uninformed and intelligent among us, may be the subjects of a future number.

A COLORED BALTIMOREAN

Colored American (New York, N.Y.), 17 June 1837.

1. Watkins quotes from 2 Corinthians 3:6 in defense of a contextual, rather than a literal, interpretation of the Bible.
2. Watkins paraphrases Matthew 10:19.
3. Watkins quotes from 1 Corinthians 1:26–27.
4. Watkins paraphrases 2 Timothy 2:15.
5. Watkins paraphrases Titus 2:1.

24.
"A Colored American" to Samuel E. Cornish
2 August 1837

The black press offered a unique forum for the discussion of racial issues ignored or judged too controversial by white reform journals. Letters and editorials in the *Colored American* debated black identity, charges of apathy and disunity in the black community, the origins and nature of racial prejudice, and other sensitive issues, including color prejudice among northern mulatto elites. White racism encouraged many mulattoes to draw distinctions based on shades of skin color. In older black communities, complexional differences often affected social standing, occupational status, and choice of marriage partners. One correspondent of the *Colored American* believed that light-skinned blacks were the "greatest persecutors and villifiers" of their darker brethren. A 2 August 1837 letter from a Boston reader, written under the pseudonym "A Colored American," explored the problem of prejudice among free blacks. Although the correspondent admitted that the subject was "a very delicate one," he insisted on raising the issue because it diverted black Americans from their common fight. He applauded the renaming of the *Colored American*, noting that the title symbolized the unity of all Americans of African descent. Cottrol, *The Afro-Yankees*, 136–39; Horton and Horton, *Black Bostonians*, 11, 21–23; *CA*, 15 September, 20 October 1838 [2:0591, 0621].

Boston, [Massachusetts]
August 2nd, 1837

Brother Cornish,

I have read with much interest and gratification, all the numbers of your small but invaluable journal, and am anxiously waiting to see it receiving such patronage as will warrant its enlargement. It has done much good in enlightening the minds of the community, upon a variety of subjects relative to the interests of the colored man, and the duties of all professors of religion. It has nobly and successfully made war upon that prejudice which the whites of this country generally have entertained against their colored brethren, and which has led them to practice the most sinful and cruel oppression. I hold prejudice of color as the most groundless of all prejudices, inasmuch as color is the least difference that exists between men.

Preference of color is a mere matter of taste, in which there is a great variety of opinions—some preferring one color, and some another, and it is impossible to say which, upon the whole, is preferable. Certain it is, that there are handsome and ugly persons of every color, and if it be allowed that the white has the advantage in youth, it cannot be denied that the black has the advantage in age, as it preserves longer a fresh and wholesome appearance, and gives a beauty and dignity to gray hairs, which connoisseurs in coloring have universally admired. Partial as are the whites of these parts to their own complexion, how often do we see them, preferring to have the statues of their great men, and even of their own relatives, sculptured in black marble, and how generally do they admire marble statues with black busts, and white hair. These are every-where considered as the most beautiful specimens of statuary. They have a grace and grandeur in them, which cannot be given to statues wholly white, and as to statues with white faces, and black, auburn, or brown hair, it is what no man of taste ever thinks of attempting. I make these remarks, merely to show that much can be said in favor of the black complexion, as well as the white, and that the prejudices which have been entertained here against men, because they are black, are ridiculous.

I repeat, that I have felt great pleasure in reading your powerful at-tacks upon these prejudices, and know that they have convinced many that they are foolish and sinful. But there is a species of prejudice of color, which you have hitherto passed by in silence, although it cannot have escaped your observation, and if report says true you have been assailed by it in your own person—I mean a prejudice of color existing among colored men on account of different shades of complexion. Brother Cornish, when I first looked at the title of your paper, I was so displeased that I was on the eve of laying it aside unread, and of resolv-ing not to be one of its subscribers. But after reflecting upon the various appellations by which our people are distinguished, I found none but what was more inappropriate and objectionable. The title "COLORED AMERICAN," is one of which no colored man need be ashamed and fully embraces all colored persons of this country. We should know our people only as colored people, whatever their hue—*however fair or, however dark*. It is a title of brotherhood, which should unite our hearts in the kindliest affections, as those who are alike subject to the same persecution and oppression, and have sprung from a common and deeply injured parentage. To class them as blacks and mulattoes, is to make the most unhappy divisions, to sow among them the seeds of discord and strife, jealousy and hatred, and to hinder the advancement of the whole. He who does this, whatever his complexion, or pretensions, is the com-mon enemy of the people of color, and ought to be banished from the society of all who desire their welfare. He is an incendiary of the very worst kind, who ought to be thrown into the fire which he kindles. What would you think of such conduct in a black man who has a mulatto wife?

Shall colored men strive to make colored men hate each other on account of color? Are they not all brethren, all afflicted, persecuted, proscribed? What privileges, what rights does one portion of them enjoy, that the other does not? What difference does law of custom make between them? What cause then can there be of division or jealousy among them?

They are our true friends, our only true friends, who are laboring for the entire abolition of the cord of caste, and shall there be cords of caste formed among ourselves! That colored man who is prejudiced against another colored man on account of color, should never complain of the prejudices of the whites.

I could mention some very lamentable instances of the effects of this prejudice in times past, and I cannot but rejoice, that at the present, our people generally have a more correct view of this matter. The enemies, who wished to strengthen the bonds of slavery, were very active in striving to excite it, but our people have become enlightened, they have discovered the baseness of their attempts, and pursued an opposite course. I consider it as one of the greatest proofs of their improvement, that they consider themselves now more than formerly as one people. Still there are always to be found some little, jealous minds, who seek to disseminate this prejudice among them—who would make one description of colored persons believe, that the other dislikes them, looks upon them with contempt, and would not have them placed on an equality with themselves!

These efforts must be discountenanced, or they will result in incalculable mischief. Men should be esteemed and treated, not according to their color, but their merits. In selecting them for places of trust and honor, color should never be thought of, but only their moral and intellectual qualifications.

I wish, brother Cornish, that you would occasionally employ your pen on this subject, or that it may engage the talents of some of your able correspondents. I am conscious that it is a very delicate one, but there is danger in letting it be passed in utter silence, and as a faithful sentinel, whenever you see this or any other enemy approaching, I hope you will not fail to sound the alarm. Yours faithfully,

A COLORED AMERICAN

Colored American (New York, N.Y.), 19 August 1837.

25.

Speech by William Whipper

Delivered at the First African Presbyterian Church
Philadelphia, Pennsylvania
16 August 1837

Many antebellum abolitionists advocated nonresistance. Arguing that divine law precluded the use of force, they opposed capital punishment, military service, lawsuits, the use of violence in self-defense, revolution (including slave revolt), and allegiance to governments. During the 1830s, most black abolitionists accepted pacifist principles and moral suasionist tactics. William Whipper, William P. Powell of New Bedford, Robert Roberts of Boston, and other black leaders argued that both war and slavery were based on a faith in the legitimacy of violence. Powell, one of the few black members of the New England Non-Resistance Society, "believed the principles of non-resistance heaven-born." Aging black abolitionist James Forten, Sr., presided over a 16 August 1837 session of the American Moral Reform Society, which convened at the First African Presbyterian Church in Philadelphia. William Whipper addressed the society, characterizing violence as unchristian and exposing the nexus between war and slavery. "The love of power," he claimed, "is one of the greatest of human infirmities, and with it comes the usurping influence of despotism, the mother of slavery." John Demos, "The Anti-Slavery Movement and the Problem of Violent Means," *NEQ* 37:501–26 (December 1964); Horton and Horton, *Black Bostonians*, 86–88, 103, 115; *NRB*, 5 October 1839; *Lib*, 18 April 1835; Porter, *Early Negro Writing*, 216–19, 224.

> *Resolved*, That the practice of non-resistance to physical aggression, is not only consistent with reason, but the surest method of obtaining a speedy triumph of the principles of universal peace.

Mr. President:

The above resolution presupposes, that if there were no God, to guide, and govern, the destinies of man on this planet, no Bible to light his path through the wilds of sin, darkness and error, and no religion to give him a glorious, and lasting consolation, while traversing the gloomy vale of despondency, and to light up his soul anew, with fresh influence from the fountain of Divine grace—that mankind might enjoy an exalted state of civilization, peace, and quietude, in their social, civil, and international relations, far beyond that which christians now enjoy, who profess to be guided, guarded and protected by the great Author of all good, and the doctrines of the Prince of Peace.

But, sir, while I am assuming the position, that the cause of peace amongst mankind, may be promoted without the scriptures, I would not, for a single moment, sanction the often made assertion, that the doctrines of the holy scriptures justify war—for they are in my humble opinion its greatest enemy. And I further believe, that as soon as they become fully understood, and practically adopted, wars and strifes will cease. I believe that every argument urged in favor of what is termed a "just and necessary war," or physical self-defence, is at enmity with the letter and spirit of the scriptures, and when they emanate from its professed advocates should be repudiated as inimical to the principles they profess, and a reproach to christianity itself. I have said this much in favor of the influence of the scriptures, on the subject of peace. It is neither my intention, nor my province, under the present resolution, to give proofs for my belief by quotations from holy writ. That portion of the discussion, I shall leave to the minister of the *altar* and the learned and biblical theologian. Though I may make a few incidental quotations hereafter, I shall now pass on for a few brief moments to the resolution under consideration.

The resolution asserts, that the practice of non-resistance to physical aggression is consistent with reason. A very distinguished man asserts "that reason is that distinguishing characteristic that separates man from the brute creation," and that this power was bestowed upon him by his Maker, that he might be capable of subduing all subordinate intelligences to his will. It is this power when exerted in its full force, that enables him to conquer the animals of the forest, and which makes him lord of creation. There is a right and a wrong method of reasoning. The latter is governed by our animal impulses and wicked desires, without regard to the end to be attained. The former fixes its premises in great fundamental and unalterable truths—surveys the magnitude of the objects, and the difficulties to be surmounted, and calls to its aid the resources of enlightened wisdom, as a landmark by which to conduct its operations.

It is self evident, that when the greatest difficulties surround us, we should summon our noblest powers. "Man is a being formed for action as well as contemplation." "For this purpose there are interwoven in his constitution, powers, instincts, feelings and affections, which have a reference to his improvement in virtue, and which excite him to promote the happiness of others." When we behold them by their noble sentiments, exhibiting sublime virtues and performing illustrious actions, we ascribe the same to the goodness of their hearts, their great reasoning powers and intellectual abilities. For were it not for these high human endowments, we should never behold men in seasons of calamity, displaying tranquility and fortitude in the midst of difficulties and dangers, enduring poverty and distress with a noble heroism, suffering injuries and affronts with patience and serenity, stifling resentment when they have it in their power to inflict vengeance, displaying kindness and generosity towards enemies and slanderers, submitting to pain and disgrace in order to promote the prosperity of their friends and relatives, or the great interests of the human race.

Such acts may be considered by persons of influence and rank as the offspring of pusillanimity, because they themselves are either incapable of conceiving the purity of the motives from which they emanate, or are too deeply engulfed in the ruder passions of our nature, to allow them to bestow a just tribute to the efforts of enlightened reason.

It is happy for us to contemplate, that every age, both of the pagan and the christian world, has been blessed, that they always have fastened their attention on the noblest gifts of our nature, and that they now still shine as ornaments to the human race, connecting the interests of one generation with that of another. Rollin, in speaking of Aristides the Just,[1] says "that an extraordinary greatness of soul made him superior to every passion. Interest, pleasure, ambition, resentment and jealousy were extinguished in him by the love of virtue and his country," and just in proportion as we cultivate our intellectual faculties, we shall strengthen our reasoning powers, and be prepared to become his imitators.

Our country and the world have become the munificent patron of many powerful, existing evils, that have spread their devastating influence over the best interests of the human race. One of which is the adopting of the savage custom of wars, and fighting as a redress for grievances, instead of some means more consistent with reason and civilization.

The great law of love forbids our doing aught against the interests of our fellow men. It is altogether inconsistent with reason and common sense for persons, when they deem themselves insulted by the vulgar aspersions of others, to maltreat their bodies for the acts of their minds. Yet how frequently do we observe those that are blest by nature and education (and if they would but aspire to acts that bear a parallel to their dignified minds, they would shine as illustrious stars in the created throngs), that degrade themselves by practising this barbarous custom, suited only to tyrants—because in this they may be justly ranked with the untutored savages or the animals of the forest, that are impelled only by instinct.

Another fatal error arises from the belief that the only method of maintaining peace is always to be ready for war. The spirit of war can never be destroyed by all the butcheries and persecutions the human mind can invent. The history of all the "bloody tragedies," by which the earth has been drenched by human blood, cannot be justified in the conclusion, for it is the spirit of conquest that feeds it. Thomas Dick, after collecting the general statistics of those that have perished by the all-desolating pestilence of war, says "it will not be overrating the de-struction of human life, if we affirm, that one tenth of the human race has been destroyed by the ravages of war"[2]—and if this estimate be admitted, it will follow that more than fourteen thousand millions of beings have been slaughtered in war since the beginning of the world, which is about eighteen times the number of its present inhabitants. This calculation proceeds from a geographical estimate, "that since the Mosaic creation one hundred and forty-five thousand millions of beings have existed."

But, sir, it is not my intention to give a dissertation on the subject of national wars, although it appropriately belongs to my subject. I decline it only for the simple reason that it would be inapplicable to us as a people, while we may be more profitably employed in inveighing against the same evil as practised by ourselves, although it exists under another form, but equally obnoxious to the principles of reason and christianity. My reason for referring to national wars, was to exhibit by plain demon-stration, that the war principle, which is the production of human pas-sions, has never been, nor can ever be, conquered by its own elements. Hence, if we ever expect the word of prophecy to be fulfilled—"when the swords shall be turned into plough-shares, and the spears into pruning-hooks, and that the nations of the earth shall learn war no more,"[3] we must seek the destruction of the principle that animates, quickens, and feeds it, by the elevation of another more powerful, and omnipotent, and preservative; or mankind will continue, age after age, to march on in their mad career, until the mighty current of time will doubtless sweep thousands of millions more into endless perdition, beyond the reach of mercy and the hope of future bliss. Thus the very bones, sinews, muscles, and immortal mind, that God, in his infinite mercy has bestowed on man, that he might work out his own glory and extend the principles of "Righteousness, justice, peace on earth, and good will to their fellow men," are constantly employed in protracting the period when the glori-ous millennium shall illumine our world, "and righteousness cover the earth as the water of the great deep."

Now let us solemnly ask ourselves, is it reasonable, that for the real or supposed injuries that have been inflicted on mankind from the begin-ning to the present day, that the attempted redress of the same should have cost so much misery, pain, sweat, blood, tears, and treasure? Most certainly not; since the very means used has measurably entailed the evil a thousand fold on coming generations. If man's superiority over the brute creation consists only in his reasoning powers and rationality of mind, his various methods of practising violence towards his fellow-creatures has in many cases placed him on a level with, and sometimes below, many species of the quadruped race. We search in vain amongst the animal race to find a parallel for their cruelties to each other on their own species, that is faithfully recorded in the history of wars and blood-shed, that have devoured empires, desolated kingdoms, overthrown governments, and well nigh aimed at the total annihilation of the human race. There are many species of animals that are so amiable in their disposition to each other, that they might well be considered an eminent pattern for mankind in their present rude condition. The sheep, the ox, the horse, and many other animals exist in a state of comparative quietude, both among themselves, and the other races of animals when compared with man. And if it were possible for them to know the will of their Author, and enjoy that communion with the Creator of all worlds, all men and all animals, they might justly be entitled to a distinction above all other species of creation, that had made greater departures from the will of the divine government.

It is evidently necessary that man should at all times bear in mind his origin and his end. That it is not because he was born a ruler, and superior to all other orders of creation, that he continually reigns above them—it is because he has made a right use of the powers that God has given him of rising in the scale of existence. The rich bequest of Heaven to man was a natural body, a reasonable soul, and an immortal mind. With these he is rendered capable, through the wisdom of Providence, of ascending to the throne of angels, or descending to the abyss of devils. Hence there seems to be a relation between man and the animal creation that subsists, neither in their origin nor their end, but satisfactorily exhibits that man may exist in a state of purity, as far *superior* to theirs as future happiness is to this world, and as far *inferior* as we are distant from future misery.

There is scarcely a single fact more worthy of indelible record than the utter inefficiency of human punishments to cure human evils. The history of wars exhibits a hopeless, as well as a fatal, lesson to all such enterprises. All the associated powers of human governments have been placed in requisition to quell and subdue the spirit of passion, without improving the condition of the human family. Human bodies have been lacerated with whips and scourges—prisons and penitentiaries have been erected for the immolation of human victims—the gibbet and halter have performed their office—while the increase of crime has kept pace with the genius of punishment, and the whole march of mind seems to have been employed in evading penal enactments and inventing new methods of destroying the blessings of the social state, not recognised by human codes.

If mankind ever expect to enjoy a state of peace and quietude, they must at all times be ready to sacrifice on the altar of principle, the rude passions that animate them. This they can only perform by exerting their reasoning powers. If there be those that desire to overlook the offences of others, and rise above those inflictions that are the offspring of passion, they must seek for protection in something *higher* than human power. They must place their faith in Him who is able to protect them from danger, or they will soon fall prey to the wicked artifices of their wicked enemies.

Human passion is the hallucination of a distempered mind. It renders the subject of it like a ship upon the ocean, without ballast or cargo, always in danger of being wrecked by every breeze. Phrenologically speaking, a mind that is subject to the fluctuating whims of passion, is without the organ of order,[4] "which is nature's first law." Our reasoning powers ought to be the helm that should guide us through the shoals and quicksands of life.

I am aware that there are those who consider non-resistance wholly impracticable. But I trust that but few such can be found that have adopted the injunction of the Messiah for their guide and future hope, for he commands us to "love our enemies, bless them that curse you, pray for them that despitefully use you, and persecute you."[5] These words were peculiarly applicable at the period they were uttered, and had a direct reference to the wars and strifes that then convulsed the world, and they are equally applicable at this moment. If the christian church had at her beginning made herself the enemy of war, the evil would doubtless have been abolished throughout christendom. The christians of the present day do not seem to regard the principles of peace as binding, or they are unwilling to become subject to Divine government. Human governments then, as well as now, were too feeble to stay the ravages of passion and crime, and hence there was an evident necessity for the imperious command, "Whomsoever shall smite thee on thy right cheek, turn unto him the other also."[6]

And now, Mr. President, I rest my argument on the ground, that whatever is *scriptural* is *right* and, that whatever is right, is reasonable, and from this invulnerable position I mean not to stray, for the sake of any expediency whatever. The doctrine evidently taught by the scriptural quotation, evidently instructs us that resistance to physical aggression is wholly unnecessary as well as unrighteous, and subjects the transgressor to the penalty due from a wilful departure from the moral and Divine law. Therefore every act of disobedience to the commands of christian duty, in relation to our fellow men, may fairly be deemed unreasonable, as it is at enmity with our true interests and the welfare of human society. We are further instructed to turn away from the evil *one*, rather than waste our strength, influence, and passions in a conflict that must in the end prove very injurious to both.

But someone perhaps is ready to raise an objection against this method of brooking the insults of others, and believes it right to refer to the maxim "that self defence is the first law of nature." I will readily agree that it is the unbounded duty of every individual to defend himself against both the vulgar and false aspersions of a wicked world. But then I contend that his weapons should be his reasoning powers. That since a kind Providence has bestowed on him the power of speech, and the ability to reason, he degrades his Creator by engulfing himself in the turmoils of passion and physical conflict, a mode of warfare practised by barbarous tribes in their native forests, and suited only to those animals that are alone endowed with the powers of instinct. Nor is it possible to suppose that men can pursue such a course, without first parting with their reason. We often see men, while under the reigning influence of passion, as fit subjects for the lunatic asylum, as any that are confined in the lunatic asylum on account of insanity. In every possible and impartial view we take of the subject, we find that physical conflict militates against the interest of the parties in collision. If I, in conflict with mine enemy, overcome him with my superior physical powers, or my skill in battle, I neither wholly subdue him, or convince him of the justice of my cause. His spirit becomes still more enraged, and he will seek retaliation and conquest on some future occasion that may seem to him more propitious. If I intimidate him I have made him a slave, while I reign a despot; and our relation will continue unnatural, as well as dangerous to each other, until our friendship has become fully restored. And what has been gained by this barbarous method of warfare, when both parties become losers thereby? Yet this single case illustrates the value of all personal conflicts.

But let us pursue this subject in a more dignified view, I mean as it respects the moral and Divine government. Is it possible that any christian man or woman, that will flog and maltreat their fellow beings, can be in *earnest* when they, with apparent devotion, ask their heavenly Father to "forgive their trespass as they forgive others?" Surely they must be asking God to punish them—or when they say "lead us not into temptation, but deliver us from evil,"[7] do they mean that they should run headlong into both, with all their infuriated madness? Certainly not. Who would not be more willing to apply to them insincerity of motive, and that they knew not what they were doing, rather than suppose that intelligent minds would be capable of such gross inconsistency. Would it not prove infinitely better in times of trials and difficulties, to leave the tempter and temptation behind, and pursue our course onward? But says the objector, there will be no safety nor security in this method, from the insults of the vulgar and the brutal attacks of the assassin. I am inclined to believe to the contrary, and will be borne out in that belief by the evidence of those that have pursued this christian course of conduct.

A writer under the signature of Philopacificus, while "taking a solemn view of the custom of war," says, "There are two sets of professed christians in this country, which, as sects, are peculiar in their opinions respecting the lawfulness of war, and the right of repelling injury by violence." These are the Quakers and Shakers. They are remarkably pacific. Now we ask, does it appear from experience, that their forbearing spirit brings on them a greater portion of injury and insults than what is experienced by people of other sects? Is not the reverse of this true in fact? There may indeed be some such instances of gross depravity as a person taking advantage of their pacific character, to do them an injury with the hope of impunity. But in general it is believed their pacific principles and spirit command the esteem, even of the vicious, and operate as a shield from insult and abuse.

The question may be brought home to every society. How seldom do children of a mild and forbearing temper experience insults or injury, compared with the waspish, who will sting if they are touched? The same inquiry may be made in respect to persons of those opposite descriptions of every age, and in every situation of life, and the result will prove favorable to the point in question.

When William Penn took the government of Pennsylvania, he distinctly avowed to the Indians his forbearing and pacific principles, and his benevolent wishes for uninterrupted peace with them. On these principles the government was administered while it remained in the hands of the Quakers.[8] This was an illustrious example of government on religious principles, worthy of imitation by all the nations of the earth.

I am happy to state that there are various incidents related by travellers, both among the native Africans and Indians, where lives have been saved by the presentation of a pacific attitude, when they would have otherwise fallen prey to savage barbarity.

It has been my purpose to exhibit reason as a great safeguard, at all times capable of dethroning passion and alleviating our condition in periods of the greatest trouble and difficulty, and of being a powerful handmaid in achieving a triumph of the principles of universal peace. I have also thus far treated the subject as a grand fundamental principle, universal in its nature, and binding alike on every member of the human family. But if there be a single class of people in these United States on which these duties are more imperative and binding than another, that class is the colored population of this country, both free and enslaved. Situated as we are, among a people that recognize the lawfulness of slavery, and more of whom sympathize with the oppressor than the oppressed, it requires us to pursue our course calmly onward, with much self-denial, patience and perseverance.

We must be prepared at all times to meet the scoffs and scorns of the vulgar and indecent—the contemptible frowns of haughty tyrants and the blighting mildew of a popular and sinful prejudice. If amidst these difficulties we can but possess our souls in patience, we shall finally triumph over our enemies. But among the various duties that devolve on us, not the least is that which relates to ourselves. We must learn on all occasions to rebuke the spirit of violence, both in sentiment and practice. God has said, "vengeance is mine, and I will repay it."[9] The laws of the land guarantee the protection of our persons from personal violence, and whoever for any cause inflicts a single blow on a fellow being, violates the laws of God and of his country, and has no just claim to being regarded as a christian or a good citizen.

As a people we have suffered much from the pestilential influence of mob violence, that has spread its devastating influence over our country.[10] And it is to me no matter of astonishment that they continue to exist. They do but put in practice a common everyday theory that pervades every neighborhood, and almost every family, viz: That it is right, under certain circumstances, to violate all law, both civil and national, and abuse, kick and cuff your fellow man, when they deem that he has offended or insulted the community in which he resides.

Whenever the passions of individuals rise above all laws, human and divine, then they are in the first stages of anarchy, and then every act prosecuted under the influence of this spirit necessarily extends itself beyond the boundary of our laws. The act of the multitude is carried out on the principle of combination, which is the grand lever by which machinery as well as man is impelled in this fruitful age. There is no difference in principle between the acts of a few individuals, and those of a thousand, while actuated by the spirit of passion, dethroning reason, the laws of our country and the liberty of man. Hence every individual that either aids or abets an act of personal violence towards the humblest individual is guilty of sustaining the detestible practice of mobocratic violence. Yet such is the general spirit that pervades our common country, and receives its sanction from places of high honor and trust, that it is patriotism to disregard the laws. It is but reasonable to suppose that individuals, guided by like views and motives, will on some occasions concentrate their power, and carry on their operations on a large scale. Unless the hearts and reasoning powers of man become improved, it is impossible for the most sagacious mind to augur the consequences. The spirit of passion has become so implanted in human bosoms, that the laws of our country give countenance to the same, by exhibiting lenity for those who are under its influence.

This is doubtless a great error in legislation, because it not only presupposes the irrationality of man, but gives him a plea of innocence in behalf of his idiotism. The only sure method of conquering these evils is to commend a reform in ourselves, and then the spirit of passion will soon be destroyed in individuals, communities, and governments, and then the ground-work will be fully laid for a speedy triumph of the principles of universal peace.

The love of power is one of the greatest of human infirmities, and with it comes the usurping influence of despotism, the mother of slavery.

Show me any country or people where despotism reigns triumphant, and I will exhibit to your view the spirit of slavery, whether the same be incorporated in their government or not. It is this principle of despotism (which is nothing but an exercise of the corrupt passions) that sends forth its poignant influence over professedly civilized nations, as well as the more barbarous tribes. It is alike in its effects on human interests, whether it emanates from the Czar of Russia, the mild influence of Great Britain, the hotspurs of the South,[11] or the genial clime of Pennsylvania—from the white, the red or the black man—whether he be of European or African descent, or the native Indian that resides in the wilds of the West. The combined action of all these are at war with the principles of peace and the liberty of the world, and retard the period when righteousness shall cover the earth like the waters of the great deep. How different is the exercise of this love of power, when exercised by men or enforced by human governments, to the exercise of Him who holds all power over the heavens, earth and seas, and all that in them is. With God all is order, with man all confusion. The planets perform their annual rotations, the tides ebb and flow, the seas obey his command, the whole government of universal worlds is sustained by his wisdom and power, each unvaryingly performing the course marked out by their great Author, because they are impelled by his love. But with man, governments are impelled by the law of force: hence despotism becomes an ingredient in all human governments.

The power of reason is the noblest gift of heaven to man, because it assimilates man to his Maker, and were he to improve his mind by cultivating his reasoning powers, his acts of life would bear the impress of the Deity indelibly stamped upon them. Governments would be mild in their operation, and the principles of universal peace would govern every heart, and be implanted in every mind. Wars, fighting and strifes would cease; there would be a signal triumph of truth over error; the principles of peace, justice, righteousness and universal love would guide and direct mankind onward in that sublime path marked out by the Great Prince of Peace.

And now my friends, let us cease to be guided by the influence of a wild and beguiling passion—the wicked and foolish fantasies of pride, folly and lustful ambition—the alluring and detestable examples of despotism and governments—the sickly sensibility of those who from false notions of honor, attempt to promote the ends of justice, by placing "righteousness under their feet," and are at all times ready to imbue their hands in a fellow creature's blood, for the purpose of satisfying their voracious appetites for crime, murder and revenge. I say from them let us turn away, for a terrible retaliation must shortly await them, even in this life. The moral powers of this nation and the world is fast wakening from the sleep of ages, and wielding a swift besom that will sweep from the face of the earth error and iniquity with the power of a whirlwind. But a few years ago and duelling was considered necessary to personal honor, and the professional christian or the most upright citizen might barter away the lives and happiness of a nation with his guilty traffic in ardent spirits, with impunity. But now a regenerated public sentiment not only repudiates their conduct, but consigns them with "body and soul murderers." Though the right to be free has been deemed inalienable by this nation, from a period antecedent to the declaration of American Independence, yet a mental fog hovered over this nation on the subject of slavery that had well nigh sealed her doom, were it not that in the Providence of God a few noble spirits arose in the might of moral power to her rescue. They girded on the power of truth for their shield, and the principles of peace for their buckler, and thus boldly pierced through the incrustations of a false and fatal philosophy, and from the *incision* sprang forth the light of glorious liberty, disseminating its delectable rays over the dark chasms of slavery, and lighting up the vision of a ruined world. And the effect has been to awaken the nation to her duty with regard to the rights of man—to render slaveholders despicable and guilty of robbery and murder—and in many places, those that profess christianity have been unchurched, denied the privilege of christian fellowship. And the same moral power is now awakening in the cause of peace, and will bring disgrace and dishonor on all who engage in wars and fighting.

The period is fast approaching when the church, as at present constituted, must undergo one of the severest contests she has met with since her foundation, because in so many cases she has refused to sustain her own principles. The moral warfare that is now commenced will not cease if the issue should be a dissolution of both church and state. The time has already come when those [who] believe that intemperance, slavery, war, and fighting is sinful, and it will soon arrive when those who practice either their rights to enjoy christian fellowship will be questioned.

And now Mr. President, I shall give a few practical illustrations, and then I shall have done. It appears by history that there have been many faithful advocates of peace since the apostolic age, but none have ever given a more powerful impetus to the cause of peace than the modern abolitionists. They have been beaten and stoned, mobbed and persecuted from city to city,[12] and never returned evil for evil, but submissively, as a sheep brought before the shearer, have they endured scoffings and scourges for the cause's sake, while they prayed for their persecutors. And how miraculously they have been preserved in the midst of a thousand dangers from without and within. Up to the present moment not the life of a single individual has been sacrificed on the altar of popular fury. Had they set out in this glorious undertaking of freeing 2,500,000 human beings, with the war-cry of "liberty or death," they would have been long since demolished, or a civil war would have ensued; thus would have dyed the national soil with human blood. And now let me ask you, was not their method of attacking the system of human slavery the most reasonable? And would not their policy have been correct, even if we were to lay aside their christian motives? Their weapons were reason and moral truth, and on them they desired to stand or fall—and so it will be in all causes that are sustained from just and christian principles, they will ultimately triumph. Now let us suppose for a single moment what would have been our case if they had started on the principle that "resistance to tyrants is obedience to God?"[13]—what would have been our condition, together with that of the slave population? Why, we should have doubtless perished by the sword, or been praying for the destruction of our enemies, and probably engaged in the same bloody warfare.

And now we are indebted to the modern abolitionists more than to any other class of men for the instructions we have received from the dissemination of their principles, or we would not at this moment be associated here to advocate the cause of moral reform—of temperance, education, peace and universal liberty. Therefore let us, like them, obliterate from our minds the idea of revenge, and from our hearts all wicked intentions towards each other and the world, and we shall be able through the blessing of almighty God, to do much to establish the principles of universal peace. Let us not think the world has no regard for our efforts—they are looking forward to them with intense interest and anxiety. The enemies of the abolitionists are exhibiting a regard for the power of their principles that they are unwilling to acknowledge, although it is everywhere known over the country that abolitionists "will not fight," yet they distrust their own strength so much that they frequently muster a whole neighborhood of from 50 to 300 men, with sticks, stones, rotten eggs and bowie knives, to mob and beat a single individual, probably in his "teens," whose heart's law is non-resistance. There is another way in which they do us honor—they admit the right of all people to fight for their liberty, but colored people and abolitionists—plainly inferring that they are too good for the performance of such unchristian acts—and lastly, while we endeavor to control our own passions and keep them in subjection, let us be mindful of the weakness of others; and for acts of wickedness committed against us, let us reciprocate in the spirit of kindness. If they continue their injustice towards us, let us always decide that their reasoning powers are defective, and that it is with men as the laws of mechanics—large bodies move slowly, while smaller ones are easily propelled with swift velocity. In every case of passion that presents itself, the subject is one of pity rather than derision, and in his cooler moments let us earnestly advise him to improve his understanding, by cultivating his intellectual powers, and thus exhibit his close alliance with God, who is the author of all wisdom, peace, justice, righteousness and truth. And in conclusion, let it always be our aim to live in a spirit of unity with each other, supporting one common cause, by spreading our influence for the good of mankind, with the hope that the period will ultimately arrive when the principles of universal peace will triumph throughout the world.

Colored American (New York, N.Y.), 9, 16, 23, 30 September 1837.

1. Whipper quotes from *The Ancient History of the Egyptians, Carthaginians, Assyrians, Babylonians, Medes and Persians, Macedonians and Grecians* (1730–38), a thirteen-volume work by French historian Charles Rollin. In book 6 Rollin discusses Aristides the Just, a political leader in ancient Athens, who was ostracized for his opposition to the construction of two hundred warships.

2. Thomas Dick (1774–1857), a Scottish scientific writer and moral philosopher, reached a broad audience in Britain and the United States. Many of Dick's writings discuss warfare, but Whipper refers to *An Essay on the Sin and Evils of Covetousness* (1836), his most thorough examination of the subject. *DNB*, 5:923.

3. Whipper paraphrases Isaiah 2:4.

4. Phrenology, a nineteenth-century pseudoscience, originated in Europe and was popularized in the United States by Orson and Lorenzo Fowler during the 1830s and 1840s. It purported to understand the functioning of the human mind by charting the shape of the cranium and subdividing it into thirty-seven "faculties," which corresponded to personality traits. Each "faculty" was represented in an "organ" or position on the head, the size of which indicated the relative strength of the trait. Ronald G. Walters, *American Reformers, 1815–1860* (New York, N.Y., 1978), 156–63.

5. Whipper quotes from Luke 6:27–28.

6. Whipper quotes from Matthew 5:39, which was interpreted by many reformers as a divine command to practice nonresistance.

7. Whipper quotes a petition from Matthew 6:9–13, which is commonly called the Lord's Prayer.

8. The Quaker government of colonial Pennsylvania maintained exceptionally good relations with the indigenous Indian tribes. William Penn, the colony's founder, honored treaties signed with the Indians, respected Indian leaders, and even learned the Delaware language. Pennsylvania's peaceful Indian-white relations lasted more than fifty years and became a major theme in early American art.

9. Whipper quotes from Romans 12:19.

10. Widespread rioting and other forms of collective violence plagued American cities during the antebellum period. Between 1834 and 1860, thirty-five major riots occurred in Baltimore, Philadelphia, New York City, and Boston alone. Few American cities escaped the ravages of the mob; racial, ethnic, and religious clashes accounted for most of the violence, but gang warfare also proved endemic to antebellum urban life. Rioting—especially when directed at outcasts like blacks, abolitionists, and Catholics or other immigrants—was toler-

ated as a legitimate expression of social discontent. David Grimsted, "Rioting in Its Jacksonian Setting," *AHR* 77:362–64, 374–76 (April 1972); Hugh Davis Graham and Ted Robert Gurr, *Violence in America: Historical and Comparative Perspectives* (New York, N.Y., 1969), 50–51.

11. The term "hotspur" refers to a rash, impetuous, hotheaded man. Whipper uses it here to call attention to the cultural importance of militarism and violence in the antebellum South.

12. Between 1833 and 1838, the antislavery press recorded over 160 incidents of antiabolitionist mob violence. These attacks occurred throughout the North and were directed at individual abolitionists, antislavery meetings and meeting places, and urban blacks. Most appear to have been carefully planned and orchestrated by community leaders. Antiabolitionists were motivated by several fears. Most believed that antislavery feminism and racial egalitarianism threatened traditional values. Some worried that state and national antislavery societies jeopardized the social control by local elites. Others worried that a "foreign element" dominated the antislavery movement. Richards, *"Gentlemen of Property and Standing."*

13. Whipper quotes a popularized version of the motto on Thomas Jefferson's seal: "Rebellion to tyrants is obedience to God."

26.
Memorial by Charles W. Gardner
and Frederick A. Hinton
6 January 1838

Blacks viewed the struggle for equal voting rights as an important component of their abolitionist work. Although most states enfranchised all white men during the 1830s, blacks lost ground. The Pennsylvania Reform Convention of 1837–38, called to revise the state's constitution, debated black disfranchisement. While the convention met, Philadelphia blacks mobilized. Members of a June 1837 meeting at the Bethel African Methodist Episcopal Church selected Charles W. Gardner and Frederick A. Hinton to draft a petition defending black suffrage. When James C. Biddle, a Philadelphia Whig, read it before the convention on 6 January 1838, delegates reacted with derision, refused to print the petition, and expelled three black observers from the gallery. One month later, the convention adopted a revised constitution that limited the vote to white males. Although Pennsylvania voters ratified the document in October, blacks continued to appeal to state officials and even to Congress. By 1851 they had sent fifty-one suffrage petitions to the state legislature. Their activity sparked similar militancy elsewhere, especially in New York state, where black leaders organized a lengthy campaign to expand the franchise. David McBride, "Black Protest against Racial Politics: Gardner, Hinton, and Their Memorial of 1838," *PH* 46:149–62 (April 1979); Edward J. Price, Jr., "Let the Law Be Just: The Quest for Racial Equality in Pennsylvania, 1780–1915" (Ph.D. diss., Pennsylvania State University, 1973), 100–127; Litwack, *North of Slavery*, 84–86; *CA*, 27 January, 16 June 1838 [2:0364, 0494].

Memorial
To the Hon. Delegates of the People of Pennsylvania, in Convention at Philadelphia assembled.[1]

Your memorialists, Citizens of Pennsylvania, approach your honorable body with solicitude, and respect. We beg leave to state, that we have been informed, that a change has been proposed to be made in the constitution of this commonwealth; taking away from your memorialists, and from that portion of the citizens of this State, with whom we are identified a right, the exercise of which, they have enjoyed for forty-seven years. We have learned, that it is proposed to regulate the right of voting, by distinctions of color; against such a change, your memorialists beg leave humbly, but respectfully to remonstrate.

1st: It is making a distinction among men unknown in the law of God, and disowned by him—All arrangements of <u>His</u> Government, in respect to men, are without distinction of color.

2d: It would be a violation of the immutable principles of right, and justice, written on the hearts of all men; and at war with the living, and revolution principle, "that all men are created equal."

3d: It has been a well earned preeminence of Pennsylvania, to stand in the front rank of the assertors of Human liberty—to keep her garments unspoted—her Escutcheon pure. "It is not for us to inquire," is the solemn and expressive declaration of our act of Legislature, of this commonwealth, passed more than fifty years ago. "It is not for us to inquire," why mankind are distinguished by difference of feature, or complexion; it is sufficient for us to know, that <u>all</u> are the work of an *Almighty* hand;[2] and now after the lapse of so long a time, when the index has moved forward another half century on the <u>dial</u> of human liberty, is it to be written that Pennsylvania retrogrades? and that the shadow of her example goes backward. Will <u>she</u> whose bosom has been ever open, a refuge for all men, of all nations, will she <u>now</u> turn to crush her own children—to degrade her own home born freeman? We trust not.

4th: There is no reason for the change. There has been no general expression of the people demanding it; nothing has occured to render it necessary. Have the rights we now possess, been abused? The domestic History of Pennsylvania answers the question in the negative. We are a people "more sinned against than sinning."[3] We have been the innocent sufferers of wrong; our persons, and houses have been assailed; our families compelled to fly for shelter, and protection; but no where on the page of History does it appear that insurrection, or similar violence, originated with us. Why then should we, without crime or misdoing on our part, be deprived of our rights, and disowned as citizens.

5th: In determining how many representatives this commonwealth is entitled to in the Congress of the United States, the whole free male population of the State, without distinction of color, is taken as a basis upon which to graduate the number. The colored people therefore in common with other citizens, are represented in Congress. But <u>how</u> can they be represented if they are not allowed to vote for representatives?

6th: The distinction is unwise, and impolitic. It is fostering antagonist[ic] interests, in the bosom of society; and arraying one class of the community, against another. The Government of this commonwealth, is a government of the people, upheld by public sentiment—to be safe, the people should be one in feeling, and interest. We submit therefore, whether by creating this distinction, you would not compel 40,000 of the people, and their posterity, forever to view the Government as their Enemy, and to regard its institutions, with distrust, and jealousy.

7th: Is it alleged that we do not share our equal part of the burdens of Government? To this we reply, that we do, and always have paid taxes according to our property as other citizens. If however, the principle proposed, of limiting the right of voting, to the mere accident of complexion, be adopted, in the present state of things, it is virtually avowing the doctrine of "taxation without representation."

8th: Is it alleged that we do not serve in the militia? On this head we ask, Have we ever refused to do it; when called on by our Country in an hour of danger, were we ever found wanting? Did not many of our number serve in the war of the revolution—and when our state constitution was formed, were they not incorporated as citizens in the body politic? Some of these are yet living; and now, are these to be torn from the citizenship of the commonwealth and disowned? And in the late war colored men helped achieve our most splendid victories. Witness Champlain, and New Orleans. When on the Banks of the Mobile, says General Jackson, in his proclamation to the free people of color, in 1814. "I called you take up arms, inviting you to partake the perils, and glory, of your white fellow citizens, I expected much from you; for I was not ignorant that you possessed qualities most formidable to an invading foe. I knew with what fortitude you could endure hunger, and thirst, and all the fatigues of a campaign. I knew well how you loved your native country, and that as well as ourselves, you had to defend what man holds most dear—parents, relatives, wife, children, and property. You have done more than I expected; I found among you a noble enthusiasm, which leads to the performance of great things."[4]

9th: One of the difficulties which most embarrasses the condition of the people of color, is the existing, and popular prejudice against the complexion, which it has pleased God to give them. It is this which meets us everywhere, and throws stupendous obstacles in our way; which excludes so many from schools, and from opportunities of learning useful trades. Your memorialists therefore submit, whether in the exercise of that paternal regard, which your honorable body, we are persuaded cherishes for the welfare of the humblest citizens, you can consent to give to a prejudice, of such wicked, and malignant influence, the additional strength it will derive from the influence of your high example, and sanction.

10th: It is often alleged, that we are degraded; on this subject we would say, unhappily, we have been much misrepresented, and the facts necessary to just appreciation of the matter, little known. We protest against being judged of, as a people by those degraded specimens of humanity; some of which are to be found in every community, and among every people; and we claim only the same candid examination into our condition, and the same allowances to be made for circumstances, which are extended to other classes in the humble walks of life.

Further, we unhesitatingly affirm, that under the influence of the spirit of the age—the preaching of the Gospel—the establishing of schools, and Sabbath Schools—of literary and benevolent Societies—the circulation of periodicals, and an increasing conviction of the advantages of mechanic pursuits, and agricultural occupations, the colored people are a rising, a rapidly rising people, both in morals, in intelligence, in respectibility, in the comforts, and the refinements of life; and many of them in wealth and that advances have already been made, almost incredible to those who have not had the evidence of personal observation.

Signed, in behalf of the people of color in the city and county of Philadelphia.

Charles W. Gardner
Fred'k A. Hinton
Comt.

John Strohm Papers, Pennsylvania State Archives, Harrisburg, Pennsylvania. Published by permission.

1. The Pennsylvania Reform Convention initially met in Harrisburg during May and June of 1837 but reconvened in Philadelphia from November through January 1838. Delegates voted seventy-seven to forty-five to disfranchise the state's black residents. The Pennsylvania Act for the Gradual Abolition of Slavery (1780) and the 1790 state constitution had left the question of black suffrage to the discretion of local officials. A few blacks had voted. But emboldened by the ruling of the state supreme court in *Hobbs* v. *Fogg* (1837) that the state constitution did not guarantee suffrage for blacks, the convention adopted universal white male suffrage. Blacks around the state vigorously protested, but several widely circulated pamphlets—especially Robert Purvis's *Appeal of Forty Thousand* (1838)—and mass rallies failed to halt adoption of the new constitution on 9 October 1838. Winch, *Philadelphia's Black Elite*, 134–42; Edward Price, "The Black Voting Rights Issue in Pennsylvania, 1780–1900," *PMHB* 100:356–65 (July 1976).

2. Gardner and Hinton quote from the Act for the Gradual Abolition of Slavery approved by the Pennsylvania General Assembly in 1780. Mathew Carey and J. Bioren, eds., *Laws of the Commonwealth of Pennsylvania*, 6 vols. (Philadelphia, Pa., 1803), 2:247.

3. Gardner and Hinton quote from a line in act 3, scene 2, of William Shakespeare's *King Lear* (1606): "I am a man more sinn'd against than sinning."

4. Black soldiers fought bravely in the American army at several battles during the War of 1812, including battles at Lake Champlain and New Orleans. Gardner and Hinton quote from "To the Free Coloured Inhabitants of Louisiana," a September 1814 address by Andrew Jackson. In the address, Jackson honored black volunteers as brave "fellow citizens" and promised them the same pay, bounties, supplies, and 160-acre land grant given to white soldiers. William C. Nell, *The Colored Patriots of the American Revolution* (Boston, Mass., 1855; reprint, Salem, N.H., 1986), 286–88.

27.
Lewis Woodson to Samuel E. Cornish
7 February 1838

Antebellum Americans often contrasted the virtues of agrarian life with
the corruption of the city. For blacks, agriculture offered an opportunity
to demonstrate self-reliance and to refute racist myths of black inferiority and dependency. Several black rural settlements were established in
the United States and Canada West (now Ontario). In 1838 the *Colored
American* opened its columns to a discussion of the virtues of black
agrarianism. Correspondents offered ambitious plans for organized
black farming communities. Lewis Woodson, writing under the pseudonym "Augustine," responded to white abolitionist Augustus Wattles's
call for black settlements in the West. Woodson's 7 February letter was
the first of four he wrote to the *Colored American* on the subject of
black agrarianism. Woodson, who had helped found a black rural settlement in Jackson County, Ohio, eight years earlier, emphasized the
complexity of the issue. In response to the discussion, the American
Anti-Slavery Society appointed a committee to investigate "the importance of agricultural pursuits for free colored men." *CA*, 27 January, 22
March, 19 April, 3 May, 23 June, 28 July, 8 September 1838 [2:0363,
0441, 0461–62, 0465, 0542, 0577]; Ellen Nikenzie Lawson and Mar-
lene D. Merrill, *The Three Sarahs: Documents of Antebellum Black
College Women* (New York, N.Y., 1984), 152; *Lib*, 18 May 1838.

Pittsburgh, [Pennsylvania]
Feb[ruary] 7th, 1838

MR. EDITOR:

In your paper of the 27th January, I see a letter from Mr. Wattles,
dated at Columbus, in the State of Ohio, on the important subject of our
"dashing out in the country" and becoming the *owners* and *cultivators*
of the soil. Mr. Wattles was in our city some time since, and from the
short acquaintance which I then made with him, I should judge him to be
a young man of intelligence and integrity, and a devoted friend of our
people. Consequently, the sentiment and recommendations contained in
his letter, are worthy of serious consideration.[1]

I believe that his plan is, for colored men to purchase lands contiguous
to each other, so as to have the benefit of schools and society of their
own. And as he has observed in his letter, there is at present no apparent
obstacle in the way of its accomplishment, the lands of government being
open to the selection and purchase of all, at the same price. The utility of
the plan must be apparent to everyone who appreciates the *unmolested*
enjoyment of the privileges of social life. It is well adapted to our present

case; obviating all the difficulties of our settling alone among those by whom we should be cut off from all privileges and advantages, which render life desirable.

But whether it is prudent to commence such settlements within the jurisdiction of the United States, or any of the individual states, is a question, I think, deserving of serious attention. May we safely suppose that a government which has shown such decided hostility towards us as individuals, would regard us with a more indulgent eye, when formed into communities, acquiring intelligence, wealth, and power? Would she put forth her powerful arm to foster our interests and prosperity, or to thwart and cripple them? What is the general policy of this government towards those composed of colored men? What has been her conduct towards Hayti and Mexico? And what is now her conduct towards the ignorant and hopeless aborigines of the land? The solution of these questions will lead us to anticipate what ourselves might expect, under similar circumstances.[2]

It is true that nothing has been said, as yet, against our purchasing large bodies of land, and forming distinct communities; but for this there exists a very good reason. Our people have shown a disposition adverse to settling in the country. They have heretofore been in the habit of crowding into the large towns and cities, and settling there, for no other reason, of which I can conceive, than the enjoyment of each other's society. This circumstance has, all along, been quite sufficient to silence any apprehension of our forming powerful settlements in the country.

A more powerful means of changing our present dependent and precarious condition, into one of comfort and independence, could not be devised, than of our settling in the country and becoming the owners and cultivators of the soil. The possession of houses and lands, and flocks and herds, inspires the possessor with a nobleness and independence of feeling, unknown to those in any other business. Every thing by which he is surrounded tends to the preservation of his morals, and the integrity and elevation of his soul. The lofty hill, the deep valley, the golden fields of waving grain, the green carpeted meadows of luxuriant grass, the bleating flocks and herds of cattle, the beautiful landscape, the painted flowers, the rich odours of the balmy breeze, are scenes and associations amongst which to dwell without the most exalted emotions, we must be either more or less than human.

Hence, were our people to turn their attention to this business, and unite with it the proper amount of intelligence and enterprise, their condition would be entirely changed. They would soon regard themselves, and be regarded by others, in an entirely different light from what they now are.

But farming is a *trade*, which, like all others, to be prosecuted successfully, must be *understood*. Those who suppose it to be so simple and natural, that one who has had no knowledge of it, may at once enter upon its successful prosecution, are mistaken. The art of farming involves as many and as intricate mysteries, as any other. And their complete developement requires no ordinary skill and attention.

One who contemplates living comfortably by farming should understand the *nature* and *quality* of the soil; and be able to judge from the *timber* which grows upon it, of its *strength* and *durability*; and of the different grains and vegetables which it is calculated to produce. In addition to this, he should avail himself of such books as have been written upon the subject, by the best practical farmers; and take the best agricultural newspaper which he can obtain. Thus he will not only have the benefit of his own resources and discoveries, but all those of the most intelligent and enterprizing of his profession. Such a man would not merely *stay* upon his land, as many do, but *live*, in all the comforts and enjoyments which wealth can bring.

Those who are doing well, in the large towns and cities, in mechanical and other pursuits, I would not advise to leave them with too much precipitancy. One who is a successful mechanic or dealer, may not be a successful farmer. Many who have been successful in one business, turned to another, and have been soon reduced to poverty and wretchedness, for want of the requisite qualification to conduct it with success.

But those who are living in these places, *and have no trades*, who depend for a precarious subsistence upon their daily labor, should immediately turn their attention to the country. Their condition cannot be worsted; but very probably much bettered. Their children would be taken from the degrading drudgery and domineering of others; and from their exposure to the pollutions of idleness, vice, and crime, to constant, useful, and profitable employment.

Before I conclude, I would beg leave to direct the attention of Mr. Wattles, and all others who feel interested in this matter, to a class of our people who are already in the country. I allude to those who live amongst prejudiced white persons, by whom they are cut off from the privileges of schools, &c. These, if they desire to bring up their children in a proper manner, must be very unhappily situated. Would it not be advisable to visit these, and apprize them of the utility of emigrating to colored settlements?

AUGUSTINE[3]

Colored American (New York, N.Y.), 17 February 1838.

1. Augustus Wattles's 27 January 1838 letter to the *Colored American* sought to convince eastern blacks to settle in the Midwest and Canada. Wattles (1807–1883) was born in Connecticut and attended the Oneida Institute. At Lane Seminary in 1834, he joined with Theodore Dwight Weld and Marius Robinson to promote Garrisonian abolitionism among Cincinnati's black poor. An agent of

both the American and Ohio antislavery societies, he eventually founded twenty-five black schools around Ohio and convinced Lewis and Arthur Tappan to fund his educational schemes and to hire female assistants, one of which he married. He organized an agrarian movement to shield blacks from white racism and the "contaminating influences" of urban life. Serving as land agent, Wattles pooled black funds to purchase about thirty thousand acres in Ohio by 1835, particularly in Mercer County, where several hundred blacks—mostly former slaves—settled. His Carthagena community possessed a manual labor school with over one hundred students. Wattles moved in 1854 to Kansas, where he edited the *Herald of Freedom*, assisted John Brown, and worked as an inspector for the Bureau of Indian Affairs. *CA*, 28 October 1837, 27 January, 17 February, 15 December 1838, 2 March 1839 [2:0246, 0363, 0380, 0385, 3:0016]; Lesick, *Lane Rebels*, 173–93; "Transplanting Free Negroes to Ohio from 1815–1858," *JNH* 1:302–17 (July 1916); Pease and Pease, *Black Utopia*, 38–41; Barnes and Dumond, *Letters of Theodore Dwight Weld*, 1:90–91, 134, 178–79, 285; O. E. Morse, "Sketch of the Life and Work of Augustus Wattles," *CKSHS* 17:290–99 (1928).

2. Woodson is made nervous by the racist policies of the U.S. government. Largely because of southern opposition, the U.S. Congress refused to recognize the black republic of Haiti until 1862. Abolitionists blamed the United States for the Texas Revolution of 1835–36, charging that southerners had fomented it in order to strengthen slavery by expanding it into the borderlands of the Southwest. Native Americans were removed by the federal government from valued lands in the Southeast during the 1830s. Rayford W. Logan, *The Diplomatic Relations of the United States and Haiti, 1776–1891* (Chapel Hill, N.C., 1941), 112, 191–207, 277, 298, 302–3; David M. Pletcher, *The Diplomacy of Annexation* (Columbia, Mo., 1973), 69–72.

3. Lewis Woodson (1806–1878) was born in Greenbriar County, Virginia, and served as a cabin boy on a privateer during the War of 1812. His family resettled in Chillicothe, Ohio, in 1820. Woodson became involved with the antislavery movement in Ohio at the age of seventeen, the first step in a life devoted to education, religion, and reform. He worked with the local underground railroad, once venturing into Kentucky to rescue a fugitive slave kidnapped from Ohio. Between 1826 and 1830, he taught at black schools in Chillicothe, Columbus, and Gainesville, Ohio, and founded the African Education and Benevolent Society to provide for black children denied access to public schools. In 1831 he moved to Pittsburgh, where he worked as a barber, taught school, and supplemented his income by lecturing on physiology and hygiene. His commitment to education extended beyond teaching. He founded the Pittsburgh African Educational Society with John B. Vashon in 1832 and later served as a trustee of Wilberforce University. Woodson, who had been ordained in 1828, ministered to a local African Methodist Episcopal congregation for much of the next three decades; he also served briefly as an elder of the True Wesleyans, an interracial antislavery church. Active in state and local concerns, he organized Pittsburgh's first black temperance society in 1834, joined the struggle to defend black voting rights in Pennsylvania, and attended the 1841 black state convention.

Woodson is considered a pioneer of black nationalism because of his early advocacy of black separatism. He participated in the black national convention movement in the 1830s. After serving as corresponding secretary of the Pittsburgh auxiliary of the American Moral Reform Society, he broke with AMRS leaders over their stated preference for integrated reform organizations. Woodson felt that black unity and identity would be strengthened through the development of distinctly black organizations and institutions. His ideas on black identity and moral reform reached black readers through a series of letters to the *Colored American*, many of which appeared under the pseudonym "Augustine" (after the fourth-century North African theologian). Woodson championed several black national organizations—especially the American League of Colored Laborers and the National Council of the Colored People—during the early 1850s. A leading proponent of a separate black press, he promoted the *Rights of All* and the *Colored American* and helped Martin R. Delany, a former student, publish the *Mystery* in Pittsburgh. Although critical of the American Colonization Society, he endorsed black settlement in Canada and the Caribbean. He also encouraged the growth of African missions, particularly as a member of the board of managers of the Union Missionary Society. Throughout his reform career, Woodson defended separate black settlements, black emigration, and separate schools and churches. This separatism evoked criticism from Frederick Douglass and some black Garrisonians, but his ideas prepared the way for the black nationalism of Delany and others in the 1850s. Floyd J. Miller, " 'The Father of Black Nationalism': Another Contender," *CWH* 17:310–19 (December 1971); Pease and Pease, *They Who Would Be Free*, 261n; Daniel A. Payne, *Recollections of Seventy Years* (Nashville, Tenn., 1888; reprint, New York, N.Y., 1969), 225–26; Payne, *African Methodist Episcopal Church*, 97, 284; Lawson and Merrill, *The Three Sarahs*, 150–52; *Minutes of the Second National Convention* (1832), 25 [1:0182]; *Proceedings of the Colored National Convention, Held in Rochester, July 6th, 7th, and 8th, 1853* (Rochester, N.Y., 1953), 25 [8:0338]; Foner and Walker, *Proceedings of the Black State Conventions*, 1:108–16; Lewis Woodson to Lewis Tappan, 31 January 1842, Weld-Grimké Papers, MiU [4:0353–54]; *CR*, 7 February 1878; *FJ*, 6 April 1827, 31 January 1829; *RA*, 18 September 1829; *CA*, 1, 22 July, 2, 9 December 1837, 25 August, 29 November 1839, 18 July 1840, 17 February, 7 August 1841 [2:0098, 0122, 3:0192, 0344, 0526, 0929, 4:0148]; *NSt*, 13 June 1850 [6:0526]; *WAA*, 3 September 1859 [12:0010].

28.
Editorial by Samuel E. Cornish
10 February 1838

Black leaders of the 1830s were painfully aware that many blacks fell short of the standards set by white society. Believing that black moral and mental elevation would lessen racial prejudice, they founded hundreds of organizations and institutions dedicated to self-improvement—schools, lyceums, literary societies, library companies, debating clubs, and lecture series. Many books, pamphlets, and journals were unavailable to blacks because of their exclusion from public libraries and other literary institutions. In a 10 June 1838 editorial, Samuel Cornish reported that the *Colored American* was contemplating opening a "reading room" in New York City that would provide moral reform and antislavery literature. Before the month was out, David Ruggles opened a "reading room" in the offices of the New York Committee of Vigilance. Less than two months later, the *Colored American* opened another one next to its offices at 161 Duane Street. It provided patrons with foreign and domestic newspapers on a wide range of subjects. Porter, *Early Negro Writing*, 212; *CA*, 16 June, 28 July, 4 August 1838, 19 January 1839.

A Reading Room

The Committee of Publication[1] have in contemplation the opening of a *Reading Room*, in connection with this Paper. Our large exchange list, together with the pamphlets and other literary productions, which are presented and furnished us, weekly, will give great facilities to such an enterprise; and there is nothing so much needed by all classes of our people, as a well-furnished and well-selected reading establishment. Such an institution would be productive of the greatest good. Its influence and effects would be two-fold. While it would, *directly*, produce much good to our community, it would also be a preventative of much evil.

The reason why we have so many empty minds and idle hands, is our deficiency of literary and scientific institutions. Where the acquirement of knowledge, mental and moral, is neglected, there the vices grow and luxuriate. As an evidence of this fact, we have only to go into certain parts of our city, which are cursed with tippling and gaming-houses, instead of being blessed with institutions of science and literature, and there we find all sorts and complexions of people, living in ignorance and given up to the practice of EVERY VICE.

But take any portion of our city, or any other city or town, where the institutions of learning, and establishments for the arts are maintained, and there you will find the morals and manners of the people improved and elevated.

Then, brethren, if such be the influence of institutions of knowledge and refinement, of all people, we should avail ourselves of every chance of procuring them. We need all the moral character and the mental resources we can possibly husband. We are barbarously oppressed by a refined and christian people, and need more than *common intelligence and grace*, to sustain us; and we know of no better way of procuring these blessings for ourselves and our posterity, than by establishing and maintaining moral and literary institutions.

In this way we may fill up the years of our oppression, and pass the days of our pilgrimage profitably, and comparatively happily. In this way, we may train up our offspring to virtue and religion, and prepare them to be a blessing to future generations. And in this way, we may prevent worlds of vice, and save thousands of the young and thoughtless from those evil practices, which accumulate miseries, and lead to ruin and death.

The expense of the room will be two dollars a year, to subscribers. This sum will be necessary to meet the rent, and other expenses of the establishment. Subscriptions will be received at this office, in all the next week. Our brethren who intend patronizing the enterprise, and availing themselves of its privileges, will please to call without delay. We hope also that our people in other towns and cities, will adopt the same measure, for mutual improvement and benefit. We shall be glad to send papers, and give other facilities to all such establishments.

Colored American (New York, N.Y.), 10 February 1838.

1. The Committee of Publication, which was chaired by Thomas L. Jinnings, consisted of twenty-eight prominent New York City blacks. The committee acted as proprietor of the *Colored American* from November 1837 to June 1838 and exercised executive authority over all aspects of the publishing process. *CA*, 13 January, 16 June 1838 [2:0345].

29.
Editorial by Samuel E. Cornish
15 March 1838

Black abolitionists grew concerned about black institutions and identity during the 1830s. They feared that drawing attention to racial differences by promoting separate black organizations or by including words such as "Afric," "African," and "colored" in their institutions' names would encourage the colonizationist movement and increase racial prejudice. William Whipper persuaded delegates at the 1835 black national convention to approve a resolution asking blacks to avoid use of the term "colored" and to remove the title "African" from the names of their churches, schools, and social institutions. Leaders of the Philadelphia-based American Moral Reform Society debated the issue of racial nomenclature. Their public discussion revolved around the naming controversy, but the actual struggle was over the purpose and program of the AMRS. Whipper and Robert Purvis wanted the AMRS to be an integrated organization. Junius C. Morel, Frederick Hinton, and others preferred an organization specifically identified with black concerns and issues. A 15 March 1838 editorial by Samuel Cornish in the *Colored American* expressed exasperation at the debate. He criticized the idea of avoiding racial language and characterized the whole issue as trivial compared to the larger battles that blacks faced. Sterling Stuckey, *Slave Culture: Nationalist Theory and the Foundation of Black America* (New York, N.Y., 1987), 200–211; *Lib*, 2 July 1836; *CA*, 4 March 1837 [1:0993].

Our Brethren In Philadelphia

The good sense of some of our brethren in Philadelphia, seems to have forsaken them. They are quarrelling about trifles, while their enemies are robbing them of diamonds and of gold. Nothing can be more ridiculous nor ludicrous, than their contentions about NAMES—if they quarrel it should be about THINGS.

But what caps the climax is, that while these sages are frightened half to death, at the idea of being called COLORED, their FRIENDS and their FOES, in the convention, in the Assembly and in the Senate; through the pulpit and the press, call them nothing else but NEGROES, NEGROES, THE NEGROES of Pennsylvania.

To us, and we should think to anyone of good sense, laboring under such persecutions as the colored citizens of Philadelphia are, to be called "Colored Americans" would be like a ray of *Heavenly light*, shining amidst the blackness of darkness.

Oppressed Americans! *who are they?* nonsense brethren!! You are

COLORED AMERICANS. The Indians are RED AMERICANS, and the white people are WHITE AMERICANS and *you are as good as they, and they are no better than you*—God made all of the same blood. Do not fool away anymore of your time nor fill up any more of your papers with SUCH NONSENSE.

Colored American (New York, N.Y.), 15 March 1838.

30.
Editorial by Samuel E. Cornish
9 June 1838

By the late 1830s, black leaders sensed a growing distinction between black and white abolitionism. When the immediatist movement began, white abolitionists pledged to fight racial prejudice and improve the condition of free blacks, as well as end slavery. But prejudice and black elevation became secondary issues even among well-meaning whites. Faced with an alarming increase in discriminatory enactments and racial violence, blacks challenged white abolitionists to reaffirm their original commitment to fight racism in the North. Samuel Cornish's 9 June 1838 editorial in the *Colored American* summoned his white colleagues to pay more attention to racial prejudice. Calling it the more important issue, he urged that it become the "test question" for all abolitionists— simple opposition to slavery would not suffice. Pease and Pease, *They Who Would Be Free*, 3–16.

HINTS ABOUT PREJUDICE

Now is the time for abolitionists to gird up the loins of their minds for a conflict with prejudice against color—to burnish the armour of truth, to supply themselves with the appropriate tracts and books which are the ammunition necessary for our warfare—for now their use is called for. The signs of the times indicate this. The recent outbreak of popular violence in Philadelphia[1]—the recent affair in Newark, where a worthy Minister has been hunted from his charge, because he presumed to walk to meeting with a colored woman, and to seat her in a pew with his wife and family, one who was his own domestic, and a sister in the church (a most horrible sin truly!)—and the recent demonstration of sentiment in New Brunswick, because the Baptist Convention held at that place chose Brother Raymond[2] of this City, to preach the introductory sermon. All these things place the question of prejudice against color, and the duty the abolitionists owe to their colored brethren, so prominently before the public, that it will be hard work, even should any be inclined to do it, to get around it or to dodge it. The time has come when the question has got to be met. When our friends must face it, if they are our friends; or do as some will, take to their heels and run. Prejudice against color, after all, is the test question—at least among us. The mere and direct question of slavery is not. For every man here says—"I am as much opposed to slavery as you are. But as for these *Niggers*, we don't want them here— let them go home to their own land." This is what we hear, and this is the feeling. Here comes the tug; and here our friends have to grapple with slavery, not at arms length, but with a back-hold. Here the slimy serpent is among them, coiled up in their own hearts and houses.

We see it, and have long seen it—that the real battleground between liberty and slavery is prejudice against color. The friends of humanity have as yet but possessed a few out-posts upon its frontiers. They have not yet undisputed possession of the field, even in their own hearts, as time will show; and we have been a little surprised that the phalanx of our friends have been so slow to see this.

We do not object of course to the tremendous cannonading which has been kept up on the citadel of slavery with the big ordinance and long-toms of our cause. Such as Emancipation in the West Indies—Bible *vs.* Slavery—Powers of Congress, and the like.[3] But we suggest, whether the drill officers and the file leaders should not have inculcated a little more the importance and use of our abolition side arms and pocket weapons. That all may be as well prepared for the controversy, in close quarters as at a distance. Our abolition magazine is pretty well stocked. But yet there should be no slacking up in forging more. Brother Lewis' tract ON CASTE,[4] is a pocket pistol that no one should be without. "Goodell's Speech on Prejudice,"[5] and the *Appeal of the 40,000,*[6] are both polished toledoes. *Rights of Colored Men*[7] is a broad-sword; and *The Negro Pew*[8] an iron spear. Get your pistols and broad-swords brethren, and go to work.

Our figures are clumsy, and perhaps out of place. But our readers will understand what we mean. Now is the time to circulate books and tracts of the description we have spoken of. The public mind should be saturated with them.

Colored American (New York, N.Y.), 9 June 1838.

1. Cornish refers to the destruction of Pennsylvania Hall, a building erected by Philadelphia abolitionists to house antislavery meetings and provide office space for their societies. Outraged by the racially integrated meetings held there, an antiabolitionist mob burned the hall on the evening of 17 May 1838, three days after it had first opened. On 19 May, the mob destroyed a shelter for black orphans and damaged the Bethel African Methodist Episcopal Church. Foner, *History of Black Americans,* 2:430–32.

2. John T. Raymond, a black Baptist minister, described himself as a Virginian of "French descent." During the early 1830s, he spent time in New York and was effectively banished from his home by a Virginia law that prohibited free black residents from reentering the state after being away for a year or more. He settled in New York City where in 1832 he founded the Zion Baptist Church. After a brief assignment as pastor of the African Church in Albany (1840), Raymond took charge of the First Independent Baptist Church in Boston. Parish factionalism and health problems led him to leave for Philadelphia in 1843, but by 1845 he had returned to the Boston congregation. Upon his return, his eyesight began

to deteriorate rapidly, and he was obliged to resign his post. Although partially blind, he revived his ministerial career in 1848 at the Abyssinian Baptist Church in New York City. In 1855 he returned to his first church, the Zion Baptist congregation.

Raymond's abolitionist activities began in the 1830s. He was vice-president of the New York Young Men's Anti-Slavery Society and a member of the Roger Williams Anti-Slavery Society, and he attended the 1840 black state convention at Albany. In Boston he brought the antislavery and temperance message to his pulpit, opening his church to "lecturers on various reforms." A member of the Committee of Thirteen in the 1850s, he frequently presided over antislavery meetings in New York City. At a public rally against the Fugitive Slave Law of 1850, he denounced the law as a "hell-concocted scheme" and urged black resistance. He remained active in black community affairs well into the 1860s. *E*, 14 March 1839, 13 April 1843, 3 September 1845; *Lib*, 2 December 1842, 7, 28 April 1843, 14 May 1852; *FDP*, 15 January 1852 [7:0356]; *CA*, 5 December 1840; *NASS*, 10 October 1850 [6:610–11]; *VF*, 3 June 1852; *WAA*, 21 December 1861, 1, 22 March 1862; *PP*, 18 May, 28 December 1861; Mechal Sobel, *Trabelin' On: The Slave Journey to an Afro-Baptist Faith* (Westport, Conn., 1979), 262, 266–67; Horton and Horton, *Black Bostonians*, 42, 46–47; Foner and Walker, *Proceedings of the State Black Conventions*, 1:5, 15, 24; Abajian, *Blacks in Selected Newspapers*, 2:142; George Levesque, "Inherent Reformers, Inherited Orthodoxy: Black Baptists in Boston, 1800–1873," *JNH* 60:512–21 (October 1975); Lewis Tappan, *The Life of Arthur Tappan* (New York, N.Y., 1870; reprint, New York, N.Y., 1970), 181; Freeman, "Free Negro in New York City," 199.

3. Cornish mentions three of the many arguments that abolitionists employed against slavery. They pointed to a successful example of emancipation—the end of slavery in the British Empire (including the British West Indies) on 1 August 1834. They charged that slavery violated biblical teachings about equality, love, purity, and compassion and contradicted biblical injunctions against "man stealing." Many abolitionists argued that the U.S. Congress had constitutional authority over slavery. In reality Congress's control over the institution was limited to ending the importation of slaves and regulating bondage in Washington, D.C., and the territories. James Brewer Stewart, "Abolitionists, the Bible, and the Challenge of Slavery," in *The Bible and Social Reform*, ed. Ernest R. Sandeen (Philadelphia, Pa., 1982), 31–58.

4. Cornish probably refers to "Caste," the second in a series of *Miniature Anti-Slavery Tracts* published by Ransom G. Williams in 1837 for the American Anti-Slavery Society. The pamphlet, which was a compilation of excerpts from the *Emancipator*, traced the origins of caste and discussed the nature and effects of racial discrimination. No author is listed on the tract. *E*, 11 May 1837; "Caste," *Miniature Anti-Slavery Tracts*, no. 2 (New York, N.Y., 1837).

5. Cornish refers to a powerful attack on American racism delivered by William Goodell before the Lewis County Anti-Slavery Society in Lowville, New York, on 10 January 1837. Goodell (1792–1878), a New York abolitionist and reformer, edited the *Emancipator*, the *Friend of Man*, the *Radical Abolitionist*, and the *National Principia*. He helped found the American Anti-Slavery Society

in 1833, the Liberty party in 1840, and the Liberty League in 1847 but is usually remembered for his writings on the antislavery character of the Constitution. *DAB*, 7:384–85; *CA*, 11, 18 March 1837; *FM*, 26 January 1837.

6. *The Appeal of Forty Thousand Citizens, Threatened with Disfranchisement, to the People of Pennsylvania* (1838), written by a committee headed by Robert Purvis, rejected the new state constitution adopted by the Pennsylvania Reform Convention of 1837–38, which disfranchised blacks. In the pamphlet, Pennsylvania blacks defended their right to suffrage, which they had exercised for forty-seven years, by appealing to natural rights theory and attacking the convention's racist assumptions. The *Appeal of Forty Thousand* catalogued black accomplishments in the state, including the value of all black-owned property, and reminded whites of the black contribution to the American Revolution.

7. William Yates's *Rights of Colored Men to Suffrage, Citizenship and Trial by Jury* (1838), was written in response to growing black disfranchisement in New Jersey, Connecticut, New York, and Pennsylvania. A compendium of laws and legal opinions relating to black suffrage, citizenship, and the right to a jury trial for those accused of being fugitive slaves, it sought the repeal of all laws that discriminated on the basis of race.

8. *The Negro Pew* (1837), reputedly written by Boston clergyman Harvey Newcomb, assaulted racism in the American church, as symbolized by separate seating.

31.
Benjamin F. Roberts to Amos A. Phelps
19 June 1838

The leadership of the antislavery movement remained almost entirely white through the late 1830s. More and more, black abolitionists examined the significant contributions blacks were making to the crusade, questioned their exclusion from policy-making positions, and concluded that whites were deliberately obstructing the emergence of a black leadership within the movement. Benjamin F. Roberts's experience typified the problems faced by assertive blacks. In May 1838, he began publishing the *Anti-Slavery Herald*, a paper owned and operated by Boston blacks. At the start, Roberts found strong support among white abolitionists. William Lloyd Garrison wished the *Anti-Slavery Herald* "abundant success," and Amos A. Phelps, an agent of the Massachusetts Anti-Slavery Society, praised the paper and provided Roberts with a letter of recommendation. But within a month, white enthusiasm turned to hostility. Garrison began to undermine local black support for the paper, Phelps objected to the paper's militant tone and asked that his letter be returned, and other white abolitionists spread rumors that Roberts was acting on selfish, personal motives. In an angry 19 June reply to Phelps, Roberts called his opponents hypocrites and charged that there had been "a combined effort on the part of certain professed abolitionists to muzzle, exterminate and put down" black endeavors. He discontinued publication of the *Anti-Slavery Herald* within six months. Pease and Pease, *They Who Would Be Free*, 70–71; *NSt*, 25 February 1848; *Lib*, 14 December 1833, 4 May, 12 October 1838; Horton and Horton, *Black Bostonians*, 76, 82–83; Amos A. Phelps to Whom it May Concern, 16 May 1838, Anti-Slavery Collection, MB.

Boston, [Massachusetts]
June 19, 1838

Rev A. A. Phelps[1]
Dear Sir:

At 25 Cornhill,[2] I found a note addressed to myself, which on opening I was surprised to learn that you felt much dissatisfied with the recommendation you furnished[3]—the impression I got showed it was undeserving. I return it as requested. But as it respects the facts alluded to, I am aware there has been and now is, a combined effort on the part of certain professed abolitionists to muzzle, exterminate and put down the efforts of certain colored individuals effecting the welfare of their colored brethren. The truth is respecting myself, my whole soul is engaged in the cause of humanity. I am for improvement among this class of people, mental and <u>physical</u>. The arts and sciences have never been introduced to any extent among us—therefore they are of the utmost importance. If anti-Slavery men will not subscribe to the advancement of these principles, but <u>rail out</u> and <u>protest against</u> them when took up by those who have a darker skin, why we will go to the <u>heathen</u>. The principle ground on which the anti-slavery cause is said to be founded (and <u>boasting</u> are not a few) <u>are the elevation of the free colored people here</u>. Now it is altogether useless to pretend to affect the welfare of the blacks in this country, unless the chains of prejudice are broken. It is of no use [to] say with the mouth we are friends of the slave and not try to encourage and assist the free colored people in raising themselves. Here is sir the <u>first</u> efforts of the colored man in this country of the kind, vis. the paper <u>published</u>, <u>printed</u> and <u>edited</u> by colored persons in Massachusetts—shall <u>this</u> be defeated? But it is contended the <u>individual</u> who started the enterprise has not taken it up from principle—<u>he</u> don't intend what he pretends. Base misrepresentations! false accusations!—I was not aware that so many hypocrites existed in the Anti slavery society.[4] According to what I have seen of the conduct of some, a black man would be as unsafe in their hands as in those of Southern slaveholders. I have found a few <u>true</u> to the righteous cause, and those were practical abolitionists as well as abolitionists by profession. I should like to become acquainted with some of the stories in circulation. Those in haste

B. F. Roberts[5]

1. Amos Augustus Phelps (1804–1847) was born in Farmington, Connecticut, attended Yale Divinity School, and ministered to several Boston Congregational churches from 1832 to 1845. A founder of the American Anti-Slavery Society, Phelps also served as general agent for its Massachusetts auxiliary. He was a devoted Garrisonian until 1837 when he broke with the AASS over nonresistance and women's rights. Merrill and Ruchames, *Letters of William Lloyd Garrison*, 2:xxviii.

2. The Massachusetts Anti-Slavery Society and the *Liberator* shared an office at 25 Cornhill in Boston from 1837 to 1846. *Lib*, 2 January 1837, 13 November 1846.

3. On 16 May 1838, Amos A. Phelps wrote a letter of recommendation endorsing Benjamin Roberts's plans to establish a printing office in Boston that would publish an antislavery newspaper and offer instruction in the printing business to young blacks. Phelps acknowledged that he did not know Roberts well but characterized him as an enterprising young man of good character. Amos A. Phelps to Whom it May Concern, 16 May 1838, Anti-Slavery Collection, MB.

4. Roberts refers to the Massachusetts Anti-Slavery Society, which Phelps

served as a general agent from June 1837 to December 1838. Merrill and Ruchames, *Letters of William Lloyd Garrison*, 2:xxviii.

5. Benjamin F. Roberts, a Boston printer, established the *Anti-Slavery Herald*, a short-lived newspaper "edited and published entirely by colored men," in 1838. His paper drew hostility from white abolitionists and little support from Boston blacks. Fifteen years later, his efforts to publish the *Self-Elevator* proved equally futile. As a printer, Roberts was involved in a broad range of abolitionist activities. He published speeches, reports, pamphlets, and placards for black and antislavery organizations. During the 1844 elections, he worked to generate local black support for Whig party candidates. With the passage of the Fugitive Slave Law of 1850, he abandoned the Whigs and participated in public meetings on the fugitive issue. In 1850 he accompanied Henry "Box" Brown on an antislavery tour of New England, narrating the illustrated scenes in a diorama of Brown's dramatic escape from slavery and lecturing the public on the "Condition of the Colored Population in the United States."

Roberts's most notable contribution to Boston's black community came in the late 1840s when he challenged segregated education. With William C. Nell and others, he led the protest and boycott against the all-black Smith School. After four unsuccessful attempts to enroll his daughter, Sarah, in white classrooms, he sued the city for $600 in damages. Charles Sumner, assisted by black attorney Robert Morris, argued the case. The Massachusetts Supreme Court ruled against Roberts in 1850, establishing the "separate but equal" doctrine later cited in *Plessy v. Ferguson* (1896) and in other judicial rulings that upheld racial segregation. *Lib*, 23 December 1842, 7 September 1849, 5 April 1850, 4 April 1851 [4:0496, 6:0435, 0871]; *CF*, 17 October 1844; "The Smith School," 1848, "Anti–Smith School Petition," 11 August 1848, Benjamin F. Roberts to Amos A. Phelps, 19 June 1838, Anti-Slavery Collection, MB [2:0498, 5:0549, 0749–50]; Donald M. Jacobs, "The Nineteenth-Century Struggle over Segregated Education in the Boston Schools," *JNE* 39:76–85 (Winter 1970); Horton and Horton, *Black Bostonians*, 72, 75–76, 82–83, 93; Pease and Pease, *They Who Would Be Free*, 36, 115.

32.
Editorial by Samuel E. Cornish
30 June 1838

Few black or white abolitionists encouraged interracial sex and marriage, although they urged the repeal of state laws outlawing either
practice. Many black abolitionists opposed amalgamation because they
believed that it would destroy racial pride. Yet among most antiabolitionist whites, support for amalgamation was practically synonymous
with abolitionism. Opponents of racial equality invoked the image
of race mixing to ignite racist sentiment. In a 30 June 1838 editorial
in the *Colored American*, Samuel Cornish called the amalgamation
threat a sham argument. He observed that there seemed to be no fear of
this "bleaching process" in northern brothels or southern slave quarters. The "cry of amalgamation! amalgamation!" had a personal ring
for Cornish, a light-skinned black with a son who passed for white.
Quarles, *Black Abolitionists*, 38–39; *CA*, 2 September 1837, 7, 14, 28
July 1838; Pease and Pease, *They Who Would Be Free*, 105.

Tired With Nonsense

We are heartily disgusted with the ridiculous cry of amalgamation!
amalgamation!! It is a mean, dishonest, ungodly resort of colonizationists, knaves, and fools, and seems to be the only argument they are
capable of using in defence of their corrupt system of slavery, their oppression and tyranny. Jehovah has no attribute which will take sides with
such men, and there are no principles in his moral code which can justify
a single act of their ludicrous conduct.

The wicked and false cry (amalgamation) is raised with the view, if
possible, of worrying inoffensive and defenceless colored citizens out of
their senses, and driving them into the cruel, utopian, heathen scheme of
colonization, and with the further view of wearing out and driving abolitionists from their humane and righteous efforts, in behalf of the slave. It
will not do—God is stronger than the devil, and the foolish authors of
this foolish scheme, will assuredly find themselves in the result, on the
weak side.

Why do not these "eagle eyed" beings, who have set themselves up to
prevent amalgamation, turn their attention to the south? Are they not
aware of the mixing up, bleaching process of amalgamation carried on in
that ill-fated region, where the slaves are fastly growing as white as their
masters? And why do not these little minded "amalgamation trumpet-
ers," draw aside the curtain in New York, Philadelphia and other cities,
and reform the houses of assignation which are kept, *wholly*, for the
amalgamation of white males and colored females—if driven to it, we

11. Samuel E. Cornish
Courtesy of Moorland-Spingarn Research Center, Howard University

can give volumes with names and numbers on this subject.[1] Yet all these things are overlooked—nobody gives the alarm. But let a colored Christian be seated in the house of God; let him be given a berth, and a comfortable place in a Steam Boat cabin, or an inside passage in a Rail Road car or a stage coach; and the cry amalgamation!! amalgamation!!! is at once raised by ten thousand polluted tongues. This conduct is unworthy [of] the American or any other civilized people, and we hope every virtuous, enlightened citizen will at once set his face against it. Let such nonsense be buried with the abominations of the barbarous ages.

In conclusion, we are grieved to the heart with the fatal influence this wicked scheme of colonizationist and pro-slavery men has over Christians and the Christian ministry. The successors of the holy Jesus and his humble apostles, in America, have actually become almost as afraid of showing the common courtesies of life to a colored Christian brother, as the Pharisees of old were of mingling with uncircumcised Publicans[2] and sinners, and all forsooth, because they fear public opinion, *more than they fear God.*

Colored American (New York, N.Y.), 30 June 1838.

1. While often illegal and seldom acceptable, sexual relations in antebellum America crossed the color line. In the South, the process frequently involved white planters and black slaves, a circumstance that contributed to the growth of a mulatto population. By 1850 mulattoes numbered 350,000 and comprised 3.6 percent of the region's population. In northern cities, black prostitutes frequently served a white clientele. Many brothel keepers maintained biracial staffs. At brothels in the infamous Five Points district of New York City, white customers could select from women "of all colors, white, yellow, brown, and ebony black." Joel Williamson, *New People: Miscegenation and Mulattoes in the United States* (New York, N.Y., 1980), 5–91; Curry, *Free Black in Urban America*, 117–18.

2. Cornish compared the treatment of blacks by white Christians to that of Publicans by the Pharisees, a strictly orthodox Jewish sect in ancient Palestine. The Pharisees refused to associate with non-Jews and despised Publicans—Jews who collected taxes and tolls for the Roman authorities—because their frequent contact with non-Jews made them ritually unclean. The Pharisees are frequently criticized in the New Testament. Matt. 23:23–33; Luke 18:9–14.

33.
"Junius" to Samuel E. Cornish
[July 1838]

Moral reformers of the 1830s urged blacks to work hard and learn trades as a way of improving their material condition. But by the end of the decade, black workers—already suffering from a national economic recession—faced increasing competition from Irish immigrants, who arrived in northern cities in such numbers that they threatened to displace blacks from traditional areas of employment. Writing as "Junius" in the 28 July 1838 issue of the *Colored American*, an anonymous New York City black questioned the assumptions of the moral reformers. He called black economic prospects "dark and discouraging," noted the hardships that the Irish influx was creating in the black community, and asked white abolitionists to demonstrate their concern for black economic progress by employing black workers. Like other black leaders, he asked why none of them had yet "placed one of our intelligent and respectable citizens in a conspicuous place in their stores or counting houses." Litwack, *North of Slavery*, 162–63; David Hellwig, "Black Attitudes toward Irish Immigrants," *MA* 59:39–49 (January 1977); *NSFA*, 3 March 1842 [4:0371–72]; *E*, 29 November 1839.

MR. EDITOR:

For many years I have been watching over the interests of our people with the most anxious solicitude. I have heard the predictions of many of our warmest friends, who long since foretold that many avenues to respectability, wealth, and usefulness would shortly be opened, and I have listened to the voice of the press, and the voice of the philanthropist who have confidently proclaimed, that a few years would see us in the complete restoration of our civil and political rights. But years have glided along, and yet the prospect looks dark and discouraging. Our political elevation, come as it will, come as it must, yet from a rational view of things as they are, must not be considered as a period nigh at hand. And my observation on the *private* condition and hopes of the man of color, teaches me that his situation in this country, is alarming enough to rouse the attention, and demand instantly and imperiously the aid of every man who pretends to be concerned for his welfare. I say that our private condition is lamentable, though it may not be desperate. Facts justify the assertion. The introduction of foreigners into this country is a sore and grievous evil to our people. These impoverished and destitute beings, transported from the trans-atlantic shores, are crowding themselves into every place of business and of labor, and driving the poor colored American citizen out. Along the wharves, where the colored man once did the whole business of shipping and unshipping—in stores where his services were once rendered, and in families where the chief places were filled by him, in all these situations there are substituted foreigners or white Americans.[1]

Now, whether this unfortunate transfer of employment from the hands of honest, industrious and intelligent colored men, into the hands of intruding foreigners, be the result of a settled policy among the enemies of our race, or whether it will be from a principle of self-interest on the part of the employers, the event is the same to our people—they are deprived of their only means of substinence. If now there are no ways opened for their employment, I need not say what dreadful effects will follow upon this very large class of our citizens. Man can be patient to a certain point, but when hope is cut off, he grows desperate.

You, I believe, Mr. Editor, were the first man, or among the first of those keen-sighted men, who years ago, apprehending the present state of things, advocated the pursuit of agriculture. In your present paper you have strenuously urged the same subject upon the people.[2] But how few, since the first article was written twelve years ago, have become the steady cultivators of the soil! Our people really seem to be the firm and determined opposers of colonization, in any of its forms. If, then, from whatever reasons may be alleged, either of ignorance of agricultural science, or pecuniary inability, our people cannot become farmers, and are hence obliged, from the circumstances of the case, to remain in the city, what must be done? The only remedy that I see is, that every man who pretends to be a friend of the oppressed—every man who calls himself an abolitionist, and who is in reality such, should combine to seek situations and furnish employment for every honest and worthy unemployed man of color. I know it may be said, that the abolitionists are exceedingly busy in agitating the great question of our constitutional rights, and using all their efforts to break asunder the bonds which fetter the poor slave. I am aware of all this, and hence honored be the names of all who are engaged in a cause so sacred, and ten thousand blessings be showered upon their heads by every colored American.

But, while they are agitating and discussing the all absorbing question, let them not forget that there is a duty at home to perform—a duty, which, if they would act consistent with their benevolent principles, they ought to perform. I would not willingly or falsely charge upon these distinguished philanthropists an indifference to the domestic interests of our people: but I must boldly confess, that I think they have the means and the opportunity of benefiting the colored man, which they have not yet embraced. There is not an abolitionist in our city who has placed one of our intelligent and respectable citizens in a conspicuous place in their stores or counting houses—not one that I have heard of, who has offered a good inducement to any to fit themselves for such a station. Why is there not, I would ask, one colored man holding a conspicuous place in the N.Y. Anti-Slavery Office?[3] If such places were occupied by respectable, talented and competent men of color, and liberal salaries given them, there would be a glorious proof of abolition consistency, and incalculable benefit to the many able and talented men among us, who are now in wretched circumstances.

JUNIUS

Colored American (New York, N.Y.), 28 July 1838.

1. "Junius" refers primarily to the large number of Irish immigrants that entered northern cities like Philadelphia, New York City, and Boston during the antebellum period. Frequently unskilled, Irish immigrants flooded the work force, depressed wages, and displaced black competitors in numerous service occupations, which included barbers, domestic servants, cooks, coachmen, and stevedores. Litwack, *North of Slavery*, 159, 163–66.

2. Samuel Cornish advocated agriculture as a means by which blacks could improve their moral and material condition. He praised the virtues of agrarian life as early as 1827 in *Freedom's Journal* and continued the practice in the *Rights of All*. As an incentive, he offered to distribute two thousand acres of land on the banks of the Delaware River in New Jersey to blacks who would leave the city to become farmers. He later opened the columns of the *Colored American* to a wide-ranging debate on the issue of black agrarianism. *FJ*, 23 March, 22 June, 31 August, 9 November 1827; *RA*, 29 May 1829; *CA*, 12, 19 April 1838, 22 June 1839 [2:0457, 0461–62, 3:0123].

3. "Junius" refers to the New York City office of the American Anti-Slavery Society which was located at 143 Nassau Street. *E*, 1 March 1838 [2:0392].

34.
William Watkins to John P. Burr
13 August 1838

William Whipper, Robert Purvis, and other leaders of the American
Moral Reform Society hoped to make the organization a racially integrated body devoted to universal reform principles. But many black
abolitionists disapproved, arguing that separate organizations were
needed to fight discrimination and encourage black progress. When failing health prevented William Watkins from attending the annual meeting
of the AMRS, he outlined this argument in a 13 August 1838 letter to
John P. Burr, the chairman of the organization's board of managers. He
defended the use of the term "colored" and argued that black organizations should address the unique situation of oppression that blacks faced.
"*Under these peculiar circumstances*," he argued, "it is my duty to give
all my aid to the colored man." He informed Burr that if he were able to
attend, he would submit a resolution calling for the AMRS to turn its
attention to black concerns. When Burr failed to bring these remarks
before the convention, the *Colored American* charged that the letter
had been deliberately suppressed. The AMRS board later published it in
the *Pennsylvania Freeman*. *CA*, 26 August, 2 September 1837, 10 February, 15, 29 March, 15 September 1838 [2:0160, 0169, 0172, 0375,
0437, 0448–49, 0590]; Bell, "American Moral Reform Society," 34–41;
Winch, *Philadelphia's Black Elite*, 117–19.

                                    BALTIMORE, [Maryland]
                                    August 13th, 1838

Friend Burr:

   I rise this morning very early to discharge a duty which I have been
compelled to delay to the last hour, but which, if totally neglected,
would, I am sure, bring down upon me the ire of you and friend Whipper, which I cannot but deprecate this hot weather. I see clearly (what I
am very reluctant to communicate) that I shall not be with you at your
approaching anniversary.[1] This disappointment to you and some of my
too partial friends, whom I should rejoice to see once more, is a source of
unfeigned regret to me. Indeed, nothing but circumstances of an unusu-
ally forbidden character, could influence me to forgo the happiness
which I should realise from a visit to friends distinguished for their
intelligence, respectability, and warm-hearted hospitality. But though it is
not my privilege to bear some humble part in your deliberations, yet, I
assure you, I still take an intense interest in your doings, especially, such
of them as evince a determination to repudiate the word "colored," as
inapplicable to us as individuals, associations, or as a people. I am also

of the opinion that so much of your past doings as go to decry, in effect, the existence of a distinct organization by ourselves of a society specifically devoted to the interests of the colored population of our country, have, with all due deference, been rather hastily adopted; and should, I think, be reconsidered. First, as to the distinguishing epithet "colored," I would ask, what is there in the term, exceptionable? Does it convey an idea of degradation? Does it cast odium upon those whom it designates? None, I presume, will affirm this. Are you afraid, then, that the *use* of the word will *remind* the white people of this nation that one sixth portion of their fellow countrymen may, by certain physical peculiarities, be distinguished from themselves? Surely, you are not so much like those who fear that the *mere sight,* by the slaves, of pictorial representations of their *actual* sufferings, will excite them to deeds of violence. Will any say that the applicability of this term to us as a people is not philosophically correct? Let those prove it who can. Without stopping, however, to contend with our hair-splitting hypercritics, on this point, permit me to say that words are used as the signs of our ideas, and whenever they perform this office, or are truly significant of the ideas for which they stand, they accomplish the object of their invention. In vain do we carp at some supposed inapplicability of a term as applied to a certain object, when imperious custom, or common consent has established the relation between the sign or word and the thing signified, that as soon as the sign or word presented to the eye, or its sound conveyed to the ear, the idea which it represents is immediately and distinctly brought to the mind. This is the case with the word in question. Custom has fixed its meaning in reference to a particular people in this country, and from this decision, however arbitrary, there is, I am sure, no successful appeal. Again, to decry the use of the word "colored," on account of some questionable inaccuracy in its applicability to us, is an argument, which, if successful, would blot out from our English vocabularies, certain words which are of established usage, or which have received the sanction of the best speakers and writers of the language. As an illustration: we correctly say (yielding to the imperious dictates of custom) that a thing is *good,* a second, *better,* a third, *best;* that the pen I had was *bad,* the one with which I now write is *worse,* and the one before me is the *worst.* This is the established mode of speech; but suppose that some of our innovating hypercritics were to affirm that these epithets should no longer be so irregularly compared—that according to the genius and analogy of our language, we ought to say, *good, gooder, goodest; bad, badder, baddest.* What advantage, I ask, would be gained by insisting upon the adoption of this uncouth phraseology? What success, think you, would attend this proposed innovation? Precisely that which awaits all resolutions calling upon us to blot from our institutions, periodicals, &c., not the word *African,* but the appropriate, and, may I not say, the endearing epithet—

"*colored.*" The truth is, while I am unfriendly to a prodigal use, or unnecessary parade of the word, I must say it is too convenient in practice to be dispensed with, unless you furnish us a substitute of paramount utility.

Once more. If I am not mistaken, the "American Moral Reform Society" assumes the ground, or has virtually decided that an organization for the *exclusive* benefit of the colored population of the country, is selfish, and totally at variance with the moral obligation to do good to all men agreeably to the principles of universal benevolence. Now, I hold to those principles, that is, I believe we should do good to all irrespective of color, &c., but I deny that an organization of the exclusive cast alluded to, *necessarily* militates against these principles. I believe they are perfectly reconcilable. On this point, it seems we are at issue. Let me illustrate my position. On my passage to Philadelphia, two men, the one white and the other colored, fall overboard—five passengers, all white men, and myself, behold the heart-rending scene—the drowning men cry for help—the five white men having contracted a deep-rooted hatred against a sable hue, and actuated by a sympathy of color, and a supposed identity of interest with the drowning [white] man, run *en masse*, to succor him; I, finding the colored man neglected from an unworthy principle, spring to his rescue, and stretch out, not one hand to the white man (who has already abundant help) and the other to the colored man, but I reach out both hands to him who has none to help him—I concentrate all my energies in one vigorous effort to extricate him, who, under these circumstances, most needs help. Is this, in the language of your Circular,[2] "to be governed by the most invidious of all creeds that ever regulated human duty, viz. the complexion of the human body?"

Can you find it in you to stigmatize such humanity as "*selfishness?*" I should well deserve the opprobrium, were I actuated by the same narrow-minded views which impelled the white men to rush to the rescue. But I was actuated by a holier impulse. I ran to the relief of the sable sufferer, *not because of his color*, (mark that), but because *being colored*, he was despised and neglected by those whose timely aid, properly apportioned, would have been most efficient. You perceive, that *under these peculiar circumstances*, it is my duty to give *all* my aid to the colored man, and this I could do for him, without feeling the least want of compassion for the white man; nay, you see clearly, that were all the circumstances of the case reversed—that is, had five colored men ran to the relief of the colored man, I would, on the principles laid down, have sprung to the rescue of the white man. Now, sir, in the candor of your soul, make the application, and then show me, if you can, the difficulties in the way of organizing a Moral Reform Society (on the principles suggested) for the exclusive benefit of our own people. Harmony in our deliberations is of the utmost consequence. Our honest differences should, if possible, be amicably adjusted. No pride of opinion—no disposition to contend for mere victory, should find place among us for a moment. Whatever sacrifices we can make without a renunciation of principle, or a dereliction of duty, should be cheerfully made for the general good. If, then, we can fall upon some plan that will leave unimpaired those sublime principles of action which embrace, without respect or partiality, the whole brotherhood of mankind—principles we all profess to admire—and, at the same time, will limit, for the present, our action to the elevation of our own people, I think we shall accomplish incomparably more good than can be achieved by a tenacious adherence to non-essentials. I hope that the society will, at this session, adopt some pacificatory course. Were I among you, I should labor for the adoption of the following, or a similar resolution:

> *Resolved*, That the object of *this Society*, is to improve the condition, mental and moral, of the colored population of our land, not because they are *colored*—but because, being colored, they are, for the most part, despised, neglected, and denied the facilities enjoyed by others, to aspire to the true dignity of rational, intelligent creatures, created in the image of God.

The adoption of a resolution like this, would be as tranquilizing as the pouring of oil upon the troubled waters.

The title of our Society, I have always thought, is rather too sweeping. It embraces, as the founders of it doubtless intended, all the inhabitants of the United States. Now, there is such a thing as propriety; and it seems to me, that, for a people in our condition, just emerging from darkness and degradation, to assume the office of reforming the whole country, betrays, to say the least, a want of modesty. We promote *"education"* among those who enjoy all its facilities, and from whom we are, in this our day of small things, soliciting the crumbs of knowledge! We promote the spread of principles of *"universal liberty"* among a people thoroughly indoctrinated in those principles!

But, upon second thoughts, we need not grasp at visionary theories here; the object at which we aim is both tangible and practicable: we can *"appeal"* to the *"people"* against, not only the injustice of our present privations and disabilities, but, also, against contemplated, additional *disfranchisements*, and can thereby inculcate the principles of *"universal liberty."* Go on, in this commendable work. Your *"Appeal"* is a masterly document.[3] My limits remind me that it is time to conclude, which I do abruptly, lest I amplify to tediousness.

Your friend,

WM. WATKINS

Pennsylvania Freeman (Philadelphia, Pa.), 6 September 1838.

1. Watkins alludes to the annual meeting of the American Moral Reform Society, which convened in Philadelphia during 14–17 August 1838.

2. Watkins quotes from a circular issued by the board of managers of the American Moral Reform Society on 12 June 1838, which was published in the 5 July 1838 edition of the *Pennsylvania Freeman*. It challenged the popular impression that the society was race-oriented in its character and objectives.

3. Watkins probably refers to a manifesto entitled "To the American People," which was coauthored by William Whipper, Alfred Niger, and Augustus Price and issued by the 1835 black national convention in conjunction with the founding of the American Moral Reform Society. The appeal outlined reasons for establishing a national reform organization and described the methods and goals of the new society. *Minutes of the Fifth Annual Convention* (1835), 25–31 [1:0598–601].

35.
Augustus W. Hanson to William Lloyd Garrison
3 November 1838

By the late 1830s, black abolitionists began to question the utility of nonresistance doctrine. The escalation of racial violence—kidnappings, individual assaults, and rioting mobs—prompted many to justify the use of force in self-defense. As early as 1837, black leaders in New York City announced their unwillingness to "recommend non-resistance to persons who are denied the protection of equitable law, and when their liberty is invaded and their lives endangered by avaricious kidnappers." Samuel Cornish could not understand why any black would advise using "moral weapons, in defense against a kidnapper or a midnight incendiary with a lighted torch in his hand." David Ruggles's work on the New York Committee of Vigilance convinced him that nonresistance was neither sound religious doctrine nor a practical method of rescuing fugitive slaves. "What efficacy is there in peace?" he asked. Augustus W. Hanson challenged nonresistance principles in a 3 November 1838 letter to pacifist William Lloyd Garrison. He revealed that in a recent assault, probably suffered on a public conveyance, he had challenged his attacker and appealed to the legal authorities. Robert C. Dick, *Black Protest: Issues and Tactics* (Westport, Conn., 1974), 129–34; *CA*, 9 September 1837 [2:0177]; *E*, 1 March 1838 [2:0393].

Saturday, 3rd November 1838

My dear Sir:

   With inexpressible feelings I now take up my pen to address you; and as a multiplicity of Subjects urge themselves upon my mind I hardly know with which to commence, but as the most recent occurrence is the most fresh undoubtedly upon your mind as well as my own, I will endeavor first to treat briefly upon that. Not having it in my power to avail myself of the conversation of men of such exalted and enlightened views of morality and Christianity as yourself, and being necessitated to rely solely upon my own feeble resources, I consequently have not probably arrived at the conclusion touching some Subjects which probably under other circumstances I might have done. In this manner am I Situated respecting the doctrine of no Civil Government; with all becoming deference would I speak of your opinions on this Subject if at any time I may occasionally recur to them. On mentioning to you the other day the circumstance of the outrageous assault committed upon me, my object really was to procure advice—and to be governed thereby in case my own reason[s] should accord thereto—and strange as it may seem to you that I should have acted in opposition to the advice given by you, I know you will allow me a few moments of your precious time to give my reason[s] for so doing. In the first place however, it is necessary that I should [assert] my belief that "the <u>powers</u> that be <u>are</u> ordained of God," as "a praise to them that do good, and a terror to Evildoers." Although therefore I would under no circumstances exercise physical force to the infliction of injury upon any fellow being. I do not believe that I should commit sin—that is transgress the law of God—by the exercise of the same physical powers merely to restrain that fellow being from inflicting an injury upon me. For instance a man comes with the avowed intention of striking me, and if possible by that blow to terminate my existence—no one will deny that he is thereby be doing wrong—and consequently if I return him the <u>like</u> injury—even though with the view to save my own life—I should be guilty of the <u>like</u> wrong. But Supposing that instead of retaliating blow for blow I merely put forth my arm to avert the intended injury—should I in this case be doing wrong? In my humble conception it appears not. Consequently the sin consists not merely in the application of physical force—but in the application thereof with a bad motive to gain a certain end at all hazard. If I be right in my view of this subject I think my course in this late affair of assault upon me with evident intent to injure will be perfectly justifiable—for my reason for appealing to the strong arm of the law for protection arose from the settled conviction that my life was in danger. And as I hold it my duty to protect and preserve that life as far as may be without infringing upon the laws of God—and also to prevent at any time the Commission of crime whenever it lies in my power so to do—I entered my protest that the law restrains that individual, and protect my life—not any more for the sake of my life than to prevent the commission of crime—and the periling of an immortal Soul to irretrievable and inevitable ruin. Self knowledge is undoubtedly the knowledge in which man has yet arrived at the least perfection but as far as I know myself this was my true and only motive in appealing to the law. I feel no personal enmity—nor have I at any time felt any against that individual. I am not aware that I have at any time infringed upon any perogative of his—for with Cowper I hold that "a disputable point is no man's ground"[1]—much therefore as I contemn and repudiate the [word illegible] sin-like conduct of this / disgrace to / man—I can freely forgive him. My aim is to arrive at the truth concerning the divine Sanction concerning human governments—and "j'espere que nous [ne] contredisons pas."[2]

The next point to which I would advert is the studiousness with which my name seems to have been shut out of the proceedings of the two last AntiSlavery Conventions (I allude to those in Worcester Co. & holden in the towns of Worcester & Northampton / which I attended). In this private epistle I request to be informed by you of the reason for these proceedings. In Worcester the resolution I introduced in behalf of the

"Mirror of Liberty"[3] was not only not acted upon but Wendell Phillips deputed a Committee to take the unusual step of returning my resolution, on the false ground that the Mass. AntiSlavery Society never in their Conventions recommended any periodicals or other publications not published in New England. Need I say to you Sir that I am convinced this is not true fo[r] in the case of the Color'd American—and others which cant be mentioned they have acted upon publications out of New England. In Worcester my name was given in as a member of the Convention and my money—one dollar in amount—paid towards defraying the expences of the Convention. Yet altho. my name was there read on the [note] it was shut out of the Liberator—tho. not I am convinced by you. [In the] minutes of the Northampton Convention published this week[4]—everyone that made any remarks is mentioned excepting your humble Servant—not that I wish to be mentioned but I cannot help noticing and feeling the evident design in these proceedings. Altho. we are told that "there is Joy in the presence of the angels of God in heaven over one Sinner that repents"—men are not willing to cooperate with one however penitent for the errors of past ways. It is impossible for me to place the one twentieth part of my thoughts on paper—and I have no friend like yourself to whom I can disburden my mind of its many encumberances. This of course does not concern the public & if at any time you can spare me or permit me one hour's interview whereever it may suit your convenience you will exceedingly oblige.

My dear Sir, Your most obedient and humble Servant

Augustus William Hanson[5]

1. William Cowper (1731–1800), an English author and poet, was noted for his many hymns and translations of classical Greek literature. Hanson quotes from Cowper's poem on controversy entitled "Conversation":

> A disputable point, is no man's ground;
> Rove where you please, 'tis common all around.

DNB, 4:1319–27; H. S. Milford, ed., *The Poetical Works of William Cowper* (London, 1934), 92.

2. This translates from the French as "I hope we don't disagree."

3. The *Mirror of Liberty*, edited by David Ruggles, was the nation's first black magazine. Intended as a quarterly, it appeared irregularly between July 1838 and July 1841 and operated on funds raised by blacks or donated by white philanthropists. Although few blacks besides Ruggles actually wrote for the journal, the *Mirror of Liberty* was an important source of abolitionist propaganda and served the interests of the black community across the North. Ruggles operated a reading room in his New York editorial office, providing blacks with access to abolitionist papers from around the country. As the voice of the New York

Committee of Vigilance, it disseminated vital information about the kidnapping rings that plagued the city and exposed the link between city officials and the kidnappers.

The *Mirror of Liberty* and its editor became symbols of black racial pride, proving "that a sable skin shrouds a mind bold and fearless, that yields no principle, and pays homage to none but to God and Liberty." Unfortunately, the journal fell victim to difficulties resulting from a lawsuit involving Ruggles, the *Colored American*, and the New York Committee of Vigilance. With failing eyesight, nearly penniless, and alienated from his former colleagues, Ruggles resigned from the committee in 1839 and suspended publication of the *Mirror of Liberty* in 1841 after local blacks failed to raise the necessary operating funds. *CA*, 10 November 1838 [2:642]; *Lib*, 19 June 1840, 24 May 1844 [3:0460, 4:0813]; Ruggles, *A Plea* [2:0702–706]; *E*, 23 January 1840 [3:0323]; Penelope Bullock, *The Afro-American Periodical Press, 1838–1909* (Baton Rouge, La., 1981), 1, 13, 25–33.

4. Hanson attended the Worcester Young Men's Anti-Slavery Convention of 2–3 October 1838 and the Convention of Western Massachusetts Counties, which met in Northampton on 5 October. The *Liberator* published the proceedings of both gatherings but mentioned neither Hanson's resolution at Worcester nor his remarks at Northampton. *Lib*, 14 September, 5, 12, 26 October, 2 November 1838.

5. Augustus W. Hanson (1815–1862) was born in the British settlement of Accra on the West African coast. His father, John W. Hanson, was a merchant and a government official. His mother was the daughter of a local tribal ruler. Educated in England, Hanson returned to Africa after completing his studies in 1827. In the spring of 1837, Hanson arrived in the United States with assurances of a position in a commercial firm, but to his dismay, he received neither the employment he had been promised nor the egalitarian treatment that he had enjoyed in England. Despite these disappointments, he remained in New York City and became active in the black community, serving as financial agent for the New York Committee of Vigilance and the *Mirror of Liberty*. His reform interests also included temperance, improving black education, and ending discrimination on public conveyances. Hanson began tutorial studies in theology in Hartford, Connecticut, in 1840. One year later, he joined J. W. C. Pennington and others to found the Union Missionary Society. Immediately thereafter he toured several states promoting the society's program for African missions. Blacks applauded Hanson's oratorical and literary skills, but some were suspicious of his contacts with the American Colonization Society. Writing under the pseudonym "Africanus," he played on colonizationist sympathies by questioning the idea of racial equality. His comments on race relations and African missions provoked strong criticism in the black press.

Ordained an Episcopal clergyman in 1842, Hanson translated the books of St. Matthew and St. John into a West African language for the Church Missionary Society, while awaiting an African missionary assignment. He returned to England in December 1842, then departed for mission work in Africa early in 1844. Two years later, he became the government chaplain for the British settlements and forts on the Gold Coast. In 1850 he received an appointment to the British consulate in Monrovia, Liberia, thereby becoming the first black British consul.

Hanson's reports on corruption and misgovernment strained his relations with Liberian president Joseph J. Roberts. He left his consular post in 1852 and after a brief stay in England, was reassigned to the consulate on Sherbro Island. There he came under criticism for being an advocate for the indigenous tribes rather than a representative of British interests. After his position was abolished in 1861, he retired on a government pension. He drowned one year later while trying to swim to a shipwreck off the coast of Sherbro Island. *CA*, 3, 15, 29 September 1838, 2, 9, 14 November 1839, 15 May, 24 July, 14 August, 4, 25 September 1841 [2:0586–87, 3:0201–202, 0251, 0260–61, 4:0184, 0214]; *Lib*, 26 January, 5, 12 October 1838 [2:0602–603, 0612]; *E*, 22 July 1841 [4:0118]; *P*, 20 February 1838, 3 September 1839; *WAA*, 16 November 1861; Augustus W. Hanson to Amos A. Phelps, 7 July, 3 August 1838, Augustus W. Hanson to Francis Jackson, 22 October 1838, Anti-Slavery Collection, MB [2:0520, 0545, 0624–25]; Augustus W. Hanson to Thomas Hodgkins, 4 August 1851, British Empire MSS., UkOxU-Rh [7:0032], Kenneth W. Cameron, ed., *American Episcopal Clergy* (Hartford, Conn., 1970), 14; Randall K. Burkett, "Chronology/ Correspondence: Augustus W. Hanson," unpublished ms, copy in author's possession.

36.
Speech by Peter Paul Simons
Delivered before the African Clarkson Association
New York, New York
23 April 1839

By the late 1830s, with slavery, discrimination, and racial violence all
on the rise, many black leaders began to question the value of moral
reform for racial advancement. In a 23 April 1839 address to the African Clarkson Association of New York City, Peter Paul Simons challenged moral reform. He argued that black leaders continually called
for "OUR MORAL ELEVATION," yet no race was "given more to
good morals and piety than we are." Simons charged that moral reform
had made blacks servile, timid, and passive. He demanded more aggressive strategies and tactics, questioning why black leaders never urged
"physical or political elevation." Simons's remarks were so controversial
that the *Colored American* repudiated them and refused to print them
except as a paid advertisement. *CA*, 8 June 1839.

My Brother Clarksons,[1] I have on all occasions where I have had the
honor to address an assemblage of our people,[2] advocated in most strongest terms the benefit of our benevolent institutions and the object of our
moral elevation. The reason why I advocated the first was that we have
had practical proof of its benefit, while the latter has now carried its
good to a climax.

In particular reference to our people, my language is inadequate to
express the honor due to those who first introduced these institutions
among us, all that I can say to those who still remain among us is, that
heaven alone can justly pay them for their labors. It would be vain to
endeavor the useless task to trace up the very many practical proofs
derived from our benevolent associations, but there is one I cannot pass
over, which is unity. Unity alone has elevated us to our present stand, and
benevolent societies was the father of it; some thirty years back there was
nothing to guide us but discord and enmity, but with the introduction of
institutions, came virtue, benevolence, sympathy, brotherly affection,
unity. It was this, exertions of our feeble selves (independent of other
sources) that has brought us to our present stand.

But hark to the trumpet sound from the pulpit. Again its thundered
from the press, now its the topic of our common arguments. What is this
discording tone? MORAL ELEVATION. OUR MORAL ELEVATION.

It is sounded to be the prolific parent of all virtue, and he who would
dare whisper in the faintest breath against it, is thought no less than the
parent of all vice, crime, and degradation, that possibly could afflict

humanity. But I my Brother Clarksons will venture to say that this long talk of our moral elevation, has made us a moral people, but no more. There is no nation of people under the canopy of heaven, who are given more to good morals and piety than we are. Show up to the world an African and you will show in truth morality. It is stamped in his countenance, it is in his word an act-on, he uses it mechanically for his principal tool to work by. But as it has progressed, it has carried along with it blind submission. Yes brothers, our soft manners when particularly addressing those of pale complexions, this very great respect which is particularly shown to them also, moral elevation carries these which are roots of degradation with it. As my proof to this fact our children by having so much of this folly for their institutions, taught by example from its parent, to submit to any decision that comes from a white quarter; this cherishes a natural timidity, and white children can with ease coward down colored children of the same age. Why is this? The difference of their bringing up, my worthy brothers is the sole cause. The parent of the one although he may be extremely poor, thinks himself a poor finite being, and knows too well that all mankind are the same, he knows nothing, and will acknowledge nothing superior, but the Almighty God. He shows this as an example for his child, which it carries out through life. While the parent of the other takes morality for his guide (although morality when uninterrupted is a strong step to piety, I must confess, but when harassed by prejudice it makes a slave of itself), and this morality links on those evils, and we chain on ourselves oppression. Yes it's nothing but this moral elevation that causes us to have so little confidence in one another, it is this alone that puts white men at the head of even our private affairs, they are both judge and council for some of our people's transactions, and they can fill all offices where they can gain their ends. Yes Brothers, this moral elevation of our people is but a mere song, it is nothing but a conspicuous scarecrow designed expressly, I may safely say, to hinder our people from acting collectively for themselves. For long as it continues we will have a lack of confidence in one another, and if we suspect each other, how can we act together. No, we must lose sight of it entire, for it will deceive you if practised any longer. I wonder much how our people could be regurgitated by this false philanthropy so long, for there is no such a thing as elevating a nation of people by good morals, it is contrary to common sense or any plan of elevation laid down in record. But it is practised on our people as a means for to hinder them from acting in another way to obtain their rights. The basis of the manumission society was to elevate Africans by morals, and this has been formed upwards of a half century,[3] and what has been done? Our people were slaves then and are the same today; this northern freedom is nothing but a nickname for northern slavery, and it was but a speculative policy in making us the free slaves of the north, being the climate would not suffer a sugar plantation, a coffee or a rice field, the master found it to be a good speculation in making us the free slaves of the north. We have been a people more deceived than any nation of people under the sun; we have always mistaken speculation for benevolence, like the slave trade, it was not benevolence that roused England, France, and America, to send out naval forces to stop the importation of slaves, no such a thing, it was their policy.[4] For they knew that the annual importation, together with the natural increase of slaves, that in time they would double outnumber the white population, and it would bring about too soon that very dark day, when God would raise up the ghosts of our forefathers from their *graves*, to rouse us all to revenge.

But I am intruding on your patience by dwelling too long on this one topic, I will carry you to the next which is also hashed up for us to feast on, it is intellectual elevation. In my schoolboy days parents were much infatuated with the idea of educating their children, that they might fill easy situations in life, but they have found themselves now, bitterly disappointed. It was said then by those who were called our friends, educate your children, and when they become men they can fill easy situations in life, this was the language then used, and it is used now by those who are our friends.

But we all know well that their sayings in this particular has not proved itself. For we see men of the highest standing among us filling very low stations. Men educated, and are preachers of the gospel, filling the meanest occupations in life from extreme necessity. But our friends tell us we must not fill low stations, for it degrades us the more, but they take good care not to adopt the means that some of our talented men might fill respectable stations.

The Colonizationist or pro-slavery men as they are called, say to us go to Africa, the land of your forefathers, for I hold a prejudice within my breast, I can no way get rid of, I was born with it, in infancy taught it, in my boyhood practised upon it, and now I am a man it has become an innate principle, go to Africa, but if you insist on staying here, I will give you only such employment to do, as to make you a poor wretch all your lifetime.

Our friends to the contrary say stay here brother, our principles are all men are equal, but my brother do not domesticate yourself, do not be any man's servant, for it helps to degrade you. But mark ye, the friend has not adopted a plan yet for us to do anything else. And let me ask this generous public, who of these two speaks most conscientious, or gives the full development of his heart? You can answer that best yourselves. But we have been waiting for better prospects this great while, but we will never see better prospects until we give up all parties, acknowledge none as our friends, until they carry out their views to a letter, and have practical proof of some truth in their great declarations.

I think it is high time for us to act, for we must certainly see this deception, and all that is left for us to do is simply collective action, and we will profit our desires.

Parents I have perceived of late, act quite to the contrary from what was practised some few years back. It was then education of children, and both the means of the parent and time of the child went to accomplish the great end. But parents at present set them to some employment early that they might thank God for putting it in the parent for adopting the best means for a welfare. As a proof to this let me ask my auditors, who are they in the best circumstances among us the learned or the unlearned? How many men of education among us has accumulated anything at all? I will take the responsibility and answer none. It has been those who toil daily at the rough and most laborous work that has accumulated the means to benefit them while living, then to bequeath a legacy when dead. The reason those who are considered the most literate among us do not reap the sweets of the harvest, is that this cry of intellectual elevation has caused them to be proud, and they will not be no man's servant, they carry our friends' views out to a letter in this particular, they form classes of distinction, so as to be known from those who get an honest living by labor. These individuals to keep up their rank of distinction by intellectual capacity, and having no means to back it, they degrade themselves the more for they are nothing but learned paupers. It is a wrong idea in our people that because they have education, they must do only such employment to meet their large views, seek for means first, all, or principal part of the means that is among us, you will find among the laboring class. Those who first introduced this phantom of imagination among us will not give a help in time of need, no, for this reason I say, let everyone study his own interest, and let everyone's interest be self. Why is it, that we never hear of a physical and a political elevation, because they both call for united strength. And these two must go together, for if you destroy the one you must unquestionably shock the other, and even when taken separately they require action, and we must act before we can be an independent people.

Physical and political efforts are the only methods left for us to adopt. Yes my Brothers, and it may appear very singular, but it is a true trait in the African character, that there is a natural timidity, a great lack of physical courage.

We act like infidels. The time when France in her infidelity, believing that death was an eternal sleep, this caused them to be complete cowards.[5] They started at their own moonlight shadow, fearing that some assassin were at their heels to end their eternal career. So it is with us, we seem to have lost all sight of the splendid mirror of immortality, we act like when this miserable life is ended, it will be to an eternal nonentity. Our actions do not show well the belief that this world was but a turnpike for us to travel through, and at the end of which lies life eternal. No, and if our forefathers held the truths of immortality of the soul before their eyes, there would have been no such thing as African slavery, for they all would have died one by one, before they would remain one day in the clutches of captivity. Oh! that we could picture to our views the splendor of an after existence, Oh that I could rouse my brethren, even to the last struggle. Who would sicken years away of servitude and oppression? Who, at this age of intellect, would not rather cling to immortality? What boots this miserable life since it is to pass away, even if it is lost by disease or strife?

Is it possible that this foolish thought of moral elevation suffers us to remain inactive? If so, than remain inactive, and you but raise another generation of slaves, and your children's children to the last posterity will spend their lives in as bitter oppression as ye do now today.

Remain inactive and your children will curse the day of their birth.

Remain inactive, and you will be the cause of rearing children for an eternal torment, for they in an ecstacy of despair will curse their maker for suffering such bitter oppression to be practised upon them.

Remain inactive, and the almighty himself will spurn you, for lack of courage and not using properly your agency. No, we must show AC-TION! ACTION! *ACTION!* and our will to be, or not to be; this we study, this we must physically practice, and we will be in truth an independent people.

Colored American (New York, N.Y.), 1 June 1839.

1. The African Clarkson Association was one of many mutual aid societies organized by New York City blacks. Founded in 1825, it offered financial assistance to widows, orphans, and infirmed members; promoted education; and helped pay members' burial expenses. Blacks between the ages of twenty-one and forty who had been in good health for one year prior to enrollment were eligible for membership. The association met monthly and remained in operation until the 1850s. Porter, *Early Negro Writing*, 45–50; Daniel Perlman, "Organizations of the Free Negro in New York City, 1800–1860," *JNH* 56:186 (July 1971); Freeman, "Free Negro in New York City," 240–41.

2. Peter Paul Simons, a black porter, addressed benevolent societies in New York City on several occasions during the late 1830s. His early criticisms of moral reform and his personal attacks on Philip Bell, the publisher of the *Colored American*, made him a controversial figure in the local black community. A vocal advocate of the rights of women and blacks, he worked in the campaign for equal suffrage in New York state during the late 1830s and coordinated petition drives in his neighborhood. Simons was a delegate to the 1841 convention of New York City blacks. His reform activities subsided until the 1860s, when he became an outspoken critic of the African Civilization Society, characterizing it as "kin to the old colonization scheme." After the Emancipation Proclamation, Simons worked hard to encourage black enlistment in the Union army. *New York*

City Directory, 1850–61; *CA*, 19 August, 2 September, 30 December 1837, 13 January, 20 October 1838, 1 June 1839, 2 October 1841 [2:0152, 0167, 0311–12, 0344, 0622, 3:0075–76, 0078, 4:0232]; *WAA*, 21 April 1860 [12:0646]; *Lib*, 22, 29 May 1863 [14:0868, 0875].

3. Simons refers to the New York Manumission Society, which was founded in 1785.

4. Britain led the Western world in suppressing the African slave trade. France and the United States contributed token naval forces to the effort, but despite diplomatic pressure, both repeatedly denied the British navy the right to search vessels flying their country's colors. Because of lax American enforcement, most slave traders sailed under the U.S. flag after 1830. W. E. F. Ward, *The Royal Navy and the Slavers: The Suppression of the Atlantic Slave Trade* (New York, N.Y., 1969), 121, 126, 138–39, 141.

5. Simons probably refers to the popular influence of deism, atheism, and rationalist philosophy during the era of the French Revolution.

37.
Speech by Andrew Harris
Delivered at the Broadway Tabernacle
New York, New York
7 May 1839

At the heart of the black abolitionist message lay an understanding of the connection between slavery and racial prejudice. According to many black leaders, slavery promoted racism, which in turn was used to justify inequality in the North as well as slavery in the South. Black abolitionists denounced this link as the wellspring of oppression. This understanding strengthened free black identification with the slave. By ending slavery, northern blacks expected to increase their own freedom. Andrew Harris's remarks at the annual meeting of the American Anti-Slavery Society on 7 May 1839 underscored the relationship between slavery and racism. Addressing nearly five thousand abolitionists at the Broadway Tabernacle in New York City, Harris spoke in support of a resolution blaming slavery for the condition of free blacks. During this time, when internecine battles over women's rights, nonresistance, and political antislavery were destroying antislavery unity and moving abolitionism away from black concerns, his comments reminded white reformers that the fight was not just about slavery but also about its effects on free blacks. *E*, 16 May 1839; *Lib*, 17, 24 May 1839; *AF*, 30 May 1839.

It is with no pleasant feelings, said he, that I stand here to speak in relation to the wrongs of a portion of the inhabitants of this country, who, by their complexion, are identified with myself. It is with feelings of great responsibility that I stand here as their representative.[1]

Who of our Pilgrim fathers, when they entered ship, and committed themselves to the waves—when the breeze carried back the echo of their songs, even though the day would come, when an assembly like this would meet on the island of Manhattan, for such an object? Who would then have supposed, that the oppression and wrongs of millions in this country, would have been so great as to call together an audience like this? If an inhabitant of another world should enter one of these doors, and look abroad upon these thousands, and ask, "For what are you assembled?" and the voice of this multitude should be heard in answer, "We have come to hear and converse about the wrongs of our fellow men;" would he esteem it a light or trifling thing, which has brought this audience together?

But from whence spring these wrongs? The original source from which they spring, is the corruption of the human heart. The beginning of its development is *slavery*. Shall I again point to the South, and depict the sufferings of the slave? If the groans and sighs of the victims of slavery could be collected, and thrown out here in one volley, these walls would tremble, these pillars would be removed from their foundations, and we should find ourselves buried in the ruins of the edifice. If the blood of the innocent, which has been shed by slavery, could be poured out here, this audience might swim in it—or if they could not swim they would be drowned. If the tears that slavery has caused to be shed, were poured out here, there might be a sea on which to ply the oar in exercise of sport and diversion. But this is not all—the anguish produced by separation of husband and wife, children and parents, and the scourges of the defenseless and unoffending slave, are a fathomless sea, and an ocean without a shore.

But slavery does not stop here. It presses down upon the free people of color. Its deadly poison is disseminated from the torrid regions of the South to the frigid North. We feel it here. Yet, with all this, if the colored man is vicious, or if he is not elevated, it is set down to his natural stupidity and depravity, and the argument is raised that he belongs to an inferior race. The colored people are also charged with want of desire for education and improvement; yet, if a colored man comes to the door of our institutions of learning, with desires ever so strong, the lords of these institutions rise up and shut the door; and then you say we have not the desire nor the ability to acquire education. Thus, while the white youth enjoy all these advantages, we are excluded and shut out, and must remain ignorant. It is natural to suppose, then, that there should be more crime among us. But is this crime properly chargeable to the colored man, as evidence of the vicious propensities of his race?

Again, in the social relations of life, wrongs are inflicted upon us that are grievous and heavy to be borne, and we must fold our arms and bear it. But even this is thrown out as a taunt against us, that we do not speak of our wrongs, as evidence that we are too stupid and degraded to feel them: while, if we rise to defend ourselves and to plead our cause, the torch and the brick-bat are poured out as arguments on the other side. As a specimen, I will mention what I experienced in my passage to this city, from the city of "brotherly love," so called; but as to the claim it has upon that title, I leave the ruins of Pennsylvania Hall to answer.[2] On the way, they refused to give the colored man a seat, but put him up in boxes, as they would monkeys or wild geese. And why was this? Was it because he had no money? No. Was it because he was not decently clad? No. Was it because he was an idiot, and they feared he would annoy the company with his foolishness? No—it is because he has *the complexion which God has given him*. The bible says the love of money is the root of all evil; and if the love of money is a predominant passion anywhere, it is in this land. Yet, without disputing the correctness of the declaration, it seems to me that slavery has developed a passion in the human heart that is stronger than the love of money; for they refuse to gratify this disposition which the bible says is the root of all evil, through the influence of that still deeper root of evil, *prejudice.*

Again: the colored man is deprived of the opportunity of obtaining those situations in society which his enemies say he ought to hold, if capable. If he wishes to be useful as a professional man, a merchant or a mechanic, he is prevented by the color of his skin, and driven to those menial employments which tend to bring us more and more into disrepute.

The church itself was not free from participation in the general guilt of oppressing the black man. He feared that some of her pastors would in the great day, have the Judge say to them, "though ye have cast out devils in my name, yet this devil of prejudice you have not cast out of your own hearts—and though you may have done many wonderful works, one great work, that of emancipating the slave, ye have left undone."

Time would fail me, said he, to depict all these wrongs. Yet, with all the oppression and odium that is heaped upon us here, I for one would rather stand and endure it all, choosing rather to suffer affliction with my people, than to emigrate to a foreign shore, though I might there enjoy the pleasures of Egypt. And while I live, let my prayer be, that the same soil which cherished my father may cherish me; and when I die, that the same dust may cover me that covered the ashes of my father.

Emancipator (New York, N.Y.), 16 May 1839.

1. Andrew Harris (1810–1841) was born in New York. Little is known about his parentage, except that he was raised in a religious foster household. After attending the Geneva Lyceum, he was refused admission to Union and Middlebury colleges because of his race and finally enrolled at the University of Vermont, where he graduated in 1838. While pursuing his studies, Harris took charge of a black school in Troy, New York. He also succeeded Daniel A. Payne as the pastor of the local Liberty Street Presbyterian Church and helped organize the Union Society of Albany and Troy. Once he received his degree, Harris settled in Philadelphia and continued theological studies under abolitionist Albert Barnes. After serving as a licentiate for the Second African Presbyterian Church, he was ordained and installed as pastor in April 1841. Harris was a member of the American Moral Reform Society and participated in local antislavery, anticolonization, and vigilance committee work. As a speaker, he seemed "more a discriminating logician than a fanciful poet," according to one contemporary observer. He addressed the 1839 annual meeting of the American Anti-Slavery Society on the subjects of slavery and racial prejudice. Like many other black Congregational and Presbyterian ministers, Harris grew uncomfortable with Garrisonianism and turned to the newly formed American and Foreign Anti-Slavery Society in 1840. His death in December 1841 ended a promising ministerial and reform career. *E,* 1 December 1836, 16 May 1839 [1:0743, 3:0060];

CA, 15 April 1837, 15 September 1838, 5 December 1840, 8, 22 May, 11 September 1841 [2:0027, 0588, 3:1025, 4:0029, 0191–96]; *Lib*, 10 November 1848; *NASS*, 13 March 1841; *RDA*, 17 December 1841; *WAA*, 14 October 1865; Winch, *Philadelphia's Black Elite*, 84, 118, 120; Payne, *Recollections of Seventy Years*, 326–27.

2. Harris refers to the burning of Philadelphia's Pennsylvania Hall by an antiabolitionist mob in 1838.

38.
Boston Blacks Defend William Lloyd Garrison

William P. Powell to William Lloyd Garrison
10 July 1839

Resolutions by a Committee of Boston Blacks
Presented at the First Independent Baptist Church
Boston, Massachusetts
19 March 1840

The fracture of the Massachusetts Anti-Slavery Society in 1839 fore-shadowed the breakup of the American Anti-Slavery Society the following year. Passionate clashes over strategies, tactics, and reform principles drove conservatives from both organizations. Several white clergymen broke with the MASS, describing it as a *"women's-rights, non-government Anti-Slavery Society."* They organized the rival Massachusetts Abolition Society and began publishing the *Massachusetts Abolitionist.* The schism forced Massachusetts blacks to choose sides. In a 10 July 1839 letter, William P. Powell spoke for a majority of Boston blacks who remained fiercely loyal to Garrison and his principles. Using a medical metaphor, Powell traced the rise of the immediatist movement and defended Garrisonianism as "the genuine medicine." Between June 1839 and April 1840, Boston blacks held a series of meetings devoted to the growing conflict among Massachusetts abolitionists. They equated support for Garrison with true abolitionism and unanimously condemned "new organization men" as colonizationists at heart. On 19 March 1840, a large crowd of Boston blacks crammed into the city's First Independent Baptist Church to respond to a letter published six days earlier in the *Massachusetts Abolitionist* by "A Colored Man." They disputed the letter's claim that local blacks supported the "new organization" and approved a series of resolutions by John T. Hilton, Joel W. Lewis, James G. Barbadoes, Joshua B. Smith, and Christopher Weeden expressing support for Garrison and the MASS. Kraditor, *Means and Ends in American Abolitionism,* 50–51; Ripley et al., *Black Abolitionist Papers,* 2:190–91; *Lib,* 7, 14 June, 1 November 1839, 20 March, 3, 10 April 1840; *MAb,* 13 March 1840.

BOSTON, [Massachusetts]
7th mo. 10, 1839

DEAR FRIEND:

Circumstances entirely beyond my control constrained me to forego the pleasant interview that I expected to have had with you on Tuesday evening, previous to my leaving the city, consequently I embrace this opportunity of expressing my regret at the unexpected disappointment. But before leaving the city: allow me, through the medium of this letter, to indulge myself in a few remarks concerning the advancement of the *holy cause of Abolition*.

"When doctors disagree, who shall decide?" says the moralist.[1] And when abolition doctors disagree about prescribing medicine to cure the infectious *disease* of slavery, who shall we look to for a decision? My answer is—to the *patient*. And professing to be one who has been sick *all* his days, and knowing that the *disease* still continues to make sad havoc among my colored countrymen, I venture to decide for myself.

Before examining the disagreement of abolition doctors, allow me to notice the experimental medicine used by the Colonization Society. These doctors proposed to remove such free colored people as were convalescent to a purer air, where the scorching rays of an African sun would make them a healthy nation of *Freemen*. But some how or other, they very imprudently furnished them with "the cordial for all our fears," rum, which, when mixed with a little gunpowder, and taken in strong doses, soon brought on a *relapse*; and dreadful to relate, many died or— were decently *killed*! Things went on this way for some years, when a young printer proposed to try a new medicine, immediatism, which, when rightly applied, would cure the disease without *bleeding*. So confident was he of the efficacy of his medicine, that he applied some of the same to a slave-trader in Maryland, which threw him into such a fit that with the assistance of twelve jurymen and others, the printer was pronounced a *quack* and thrown into close confinement. But, if I am rightly informed, through the liberality of a *Gothamite*, he was soon after released. Afterwards, he established a *school* in Boston, consisting of eleven or twelve pupils, and astonishing to relate, the whole country is now overrun with schools to the number of 2000, and pupils without number.[2] Certificates were coming in from all quarters, testifying to the astonishing cures effected by using his *life*-preserving medicine.

But after all, this printer entertained two or three *ultra notions*, viz: that in the nineteenth century, women were to all intents and purposes— *persons*—entitled to be respected as such in *all* the relations of life. That divine government is preferable to human governments, &c. Consequently, "the staff of accomplishment" must be taken from him and others, and placed in the hands of an electioneering and time-serving clergy. Now, dear friend, as they are about to administer strange medicine, I, for one (and I know I speak the sentiments of *all* my colored brethren) will neither touch, taste nor handle the unclean thing; and I warn all true-hearted abolitionists to buy and circulate the genuine medicine to cure the "infectious disease of slavery" to be had only at No. 25 Cornhill.[3] I would like to say more, but time and paper fails me. Go on in the good cause and heaven will be your reward.

Yours truly,

WILLIAM P. POWELL[4]

Liberator (Boston, Mass.), 19 July 1839.

Resolved That whereas, the Mass. Abolitionist of the 13th inst. contains an article over the signature of "A Colored Man," charging the old Massachusetts Anti-Slavery Society, and the editor of the Liberator, with recreancy to the first principles of abolition; and whereas he claims to give utterance to the sentiments and feelings of the colored population of Boston;[5] therefore we feel called upon, out of respect for ourselves, and to the old society to whose principles of equal rights, liberty, and humanity, we subscribe, to register our united and unqualified denial of the truth of these unwarranted assertions.

Resolved, That the position taken by the author, where he says, "Touch one colored man and you touch all," would not seem to be true in all cases; for the poor slaves are daily touched, and there are some, we regret to say, among us, who have little or no sympathy for them, if we judge them by the scripture standard "Out of the abundance of the heart, the mouth speaketh."[6] Again—were there no exceptions to this rule, persons might be sheltered from justice, who are guilty of crimes of the deepest dye, and that simply because they are colored.

Resolved, That whereas the same writer has said that were a meeting called of the colored people to lay their votes on the merits of the two societies in question,[7] they would give their hearty amen in favor of the new—we pronounce it a wholesale falsehood, and feel justified in saying that the spirit which prompted him in penning said article was dictated neither by truth nor self-respect.

Resolved, That so far from our confidence being shaken in the integrity of the Massachusetts Anti-Slavery Society, or that of the veteran editor of the Liberator, as stated in the article above alluded to, daily proofs of their real merits increase our attachment, and bind us stronger to them; and of Mr. Garrison we can truly add, that we doubt not that the day will come, when many an emancipated slave will say of him, while weeping over his monument, "This was my best friend and benefactor. I here bathe his tomb with the tears of that liberty, which his services and sufferings achieved for me."

Resolved, That to slander Garrison, and pronounce him a hypocrite, is certainly the most unkind and ungrateful expression that could ever escape the lips of any colored man, and is what we least expected to hear, after so much toil and suffering in our behalf, and we rejoice that such spirits are few and far between.

On the adoption of the resolutions a discussion ensued, in which the following gentlemen participated—Geo. Washington,[8] John Levy,[9] Joshua B. Smith,[10] J. H. Gover,[11] J. T. Hilton,[12] and J. G. Barbadoes,[13] when they were unanimously adopted by a rising vote.

John Levy suggested the propriety of affording an opportunity to those who did not concur in the adoption of the resolutions, to present their objections. None were offered.

Joshua B. Smith offered the following resolution, which was unanimously adopted:

Resolved, That the man or men who wrote the article against Mr. Garrison, are like unto the new organization, seeking nothing more than personal interest; and we, as a body, do detest their conduct, for it is founded on deceptions; and if we follow them, they will lead us to destruction, instead of elevation.

Christopher R. Weeden[14] offered the following resolution which was unanimously adopted:

Resolved, That we will, while life remains, prove steadfast and true to the old Massachusetts Anti-Slavery Society and its auxiliaries, while they continue to plead the cause of the down-trodden sons of America, with their past zeal, and also our claim to the rights and privileges of independent citizens of the United States, irrespective of color.

On motion of J. T. Hilton, a committee was appointed to obtain the publication of the proceedings in the Massachusetts' Abolitionist, Liberator and Colored American;[15] and also to request of the editor of the Abolitionist,[16] the name of the author of the communication alluded to. The committee consisted of J. C. Barbadoes, J. T. Hilton, J. E. Scarlett,[17] Wm. C. Nell,[18] and John P. Coburn.[19] J. T. Hilton spoke in reply to the query, what has the old society done?

Among other remarks he said, the old Society overthrew the Colonization Society.[20] It has quelled the mobocratic spirit and given birth to the American Anti-Slavery society. It has uniformly elected colored men as members of the Board of Managers.[21] It has secured the right of a trial by Jury for fugitive slaves—gained equal rights for colored people in Providence and Worcester cars. Through its influence, four colleges have opened their doors for the admission of colored youth on equal terms with the whites. And, finally, it has obtained in the Massachusetts Legislature the passage of resolutions in favor of immediate emancipation.[22] Messrs Garrison and Knapp[23] have, at different times, appropriated over six hundred dollars, towards assisting colored persons, &c.&c.

Great enthusiasm was manifested at the close of the meeting, in view of the proceedings, which were concluded by singing "From all that dwell below the skies" to the tune of Old Hundred[24]

John B. Cutler,[25] Chairman
William C. Nell, Christopher
Weeden, Secretaries.

Elizur Wright Papers, Library of Congress, Washington, District of Columbia. Published by permission.

1. Powell freely quotes from "To Lord Bathurst," a series of couplets in epistle 3 of *Moral Essays* (1735) by English poet Alexander Pope: "Who shall decide when doctors disagree?"

2. Powell provides a metaphorical account of William Lloyd Garrison's role in the rise of an immediatist antislavery movement. As junior editor of Benjamin Lundy's Baltimore weekly, the *Genius of Universal Emancipation*, Garrison criticized a Massachusetts merchant named Francis Todd for allowing his ship to be used in the domestic slave trade. Todd sued Garrison for libel and in early 1830, Garrison was brought to trial, found guilty, and fined $100. When he could not pay, he was incarcerated in Baltimore Jail for forty-nine days until New York City abolitionist Arthur Tappan paid his fine. Garrison soon left Baltimore for Boston, where in 1832 he and a small circle of local abolitionists organized the New England Anti-Slavery Society. Thereafter, the antislavery movement grew quickly. By 1838 the American Anti-Slavery Society officially claimed that 1,350 antislavery societies with 250,000 members had been founded. David K. Sullivan, "William Lloyd Garrison in Baltimore, 1829–1830," *MHM* 68:66–77 (Spring 1973); Filler, *Crusade against Slavery*, 87.

3. Powell continues his metaphorical account of William Lloyd Garrison, focusing on those antislavery tenets that alienated more conservative abolitionists by the late 1830s. Garrison supported the equal participation of women in the movement, criticized American churches for their moderation on the slavery issue, and opposed political action against slavery. These stands antagonized many abolitionists, particularly clergymen, and divided the antislavery movement in 1840. Powell advises abolitionists to cling to Garrisonian principles and to support Garrison's paper, the *Liberator*, which was published at 25 Cornhill in Boston. Kraditor, *Means and Ends in American Abolitionism*, 39–141.

4. William P. Powell (1807–ca. 1879) was born free in New York state and was later described on his passport application as "of a mulatto colour but of Indian extraction." Powell's grandmother was Elizabeth Barjova, a cook for the Continental Congress, and his father was a slave named Edward Powell, who was freed when New York abolished slavery in 1827. Powell received considerable education before serving as an apprentice sailor. He settled in New Bedford, Massachusetts, married Mercy O. Haskins from nearby Plymouth (who was probably part Indian), and established a boardinghouse for sailors.

Powell was an early Garrisonian abolitionist. He signed the constitution of the American Anti-Slavery Society in December 1833, helped found a local antislavery society in the New Bedford area, and was one of the first members of the New England Anti-Slavery Society. An anticolonizationist, he believed that blacks should participate fully and equally in American society. In 1837 Powell and other free blacks appeared before the Massachusetts legislature to protest racial discrimination in the state. Their efforts began a long struggle, which culminated in 1855, when blacks won the statewide right to send their children to integrated public schools.

Powell promoted women's rights and black self-help. He was chairman of New Bedford's Young Men's Wilberforce Debating Society and supported the temperance crusade. In 1839 Powell moved to New York City and opened an employment agency and home for sailors under the auspices of the American Seamen's Friend Society. Powell continued his antislavery activity by founding the Manhattan Anti-Slavery Society (1840) and by using the sailors' home to host abolitionist gatherings. Throughout his antislavery career, Powell maintained his allegiance to the American Anti-Slavery Society and Garrisonian principles. He served on the society's executive committee, opposed political abolitionism, and criticized the slaveholding American church. When the Fugitive Slave Law of 1850 was passed, Powell led black efforts to prevent state and local police involvement in extraditions.

Powell's concern about the law and his desire to insure an adequate education for his seven children prompted a ten-year residence in Liverpool, England. While living there, Powell worked for a trading company and continued his antislavery efforts by hosting black abolitionists during their British tours, serving as a conduit between reform allies in the United States and Britain, and coordinating shipments of British goods to the Boston Anti-Slavery Bazaar.

Powell returned home during the secession crisis. His son William, Jr., was commissioned as a surgeon for the Union army. In 1862 Powell reopened his seamen's home in New York City; a year later, the home was ransacked and his family threatened by draft rioters. Powell helped found the American Seamen's Protective Union Association (1863); he served as a delegate to the National Colored Labor Convention held in Washington, D.C. (1869); and he was chairman of the New York Civil Rights Committee (1873). Powell was a participant at a William Lloyd Garrison Memorial meeting held in San Francisco during June 1879. Philip S. Foner, *Essays in Afro-American History* (Philadelphia, Pa., 1978), 88–111; George W. Forbes, "William P. Powell," Biographical Sketches of Eminent Negroes, William Powell to Maria Weston Chapman, 30 October 1857, 12 January 1859, William Powell to Samuel J. May, 21 October 1859, Anti-Slavery Collection, MB [10:0880, 11:0545, 12:0142]; Constitution of the American Anti-Slavery Society, American Anti-Slavery Society Papers, DLC [1:0352]; *Lib*, 24 May 1834, 13 June 1835, 19 July, 27 September 1839, 21 July 1843, 7 February 1845, 13 March, 24 July 1863, 29 September 1865 [1:0456, 0609, 3:0141, 0207, 4:0613, 0987, 14:0762, 0974, 16:0236]; *NASS*, 6 May 1841, 24 February 1842, 28 March 1844, 3 May 1845, 10 August, 10 September, 29 October 1846, 9 January, 6 February 1851, 12 February 1859, 23, 30 July 1863 [3:1022, 4:0369, 0774, 5:0267, 1071, 6:0726, 11:0585]; *NSt*, 7 April 1849, 24 October 1850 [5:1051]; *ASA*, August 1853; *WAA*, 10 August 1861 [13:0685]; *PP*, 17 August 1861 [13:0693, 0694].

5. The resolution refers to a piece in the 13 March 1840 issue of the *Massachusetts Abolitionist*, the organ of the Massachusetts Abolition Society and a

vocal opponent of Garrisonian principles. First published in February 1839, the paper was edited throughout much of it brief existence by Elizur Wright, Jr., despite his ongoing ideological disputes with society leaders. Renamed the *Free American* in March 1841, it merged with Joshua Leavitt's *Emancipator* at the end of the year. Lawrence B. Goodheart, "Elizur Wright, Jr., and the Abolitionist Movement, 1820–1865" (Ph.D. diss., University of Connecticut, 1979), 153–71.

6. The authors of the resolution quote from Matthew 12:34.

7. The two societies referred to are the Massachusetts Anti-Slavery Society and the Massachusetts Abolition Society. The MAS was formed when a conservative faction of the MASS broke with the Garrisonians in May 1839. It briefly published its own paper, the *Massachusetts Abolitionist*. Reflecting the sentiments of conservative abolitionists, the society rejected Garrisonian principles. The division of the MASS sparked similar schisms within local societies in Massachusetts and presaged the splintering of the American Anti-Slavery Society the following year. The MAS dissolved by December 1839. Kraditor, *Means and Ends in American Abolitionism*, 50–51; Thomas, *Liberator*, 274–80.

8. George Washington (1795–?), a Boston barber, served for over thirty years as a deacon of the black First Independent Baptist Church. He was active in local struggles for equal rights, including the efforts to integrate Boston's public schools and attempts to organize a local black militia called the Massasoit Guards. Washington, a devout Garrisonian, participated in several pro-*Liberator* meetings and joined the public protest against the Fugitive Slave Law. *Lib*, 20 April 1838, 14 June, 1 November 1839, 3 April 1840, 4 August 1843, 10 August, 21 September 1849, 5 April 1850, 4 April 1851 [2:0463, 3:0113, 0248, 0374, 4:0621, 6:0074, 0163, 0435, 0871–72]; "To the School Committee of the City of Boston," 1844, Anti-Slavery Collection, MB [4:0723–27]; Horton and Horton, *Black Bostonians*, 33, 44, 52, 120; George A. Levesque, "Black Boston: Negro Life in Garrison's Boston, 1800–1860" (Ph.D. diss., State University of New York at Binghamton, 1976), 374–78; U.S. Census, 1850.

9. John Levy was originally from St. Thomas in the Caribbean. Settling in Boston by the mid-1820s, he worked as a waiter before opening a refreshment concession, then a hairdressing establishment. Levy served as the Boston agent for the Providence-based New England Union Academy in the 1830s, joined other prominent Boston blacks in generating support for the Colored Orphan Asylum, and regularly attended anticolonization rallies, First of August celebrations, and New England Colored Temperance Society meetings. He lived in Massachusetts and was an agent and frequent correspondent of the *Liberator* during the 1840s. A loyal Garrisonian, he sent issues of the newspaper to abolitionists on St. Croix in the Caribbean, defended Garrison from detractors within the black community, and spoke against black separatism in the abolitionist movement. *Lib*, 27 August 1836, 5 October, 14 December 1838, 8 March, 14 June, 26 July, 30 August, 1, 29 November 1839, 20 March, 3, 10 April 1840, 21 July, 4 August 1843, 16 October 1846, 28 January 1848, 27 December 1850 [1:0698, 2:0604, 0674, 3:0022, 0113, 0150, 0185, 0248, 0347, 0374, 4:0621]; *PF*, 22 August 1839; *Boston City Directory*, 1825, 1839.

10. Joshua B. Smith (1813–1879), a black Boston caterer, was born in Coatesville, Pennsylvania, where he attended public school through the assistance of a

Quaker woman. He resettled in Boston in 1836, worked as a headwaiter, and then in 1849 established his own restaurant business. During the following twenty-five years, he became known locally as "the prince of the caterers." Smith used his business to complement antislavery and civil rights activities in Boston. He employed fugitive slaves during their sojourns in the Boston area and frequently provided dinners and refreshments for antislavery fairs, antislavery conventions, and other public gatherings. Well-known and respected by Boston abolitionists, Smith remained loyal to William Lloyd Garrison throughout his life. He was a vice-president of the New England Freedom Association, a vigilance committee active in the mid-1840s, and later served on the executive board of the Boston Vigilance Committee. Outraged by the passage of the Fugitive Slave Law of 1850, he urged the fugitive slave to arm himself with "bowie knife and revolver." As a personal protest, he refused Daniel Webster's request for his catering services.

Smith was involved in a variety of civic affairs. For over a decade, he participated in the struggle to end segregation in Boston public schools. In the 1850s, he petitioned the state legislature for a monument to honor Crispus Attucks. After the Civil War, he collected subscriptions for a memorial to Robert G. Shaw, commander of the Fifty-fourth Massachusetts Regiment. He became the first black Freemason accepted by St. Andrew's Lodge. His involvement in Republican politics led to a term in the state senate in 1873.

Smith was financially ruined by business dealings with the government during the Civil War. Although he supplied provisions for the Twelfth Massachusetts Regiment, both the state and federal governments refused to take responsibility for the contract. After a protracted legal battle, he received only partial compensation. He died in 1879, leaving his estate heavily in debt. *DANB*, 565–66; Horton and Horton, *Black Bostonians*, 100, 110; Merrill and Ruchames, *Letters of William Lloyd Garrison*, 4:334n; *Lib*, 3 April 1840, 12 December 1845, 7 August 1846, 11 October 1850, 4 April 1851 [3:0374, 5:0116, 0252, 6:0611–13, 0871]; William Lloyd Garrison to Joshua B. Smith, 23 March 1855, Anti-Slavery Collection, MB [9:0502].

11. Joseph H. Gover, a Boston laborer, helped organize a black national convention in 1840. *Lib*, 19 June 1840 [3:0460]; *CA*, 25 July 1840 [3:0534]; *Boston City Directory*, 1838, 1840–42.

12. John Telemachus Hilton (1802–1864), a black Boston hairdresser, was born in Pennsylvania and moved to Massachusetts as a young man. Literate, articulate, and energetic, Hilton played a prominent role in several black organizations, beginning in 1826 with the founding of the Massachusetts General Colored Association. His commitment to moral reform grew in the 1830s. Active in the New England Colored Temperance Society, he also served as president of the Adelphic Union, secretary of the Infant School Association, and grand master of the Prince Hall Masonic Lodge in Boston. Hilton worked diligently on behalf of the antislavery press, rallying local support for *Freedom's Journal* and contributing articles to the *Liberty Bell*—an annual antislavery journal. In 1835 he became president of the Colored Liberator Aiding Association. A recognized leader in the local black community, he led demonstrations against colonization, discrimination, and fugitive slave laws. He frequently organized civic functions—

from receptions for prominent abolitionists to First of August celebrations and black conventions. His most visible role in the antislavery movement was as the only black manager of the Massachusetts Anti-Slavery Society.

In 1840 Hilton joined a short-lived effort to settle free blacks in British Guiana. Along with James G. Barbadoes, Thomas Cole, and others, he acted as a recruiting agent for the colonial government. Later in the decade, he helped organize the petition campaign against segregated schools in Boston. His antislavery work included membership on the Boston Vigilance Committee in the early 1850s. Later he served on the Massachusetts State Council of the Colored People and attended the New England Colored Citizens Convention (1859). From his early opposition to colonization to his death in 1864, Hilton remained loyal to William Lloyd Garrison, defending the *Liberator* and its editor against critics. In turn, Garrison was gratified by Hilton's "right hand of fellowship" and recognized it as a symbol of his following in Boston's black community. *Lib*, 12 February 1831, 26 March, 29 October 1836, 15, 29 September 1837, 10 August, 14 December 1838, 1 March, 7, 14 June 1839, 10 April, 8 May, 14, 28 August 1840, 8 July, 16 September, 23 December 1842, 4 August 1843, 28 January 1848, 10 August 1849, 26 April, 29 November 1850, 10 October 1862, 25 March 1864 [1:0030, 0722, 2:0185, 0201, 0551, 0674, 3:0013–15, 0112–13, 0384, 0557, 0585, 4:0451, 0469, 0496, 0621, 5:0569]; *FJ*, 25 April, 7 November 1828 [17:0548, 0578–80]; Merrill and Ruchames, *Letters of William Lloyd Garrison*, 1:127n, 2:118–19, 685; Horton and Horton, *Black Bostonians*, 40–41, 60, 71, 74, 90, 101; John Daniels, *In Freedom's Birthplace: A Study of the Boston Negroes* (Boston, Mass., 1914; reprint, New York, N.Y., 1969), 36n; Foner and Walker, *Proceedings of the Black State Conventions*, 2:94, 208; *BMC*, 29 June 1844 [4:0835]; Donald M. Jacobs, "William Lloyd Garrison's *Liberator* and Boston's Blacks, 1830–1865," *NEQ* 44:259–77 (June 1971).

13. James G. Barbadoes (1796–1841), a clothier and barber, was a prominent figure in the Boston black community during the 1820s and 1830s. In 1826 he helped organize the Massachusetts General Colored Association and served as the association's secretary. He participated in the black national convention movement, representing Boston at the 1833 and 1834 assemblies. Barbadoes supported black education and temperance. He backed William Lloyd Garrison in the campaign against colonization in the early 1830s and, like many black Bostonians, held Garrison in high regard, even naming one of his sons after him. A founding member of the American Anti-Slavery Society, he served on the society's board of managers from 1833 to 1836. He also attended the New England Anti-Slavery Convention in 1834. Barbadoes understood the dangers that slavery posed for free blacks. His brother, a Boston seaman, was kidnapped and jailed in New Orleans and was saved from enslavement only by the fortuitous intervention of friends and family.

Although an outspoken critic of colonization, Barbadoes became involved in a British Guiana immigration scheme in early 1840 when he acted as secretary for the group of Boston blacks authorized by the colonial government to recruit free black settlers. This short-lived effort fired his interest in emigration. In the spring of 1840, much to the surprise of his friends, he resettled his family in Jamaica. Barbadoes had hopes of developing a silkworm industry in Jamaica, but two of his children died from malaria shortly after arriving there, and he succumbed to the same malady on 22 June 1841. Completely destitute, the surviving family members returned to the United States. *Lib*, 22 January, 12 February, 12 March, 22 October 1831, 5 May, 2 June, 21 July 1832, 20 April 1833, 7 June 1834, 26 March 1836, 5, 19 May 1837, 3 May, 9 August 1839, 21 February, 11 September 1840 [1:0020, 0029, 0039, 0128, 2:0059, 3:0331, 0614]; *PF*, 4 August 1841; *DANB*, 26–27; Horton and Horton, *Black Bostonians*, 88, 90; *Minutes of the Second Annual Convention* (1832), 25 [1:0182]; *Minutes of the Third Annual Convention* (1833), 4, 24 [1:0295, 0305]; *Minutes of the Fourth Annual Convention* (1834), 8, 10, 13, 16 [1:0466–67, 0469–70].

14. Christopher Weeden, a black Boston clothier, held a business partnership in the late 1830s with Benjamin Weeden, an older relative. A loyal Garrisonian, he supported the *Liberator* and its editor, participated in local protests against colonization and fugitive slave extraditions, and joined the petition campaign to end school segregation in Boston. He endorsed the call for a black national convention in 1840. Weeden apparently left Boston in the late 1840s, eventually settling in San Francisco. *Lib*, 24 November 1837, 23 March 1838, 19 June 1840, 23 December 1842 [2:0278, 0446, 3:0460]; *CA*, 25 July 1840 [3:0534]; "To the School Committee of the City of Boston," 1844, Anti-Slavery Collection, MB [4:0723]; Abajian, *Blacks in Selected Newspapers*, 2:263; *Boston City Directory*, 1838, 1840.

15. The proceedings of this meeting were published in the 2 April 1840 issue of the *Massachusetts Abolitionist*, the 3 April issue of the *Liberator*, and the 11 April issue of the *Colored American*.

16. Hilton refers to Elizur Wright, Jr. (1804–1885). As a secretary in the American Anti-Slavery Society's New York City office from 1833 to 1839, Wright helped organize a system of antislavery agents and edited many of the society's publications. After breaking with the Garrisonians, he edited several antislavery and reform journals—the *Massachusetts Abolitionist*, the *Free American*, the *Chronotype*, and the *Commonwealth*—in Boston during the 1840s. Wright was a pioneer in the development of life insurance. Goodheart, "Elizur Wright, Jr.," 1–14, 153–71.

17. John E. Scarlett (1785–1844), a black grocer, worked as a chimney sweep before opening his Boston store in 1828. He became involved in antislavery activities in the 1820s as a member of the Massachusetts General Colored Association. A loyal Garrisonian, he supported the *Liberator*, joined the protest against colonization, and served as a delegate to the 1834 black national convention. *Lib*, 7, 14 December 1838, 3 April 1840, 16 February 1844 [2:0667, 0674–75, 3:0374]; Daniels, *In Freedom's Birthplace*, 36n; *Minutes of the Fourth Annual Convention* (1834), 8 [1:0867]; *Boston City Directory*, 1827, 1828, 1841, 1842.

18. William Cooper Nell (1816–1874) was born in Boston, the son of local black leader William G. Nell, a tailor, who had fled north from Charleston during the War of 1812. In 1826 the elder Nell helped found the Massachusetts General Colored Association—the first black antislavery society. William C. Nell graduated from Boston's African School with honors, but despite his achievements, he was excluded from citywide ceremonies honoring outstanding schol-

ars. That incident inspired his involvement in the lengthy movement to integrate Boston public schools during the 1840s and early 1850s. Nell read law with abolitionist William I. Bowditch during the 1830s but abandoned a potential legal career to devote his energies to fighting for antislavery and the civil rights of his race.

Nell was an early member of the American Anti-Slavery Society and a close associate of William Lloyd Garrison. When the antislavery movement divided in 1840, he joined other Boston blacks in affirming allegiance to the Garrisonian principles of moral suasion and nonresistance. Nell began a lengthy association with the *Liberator* in the early 1840s. He operated the paper's Negro Employment Office, organized antislavery meetings, and corresponded frequently with other abolitionists. Nell represented local blacks at several state and national conventions during the decade. He moved to Rochester, New York, in the late 1840s and helped Frederick Douglass publish the *North Star*, until conflict between Garrison and Douglass forced him to choose sides. Nell returned to Boston and Garrison.

Nell tempered his moral suasion and nonresistance views in response to events of the 1850s. He made an unsuccessful bid for the state legislature as a Free Soil candidate and fought enforcement of the Fugitive Slave Law as a member of the Boston Vigilance Committee. When illness curtailed his antislavery activities in 1851, he turned to writing and composed a pamphlet of black history entitled *The Services of Colored Americans in the Wars of 1776 and 1812*. He later expanded this into *Colored Patriots of the American Revolution* (1855). Both works reflected Nell's belief that black history and memory influenced Afro-American identity and advanced the struggle against slavery and racism. His careful scholarship and innovative use of oral sources contributed in important ways to the development of black history. Nell responded to the *Dred Scott* decision by organizing annual Crispus Attucks celebrations to commemorate black contributions to the American Revolution and to justify black claims to American citizenship. He also promoted plans for an Attucks monument. When the Civil War came, he encouraged blacks to participate in the struggle for their liberation and applauded the formation of the Fifty-fourth and Fifty-fifth Massachusetts regiments. In 1861 he became the first black appointed to a position in the federal government when he was named a postal clerk in Boston. Nell withdrew from reform activities after the war. During his last years, he compiled a history of black soldiers in the Civil War. *DAB*, 13:413; *DANB*, 472–73; Robert P. Smith, "William Cooper Nell: Crusading Black Abolitionist," *JNH* 55:183–99 (July 1970); Levesque, "Black Boston," 157–236; Horton and Horton, *Black Bostonians*, 57–59, 68–76, 118–22; *PA*, 18 July 1874.

19. John P. Coburn (1811–?), a black Boston merchant, was born in Massachusetts. After working as a housewright in the 1820s, he established a clothing business and eventually accumulated $3,000 in real estate. Coburn embraced Garrisonian principles in the 1830s. He helped organize First of August celebrations, served as treasurer for the New England Freedom Association, and participated in the petition campaign to end school segregation in Boston. A member of the Boston Vigilance Committee, he was arrested, tried, and acquitted for his involvement in the 1851 rescue of the fugitive slave Shadrach. Later in the 1850s,

he became a cofounder and captain of the Massasoit Guards, a black militia company. Horton and Horton, *Black Bostonians*, 120, 152n; *Lib*, 3 April 1840, 8 July 1842, 12 December 1845, 14 March 1851 [3:0374, 4:0451, 5:0116]; *NSt*, 17 April 1851; *FDP*, 24 August 1855; U.S. Census, 1850; *Boston City Directory*, 1821, 1830–42.

20. Hilton refers to the American Colonization Society.

21. Between the founding of the American Anti-Slavery Society in 1833 and the abolitionist schism of 1840, thirteen blacks were elected to the society's board of managers. They were James G. Barbadoes, James McCrummill, Robert Purvis, Abraham D. Shadd, John B. Vashon, Joseph Cassey, Samuel E. Cornish, Christopher Rush, Peter Williams, Theodore S. Wright, James Forten, Sr., Jehiel C. Beman, and Charles W. Gardner. After 1840 few blacks were elected to the board. McKivigan, *War against Proslavery Religion*, 203–20.

22. Hilton credits the American Anti-Slavery Society with influencing four improvements in the condition of northern blacks by the late 1830s. Several northern states had passed personal liberty laws, which sought to circumvent the Fugitive Slave Law of 1793 by restricting slave catchers and protecting the rights of fugitive slaves. Massachusetts provided the greatest protection, restoring the writ *de homine replegiando* in 1837, which offered a jury trial to accused runaways. Some railroads began to reserve first-class seats for blacks on trains bound from Boston for Worcester or Providence. A few abolitionist schools and colleges—Oberlin College in Oberlin, Ohio, Oneida Institute in Whitesboro, New York, and Western Reserve College in Hudson, Ohio—admitted blacks. Reacting to abolitionist pressure, the Massachusetts legislature passed resolutions in April 1838 asking Congress to abolish slavery in the District of Columbia, to end the interstate slave trade, and to outlaw slavery in new states admitted to the Union. Morris, *Free Men All*, 44–90, 104–25; *Lib*, 21 August 1840 [3:0576]; *Minutes of the Fifth Annual Convention* (1835), 17; *CA*, 3 May 1838.

23. Isaac Knapp (1804–1843), a printer, was William Lloyd Garrison's boyhood friend and one of his earliest collaborators. They founded the *Liberator* in 1831 and copublished it through 1835, when Knapp assumed all publishing and financial responsibilities for the paper. He relinquished control of the *Liberator's* business management in 1838 when his finances and health began to deteriorate. Knapp broke with Garrison in 1841 and published one issue of a rival newspaper, *Knapp's Liberator*. An active abolitionist, he helped organize the New England Anti-Slavery Society in 1832. Merrill and Ruchames, *Letters of William Lloyd Garrison*, 2:xxvi.

24. "From All That Dwell Below the Skies," by English hymnist Isaac Watts, first appeared in Watts's *Psalms of David* (1719) and was widely reprinted. At this meeting, it was sung to the music of "Old Hundredth," a Psalter tune frequently used with reform hymns. John Julian, *Dictionary of Hymnology*, 2 vols. (London, 1908; reprint, Grand Rapids, Mich., 1985), 1:398.

25. John B. Cutler (1805–1844), a Boston barber and nephew of Nathaniel Paul, was among William Lloyd Garrison's staunchest supporters in the local black community. He figured prominently at several pro-Garrison and anticolonization meetings and served as secretary of the Colored Liberator Aiding Association. Cutler also helped organize First of August celebrations in Boston and

participated in the Adelphic Union—a black literary society. *Lib*, 14 February 1835, 22 September, 6 October, 24 November 1837, 5 October 1838, 26 July, 1 November 1839, 20 March 1840, 9 February 1844 [1:0564, 2:0194, 0209, 0278, 0604, 3:0150, 0248, 0347]; *CA*, 14 October 1837 [2:0229]; John B. Cutler to William Lloyd Garrison, 2 April 1833, Anti-Slavery Collection, MB [1:0264–65].

39.
Editorial by Charles B. Ray
13 July 1839

The antislavery movement offered blacks unprecedented opportunities to create new organizations, to develop leaders, and to publicize
their concerns. It also imparted a spirit of hope and optimism to the
black community. In a 13 July 1839 editorial in the *Colored American*,
Charles B. Ray disputed the idea that the movement had done little for
blacks. *CA*, 17 August, 9 November 1839.

WHAT HAVE THEY DONE?

The question "what have abolitionists done for the colored man?"
is often asked, and as often sneeringly answered by the inquisitor,
NOTHING.

Having some knowledge on this subject, and being not a little interested in these matters, we beg leave to give our candid, unbiased opinion,
and this opinion is the result of close observation and long experience.
Abolitionists, apart from what they have done in waking up our guilty
nation to its sin and danger, and apart from what they have done towards breaking the shackles of the slave, and towards procuring for him
rights, privileges, and the Bible, have carried our population forward, in
the scale of *improved humanity*, at least, half a century.

Had there been no Anti-Slavery organization or efficient Anti-Slavery
action, similar to the organization and action of the American Anti-
Slavery Society for fifty years to come, our free colored population
would not have been as efficient and as capable of taking care of themselves, and acting the part of enlightened men and citizens as they *now
are*. The concessions made by abolitionists, *willingly*, and by their opponents, of *necessity*, to principle and to human rights, have almost
effected among our colored brethren a *new creation*. Think for a moment what must have been the influence of the proclamation of our
Declaration of Independence upon the mind and energies of our oppressed nation, in 76? Why it was like proclaiming LIFE to a valley of
dry bones.[1] Just so, did the publication of the first document of the
abolitionists, which conceded to colored men *humanity and rights* effect
our brethren. It seemed to give a new existence and to call forth energies
and powers which they were not aware of possessing.

With increased humility before God and increased love and respect for
men, the free population of our people, throughout the country, possess
feelings of *manhood, energy, enterprise and virtue* which nothing but
principles and measures of liberty could inspire. Without the abolition
movement our colored citizens would have dragged out an intolerable

12. Charles B. Ray
Courtesy of Moorland-Spingarn Research Center, Howard University

existence of, at least, fifty years more, without energy, efficiency or elevation. More than this, slavery and colonization were exerting an influence
of deterioration over the free colored population and effecting in them
feelings of pusillanimity and discouragement, which we dare prophecy,
would have eventually sought relief in universal and perpetual bondage
or in banishment. "ABOLITION" has awoke this dispirited people to the
dignity of manhood and to the energy and enterprize of freemen. With
the same zeal and skill, which they now contend for "inalienable rights"
do they also seek affluence and cultivation.

Colored American (New York, N.Y.), 13 July 1839.

1. Cornish refers to a vision in Ezekiel 37:1–14, in which a godly voice brings
to life a valley of dry bones.

40.
Charles Lenox Remond to Austin Willey
27 October 1839

By the late 1830s, the American Anti-Slavery Society was making a
concerted effort to recruit black speakers, having learned that "a colored man who is eloquent will in all parts of the north draw larger audiences than a white, in most places far larger." Audiences flocked to
hear blacks who spoke about slavery with the authoritative voice of
personal experience. The AASS commissioned Charles L. Remond as its
first black lecturing agent in 1838. He spent much of the next two years
traveling throughout New England giving antislavery speeches, recruiting AASS members, soliciting donations, selling subscriptions to anti-
slavery journals, and organizing local antislavery societies. His 27 October 1839 letter to Austin Willey, the editor of the *Advocate of Freedom*,
described the vicissitudes of a lecture tour in Maine. As the first black
that many of his listeners had seen, Remond attracted considerable attention. His early successes confirmed the value of employing black
speakers and opened the way for other black lecturing agents, including
John W. Lewis, Samuel R. Ward, Frederick Douglass, William Wells
Brown, and Henry Bibb. Pease and Pease, *They Who Would Be Free*,
33–37; William E. Ward, "Charles Lenox Remond: Black Abolitionist,
1838–1873" (Ph.D. diss., Clark University, 1977), 31–40.

BANGOR, [Maine]
Oct. 27th, 1839

My Dear Friend Willey:[1]

Upon the eve of setting out for Washington Co.,[2] you will be somewhat surprised to learn that Hampden has disgraced herself, and advanced the abolition cause. On the 16th inst., I lectured in the congregational meeting house in Hampden.[3] The Rev. Mr. Tappan[4] was present,
but prayer was offered on the occasion by Rev. Mr. Robinson, the baptist
minister. On the following evening, I again lectured in the baptist meeting house,[5] to a large and attentive assembly. At the close of my talk, a
request was made that all those favorable to the formation of a society
should stop after the audience was dismissed. When, in consequence of
some little confusion, it was thought advisable to postpone the meeting
until the following thursday evening, to be held at the Academy building;[6] on which evening I agreed to be present. On going to the place on
the appointed evening, as I passed towards the house, I noticed three or
four individuals near the door, and before I entered the house, was
besmeared with eggs. I took no notice of the insult, but went in and sat
down; some sensation was discoverable, when the chairman of the meet-

ing rose, saying, the question upon the propriety or impropriety of forming an anti-slavery society[7] was before the audience; when Mr. Hamlin,[8]
the Representative elect, observed, that he believed it to be customary on
such occasions, for those, who proposed the formation of a society, to
open a discussion in the affirmative, at least, it was agreeable to common
sense; upon which Mr. Bartlett,[9] my friend, moved that I be invited to
open the discussion, upon which I rose, saying that before I could take a
part in the discussion, I wished to have an expression of the audience
whether I came within the call for the meeting; being myself a stranger, I
did not wish to intrude my opinion, or a single thought upon the hearing
of the audience, but simply wished to say, before sitting down, that when
entering that house, I was insulted in a manner I had never before been
under the painful necessity of relating. At this moment some inhuman
fellows aimed a number of stones and eggs at my head—which—thank
GOD, missed the mark, and passed with great swiftness through the
window behind me. Immediately there was screaming and a simultaneous rush for the door—the ladies were apparently much alarmed.
Without moving from my position, I requested the audience to resume
their seats, as there was no harm intended to any person but myself; and
if in order to put down the cause in which I was engaged, it was necessary I should be pelted with eggs, be it so; that if I must be stoned, be
it so; that if they must walk over my prostrate and bleeding body, be it
so; for while I lived, and a single slave clanks his chain upon the soil
which gave me birth, I will exercise the prerogative of thinking and
speaking in his behalf, though slaveholders, mobocrats, eggs and brick-
bats multiply as fast and as thick as the locusts of Egypt. I then took my
seat, and the motion was put and unanimously carried in favor of my
speaking. I then endeavored to argue the necessity of forming a society
on the ground of its being a question which interested every individual,
composing that intelligent assembly; I occupied some twenty five or
thirty minutes. On taking my seat, Mr. Hamlin rose and answered me in
a speech some one hour, bringing forward every objection which has
been stated from the time of William Lloyd Garrison's incarceration in
the prison at Baltimore, down to the capture of the noble Cinque;[10]
beginning with the charge, that we scruple not at the most gross violation of the Federal Constitution, and ending with his solemn conviction
and opinion, that all that was wished by the abolitionists, was to bring
about a general amalgamation of the blacks and whites etc. etc. When I
again answered the gentleman in a speech of eight or ten minutes, and
was again replied to by him, and Mr. Mathews, who also spoke against
the formation of an anti-slavery society—attempting to show that the
efforts of the abolitionists have put back emancipation fifty years, and
that emancipation was about to take place a few years since, when the
formation of anti-slavery societies completely defeated the objects and

wishes of the friends of emancipation in Kentucky &c.[11] It being now ten o'clock, a motion to adjourn one week prevailed, and Mr. Hamlin, and his party retired, evidently convinced that the opponents to abolition had lost ground, eggs, stones and his eloquent arguments to the contrary notwithstanding.

On the following evening, agreeable to appointment, I went to Orring-ton[12] and addressed the friends on the duty and necessity of forming an anti-slavery society, in that village; at the close of the lecture, the sense of the audience was taken by the rising of a very large number of friends, who I was informed by Rev. Mr. Young,[13] composed the respectability and piety of the place. A committee was appointed to draft a constitu-tion, and a time appointed for another lecture and the organization of a society. Intending to return to Bangor the same evening, my friends went to the fence for my horse and chaise, when it was discovered that some evil minded persons had cut my harness in pieces, and also the top and lining of the chaise, thus disappointing me in my plans, and subjecting me to $30 or $35 expense.

It was ascertained that these mischievous beings crossed the river from Hampden, with their faces painted black, and were doubtless the same who insulted me the evening before; but for each offence I can forgive them. If the friends of order and truth in Orrington will detect the perpe-trators, and thus fix the stigma where it belongs, the cause of the poor slave will be advanced. I shall write you soon again, and give some accounts of my labors prior to the outrage. Yours truly,

C. LENOX REMOND[14]

Advocate of Freedom (Augusta, Maine), 2 November 1839.

1. Austin Willey (1806–1896), a Maine abolitionist and temperance advocate, edited several reform newspapers, including the *Advocate of Freedom* (1839–41), *Liberty Standard* (1842–48), and *Free Soil Republican* (1848–49). He also lectured widely for the Liberty party during the 1840s. Willey resettled in Northfield, Minnesota, in 1855 and later published his *History of the Anti-Slavery Cause in State and Nation* (1886). *ACAB*, 6:518; Edward O. Schriver, *Go Free: The Antislavery Impulse in Maine* (Orono, Maine, 1970), 31n, 50, 65.

2. On 28 October 1839, Remond left Bangor for an antislavery lecture tour of Washington County, which includes the easternmost townships of Maine. He remained there about two weeks, speaking in local schoolhouses and recruiting subscribers for the *Advocate of Freedom*. Remond attended the annual meeting of the Washington County Anti-Slavery Society in Pembroke (29–30 October), then lectured in Calais, Alexander, Cooper, and Charlotte Village. Although heckled and pelted with volleys of stones in Calais, he was well received in the other villages. *AF*, 9, 16 November, 21 December 1839 [3:0302].

3. The Hampden Congregational Church was founded by colonizationist Je-hudi Ashmun in 1817. The congregation's first meetinghouse was constructed in 1835 and served the congregation into the twentieth century. Calvin M. Clark,

History of the Congregational Churches in Maine, 2 vols. (Portland, Maine, 1926–35), 306–8.

4. Benjamin Tappan (1788–1863), a Massachusetts-born cousin of abolitionists Arthur and Lewis Tappan, was educated at Harvard College. A Congregationalist clergyman and a leading figure in the Maine Missionary Society, he served South Church in Augusta, Maine, from 1811 until 1850, when he was named to the faculty of Bangor Theological Seminary. An antislavery gradualist and colonizationist, Tappan helped found and lead the conservative Maine Union in Behalf of the Colored Race, until joining the Maine Anti-Slavery Society in the late 1830s. He helped move Maine Congregationalists in an antislavery direction. *ACAB*, 6:32–33; Calvin M. Clark, *History of Bangor Theological Seminary* (Boston, Mass., 1916), 107–8, 114; Calvin M. Clark, *American Slavery and Maine Congregationalists* (Bangor, Maine, 1940), 20–21, 50, 58, 62, 69, 181; *AF*, 8 March 1838; Schriver, *Go Free*, 87n, 103n, 105n.

5. A Baptist congregation was organized at Hampden in 1809. Rev. Thomas B. Robinson was serving as pastor at the time of Remond's visit. Robinson served congregations in several Penobscot and Kennebec County villages from the 1820s through the 1870s. Converting to abolitionism in the 1830s, he was a founding member of the Maine Anti-Slavery Society. During the 1840s, he helped arouse antislavery sentiment among Maine Baptists and played a leading role in the Maine Anti-Slavery Baptist Convention, generating ministerial protests and persuading local Baptist associations to disfellowship slaveholders. Henry S. Burrage, *History of the Baptists in Maine* (Portland, Maine, 1904), 148, 305, 313, 316, 333, 436, 444; Fay M. Graham, "Maine Baptists and the Antislavery Movement, 1830–1850" (M.A. thesis, University of Maine, Orono, 1962), 103–4, 117, 119; *AF*, 12 October 1839 [3:0226].

6. The Hampden Academy was established in 1803 through the donations of local civic leaders. One of the most expensive private academies in antebellum Maine, it trained local students as well as boarders from surrounding villages. Ava H. Chadbourne, *The Beginnings of Education in Maine* (New York, N.Y., 1928), 87–90, 99, 111.

7. As a result of Remond's activities, and the efforts of the Bangor Anti-Slavery Society, a Penobscot County Anti-Slavery Society was organized in 1839. It helped forge the county into one of the most prominent areas of antislavery enthusiasm in Maine. *AF*, 21 February 1839; Schriver, *Go Free*, 32, 124.

8. Hannibal Hamlin (1809–1891), a lawyer, represented the Hampden district in the Maine legislature from 1836 to 1841, before embarking on a national political career. After serving as a Democrat in the House of Representatives (1843–47) and the Senate (1848–57), he broke with the party over the slavery issue. Later joining the Republicans, he became Abraham Lincoln's vice-president during the Civil War. *DAB*, 8:196–98.

9. Daniel W. Bartlett (ca. 1812–?), a Hampden joiner born in New Hampshire, is listed as a subscriber to the *Advocate of Freedom*. U.S. Census, 1850; *AF*, 19 October 1839.

10. Remond refers to Joseph Cinqué, the leader of the July 1839 mutiny on the *Amistad*, a Spanish slave ship. Cinqué and his comrades were kidnapped from West Africa and illegally transported to Cuba, where fifty-three of them were sold and loaded on the *Amistad*. Two days out of Havana, they took control of

the ship in a bloody revolt. The vessel wandered for weeks along the North American coast until seized by the American navy off Long Island, New York. The trial of the *Amistad* captives became an abolitionist cause célèbre and an international diplomatic incident. In March 1841, the U.S. Supreme Court granted the mutineers their freedom. Through the efforts of abolitionists, they were returned to West Africa. Howard Jones, *Mutiny on the Amistad* (New York, N.Y., 1987).

11. Mathews overstated the case. From 1800 to 1823, a small number of Baptists, Methodists, and Presbyterians opposed slavery. David Barrow, a dissident Baptist, organized the Kentucky Abolition Society in 1808. The society published John Finley Crowe's moderate *Abolition Intelligencer* in 1821, one of the nation's earliest antislavery newspapers. But Kentuckians rejected abolitionism in favor of colonization. The single abolition society never attracted more than a hundred members, and it was overwhelmed by the state's thirty-one colonization societies. With the rise of militant abolitionism in the 1830s, tolerance for dissent evaporated and Kentucky's limited antislavery movement disappeared. Lowell H. Harrison, *The Antislavery Movement in Kentucky* (Lexington, Ky., 1978), 18–37; Gordon E. Finnie, "The Antislavery Movement in the Upper South before 1840," *JSH* 35:319–42 (August 1969).

12. The villages of Hampden and Orrington were located about two miles apart in southern Penobscot County, Maine. They were separated by the Penobscot River.

13. John Young (1799–1867), who first came to public attention as a successful revivalist, served small Methodist churches in southern and central Maine (including Orrington, 1838–39) from 1830 until his death. He was also an agent for the American Bible Society (1848–52) and chaplain of the Maine Insane Hospital (1865–67). Stephen Allen and W. H. Pilsbury, *History of Methodism in Maine, 1793–1886*, 2 vols. (Augusta, Maine, 1887), 1:461–62.

14. Charles Lenox Remond (1810–1873) was born in Salem, Massachusetts. He was the eldest son of John and Nancy Remond, who had eight children. John Remond immigrated to the United States from Curaçao in 1798 and became a successful hairdresser and merchant. An abolitionist and community leader, the elder Remond led a successful campaign to desegregate Salem's public schools. Charles Remond was educated in those schools as well as by a private tutor. He also learned a great deal in the comfortable and exciting Remond household, which was often filled with visiting reformers. Remond followed his parents into the antislavery movement, becoming a founding member of the American Anti-Slavery Society. A year after he first spoke at an abolitionist gathering (the 1837 meeting of the Rhode Island Anti-Slavery Society), he was appointed as a full-time lecturing agent for the Massachusetts Anti-Slavery Society. Between 1838 and 1840, he toured Massachusetts, Maine, and Rhode Island, lecturing and organizing dozens of local antislavery societies.

Remond attended the World's Anti-Slavery Convention in London in early 1840, then undertook an eighteen-month British sojourn, which revealed some of the fundamental organizational elements of a black lecture tour abroad. He also forged an essential link between women abolitionists in Britain and the American women who directed the Boston Anti-Slavery Bazaar. Remond's appearance at the London convention was a dramatic and influential moment in

the antislavery movement. When the convention refused to seat women delegates, he declined to participate in the proceedings and delivered a powerful
address rebuking female exclusion.

Remond returned home in December 1841 and resumed his antislavery work.
He frequently toured with Frederick Douglass, and they led the opposition to
Henry Highland Garnet's call for slave violence at the 1843 black national convention. They remained friends until 1850 but later engaged in a protracted and
bitter dispute fueled by personal rivalry and a variety of ideological disagree-
ments. Initially a committed Garrisonian, Remond flirted with political antislavery as president of the Essex County (Mass.) Anti-Slavery Society in the late
1840s. In the wake of the Kansas-Nebraska Act and the Dred Scott decision, he
abandoned nonresistance. He defended slave insurrections in August 1858 and a
year later at a black convention in Boston, he predicted that American slavery
would "go down in blood." Declining health restricted Remond's reform activities during the Civil War, but he did recruit black troops for the Fifty-fourth and
Fifty-fifth Massachusetts regiments. When the war ended, he called for the
American Anti-Slavery Society to continue its reform work, which further alienated him from Garrison, who argued that the AASS should disband once emancipation was achieved. After attending the 1867 meeting of the American Equal
Rights Association, Remond retired from reform, spending his last years as a
stamp clerk at the Boston Customs House. Miriam L. Usrey, "Charles Lenox
Remond, Garrison's Ebony Echo: World Antislavery Convention, 1840," *EIHC*
106:113–25 (April 1970); Ward, "Charles Lenox Remond," 1–262.

41.
David J. Peck and George B. Vashon to
Charles B. Ray and Philip A. Bell
14 November 1839

Black abolitionism was a community venture that involved men and
women of all ages and social stations. Beginning in 1838, juvenile anti-
slavery associations were organized in several black communities as a
way to encourage antislavery sentiment among black males. Often affiliated with black churches, these organizations collected donations for
antislavery societies and the black press, staged First of August celebrations, and sponsored public meetings where boys as young as eleven
years old delivered antislavery speeches. The societies proved to be
training grounds for future black leaders. Organized on 7 July 1838, the
Pittsburgh Juvenile Anti-Slavery Society promoted abolitionism among
the city's rising generation of blacks. In a 14 November 1839 letter,
officers David Peck and George B. Vashon—both the sons of prominent local black abolitionists—forwarded a small contribution to the
Colored American and discussed the origins of the society, the first juvenile association west of the Appalachian mountains. The society continued for at least another year. *PF*, 23 May 1839; *CA*, 1 September, 20,
27 October 1838, 23 November 1839, 25 September 1841 [2:0622,
4:0216]; Quarles, *Black Abolitionists*, 30; Catherine M. Hanchett,
"George Boyer Vashon, 1821–1878: Black Educator, Poet, Fighter for
Equal Rights," *WPHM* 68:206 (July, October 1985).

Pittsburgh, [Pennsylvania]
Nov. 14, 1839

Gentlemen:

At a meeting of the Juvenile Anti-Slavery Society, held November 11,
it was unanimously resolved that five dollars should be given to the
support of the *Colored American*, a paper, which, of all others we ought
to support. We hope that this small donation may be the means of doing
good, and we pray you in the name of the members of the Juvenile Anti-
Slavery Society, to accept it as a small token of the esteem we have for
your paper. The Juvenile Anti-Slavery Society (of which we have the
honor of being members) was formed on the seventh of July, 1838. It is a
"cent a week" society, and is the first and only of the kind formed this
side of the mountains. The Society now consists of about forty members:
several of whom have addressed the Society, at different times. We con-

clude, by expressing our hope, that our little mite may be of some service in the cause, in which you are engaged.

Very respectfully, Your obdt. servants,

DAVID PECK[1] Pres. J.A.S.S.
GEO. B. VASHON,[2] Sec

Colored American (New York, N.Y.), 23 November 1839.

1. David J. Peck, a Pennsylvania physician, was the son of black abolitionist John Peck of Pittsburgh. He lived in Toronto briefly before enrolling in Oberlin College in 1840. After graduating from Rush Medical College in Chicago in 1847, he established a medical practice in Philadelphia. As the city's first formally trained black doctor, Peck became prominent in the local black community. He participated in antislavery meetings, attended the 1848 state convention, and served as corresponding secretary for the short-lived American League of Colored Laborers. Encounters with racial prejudice and business difficulties apparently prompted Peck to leave Philadelphia in 1850. He intended to settle in California, but after meeting with Martin R. Delany in New York City, he went to Central America instead and practiced medicine in San Juan del Norte, a port city on the Mosquito coast. There he became active in local politics, helping to organize a representative municipal government and opposing the impositions of American cotton growers. Peck eventually returned to Pennsylvania, and after the Civil War, he served as vice-president of the Pennsylvania State Equal Rights League. *NSt*, 4 February, 6 October, 10 November 1848, 5 January, 15 June, 3, 31 August, 21 September 1849 [5:0802–3, 6:0134, 0171]; *NASS*, 1 April 1847, 24 February 1848; *PF*, 28 September 1848 [5:0797]; Delany, *Condition of the Colored People*, 122; Foner and Walker, *Proceedings of the Black State Conventions*, 1:104, 119, 121–22; "Black Organizational Members Sorted by Name," Philadelphia Social History Project, PU; Herbert M. Morais, *The History of the Afro-American in Medicine* (Cornwell Heights, Pa., 1978); Victor Ullman, *Martin R. Delany: The Beginnings of Black Nationalism* (Boston, Mass., 1971), 138–39; Dorothy Sterling, *The Making of an Afro-American: Martin Robinson Delany, 1812–1885* (Garden City, N.Y., 1971), 143–45.

2. George Boyer Vashon (1824–1878) was the son of John B. and Anne Vashon of Carlisle, Pennsylvania. In 1829 the Vashon family settled in Pittsburgh. Under the guidance of his father, young George became involved in the abolition movement and served as secretary of the Pittsburgh Juvenile Anti-Slavery Society. In 1844 he received the first bachelor of arts degree awarded by Oberlin College to a black student. Vashon then returned to Pittsburgh, assisted Martin R. Delany in publishing the *Mystery*, and read law with a local judge. Because of his race, he was twice denied the opportunity to take the Pennsylvania bar examination but passed the New York bar and became the state's first licensed black attorney. With little hope of practicing law in the United States, he accepted a teaching position at Collège Faustin in Haiti, where he fulfilled a variety of academic duties from 1848 to 1850. He also may have served briefly in the government of Emperor Faustin I. Haiti's "unsettled state" eventually de-

terred him from his original intent of becoming a Haitian citizen and practicing law there.

Vashon returned to the United States in 1850 and established a law practice in Syracuse, New York. His professional status gave him instant stature in antislavery circles. He worked on the Syracuse Vigilance Committee, attended local antislavery gatherings, and lectured throughout the state. Vashon coauthored the public address issued by the 1853 black national convention at Rochester. He also participated in Liberty party politics and twice received the party's nomination for state attorney general. Vashon's law practice never flourished, despite the encouragement and financial support of Gerrit Smith and other antislavery colleagues. His situation improved somewhat when he accepted a temporary teaching position at New York Central College in 1854. The college trustees dismissed Vashon in 1856, ostensibly as an austerity measure, but he contended that racial prejudice had once again hindered his professional career. Returning to Pittsburgh in 1857, he accepted a less prestigious (but better-paying) position as principal and teacher at a black public school. Two years later, he married Susan Paul Smith of Boston. In 1864 Vashon assumed the presidency of Avery College.

Vashon's erudition and scholarship made him a respected intellectual in the black community. The *North Star* published his correspondence from Haiti under the pseudonym "Harold." While in Syracuse, he contributed regularly to *Frederick Douglass' Paper*. He also composed several notable poems, including "Vincent Ogé" (1853), an epic verse on the Haitian Revolution. His essay on astronomy appeared in the *Anglo-African Magazine*, and the antislavery press published many of his other pieces. Although Vashon's literary work was generally well received, his shifting views on black emigration provoked criticism. Upon his return from Haiti, he joined Frederick Douglass in attacking emigration programs. Commenting on the National Emigration Convention of 1854, he called for an integrationist solution—blacks should become "an essential constituent in the ruling element." He moderated his position on emigration during the Civil War, but in a letter to Abraham Lincoln, he strongly opposed plans for government-sponsored colonization. Vashon had a prominent role in the 1864 and 1867 black national conventions and participated in the Pennsylvania State Equal Rights League. After the war, he worked as a solicitor for the Freedmen's Bureau and received permission to argue cases before the U.S. Supreme Court. In 1867 he became the first black instructor at Howard University. When his efforts to obtain a consular post in Haiti failed, he went to Alcorn University in Mississippi. He died there of yellow fever during the epidemic of 1878. *DANB*, 617; *FDP*, 17 November 1854, 1 January, 5 September 1855 [9:0235]; *PP*, 3 August 1861 [13:0676]; Hanchett, "George Boyer Vashon," 205–19, 333–49.

42.
Essay by Lewis Woodson
29 November 1839

Although blacks avoided the disunity that plagued the antislavery movement in the late 1830s, they did debate antislavery tactics. As black
abolitionism entered the 1840s, a younger generation found promise in
political antislavery. If moral suasion was ineffectual, one black abolitionist declared, "[we] have the right and we are bound in conscience,
to use the ballot box." Older leaders like Pittsburgh's Lewis Woodson
urged caution. In a 29 November 1839 essay in the *Colored American*,
written under the pseudonym "Augustine," he argued that political action, while important, could not take precedence over moral suasion.
Politics, he warned, could not change men whose hearts were corrupted
by slavery. Writing from the West, Woodson criticized the bickering
among black abolitionists in Massachusetts, warning that they could
not afford internecine warfare. "Have we so much power on hand," he
asked, "that we can afford to throw some away?" *CA*, 24 November
1838 [2:0660].

Pittsburg[h], [Pennsylvania]

Nov. 29, 1839

MEASURES

By the above term I understand, the *means* by which a certain *end* is to
be attained.

Of late this question has caused some agitation in the Anti-Slavery
ranks, the result of which, it appears, may have an important influence
upon the interest of our people in the United States. For if our friends
divide among themselves, and exhaust their energies in combatting each
other, what is to become of the object in whose behalf they first enlisted?
He will be left in the power of the enemy, having added to his former
woes, the anguish of disappointed hope.

But much as I regret the present state of things, my mind *has*, some
time since, been prepared for it. Because, notwithstanding all the measures adopted by Anti-Slavery men were legitimate, yet some of them at
least, and these most attended to, were entirely out of *tune*, among which
is the late measure of *"political action."*

That abolitionists must resort *ultimately* to political action, every one
must admit; because slavery has been sanctioned and regulated by law,
and the laws which have thus sanctioned and regulated slavery must be
repealed, before slavery can be abolished. But that it should constitute
the chief part of their *primary* work, I think is questionable.

If slavery had its *source* in the political compact of our country, then to

begin with political action would be the proper course to attain its abolition. But this is not the fact. Slavery has its source in the *corrupt moral
sentiment* of the country, and the great *primary* means, and as we may
see presently, the almost entire means of its abolition, is the correction of
this corrupt moral sentiment.

Slavery is the result of violence and force. It is the creature of unrighteous action. All actions spring from the impulse of the mind. No action
can take place without first involving the determination and consent of
the moral powers. It is a settled principle in human nature, that a morally
good man cannot do a physically bad deed, any more than a good tree
can bring forth bad fruit, or a sweet fountain can send forth bitter waters. Hence then it follows as a matter of course, that if the moral sentiment of the community were corrected, slavery must cease; because the
great source from whence it springs would be dried up.

The CREATOR of all things has made the *Church* the source or foundation of morals. He has deposited in the Church that salt which saves
the world from moral putrefaction; and all who would labor successfully
for the reformation of public morals, must labour in, through, or with
the Church. Hence we see the bad policy of those of our friends, who
have broken ground with the Church and the clergy.

In the present state of the Anti-Slavery cause, the chief object should
be the reformation of the Church. The Church should be made to feel
right, to vote right, to act right in every way on this great question.
Petitions should be sent into the Church, and from the whole Church up
to Almighty God, instead of sending so many into Congress. The Church
should be made to cast out this bloody and unclean spirit from her
midst, and no longer shield it with her sacred veil, but leave it exposed in
all its hideousness, in the ranks of the ungodly and sinners.

But now when Congress is called upon to put an end to slavery in all
places under her jurisdiction, and that chiefly on account of its enormous
criminality, she steps behind the Church, and tells you that slavery is an
institution sanctified by the Church of God, and that to abolish it would
be sacrilege. The Church must be made to stand out of the way, and then
shall the arrows from the bow of humanity tell upon this monster.

Again I repeat it, that *moral* action must *first* be had on this question,
and *then political action*. A right state of moral feeling must be brought
about, and then a right course of political action will take place, as
naturally as any other effect results from its natural cause.

And now if the *time* for political action has not come, and the time for
moral action is upon us, where is the wisdom of our dividing and falling
out among ourselves, about politics? Have we so much power on hand
that we can afford to throw some away? Do our numbers and strength
give such an assurance of victory, that we may turn from combatting the
common enemy, to fight among ourselves? Surely wiser and better things

might be expected of the leading men of the free people of color of the United States.

I ardently hope that our brethren in the East will ponder and pray over this matter, and come to the right conclusion, of laboring for the object on which labor will tell, and which can be attained now, and leaving that on which labor will not tell, and which cannot be attained now, to be attended to at the proper time.

AUGUSTINE

Colored American (New York, N.Y.), 14 March 1840.

43.
Essay by "A Colored Woman"
[November 1839]

Black women advanced the antislavery movement through a variety of means. They formed antislavery societies, raised funds, and aided fugitive slaves. Antislavery women of both races viewed the campaign to flood Congress with antislavery petitions in the late 1830s as their "only means of direct political action." Between December 1838 and March 1839, nearly fifteen hundred petitions, bearing more than 163,000 signatures, poured into the Capitol. They protested against the interstate slave trade, the expansion of slavery into the territories, the admission of new slave states (especially Texas), the gag rule, and the continued existence of slavery in the District of Columbia. Fifty-eight petitions came from Connecticut alone. In a 1839 essay in the *Charter Oak*, a Hartford reform journal, an anonymous black woman explained the importance of the petition campaigns and encouraged women to become involved in them. *AF*, 7 December 1839; *PF*, 19 December 1839; Dwight L. Dumond, *Antislavery: The Crusade for Freedom in America* (New York, N.Y., 1966), 243–48.

Free women of Connecticut (for I speak not now to slaves, to the servile minions of pride, selfishness and prejudice), have you this fall signed the petitions in behalf of the dumb, and entreated *all* the women in your town to do the same? If you have not, I implore you to drop the work you have in your hand, or this paper, as soon as you shall have finished this article, and go to the work *now*, nor leave it till not one woman in your town shall have for excuse in the day of accounts, that she has not been *asked* to pray for the perishing.

Do you say you have so many family cares you cannot go? Thousands of your sisters may never hear the word *family* but to mock their desolation. But you must prepare your beloved children's *warm, winter clothing*. Look yonder. Do you not see that mother toiling with her *almost, or quite naked children, shivering in the keen blast?* Yet you cannot go, you must prepare the table for your family. The slave spends but little time in dressing her "*peck of corn per week*." Does your house need putting in order? Had you a house but "*fifteen feet by ten*," furnished with a rough bench, a stool and a bunk, with a little straw and a blanket, and then, for cooking and table apparatus, a kettle, a spoon and a knife, it might not take you so long to set them in order. Why do you delay, and take up a book to read? Is it in derision of blighted intellect? Ah! throw it down in remembrance of the millions in whose bodies immortality has well nigh found a sepulchre. Do your precious babes demand your tender watchings, so that you cannot leave them? Hark! That shriek!! It proclaims the bursting of a heart, as the babe is torn from the frantic mother, and *sold for "five dollars the pound."* Still do you say "I have not time?" O! I pity you. You are yourself almost qualified to be a slave. Ay, *you are a slave—* a slave to hardness of heart. You have got a stone in your bosom; there is no flesh there; you are consumed by selfishness. Is this hard talk? How would *you* talk of *me*, were you allowed to speak, if I should wrap myself up in "my own concerns" and see your relatives and friends sold under the hammer, your clothing stripped from you, except, perhaps, a mere rag, your mind smothered to almost utter extinction, and then the defaced remnant of your former self driven before the gory lash, till, exhausted, you cannot finish your task, and are bound down, shamelessly exposed, and a cat hauled up and down your back to gratify the revenge of some lustful brute of an overseer. I see all this, and know that our GREAT and WISE men (?) in the nation's BLACK LAW FACTORY have decided that *you have no right to ask for mercy* in their behalf.[1] You know all this, and whine out, "O how I pity the poor creature. I can't bear to hear of such treatment. My feelings are so acute I cannot read such horrible cruelties; but I have so much to do, that I cannot carry this petition all around town; it will take so much time I shan't be able to finish this ruffle, or put the ribbon on this bonnet."

Women of Connecticut, I shall blush to acknowledge myself a woman, if women's souls have become so sear, so blighted, so shrunk to nonentity, as to neglect this labor of humanity. But I cannot think it will be neglected. I cannot think there will be a falling off in this important work.

Let us rouse ourselves and pour an overwhelming flood of rebuke upon those beings who claim to be men, agents of those who style themselves the "FREEST NATION ON THE EARTH," and use their freedom to say, "For Four Hundred Dollars WASHINGTON may be a *Guinea coast for Texas.*"—"For Four Hundred Dollars any wretch may trade in human flesh and bones, in slaves and the souls of men, in the Capital of 'THE REFUGE OF THE OPPRESSED.' "—"For Four Hundred Dollars any human hyena may FATTEN ON THE BLOOD OF MEN, WOMEN AND CHILDREN, under the walls of our CAPITOL."[2] Yes, worse still, they have made *robbery, adultery*, and murder, free game—ay, honorable sport—and he who holds the greatest number of trophies is deemed most noble. Up, my sisters, speak while there is time. Millions are perishing, victims of your delay.

A COLORED WOMAN

Charter Oak (Hartford, Conn.), November 1839.

1. The author refers to the "gag rule" adopted by the U.S. House of Representatives in 1836 in response to the abolitionist petition campaign designed to pressure Congress to abolish slavery in the District of Columbia and the federal territories. Beginning in 1828, antislavery petitions arrived in such quantities during the next decade that they threatened to disrupt the congressional agenda. Antagonized southern congressmen reacted by passing the "gag rule," which automatically tabled such petitions. Passage of the rule broadened and strengthened the antislavery crusade by tying it to the constitutional issue of free speech and the right to petition. The rule was rescinded in 1844.

2. The author compares Washington, D.C., a leading center of the domestic slave trade by the 1830s, to the Guinea coast, an important African source of the transatlantic slave trade. Washington served as a convenient depot for slaves purchased in the Chesapeake region for shipment to the developing cotton lands of the Southwest, including the newly independent Republic of Texas. A city ordinance required slave dealers to pay a $400 license fee in order to conduct their trade. Federal courts declared the statute unconstitutional in 1847. William T. Laprade, "The Domestic Slave Trade in the District of Columbia," *JNH* 11:27–30 (January 1926).

44.
Thomas Van Rensellaer to "Colored Abolitionists"
[April 1840]

Nearly four years of feuding among white abolitionists over women's rights, nonresistance, and political antislavery prior to the May 1840 annual meeting of the American Anti-Slavery Society in New York City threatened to destroy the society. Black abolitionists were divided over these contentious issues, but they opposed the growing discord, believing that the conflict diverted abolitionist attention from the issue of slavery. In an open letter to fellow black abolitionists, published ten days before the convention began, Thomas Van Rensellaer, a steadfast Garrisonian, urged black communities throughout the North to send representatives to the gathering. He hoped that "a little *right* action on *our* part" could avert a complete rift. Yet when the delegates at the meeting elected a woman to the AASS business committee, Tappanites walked out and established the rival American and Foreign Anti-Slavery Society. Kraditor, *Means and Ends in American Abolitionism*, 50–52, 69; Pease and Pease, *They Who Would Be Free*, 73; CA, 10, 24 October 1840.

To Colored Abolitionists:
Dear Brethren:
  I have been waiting for someone, better qualified than myself, to call your attention to this subject, of such *vital* importance to every colored American. The approaching Anniversary of the American Anti-Slavery Society, on the 12th of May next,[1] will be one of the most important meetings (to us) ever held in this country: and therefore, we, in a special manner, are called upon to inform ourselves thoroughly on all subjects of interest that will be brought up and acted upon by the Society.
  Brethren, it is well known to us that a few years ago our Abolition friends were laboring zealously and *harmoniously* for the deliverance of the *Slave*, and the removal of obstacles out of the way of *our* elevation; but, unfortunately, these *friends* have fallen out by the way, and unhappily, divisions have crept into their ranks, and their attention has been, to some extent, diverted from their noble object.
  Finding such a state of things existing among the *friends* of human rights: and knowing, as I do, the favorable situation in which the colored people are placed to exert a salutary influence over the minds of these alienated brethren, I take the liberty of urging the people of color in different parts of the country, to see to it, that they are represented in this meeting; let there be immediate steps taken to appoint delegates, and to raise means to send them. Let every male and female Anti-Slavery

Society among our people, send up here their best and most talented men and women, to watch the movements, and save the Society from destruction.

It does appear to me that a little *right* action on *our* part, just at this crisis in the history of our sacred cause, will save it. Bear with me, my brothers and sisters, while I again urge upon you, by your regard for invaluable Human Rights, by your love for the slave, by your love of country, and by your regard for those friends who have been faithful up to the present hour, be present at the coming Anniversary on the 12th of May.

T. Van Rensellaer

Colored American (New York, N.Y.), 2 May 1840.

1. The American Anti-Slavery Society held its 1840 annual meeting in the Fourth Free Church in New York City during 12–15 May. Anticipating conflict, both Garrisonians and conservatives attempted to pack the convention. Since 1837 the two factions had become increasingly divided over the issues of women's rights, political antislavery, and nonresistance. When delegates elected Abby Kelley Foster to the AASS executive committee, most conservatives resigned from the organization. Followers of Lewis and Arthur Tappan soon organized the rival American and Foreign Anti-Slavery Society, while others joined with Gerrit Smith to create the Liberty party. *Lib*, 22 May 1840; Kraditor, *Means and Ends in American Abolitionism*, 69n.

45.
Charles B. Ray to James G. Birney
and Henry B. Stanton
20 May 1840

Black abolitionists regretted the division of the American Anti-Slavery Society. They urged whites not to put ideological purity above the interests of the slave. But the spreading conflict placed blacks in a difficult situation. Some stayed with William Lloyd Garrison and the old American Anti-Slavery Society; others allied with the "new organization"; and many looked for neutral ground, despite pressure from white abolitionists to choose sides. Charles B. Ray's 20 May 1840 letter to "new organizationists" James G. Birney and Henry B. Stanton described the impact of the conflict on New York City's black leaders. Ray described a meeting at the First Colored Presbyterian Church that had rejected an attempt by Thomas Van Rensellaer to rally local blacks behind Garrisonian delegates to the 1840 World's Anti-Slavery Convention in London while ignoring Birney and Stanton who were also delegates. Ray opposed supporting one faction over another and, like most local blacks, sought an independent position in the antislavery movement. *CA*, 2, 9, 23, 30 May, 4 July 1840 [3:0440, 0443, 0509]; Pease and Pease, *They Who Would Be Free*, 45, 75.

New York, [New York]
May 20th, 1840

Dear friends coadjutor[1] in the great cause of human Freedom:

I improve the detention of our brethren by a contrary mind, transmit to you a circumstance, which I hope may not be called for, but which from evidence received I have reason to think may be. It refers to the results of a meeting held by some of us, on the evening of the 18 inst. & which I am informed, our esteemed friend N. P. Rogers,[2] intends to use at the worlds convention,[3] to show the effect New Organization[4] has had upon the colored people of our City. My object in writing is to repudiate the idea, & to furnish you with the true state of the case, being rather apprehensive that our friend may be wrongly informed, as to the history of the matter.

On the 17th ultimo, Bro T. Van Ranselaer[5] between meetings, (it being Sunday) suggested to me the propriety as he thought, of having a meeting of the colored people, to hear an address from our old and tried Friend Mr. Garrison, & as he was to leave us the ~~next~~ day following, for London to attend the worlds convention, to pass some resolutions expressive of our confidence in him, as a delegate, to said convention. I objected to aid him in getting up a meeting for that object alone, on the grounds as I

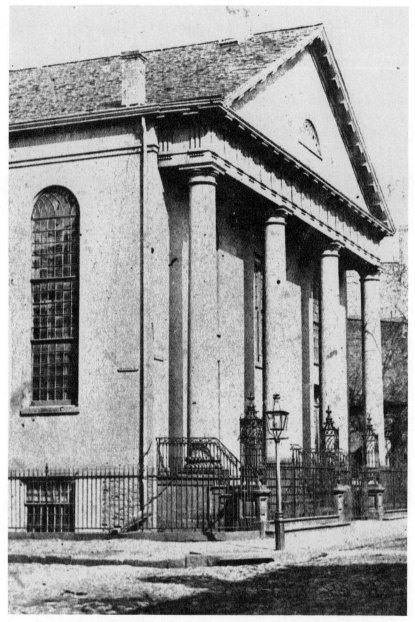

13. First Colored Presbyterian Church of New York City
Courtesy of The New-York Historical Society, New York City

stated to him, that other men had gone, who were dear to us as a <u>colored community</u> & if we were going to express our confidence in one as a delegate, we should do the same to all, & not make such an insidious distinction, which in my opinion was unjust. The Rev <u>Theo S. Wright</u> concurred with my views. Mr Van Ranselaer deemed them satisfactory & Judicious, as we thought, whereupon the House was ~~obtained~~ granted, & I exerted myself to notify the meeting. Three of us, Mr Van Ranselaer, being one, resolved ourselves into a committee, to draft resolutions for the meeting & ~~to~~ move to meet at my office[6] at 4 o'clock. Upon presenting our resolutions in committee, Mr Van Ranselaer presented but one, & that expressive of our views of the Convention to be held & our confidence in four only of the delegation,[7] those who were taken up by the <u>American Society</u>, upon the third day of the meeting. We objected to the resolution as perverting the meeting from its avowed object & contrary to the notices given, & a violation of the condition upon which the House was obtained, & I had consented to cooperate in getting up the meeting, & because it was a negative disapproval of all the other delegates to be present from this country, who were alike entitled to our approbation & love, & as the resolution if passed would be presented to the convention, it would place those other delegates in awkward position, & be both unfair & unjust. Mr Van Ranselaer determined to accept no amendment, we waived the matter until it should be presented to the meeting, informing him that then, it should be amended if passed, or else it should be laid aside.

The meeting convened in the Rev <u>Mr Wrights Church</u>,[8] a very respectable attendance both as to numbers and character. The Rev Bro Wright in the chair & myself appointed secretary.

After an address of some length, from our <u>Friend</u> Mr. <u>Garrison</u>, <u>Mr Van Ranselaer</u>, immediately arose & presented his resolution.

Bro H H Garnett[9] of <u>Oneida Institute</u>,[10] seconded the resolution, & moved an amendment to insert your names as delegates also virtually appointed, by the <u>American Society</u>. This not meeting any objections, Mr J J Zuille[11] a clerke in our Office, moved an amendment to Mr Garnetts amendment, & I suggested an improvement to his, so that it should read "we approve of the American delegation, sent out by American Abolitionists" for we know them all, either personally or by reputation. The whole matter elicited some considerable debate, all excepting Mr. Van Ranselaer, in favor of the amendments. Some however thought we had better take no action ~~in~~ upon the matters & after hearing some remarks from Mr. <u>Garrison</u> in which he objected to have his name associated with yours, & Mr. Colvers,[12] remarks which the meeting were very sorry to hear, & which they were not prepared to receive, & it being late, I moved the indefinite postponement of the whole subject, which was carried.

We could easily have passed a resolution, approving of the entire delegation, had it not been so late, but any other insidious resolution, could not have been passed by that meeting, not because we were wanting in respect for any, but because we had too ~~respect~~ much real regard for all.

Now this refusal to pass an <u>illiberal</u> resolution (taken in its relation to this delegation) expressing our confidence, in & approval of a few of the delegation, of which ~~he~~ Bro Garrison was one, to the rejection of the many, Bro Rogers regards as an alienation of feeling, & respect towards Mr. Garrison and this alienation of affection as he regards it, Bro Rogers is going to show as he says, & as I am informed by Bro Van Ranselaer as one of the fruits of New Organization as tho. nothing else could effect our minds toward Mr. Garrison if affected at all, but New Organization, a conclusion more unfounded & more unfair, in relation to us, could hardly have been arrived at.

If the colored people of this City, or any section of this country, ~~have~~ do manifest less warmth of feeling than formerly towards <u>Mr. Garrison,</u> it is in part owing, to our <u>Friends</u> having multiplied who are equally active, & equally efficient with Mr. <u>Garrison</u>, & as a necessary consequence our good feeling is scattered upon all, instead of being concentrated upon one, as when Mr. Garrison stood alone. But there is another reason, & which I intended to have mentioned to Mr. <u>Garrison</u> personally, but had not the time when I saw him, nor the spirit with which Bro Garrison has conducted his own <u>Paper</u> since this controversy commenced, especially the repeated use which he made of Bro. <u>Wright</u> letter to yourself.[13]

These things affected some of our intelligent brethren, ~~who [word illegible] of Bro~~ as they have informed me, & not <u>New Organization</u> however much that may have a tendency to alienate feeling from Bro Garrison. I give you this history of the meeting by no means in defence of New Organization, but that you may have the facts, to prevent any wrong impressions that might be made, by B. Rogers ~~by~~ from his want of a knowledge of the true state of the case, & that it might not appear in England that we have forsaken our friends, but are consistent & [cleave] to all. We look forward to the worlds convention, with great interest— we anticipate the happiest results from its proceedings, especially if you do not drag in foreign matters which may God prevent. We are proud, in a proper sense, of our American delegation & no man is an exception, we know you as men having passed through the ordeal that tried mens souls, & now hardly having escaped, you are not going to form an alliance with the enemy. We regret that some more of us ~~could not~~ cannot be with you. We hope[,] we pray that the enslaved of the world those held in a chattel sense, of all colors & of all claims, may be the object of your deliberations, & that the result of them may be to raise up mankind to all the dignity of free men. We hope our American delegation will meet together in London & altho. they have differed here, that they will bury the hatchet, & do nothing to ~~[illegible word]~~ reflect upon our holy cause in this our beloved tho. slavery ridden country.

You will please remember me to Bro Keep and Dawes,[14] J C Fuller,[15] to James & Lucretia Mott,[16] to Elder Galusha,[17] Mr. Colver, the only delegates with whome I am personally acquainted.

Excuse this epistle, I am aware that is as weak as may be the occasion for it. I commend to you our Friend C Lenox Remond.

Birney Papers, William L. Clements Library, University of Michigan, Ann Arbor, Michigan. Published by permission.

1. Ray is writing to James Gillespie Birney and Henry Brewster Stanton, prominent abolitionists who broke with William Lloyd Garrison and the American Anti-Slavery Society in 1840 over the question of political action. Birney (1792–1857), a former Kentucky slaveholder and leading colonizationist, was converted to immediate emancipation in 1834. He served for a time as agent and corresponding secretary of the AASS and published the *Philanthropist* in 1836. After abandoning the AASS, he ran as the Liberty party's presidential candidate in 1840 and 1844. Stanton (1805–1887), one of the Lane Rebels, married well-known feminist Elizabeth Cady. After breaking with Garrison, he joined the American and Foreign Anti-Slavery Society. Stanton became a New York state senator in 1849 and promoted antislavery through the Liberty, Free Soil, and Republican parties. Barnes and Dumond, *Letters of Theodore Dwight Weld*, 1:150; Merrill and Ruchames, *Letters of William Lloyd Garrison*, 3:269, 4:233.

2. Nathaniel Peabody Rogers (1794–1846) served as editor of the *Herald of Freedom*, a Concord, New Hampshire, antislavery newspaper and the official organ of the New Hampshire Anti-Slavery Society. Active in the New England Non-Resistance Society, Rogers opposed all forms of organization, even formal meetings; this eventually created conflict with the New Hampshire Anti-Slavery Society and William Lloyd Garrison. *NCAB*, 2:320.

3. The World's Anti-Slavery Convention met during 12–23 June 1840 at Freemasons' Hall in London. Organized primarily through the efforts of Joseph Sturge and the British and Foreign Anti-Slavery Society, it was the first international reform convention. Sessions were attended by 409 delegates, mostly from the British Empire, although small delegations also attended from France and the United States. Efforts at international unity were seriously damaged at the initial session when the majority refused to seat eight American women delegates. Thereafter, the women and several protesting male Garrisonian delegates, including William Lloyd Garrison himself, viewed the proceedings from the gallery. Despite this, other issues received lengthy discussion, particularly the role of churches in the antislavery crusade and endorsement of the free produce movement as a means of combating slavery. Douglas H. Maynard, "The World's Anti-Slavery Convention of 1840," *MVHR* 47:452–62 (December 1960).

4. "New organization" refers to the American and Foreign Anti-Slavery So-

ciety, which was founded in May 1840 by Lewis Tappan and some thirty other disaffected American Anti-Slavery Society members, including Samuel Cornish, Theodore S. Wright, J. W. C. Pennington, and five other leading black abolitionists. The association hoped to expand the arena of abolitionist activity by endorsing the idea of antislavery political action. Although the AFASS met annually throughout the 1840s, the society did not flourish. The organization was administratively top-heavy, lacked vigorous local affiliates, was financially troubled, did not sharply define its goals, and failed to attract a large membership. The AFASS's white leaders divided over whether or not the organization should attach itself to a political party. Black leaders were alienated by the association's eventual support of a third political party and its 1852 endorsement of African settlement. Finally, the society never developed an effective newspaper. In 1855 Tappan abandoned the virtually defunct AFASS and joined with William Goodell and Gerrit Smith to form the American Abolition Society. Gerald Sorin, *Abolitionism: A New Perspective* (New York, N.Y., 1972), 61, 87, 92, 101; Wyatt-Brown, *Lewis Tappan*, 193–200, 213, 215, 249, 252, 279, 282, 315, 332, 516; Pease and Pease, *They Who Would Be Free*, 41, 73–79, 80–85, 196, 259; Kraditor, *Means and Ends in American Abolitionism*, 7, 52–57, 63, 107, 118, 129, 141, 142, 148, 152.

5. Thomas Van Rensellaer.

6. Ray refers to his third-floor office at 9 Spruce Street in New York City. After reviving the *Colored American* in March 1840, he published the journal from this office. *CA*, 7 March 1840.

7. Forty Americans, representing various antislavery organizations and their auxiliaries, attended the 1840 World's Anti-Slavery Convention in London. William Lloyd Garrison, Charles L. Remond, Lucretia Mott, and Nathaniel P. Rogers attended as official delegates of the American Anti-Slavery Society. Maynard, "World's Anti-Slavery Convention," 452–57.

8. Theodore S. Wright was pastor of the First Colored Presbyterian Church in New York City, commonly known as the Shiloh Church, from 1828 until his death in 1847.

9. Henry Highland Garnet (1815–1882) was born in Maryland to slave parents. In 1824 Henry's father, George Garnet, led ten family members to freedom in the North, finally settling in New York City. Between 1826 and 1833, Garnet received an intermittent education in New York's African Free School, enrolled in the Phoenix High School for Colored Youth, and met Rev. Theodore S. Wright, a leader of New York's black community, who became his mentor. In 1835 Garnet, Alexander Crummell, Thomas Sidney, and four other blacks were driven from Rev. William Scales's integrated Noyes Academy in Canaan, New Hampshire, by an antiintegration mob.

After graduating from Beriah Green's Oneida Institute in 1839, Garnet began an eight-year residence (1840–48) in Troy, New York, where he ministered to a black congregation (the Liberty Street Presbyterian Church), edited two short-lived reformist newspapers (the *Clarion* and the *National Watchman*), and founded a school for black children in nearby Geneva. Garnet also assisted the suffrage struggle of New York blacks and was active in Liberty party deliberations. His considerable reputation as an antislavery reformer was enhanced at the 1843 black national convention in Buffalo, where he gained notoriety as a strident black voice for freedom by delivering his "Address to the Slaves of the United States"—a speech generally perceived as a call for slave violence. A supporting resolution was narrowly defeated.

In 1850 Garnet's support of the free produce movement brought an invitation from Henry and Anna Richardson, leaders of the British movement, to lecture on the subject. After a two-year stay in Britain, Garnet accepted an appointment by the United Presbyterian Church of Scotland to serve as a missionary in Jamaica. During his stay on the island (1853–55), Garnet established two elementary schools for black children and a female industrial school, which was directed by his wife, Julia. Illness forced Garnet to resign his post. He returned to New York City in 1856 to pastor the Shiloh Presbyterian Church. Although Garnet had spoken positively about limited black emigration as early as 1849, he institutionalized these beliefs in the late 1850s by helping found the African Civilization Society—an organization that did not repudiate a black presence in the United States but encouraged black missionary work and entrepreneurship in Africa. He traveled to England again in 1861 to promote the society. During the Civil War, Garnet recruited black troops for the Union army and afterwards became the first black man to preach a sermon in the House of Representatives (1865).

In 1868, after serving the Fifteenth Street Presbyterian Church in Washington, D.C., and directing African Civilization Society efforts to educate newly freed black children, he was appointed president of Avery College, a black college established by influential Pittsburgh cotton merchant Charles Avery. Garnet returned to his Shiloh pastorate in 1870. He was appointed U.S. minister to Liberia in 1881. Joel Schor, *Henry Highland Garnet: A Voice of Black Radicalism in the Nineteenth Century* (Westport, Conn., 1977), 3–217; Martin Burt Pasternak, "Rise Now and Fly to Arms: The Life of Henry Highland Garnet" (Ph.D. diss., University of Massachusetts, 1981), 1–269; *DANB*, 252–53.

10. The Oneida Institute, located near Utica, New York, developed out of the Oneida Academy established by Presbyterian minister George W. Gale in 1827. Encouraged by the success of his students, Gale expanded the school and changed its name in 1829. Rev. Beriah Green replaced Gale in 1832 and immediately transformed the school into a center of abolitionism. Oneida became one of the nation's few colleges to admit black and white students on an equal basis. At least fourteen blacks, including Henry Highland Garnet, Alexander Crummell, and Jermain W. Loguen, attended the school. The institute flourished during its early years, admitting 140 students in 1835. Operating upon manual labor principles, Oneida emphasized preparation for the Presbyterian ministry and spreading abolitionist doctrines. Students printed William Goodell's *Friend of Man*. Oneida closed in 1844 because of Green's controversial administration and a sharp decline in revenue resulting from the panic of 1837. Milton C. Sernett, *Abolition's Axe: Beriah Green, Oneida Institute, and the Black Freedom Struggle* (Syracuse, N.Y., 1986), 31–67, 91–106; Carleton Mabee, *Black Education in New York State: From Colonial to Modern Times* (Syracuse, N.Y., 1979), 25, 166–71.

11. John J. Zuille (1814–1894), a black printer and teacher, was born in Bermuda. After settling in New York City in the 1830s, he worked as an apprentice for the *Colored American* and gradually assumed greater responsibility for its publication; he contributed articles and occasionally managed the paper in the

editor's absence. Zuille taught at Colored Public School No. 2 in the 1840s. During the early 1850s, he established a successful printing business, which provided a valuable means of communication for the black community. Zuille played a prominent role in several black organizations and causes: he was a member of the New York Political Association, the Phoenix Society, and the United Anti-Slavery Society, and served as secretary for the African Society for Mutual Relief. From the 1830s through the Civil War, he participated in efforts to protect and expand black voting rights by promoting state conventions and petition drives. Zuille's political activism generated controversy, particularly when his commitment to Whig candidates drew fire from blacks loyal to the Liberty party in the late 1840s. In the 1850s, he chaired the Committee of Thirteen—a group of New York black leaders in the struggle against the Fugitive Slave Law, colonization, and racial discrimination. When Zuille suffered property losses and narrowly escaped personal injury in the 1863 draft riots, he fled with his family to Hartford. After the Civil War, he worked as cashier of the New York City branch of the Freedman's Savings Bank from 1866 to 1874. *CA*, 29 April 1837, 12 October, 17 August 1839, 20 June 1840, 13 February 1841 [2:0037, 3:0173, 0231, 0461, 0884]; *NSt*, 4, 18 May 1849 [5:1085, 1092]; *IC*, 5 December 1849 [6:0235–36]; *FDP*, 15 January 1851, 26 February 1852 [7:0356, 0439–40]; *WAA*, 31 March 1860, 12 April 1862, 1, 8 August 1863 [12:0600, 14:0237]; *PA*, 30 May 1863 [14:0878]; *DM*, October 1860 [12:1022]; *ESF*, 17 November 1865; Walker, "Afro-American in New York City," 134, 167–68, 172, 221n; Alexander Crummell to John Jay, 24 October 1839, Jay Family Papers, NNC [3:0242]; Charles B. Ray to James G. Birney, 20 May 1840, James G. Birney Collection, MiU [3:0431]; George T. Downing to Alexander Crummell, 19 April 1860, Alexander Crummell Papers, NN-Sc [12:0642]; Carl R. Osthaus, *Freedmen, Philanthropy, and Fraud: A History of the Freedman's Bank* (Urbana, Ill., 1976), 232.

12. Nathaniel Colver (1794–1870), a former lecturer for the American Anti-Slavery Society, split with the Garrisonians in 1839 over the question of women's rights and nonresistance. He became a vocal critic of the anticlericalism and social radicalism of Garrison and his followers. Colver attended the 1840 World's Anti-Slavery Convention in London, voicing his opposition to the seating of female delegates. A Baptist clergyman, he served from 1839 to 1852 as the pastor of Boston's interracial Tremont Temple. After the Civil War, he established the Colver Institute for the training of black ministers in Richmond. *DAB*, 4:324; Merrill and Ruchames, *Letters of William Lloyd Garrison*, 2:336, 412, 415, 3:17, 23.

13. Ray refers to Elizur Wright, Jr.'s, October 1839 letter to Henry B. Stanton, which Garrison published several times in the *Liberator*. The letter advocated the creation of an abolitionist political party and encouraged Stanton to lead the AASS into antislavery politics. Garrison accused Wright and his clerical associates of attempting to force radicals like Garrison out of the movement. The controversy exacerbated the tensions that led to the breakup of the AASS in May 1840. *Lib*, 13, 27 December 1839, 3, 17 January 1840; Merrill and Ruchames, *Letters of William Lloyd Garrison*, 2:111; Goodheart, "Elizur Wright, Jr.," 149–62.

14. John Keep and William Dawes conducted an English fund-raising tour that

netted $30,000 for Oberlin College. Keep (1781–1870), a Congregational minister, filled a number of pulpits in Massachusetts, New York, and Ohio. He donated $10,000 to Oberlin College, became president of the board of trustees, and cast the deciding vote that admitted black students. Dawes (1799–1888) was a peace advocate and member of Oberlin's board of trustees from 1839 to 1851. Merrill and Ruchames, *Letters of William Lloyd Garrison*, 3:525; *ACAB*, 3:501.

15. James Canning Fuller (1793–1847), an English Quaker and Garrisonian abolitionist, settled in Skaneateles, New York, in 1834. Fuller helped found the black Dawn settlement in Canada West and attended the 1840 and 1843 World's Anti-Slavery Conventions in London. Merrill and Ruchames, *Letters of William Lloyd Garrison*, 3:46–48, 146–47; Pease and Pease, *Black Utopia*, 64.

16. James Mott (1788–1868), a wealthy wool merchant, and Lucretia Coffin Mott (1793–1880) were well-known Philadelphia Quaker reformers. They advocated antislavery, temperance, and peace, and their home was a frequent stop on the underground railroad. James was a founding member of the American Anti-Slavery Society and Lucretia helped establish both the Philadelphia Female Anti-Slavery Society and the Anti-Slavery Convention of American Women. Both attended the 1840 World's Anti-Slavery Convention in London, but Lucretia was rejected as a delegate because of her gender. They were early feminists, and Lucretia helped organize the Seneca Falls Convention of 1848. With the coming of the Civil War, the Motts turned their attention to black suffrage and freedmen's education. *DAB*, 8:288–90; *NAW*, 2:592–95.

17. Elon Galusha (1790–1856), the son of Vermont governor Jonas Galusha, ministered to Baptist congregations in Rochester and Perry, New York. In 1840 he served as president of the National Baptist Anti-Slavery Convention and represented the American and Foreign Anti-Slavery Society at the World's Anti-Slavery Convention. Galusha's antislavery activities provoked Southern Baptists to exclude him from the American Board of Commissioners for Foreign Missions. Merrill and Ruchames, *Letters of William Lloyd Garrison*, 2:100n; John W. Blassingame, *The Frederick Douglass Papers*, ser. 1, 3 vols. to date (New Haven, Conn., 1979–), 1:110n.

46.
Samuel Ringgold Ward to Nathaniel P. Rogers
27 June 1840

White abolitionist prejudice helped convince blacks that independent
black action offered the best hope for attacking slavery, securing civil
rights, and improving the condition of the free black community. Although white abolitionists opposed some Jim Crow practices—the "Negro pew," segregated railroad cars, and laws against interracial marriage
—most were cautious about racial matters, refusing to openly associate
with blacks until "the public mind and conscience [are] more enlightened on the subject." For whites, equal rights became a secondary issue
in the antislavery struggle. Many black leaders accused white abolitionists of failing to conquer their own prejudices. Samuel R. Ward raised
this sensitive issue in a 27 June 1840 letter to Nathaniel P. Rogers, the
editor of the *National Anti-Slavery Standard*. He argued that too many
white abolitionists "have yet to learn what it is to crucify prejudice
against color within their own bosoms." He charged that there were
"too many who best love the colored man at a distance." Ward wrote in
response to an editorial by Rogers that criticized racially exclusive action. By the close of the 1830s, black leaders increasingly supported
separate action and black-dominated institutions, arguing that they
must take the lead if racial equality was to remain a goal of the antislavery movement. Foner, *History of Black Americans*, 2:518, 532–33;
Pease and Pease, *They Who Would Be Free*, 97–98; *NASS*, 18 June
1840.

PETERBORO, [New York]
June 27, 1840

MR. EDITOR:

With all that has been done by our friends, we see ample reasons for
efficient action on our own part. Abolitionists have met frequently, and
held Town, County, State, and National Conventions. They have generally remembered us, scattered, peeled, disfranchised, and downtrodden,
as we are. They have done much, very much, for the reformation of
public opinion concerning us and our rights. Some of them have refused
to sustain pro-slavery political parties, to give their suffrages to those
who would not remember us in the halls of legislation. Yet the fact
ought not to be concealed, that there are too many Abolitionists in
profession, who have yet to learn what it is to crucify prejudice against
color within their own bosoms. Too many who best love the colored man
at a distance.

A fact or two in proof. From my own observation and painful experience, I am enabled to say, that a large proportion of the professed friends

of the slave, the professed and recorded believers in the doctrine of immediate emancipation, give encouragement to prejudice against color, at the polls, in the social circle, and in the church.

At the polls, they sustain the pro-slavery laws which disfranchise us, and the pro-slavery parties that uphold and sanction those laws.

In the social circle, in company with white persons, they find it difficult to see a colored man, though they have spectacles on their noses.

In the church, they refuse to remonstrate against negro-pewism,[1] and suffer colored persons to wander about the aisles unseated, till the sexton seats them *near the door.* A white person, of no greater respectability in appearance, enters next, and they offer him a good pew, with proper respect. Indeed, brother Gardner,[2] of Newark, lately wrote me, that for seating and sitting with Rev. Mr. Williams (the pastor of the colored Methodist church of that city),[3] in the free church of Newark,[4] he was *reproved* by one of the *earliest Abolitionists* of New Jersey, [at] one of the sessions of that church.

Besides, Abolitionists have not so much regard for the rights of colored men as they think they have. When press, speech, and others of *their own rights* were jeopordized by the spirit of slavocracy, they raised their united voice, as men should, in self-defence. But now, when their own rights are somewhat secure, they appear to cease to feel identified with us. I know not how else to account for their strong and determined action in defence of their own rights, while now they are comparatively mute concerning *ours.*

I repeat, that these are facts which have come under my own observation; facts that are facts concerning a large proportion of the professed Abolitionists of this State and other States. Happy for us, however, there are many honorable exceptions, especially in Western New York.[5] But viewing these facts as they are, and feeling their malign influence as we do, I must beg leave to dissent from the views expressed in an editorial article in the *Standard* of the 18th instant, concerning a Convention of colored people.[6] I know that your intentions are correct; but had you worn a colored skin from October '17 to June '40, as I have, in this pseudo-republic, you would have seen through a very different medium.[7] The continuation of wrongs, injustice, and ingratitude, inflicted upon us by the State government, the small share of sympathy evinced towards us by many of our professed friends, and the still smaller amount of efficient action put forth by them in our behalf, all render it indispensably necessary that the colored people of this State should convene and act for themselves.

Yours, for pure and impartial Abolitionism.

SAMUEL R. WARD[8]

National Anti-Slavery Standard (New York, N.Y.), 2 July 1840.

1. Northern free blacks attending antebellum white churches were generally segregated into inconspicuous sections, either in an "African corner," a "Negro pew," on seats marked "B.M." (for black members), or in a balcony or loft referred to as "Nigger Heaven." Sabbath schools often provided separate quarters for white and black children. The "Negro pew" most dramatically symbolized the inferior status of blacks in white churches and made separate black churches attractive to many blacks. Litwack, *North of Slavery*, 191, 196–97, 206–7, 213.

2. William F. Gardner, a white bookkeeper and bill collector in Newark, was a friend and business associate of Samuel Ringgold Ward. He participated in the campaign for black voting rights in New Jersey during the 1840s. *CA*, 29 June 1839, 6 January 1841 [3:0871]; *Newark City Directory*, 1836–50.

3. Ward refers to John A. Williams (1805–?), who was pastor of the First African Methodist Church of Newark, an African Methodist Episcopal Zion congregation, from 1840 to 1844. Williams was born in slavery near Baltimore but escaped in the mid-1820s. After joining the AMEZ ministry in 1834, he itinerated throughout New York and New Jersey. He later served several settled pastorates, including the one in Newark and the Sixth Street AMEZ Church in New York City (1849–60), before assuming pastoral duties at the Union Wesley Church in Harrisburg, Pennsylvania, and the Brick Wesley Church in Philadelphia during the 1860s. Wherever his ministry took him, Williams became involved in local antislavery and civil rights efforts. Under his leadership, Newark's First African Methodist Church was a local center for the antislavery and black suffrage campaigns. Williams later opened his Philadelphia church to agents of the Haitian immigration movement. During the Civil War, he encouraged black enlistment in the Fifty-fourth Massachusetts Regiment. *PP*, 31 August, 5 October 1861, 6 February 1862 [13:0715, 0739]; *Newark City Directory*, 1840–44; William J. Walls, *The African Methodist Episcopal Zion Church: Reality of the Black Church* (Charlotte, N.C., 1974), 127; *WAA*, 1 October 1859, 17 March, 28 April, 5, 26 May, 9, 16, 23 June 1860, 12 April 1862 [12:0688, 0766–67, 0795, 0809, 0811]; *PA*, 16 May 1863 [14:0863]; "Call to Arms," 6 July 1863, Leon F. Gardiner Collection, PHi [14:0945]; *E*, 14 April 1842 [4:0414]; *CA*, 20 July 1839, 25 July 1840, 6 February 1841 [3:0534, 0871]; *FDP*, 10 June 1852 [7:0623].

4. Ward refers to the First Free Presbyterian Church, which was located at 15 Clinton Street in Newark. Organized in 1834, it became a Congregationalist parish in the early 1850s. Charles Fitch was the pastor in 1840. *Newark City Directory*, 1835–61.

5. Ward refers to the antislavery efforts of Gerrit Smith and his followers in western New York. Men like Smith, Lysander Spooner, William Goodell, and James G. Birney worked closely with blacks through the Liberty party and other organizations. Friedman, *Gregarious Saints*, 96–126.

6. An editorial in the 18 June 1840 issue of the *National Anti-Slavery Standard* expressed opposition to the New York black state convention, which was to be held in Albany in August. The paper condemned racially exclusive meetings and all social distinctions based upon race. Although the *Standard* reprinted the call for the convention, it advised blacks to display more patience with the pace of

reform and warned them to "be careful that you do not tear down what you build up." *NASS*, 18 June 1840.

7. Ward, who was born in October 1817, refers to his lifelong encounters with prejudice, suggesting that black and white abolitionists viewed American race relations differently.

8. Samuel Ringgold Ward (1817–ca. 1866) was the second son of slave parents who fled to freedom in 1820. The Ward family lived in New Jersey for six years until the threat of kidnapping by slave catchers prompted them to resettle in New York City. Ward received the rudiments of an education from his father, attended New York's African Free School, and clerked for two leading black activists, David Ruggles and Thomas L. Jinnings. He moved to Newark in 1835 and taught school until 1839; he and his wife then relocated to Poughkeepsie, New York, where he was employed at the Colored Lancastrian School. That same year, Ward became a licensed minister in the New York Congregational Association. At the end of the year, his growing reputation as a forceful and articulate antislavery spokesman earned him an appointment as lecture agent for the American Anti-Slavery Society. When the society divided in 1840, Ward left his agency and joined the American and Foreign Anti-Slavery Society because he believed slavery should be attacked with political weapons as well as moral suasion.

Throughout the 1840s, Ward led New York blacks in their efforts to acquire the right to vote. He returned to the ministry, first as pastor of a church in South Butler, New York (1841–43), and then as leader of a white congregation in Cortland, New York (1846–51), while continuing his antislavery activity. Perhaps more than any other black abolitionist, Ward was angered by the hypocrisy of white reformers, and he often cautioned his listeners that there were many abolitionists "who best love the colored man at a distance." Ward founded and edited several reform newspapers: first the short-lived *True American* in 1847–48 and later the more successful *Impartial Citizen*, which lasted from mid-1849 until well into 1851 and which allowed Ward to display his Liberty party commitment and his interpretation of the U.S. Constitution as an antislavery document.

He joined the Syracuse Vigilance Committee, Gerrit Smith, and his longtime friend, black minister Jermain W. Loguen, in rescuing the fugitive slave William "Jerry" McHenry from federal officers in October 1851. Difficulties resulting from the Jerry rescue sent Ward to Canada, where he remained for over two years, serving as an agent for the Anti-Slavery Society of Canada. Early in 1853, he founded the *Provincial Freeman*, a newspaper meant to serve the Canadian black community. A few months later, he accepted a commission from the society to seek British funds for Canadian fugitives, and he remained abroad for two and a half years, touring successfully (he impressed British audiences with his eloquence, humor, and imposing black presence) and publishing his narrative, *Autobiography of a Fugitive Negro: His Anti-Slavery Labours in the United States, Canada and England* (1855).

When Ward left England, he sailed not to Canada, but to Jamaica, where he ministered to a Kingston congregation for the next five years. In 1860 he settled on a small piece of land in Jamaica he had received as a gift while in England. In

Document 46

the wake of the Morant Bay Rebellion in Jamaica (October 1865), Ward wrote *Reflections on the Gordon Rebellion* (1866), a critical examination of George William Gordon, the leader of the island's black revolutionary forces. Samuel Ringgold Ward, *Autobiography of a Fugitive Negro* (London, 1855; reprint, New York, N.Y., 1968); Ronald Kevin Burke, "Samuel Ringgold Ward, Christian Abolitionist" (Ph.D. diss., Syracuse University, 1975), 12–98; Winks, *Blacks in Canada*, 206–7, 218, 227, 235, 241, 249, 255–59, 265–66, 361, 441; *NASS*, 2 July, 10, 17 September 1840, 11 March 1847 [3:0478, 0612, 0619, 5:0391]; *IC*, 14 March, 11 April, 27 June 1850, 13, 20 February 1851 [5:1003, 1054, 6:0021, 0023, 0398, 0404]; *NSt*, 27 June 1850 [6:0026]; *WAA*, 20, 27 August 1859 [11:0944, 0972]; *DANB*, 631–32.

47.
Reviving the Black Convention Movement

James McCune Smith to Charles B. Ray
12 August 1840

Editorial by Charles B. Ray
12 September 1840

New enthusiasm for reviving the black convention movement prompted a debate on the subject in 1840. Some activists opposed separate black conventions, insisting that integrated action was the best avenue to racial progress. But most black leaders had faith in the convention idea and defended "exclusive action." Advocates of conventions divided over whether they should be national or state gatherings. David Ruggles's call for a National Reform Convention of Colored Citizens drew only five delegates to New Haven in September 1840. State conventions gained more support because they were easier to attend and they offered the opportunity to devise specific strategies addressing particular local problems. The issue filled the columns of the *Colored American* during the summer of 1840. James McCune Smith's 12 August letter to editor Charles B. Ray criticized plans to hold a state convention of New York blacks in Albany later in the month. He argued that all-black assemblies wasted financial resources, created white hostility, and hindered integrated action. A 12 September editorial by Ray, written several weeks after the Albany gathering, offered a more positive assessment. He suggested that the unique oppression that blacks faced demanded a separate fight, and he recommended state conventions, arguing that racial discrimination could best be fought at the state and local level. Pease and Pease, *They Who Would Be Free*, 180–82; CA, 6, 13, 20, 27 June, 25 July, 15 August, 12 September 1840 [3:0449, 0455, 0458, 0462, 0472–73, 0534, 0561, 0618]; E, 12 June 1840 [3:0454].

New York, New York
August 12th, 1840

MR. EDITOR:

In your last paper, in the accounts of two meetings held in this city in relation to the "Colored Convention to be held in Albany on the 18th inst.,"[1] it is stated that in company with several gentlemen of this city, I opposed the Convention. As the grounds of opposition are not even alluded to in your paper, I have to request that you will, as an act of justice allow me briefly to state the views which led me to oppose the movement.

I opposed the Convention—

1st. Because the difficulty of the times is a reason why all men, and especially we, who are *proverbially poor*, should husband our means so as to meet our actual physical wants, and thus destroy the charge of improvidence and penury, which is trumpeted against us.

2d. Because the absence of principle, obtains so largely in this State at present, that the Convention, distinguished by complexion, would be likely to excite that prejudice to our detriment, as was the case in the State of Pennsylvania, where, in consequence of a similar movement, the colored people, from possessing the elective franchise, were entirely disfranchised.[2]

3d. Because the Convention aims to do by separate action what can better be done by a movement based on principle, and carried on by all the influences, irrespective of complexion, that can be brought to bear: this separate action, distinguished by the complexion of the skin, being a virtual acknowledgement that there are rights peculiar to the color of a man's skin; thus fostering prejudice against complexion; separate action the more to be condemned, because entirely voluntary on the part of the callers of the Convention.

4th. Because a colored Convention of the kind in question "does evil, that good may come"[3]—violates the principles of equal rights in the attempt to attain equal rights. For example, Isaac T. Hopper,[4] William M. Chace,[5] James S. Gibbons[6] and others, oppressed citizens of this State—oppressed from *the same cause* which oppresses us—are anxious to join with us in this movement, yet the call for the Convention shuts them out, not on account of difference in principles, but because their complexion is different.

In conclusion, I beg to state, that I still entertain these views in regard to the Convention, and said so at the meeting on Friday night—which meeting appointed Mr. Hudson and myself,[7] with the understanding that we should lay our views before the Convention.

I am not at all opposed to all action on the part of the colored people, but am opposed to action based upon complexional distinction; believing that whilst a movement based on principle will effect our enfranchisement, that, on the other hand, a movement based on the complexion of the skin, will end in riveting still more firmly the chains which bind us.

Your obedient servant,

JAMES McCUNE SMITH[8]

Colored American (New York, N.Y.), 15 August 1840.

STATE CONVENTIONS

Having attended our own State Convention at Albany, and having endeavored to aid in its proceedings as we thought duty required, as we had endeavored to do what we could towards getting it up. And it having passed off much to the satisfaction of all who attended, and we hope much to the credit, and the influence of which so far as felt, having been good, and as it shall extend itself still to be good. If the citizens of other States see as we saw, and feel as we felt upon local subjects which concern them, as ours concerned us, we are prepared to recommend State Conventions as having in themselves a tendency to do good, to those who attend, and through them to benefit doubtless the people.

We recommend them upon the same basis upon which ours was called and held, and for the same reasons, notwithstanding the strong opposition of the *National Anti-Slavery Standard*, resorting to various arguments to oppose it.

The last and certainly the least the *"aristocracy of the skin,"* by no means a new kind of aristocracy but which exists all on their side of the house; *a lily skin* is the *real simon pure* in this country. A skin colored like our own, has no right to say much, or do much, not even to hold a Convention.

It is not in every free state where local matters exist, oppressing the colored people sufficiently, to make it necessary to hold a Convention, to take them into consideration. It is no use to do a thing for which there is no special call, or necessity; when there is necessity it becomes duty, and ought to be attended to. It would be useless as to the good to be affected, to come together for any such purpose, unless the people were prepared for it. To come together and not to harmonize, and proceed, and break up in confusion it were better never to meet, than to meet under such circumstances; the tendency would be, to defeat the object rather than to further it, to put back the cause, rather than to advance it.

Where then the people can fix upon the object or objects, if more than one exist, alike oppressive to the people, and can agree upon a measure to effect that or those objects, and come together in a proper spirit, State Conventions can but be beneficial to the people.

It may be, that the people generally are not sufficiently under the influence of correct principles, to allow such a Convention peaceably to proceed with their business, as is doubtless the case in some of the States, in which case the people would pause before attempting to hold such a meeting.

Where all things are favorable, and the people are laboring under proscriptive legal disabilities, they ought to meet together, embody views, and express their opinion in the case, adopt some measures to affect the object, and enlist to a greater extent the co-operation of others. Such a state of things do exist in *old Connecticut*, where the people are proscribed, are laboring under legal disabilities, greater than our own, and where they have a property, talent and piety, and may convene in a number of places peaceably, and discuss their disabilities, much to their honor, and in our opinion if they are prepared for it ought to do so. In other states equal reasons exist for such a measure, where if practicable and the people are ready for it, might be adopted to great benefit.[9]

State Conventions called for a local and special object, fixed upon by the people, would be likely to be regarded as matters especially their own, matters with the continuance or overthrow of which, depended their own rise or fall, and they would be likely to adopt measures with greater harmony, and carry them out with more efficiency, than in our opinion, would be done by a National Convention, and each State taking into consideration their own local disabilities, would answer all the purposes of a National Convention.

A Convention of the latter sort, would have to be made up, to make it National, of delegates from all the States from which it would be safe to come, who would come together with more or less of the jealousies peculiar to our country, and with their local prejudices, and interests, and conflicting views and thus make it almost impossible to fix with all that unanimity upon measures, and to harmonize together in adopting them, as what might apply to one section of the country, might not to another and what might be safe and practicable in one, might not be in another. All this difficulty with State Conventions would be very much obviated.

We have not seen all that necessity for a National Convention which, some of our fellow laborers seem to suppose to exist. We would oppose a Convention of this kind, if we thought the whole people wheresoever practicable, would not be represented in it. The greatest reason that we can see for a National assemblage of our people is, to have the whole represented, and make a noble expression of opinion as to our relation to the American soil, and the American government, as men and citizens, and to take a stand for our rights as such, more firm and decisive, than that taken by Patrick Henry,[10] and the fathers of the revolution.

We have written as much as we have upon State Conventions because we know the mass of the more intelligent of our people, are ripe for a Convention, and as with the people of this State, will not be satisfied until they have had a Convention, and because we wish to turn their attention towards State Conventions, where practicable as answering a better purpose than the National. And we will aid towards getting them up.

No friend of our people, could he but place himself under the political, moral and social disabilities, under which we are placed, and could he feel under these circumstances as we feel, would raise any opposition to any judicious measure, we in our anxiety for relief might adopt, calculated in any sense to lead towards a relief. We have now perhaps written enough about Conventions for the present.

Colored American (New York, N.Y.), 12 September 1840.

1. Smith refers to two meetings held by New York City blacks in support of the black state convention that met in Albany during 18–20 August 1840. The Albany gathering, the nation's first black state convention, was organized to work for repeal of the discriminatory property requirement for black suffrage in New York. It attracted most of the leading black abolitionists from around the state. Smith, who opposed racially separate conventions, first voiced his disapproval at a 27 July 1840 meeting held at Philomathean Hall. The *Colored American* reported his opposition but failed to print Smith's resolutions against the Albany convention. Smith also attended a 4 August meeting at the First Colored Presbyterian Church. The paper noted Smith's opposition but again failed to publish his remarks. *CA*, 8 August 1840; Foner and Walker, *Proceedings of the Black State Conventions*, 1:5–26.

2. The Pennsylvania Reform Convention of 1838 proposed eliminating black suffrage and dropping property requirements for whites. Despite opposition by black and white abolitionists, Pennsylvania voters approved black disfranchisement in the fall election.

3. Smith paraphrases Romans 3:8.

4. Isaac Tatem Hopper (1771–1852), a Quaker tailor, was active in abolitionism, prison reform, and poor relief efforts. He joined the Pennsylvania Abolition Society in 1795. In Philadelphia, and later in New York City, Hopper aided fugitive slaves and provided them with legal assistance. He worked closely with the New York Committee of Vigilance. From 1841 to 1845, Hopper served the American Anti-Slavery Society as treasurer and book agent. Merrill and Ruchames, *Letters of William Lloyd Garrison*, 4:15; Lydia Maria Child, *Isaac T. Hopper: A True Life* (Boston, Mass., 1853).

5. William M. Chace (1814–1862), a Providence wool merchant, helped found the Rhode Island Anti-Slavery Society. An early supporter and agent for the *Liberator*, he rejected all antislavery organizations in 1840 because of abolitionist infighting. For a time, he cooperated in a utopian community scheme. He later practiced law in New York, joined the Republican party, and aided the Union cause as a civilian during the Civil War. Merrill and Ruchames, *Letters of William Lloyd Garrison*, 2:8, 3:8–10, 38; Garrison and Garrison, *William Lloyd Garrison*, 3:23–27.

6. James Sloan Gibbons (1810–1892), a Quaker born in Wilmington, Delaware, moved to New York in 1835, where he became a successful banker and financier. He married Abigail Hopper, daughter of Isaac T. Hopper, and staunchly supported Garrisonian abolitionists and the *National Anti-Slavery Standard*. The New York Friends disowned him for his abolitionist activities, and his home was sacked during the 1863 draft riots. *DAB*, 7:242; *ACAB*, 2:636.

7. On 7 August 1840, a Friday night, New York City blacks again met at Philomathean Hall to express support for the controversial Albany convention. Smith repeated his opposition to racially exclusive gatherings and declined his selection as a delegate. He named James Hudson as his replacement, but neither

man attended the Albany meeting. Hudson, who was active in the campaign for equal suffrage in New York state, did attend the black state convention at Troy the following year. *CA*, 15 August 1840, 28 August, 11 September, 9, 30 October, 20 November 1841 [3:0564, 4:0180, 0196, 0246, 0273–75, 0308].

8. James McCune Smith (1813–1865) was born in New York City, the son of former slaves. He excelled at the city's African Free School but was denied admission to American colleges. With the aid of black clergyman Peter Williams, Jr., he enrolled at Glasgow University in 1832, eventually obtaining three academic degrees, including doctorate of medicine. While there he played an active role in the Scottish antislavery movement as an officer of the Glasgow Emancipation Society. After a brief internship in Paris, he returned to New York City in 1837 and established a successful, integrated medical practice and the first black-owned pharmacy. His professional status, intellect, and civic-mindedness soon made him a prominent spokesman for the city's black community, which he frequently represented at black national conventions.

Smith helped define many of the themes of the black abolitionist movement. A lifelong opponent of colonization and defender of black claims to American citizenship, he became a leading critic of West African and Haitian immigration schemes in the 1850s. He was convinced that blacks should fight for racial integration in the United States but recognized the need for independent black initiatives and separate black organizations. Smith defended the autonomous black press and directed efforts to establish the National Council of the Colored People in the early 1850s. He promoted black education and self-help principles through his writings and his work with the Philomathean Society, the Colored Orphan Asylum, New York Central College, the proposed American Industrial School, and other black organizations. Although Smith wrestled with the issue of political antislavery for more than a decade, initially rejecting the Liberty party, he helped lead the campaign for unrestricted black suffrage in New York state. By the mid-1850s, he had firmly embraced political abolitionism, defended the U.S. Constitution as an antislavery document, and called for federal intervention to end slavery. His growing involvement in electoral politics led the Radical Abolition party to nominate him in 1857 for New York secretary of state.

Because of his perceptive social insights and numerous contributions to Afro-American culture, Smith ranks as one of the foremost black intellectuals of the antebellum period. He is best remembered for his essays and editorial work. Smith briefly edited the *Colored American*, the *Northern Star and Freeman's Advocate*, and *Douglass' Monthly*; helped revive the *Weekly Anglo-African* as an antiemigration newspaper in 1861; and was a leading contributor to the *Anglo-African Magazine*. As the New York City correspondent for *Frederick Douglass' Paper* (often writing under the pseudonym "Communipaw"), he commented on a variety of issues, including black economic and social life, scientific theories of race, antislavery strategies, and racial prejudice among white abolitionists. The eclectic nature of his interests was reflected in such essays as "On the Influence of Opium on Catamenial Functions" (1844), two pamphlets entitled *A Lecture on the Haytian Revolution* (1841) and *The Destiny of the People of Color* (1843), and eloquent introductions to Frederick Douglass's second autobiography and Henry Highland Garnet's *Memorial Discourse* (1865). Smith's distinction as a writer and the first university-trained black American physician made him a model of black achievement. David W. Blight, "In Search of Learning, Liberty, and Self-Definition: James McCune Smith and the Ordeal of the Antebellum Black Intellectual," *AANYLH* 9:7–25 (July 1985); *DAB*, 17:288–89; *Convention of Colored People . . . in Troy* (1847), 18–21; *Colored National Convention . . . in Rochester* (1853), 18–20; *Proceedings of the Colored National Convention, held in Philadelphia, October 16th, 17th, and 18th, 1855* (Salem, N.J., 1856), 30–33; *CA*, 9 February 1839, 15 August 1840 [2:0998, 3:0561]; *NASS*, 10 October 1857, 25 November 1865; *AP*, 29 May 1844; *FDP*, 16 July 1852, 3, 17 November, 23 December 1854, 26 January, 9 February, 27 April, 11, 18 May 1855, 13 November 1856; *E*, 20 December 1838, 17 January, 28 November 1839; *PF*, 24 January, 10 October 1839 [2:0982]; *P*, 17 October 1837, 22 May 1838, 19 January 1842; *AAM*, May, August, September 1859 [11:0708, 0888, 12:0029]; *DM*, March 1859, October 1860 [12:1022]; *WAA*, 5, 12 January, 23 March 1861 [13:0174, 0190, 0362].

9. Ray compares the complete disfranchisement of Connecticut blacks to the limited suffrage allowed blacks in New York state. Although Connecticut did not officially bar blacks from voting, the state constitution only provided for white suffrage. Ray argues that Connecticut's black leaders should gather in a state convention to protest their disfranchisement. Litwack, *North of Slavery*, 79–84.

10. Patrick Henry (1736–1799) of Virginia, a leading political figure during and after the American Revolution, helped consolidate southern support for independence. He is best remembered for his credo: "Give me liberty or give me death." *DAB*, 8:554–59.

48.

John W. Lewis to the Executive Committee
of the New Hampshire Anti-Slavery Society
28 December 1840

Continuing conflict among white abolitionists left black leaders disillusioned with their white allies. By late 1840, blacks limited their involvement in white-dominated antislavery societies and turned their
attention to separate black efforts. The ongoing battle between Garrisonians and "new organization" supporters eventually prompted John
W. Lewis to leave his position as a lecturing agent for the New Hampshire Anti-Slavery Society. His 28 December 1840 letter of resignation
to the NHASS executive committee outlined his reasons for pursuing an
independent course. Lewis claimed that abolitionist infighting discredited and weakened the movement. It was time, he charged, to again
make the cause of the slave "the paramount question." White Garrisonians, who had boasted of Lewis's loyalty to dissuade blacks from deserting to the "new organization," now resented his resignation, rejected his
criticisms, and charged him with "deserting his post." The *Herald of
Freedom*, a NHASS publication, accused Lewis of fraud and of lacking
the stamina for antislavery work. He spent the next two decades conducting independent lecture tours and recruiting subscribers for three
black newspapers. *Lib*, 15 January 1841; *CA*, 25 July 1840; *HF*, 11
January 1840, 22 January 1841; Ripley et al., *Black Abolitionist Papers*,
2:314–15.

CONCORD, [New Hampshire]
Dec. 28th, 1840

GENTLEMEN:

As I have concluded to resign to you my agency to your society,[1] I feel
it my duty to give the reason why. I have for a long time past felt it my
duty, in view of the useless controversy going on between the N.H. Anti-
Slavery and Abolition Societies,[2] to assume a strict neutral ground, not
on the subject of slavery, but on a contentious spirit and action going on,
in my view, to the great disadvantage of the anti-slavery cause. I am
aware there are those in both societies, who are uncompromising and
inflexible opponents of the foul system of slavery, and decided friends to
the colored man. And, as a colored man, and representative of my people, I feel it a duty to make the advocacy of the cause the paramount
question. Thus, in assuming a strict conservative ground, I do not dis-
card the merits of the old platform on which the genuine *anti-slavery*
rests. And I do not give up my agency with the intention of quitting the
anti-slavery field, for I shall go on and lecture whenever and wherever

the way is open to me, and hold myself amenable to God for the faithful discharge of my duty. But I shall not at any time attempt to discuss the merits or demerits of new or old organization. I do feel truly conscientious in taking this position, and think I can do more for the abused slave than to hold my agency with any society, unless one that agrees with me on the ground of neutrality; and, further, it is my humble opinion (and I value my own opinion as much as of others in guiding me to duty), that for the two societies to act as antagonists, and trying to build itself up on the ruins of the other, instead of spending all the moral strength to pull down slavery, has a direct tendency to bring our cause into disrepute before our enemies, and thus counteract all the good that is attempted to be done, and lead to alienation of feeling among those who ought to be an undivided host. I do not take this step through any sinister motive. I love the cause—it always has had, and still has the warmest affection of my heart. For while it tends to emancipate the slave, it also tends to enfranchise the nominally free colored man. Of course, I have some great interest in the cause, and have long learnt to trust those interests on the altar of freedom; then I cannot be recreant to anti-slavery; and I regret that any should. And while I fear there is an alarming degeneracy from genuine principles, I am wishing to stand in the breach, and use my influence to check the evil. Again my ideas of carrying on this work differ from some of the prominent men in your society. I think the preaching of the Gospel, as it is technically called, will open the way in those places where there is an aversion to hear anti-slavery. I have pursued this course, and for it have been censured as wasting time. I think if I am acting on my own hook, I can consult my own way and plan of operation; this is the main ground of my taking this stand. I hope your society will do much; and the new society do all they can. I bid both God speed to the rescue of suffering, bleeding humanity; and may both act for the slave, so that both may join in the general enthusiasm when the bondman shall go free. Yours truly, for human rights,

JOHN W. LEWIS[3]

Liberator (Boston, Mass.), 15 January 1841.

1. In 1840 the executive committee of the New Hampshire Anti-Slavery Society consisted of Carleton Heath and Samuel Burnham of Bow, Moses Sawyer and John Q. Eaton of Weare, Phillip Brown of London, David Morrill, Jr., of Canterbury, William Chamberlain of Boscawen, and four Concord abolitionists—John R. French, John B. Chandler, George Kent, and Nathaniel P. Rogers. The NHASS had been founded in November 1834 by a small group of Garrisonian reformers led by Rogers. It raised funds for the American Anti-Slavery Society, supported lecturing agents, helped organize local auxiliaries, and sponsored the *Herald of Freedom*, which Rogers edited. The NHASS became one of the most energetic state antislavery organizations in the nation until a dispute

between Rogers and the executive committee over the former's extreme nonresistance doctrines splintered the society in 1844. *HF*, 13 June 1840; Merrill and Ruchames, *Letters of William Lloyd Garrison*, 2:27n, 33n, 264–66, 461–64, 3:16n, 120–21, 252n, 267, 269–70n, 273, 285, 287.

2. Controversy engulfed the New Hampshire Anti-Slavery Society in late May 1840, resulting in the formation of a rival state antislavery organization. Events in New Hampshire mirrored the split that had occurred within the American Anti-Slavery Society a few weeks earlier. At the annual meeting of the NHASS in June, about fifty members—including many clergymen—tried to steer the society toward political antislavery and the American and Foreign Anti-Slavery Society. These members also sought to restrict the role of women in the NHASS and to seize control of the *Herald of Freedom*, the society's newspaper. After being rebuffed by a majority vote, they withdrew and formed the short-lived New Hampshire Abolition Society. *Lib*, 29 May, 18 September, 4 December 1840; *HF*, 13 June 1840.

3. John W. Lewis (1810–1861) of Providence, Rhode Island, was ordained into the African Methodist Episcopal Zion ministry in 1832, but he later served local Freewill Baptist congregations. An amateur denominational historian, he wrote biographies of several Freewill Baptist clergymen, most notably *The Life, Labors, and Travels of Elder Charles Bowles* (1852), a book with antislavery overtones. Lewis established and taught at the black New England Union Academy in Providence during the mid-1830s but thereafter devoted most of his energy to antislavery, temperance, and other reform causes. Increasingly concerned about the use of alcoholic beverages among the northern, urban black population, he organized the Providence Temperance Society and called for the formation of the New England Colored Temperance Society in 1836; he served as the latter organization's president during its first three years. He urged blacks to adopt temperance practices as an avenue to both economic survival and moral salvation. Lewis first attracted the attention of white abolitionists in 1837, when a series of his letters to the Concord (New Hampshire) Juvenile Anti-Slavery Society was published in the *Herald of Freedom*. The pro-Garrisonian New Hampshire Anti-Slavery Society employed him as a lecturing agent by 1839; he lectured and solicited funds for the society throughout the state. When the antislavery movement splintered in 1840, Lewis, a moral suasionist, initially supported the Garrisonians, but he later informed the NHASS executive committee that he planned to avoid antislavery infighting and considered it his "duty to make the advocacy of the [slave's] cause the paramount question." The NHASS responded vituperatively, questioning Lewis's antislavery commitment and charging him with keeping a portion of the funds he had raised for the society. Lewis resigned and for the next few years, was a traveling agent for the Albany *Northern Star and Freeman's Advocate* and the *Colored American*, two black papers. Then throughout the late 1840s and early 1850s, he did independent antislavery lecturing throughout northern New England. Lewis moved to St. Albans, Vermont, by the early 1850s. In 1855 he was appointed a traveling agent for *Frederick Douglass' Paper* and solicited subscriptions throughout northern New England, upstate New York, and southern Canada East. He proved to be an indefatigable lecturer.

Lewis had favored the formation of a black national organization as early as

1840, and in the 1850s, he played a role in attempting to form such an organization. He entered the black convention movement and served on the National Council of the Colored People—a national black coordinating body formed at the 1853 black Colored National Convention in Rochester. About the same time, he abandoned his moral suasionist ideals and joined the Liberty party remnant. Lewis moved to New York City around 1860 but soon became disillusioned by black prospects in the United States. Believing that blacks could "better develope [*sic*] their manhood" in a black nation, he became attracted to the Haitian immigration movement. In February 1861, shortly after the death of his wife, he sailed to Haiti as minister and leader of the black Lawrence Association colony. Lewis settled near St. Marc but died of neuralgia and inflammation of the kidneys within six months of his arrival. *PP*, 26 October 1861; *Lib*, 7 July 1832, 27 August, 3 September, 29 October, 26 November 1836, 15 September 1837, 14 September, 5 October 1838 [1:0698, 0701, 0723, 0741, 2:0185, 0585, 0604]; *HF*, 3, 24 June 1837, 11 January 1840, 1 January, 30 July 1841 [2:0067, 0086, 3:0322, 4:0132]; Pease and Pease, *They Who Would Be Free*, 33, 77–78, 126; *Minutes of a Convention of People of Color, for the Promotion of Temperance in New England* (Providence, R.I., 1836), 3 [1:0710]; *CA*, 25 July 1840, 30 January, 3 July, 4 September 1841 [3:0533, 4:0093]; *NSFA*, 10 February, 8 December 1842; *FDP*, 2 December 1853, 5 May, 28 July 1854, 16 February, 30 March, 27 April, 8 June 1855 [8:0770, 0941, 9:0560, 0686]; Foner and Walker, *Proceedings of the Black State Conventions*, 2:207–8, 217, 224–25; John W. Lewis to Gerrit Smith, 20 December 1860, Gerrit Smith Papers, NSyU [13:0049]; John W. Lewis to George Whipple, 30 January 1861, AMA-ARC [13:0250]; *WAA*, 2, 9 February, 4 May 1861 [13:0256, 0502].

49.
Essay by "Sidney"
[February 1841]

The changes in black abolitionism during the early 1840s provoked vigorous debates among black leaders. During the first few months of 1841, the *Colored American* provided the forum for an exchange between William Whipper and "Sidney" (most likely Henry Highland Garnet). Whipper repeated his call for an integrationist solution based on moral reform. He argued that racially exclusive institutions and efforts reinforced racism. Speaking for younger activists, "Sidney" challenged Whipper's assumptions in a four-part series entitled "William Whipper's Letters." He defended race consciousness and independent action and emphasized the need for black initiative and leadership in the antislavery movement. In his third essay, which was published in the 6 March issue, he concluded that the battle against slavery was essentially a black one, which required "several important and indispensable qualifications, which the oppressed alone can possess." He argued that oppression gave blacks insights and a determination that could not be matched by "abstract disquisitions from sympathizing friends." "Sidney"'s appeal for a black-directed, black-centered antislavery movement marked a critical juncture in the development of black abolitionist thought. Stuckey, *Slave Culture*, 211–22; *CA*, 30 January, 6, 13, 20 February 1841 [3:0859, 0864, 0882, 0896–97].

WILLIAM WHIPPER'S LETTERS
NO. III

Ought they not (the free people of color) to make one weak effort; nay, one strong, one mighty, moral effort to roll off the burden that crushes them?—*Wm. Hamilton*[1]

The correctness of our views will further appear from a consideration of the essentially peculiar ability of the oppressed, and the necessary incapability of all others, even of the best of friends.

In an effort for freedom, there are several important and indispensable qualifications, which the oppressed alone can possess.

There must be, primarily, a keen sense of actual suffering, and a fixed consciousness that it is no longer sufferable. These are requisite, both to unite the entire feeling and purpose of those who suffer, and likewise to awaken the sympathy of those in power. It is absolutely important that there should be *such* a presentation of wrongs as may reveal to the power-holding body the enormity of their oppression; and at the same time, acquaint them that their outrages have so proved the vital seat of suffering, as to arouse the deepest feelings and most inflexible determination of their insulted victims. Now, from the nature of the case, this statement of grievance in all its fulness and power, can come from none other than those conscious of suffering. How is it possible, we ask, for men who know nothing of oppression, who have always enjoyed the blessedness of freedom, by an effort of imagination, by any strength of devotedness, by any depth of sympathy, so fully and adequately to express the sense of wrong and outrage, as the sorrowful presence and living desire of us who have drank the dregs of the embittered chalice?

The oppressed are ever their best representatives. Their short and even abrupt expression of intense feeling, is more effectual than the most refined and polished eloquence, prompted though it be, by deep humanity and strong human-heartedness. Sterne's description of slavery has always been considered very graphic;[2] we can bring three millions of men who can give one still more natural and touching. Hence the expression of Mr. Buxton, in his recent letter upon Colonization, in which he calls us "the *natural* allies, and ABLEST CHAMPIONS of the slave!"[3] And why? Because we are oppressed, and know what slavery is.

Again, it is one of the most malignant features of slavery, that it leads the oppressor to stigmatize his victim with inferiority of nature, after he himself has almost brutalized him. This is a universal fact. Hence the oppressed must vindicate their character. No abstract disquisitions from sympathizing friends, can effectually do this. The oppressed themselves must manifest energy of character and elevation of soul. Oppression never quails until it sees that the downtrodden and outraged "know their rights, and knowing, dare maintain."[4] *This* is a radical assurance, a resistless evidence both of worth and manliness, and of earnest intention and deep determination.

We maintain that these evidences—these feelings, desires, and capacities, must stand out prominently, as coming from their proper source, to have their rightful influence. Thus exhibited, they can be employed with prodigious effect. But on the other hand, experience proves, that they lose by retailment or admixture. Let an expression of our wants and feelings be produced by others, and should there be anything of character, intellect, or dignity connected with it, it is not predicated of our ability. How pregnant with verification are facts in our history! where documents setting forth our views and demanding our rights, which were ostensibly the productions of colored men, have proved to have been written by whites. The base suspicion (to say nothing of the real knowledge of the fact) has caused the effort to fall powerless to the ground.

The elevation of a people is not measurably dependant upon external relations or peculiar circumstances, as it is upon the inward rational sentiments which enable the soul to change circumstances to its own temper and disposition. Without these, the aids of sympathizing friends, the whisperings of hope, the power of eternal truth, are of but little advantage. We take the case of an individual. His ancestors have been the objects of wrong and violence. In consequence, they become degraded. At the season of thought and reflection he feels a desire to escape from the degradation of his sires, and the oppressions of the many. The sympathy of friends is excited, and they make active exertions.

Now we affirm that their efforts and influence may be as potent as angels; yet vain that influence, vain their efforts, vain

> The sayings of the wise,
> In ancient and in modern books enrolled.
> * * * * *
>
> Unless he feel within himself,
> Secret refreshings that repair his strength
> And fainting spirits uphold.

It must exist in the man. The spirit that would elevate him above his circumstances, and gain him respect and manhood, must have all the strength of personal character.

And the same it is with a people. Our friends, abolitionists, may redouble their efforts, they may lavishly expend their means, they may strew their pamphlets over the country, thick as the leaves in some primeval forest, where the soil is undistinguishable from their thickly bedded masses—they may add to their numbers, and fill up their ranks, until they become as numerous as that

> Pitchy cloud
> Of locusts,
> That o'er the realm of impious Pharaoh hung
> Like Night.

Yet our condition will remain the same, our sufferings will be unmitigated, until we awaken to a consciousness of a momentous responsibility, which we shall manifest by giving it actuality. We occupy a position, and sustain relations which they cannot possibly assume. *They* are our allies—Ours is the battle.

In coming forth as colored Americans, and pleading for our rights, we neither preclude the necessity, nor forbid the action of our friends, no more than the Americans forbade the help of their French allies. We ask their sympathy, and entreat their prayers and efforts. The Americans received the aid and co-operation of their French allies;[5] but they kept the idea of *American* resistance to oppression distinct and prominent. As wise men, they knew much depended upon that. They know not what evils—perhaps failure—might result from an admixture of extraneosities.

So the convention at Albany acted.[6] They interdicted the presence and co-operation of no set of men, but they called for the exertion of a people peculiarly interested in its objects.

The necessity, nay, the DUTY of peculiar activity on the part of an aggrieved people, we conclude, is the dictate of reason and common sense, and the testimony of history.

And thus thought our fathers. In this way they acted for years. It was this conviction that led to the concentration of their energies in the annual conventions. The people generally acquiesce in their judgement, and follow in their wise and rational footsteps. Thus, throughout the country, we hear the sounds of their hearty, earnest labor. But lo! in the midst of our energetic and effectual exertions, we are called off from our efforts, when we have made considerable progress in undermining our great Bastille,[7] a LEADER informs us, that not only we, but our fathers, yea, all mankind, have gone wrong, and that he has found out a better plan—a new *theory*.

He bids us disregard the voice of principle, to pay no heed to its historic affirmations, to repudiate the dictates of *reason* and common sense, to leave the path of our sires, and adopt a new theory, alike unsupported by reason, and unaffirmed by experience.

In speculating upon "heaven born truth," he comes to despising all specific actions or means, and can deal in nothing but generalities—universalities.

We differ from him. We do not think that by watering and preserving the plant that perfumes our room, that therefore we dislike all other plants in the world. We do not believe that in loving our own mother's sons, our brothers, that therefore we create a cord of caste, and exclude mankind from our rights. In fine, we have no sympathy with that cosmopoliting disposition which tramples upon all nationality, which encircles the universe, but at the same time theorizes away the most needed blessings, and blights the dearest hopes of a people.

And pray, for what are we to turn around and bay the whole human family? In the name of common sense, we ask for what have we to make this great radical change in our operations? Why are we to act different from all others in this important matter? Why, because we *happen* to be—COLORED—which we shall endeavor to look into by and by.[8]

SIDNEY

Colored American (New York, N.Y.), 6 March 1841.

1. "Sidney" quotes from a speech delivered by William Hamilton (1773–1836) at the 1834 black national convention. Hamilton, reputed to be the son of Federalist statesman Alexander Hamilton, worked as a carpenter in New York City. An early leader of the city's black community, he was involved in antislavery, self-help, education, and anticolonization. He cofounded and directed the African Society for Mutual Relief and supported black education through the Phoenix

and Philomathean societies. He contributed to the movement to abolish slavery in New York in the 1820s. During the 1830s, he coordinated local opposition to the American Colonization Society, mustered support for William Lloyd Garrison's *Liberator*, and participated in five of the six black national conventions. Hamilton was a forceful, eloquent orator; several of his addresses were published as pamphlets. His sons, Thomas and Robert Hamilton, achieved prominence as editors and publishers of the *Weekly Anglo-African*. *FJ*, 20, 27 April, 12 October 1827; *Lib*, 30 August 1834, 8 August, 12 September 1835 [1:0507]; *E*, 29 December 1836 [1:0761]; *WA*, 7 January 1837 [1:0883–85]; *NYE*, 24 September 1836 [1:0704]; *DM*, March 1859; *WAA*, 15 October 1859, 10 June 1865; *Minutes of the First Annual Convention* (1831), 3 [1:0077]; *Minutes of the Second Annual Convention* (1832), 3 [1:0171]; *Minutes of the Third Annual Convention* (1833), 4, 26–28 [1:0295, 0306–7]; *Minutes of the Fourth Annual Convention* (1834), 1–9 [1:0459–68]; *Minutes of the Fifth Annual Convention* (1835), 15 [1:0593]; Mabee, *Black Education in New York State*, 22, 65; Porter, *Early Negro Writing*, 33–41, 96–104, 391–99.

2. Henry Sterne's *Statement of Facts ... With An Exposure of the Present System of Jamaica Apprenticeship* (1837) graphically revealed widespread judicial violations of the Emancipation Act of 1833 and the physical mistreatment of black apprentices in Jamaica. The English-born Sterne, who operated a sugar plantation and wharf at Buff Bay, Jamaica, published the volume because of legal troubles with local authorities; his book inadvertently contributed to ending the apprenticeship system.

3. "Sidney" refers to a 9 October 1840 letter from Sir Thomas Fowell Buxton to Ralph R. Gurley, the secretary of the American Colonization Society. Abolitionists viewed the letter, which condemned the ACS as an enemy of abolitionism and a bulwark of slavery, as a major victory. Buxton (1786–1845) was well known as a philanthropist, reformer, and leading British parliamentary opponent of the African slave trade. He penned *The African Slave Trade and Its Remedy* (1839), an influential treatise on the subject. *DNB*, 3:559–61; Charles Buxton, ed., *The Memoirs of Sir Thomas Fowell Buxton* (London, 1848); *Lib*, 5 February 1841.

4. "Sidney" quotes from *An Ode in Imitation of Alcaeus* (1781) by William Jones:

> Men who their duties know,
> But know their rights, and,
> Knowing, dare maintain.

5. The government of France, seeking to weaken the British Empire, aided the Americans during the Revolution. A few private individuals, like the Marquis de Lafayette, joined the American army, and beginning in 1775, the French secretly provided the new government with desperately needed funds. On 6 February 1778, France signed a Treaty of Amity and Commerce, which committed them to an American victory.

6. "Sidney" refers to the New York black state convention, which met at Albany from 18–20 August 1840.

7. The Bastille in Paris, a fortified prison, was a symbol of the tyranny of the

French monarchy during the French Revolution. "Sidney" employs Bastille here as a metaphor for racial prejudice in the United States.

8. One week later, in the 13 March 1841 issue of the *Colored American*, a second essay by "Sidney" appeared under the title "William Whipper's Letters." It defended race consciousness and criticized Whipper for avoiding color distinctions. "Sidney" argued that since blacks were oppressed due to their race, all-black organizations and actions were required to fight that prejudice. *CA*, 13 March 1841 [3:0941].

50.
William C. Nell to William Lloyd Garrison
July 1841

Black abolitionists regularly attempted to free slaves brought into the
North, even in places where no vigilance committee existed. The effort
of New Bedford blacks to rescue the slave Lucy Faggins typified the response of most black communities. Henry Ludlam, a Richmond, Virginia, merchant, brought Faggins into the city on a visit to his ailing father-in-law. When Thomas James, a local African Methodist Episcopal
Zion clergyman, attempted to interview Faggins, he was rebuffed by
Ludlam. James obtained a writ of habeas corpus for Faggins from the
state supreme court. Accompanied by a sheriff, he served the writ and
headed with Faggins to Boston. Ludlam and a dozen supporters tried to
seize the slave but were thwarted by a guard of more than twenty New
Bedford blacks. Once in Boston, Faggins was granted her freedom by a
state supreme court justice. A July 1841 letter by William C. Nell described the incident, which raised a firestorm of "Anti Abolition excitement." *E*, 15 December 1836; *Lib*, 23, 30 July 1841; Joseph W. Barnes,
ed., "The Autobiography of Rev. Thomas James," *RH* 37:10–12 (October 1975); Jeremiah B. Sanderson to William C. Nell, 20, 25 April, 16
July 1841, Post Papers, NRU [3:0998–1000, 1004–6, 4:0105–7].

MR. EDITOR:

The following facts in relation to the case of habeas corpus, heard
before Judge Wilde[1] on Saturday last, may not be uninteresting to the
readers of the *Liberator*, especially as the pro-slavery press is industri-
ously circulating stories which have no proximity to truth, and are therefore calculated to deceive many who may not have an opportunity to
learn both sides of the question.

Henry Ludlam, of Richmond, Va., having urgent business that called
him to the North,[2] secured the services of the said Lucy, as a servant,
making a contract with her owner, it is said, for the term of one year. On
their arrival at New Bedford, some of the vigilant friends of liberty soon
ascertained that Lucy was held as a slave, contrary to the statute provision of the Old Bay State;[3] and further learned from her own lips, that
she desired to be free. It would be well to state here that as soon as it was
found that she had been conversing with colored persons, efforts were
immediately made by the family to put an end to what they deemed a
"foreign" interference, though it has been asserted that she was subject
to no restraint while in New Bedford. The attempt, however, to deny her
the opportunity to see and converse with friends, proved unsuccessful,

for they, doubtless remembering that eternal vigilance was the price of liberty, were not to be deterred from their mission by any influences exerted to restrain a fellow being in bondage, and, that too, when the unhappy victim herself was panting for the invigorating atmosphere of liberty. Many strange stories are told of her being dragged from under Mr. Dunbar's bed,[4] and of there being a great noise about the house, but they are *pro-slavery* facts. There was no noise. It was not generally known, even amongst abolitionists, the course that was to be taken to secure her right to freedom, and consequently but few were gathered near the house. Those without were quietly listening to the doings within. The Sheriff,[5] however, served the writ of habeas corpus, and she was conveyed to Boston, where on Saturday morning Judge Wilde pronounced her FREE.

She retired from the court-house accompanied by a large concourse of friends, who proceeded with her to the Rev. Mr. Cannon's chapel in West Centre street,[6] where she received their congratulations. Prayers were offered in gratitude to God, followed by remarks from several individuals. A collection was taken for her benefit, and the exercises concluded with a hymn of Praise for her escape from the "*delectable land of slavery.*"

W. C. N.

Liberator (Boston, Mass.), 16 July 1841.

1. The case of Lucy Faggins was heard by Samuel Sumner Wilde (1771–1855), a justice of the Massachusetts Supreme Court from 1815 to 1850. A Massachusetts native, Wilde had practiced law and served in the state legislature before being appointed to the bench. He possessed a reputation for unquestioned integrity and extensive legal knowledge. *ACAB*, 6:505–6.

2. Henry Ludlam was in New Bedford visiting his ailing father-in-law Joseph Dunbar. Ludlam was a white commission merchant in Richmond, who in the mid-1840s became the Virginia agent for the National Loan Fund Life Insurance Society of London. *Lib*, 23 July 1842; *Richmond City Directory*, 1845–46, 1850–51.

3. Masters who traveled to free states with their slaves fell into one of three categories: transient, visitor, or sojourner. Prior to 1836, slaveholders enjoyed legal entry in Massachusetts and could retain their slaves if they did not become permanent residents. In *Commonwealth v. Aves* (1836), Chief Justice Lemuel Shaw decided that because slavery depended upon local, not national, law, and because no Massachusetts statute granted slaveholders the right to another person's liberty, slaves would be free upon reaching Massachusetts. Shaw's ruling did not affect fugitive slaves. Paul Finkelman, *An Imperfect Union: Slavery, Federalism, and Comity* (Chapel Hill, N.C., 1981), 9, 41, 81–82, 101–25.

4. Joseph Dunbar, a former ship's captain and merchant, lived at 26 South Sixth Street in New Bedford. Although seriously ill at the time of Henry Ludlam's

visit, he recovered. *New Bedford City Directory*, 1836–45; Zephaniah W. Pease, ed., *Life in New Bedford One Hundred Years Ago* (New Bedford, Mass., 1922), 64.

5. The writ of *habeas corpus* was served by Joseph Eveleth, the sheriff of Suffolk County, Massachusetts, during the early 1840s. *Boston City Directory*, 1841–46.

6. Noah C. W. Cannon (1806–1850) ministered to Boston's Bethel Society, which met in a small chapel on West Centre Street, in the early 1840s. Cannon, a prominent black pastor, revivalist, controversial author, and abolitionist, simultaneously served as African Methodist Episcopal missionary to the black communities in Providence, Rhode Island, and Boston and Springfield, Massacusetts, and later organized AME congregations in Canada West. His Boston congregation was formed in 1836 when secessionists broke away from the black May Street Methodist Church. One year later, the group petitioned to join the AME denomination. In 1876 the Bethel Society became the Charles Street AME Church, which still exists. *Lib*, 6 October 1837, 28 August 1840, 28 April 1843; Wayman, *Cyclopaedia of African Methodism*, 23; Payne, *African Methodist Episcopal Church*, 120, 124, 127, 252–55; Edward D. Smith, *Climbing Jacob's Ladder: The Rise of Black Churches in Eastern American Cities, 1740–1877* (Washington, D.C., 1988), 55–56.

51.
Lewis Woodson to [Lewis Tappan]
31 January 1842

Many black abolitionists believed that Christian missions on the African continent would contribute to the demise of slavery and the slave trade. In August 1841, a group of black clergymen met in Hartford and founded the Union Missionary Society to encourage the evangelization of African blacks. Lewis Woodson sought to rally Pittsburgh blacks behind the UMS, which he served as a nominal agent. On 31 January 1842, Woodson wrote an advocate of African missions, probably Lewis Tappan, to ask for his opinion and recommendations. Both men joined the leadership of the UMS later in the year. Clara Merritt De Boer, "The Role of Afro-Americans in the Origin and Work of the American Missionary Association, 1839–1877" (Ph.D. diss., Rutgers University, 1973), 25–27, 39–40; Clifton H. Johnson, "American Missionary Association, 1846–1861: A Study of Christian Abolitionism" (Ph.D. diss., University of North Carolina, 1959), 57–60; *MCJ*, October 1847 [5:0484].

Pittsburgh, P[ennsylvani]a
January 31st, 1842

My Dear Sir:[1]

It is taken for granted that you are aware of the organization of the Union Missionary Society at Hartford Conn. in August last;[2] and that you are acquainted with the general character of those who originated it, and assisted in its organization.

So far as the nature and design of the Society is understood in this region, it is generally approved of by all opposed to slavery; especially in regard to its educating and sending out, as missionaries, persons of African extraction. It is supposed that several causes combine to make these the most proper persons for propagating the gospel in Africa, among which are their national consanguinity, national identity, and a national sympathy. It is true that these causes must be greatly modified, if not annihilated in those who for many generations have inhabited the northern regions of the United States; but they are certainly very applicable to those of the extreme south.

A strong desire to do something for the conversion and civilization of Africa, is felt by several persons in this region; and they are now ready and willing to co-operate with any organization of known integrity and efficiency. Residing at so great a distance from the seat of its operations, we need scarcely inform you, that as yet, our knowledge of the general character of the Hartford Society is quite imperfect. We wish it however to be understood, that we have never heard any thing said against it; but not quite enough for it, to fully warrant its friends in demanding for it that support which it requires for the great object which it proposes to accomplish.

All the colored people know you, and all their friends know you, and all have confidence in you, in consequence of your past services; and some in this city are anxious to know your views of the Union Missionary Society organized at Hartford in August last. Among those who are anxious to know your opinion are some of the most wealthy and influential Abolitionists in this city.

I should be much obliged to you, to answer this letter at your earliest convenience, as there is to be a meeting of the West Pennsylvania Anti-Slavery Society[3] in this city on the 23rd of Feby. and some wealthy friends from the adjoining counties would like to see it.

My reluctance at troubling you with this letter is only overcome by my more ardent desire to promote the interests of my brethren in this country and in Africa. Your favourable opinion would bring to the assistance of the Society several additional friends, and it is therefore respectfully solicited. Your most sincere friend And humble servant,

Lewis Woodson

Weld-Grimké Papers, William L. Clements Library, University of Michigan, Ann Arbor, Michigan. Published by permission.

1. Lewis Tappan (1788–1873), a successful New York City businessman and philanthropist, was a primary figure in a variety of antebellum religious and social reform movements. During the 1830s, he befriended William Lloyd Garrison and helped organize the New York Anti-Slavery Society and the American Anti-Slavery Society. Tappan helped fund several antislavery newspapers, including the *Liberator* and the *Emancipator*. He broke with Garrison in 1840 over the participation of women in the movement and the use of political action and joined other anti-Garrisonians in founding the American and Foreign Anti-Slavery Society and supporting the 1840 Liberty party campaign. As AFASS corresponding secretary, Tappan maintained close ties with British abolitionists during the 1840s. Tappan also filled executive positions with the Amistad Committee and the American Missionary Association. In 1855 he abandoned the AFASS to join the more radical American Abolition Society. After the Civil War, he published *Is It Right to Be Rich?* (1869), an apologia for his philanthropic endeavors, and *The Life of Arthur Tappan* (1840), a biography of his brother. Merrill and Ruchames, *Letters of William Lloyd Garrison*, 2:xxix; *DAB*, 18:303–4.

2. The Union Missionary Society was organized in August 1841 by a gathering of black clergymen in Hartford, Connecticut. The plight of the *Amistad* captives sparked these ministers to consider their missionary obligations to Africa. The UMS publicized its activities through Josiah Brewer's *Union Missionary Herald* and appointed agents in five states. Although Lewis Tappan controlled most of

the society's finances, black abolitionists dominated its executive committee. They hoped to train young black men to distribute Bibles, to preach to free and enslaved blacks, and to fill crucial leadership roles in the South once emancipation arrived. Instead the society funded the Mendi Mission in Africa, Charles B. Ray's New York City mission, two Hawaiian missionaries, and Isaac J. Rice's work in the black settlements of Canada West.

The UMS was short-lived. Black Methodists departed when the African Methodist Episcopal church created a mission department in 1844. In 1846 the UMS merged with white evangelicals disaffected from the American Board of Commissioners for Foreign Missions to form the American Missionary Association. Blacks failed to dominate the AMA as they had the UMS. During its brief existence, the UMS established the pattern for the AMA's missionary work after the Civil War. De Boer, "Afro-Americans in American Missionary Association," 22–79.

3. The Western Pennsylvania Anti-Slavery Society began as a division of the Pennsylvania Anti-Slavery Society, which was founded in 1837. The eastern division so dominated the state organization that it wrote the western group out of its 1839 constitution. The WPASS reorganized in March 1842 and absorbed the black-dominated Pittsburgh Anti-Slavery Society, which had been founded in 1833 by John B. Vashon, Lewis Woodson, A. D. Lewis, and Martin R. Delany to work for black suffrage, civil rights, education, and uplift. The refurbished society advocated black suffrage and published the *Spirit of Liberty*. It often met at the house of John Peck, a local black leader and a member of its executive committee. The WPASS dissolved by the late 1840s, and most members joined Ohio's Western Anti-Slavery Society, an American Anti-Slavery Society auxiliary. Robert S. Hochreiter, "The Pennsylvania Freeman, 1836–1854" (Ph.D. diss., Pennsylvania State University, 1980), 72–79; Ann G. Wilmoth, "Pittsburgh and the Blacks: A Short History, 1780–1875" (Ph.D. diss., Pennsylvania State University, 1975), 71–80, 85–89, 130; William B. Gravely, Research Log, 1981–82, for "Institutional History of Northern Black Churches, 1787–1860," unpublished ms.

52.

Testimony by Charles Lenox Remond
Delivered at the Massachusetts State House
Boston, Massachusetts
10 February 1842

Abolitionists frequently initiated petition campaigns to combat racial discrimination at the state and local levels. In early 1842, Massachusetts blacks and their Garrisonian allies petitioned the state legislature to outlaw segregated seating on public conveyances. A legislative committee heard testimony on the issue. On 10 February, Charles L. Remond spoke before the committee at the Massachusetts State House. The noted antislavery lecturer gave a personal account of encounters with racial prejudice on American railroads and passenger ships. He contrasted this discrimination with the equitable treatment he had received during a recent trip to Britain. Remond's address—the first delivered by a black before the Massachusetts legislature—was well received. The committee expressed support for the petitions, but the legislature delayed action on the issue for more than a decade. *Lib*, 18, 25 February, 4, 11 March 1842; Louis Ruchames, "Jim Crow Railroads in Massachusetts," *AQ* 8:61–75 (Spring 1956).

Mr. Chairman, and Gentlemen of the Committee:[1]

In rising at this time, and on this occasion, being the first person of color who has ever addressed either of the bodies assembling in this building, I should, perhaps, in the first place, observe that, in consequence of the many misconstructions of the principles and measures of which I am the humble advocate, I may in like manner be subject to similar misconceptions from the moment I open my lips in behalf of the prayer of the petitioners for whom I appear, and therefore feel I have the right at least to ask, at the hands of this intelligent Committee, an impartial hearing; and that whatever prejudices they may have imbibed, be eradicated from their minds, if such exist. I have, however, too much confidence in their intelligence, and too much faith in their determination to do their duty as the representatives of this Commonwealth, to presume they can be actuated by partial motives. Trusting, as I do, that the day is not distant, when, on all questions touching the rights of citizens of this State, men shall be considered *great* only as they are *good*—and not that it shall be told, and painfully experienced, that, in this country, this State, ay, this city, the Athens of America, the rights, privileges and immunities of its citizens are measured by complexion, or any other physical peculiarity or conformation, especially such as over which no man has any control. Complexion can in no sense be construed into crime, much less be rightfully made the criterion of rights. Should the people of color, through a revolution of Providence, become a majority, to the last I would oppose it upon the same principle; for, in either case, it would be equally reprehensible and unjustifiable—alike to be condemned and repudiated. It is JUSTICE I stand here to claim, and not FAVOR for either complexion.

And now, sir, I shall endeavor to confine my remarks to the same subject which has occupied the attention of the Committee thus far, and to stand upon the same principle which has been so ably and so eloquently maintained and established by my esteemed friend, Mr. Phillips.[2]

Our right to citizenship in this State has been acknowledged and secured by the allowance of the elective franchise and consequent taxation;[3] and I know of no good reason, if admitted in this instance, why it should be denied in any other.

With reference to the wrongs inflicted and injuries received on railroads, by persons of color,[4] I need not say they do not end with the termination of the route, but, in effect, tend to discourage, disparage and depress this class of citizens. All hope of reward for upright conduct is cut off. Vice in them becomes a virtue. No distinction is made by the community in which we live. The most vicious is treated as well as the most respectable, both in public and private.

But it is said, we all look alike. If this is true, it is not true that we all behave alike. There is a marked difference; and we claim a recognition of this difference.

In the present state of things, they find God's provisions interfered with in such a way, by these and kindred regulations, that virtue may not claim her divinely appointed rewards. Color is made to obscure the brightest endowments, to degrade the fairest character, and to check the highest and most praiseworthy aspirations. If the colored man is vicious, it makes but little difference; if besotted, it matters not; if vulgar, it is quite as well; and he finds himself as well treated, and received as readily into society, as those of an opposite character. Nay, the higher our aspirations, the loftier our purposes and pursuits, does this iniquitous principle of prejudice fasten upon us, and especial pains are taken to irritate, obstruct and injure. No reward of merit, no remuneration for services, no equivalent is rendered the deserving. And I submit, whether this unkind and unchristian policy is not well calculated to make every man disregardful of his conduct, and every woman unmindful of her reputation.

The grievances of which we complain, be assured, sir, are not imaginary, but real—not local, but universal—not occasional, but continual— every day matter of fact things—and have become, to the disgrace of our common country, matters of history.

Mr. Chairman, the treatment to which colored Americans are exposed in their own country, finds a counterpart in no other; and I am free to declare, that, in the course of nineteen months' travelling in England, Ireland and Scotland, I was received, treated and recognized, in public and private society, without any regard to my complexion. From the moment I left the American packet ship in Liverpool, up to the moment I came in contact with it again, I was never reminded of my complexion; and all that know anything of my usage in the American ship, will testify that it was unfit for a brute, and none but one could inflict it.[5] But how unlike that afforded in the British steamer *Columbia*! Owing to my limited resources, I took a steerage passage. On the first day out, the second officer came to inquire after my health; and finding me the only passenger in that part of the ship, ordered the steward to give me a berth in the second cabin; and from that hour until my stepping on shore at Boston, every politeness was shown me by the officers, and every kindness and attention by the stewards; and I feel under deep and lasting obligations to them, individually and collectively.

In no instance was I insulted, or treated in any way distinct or dissimilar from other passengers or travellers, either in coaches, rail-roads, steam packets, or hotels; and if the feeling was entertained, in no case did I discover its existence.

I may with propriety here relate an incident, illustrative of the subject now under consideration. I took a passage ticket at the steam packet office in Glasgow, for Dublin; and on going into the cabin to retire, I found the berth I had engaged occupied by an Irish gentleman and merchant. I enquired if he had not mistaken the number of his berth? He thought not. On comparing tickets, we saw that the clerk had given two tickets of the same number; and it appeared I had received mine first. The gentleman at once offered to vacate the berth, against which I remonstrated, and took my berth in an opposite stateroom. Here, sir, we discover treatment just, impartial, reasonable; and we ask nothing beside.

There is a marked difference between social and civil rights. It has been well and justly remarked, by my friend Mr. Phillips that we all claim the privilege of selecting our society and associations; but, in civil rights, one man has not the prerogative to define rights for another. For instance, sir, in public conveyances, for the rich man to usurp the privileges to himself, to the injury of the poor man, would be submitted to in no well regulated society. And such is the position suffered by persons of color. On my arrival home from England, I went to the railway station, to go to Salem, being anxious to see my parents and sisters as soon as possible—asked for a ticket—paid 50 cents for it, and was pointed to the American designation car. Having previously received information of the regulations, I took my seat peaceably, believing it better to suffer wrong than do wrong. I felt then, as I felt on many occasions prior to leaving

home, unwilling to descend so low as to bandy words with the superin-
tendents, or contest my rights with conductors, or any others in the
capacity of servants of any stage or steamboat company, or rail-road
corporation; although I never, by any means, gave evidence that, by my
submission, I intended to sanction usages which would derogate from
uncivilized, much less long and loud professing and high pretending
America.

Bear with me, while I relate an additional occurrence. On the morning
after my return home, I was obliged to go to Boston again, and on going
to the Salem station, I met two friends, who enquired if I had any objection to their taking seats with me. I answered, I should be most happy.
They took their seats accordingly, and soon afterwards one of them
remarked to me—"Charles, I don't know if they will allow us to ride
with you." It was some time before I could understand what they meant,
and, on doing so, I laughed—feeling it to be a climax to every absurdity I
had heard attributed to Americans. To say nothing of the wrong done
those friends, and the insult and indignity offered me by the appearance
of the conductor, who ordered the friends from the car in a somewhat
harsh manner—they immediately left the carriage.

On returning to Salem some few evenings afterwards, Mr. Chase, the
superintendent on this road,[6] made himself known to me, by recalling
by-gone days and scenes, and then enquired if I was not glad to get
home, after so long an absence in Europe. I told him I was glad to see my
parents and family again, and this was the only object I could have,
unless he thought I should be glad to take a hermit's life in the great
pasture; inasmuch as I never felt to loathe my American name so much
as since my arrival. He wished to know my reasons for the remark. I
immediately gave them and wished to know of him, if, in the event of his
having a brother with red hair, he should find himself separated while
travelling because of this difference, he should deem it just. He could
make no reply. I then wished to know if the principle was not the same;
and if so, there was an insult implied by his question. In conclusion, I
challenged him, as the instrument inflicting the manifold injuries upon
all not colored like himself, to the presentation of an instance in any
other christian or unchristian country, tolerating usages at once so dis-
graceful, unjust and inhuman. What if some few of the West or East
India planters and merchants should visit our liberty-loving country,
with their colored wives—how would he manage? Or, if R. M. Johnson,
the gentleman who has been elevated to the second office in the gift of
the people, should be travelling from Boston to Salem, if he was prepared
to separate him from his wife or daughters.[7] (Involuntary burst of applause, instantly restrained.)

Sir, it happens to be my lot to have a sister a few shades lighter than
myself;[8] and who knows, if this state of things is encouraged, whether I

may not on some future occasion be mobbed in Washington street, on the supposition of walking with a white young lady! (Suppressed indications of sympathy and applause.)

Gentlemen of the Committee, these distinctions react in all their wickedness—to say nothing of their concocted and systematized odiousness and absurdity—upon those who instituted them; and particularly so upon those who are illiberal and mean enough to practise them.

Mr. Chairman, if colored people have abused any rights granted them, or failed to exhibit due appreciation of favors bestowed, or shrunk from dangers or responsibility, let it be made to appear. Or if our country contains a population to compare with them in loyalty and patriotism, circumstances duly considered, I have it yet to learn. The history of our country must ever testify in their behalf. In view of these and many additional considerations, I unhesitatingly assert their claim, on the naked principle of merit, to every advantage set forth in the Constitution of this Commonwealth.

Finally, Mr. Chairman, there is in this and other States a large and growing colored population, whose residence in your midst has not been from choice (let this be understood and reflected upon), but by the force of circumstances, over which they never had control. Upon the heads of their oppressors and calumniators be the censure and responsibility. If to ask at your hands redress for injuries, and protection in our rights and immunities, as citizens, is reasonable, and dictated alike by justice, humanity and religion, you will not reject, I trust, the prayer of your petitioners.

Before sitting down, I owe it to myself to remark, that I was not apprised of the wish of my friends to appear here until passing through Boston, a day or two since; and having been occupied with other matters, I have had no opportunity for preparation on this occasion. I feel much obliged to the Committee for their kind, patient and attentive hearing. (Applause.)

Liberator (Boston, Mass.), 25 February 1842.

1. As petitions demanding legislative action to end segregated railroad cars flooded the Massachusetts legislature, a joint committee of both houses was appointed to study and report on the issue. It was chaired by Seth Sprague, Jr., of Boston. The committee unanimously condemned racial distinctions on the railroads and submitted a bill designed to outlaw the practice. The bill was defeated in the state senate. *Lib*, 25 February, 4 March 1842.

2. Remond refers to Wendell Phillips's 10 February 1842 remarks before the Massachusetts House of Representatives denouncing segregated railcars. Phillips admitted that a conflict of individual interests existed, but he argued that the legislature had a higher obligation to compel corporations to obey constitutional law. Phillips (1811–1884), the son of a patrician Massachusetts family, was edu-

cated at Harvard College and Harvard Law School. Early in 1837, he declared his commitment to the antislavery cause and to the moral suasionist principles of his friend William Lloyd Garrison. For the next twenty-four years, he made vigorous antislavery efforts. He was a member of the Boston Vigilance Committee, supported aid to Kansas free-state settlers, and advocated the disunion of the North and South as a way of ending slavery. After the Civil War, he opposed Garrison's effort to disband the American Anti-Slavery Society and used the organization to support passage of the Fourteenth and Fifteenth amendments. In the 1870s, Phillips devoted himself to temperance, penal, and labor reform. *Lib*, 18 February 1842; *DAB*, 14:546–47.

3. The Massachusetts state constitution of 1780 had no racial restrictions on voting rights. But in practice, since the voting lists were derived from the tax rolls, blacks deliberately omitted from the rolls were prevented from voting. Litwack, *North of Slavery*, 16, 91–92.

4. Prior to the mid-1840s, blacks were regularly discriminated against on common carriers in Massachusetts. They were seated in separate "Jim Crow" cars until a concerted abolitionist campaign integrated Massachusetts railroads by 1843. Ruchames, "Jim Crow Railroads," 61–75.

5. In mid-May 1840, Charles L. Remond attempted to book passage on the ship *Columbus* for London and the World's Anti-Slavery Convention, but the ship's ticket agent refused his request until William Adams, a white abolitionist attending the convention, agreed to share a berth with Remond. The vessel's second mate refused to allow Remond to associate with white passengers and, instead, prepared a narrow and uncomfortable bunk for him in the steerage. When Adams protested, both he and Remond were removed from the berth for which they had paid and were given "quarters" at the bottom of a gangway in the open air, where they were subjected to occasional taunts by crew members. Usrey, "Charles Lenox Remond," 112–25; Garrison and Garrison, *William Lloyd Garrison*, 2:360–61.

6. Stephen A. Chase, a Quaker from Salem, Massachusetts, was general superintendent and manager of the Eastern Railroad during the 1840s and 1850s. He first came to abolitionists' attention on 8 September 1841, when an Eastern Railroad conductor ejected Frederick Douglass from the white car of a train. Chase defended the action and ordered that no passenger trains stop in Lynn, where Douglass lived. Under Chase's leadership, the Eastern Railroad continued to assign blacks to "Jim Crow" cars until 1843, when public protest finally forced the company to abandon the policy. *CA*, 30 October 1841 [4:0275]; Peter Still Account Book, 26 July 1853, William Still Papers, NjR; Frederick Douglass, *Life and Times of Frederick Douglass*, rev. ed. (Boston, Mass., 1892; reprint, New York, N.Y., 1962), 225; Foner, *History of Black Americans*, 2:325–26.

7. Richard M. Johnson (1780–1850), a Kentucky lawyer, planter, and U.S. congressman (1807–37), is best remembered as vice-president in the administration of Martin Van Buren (1837–41). He was the only vice-president elected to office by vote of the U.S. Senate, an event occasioned by his failure to receive a majority of the electoral vote, probably due to public charges that he was an amalgamationist. For twenty years, Johnson openly acknowledged Julia Chinn (d. 1833), a mulatto house servant, as his mistress. She bore him two daughters, Imogene and Adaline, who later inherited his estate. *DAB*, 10:114–16; Leland

Winfield Meyer, *The Life and Times of Colonel Richard M. Johnson of Kentucky* (New York, N. Y., 1932), 317–22, 393, 421–22.

8. Remond refers to his sister, Sarah Parker Remond (1826–1894). Born in Salem, Massachusetts, to a family of black abolitionists, she was active in the antislavery movement by the early 1840s. Appointed an agent of the American Anti-Slavery Society in 1856, Remond became one of the first black women to lecture regularly before antislavery audiences. She lectured in the British Isles for the AASS from 1859 to 1861, successfully taking the antislavery message to all classes of British society. Remond remained in England throughout the Civil War but moved in 1866 to Florence, Italy, where she lived for the remainder of her life. She earned a medical degree in 1868 and established a successful medical practice. Remond married Lazzaro Pintor in 1877. *DANB*, 522–23.

53.
Editorial by Stephen A. Myers
3 March 1842

The hypocrisy of white abolitionists irritated black leaders. Prominent antislavery businessmen such as Lewis Tappan refused to hire blacks. William Wilson of New York City reported with rancor that white abolitionists would not hire him, his children, or any black in their "counting room, nor work bench nor to any other respectable station." Black leaders grumbled that white associates had spent "not one dollar to make a practical example of the capacity of a single colored man." Stephen A. Myers, a popular black journalist in Albany, New York, called on white reformers to hire black workers as a demonstration of their principles. He reminded them that northern prejudice was "akin to the slavery of the south" and that their bad example crippled black aspirations. In a 3 March 1842 editorial in his *Northern Star and Freeman's Advocate*, Myers warned white abolitionists that they could not expect support from the black community until they "*eradicate[d] prejudice from their own hearts.*" CA, 12 September, 17 October 1840, 19 June 1841 [3:0615, 0657, 4:0064]; Pease and Pease, *They Who Would Be Free*, 85–86.

For several years we have been astonished at the indifference manifested by abolitionists, in regard to the adoption of some effectual measures for advancing the welfare of free people of color. In observing the principles set forth by the abolition presses, the declarations of lecturers, and the sentiments expressed to us in private in relation to these things, and contrasting them with their daily practises we discover many gross inconsistencies. They profess to possess the most generous and benevolent feelings towards us, and deeply lament the unhappy situation in which we are placed by unjust laws and a cruel and oppressive prejudice. They regret and acknowledge that we labor under a thousand disadvantages from which every other class of community are exempt, and wonder that with all the accumulated hindrances to our progress to become intelligent and respectable members of society, we possess moral fortitude sufficient to rise above the surges of persecution.

Twenty-two thousand abolition votes were polled during the last year in the states,[1] in favor of persons opposed to southern slavery, and a large number of those opposed to political action withheld theirs. Large numbers in this and other states, have also with us petitioned the legislatures, for the repeal of those laws which were unjust, oppressive, anti-republican, and inimical to the interests of the colored portion of community. Now with all this array of sentiment and feeling, and political action before us, the natural inference would be, that the united wisdom, wealth, influence, benevolence, and sympathy of so large a portion of our citizens, could and would have devised some efficient means for bettering the condition of at least a portion of the people of color.

Some twelve or fifteen years ago, when the spirit of immediate emancipation sundered the bonds by which it was bound, and arrayed itself with the immutable truth that all men are born free and equal, the veil which had covered the horrors of slavery and an unholy prejudice, was rent in twain; the corruption of almost the entire community was made palpable, and the hearts of men were found susceptible to the impressions of truth. The hopes of our people became exalted; their anticipations of future happiness and prosperity were high, and they believed that in a few years they should realize what for ages their fathers had fervently prayed for. But sad experience has taught us, that "it is a vain thing to trust in man." But yet amid all our expectations there are some things asserted of us, which we never expected nor ever desired. We never expected that abolitionists would place themselves upon a level even with the most intelligent and respectable of our people; neither did we desire their daughters in marriage. We did not expect to ride in their carriages, nor desire to mix in their parties of pleasure; but we did HOPE that they would do for us some things, which they have not only neglected, but what appears to us to have been foreign from their intentions. We supposed that while they advocated the rights of man and the cause of suffering humanity, that they would have been foremost in opening every avenue, and destroying every barrier in their power that was closed against us, or that retarded our progression; and that by doing so they would be enabled to present those with whom they plead for the restoration of the inalienable rights of man, a class of individuals rising from degradation, and striving to become good, intelligent, economical and industrious citizens. Probably there are no less than thirty thousand abolitionists in the states, and doubtless among them there are mechanics of every description;[2] who, instead of endeavoring to break down prejudice and make a powerful thrust at slavery, by taking our youth and instructing them in the various branches, content themselves and suppose that *we* also are contented, by having them disseminate what they call *their* principles from one end of the country to the other. They profess to be opposed to slavery, but with the greater portion of them *we* believe that it is that slavery only which exists at the south.

Now we ask if the prejudice which exists at the north is not akin to the slavery of the south? *We* firmly believe it to be so, and if the prejudice of the northern abolitionists will not permit them to take as apprentices colored boys, or if their regard for the prejudices of others will not allow them so to do, *we also believe* that the influence of their example is more injurious to colored people at large, than the disinclination of the slave holder to release the victims of his avarice. And until abolitionists *eradicate prejudice from their own hearts*, they never *can* receive the unwavering confidence of the people of color. We do not ask for money, neither do we wish them to educate our children; these we will endeavor to provide for by the sweat of our brow, but we *do* ask that their workshops may be opened to our youth, and that those of us who are already in business may be patronized. These things (if there be any meaning in their language) we think we have a right to ask of those who are our professed friends, and if they will grant what we actually want (and what we know they can give) we shall the more readily believe them sincere in their professions.

The question is frequently asked us, why abolitionists do not give practical demonstrations of the sincerity of their regard for colored people, by making apprentices of our boys, &c., and the only answer which we have been able to give without exposing *what we* believe to be the real cause has been that we were unable to tell. We know a professed abolitionist of this city, upon whom a friend of ours called for the purpose of hiring a frame tenement which he owned in the lower part of the city, who refused to let him have it, for fear the neighbors would not like to have colored people living so near them; and at the same time this man was called by abolitionists a staunch friend of the cause, he could exclaim as loudly against southern oppression as the best of the party, and denounce others for developing in a different manner the very same principles which were dominant in his own bosom.

We hope that our friends will not be hasty and conclude that we are opposed to abolitionists because we express ourselves in a free and candid manner; we believe it to be a duty which we owe them and ourselves; and if others have neglected and feared to speak the truth, *we are determined* not to follow into their footsteps.

We are aware of and acknowledge that some very great sacrifices have been made for our brethren in slavery; that trial, persecution and calumny have been endured by many in their endeavors to diffuse the principles of justice and truth through society; but while *they* continue to express their disapprobation and indignation of prejudice on account of complexions, and consider it cruel and unjust in others, *we* shall labor to inform them that *we* are not insensible to the prejudice which exists in their minds.

M.[3]

Northern Star and Freeman's Advocate (Albany, N.Y.), 3 March 1842.

1. Myers refers to votes cast for Liberty party candidates in the 1841 state elections. The combined tally from New York, Massachusetts, Ohio, Michigan, and Vermont was 22,437. This represented a threefold increase from 1840. Rich-

ard H. Sewell, *Ballots for Freedom: Antislavery Politics in the United States, 1837–1860* (New York, N.Y., 1976), 78, 110.

2. Myers estimates the number of active abolitionists. By 1839 the American Anti-Slavery Society and its thirteen hundred auxiliaries had about 100,000 members. Popular support for some antislavery principles is indicated by the two million signatures on antislavery petitions sent to Congress. The abolitionist leadership was culturally and economically middle class. Immediatism found its greatest strength in well-established rural areas of New England yeoman stock— New England, western New York and Pennsylvania, and Ohio's Western Reserve. Most abolitionists owned no real estate or assessable personal property. Many were clergymen, while others held church-related positions or belonged to evangelical societies. Abolitionist women generally came from Finneyite evangelical or Quaker backgrounds. Abolitionism found some support among artisans and members of the working class, who often signed antislavery petitions. But the vast majority of working men allied with the Democratic party against the antislavery movement. Sorin, *Abolitionism*, 47–69; Alan M. Kraut, ed., *Crusaders and Compromisers* (Westport, Conn., 1983), 25–43, 71–99, 205–34; John B. Jentz, "The Antislavery Constituency in Jacksonian New York City," *CWH* 27:101–22 (June 1981); Bernard Mandel, *Labor, Free and Slave: Working Men and the Anti-Slavery Movement in the United States* (New York, N.Y., 1955), 62–78, 104–5, 120–39; Edward Magdol, *The Antislavery Rank and File: A Social Profile of the Abolitionist Constituency* (Westport, Conn., 1986).

3. Stephen A. Myers (1800–?) of Albany, New York, the editor of the *Northern Star and Freeman's Advocate*, usually initialed his editorials with the letter "M." He was born in slavery in Rensselaer county, New York, but was freed by his master at age eighteen. After working for a decade as a grocer and steamboat steward, he began a career in journalism in 1842 by founding the *Northern Star and Freeman's Advocate*. Harriet Myers, his wife, the daughter of Captain Abram Johnson, provided a skilled editorial hand, transforming his writing into polished prose. The paper merged with Samuel Ringgold Ward's Cortland, New York, *True American* in 1849 to become the *Impartial Citizen*. Ward assumed the editorship, while Myers remained a business partner and general agent. Myers attempted other publishing ventures—a short-lived temperance newspaper, the *Pioneer*, appeared in 1844, and the *Telegraph and Temperance Journal* was published with some regularity between 1851 and 1855. He later worked with the *Voice of the People*, a local Republican party organ.

Myers enthusiastically embraced a variety of reforms. In addition to publishing temperance journals, he ran a temperance boardinghouse in Albany and worked as general agent for the Delevan State Temperance Union of New York. He advocated agrarian life as the practical foundation for black elevation. In the late 1840s, he founded the Florence Farming and Lumber Association, through which he hoped to organize and promote a black settlement on Gerrit Smith's lands in upstate New York. Critics questioned the credibility of the association. Myers also received harsh words from other quarters. When Ward's editorial partnership with Myers foundered, he claimed that Myers was "the most unreliable of all modern black men." Myers's activities on behalf of Whig and Republican party candidates evoked criticism from both black Garrisonians and Liberty party adherents. Even Frederick Douglass chastised him for ill-considered publishing ventures that served only to "promote strife and divide the colored people."

Despite his detractors, Myers was widely recognized for his achievements in antislavery and civil rights reform. His Albany station had the reputation of being the best-run part of the underground railroad in the state. He sheltered many fugitive slaves in his own home and personally raised funds to sustain the Albany Vigilance Committee. He helped lead the struggle to expand black voting rights in New York. Beginning in the 1830s, he coordinated petition drives, organized the Albany Suffrage Club, participated in several black state conventions, and served as president of the New York State Suffrage Association. His skillful and persistent lobbying of the state legislature in Albany strengthened the voting rights campaign. Myers also spoke out against proposals to subsidize African colonization with state funds. He sat on the executive committee of the American League of Colored Laborers in the 1850s and was a delegate to black national conventions in 1847, 1855, and 1864. During the Civil War, Myers recruited soldiers for the black Massachusetts regiments. Irving Garland Penn, *The Afro-American Press and Its Editors* (1891; reprint, New York, N.Y., 1969), 48–49; *Albany City Directory*, 1833–58; *CA*, 12 September, 17 October 1840 [3:0615, 0657]; *NSFA*, 2 January 1843 [4:0552]; *Lib*, 17 September 1831, 24 May 1844 [1:0115, 4:0954]; *NASS*, 14 November 1844, 9 October 1858 [4:0954, 11:0385]; *NSt*, 29 June 1849; *FDP*, 12 February, 15 April 1852, 25 November 1853, 4 May 1855 [7:0419, 0513, 8:0501, 9:0575]; *IC*, 14, 28 March, 23 May 1849, 13 February, 27 March, 8 May 1850 [5:1004, 1015, 1098, 6:0398, 0426, 0503]; *WAA*, 13 August 1859, 31 March, 21, 28 April, 5, 19 May 1860, 16 August 1865 [11:0927, 0928, 12:0600, 0604, 0652, 0663, 0691, 0710, 16:0127]; *PP*, 29 June 1861 [13:0607]; Foner and Walker, *Proceedings of the Black State Conventions*, 1:13, 55, 59, 76, 89, 91; Stephen Myers to Gerrit Smith, 4 December 1842, 22 March 1856, 24 March 1863, Gerrit Smith Papers, NSyU [4:0932, 10:0085, 14:0073]; *Colored National Convention . . . in Rochester* (1853), 5 [9:0897]; *Convention of Colored People . . . in Troy* (1847), 3 [5:0486]; *Proceedings of the National Convention of Colored Men, Held in Syracuse, N.Y., October 4, 5, 6, and 7, 1864* (Boston, Mass., 1864), 4 [15:0538].

54.
Editorial by Stephen A. Myers
10 March 1842

Long before the "slave power conspiracy" became an accepted idea in American antislavery circles, northern blacks understood the influence of southern slavery on American institutions and behavior. During the 1840s, a series of state and federal actions caused black abolitionists to focus more closely on slavery's impact on American political life. In a 10 March 1842 editorial in the *Northern Star and Freeman's Advocate*, Stephen Myers discussed several judicial decisions, legislative enactments, and foreign policy issues that demonstrated slavery's growing threat. He cited the claims made by the federal government after the *Creole* incident and the recent *Prigg* v. *Pennsylvania* decision of the U.S. Supreme Court as evidence of slavery's increasing influence on the federal government. Myers also explained how southern state legislatures restricted the freedom of northern blacks, particularly through passage of the black seamen's acts, which subjected free black sailors to arbitrary detention in southern ports. Litwack, *North of Slavery*, 51–53.

SOUTHERN CONSISTENCY

We will place before our readers facts not generally known to the greater portion of the northern community—and in presenting them, with an humble appeal to their kind feelings as Christians and as independent freemen, ask, if such acts should be tolerated with silent submission by our legislative assemblies. By the south our government is called upon to make the *Creole* a national claim, and Mr. Webster, from motives easily understood, stands forth as the champion of the demand upon England.[1] The colored man who is robbed of his liberty, and by the laws of the south, is made "goods and chattel," in the north has had granted him an equitable trial by jury. This law is now denounced as unconstitutional by the federal court of this session[2]—while in the south, when a vessel enters its ports, if navigated by a colored freeman of the other states, as cook, steward, or seaman, he is taken from the vessel, lodged in prison and there detained till the vessel again leaves the port. In Alabama the last legislature grants the power to the Mayor of Mobile to arrest all colored persons found on the wharfs of Mobile or in the bay. Vessels generally load in this bay 25 miles from the city, owing to the said laws, which prevent their nearer approach.

Thus the state of Alabama authorizes the forcible seizing of all colored people from their vessels and placing them in jail with common felons, there equally disgracefully to remain until the vessels are loaded and ready to depart. If by stress of weather, or any other accidental cause, the vessel is driven from her anchorage and lost, or this free colored person is shipwrecked on this coast while on a voyage to the south, he is also cast into prison, and as in other cases is liable, after certain detentions, to be sold to pay jail fees, and his price of sale is the gain of the state.[3]

Thus a free class of men, many of whom have, not unlikely, fought the battles of their country, and braved the dangers of the sea on board our national ships with credit to themselves, are, while aiding the commercial interests of their country, to be treated as slaves. Will the north take no steps to correct this evil so oppressive and so injurious to commerce, and so insulting to the free institutions of the north? Will the Christian north, whose soil presents the magnificent spectacle, scarcely ever lost sight of—of temples dedicated to God and humanity, permit such acts to remain in force? In kneeling at the altars of religion, will no appeal be made for the fate of the oppressed, because he differs in skin from his white fellow man? In times of drought, pestilence and famine, from the pulpit is heard the prayer of the pastor, petitioning the mercy of God. And does not slavery, which in all civilized Europe is denounced as inhuman, deserve commiseration? Will the great north tolerate the injustice of the south? Forbid it honor—forbid it justice. Read the following late legislative act of Maryland, and will it not create feelings of indignation in every honest, benevolent bosom?

> LAWS AGAINST COLORED PEOPLE—A bill has passed the house
> of delegates of the Maryland legislature, which provides that any
> free negro or mullatto, who shall come into the state, after the
> passage of the act, may be arrested by any person, and shall be
> adjudged to be his slave. And any free negro, who shall leave the
> state and return to it, shall be liable to the same penalty—unless, in
> both cases, they are travelling as servants of a white person. The
> fact that they are in the state, to be prima facie evidence that they
> have come into it contrary to law. The rest of the bill which con-
> tains thirty-five sections, is in the same *liberal* spirit. Every delegate
> from Baltimore voted against it. It passed, however, and is now
> before the senate.[4]

Northern Star and Freeman's Advocate (Albany, N.Y.), 10 March 1842.

1. On 7 November 1841, nineteen slaves aboard the American brig *Creole* seized control of the ship while being transported from Virginia to Louisiana. The mutineers diverted the vessel to the Bahamas and appealed to the mercy of British authorities, who freed all those slaves not involved in the revolt. Secretary of State Daniel Webster declared that the *Creole* was forced to land in the Bahamas by "disaster and distress" and asked that the slaves be returned to the United States. Britain, who had abolished slavery and maintained no extradition treaty with the United States, refused. Although Webster disapproved of the British

action, he dropped the request and sought financial compensation for the slaves. The crisis temporarily impaired relations between the two nations and threatened the talks that led to the Webster-Ashburton Treaty (1842). The *Creole* case was not resolved until 1853, when an Anglo-American claims commission awarded compensation to the owners of the slaves. Howard Jones, "The Peculiar Institution and National Honor: The Case of the *Creole* Slave Revolt," *CWH* 21:28–50 (March 1975).

2. Ward refers to the case of *Prigg* v. *Pennsylvania* (1842), in which the U.S. Supreme Court upheld the Fugitive Slave Law of 1793 and struck down existing personal liberty laws passed by northern state legislatures. The justices held that states had no constitutional authority to legislate treatment of fugitive slaves, overturning an 1837 Massachusetts law that granted a jury trial to accused runaways. But abolitionists argued that the Prigg decision released state officials from any obligation to assist in the return of fugitive slaves. This spawned a second generation of personal liberty laws, which prohibited state officials from assisting in fugitive slave cases. Stanley W. Campbell, *The Slave Catchers: Enforcement of the Fugitive Slave Law, 1850–1860* (Chapel Hill, N.C., 1968), 10.

3. In 1822 the South Carolina legislature passed a Negro Seamen's Act, which stipulated that free black seamen should be jailed while their vessels were in South Carolina ports. Their employers were liable for all detention expenses; should an employer fail to meet that responsibility, the imprisoned black could be sold into slavery to pay the expenses. Similar laws were passed in Georgia, North Carolina, Florida, Alabama, Louisiana, and Texas. The Alabama law, known as the Mobile Harbor Law (1839), required the harbor master to inform the local sheriff whenever a vessel carrying free blacks arrived in port. The free blacks were jailed until the vessel set sail. In 1841 the law was revised and strengthened. Most states continued to enforce the seamen's acts until the 1850s. *DAAS*, 657–58; Harriet E. Amos, *Cotton City: Urban Development in Antebellum Mobile* (University, Ala., 1985), 147–48.

4. The Maryland state senate rejected the bill.

55.
Samuel Ringgold Ward to Gerrit Smith
18 April 1842

Word of the *Prigg* v. *Pennsylvania* decision of the U.S. Supreme Court reverberated through northern black communities. The March 1842 action invalidated northern personal liberty laws and subjected free blacks and fugitives alike to abduction by kidnappers and slave catchers. Black abolitionists damned the decision as a threat to American liberty. New York blacks feared that "neither the constitution of the United States nor the laws of the free states can afford us any protection from the grasp of the slaveholder or his agent." Blacks throughout the North prepared for the threat. At a rally in Troy, New York, they pledged to defend themselves, even if it meant killing slave catchers. In an 18 April 1842 letter to Gerrit Smith, Samuel Ringgold Ward revealed for the first time that he was a fugitive slave, made known his fear of being captured, and discussed plans to leave for Canada West. *NSFA*, 17 March 1842 [4:0383]; *E*, 14 April 1842 [4:0414]; Morris, *Free Men All*, 96–97, 105–6.

South Butler, [New York]
18 April, 1842

Dear Sir:

I mail a letter with this to Mr. Millard Cotton[1] whom I owe $40 for which he holds a kind of a mortgage on my horse. I propose to have him take the horse, and as she is worth $70 and my note with interest does not amount to quite $40 I desire him to pay $20 to you and the remainder to Mr. Barnett.[2] Mr. Cotton desired me to preach in the church to which he belongs last spring & he endorsed $5 on my note by way of compensation. He then told me (upon my offering my horse) that in case I desired to sell, to give him the first offer. I therefore suppose that he will accept the horse and allow me the balance.

The decision of the Supreme Court alarms me. I can see no kind of legal protection for any colored man's liberty. Every thing is made as easy as possible for the kidnapper. How easy it is to seize a man & under pretense of carrying him before a U.S. Judge to take immediately south! Be a man ever free he is liable to instant seizure & enslavement. Citizens in such a case [can] do nothing but give physical resistance. This is contrary to the Constitution tending to dissolution & subjecting them to a heavy penalty. But few would run the risk. Loco Focos have only to be informed that such is the Supreme Court's decision upon & interpretation of the Constitution & they are ready to aid the hyena.[3] So I view it.

And now a word in reference to my personal interest in the matter.

Please regard this as *confidential*. On a visit this summer, my mother placed facts in the possession of my wife which I never before knew. Without troubling you with a detail of them, let it suffice to say that my being born free—legally—is not susceptible of proof. I am resolved therefore to remove immediately to Kingston, Canada.[4] The only obstacles in the way of my removal are my debts, and the lack of money to pay expenses. For the former I thank God I have sufficient property. This is one reason why I make the above proposal to Mr. Cotton. In regard to the latter, I think I can "get along." I shall dispose of my other loose property to pay my debts, and then resign my charge,[5] and remove my family trusting indeed to an uncertain living in a distant land, but being sure of my liberty in a free land.

Have the goodness to present my respects to your family and all who may inquire after my welfare. Yours respectfully,

Sam R. Ward

Gerrit Smith Papers, George Arents Research Library, Syracuse University, Syracuse, New York. Published by permission.

1. Millard Cotton (ca. 1794–?), a Vermont-born farmer, lived in Lenox Township in Madison County, New York. He had settled in New York by the 1830s. U.S. Census, 1850.

2. James Barnett (ca. 1810–?), a merchant, was born in Vermont but settled in Peterboro, New York, by the 1830s. A neighbor and antislavery confidant of Gerrit Smith's, he actively supported the Liberty party during the 1840s. Near the end of the decade, he moved to nearby Lenox Township. U.S. Census, 1840, 1850; Friedman, *Gregarious Saints*, 97; Kraut, *Crusaders and Compromisers*, 137n.

3. Ward suggests that because of their conservative antislavery principles, the Locofocos would support the Supreme Court's ruling in *Prigg* v. *Pennsylvania*. The Locofocos emerged as the radical wing of the Democratic party in New York state during the mid-1830s. Committed to economic radicalism, the Locofocos opposed banks, corporations, monopolies, tariffs, usury laws, and imprisonment for debt. Although they were hostile toward slavery, they were not active abolitionists.

4. Ward was only an infant when his slave parents, William and Anne Ward, escaped from Maryland to New Jersey in 1820. As a precaution against slave catchers, they concealed details of their past even from their children. Ward apparently believed that he was a free black until his mother revealed the family's background to his wife, Emily Reynoldson Ward, in the summer of 1841. Despite his plans to move to Kingston, Canada West, he remained in New York state throughout the 1840s. *DANB*, 631; *CA*, 3 February 1838.

5. From 1841 to 1843, Ward was the pastor of an all-white Congregationalist church in South Butler, New York. He resigned his pastorate because of a throat condition that he feared would damage his voice. *DANB*, 632.

56.
Jeremiah B. Sanderson to William C. Nell
19 June 1842

After 1830 proslavery apologists presented the institution as a "positive good" by arguing that the treatment of southern slaves was superior to that of northern factory workers. They contrasted well-cared-for slaves with exploited wage earners, benevolent slaveowners with greedy industrial capitalists, and wholesome plantations with unhealthy and hazardous conditions in northern sweatshops. Black abolitionists countered these proslavery myths whenever they could. Writing from Lowell, Massachusetts, on 19 June 1842, Jeremiah B. Sanderson commented on the factory environment there and challenged southern stereotypes of northern industrial workers. He characterized the young women who labored in the village's textile mills as happy, well treated, and filled with an independent spirit. Eugene D. Genovese, *The World the Slaveholders Made: Two Essays in Interception* (New York, N.Y., 1969), 165–234.

Lowell, [Massachusetts]
June 19th, 1842

Dear Friend William:

I have just returned from taking a walk, with a young Gentleman, Mr. George Johnson, with whom I have become acquainted since my arrival in the city. Its excessively warm, and I feel very little indeed like writing at present, but Mr. Levy[1] is coming down to the city of Boston tomorrow morning and you would hardly excuse me for neglecting so favorable an opportunity of sending you a line free of charge, as I shall not excuse you if you don't drop me a line back by him.

My health is very good indeed. The first day after I came here, if I had a mind, I might have imagined myself quite ill; I felt very lonely indeed, coming right out of the midst of so many pleasant and friendly associations as there are in New Bedford, & Boston, to bury myself for a while here in confinement to a Barber shop, its like is almost when compared with three or four months past life. However I begin to feel already more reconciled to my *new* Home. My "Foster brother"[2] is very pleasant as also his wife, thus far. I have formed a few new acquaintances since I have been here, among them Mr. Henry, Louis's two or three, & Mr. Johnson[3]—above referred to; the last I think a pleasant young gent; he will in some measure supply your place while I remain in this city, how long that will be I can't tell, he says he is acquainted with you Wm., and sends his love; you know that I send a heart full; I haven't there emptied i[t], for like a boiling spring, which, as you take away one vessel full, more flows in to supply the place of that taken away.

I have visited the Hospital here, erected for the benefit of the "Factory girls" when they are sick[4]—Will you ought to be here just at eating hours of the day, to see what a host of the "Factory girls" throng the streets then, and to pass by the Fac[t]ories at such an hour, and see them pouring out like a swarm of bees coming out of a hive, I can compare them to nothing else. The[y] seem comparatively happy; I have before now, heard their condition compared, degradingly, to the slaves of our country; I should just like to see some one of those individuals who make such a comparison, try the experiment of going up to a group of these young "Factory girls," as I was told they were, whom I saw walking out a little while ago, looking more like the Daughters of capitalists than slaves— and telling them, that they were to be compared to the slave daughters in the Southern Cotton Factories of Alabama & Georgia, and if these girls are not all non Resistents, they'd shew him, in more ways than one, that they were not to be thus insulted with impunity, or else I very much mistake the spirits they possess as indicated by the proud tossing of their heads.

I have also seen the Merrimac River the beautiful Merrimac; the city folks are quite proud of their Merrimac and frequently apostrop[h]ise i[t] tis indeed lovely. I saw it by moonlight too when walking out with Mr. Johnson, flowing on in its smooth and beautiful calmness, looking as it did, like a great Looking Glass, reflecting the face of nature, or if you please, like a great glass through which one might look, rush, into the presence of his maker; some "head over heels" in love swain, who had been disappointed. Wm. it is tea time now, and I have written enough to redeem myself from the charge of being unneighborly and besides Mr. Johnson is here in the shop waiting for me. When I've seen the Merrimack to good advantage I'll tell you more about it, also other matters. My love to all who think me worthy an inquiry after—send me a line or two. Hastily yrs. affectionally,

J. B. Sanderson[5]

P.S. Please send the accompanying as directed.

Jerry

Isaac and Amy Post Family Papers, Department of Rare Books and Special Collections, Rush-Rhees Library, University of Rochester, Rochester, New York. Published by permission.

1. John Levy.

2. Sanderson refers to Horatio W. Foster, who operated a barbershop on Centre Street in Lowell, Massachusetts, during the 1840s. He employed Sanderson in his shop during mid-1842. An ardent black abolitionist by the early 1840s, Foster helped establish a female Garrisonian antislavery society in Lowell. He later became a friend and adherent of Frederick Douglass and served as the Lowell agent for the North Star for four years. Foster moved to Pawtucket,

Rhode Island, in 1851, was elected secretary of the Rhode Island State Council of the Colored People, and became an outspoken advocate of efforts to establish a black industrial college. *Lowell City Directory*, 1840; Jeremiah B. Sanderson to William C. Nell, 25 July 1842, Post Papers, NRU; *Lib*, 12 May 1843; Horatio W. Foster to Maria Weston Chapman, 18 April 1843, Anti-Slavery Collection, MB [4:0561]; *NSt*, 3 December 1847; Liberator Mail Books, no. 1, 274–75, no. 2, 350, Anti-Slavery Collection, MB; *FDP*, 28 April 1854 [8:0755–56]; *RIF*, 10 March 1854 [8:0686].

3. Sanderson belonged to an intimate circle of black abolitionists organized around Walker Lewis's barbershop on Merrimack Street in Lowell, Massachusetts, in 1842. Lewis was the son of Thomas Lewis, a prominent figure in Boston's black community during the post-Revolutionary decades. The younger Lewis grew up in Boston, worked as a barber, and became an early convert to the antislavery cause. A close associate of David Walker, he helped Walker organize the Massachusetts General Colored Association in 1826. Lewis and his family moved to Lowell in the early 1830s, but he maintained close ties with Boston's black leaders. He employed several other barbers in his shop during the early 1840s, including George W. Johnson, a Lowell native, and William Henry, who had operated a hairdressing establishment in Boston from 1821 to 1834. *Lowell City Directory*, 1840–42; James O. Horton, "Generations of Protest: Black Families and Social Reform in Ante-Bellum Boston," *NEQ* 49:253–54 (June 1976); *Boston City Directory*, 1821–34; *Lib*, 28 May 1831, 12 October 1838 [2:0612].

4. Lowell's Corporation Hospital was established in 1841. The Boston Associates, an investment group that owned the mills in Lowell, Massachusetts, viewed the hospital as a philanthropic enterprise, although female workers paid their own medical bills. Since most of the women earned room, board, and about $2 per week, the $3 per week hospital expense made any prolonged illness financially disastrous. Benita Eisler, ed., *The Lowell Offering: Writings by New England Mill Women* (Philadelphia, Pa., 1977), 18, 64, 197–200; Thomas Dublin, ed., *Farm to Factory: Women's Letters, 1830–1860* (New York, N.Y., 1981), 7–8, 101–6.

5. Jeremiah B. Sanderson (1821–1875) was born in New Bedford, Massachusetts, of racially mixed parentage. After being educated at a local public school, he worked for a time as a barber. Beginning in the early 1840s, Sanderson demonstrated a commitment to antislavery and civil rights reform. He helped organize First of August celebrations, served as secretary of the New Bedford Anti-Slavery Society, and acted as a local agent for the *Liberator*. In 1842 he conducted antislavery lecture tours in New England and upstate New York. The American Anti-Slavery Society acknowledged his work with an invitation to address the AASS anniversary meeting in 1845. A loyal Garrisonian, Sanderson maintained close ties with William C. Nell and other Boston blacks. The 1853 black national convention appointed him to the newly formed National Council of the Colored People. The following year he settled in California, where his wife and children later joined him. Sanderson became involved in a variety of state and local black efforts. He attended the 1855 and 1856 black state conventions, participated in the campaign to end California's proscriptive black laws, and while living in San Francisco, he organized the Franchise League and the Young

Men's Union Beneficial Society. After the Civil War, he was drawn into Republican politics and served on the party's 1873 State Judicial Convention.

Sanderson's most important work in California was in education. For twenty years, he provided much-needed leadership in a state where black schools were almost nonexistent. He organized, taught, and supervised schools in Sacramento, Stockton, San Francisco, and Oakland. During these years, he also assumed a prominent role in the rapidly growing African Methodist Episcopal church in California. He ministered to congregations in San Francisco and Oakland and in 1875 was appointed secretary of the AME's California Conference. He died later that year in a railroad accident. *DANB*, 540; Rudolph M. Lapp, "Jeremiah B. Sanderson: Early California Negro Leader," *JNH* 53:321–33 (October 1968); Sue Bailey Thompson, *Pioneers of Negro Origin in California* (San Francisco, Calif., 1952), 37–42; Jeremiah B. Sanderson to William C. Nell, 26 June 1841, 25 January, 20 July 1842, Post Papers, NRU [4:0076, 0350, 0454]; *Lib*, 7 July, 11 August 1848, 24 February 1854 [5:0706, 0746, 8:0663]; *PA*, 27 September 1862 [14:0514]; *NASS*, 15 May 1845.

57.
Robert Purvis to Henry Clarke Wright
22 August 1842

Rampaging mobs regularly victimized northern black communities during the antebellum period. Philadelphia blacks endured six bloody race riots between 1829 and 1849. Each incident shattered illusions of racial progress. The 1 August 1842 riot was particularly disheartening because it occurred during an Emancipation Day celebration and resulted in the widespread destruction of the homes and meeting halls of the city's black elite. Henry Clarke Wright, a Massachusetts abolitionist who was gathering material for a British lecture tour, sought a full account of the incident from Robert Purvis. In a reply written three weeks after the riot, Purvis conveyed his deepening sense of despair, informing Wright that the racial violence had convinced him of the black community's "utter and complete nothingness in public estimation." Purvis concluded that "the bloody Will is in the heart of the community to destroy us." *Lib*, 19 August 1842 [4:0463]; Winch, *Philadelphia's Black Elite*, 150–51.

Phila[delphia], [Pennsylvania]
Aug[ust] 22nd, 1842

My Dear Friend Wright:[1]

I have been absent from this city in all of the past week. This I offer in excuse for not acknowledging the receipt of your letter before this, over date of 12th Inst.

But I am even now, in every way disqualified for making proper answers to your interrogatories in refference to one of the most ferocious and bloody spirited mobs, that ever cursed a Christian (?) Community; I know not where I should begin, nor how, or when to end in a detail of the wantonness, brutality and murderous spirit of the Actors, in the late riots,[2] nor of the Apathy and inhumanity of the Whole community in regard to the matter. Press, Church, Magistrates, Clergymen and Devils are against us. The measure of our sufferings is full. "Mans inhumanity to man, indeed make countless millions mourn."[3] From the most painful and minute investigation, in the feelings, views and acts of this community—in regard to us—I am convinced of our utter and complete nothingness in public estimation. I feel that my life and those tendrils of my heart, dearer than life to me, would find no change in death, but a glorious riddance of a life, weighed down & cursed by a despotism whose sway makes Hell of Earth—We the tormented, our persecutors the tormentors. But I must stop; I am sick—miserably sick—every thing around me is as dark as the grave. Here & there the bright countenance

14. Robert Purvis
Courtesy of Sophia Smith Collection, Smith College

of a true friend is to be seen, <u>save that</u>—nothing redeeming, nothing hopeful, despair black as the <u>pall</u> of Death hangs over us. And the bloody <u>Will</u> is in the heart of the community to destroy us.

I send you the "Freeman."[4] In it you will find much in answer to yr. enquiry. In a few days perhaps I will write you again. To attempt a reply to your letter now is impossible—I feel "I have no feeling scarce conscious what I wish." Yet never to forget my gratitude to you, and all the dear, true, and faithfull friends in the sacred cause of human freedom—Yr. brother,

Robt. Purvis

Anti-Slavery Collection, Boston Public Library, Boston, Massachusetts. Published by courtesy of the Trustees of the Boston Public Library.

1. Henry Clarke Wright (1797–1870), a Connecticut-born Garrisonian abolitionist, pacifist, and marriage reformer, ministered to the West Newbury, Massachusetts, Congregational Church until 1833. Wright joined the New England Anti-Slavery Society in 1835, becoming one of its most aggressive agents. He helped found the New England Non-Resistance Society in 1838 and coedited its organ, the *Non-Resistant*. He published dozens of pamphlets but is best known for his idiosyncratic autobiography, *Human Life* (1849), and a popular children's reform book, *A Kiss for a Blow* (1842). Lewis Perry, *Childhood, Marriage, and Reform: Henry Clarke Wright, 1797–1870* (Chicago, Ill., 1980).

2. On 1 August 1842, a "chiefly Irish" working-class mob attacked a West Indian Emancipation Day procession of the Young Men's Vigilant Association, a black temperance society centered in the Moyamensing section of Philadelphia. Two days of rioting ensued. Blacks were beaten, their homes looted, and the African Beneficial Hall and Second African Presbyterian Church burned to the ground. Order was restored by the Pennsylvania militia. Pennsylvania law held Philadelphia County liable for damages to the black-owned structures, but a local jury placed blame on the provocative nature of the black procession. In response, the owners of the hall and church sued the county for full recovery and were awarded damages by the Pennsylvania Supreme Court. Ironically, a third black hall was simultaneously destroyed by legal means when white property owners in the vicinity of the unscathed black Temperance Hall petitioned the local court of general sessions to declare the building a nuisance because it might attract future mobs. The court concurred and ordered the building's demolition. *PPL*, 2, 3, 4 August 1842; Elizabeth M. Geffen, "Violence in Philadelphia in the 1840s and 1850s," *PH* 36:387 (October 1969); Litwack, *North of Slavery*, 102; *Lib*, 26 August 1842.

3. Purvis freely quotes from stanza 7 of *Man Was Made to Mourn* (1786) by Scottish poet Robert Burns:

> Man's inhumanity to man,
> Makes countless thousands mourn.

4. Purvis refers to the *Pennsylvania Freeman*, an antislavery weekly published in Philadelphia from 1836 to 1854. Begun as the *National Enquirer and Consti-*

tutional Advocate of Universal Liberty, it was renamed in 1838 when the editorial reins passed from Benjamin Lundy to John Greenleaf Whittier. Subsequent editors included Charles C. Burleigh, James Miller McKim, Mary Grew, Oliver Johnson, and Cyrus M. Burleigh. Under their direction, the *Pennsylvania Freeman* followed the Garrisonian line on most issues, but its moderate editorial tone reflected the Quaker views of the members of the Pennsylvania Anti-Slavery Society. The PASS discontinued publication of the journal during 1842 and 1843. To fill the void, eight special issues were printed and widely distributed. Although no copies of these special issues survive, the one that Purvis mentions evidently appeared shortly after the August 1842 riot. Hochreiter, "*Pennsylvania Freeman.*"

58.
Narrative by Lewis G. Clarke
October 1842

Dozens of former slaves were lecturing to large audiences throughout the North by the mid-1840s. John A. Collins reported to the Massachusetts Anti-Slavery Society that "the public have itching ears to hear a colored man speak, and particularly a *slave*." Lewis G. Clarke, a Kentucky fugitive, toured throughout New York and New England, stirring audiences with tales of his life in bondage. In a speech delivered in Brooklyn during October 1842, Clarke used his personal story to illustrate the dehumanizing effects of slavery. Various versions of this lecture were widely reprinted by the antislavery press. Pease and Pease, *They Who Would Be Free*, 33–40; Quarles, *Black Abolitionists*, 61–62; *Lib*, 21 January 1842; *E*, 21 April 1847 [5:0413].

As a general thing, if a Kentuckian has a little money, he'd a deal rather vest it in slaves than any other property. A horse don't know that he's property, and a man does. There's a sort of satisfaction in thinking "You're a man, but you're *mine*. You're as white as I am but you're *mine*." Many a time I've[1] had 'em say to me, "You're my property. If I tell you to hold your hand in the fire till it burns off, you've got to do it." Not that they *meant* to make me put my hand in the fire, but they liked to let me know they had the *power*. The whiter a man is, the lower down they keep him.

Kentucky is the best of the slave States, in respect to the laws, but the masters manage to fix things pretty much to their own liking. The law don't allow 'em to brand a slave, or cut off his ear; but if they happen to switch it off with a cow-hide, nobody says anything about it. Though the laws are better than in other States, they ain't anyways equal. If a negro breaks open a house, he is hung for it, but if a white man does the same thing, he is put in the penitentiary, unless he has money enough to buy himself off. And there is one crime for which more black men are hung than any other, and if a white man does it, it is no crime at all. The law gives him full swing, and he don't fail to use his privilege, I can tell you. Now, if there was nothing else but this, it would make a slave's life as bad as death, many times. I can't tell these respectable people as much as I would like to, but think for a minute how you would like to have *your* sisters, and *your* wives, and *your* daughters, completely, teetotally, and altogether, in the power of a master. You can picture to yourselves a little how you would feel; but oh, if I could *tell* you! A slave woman ain't allowed to respect herself, if she would. I had a pretty sister; she was whiter than I am, for she took more after her father. When she was sixteen years old, her master sent for her. When he sent for her again, she cried, and did not want to go. She told her mother her troubles and she tried to encourage her to be decent, and hold up her head above such things, if she could. Her master was so mad, to think she complained to her mother, that he sold her right off to Louisiana; and we heard afterward that she died there of hard usage.

Now, who would like to be a slave, even if there was nothing bad about it but such treatment of his sisters and daughters? But there's a worse thing yet about slavery; the worst thing in the whole lot; though it's all bad, from the butt end to *pint*. I mean the *patter rollers* (patrols).[2] I suppose you know that they have patter rollers to go round o'nights, to see that the slaves are all in, and not planning any mischief? Now, these are just about the worst fellows that can be found; as bad as any you could pick up on the wharves. The reason is, you see, that no decent man will undertake the business. Gentlemen in Kentucky are ready enough to hire such jobs done, but if you was to ask any of them to *be* a patter roller, he would look upon it as a right down insult, and likely enough would blow out your brains for an answer. They're mighty handy with pistols down there; and if a man don't resent anything that's put upon them, they call him Poke easy.[3] The slaves catch it, too; and them as won't fight, is called Poke easy. But as I was telling ye, they hire these patter rollers, and they have to take the meanest fellows above ground; and because they are so mortal sure the slaves don't *want* their freedom, they have to put all power into their hands, to do with the niggers jest as they like. If a slave don't open his door to them, at any time of night, they break it down. They steal his money, if they can find it, and act just as they please with his wives and daughters. If a husband dares to say a word, or even look as if he wasn't quite satisfied, they tie him up and give him thirty-nine lashes. If there's any likely young girls in a slave's hut, they're mighty apt to have business there; especially if they think any colored young man takes a fancy to any of 'em. Maybe he'll get a pass from his master, and go to see the young girl for a few hours. [If] the patter rollers break in and find him, they'll abuse the girl as bad as they can, on purpose to provoke him. If he looks cross, they give him a flogging, tear up his pass, turn him out of doors, and then take him up and whip him for being out without a pass. If the slave says they tore it up, they swear he lies, and nine times out of ten the master won't come out agin 'em, for they say it won't *do* to let the niggers suppose they may complain of the patter rollers; they must be taught that it's their business to obey 'em in everything; and the patter roller knows that very well. Oh how often I've seen the poor girls sob and cry, when there's been such goings on! Maybe you think, because they're slaves, they ain't got no feeling and no shame! A woman's being a slave, don't stop her genteel ideas; that is, according to their way, and far as they *can*. They know they must submit to their masters; besides, their masters, maybe, dress 'em up, and make 'em little presents, and give 'em more privileges, while the whim lasts; but that ain't like having a parcel of low, dirty, swearing, drunk patter rollers let loose among 'em, like so many hogs. This breaks down their spirits dreadfully, and makes 'em wish they were dead.

Now, who among you would like to have *your* wives, and daughters, and sisters, in *such* a situation? This is what every slave in all these States is exposed to. Yet folks go from these parts down to Kentucky, and come back, and say the slaves have enough to eat and drink, and they are very happy, and they wouldn't mind it much to be slaves themselves. I'd like to have 'em to try it, it would teach 'em a little more than they know now. I'm not going to deny that Kentucky is better than other slave States, in respect of her laws; and she has the best name, too, about treating her slaves. But one great reason of that is, they are proud about punishing in *public*. If a man ties his slave up in the market place, and flogs him till he can't stand, the neighbors all cry out, "What a shame! The man has no regard to his character. What an abominable thing to have that nigger screaming where *everybody can hear!* Shame on him, to do such things in public!"

But if the same man flogs his slave ten times as bad, up garret or down cellar, with his mouth stopped, that he mayn't make a noise, or off in the woods, out of hearing—its all well enough. If his neighbor hear of it, they only say, "Well, of course there's no managing niggers without let-ting 'em know who's master." And there's an end of the business. The law, to be sure, don't allow such cruel floggings; but how's a slave going to get the law of his master? The law won't let him, nor any of his slaves, testify; and if the neighbors know anything about it, they *won't* testify. For it won't *do* to let the slaves think they would be upheld in complain-ing of master or overseer. I told you in the beginning, that it wouldn't *do* to let the slave think he is a *man*. That would spoil slavery, clean, en-tirely. No, this is the cruelty of the thing—A SLAVE CAN'T BE A MAN. He *must* be made a brute, but he ain't a brute, neither, if he had a chance to act himself out. Many a one of 'em is right smart, I tell you. But a horse *can't* speak, and a slave *daren't*; and that's the best way I can tell the story.

Signal of Liberty (Ann Arbor, Mich.), 23 January 1843.

1. Lewis George Clarke (1815–1897), the son of a mulatto slave woman and a white Revolutionary War veteran, was born a slave on his maternal grandfather's plantation in Madison County, Kentucky. The grandfather promised to emanci-pate the entire Clarke family by a provision in his will, but upon his death, the document could not be located, and the family was sold at auction. Sixteen-year-old Lewis, already separated from his family for ten years, became the property of a tobacco farmer, who allowed him to hire out his time. When that master

died, Clarke ran away to avoid being sold to Louisiana. In August 1841, after one abortive attempt, he gained his freedom. After a short stay in Canada West, he joined his brother Milton in Ohio and, in July 1842, helped his youngest brother Cyrus escape from slavery. During the 1840s and 1850s, Clarke devoted much of his time to the antislavery lecture circuit. He compared African colonization to the slave trade for its adverse impact on black families, and he criticized New England ministers who claimed to be abolitionists while they apologized for slaveholders and failed to pursue antislavery measures. Clarke returned to Canada West in the early 1850s, settled in Sandwich, acquired several parcels of land, and remained active in the abolitionist movement. On 1 March 1859, he helped found the Agricultural, Mechanical, and Educational Association of Canada West, a short-lived organization designed to aid fugitives in their transition to freedom; Clarke served the association as a trustee and general traveling agent. Later that same year, at the New England Colored Citizens Convention, he praised Canada as a land of opportunity and freedom for blacks and urged black parents to separate their sons from the bad influence of the cities in favor of the wholesome environment of the countryside. Clarke had sold his Canadian landholdings by 1874, and after his wife died, he moved with his children to Oberlin, Ohio. In the late 1870s or early 1880s, he returned to Kentucky. At the request of a group of planters, he lectured black agricultural laborers in the state, urging them not to immigrate to Kansas. He died in his native state and was buried at Oberlin. Jean Vacheenas and Betty Volk, "Born in Bondage: History of a Slave Family," *NHB* (May 1973), 36:101–6 (1973); *DANB*, 116; *SL*, 9 January 1843 [4:0523]; *E*, 11 May 1843 [4:0567]; *Lib*, 26 August 1859 [11:0966]; *BT*, 7, [14] December 1895; *NYSu*, 9 December 1900; Lewis G. Clark[e] et al., *The Agricultural, Mechanical, and Educational Association of Canada West* [Sandwich, Canada West, 1859], 2 [11:0625].

2. "Patter rollers" was a name slaves gave to the patrols that regulated slave conduct in the plantation South. These patrols watched the roads at night, detained blacks without passes, checked the slave quarters for arms and stolen goods, and broke up unauthorized slave assemblies. As Clarke indicated, planters and their sons frequently bought their way out of service on the patrols, leaving such duties to poor whites. Mitford M. Mathews, *Dictionary of Americanisms on Historical Principles* (Chicago, Ill., 1951), 1208; Genovese, *Roll, Jordan, Roll*, 617–19.

3. "Poke-easy" was a term used in the South to describe slow-moving or indolent persons.

59.
Annual Report of the Colored Vigilant Committee of Detroit
Delivered at Detroit City Hall
Detroit, Michigan
10 January 1843

As black abolitionists worked independently during the early 1840s, vigilance committees assumed an ever-expanding role. In addition to preventing kidnappings and aiding fugitive slaves, they championed suffrage, education, and a wide range of community concerns. Detroit blacks organized the city's Colored Vigilant Committee in 1840. The committee's annual report for 1842, read by William Lambert at a 10 January 1843 gathering at the Detroit City Hall, illustrated the committee's many functions. Under the leadership of Lambert, William C. Munroe, Madison J. Lightfoot, and George DeBaptiste, the Colored Vigilant Committee directed efforts to desegregate the city's public schools and worked with the Liberty party to gain the vote. The committee served as a link in the underground railroad throughout the decade, systematically directing fugitives to black settlements in Canada West. David Katzman, *Before the Ghetto: Black Detroit in the Nineteenth Century* (Urbana, Ill., 1973), 23, 34–38; Katherine Du Pre Lumpkin, " 'The General Plan was Freedom': A Negro Secret Order on the Underground Railroad," *Phy* 28:65–66 (Spring 1967); Saralee R. Howard-Filler, "A Place Called Safety: Detroit's Underground Railroad and the Museum of African American History," *MH* 71:28–31 (March–April 1987); Rev. Jacob Cummings interview, n.d., Siebert Collection, MH; *VF*, 3 December 1851 [7:0207]; *PFW*, 31 May 1856 [10:0172].

The committee would respectfully report, that their efforts for the past year, though few and feeble, have far exceeded our most sanguine expectations. At the time it was first proposed to organize a Committee of Vigilance from among our own people, to watch over our interests—to draft our petitions to the Legislature, praying that we may enjoy the elective franchise in common with other men, or to do any other business which they may deem of vital importance to our people. It was argued by some, that there was no necessity for such a committee, as we had friends who were already advocating our cause, and endeavoring to elevate us to our rights. Therefore, we should stand still, lest we should take a burden upon our own shoulders, that we were not able to bear, and thereby retard the great enterprize which they were about to achieve. But the more reflecting portion of us, being well satisfied that the long lost rights and liberties of our people in this community, or in any other, could only

be regained by our own exertions, elected and organized a committee of
nine persons from among ourselves, and sent them forth to act in behalf
of our whole people. As a matter of course, the want of experience in the
various duties to be performed, caused much difficulty in deciding upon
some definite plan of operating calmly, upon those difficult cases which
have hitherto heated the minds of our people with inflamed passion, and
called forth their physical force, to consummate in riot and in bloodshed,[1] that which should have been done calmly, peaceably, and with
deliberate reason. Thus have the committee learned from the past transactions of our people, as well as from history, that the spirit of physical
conquest, led on by ignorance, was always formed in enmity, pursued in
hatred, inflamed by passion, and consummated in riot and in bloodshed,
and often without accomplishing the object of its design. And as the
object of the committee was to lay the foundation for the triumph of the
just principles of liberty, and the right of all men to enjoy an equal
protection, under the government in which they live, and this to be done
under the dominion of calm and deliberate reason, have adopted morality as their shield—education, as their armor, and ungarnished truth
as their weapon to carry on this moral and political warfare.

From these instruments, the committee have learned that education is
the principle means by which an enslaved and degraded people can be
elevated; and that our moral, upright and correct deportment will be one
of the strongest arguments we can present, in favor of our universal
elevation to our civil, religious and political rights. In laying down this
plan, the committee have endeavored to impress upon the minds of our
people the great necessity of laying aside those light and frivolous amuse-
ments of the giddy and the gay, for the more calm, studious and reflecting mind of the Philosopher, and thereby bring ourselves and posterity
within the benign influence of education, temperance and morality.

The committee would now respectfully report that they have seen their
efforts abundantly blessed. They are now able to point to the names of
from 60 to 70 individuals, from our own people, the majority having no
children of their own to educate, who have resolved to contribute a
portion of their daily earnings to support a day school where all sects
and denominations may be taught free of charge.[2] The committee are
now able to enter into a day school, supported principally by our people,
and taught by a man of our color, and there behold its scholars, making
rapid strides in moral and intellectual improvement. They are also able
to count the names of a hundred individuals who have laid aside the
intoxicating bowl, and came and signed the "temperance pledge." They
can also refer to a Young Man's Society, their debating Club, their Reading Room with a Library of Historical works, all established by their own
individual exertions, to disseminate a general diffusion of knowledge
among our people. The committee have beheld, with much joy, the orga-

nization of two Female Societies, whose objects appear to be education, temperance, economy, and the universal reformation of the present, as well as the rising generations. It is true that the committee have had cause to grieve, on seeing the spirit of ignorance rising up in the midst of our people, to draw a division, and thereby presenting itself an obstacle and stumbling block in the way of our general elevation. But as ignorance is the mother of misfortune, and its wars always formed in enmity, pursued in hatred and inflamed with passion, always destroys itself and sinks to its own level, without accomplishing its designs. Such has been the fate of those obstacles which presented themselves to retard the general reformation which we are about to achieve. Thus have the committee learned from experience as well as from history, the superiority of moral and intellectual power over that of ignorance or physical force. The case of Nelson Hackett,[3] the fugitive slave from Arkansas, is a striking evidence of the superiority of calm and deliberate reason, over that of hatred and inflamed passion. When Nelson Hackett was arrested in Chatham, brought and cast into Sandwich jail, information was forwarded to our committee that a slave had been pursued into Canada by his master, who had offered five hundred dollars for his arrest, and he had been arrested and cast into Sandwich jail, to await his trial at the Court of King's Bench. A portion of our committee made it their business to attend that Court, and there learned from the presiding Judge that Nelson Hackett had been arrested on a charge of felony, and would remain in jail a certified time, and if sufficient proof should be brought within that time, the case would go before the Governor, and as there was no treaty stipulation (then) binding the two governments to deliver up fugitives, and as Nelson Hackett was a slave, it was his decided opinion that he would not be given up. The committee returned to Detroit and reported. General information of the case was circulated among our people, recommending to keep a vigilant eye upon the course pursued by British law, in the case of a slave claimed on British soil, under the charge of felony. Nelson Hackett remained in Sandwich jail for several months. Inquiry was made, time after time, by the committee, respecting Nelson Hackett's case and all the information we could receive from our people in Sandwich was, they had been informed that he had been set at liberty, yet no one had seen him. Thus the case died gradually away, and faded from the minds of many. But the mysteriousness of the case excited the suspicion of our committee, and caused them to keep an eye of vigilance to ferret out the whole proceedings.

On the night of the 8th of February 1842, at a dark and late hour of night, Nelson Hackett was taken out of Sandwich jail, conveyed across the river and lodged in our city prison, unknown to the inhabitants of Sandwich, or the good citizens of Detroit. But a vigilant eye encompassed the whole affair. General notice was circulated among our people, calm and deliberate reason was recommended as the basis of action; our friends and able counsel was consulted, who after examining the papers gave it as their opinion that they had been correctly made out, and all had been legally done, as he was a felon, it was better to let him go back to the prison house of slavery, than to bring a reproach upon the cause of emancipation by instituting a suit on his behalf. But the committee feeling themselves duty bound to act in his behalf called a general meeting of our people and resolved to publish the whole affair to the world, and thereby set a ball in motion that would roll into the British House of Commons. It had its desired effect; several letters were immediately received from distinguished persons in Canada, calling on the committee for more information upon the subject, and were all immediately answered. On the 26th of July 1842, a letter was received from England, calling on the committee for the names of all those concerned in the affair, with such other information as the committee was able to collect, such facts as the committee were in possession of were immediately forwarded. It is true that Nelson Hackett was returned to the prison house of bondage, but the name of "Nelson Hackett is now sounding upon the highest notes in the British House of Lords." Thus have the committee learned from experience, the superiority of moral and intellectual power, guided by calm, and deliberate reason, over that of ignorance and physical force, guided by heated and inflamed passion.

The committee while endeavoring to secure justice for our own people have also endeavored to impress upon their minds the great necessity of observing the law and becoming good and peaceable citizens. The committee was present themselves, before the good inhabitants of this community, to lay our people's claims upon your sympathy to act in our behalf.

[William Lambert][4]

Signal of Liberty (Ann Arbor, Mich.), 23 January 1843.

1. Detroit blacks feared that the use of violence in rescuing and protecting fugitive slaves might discredit their antislavery efforts. The city had not forgotten the Blackburn riot of June 1833, when club-wielding blacks beat a sheriff while they were attempting to free Kentucky fugitives Thornton and Rutha Blackburn. Reacting to the violence, whites imposed a curfew on local blacks and increased their efforts at preventing them from smuggling fugitives into Canada West. The following month, angered by the presence of slave catchers, blacks rioted and attempted to burn the city jail, sparking rumors that they intended to destroy the city. Federal troops were called in to quell the disturbance. Katzman, *Before the Ghetto*, 8–12.

2. When city officials took control of Detroit's black school in 1842, they fired its teacher, William C. Munroe. Black parents, led by William Lambert and Madison J. Lightfoot, boycotted the city's school, rehired Munroe, and opened

another school in the basement of the Second Baptist Church. Faced with insurmountable financial problems, this private black school closed in 1847. Katzman, *Before the Ghetto*, 22–25.

3. The extradition of fugitive slave Nelson Hackett became a celebrated incident in the transatlantic antislavery movement. Hackett, the personal servant of Alfred Wallace, a Washington County, Arkansas, merchant and land speculator, ran away in July 1841, taking with him his master's beaver overcoat, gold watch, saddle, and best horse. Traveling only at night, he reached Chatham, Canada West, within two months. But Wallace soon tracked him there, had him arrested and detained in Sandwich jail, and obtained his indictment for grand larceny in Arkansas. The governor of Arkansas formally requested Hackett's return. In January 1842, Sir Charles Bagot, the governor-general of the Canadas, ordered that the runaway be surrendered to Arkansas authorities. He was secretly ferried across to Detroit on 8 February and placed in the city jail. Detroit blacks sought legal assistance for Hackett, and C. H. Stewart, the president of the Michigan Anti-Slavery Society, attempted to obtain a writ for his release, but he was eventually returned to slavery. The case, which demonstrated that slave catchers could legally return slaves from Canada, outraged Anglo-American abolitionists and Canadian politicians, who made numerous inquiries and protests. Roman J. Zorn, "An Arkansas Fugitive Slave Incident and Its International Repercussions," *AHQ* 16:139–49 (Summer 1957).

4. William Lambert (ca. 1818–1890) was born to free black parents in Trenton, New Jersey, and received an excellent education "at the hands of Quakers." He settled in Detroit by 1840 and entered the garment trade, working first in the clothing shop of West Indian black Robert Banks, then establishing a thriving tailoring business of his own. Between the early 1840s and the Civil War, the controversial and militant Lambert devoted much of his time to the flood of fugitive slaves that poured through Detroit on their way to Canada West. He cofounded the city's Colored Vigilant Committee in the early 1840s and, as secretary of that organization, coordinated efforts to aid and protect black refugees, kept records of the hundreds he helped, and participated in several fugitive slave rescues. With the assistance of George DeBaptiste, another local black, he founded a second effort in the late 1850s that combined elements of a vigilance committee and a fraternal order. About that same time, Lambert was attracted to the revolutionary ideas of abolitionist John Brown. He attended Brown's Chatham Convention (1858) and was selected to serve as treasurer of the government that Brown intended to establish in the Appalachian mountains after the Harpers Ferry raid.

Lambert also contributed to abolitionism in more public ways. He frequently spoke out against slavery and was an active member of several state antislavery societies. During the early 1840s, he endorsed political antislavery and joined the Liberty party. He also labored for a variety of other reform causes, including civil rights, black education, and temperance. He helped lead a movement that attempted to obtain the franchise for Michigan blacks, combated racism in the Detroit press, worked for black admission to the city's public schools, and organized a black day school (1842). Lambert participated in the black convention movement, attending two antebellum national meetings and calling and organizing Michigan's 1843 black state convention. Although an early opponent of black emigration, after 1854 he advised blacks to resettle beyond the North American continent. Lambert represented Detroit blacks at the 1854 and 1856 National Emigration Conventions in Cleveland, where he rallied behind James T. Holly's plan for Haitian immigration. At the 1856 meeting, he was elected treasurer of the General Board of Commissioners, the emigration movement's administrative arm. He also worked for Holly's Protestant Episcopal Society for Promoting the Extension of the Church among Colored People, which advocated Episcopalian missionary work among Haitian blacks. Lambert continued in the movement through the early 1860s.

He remained a leader of Detroit's black community after the Civil War, when he helped to found black Masonic and Odd Fellows lodges, held prominent positions in local Episcopalian lay affairs, and represented the community at several black state conventions. A force in local Republican circles, he made unsuccessful bids for election to Detroit's board of estimates in 1875 and 1877. After a period of deteriorating mental health, Lambert hanged himself in 1890. He left an estate valued at more than $70,000. Undated newspaper clippings, William Lambert Folder, MiD-B; Katzman, *Before the Ghetto*, 3, 5, 13–14, 21, 23, 27, 32–33, 38–43, 95, 138–39, 148–49, 161, 176–77, 180; Lumpkin, " 'General Plan Was Freedom,' " 63–77; *SL*, 23 January, 25 December 1843, 23 March 1846 [4:0527, 0711]; *Lib*, 18 November 1853 [8:0495]; Foner and Walker, *Proceedings of the Black State Conventions*, 1:181–87, 190, 194; Miller, *Search for a Black Nationality*, 161, 166–67, 233; Undated newspaper clipping, Stanley Smith Collection, CaOLU; *WAA*, 31 March 1860 [12:0598].

60.
Speech by Henry Highland Garnet
Delivered before the National Convention
of Colored Citizens
Buffalo, New York
16 August 1843

Changing black attitudes toward slave violence reflected the growing breach between black and white abolitionism. After ten years of allegiance to nonresistance principles, many black abolitionists looked to different methods during the 1840s. Henry Highland Garnet's "Address to the Slaves of the United States of America," given at the 1843 black national convention in Buffalo, marked a turning point in the antislavery movement and served as a statement of independence from white abolitionists. On 16 August, more than seventy delegates and scores of black and white observers heard Garnet eloquently and passionately advocate slave resistance and insurrection. Speaking to blacks, he warned that "however much you . . . may desire it, there is not much hope of Redemption without the shedding of blood." A debate followed the speech, and then in another oration lasting over an hour, Garnet defended his views, denounced the "unreasonable and unnatural dogmas of non-resistance," and mocked Garrison's ideas as "ridiculous." His audience was spellbound. Led by Frederick Douglass, the delegates twice rejected Garnet's sentiments, the first time by only one vote. The speech was so controversial that it was universally condemned by white abolitionists and was not published until 1848—and then at John Brown's expense. Quarles, *Black Abolitionists*, 226–27; Schor, *Henry Highland Garnet*, 50–64, 293; Pasternak, "Rise and Fly to Arms," 73–74; *Minutes of the National Convention of Colored Citizens: Held at Buffalo, on the 15th, 16th, 17th, 18th, and 19th of August 1843* (New York, N.Y., 1843), 4–6, 12–13, 15–19, 23–24 [4:0633–34, 0637–38, 0639–41, 0643].

ADDRESS TO THE SLAVES OF
THE UNITED STATES OF AMERICA

BRETHREN AND FELLOW CITIZENS:

Your brethren of the north, east, and west have been accustomed to meet together in National Conventions, to sympathize with each other, and to weep over your unhappy condition. In these meetings we have addressed all classes of the free, but we have never until this time, sent a word of consolation and advice to you. We have been contented in sitting still and mourning over your sorrows, earnestly hoping that before this day, your sacred Liberties would have been restored. But, we have hoped

15. Henry Highland Garnet
Courtesy of Library of Congress

in vain. Years have rolled on, and tens of thousands have been borne on streams of blood, and tears, to the shores of eternity. While you have been oppressed, we have also been partakers with you; nor can we be free while you are enslaved. We therefore write to you as being bound with you.

Many of you are bound to us, not only by the ties of common humanity, but we are connected by the more tender relations of parents, wives, husbands, children, brothers, and sisters, and friends. As such we most affectionately address you.

Slavery has fixed a deep gulf between you and us, and while it shuts out from you the relief and consolation which your friends would willingly render, it afflicts and persecutes you with a fierceness which we might not expect to see in the fiends of hell. But still the Almighty Father of Mercies has left to us a glimmering ray of hope, which shines out like a lone star in a cloudy sky. Mankind are becoming wiser, and better—the oppressor's power is fading, and you, every day, are becoming better informed, and more numerous. Your grievances, brethren, are many. We shall not attempt, in this short address, to present to the world, all the dark catalogue of this nation's sins, which have been committed upon an innocent people. Nor is it indeed, necessary, for you feel them from day to day, and all the civilized world look upon them with amazement.

Two hundred and twenty-seven years ago, the first of our injured race were brought to the shores of America.[1] They came not with glad spirits to select their homes, in the New World. They came not with their own consent, to find an unmolested enjoyment of the blessings of this fruitful soil. The first dealings which they had with men calling themselves Christians, exhibited to them the worst features of corrupt and sordid hearts; and convinced them that no cruelty is too great, no villainy, and no robbery too abhorrent for even enlightened men to perform, when influenced by avarice, and lust. Neither did they come flying upon the wings of Liberty, to a land of freedom. But, they came with broken hearts, from their beloved native land, and were doomed to unrequited toil, and deep degradation. Nor did the evil of the bondage end at their emancipation by death. Succeeding generations inherited their chains, and millions have come from eternity into time, and have returned again to the world of spirits, cursed and ruined by American Slavery.

The propagators of the system, or their immediate ancestors very soon discovered its growing evil, and its tremendous wickedness and secret promises were made to destroy it. The gross inconsistency of a people holding slaves, who had themselves "ferried o'er the wave," for freedom's sake, was too apparent to be entirely overlooked. The voice of Freedom cried, "emancipate your Slaves." Humanity supplicated with tears, for the deliverance of the children of Africa. Wisdom urged her solemn plea. The bleeding captive plead his innocence, and pointed to

Christianity who stood weeping at the cross. Jehovah frowned upon the nefarious institution, and thunderbolts, red with vengeance, struggled to leap forth to blast the guilty wretches who maintained it. But all was vain. Slavery had stretched its dark wings of death over the land, the Church stood silently by—the priests prophesied falsely, and the people loved to have it so. Its throne is established, and now it reigns triumphantly.

Nearly three millions of your fellow citizens, are prohibited by law, and public opinion (which in this country is stronger than law), from reading the Book of Life. Your intellect has been destroyed as much as possible, and every ray of light they have attempted to shut out from your minds. The oppressors themselves have become involved in the ruin. They have become weak, sensual, and rapacious. They have cursed you—they have cursed themselves—they have cursed the earth which they have trod. In the language of a Southern statesman, we can truly say "even the wolf, driven back long since by the approach of man now returns after a lapse of a hundred years, and howls amid the desolation of slavery."

The colonists threw the blame upon England. They said that the mother country entailed the evil upon them, and that they would rid themselves of it if they could. The world thought they were sincere, and the philanthropic pitied them. But time soon tested their sincerity. In a few years, the colonists grew strong and severed themselves from the British Government. Their independence was declared, and they took their station among the sovereign powers of the earth. The declaration was a glorious document. Sages admired it, and the patriotic of every nation reverenced the Godlike sentiments which it contained. When the power of Government returned to their hands, did they emancipate the slaves? No, they rather added new links to our chains.[2] Were they ignorant to the principles of Liberty? Certainly they were not. The sentiments of their revolutionary orators fell in burning eloquence upon their hearts, and with one voice they cried, LIBERTY OR DEATH. O, what a sentence was that! It ran from soul to soul like electric fire, and nerved the arm of thousands to fight in the holy cause of Freedom. Among the diversity of opinions that are entertained in regard to physical resistance, there are but a few found to gainsay that stern declaration. We are among those who do not.

SLAVERY! How much misery is comprehended in that single word. What mind is there that does not shrink from its direful effects? Unless the image of God is obliterated from the soul, all men cherish the love of Liberty. The nice discerning political economist does not regard the sacred right, more than the untutored African who roams in the wilds of Congo. Nor has the one more right to the full enjoyment of his freedom than the other. In every man's mind the good seeds of Liberty are planted, and he who brings his fellow down so low, as to make him contented with a condition of slavery, commits the highest crime against God and man. Brethren, your oppressors aim to do this. They endeavor to make you as much like brutes as possible. When they have blinded the eyes of your mind—when they have embittered the sweet waters of life— when they have shut out the light which shines from the word of God— then, and not till then has American slavery done its perfect work.

TO SUCH DEGREDATION IT IS SINFUL IN THE EXTREME FOR YOU TO MAKE VOLUNTARY SUBMISSION. The divine commandments, you are in duty bound to reverence, and obey. If you do not obey them you will surely meet with the displeasure of the Almighty. He requires you to love him supremely, and your neighbor as yourself—to keep the Sabbath day holy—to search the Scriptures—and bring up your children with respect for his laws, and to worship no other God but him.[3] But slavery sets all these at naught, and hurls defiance in the face of Jehovah. The forlorn condition in which you are placed does not destroy your moral obligation to God. You are not certain of Heaven, because you suffer yourselves to remain in a state of slavery, where you cannot obey the commandments of the Sovereign of the universe. If the ignorance of slavery is a passport to heaven, then it is a blessing, and a curse, and you should rather desire its perpetuity than its abolition. God will not receive slavery, nor ignorance, nor any other state of mind, for love, and obedi- ence to him. Your condition does not absolve you from your moral obligation. The diabolical injustice by which your Liberties are cloven down, NEITHER GOD, NOR ANGELS, OR JUST MEN COMMAND YOU TO SUFFER FOR A SINGLE MOMENT. THEREFORE IT IS YOUR SOLEMN AND IMPERATIVE DUTY TO USE EVERY MEANS, BOTH MORAL, INTEL- LECTUAL, AND PHYSICAL, THAT PROMISE SUCCESS. If a band of hea- then men should attempt to enslave a race of Christians, and to place their children under the influence of some false religion, surely, heaven would frown upon the men who would not resist such aggression, even to death. If, on the other hand, a band of Christians should attempt to enslave a race of heathen men and to entail slavery upon them, and to keep them in heathenism in the midst of Christianity, the God of heaven would smile upon every effort which the injured might make to disen- thrall themselves.

Brethren, it is as wrong for your lordly oppressors to keep you in slavery, as it was for the man thief to steal our ancestors from the coast of Africa. You should therefore now use the same manner of resistance, as would have been just in our ancestors, when the bloody footprints of the first remorseless soul thief was placed upon the shores of our father- land. The humblest peasant is as free in the sight of God, as the proudest monarch that ever swayed a scepter. Liberty is a spirit sent out from God, and like its great Author, is no respecter of persons.

Brethren, the time has come when you must act for yourselves. It is an old and true saying, that "if hereditary bondsmen would be free, they must themselves strike the blow."[4] You can plead your own cause, and do the work of emancipation better than any other. The nations of the old world are moving in the great cause of universal freedom, and some of them at least, will ere long, do you justice. The combined powers of Europe have placed their broad seal of disapprobation upon the African slave trade.[5] But in the slave holding parts of the United States, the trade is as brisk as ever. They buy and sell you as though you were brute beasts. The North has done much—her opinion of slavery in the abstract is known. But in regard to the South, we adopt the opinion of the *New York Evangelist*—"We have advanced so far, that the cause apparently waits for a more effectual door to be thrown open than has been yet."[6] We are about to point you to that more effectual door. Look around you, and behold the bosoms of your loving wives, heaving with untold agonies! Hear the cries of your poor children! Remember the stripes your fathers bore. Think of the torture and disgrace of your noble mothers. Think of your wretched sisters, loving virtue and purity, as they are driven into concubinage, and are exposed to the unbridled lusts of incarnate devils. Think of the undying glory that hangs around the ancient name of Africa—and forget not that you are native-born American citizens, and as such, you are justly entitled to all the rights that are granted to the freest. Think how many tears you have poured out upon the soil which you have cultivated with unrequited toil, and enriched with your blood; and then go to your lordly enslavers, and tell them plainly, that YOU ARE DETERMINED TO BE FREE. Appeal to their sense of justice, and tell them that they have no more right to oppress you, than you have to enslave them. Entreat them to remove the grievous burdens which they have imposed upon you, and to remunerate you for your labor. Promise them renewed diligence in the cultivation of the soil, if they will render to you an equivalent for your services. Point them to the increase of happiness and prosperity in the British West Indies, since the act of Emancipation.[7] Tell them in language which they cannot misunderstand, of the exceeding sinfulness of slavery, and of a future judgement, and of the righteous retributions of an indignant God. Inform them that all you desire, is FREEDOM, and that nothing else will suffice. Do this, and forever after cease to toil for the heartless tyrants, who give you no other reward but stripes and abuse. If they then commence the work of death, they, and not you, will be responsible for the consequences. You had far better all die—*die immediately*, than live slaves, and entail your wretchedness upon your posterity. If you would be free in this generation, here is your only hope. However much you and all of us may desire it, there is not much hope of Redemption without the shedding of blood. If you must bleed, let it all come at once—rather, *die freemen, than live to be slaves.* It is impossible, like the children of Israel, to make a grand Exodus from the land of bondage. THE PHAROES ARE ON BOTH SIDES OF THE BLOOD-RED WATERS! You cannot remove en masse, to the dominions of the British Queen—nor can you pass through Florida, and overrun Texas, and at last find peace in Mexico.[8] The propagators of American slavery are spending their blood and treasure, that they may plant the black flag in the heart of Mexico, and riot in the halls of the Montezumas.[9] In the language of the Rev. Robert Hall, when addressing the volunteers of Bristol, who were rushing forth to repel the invasion of Napoleon, who threatened to lay waste the fair homes of England, "Religion is too much interested in your behalf, not to shed over you her most gracious influences."[10]

You will not be compelled to spend much time in order to become inured to hardships. From the first moment that you breathed the air of heaven, you have been accustomed to nothing else but hardships. The heroes of the American Revolution were never put upon harder fare, than a peck of corn, and a few herrings per week. You have not become enervated by the luxuries of life. Your sternest energies have been beaten out upon the anvil of severe trial. Slavery has done this, to make you subservient to its own purposes; but it has done more than this, it has prepared you for any emergency. If you receive good treatment, it is what you could hardly expect; if you meet with pain, sorrow, and even death, these are the common lot of the slaves.

Fellow men! patient sufferers! behold your dearest rights crushed to the earth! See your sons murdered, and your wives, mothers, and sisters, doomed to prostitution! In the name of the merciful God! and by all that life is worth, let it no longer be a debateable question, whether it is better to choose LIBERTY or DEATH!

In 1822, Denmark Vesey, of South Carolina, formed a plan for the liberation of his fellow men. In the whole history of human efforts to overthrow slavery, a more complicated and tremendous plan was never formed. He was betrayed by the treachery of his own people, and died a martyr to freedom.[11] Many a brave hero fell, but History, faithful to her high trust, will transcribe his name on the same monument with Moses, Hampden, Tell, Bruce, and Wallace, Toussaint L'Ouverture, Lafayette and Washington.[12] That tremendous movement shook the whole empire of slavery. The guilty soul thieves were overwhelmed with fear. It is a matter of fact, that at that time, and in consequence of the threatened revolution, the slave states talked strongly of emancipation. But they blew but one blast of the trumpet of freedom, and then laid it aside. As these men became quiet, the slaveholders ceased to talk about emancipation; and now, behold your condition today! Angels sigh over it, and humanity has long since exhausted her tears in weeping on your account!

The patriotic Nathaniel Turner[13] followed Denmark Vesey. He was goaded to desperation by wrong and injustice. By Despotism, his name has been recorded on the list of infamy, but future generations will number him upon the noble and brave.

Next arose the immortal Joseph Cinqué, the hero of the *Amistad*. He was a native African, and by the help of God he emancipated a whole ship-load of his fellow men on the high seas. And he now sings of Liberty on the sunny hills of Africa, and beneath his native palm trees, where he hears the lion roar, and feels himself as free as that king of the forest. Next arose Madison Washington, that bright star of freedom, and took his station in the constellation of freedom. He was a slave on board the brig *Creole*, of Richmond, bound to New Orleans, that great slave mart, with a hundred and four others. Nineteen struck for Liberty or death. But one life was taken, and the whole were emancipated, and the vessel was carried into Nassau, New Providence. Noble men! Those who have fallen in freedom's conflict, their memories will be cherished by the true hearted, and the God-fearing, in all future generations; those who are living, their names are surrounded by a halo of glory.

We do not advise you to attempt a revolution with the sword, because it would be INEXPEDIENT. Your numbers are too small, and moreover the rising spirit of the age, and the spirit of the gospel, are opposed to war and bloodshed. But from this moment cease to labor for tyrants who will not remunerate you. Let every slave throughout the land do this, and the days of slavery are numbered. You cannot be more oppressed than you have been—you cannot suffer greater cruelties than you have already. RATHER DIE FREEMEN, THAN LIVE TO BE SLAVES. Remember that you are THREE MILLIONS.

It is in your power so to torment the God-cursed slaveholders, that they will be glad to let you go free. If the scale was turned and black men were the masters, and white men the slaves, every destructive agent and element would be employed to lay the oppressor low. Danger and death would hang over their heads day and night. Yes, the tyrants would meet with plagues more terrible than those of Pharaoh. But you are a patient people. You act as though you were made for the special use of these devils. You act as though your daughters were born to pamper the lusts of your masters and overseers. And worse than all, you tamely submit, while your lords tear your wives from your embraces, and defile them before your eyes. In the name of God we ask, are you men? Where is the blood of your fathers? Has it all run out of your veins? Awake, awake; millions of voices are calling you! Your dead fathers speak to you from their graves. Heaven, as with a voice of thunder, calls on you to arise from the dust.

Let your motto be RESISTANCE! RESISTANCE! RESISTANCE! No oppressed people have ever secured their Liberty without resistance. What kind of resistance you had better make, you must decide by the circumstances that surround you, and according to the suggestion of expediency. Brethren, adieu. Trust in the living God. Labor for the peace of the human race, and remember that you are three millions.

Henry Highland Garnet, ed., *Walker's Appeal, With a Brief Sketch of His Life* (New York, N.Y., 1848), 90–96.

1. Garnet's dating is incorrect. The first twenty African blacks brought into what is now the United States were landed by a Dutch frigate at Jamestown, Virginia, in 1619.

2. Garnet notes that some leaders of the American Revolution blamed Britain for the existence of slavery in the American colonies. Thomas Jefferson's initial draft of the Declaration of Independence denounced the mother country for forcing the institution upon the colonies, for perpetuating the slave trade, and for preventing the colonies from taking any measures to halt or restrain the traffic. But the Continental Congress removed these charges from the final draft in deference to southern slaveholders and northern slave traders. Once independent, the new nation did little to control slavery.

3. Garnet's remarks are an exegetical treatment of Matthew 22:37–40, in which Jesus Christ informs Jewish leaders of his basic theology—that individuals should love God with their entire heart, soul, and mind and should love others as much as themselves. He then lists several specific rules of the Jewish faith, largely borrowed from the Ten Commandments in Exodus 20:1–17, as practical examples of observance of this basic theology.

4. Garnet paraphrases a line from canto 2, stanza 76 of Lord Byron's *Childe Harold's Pilgrimage* (1818):

> Hereditary bondsmen! Know ye not
> Who would be free themselves must strike the blow?
> By their right arms the conquest must be wrought?

5. Garnet probably refers to the Quintuple Treaty signed by Britain, Austria, Russia, Prussia, and France on 20 December 1841. It denounced the slave trade as piracy and provided for the seizure of vessels engaged in the illicit traffic. W. E. B. DuBois, *The Suppression of the African Slave Trade* (Cambridge, Mass., 1896; reprint, Baton Rouge, La., 1969), 138–48, 150.

6. Garnet paraphrases from "The Anti-Slavery Enterprise," an editorial in the 27 July 1843 issue of the *New York Evangelist*. The Presbyterian weekly, which was published in New York City from 1830 to 1902, promoted missionary work, revivalism, temperance, antislavery, and other reforms.

7. Garnet refers to the Emancipation Act of 1833, which ended slavery in the British Empire.

8. Garnet compares the situation of southern slaves to that of Jewish bondsmen in ancient Egypt. He argues that it is impractical to consider a mass exodus like that which carried the Jews out of Egypt. Even if it was possible, he notes, American expansionism threatened to annex surrounding countries like Mexico, thus cutting off reasonable avenues of escape.

9. Garnet probably refers to attempts by the slaveholding Republic of Texas to seize additional Mexican territory. Between 1839 and 1842, the young nation

conducted a series of unsuccessful border raids against Mexico and negotiated a military agreement with the government of the rebel state of Yucatán. Pletcher, *Diplomacy of Annexation*, 76–79.

10. Robert Hall (1764–1831), a Baptist clergyman serving the Broadmead Chapel in Bristol, England, made this appeal in response to Napoleon's threatened invasion of England in 1804. *DNB*, 8:969–70.

11. The foiled Denmark Vesey revolt of June 1822 revealed the slaves' determination to be free and sparked a white backlash that contributed to the nullification crisis of the 1830s. Vesey, a successful free black Charleston carpenter, convinced scores of Charleston blacks to rise up, capture the city, and eventually escape to the Caribbean. Nervous house servants exposed the plot on 14 June, throwing the city into hysteria. Vesey was captured on 22 June and hanged the next day. Charleston authorities eventually executed thirty-five blacks, banished thirty-seven others from the state, and sentenced four whites to stiff prison sentences for aiding the conspirators. Robert S. Starobin, "Denmark Vesey's Slave Conspiracy of 1822: A Study in Rebellion and Repression," in *American Slavery: The Question of Resistance*, ed. John H. Bracey, August Meier, and Elliott Rudwick (Belmont, Calif., 1971), 142–57.

12. Garnet lists a series of revolutionary heroes from ancient times to the nineteenth century—Moses led the Jewish people out of slavery in Egypt about 1200 B.C., John Hampden helped lead the Puritan opposition to Charles I before and during the English Civil War, the legendary William Tell led resistance against a tyrant in one of the Swiss cantons during the twelfth century, Robert Bruce and William Wallace captained popular resistance to the British Crown in thirteenth-century Scotland, Toussaint L'Ouverture led the Haitian Revolution, and the Marquis de Lafayette and George Washington were heroic military figures in the American Revolution. Lafayette enhanced his image as a radical leader during the French Revolution and the Revolution of 1830.

13. Nat Turner (1800–1831), a Southampton County, Virginia, slave preacher, organized and led the bloodiest slave revolt in American history. Obsessed by a messianic impulse to destroy slavery, he interpreted a solar eclipse as a long-awaited divine instruction to kill his oppressors. During 21–22 August 1831, Turner and some forty fellow slaves ravaged nearby plantations, axing and bludgeoning to death nearly sixty whites before the insurrection was crushed. A reign of terror followed. Within a year, local whites hanged or otherwise executed about two hundred blacks. The revolt sparked a brief but unprecedented statewide debate over slavery. But the appearance of William Lloyd Garrison's fiery *Liberator* the same year convinced most southerners that abolitionists were responsible for Turner's murderous spree. They responded by strengthening slave codes, repudiating emancipation schemes, and pronouncing slavery "a positive good." Stephen B. Oates, *The Fires of Jubilee: Nat Turner's Fierce Rebellion* (New York, N.Y., 1975).

61.
Henry Johnson to Austin Willey
31 August 1843

The Liberty party's commitment to emancipation and racial equality
attracted many black abolitionists. The party gained the endorsement
of the 1843 black national convention and the support of prominent
blacks such as Charles B. Ray, Samuel R. Ward, and Henry Highland
Garnet. But for other blacks, it posed a dilemma—should they support
an antislavery party that was politically weak or work with moderate
Whigs in the hope of achieving limited black goals on the local level?
Despite its ineffectiveness, black leaders rallied around the Liberty
party, the first American political organization to nominate and run
black men for office. For Henry Johnson of New Bedford, Massachusetts, there was no dilemma. His 31 August 1843 letter to Austin Willey,
the editor of the *Liberty Standard*, championed the Liberty party. *CA*,
17, 24 November 1838 [2:0654, 0660]; Quarles, *Black Abolitionists*,
184–86; Pease and Pease, *They Who Would Be Free*, 189, 197, 201–2.

Augusta, [Maine]
Aug[ust] 31, 1843

MR. EDITOR:

Having for some years been a strong supporter of first one and then
the other of the two political parties of the day—believing that they,
according to their many professions, would remove this current system
of American slavery from this our land, and finding to my satisfaction
that slavery never would be removed by these parties—I came to the
conclusion as a colored man, as a christian, as a friend to my country,
and above all, as one who but a few years since left the Prison house of
slavery to abandon them. I could not and would not go to the polls again
in support of either the Whig or Locofoco party. I have been, and still
remain, an uncompromising advocate of the Liberty party[1] principles,
believing it the duty of every true friend of liberty, and particularly every
man of color, to do the same. I lectured at the Baptist church last evening, and in my lecture[2] I stated some few reasons why I was turned out
of employment in one of these parties, and stated that it was for no other
reason than because I denounced both of these parties, and rushed
through their midst and found my way to the Liberty party—and they
give me the right hand of fellowship—not the left hand as the other two
parties do. And in making these statements it seems that I trod upon the
corns of your Whig editors, who stated, I was informed after the meeting, that these were not the reasons, that it was for some of my misconduct. I would inform that gentleman, through the columns of your Lib-

erty paper, that my moral character stands as high in the town of New Bedford, as his does in the town of Augusta, and in proof of those facts, if that gentleman will call at my boarding house, I will produce documents signed by the leading men of both parties, setting forth my true character, both moral and religious. But to the question—my object in coming to this place was not to lecture on political matters, but to lay before this people, having been a slave myself, what is the condition of those whom I left behind me—and for this only. And it has been very often the case while lecturing on this part of the subject, that many persons have desired to know what they should do to better the condition of the slave, and when this question shall be asked me, God being my helper, I shall answer according to the dictates of my own conscience, without consulting each of the two political parties of the day. If I shall consult at all, I shall consult liberty, and not slavery. The first question to be proposed by me is not what shall be profitable to me, but what is right. Duty must be primary, prominent, most conspicuous among the objects of human thought and pursuit. We can never see the right clearly and fully, but by making it our first concern. And I hold that no judgement can be just and wise but that which is built on the conviction of the paramount worth and importance of duty. This is the fundamental truth upon which I believe the foundation of the Liberty party stands. And the mind which does not start from this in its inquiries into human affairs, is in my estimation doomed to fatal error. It has been long since decided in my own mind, what my duty is to God and my fellow men. And having been made sensible of those duties, I have now come to the conclusion to perform them. I will further state, as I did last night, if there is a colored man in the town of Augusta or Hallowell, who supports either of the two political parties instead of the Liberty party, let him come out like a man and show one reason why he should support either of those corrupt parties, and I will, notwithstanding a stranger in your town, pledge myself to show for every one of his reasons, five why he should not support them. Let such come forth in public print and show himself a man by good sound reasons, through this or any other public Journal of the day, and I will never give him up until I shall prove all of his reasons before this public to be worse than folly, so long as pen, paper and ink, can be found in the town of Augusta. Yours for the downtrodden slave,

HENRY JOHNSON[3]

Liberty Standard (Hallowell, Maine), 14 September 1843.

1. The Liberty party, the nation's first antislavery political party, was founded in 1839 and quickly gained the support of prominent abolitionists like Gerrit Smith and James G. Birney. Although the party emphasized a single issue—the abolition of slavery—it attracted considerable black support by advocating racial equality, opposing Jim Crow practices, and condemning the American Coloniza-

tion Society. It ran state and national candidates from 1839 to 1848, finding its greatest strength in New York and Massachusetts. Most Liberty party adherents joined the Free Soil party by 1848, but through the leadership of Gerrit Smith, a small remnant persisted until 1860 under the banner of the Radical Abolitionists. Sewell, *Ballots for Freedom*, 47–73, 83–100, 114–20, 128–56, 162–65, 246–47, 285–87.

2. Johnson spoke on 30 August 1843 at the First Baptist Church of Augusta, Maine. At the time, the congregation was divided by the slavery issue. Although the members had approved an antislavery resolution in December 1842, a slight majority voted against disfellowshipping slaveholders the following December. After this vote, Rev. E. R. Warren and thirty-two members left the church and established the Second Baptist Church of Augusta. Ironically, Warren's replacement, Rev. N. W. Williams, proved to be a committed antislavery advocate. Burrage, *Baptists in Maine*, 314–15.

3. Henry Johnson (1812–?) was born in Richmond, Virginia, and settled in New Bedford, Massachusetts, in the early 1830s. In addition to working in New Bedford as a town crier, he became involved in local antislavery activities, anticolonization meetings, and vigilance committee work. Johnson represented the community at the 1843 annual meeting of the American Anti-Slavery Society. Following the convention, he accompanied David Ruggles on an antislavery lecture tour of Maine. Johnson attended the 1857 state convention of Massachusetts blacks and the 1859 New England Colored Citizens Convention. *Lib*, 13 October 1843, 20 September 1850, 15 August 1851, 19 August 1853, 19 August 1859 [4:0683, 6:0579–80, 7:0062, 8:0417, 11:0935–38]; *FDP*, 22 October 1852 [7:0796–97]; *WAA*, 17 December 1859 [12:0297]; *CA*, 23 May 1840 [3:0437], U.S. Census, 1850.

62.
Charles Lenox Remond to Isaac and Amy Post
27 September 1843

Antislavery lecture tours were often fraught with difficulties. Lecturers faced apathetic, indifferent, or even hostile audiences. They suffered humiliating and sometimes brutal assaults at the hands of antiabolitionist ruffians. During the fall of 1843, Charles Lenox Remond traveled through Ohio and Indiana with Frederick Douglass, Sydney Howard Gay, James Monroe, and other abolitionists as part of a much-heralded "One Hundred Conventions" campaign sponsored by the New England Anti-Slavery Society. An experienced black lecturer, Remond encountered both racial discrimination and antiabolitionist harassment, and he saw disturbing evidence of racial prejudice among his white associates. Remond described the hazards of the tour in a 27 September 1843 letter to Rochester abolitionists Isaac and Amy Post. Ward, "Charles Lenox Remond," 133–41, 148–52.

Westfield, Indiana
September 27th, 1843

My Very Dear Friends
Isaac & Amy Post:

I am sure I need make nothing in the way of apology for my seeming neglect in writing some one of your dear family[1] agreeable to my promise, other than simply intimate the accident it has been my misfortune to experience, that after my departure from Buffalo in company with our mutually dear friend Frederick.[2] You will remember that in my role connected with his reply to your very friendly letter from Rochester I expressed the desire he would accompany me as far as Oakland, Ohio and if thought best retrace his steps. Well agreeably to our expectations we reached in safety—but were subjected to very considerable expense. After our arrival and consultation with the friends, it was deemed perfectly safe and highly desireable he should meet the appointments as they had been given, and here I would not advise Frederick "pro or con," but leave him to decide as seemed best in his own judgement and he finally concluded to remain a short time and so far as that state was concerned I don't think he felt occasion for regret, but I am digressing. On the morning following our arrival in Oakland, we started in company with a large party of friends for Newport, and being fond of driving, I volunteered to drive a pair of spirited young horses attached to the carriage in which the baggage was placed & had not proceeded two miles from the residence of Dr. Brooke,[3] when one of the horses threw his bridle from his head & bit from his maith & off he went carrying his mate to the top of their speed; the young man with me jumped from the carriage without any serious injury, and [word illegible] finding myself alone and the beasts dashing off at a tremendous pace, I endeavoured to extricate myself, but in doing so was thrown upon the ground with great violence; my head— shoulder & leg was much bruised & my wrist nearly broken—in fact this is my first effort at writing since the accident occurred, this you will grant is sufficient apology and I stand fully & freely exonerated from the charge of neglect or remissness. So the next day, Frederick & myself separated joining our parties as previously arranged, and I regret to add that in Pendleton, George Bradburn[4] & Frederick and W. A. White[5] were shamefully mobbed the two latter being severely injured by clubs— stones—bars &c. They are however all in the field again. On the day before yesterday Sydney[6]—James[7] & myself were mobbed in Nobles- ville[8]—driven by threats and battle away from the court house—the audience consenting at the dictation of the ruffians in broad day light to vacate the court house, no damage was done—nor lives endangered, but liberty was murdered by the cowardly surrender of unquestionable rights on the part of those in peaceable assembly, and what made the matter more glaringly base—the mobbing villains came from a township some sixteen miles distant and actually drove the people of Noblesville from their own quiet meeting and hence I must pronounce it the coolest act of the kind within my recollection of mobocratic history or experience.

At 2 past 12 o'clock this morning Sydney and James in company with a number of friends started for the convention to be holden in India- napolis[9] tomorrow and if reports are to be relied upon sad scenes will take place there—two hundred men have been drilling for the past week on horseback with the avowed determination to burn, kill & distroy if the attempt shall be made to hold the meeting there, by the advice of the friends I remain at this place a day or [two] or until some one reports progress. So much for the capital of the Young Hoosier State, but this horrid state of things should not suprise people when they learn that the second Executive officer of the State of Indiana is himself an actual slaveholder.[10] Shame on the state of Indiana, shame on the sentiment that permits the crying disgrace—much less the hands of those who elevate to office such men, our appointment will detain us some ten or twelve days longer in this state. When we all hope to meet in Cincinnati, should our lives be spared until that time, from which place Frederick himself will in company with James Munroe & Sydney H. Gay travel the remainder of our tour together, W. A. White & George Bradburn taking the other series of conventions together being joined we trust by Jacob Ferris,[11] and the residue of our journeying we hope will be less danger- ous if not less arduous. I cannot even in view of our trials say that I am sorry [I] entered this state inasmuch as the opportunity has been allowed me of forming an acquaintance with many of the members of the Indiana

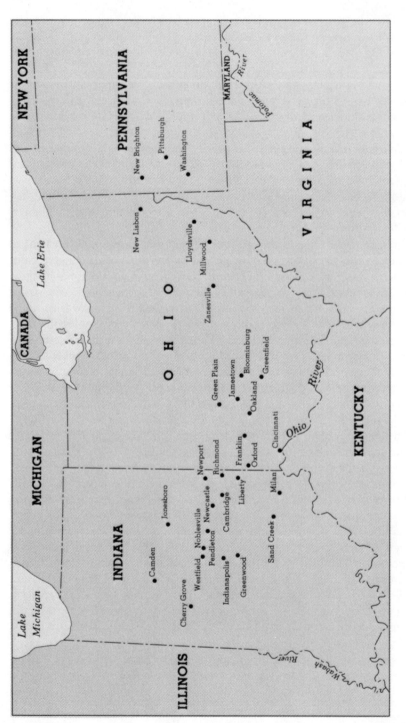

Fig. 2. Charles Lenox Remond and Frederick Douglass's "One Hundred Conventions" lecture tour in the West, 1843

Date	Location	Lecturer(s)
30–31 August	Green Plain, Ohio	Douglass
4–7 September	Oakland, Ohio	Remond & Douglass
11–12	Cambridge, Ind.	Douglass
13	Cherry Grove, Ind.	Remond
14–16	Pendleton, Ind.	Douglass
15–16	Camden, Ind.	Remond
18	Noblesville, Ind.	Douglass
21–23	Jonesboro, Ind.	Remond & Douglass
25	Noblesville, Ind.	Remond
25–26	Newcastle, Ind.	Douglass
27	Westfield, Ind.	Remond
28–29	Richmond, Ind.	Douglass
29	Indianapolis, Ind.	Remond (canceled)
30	Greenwood, Ind.	Remond
2–3 October	Liberty, Ind.	Douglass
3–4	Sand Creek, Ind.	Remond (canceled)
6–7	Oxford, Ohio	Douglass
7–8	Milan, Ind.	Remond
13–14	Franklin, Ohio	Remond & Douglass
15	Jamestown, Ohio	Remond & Douglass
17	Bloomingburg, Ohio	Remond & Douglass
19–20	Greenfield, Ohio	Remond & Douglass
22	Cincinnati, Ohio	Remond
23–24	Zanesville, Ohio	Remond & Douglass
26–27	Millwood, Ohio	Remond & Douglass
30–31	Lloydsville, Ohio	Remond & Douglass
2 November	New Lisbon, Ohio	Douglass
3–4	New Brighton, Pa.	Douglass
3–4	Washington, Pa.	Remond
6–7	Pittsburgh, Pa.	Remond & Douglass

Anti-Slavery Society of Friends[12] & I prize the acquaintances to a high degree and here I want to tell you that at the Anniversary meeting of the State Society held at Jonesboro[13] Friend Stanton[,] Editor of the *Advocate of Free Labor and Antislavery Chronicle*,[14] reported the paper to be in a sinking condition for want of support and charity owing to the large number of Bodyites[15] who have given it up since the division and feeling much interest in the little paper as the hope of the born slave, I pledged myself for five numbers of the paper at $3 each and it would not only relieve me much, but I should be highly gratified could I procure that number of subscribers in Rochester. The paper is an interesting one & especially do I believe your family would be interested in its perusal; I think friend Stanton rather sectarian but that is partially attributable to the limited circulation of his sheet, for as a true friend to the slave my confidence is unshaken in him.

I have written in much pain, but know you will excuse the imperfections. And desiring to be affectionately remembered to the several members of the dear family together with each & all of the kindred & congenial spirits who compose the band diligently laboring for the overthrow of the ever to be detested system of inequity—the counterpart of B———— the prince of devils[16]—the dear friends Burtis,[17] Curtis, Hallowell,[18] [word illegible] & families & too Miss Van Renssalaer as a matter of course. And to the interim Believe me to remain ever Faithfully,

Your Affectionate Friend,

C. Lenox Remond

P.S. I need not say that a reply from you will afford me great pleasure and be equally grateful to Frederick, who shall be a party to its perusal, and if directed in care of Dr. A. Brooke, Oakland, Ohio, will reach me in safety.

Again, Farewell,

From C. L. R.

Isaac and Amy Post Family Papers, Department of Rare Books and Special Collections, Rush-Rhees Library, University of Rochester, Rochester, New York. Published by permission.

1. The Post family was active in Rochester, New York, reform circles. Isaac (1798–1872) and Amy Kirby (1802–1889) Post, both Hicksite Quakers, helped lead the Western New York Anti-Slavery Society. Devoted friends of blacks, they sheltered a steady stream of fugitive slaves and free blacks, like Harriet Jacobs, in their Rochester home. Isaac married Amy, a sister of his deceased first wife, Hannah (?–1827), in 1828. Amy's other sister, Sarah Hallowell Willis (1818–1914), had similar interests in abolitionism and feminism. Mary Post Hallowell was Isaac's child from his first marriage. A farmer-turned-druggist, Isaac converted to Spiritualism in 1848, published the popular volume *Voices from the Spirit World* (1852), and with Amy established a Spiritualist circle. Amy organized antislavery fairs, served as a delegate to American Anti-Slavery Society

conventions, and in 1850 toured the black settlements in Canada West. A committed feminist, she labored to improve conditions for working women, attended the 1848 Seneca Falls Convention, and served as an agent for *Una*, a feminist journal, during the 1850s. "Isaac and Amy Post Family Papers Register," 17, NRU; *DAB*, 15:117; *ACAB*, 5:84; Yellin, *Life of a Slave Girl*, xvi–xvii, 289; Nancy A. Hewitt, *Women's Activism and Social Change: Rochester, New York, 1822–1872* (Ithaca, N.Y., 1984), 61, 93, 116–20, 130–36, 140–43, 167, 184, 190–96, 210–14; William F. Peck, *Semi-Centennial History of the City of Rochester* (Syracuse, N.Y., 1884), 513–18; Lucy N. Coleman, *Reminiscences* (Buffalo, N.Y., 1891), 22–23, 83–85.

2. Frederick Douglass (1818–1895) was born in Maryland and was named Frederick Augustus Washington Bailey. Douglass (the name he assumed after escaping slavery) was the son of an unknown father (possibly his master) and a slave mother, Harriet Bailey. In 1825 Douglass was sent to Baltimore, where he was hired out first as a house servant and later as a ship's caulker. During his years in Baltimore, Douglass acquired the rudiments of an education. Early in September 1838, on his second attempt, he escaped slavery, traveled to New York City, married Anna Murray, a free Baltimore black who had encouraged his flight, and settled in New Bedford, Massachusetts.

Late in 1841, Douglass was appointed as a lecture agent for the Massachusetts Anti-Slavery Society, and he began a long and sometimes controversial career in antislavery reform. Eventually he was regarded by many as the leading black abolitionist spokesman in the United States. Douglass's rapid development as a gifted orator and his growth as an antislavery thinker during the first four years of his career (1841–45) led many to doubt his slave origins. To allay their doubts, Douglass wrote *The Narrative of the Life of Frederick Douglass* (1845), the first of three autobiographies and the most widely read and highly acclaimed piece of slave literature in the nineteenth century. After publishing it, Douglass made a well-received tour of Britain (1845–47) and, during the tour, acquired funds to purchase his freedom and to begin an antislavery newspaper. In spite of contrary advice from many Garrisonians, Douglass founded the reformist weekly the *North Star* (1848–51), a journal that was succeeded by *Frederick Douglass' Paper* (1851–59) and *Douglass' Monthly* (1860–63).

Between 1848 and 1853, Douglass continued to refine his abolitionist thought and parted with essential Garrisonian doctrine by advocating political antislavery and by interpreting the U.S. Constitution as an antislavery document. Like many of his black colleagues, Douglass called for resistance to the Fugitive Slave Law of 1850 and rejected the Dred Scott decision (1857). He was one of the few abolitionists to support John Brown's attempt to stir up an insurrection at Harpers Ferry, Virginia. Although Douglass had criticized blacks who advocated emigration during the 1850s, he briefly embraced the idea in 1860.

At the start of the Civil War, Douglass urged Lincoln to enlist black soldiers in the Union army and to emancipate slaves as a war measure. He became a recruiting agent for the Massachusetts Fifty-fourth and Fifty-fifth regiments. During the 1870s, Douglass moved to Washington, D.C., edited the *New National Era* (1870–74), became an active member of the Republican party, and served as marshal of the District of Columbia (1877–81). He also continued to address the major issues of racial injustice that faced black Americans. During the 1880s,

Douglass served as the city's recorder of deeds (1881–86) and, at the end of the decade, was appointed consul general to Haiti (1890–91). *DANB*, 5:406–7.

3. Dr. Abram Brooke (1806–1867) was the U.S. postmaster of Oakland, Ohio. Brooke and Joseph Dugdale led the Garrisonian secession from the Ohio Anti-Slavery Society in 1842 and helped organize the Western Anti-Slavery Society, an organization in which women filled important leadership roles. Brooke participated in the underground railroad and erected a building on his property to house antislavery meetings. Joseph Anthony Del Porto, "A Study of American Anti-Slavery Journals" (Ph.D. diss., Michigan State College, 1953), 174; Blassingame, *Frederick Douglass Papers*, 2:394–95; Dwight L. Dummond, ed., *Letters of James Gillespie Birney, 1831–1857*, 2 vols. (Washington, D.C., 1938; reprint, Gloucester, Mass., 1966), 2:697, 722–23; Douglas A. Gamble, "Garrisonian Abolitionists in the West: Some Suggestions for Study," *CWH* 23:55–58 (March 1977).

4. George Bradburn (1806–1880), a Unitarian minister and abolitionist, was born in Attleboro, Massachusetts. He advocated women's rights, temperance, peace, and the anti–capital punishment movement. As the Whig state representative from Nantucket (1839–43), he led the fight against the Massachusetts anti-miscegenation law. An agent for the American Anti-Slavery Society, he attended the 1840 World's Anti-Slavery Convention. He accompanied Frederick Douglass during the "One Hundred Conventions" campaign and later coedited the Lynn, Massachusetts, *Pioneer*, the Boston *Chronotype*, and the Cleveland *True Democrat*. He joined the Liberty party in 1844 and campaigned for John C. Frémont in 1856. Blassingame, *Frederick Douglass Papers*, 1:112–13; Garrison and Garrison, *William Lloyd Garrison*, 2:309, 343, 353–54, 378–79, 384, 416, 428, 3:43–45, 60, 461; Merrill and Ruchames, *Letters of William Lloyd Garrison*, 3:19; Ward, "Charles Lenox Remond," 139–41.

5. William Abijah White (1818–1856), born to an established New England family, studied law under Supreme Court Justice Benjamin Curtis but abandoned legal practice for a career as a temperance advocate, reformer, and abolitionist. White edited and published three temperance journals—the *New Englander*, *Excelsior*, and *Washingtonian*. He accompanied Frederick Douglass on the 1843 "One Hundred Conventions" tour. During the Pendleton, Indiana, riot, Douglass charged the platform, club in hand, when he learned that White had been assaulted. White moved to Madison, Wisconsin, in 1854 and chaired the Republican State Committee. The unusual circumstances of his death sparked rumors of suicide. Garrison and Garrison, *William Lloyd Garrison*, 3:101; *Lib*, 5 June 1857; Benjamin Quarles, *Frederick Douglass* (Washington, D.C., 1948), 32.

6. Sydney Howard Gay (1814–1888) lectured for the American Anti-Slavery Society and became editor of the *National Anti-Slavery Standard* in 1844. In 1858 Gay went to the *New York Tribune* and became its managing editor before taking positions with the *Chicago Tribune* and then the *New York Evening Post*. In addition to his newspaper work, Gay published a four-volume history of the United States and a biography of James Madison. *DAB*, 5:195.

7. James Monroe (1821–1898) was born in Plainfield, Connecticut and attended a school taught by Prudence Crandall. Between 1841 and 1844, he lectured for the American Anti-Slavery Society and enlisted in the "One Hundred Conventions" campaign. An 1846 graduate of Oberlin College, he eventually

married a daughter of Charles G. Finney and taught at the college (1849–62, 1883–96). Monroe served in the Ohio legislature (1856–62), became U.S. consul and chargé d'affaires at Rio de Janeiro (1863–69), and sat in the U.S. Congress (1871–81). *BDAC*, 1424; James H. Fairchild, "Retirement of Professor Monroe," *OR*, 24 June 1896; James Monroe file, OO.

8. On 25 September 1843, a mob, outraged by the presence of a black speaker, drove Remond and his colleagues from the courthouse at Noblesville, Indiana. Members of the mob acted with the approval of the local sheriff and the assistance of several devout Baptists and Quakers. Raimund E. Goerler, "Family, Self, and Anti-Slavery: Sydney Howard Gay and the Abolitionist Commitment" (Ph.D. diss., Case Western Reserve University, 1975), 205–6.

9. Remond was originally scheduled to speak on 29 September 1843 at an Indianapolis antislavery convention. But several of his white colleagues on the "One Hundred Conventions" tour persuaded him to avoid the city, believing that the intensity of racist and antiabolitionist feeling there endangered his life. *Lib*, 20 October 1843.

10. Remond refers to Jesse D. Bright (1812–1875), lieutenant governor of Indiana from 1843 to 1845. Although not a slaveholder, he supported slavery and was a close friend of slaveholding Kentucky politicians Henry Clay and John C. Breckinridge. He later sat in the U.S. Senate (1845–62) but was expelled when suspected of disloyalty during the Civil War. *DAB*, 3:45–46.

11. Jacob Ferris participated in the 1843 "One Hundred Conventions" campaign, lectured in New York and the West for the American Anti-Slavery Society, and acted as lecturer and fund-raiser for the Ohio Anti-Slavery Society. His moral outrage against slavery and his attacks on the American clergy brought him attention on the lecture circuit. He adopted the position unpopular among Garrisonians in 1840 that the Constitution was an antislavery document. Ward, "Charles Lenox Remond," 133; *Lib*, 17 March, 29 September 1843; *PF*, 24 December 1840.

12. Remond refers to the Indiana Yearly Meeting of Anti-Slavery Friends, which was formed in February 1843 after the conservative leadership of the Indiana Yearly Meeting of Friends ejected eight members for their antislavery activities. Some two thousand Quakers, forming about 10 percent of the membership, seceded from the parent body to join the new organization. Centered in Newport, a hub of Quaker abolitionism in eastern Indiana, the IYMASF required its members to adhere to free produce principles and pressured them and other Quakers to join antislavery organizations and vote for antislavery candidates. As these efforts slowly radicalized their more conservative brethren, most antislavery Quakers drifted back to the parent body. The separate yearly meeting disbanded in 1857. Thomas E. Drake, *Quakers and Slavery in America* (New Haven, Conn., 1950), 165–74; Elbert Russell, *The History of Quakerism* (New York, N.Y., 1942), 365–69.

13. The fifth anniversary meeting of the Indiana State Anti-Slavery Society convened at Jonesboro, Indiana, during 21–23 September 1843. The gathering, which was characterized by "a fractious spirit," was thrown into greater turmoil by a confrontation between Remond, Frederick Douglass, and George Bradburn, ostensibly over parliamentary procedure. The society had been formed in September 1838 with two objectives—to awaken public outrage against slavery and

to elevate free blacks. Its members quickly established dozens of local societies and women's auxiliaries, particularly in the Quaker settlements of eastern Indiana. Although initially opposed to independent antislavery politics, the ISASS embraced the Liberty party in the early 1840s. But it soon waned and was moribund by 1847. *Lib*, 29 September, 20 October 1843; Abram Brooke to Maria Weston Chapman, 15 October 1843, Anti-Slavery Collection, MB; Marion C. Miller, "The Anti-Slavery Movement in Indiana" (Ph.D. diss., University of Michigan, 1938), 66–84, 125.

14. Benjamin Stanton of Newport (now Fountain City), Indiana, was a merchant, underground railroad activist, free produce advocate, and prominent figure in the Indiana Yearly Meeting of Anti-Slavery Friends during the 1840s. Stanton and Henry H. Way, a local Quaker physician, edited the *Free Labor Advocate and Anti-Slavery Chronicle* in Newport from 1841 to 1848. Established to advance the free produce cause in the West, the weekly journal published antislavery news and consistently opposed racial prejudice. Following the 1842–43 schism that divided Indiana Quakers, the *Free Labor Advocate* became the organ of the Indiana Yearly Meeting of Anti-Slavery Friends. Ruth K. Nuermberger, *The Free Produce Movement: A Quaker Protest against Slavery* (Durham, N.C., 1942), 32, 49, 104; Levi Coffin, *Reminiscences*, 2d ed. (Cincinnati, Ohio, 1880), 194, 271; *PF*, 6 November 1845, 2 November 1848.

15. Remond refers to those Quakers who remained in the Indiana Yearly Meeting of Friends, rather than joining the Indiana Yearly Meeting of Anti-Slavery Friends, during the 1842–43 schism. They were frequently called "body members." Nuermberger, *Free Produce Movement*, 105n.

16. Remond refers to Beelzebub, a demon in Christian tradition, who is called "the prince of devils" in Matthew 12:24.

17. Remond refers to Sarah A. (1810–1900) and Lewis B. Burtis (1793–1868), a stove manufacturer, who were Quaker members of the Rochester circle of abolitionists who dominated the Western New York Anti-Slavery Society. The Burtises supported women's rights, temperance, and racial equality and used their home as a refuge for fugitive slaves. They joined the Post family in the Spiritualist movement during the 1850s but dropped out of reform activities after the Civil War. Sarah Burtis, a cousin of Susan B. Anthony, served as secretary at the 1848 Seneca Falls Convention. *RPE*, 30 October 1900; *RDC*, 2 November 1900; Hewitt, *Women's Activism and Social Change*, 117, 160–69, 187, 190, 209–10, 231; Merrill and Ruchames, *Letters of William Lloyd Garrison*, 4:111.

18. William (ca. 1816–1882) and Mary Post (1823–1913) Hallowell of Rochester were active abolitionists. They belonged to the Western New York Anti-Slavery Society, and their home became a stop for fugitive slaves during the 1850s. Mary, the daughter of Isaac and Hannah Post, attended the 1848 Seneca Falls Convention and became a close friend of Susan B. Anthony. She participated in the American Equal Rights Association, the National Woman Suffrage Association, and a variety of local feminist organizations. Mary worked for the *National Anti-Slavery Standard* after the Civil War. Hewitt, *Women's Activism and Social Change*, 61, 131, 162, 209, 214; *RDC*, 8 March 1913.

63.
Antislavery and the Black Clergy

Samuel Ringgold Ward to John A. Murray
10 November 1843

Henry Highland Garnet to Charles Hall
28 June 1844

Black abolitionist ministers used their pulpits to spread the antislavery message. In the process, they often strained their relations with national churches and religious organizations. Samuel R. Ward and Henry Highland Garnet were active political abolitionists as well as clergymen. Both received small subsidies from the American Home Missionary Society, which criticized them for "preaching politics on the Sabbath." Ward and Garnet defended their conduct in letters to AHMS officials. In his 10 November 1843 letter, Ward emphasized the Christian duty to speak out against all "national sins," including slavery. Garnet wrote on 28 June 1844 that he regretted that he had not done more for the slave, and he terminated his affiliation with the AHMS. McKivigan, *War against Proslavery Religion*, 112–15; Quarles, *Black Abolitionists*, 183–85.

Geneva, [New York]
Nov[ember] 10, 1843

Rev. J. A. Murray[1]
Dear Sir:

Having heard that some objections arose in the Home Missionary Board,[2] the other day, to my appointment, on the ground of doubts as to my political sentiments, and my preaching politics on the Sabbath &c., it seemed to me, but just that I should say in a word what the truth is on this point.

In preaching now, as heretofore, I frequently speak of national sins. Of course, I mention slavery among them. I call upon the people to do all in their power at the ballot box & elsewhere for the removal of this sin, or to expect the severe judgements of God for its continuance. I frequently say that since slavery is admitted to be a sinful institution that a man is no more at liberty (morally) to vote for it than he is to pray for it.

When the duty of doing all to the glory of God is under ~~consideration~~ consideration I sometimes demand that a man should glorify God, or at least endeavor to glorify God, in his civil relations as well and as much as elsewhere.

I preach that a man has no more right to commit sin with his vote, than with any other power or instrument. I plead for no party, no candidates, against no party, against no candidates, means nor measures on the Sabbath. But what I have described in the foregoing lines I do and shall preach, because I think it duty to rebuke all sins, and to plead for righteousness every where.

If the Board deem it best not to appoint me I submit to their decision, only asking that I may have a fair and a plain statement of the reason why I am not appointed.

Your humble servant,

Saml. R. Ward

American Home Missionary Society Papers, Amistad Research Center, Tulane University, New Orleans, Louisiana. Published by permission.

Troy, N[ew] Y[ork]
June 28, 1844

Rev. C. Hall[3]
Dear Bro. Hall:

At a meeting of our Presbytery a letter which you sent to Rev. Mr. Noble was read. You state in that communication that it had been reported that I had been much engaged in political action, and you therefore hesitate to renew my commission.[4] I send this letter to [word crossed out] inform your committee that I withdraw my request.

It is true that I am an abolitionist, and when I speak of politicts I recommend all not to strengthen the Slave power. I have lifted up my feeble voice for my oppressed brethren—and what more or less could I do? My own kindred are this moment in Slavery—and I must speak for them—and do all that I can to break off their chains. This is all my crime. I hope the day will come when the American H. M. Society will not urge such an excuse. While I live I will raise my voice for Liberty. I am sorry that I have done so little. If I had a thousand lives I would spend them all for my bleeding people—for God tells me to remember them.

If it is thought that the $50. which I received the last year was improperly given I will refund the money. I have only to say that my conscience is void of offence in this matter. I have done nothing more than I would desire that others should do for me in like circumstances.

Yours truly in Christian love,

Henry H. Garnet

American Home Missionary Society Papers, Amistad Research Center, Tulane University, New Orleans, Louisiana. Published by permission.

1. John A. Murray (1800–1876), a Presbyterian clergyman and evangelist, received his ministerial training at Princeton Seminary. After serving several congregations in New York City, he functioned from 1834 to 1868 as secretary of

the Geneva, New York, agency of the American Home Missionary Society. In that capacity, he helped determine who would receive AHMS aid. With few exceptions, the New York City committee sanctioned the actions of the Geneva agency without question. Roberts, *Biographical Catalogue of Princeton Seminary*, 43; Griffin, *Their Brothers' Keepers*, 84.

2. Ward refers to the executive committee of the American Home Missionary Society. The society was organized in 1826 by a circle of Presbyterian and Congregationalist leaders. Designed to subsidize the incomes of pastors serving poorer congregations throughout the United States, the society raised funds and strictly supervised the ministers it aided. By 1837 eight hundred clergymen were affiliated with the AHMS. The society prospered until the mid-1840s, when its persistent reluctance to criticize slavery prompted abolitionists to found the rival American Missionary Association. The AHMS gradually strengthened its stance on slavery and in 1856 refused to aid congregations admitting slaveholders. The society supported missionary work in the South after the Civil War. Griffin, *Their Brothers' Keepers*, xi, 31, 46, 64–65, 77, 83–85, 114, 177–91, 262–63.

3. Charles Hall (1799–1853), an 1827 graduate of Princeton Seminary, became assistant secretary in the New York City office of the American Home Missionary Society. From 1838 until his death, he served as the society's chief secretary. In that position, he examined applications for aid, made recommendations, and kept track of aided ministers. He consistently urged the AHMS to avoid political controversy and instructed aided clergy to keep "strictly to the work of preaching the Gospel." Roberts, *Biographical Catalogue of Princeton Seminary*, 37; Griffin, *Their Brothers' Keepers*, 75, 183.

4. On 6 June 1844, Charles Hall wrote to Jonathan H. Noble, a member of the missions committee of the Troy Presbytery, asking about the propriety of renewing the American Home Missionary Society grant to Garnet. Noble (1804–1896), a Presbyterian clergyman trained at Princeton Seminary, served a congregation at Schaghticoke, New York (1837–69). In the letter, Hall voiced concern about Garnet's antislavery and civil rights activism, arguing that it was "inexpedient for ministers to be prominent actors in political matters" and expressing his unwillingness to appropriate funds for Garnet's support. Noble read the letter at the June meeting of the Troy Presbytery. De Boer, "Afro-Americans in American Missionary Association," 60, 587n; Roberts, *Biographical Catalogue of Princeton Seminary*, 46.

64.
William Jones to the United States Congress
28 December 1843

The lives of southern free blacks symbolized the precarious social and legal status of all black Americans. In the nation's capital, as in the southern states, complexion was considered prima facie evidence of one's status as a slave. Any free black could be seized as a fugitive, and responsibility was "fixed upon the person of color to prove his freedom." When William Jones, a free black sailor visited the capital in early December 1843, he was arrested and jailed as a fugitive slave. Jones claimed that he had been unjustly seized. Because Congress governed the District of Columbia, Jones petitioned the House of Representatives to prevent federal marshals from selling him into slavery to recover the cost of his imprisonment. The Ohio abolitionist and congressman, Joshua R. Giddings, introduced Jones's petition on 28 December. Southern representatives sought to dismiss the petition, but they failed and were drawn into a wide-ranging, contentious debate on slavery's relationship to the federal government. The House referred the petition to its judiciary committee, where it died the following month. Jones spent at least two months in a Washington, D.C., jail before winning his freedom without congressional assistance. *P*, 10 January 1844; *Congressional Globe*, 28 Dec. 1843, 80; 3 Jan. 1844, 85–89; 15 Jan. 1844, 144.

To the Congress of the United States:

The humble petition of, William Jones,[1] now a prisoner in the United States jail, in Washington city,[2] respectfully represents:

That your memorialist is a free citizen of the United States, born free in the State of Virginia, and has always been an industrious and honest citizen, chargeable with no crime; that, while enjoying his liberty in this city, he was seized, and, without any charge of crime, was thrown into jail, where he has been confined for several weeks, and is now advertised to be sold as a slave by the Marshal of the United States to pay the expenses of his imprisonment, unless his owner shall appear; that your petitioner has no owner but his God, and owes no service but to his country; that it is hard for him to be imprisoned without fault, and then sold to pay the expense.[3] He therefore prays that Congress will exert their powers for the protection of the weak, and procure for him that liberty and justice which are his right, and which he has a special claim for in the District, which is under the exclusive legislation of your honorable body.

his

WILLIAM   X   JONES

mark

Witness: D. A. HALL[4]

Washington Jail, *December* 28, 1843

Congressional Globe, (Washington, D.C.) 28 December 1843, 80.

1. William Jones (1818–?), a freeborn mulatto, lived near Richmond, Virginia, and worked as a hand aboard schooners that traversed the Chesapeake. *PF*, 1 February 1844.

2. The Washington County Jail on Judiciary Square was built in 1830 to house debtors, slaves awaiting resale, and those charged with violations of federal law. Although constructed to hold eighty to one hundred prisoners, frequently three times that number were crowded into the structure. Overcrowding and unsanitary conditions prompted one official to describe the jail as "little better than the black hole of Calcutta." Constance McLaughlin Green, *Washington: Village and Capital, 1800–1878* (Princeton, N.J., 1962), 90–91, 165, 252.

3. A 1719 law expressly authorized the jailing of any black unable to prove his freedom. Even free blacks who verified their status could be sold by Alexander Hunter, the presidentially appointed U.S. marshal for the District of Columbia (1834–48), if they were unable to pay the expense of their incarceration. Although blacks and white abolitionists protested this practice, it continued until the end of the Civil War. Constance McLaughlin Green, *The Secret City: A History of Race Relations in the Nation's Capital* (Princeton, N.J., 1967), 28–29; *Washington City Directory*, 1834–48.

4. David A. Hall (1795–1870) practiced law in Washington, D.C., from the 1820s through the Civil War. He also wrote several respected legal histories. Hall was a close friend and supporter of Daniel Webster and served as secretary of the Whig National Committee during the 1852 presidential election campaign. A neighbor of abolitionist editor Gamaliel Bailey, he opposed slavery, represented local free blacks threatened with enslavement, and purchased many local slaves to keep them from being sold away from their families and friends. Douglass Zevely, "Old Houses on C Street and Those Who Lived There," *RCHS* 5:166–70 (1901); Harlow, *Gerrit Smith*, 291–95.

65.
James McCune Smith to Horace Greeley
29 January 1844

Black abolitionists waged a constant battle against proslavery propaganda. One of the well-worn arguments for southern slavery was the myth of black dependency—that blacks could not adequately care for themselves and therefore could live better in slavery than in freedom. Secretary of State John C. Calhoun drew on statistics from the 1840 census to conclude that freedom had brought northern blacks "vice and pauperism" as well as increased physical and mental illness. James McCune Smith, a New York City physician and author, petitioned the U.S. Senate to review the census and correct the erroneous statistics on free blacks in the North. He also appealed to a broader, popular audience—the readership of the *New York Tribune*—with a series of essays published in early 1844 entitled "Freedom and Slavery for Afric-Americans." In these essays, Smith cited the 1840 census and other statistical sources to refute the claims of proslavery advocates. *Lib*, 31 May 1844 [4:0817–18]; *NASS*, 1 February 1844 [4:0749]; *P*, 12 March 1845.

New York, [New York]
January 29, 1844

To the editor of the Tribune:[1]

Figures cannot be charged with fanaticism. Like the everlasting hills, they give cold, silent evidence, unmoved by the clouds and shadows of whatever present may surround them. Let us see what they say of the *Vital statistics* of the slaves of the South, and of the free blacks of the North. There are one of the preliminary remarks necessary to enable us to judge of this matter: they relate to what statists call the "disturbing influences." It is generally assumed that the rigor of the northern winter is more destructive to the Afric-American constitution than the milder influence of the southern clime. How much should be allowed for this, I am at a loss to say; by the late census, however, the free colored population of the northern and southern States have nearly an equal percentage above 36 years of age not more than 1.12 per cent being in favor of the South. But this small percentage is more than balanced by the facility with which colored men and women turn white at the North. The keen and practised eyes of Southern men can instantly detect the most remote admixture of African blood; and interest and pride urge them to exercise a rigid conservatism. But here at the North, the boundary line is less distinct; the colored white has merely to change his place of abode, cut his old associates, and courtesy will do the rest—he is a white.[2] There is not a path in literature or science in our State, in which I could not point out very distinguished colored men. Of one hundred boys who attended with me the New York African Free School in 1826–7,[3] I could name six now living—all white.

There is another "disturbing influence." You have probably heard of the great Anglo-Saxon race, the Irish people and the Berserkirs. You have also heard of their indomitable energy which overwhelms all opposing obstacles—and races. During the last thirty years, the northern States have been the scene of a silent struggle. The combatants have been, and are, on the one hand the great Anglo-Saxon race, and the Irish people and the Berserkirs (I have borrowed the name from Mr. Emerson),[4] having in their possession "the arts of war and peace," their numbers swelled by an immigration of 23,000 per year, which has fallen into rank and file by naturalization and enfranchising laws—on the other hand, are the free blacks, taught to believe themselves naturally inferior, barely admitted to common school instruction, shut out from the temples of higher literature, and taunted with ignorance, barred from the jury bench, and driven from what are called churches, yet branded with impiety. This has been no trifling conflict. The Indian race have perished in a like encounter. It has severely tried the vitality of the free blacks, whilst the slaves of the South have had no such battle to fight in their struggle for bread. This should show the percentage of longevity in favor of the slaves, other things being equal.

The Texan slave trade,[5] or migration, consisted chiefly of slaves under 36. The voluntary migration to Canada of the runaway slaves[6] (about 10,000) has also consisted chiefly of a class of persons under 36 years of age. Both of these disturbing influences would throw the balance of longevity largely in favor of the slaves from the South; for the medium ages being diminished, the extremes should be greater.

Longevity is an admitted test of relative condition. Take two classes of persons, equal in other respects, and place them in like condition, their longevity will be equal; place the same classes of persons in different condition and that condition which yields less longevity will be the *worse* condition. By the census of 1840, it appears that there are of *Free colored in the free States*,

Males	Females
Aged 36 and under 55–16.12 per ct.	15.62 per ct.
" 55 and under 100–6.5 per ct.	7.1 per ct.

Slaves

Males	Females
Aged 36 and under 55–11.65 per ct.	11.22 per ct.
" 55 and under 100–4.11 per ct.	4. per ct.

That is to say:

Free colored of 36 and under 100–22.68 per cent.
Slaves of 36 and under 100–   15.49 per cent.
Difference   7.19

Here we find that whilst 22.68 per cent of the free black population of the North live beyond 36 years of age, only 15.49 per cent of the slaves of the South pass that period of life; showing a difference of 7.19 per cent in favor of the longevity, *i.e.* of the *condition* of the free blacks. And as the only difference between these classes of population is that the one is free, and the other enslaved, it follows that slavery has actually destroyed at the very least 7.19 per cent of the slave population. Had the slaves been in no worse condition than the free blacks of the North, instead of numbering only 2,487,355 in June 1840, they would have numbered 2,666,440; the difference, 179,085, having been MURDERED by the system of slavery. What mockery it is for men to talk of kindness of masters in taking care of aged slaves, when death has relieved them of so large a share of the burden! Have not the northern States a right, in view of this awful fact, to call upon the South to emancipate her slaves so that she may "do no murder?" If a hundred thousand dollars, sunk in the mire of repudiation, is sufficient cause for great and pious men to whine about, what rush of sympathy is sufficiently rapid, what language is temperate, which pleads for the loss of a hundred thousand human lives, cut off in their prime, and blasted from all usefulness? This is no accidental result of a single census; by reference to Professor Tucker's very able work on the *Progress of population,* &c. (Press of Hunt's Merchant's Magazine, N.Y.),[7] it will be seen that in the census of 1820 and 1830, the same percentage of the slave population, only 15 per cent live beyond the age of 36 years, whilst the free black population has steadily improved its percentage beyond that period of life from 17 per cent to 22.68 per cent.

Here, then, is evidence from unprejudiced witnesses, that the free blacks of the North are *not* worse off than the slaves of the South, and that the former have gradually improved in longevity; that is, in the comforts of life, since their emancipation. As a portion of these comforts must be food and clothing, it is a fair inference that they are not worse fed, nor clothed than are the slaves.

There is corroborative evidence in the annals of this city. Dr. Niles[8] states that in 1824, 5, and 6, the deaths among the free black population of this city, were 1 in 18.88. By the city inspector's report for 1840, I find that the deaths of the same class were only 1 in 32.16. Slavery was abolished, or terminated in New York in 1827; and a large proportion of those who died in 1825, &c. were slaves recently emancipated. These facts prove that within fifteen years after it became a free State, a portion of the free black population of New York have improved the ratio of their mortality 13.28 per cent, a fact without parallel in the history of any people.

It is a prevalent opinion that emancipation has made the free blacks deaf, dumb, blind, idiots, insane, &c. &c. The *Southern Literary Messenger* has quite a pretty theory on this subject, based upon certain statements, announced as facts,[9] in the census of 1840.[10] An editor at Buffalo, and subsequently Dr. Jarvis of Dorchester, Massachusetts, have demolished that theory by proving that the statements announced in the census were not facts.[11] Those statements made Maine a very mad house, yet they contradict themselves in the following manner. In that State, saith the census of 1840:

Towns	Total col'd inhab.	Col'd insane.
Limmerick	0	4
Lymington	1	2
Searboro	0	6
Poland	0	2
Dixfield	0	4
Calais	0	1
Total	1	19

To make nineteen crazy men out of one man, is pretty fair calculation even for "down east." The census is equally incorrect as to the proportion of deaf, dumb, &c. Freedom has not made us mad; it has strengthened our minds by throwing us upon our own resources, and has bound us to American institutions with a tenacity which nothing but death can overcome. Very gratefully yours,

JAMES McCUNE SMITH

No. III

In regard to the intellectual statistics of the slaves, it is well known that the laws of all the slave States, by heavy penalties—in some, *death*, for the second offense—prohibit the teaching of the slaves to read. In Ohio and the northwestern States, there is no such law, nor is there any public provision for the instruction of colored children; yet there are many schools, supported by the people of color, in those States. All the free States, east of Ohio, afford public instruction, alike to white and colored children.

Who are worse off, the slaves, whose children are doomed to brutal ignorance, or the few blacks of the North, the offspring of whom are for the most part permitted to enjoy common school education? The answer depends on the extent to which the parents of the latter embrace their superior privileges. In our own State, to a population of 50,000, there are twenty-two public schools for colored children. In this city, to a population of about 17,000, there are seven public and four private schools for colored children, with two exceptions, taught by colored teachers. The average attendance of colored children at the public schools, by the last report, was 1,031 per day. From a document issued by the board of trustees of the public schools (in March 1842), I have carefully made the following statement of the relative standing of the boys in the 8th and 9th classes: Number 1 being best, 2 good, &c. &c.

	White boys.	Colored boys.
Reading	2.18	2.50
Punctuation	2.59	1.75
Spelling	2.31	2.50
Definition	3.03	3.25
Arithmetic	1.87	2.25
Grammar	2.73	2.50
Geography	1.75	2.00
Astronomy	1.66	2.00
Slate Writing	2.46	2.00
Paper Writing	2.71	3.00
	———	
Total average	2.32	2.47

showing a difference of .15, about 1/7, in favor of the white boys.

The whole number of schools among the free black population of the North is 66. There are a large number of colored youth attending white schools; some of them are pursuing the higher branches of education at Oberlin, Western Theological Seminary, Lafayette College, Dartmouth College, and Oneida Institute.[12] There are, in the free States, sixteen colored literary societies, with libraries varying from 100 to 1,400 volumes; and there are one semi-monthly and three weekly papers, edited by colored men, and devoted to the advancement of the people of color.[13] There are also one hundred and nineteen benevolent societies. All these schools, &c. have been established within the last forty years. Have the free black population made no improvement since the emancipation? If it be true that we have not yet produced any literature worthy the name, it is because we are waiting for Anglo-Americans to lead the way. The next subject is

Religious Statistics.

African churches in the slave States   24
African churches in the free States   114

(*United States Gazette; History of the African Methodist Episcopal Church*, by the Rev. Christopher Rush, New York, 1843).[14] Including bond and free, the whole colored population of the slave States is 2,702,920; the colored population of the free States is 170,718. The African churches in the slave States are, nearly all of them, the property of the free colored population of those States; but, granting them *all* to the slaves, there are in the slave States, one church to 112,620 slaves, in the free States, one church to 1,580 free blacks. Of the colored churches in the free States, 103 have been erected within 43 years. It is true that these churches have not quite so much of the "temple made with hands," as may be seen in some Broadway edifices, yet they are endowed, in one respect at least, with a more Catholic spirit—they are "no respecters of persons."[15]

It may be thought that I underrate the religious advantages of the slaves, because the Methodist and some other churches reckon many thousands of slaves in their communion. But these churches grant nothing but *oral instruction* to the slaves, whom they do not teach to read the Bible. And may I not be excused from calling that "Christian fellowship," which expressly denies the common rights of men to those whom they have enrolled as brethren? Are those churches, wherein bishops, priests and deacons, ministers, and preachers who

Perfusi sanie vittas atroque veneno,[16]

their hands bound and their utterance choked, whilst in their ministrations before the altar, not of God, but of slavery, they croak the changes upon *"Servants obey your masters?"*[17] Such are the churches in the slave States, with one exception; let it be written upon every Protestant brow, for that one is the Roman Catholic Church—her doors, and her consolations are open alike to black and white, bond and free! She alone does not make, in the church militant, distinctions, which it were blasphemy to predicate of the church triumphant.[18]

In view of the schools, churches, and benevolent institutions organized *by her free black population, under the genial smile of emancipation,* may not the North affectionately, earnestly, and reasonably call upon the South to follow the example? This question has additional force when we find that a blessing has followed those of the free States, which have acted justly towards their free black population. New York, led on by her Murrays, Jays, and Tompkins—Massachusetts yielding to the common-sense argument of Paul Cuffe, and Rhode Island, urged by a bloodless revolution, have pre-eminently encouraged and fostered their free black population; and these are noble States and prosperous, their sons need be proud of them in either hemisphere or any clime. Pennsylvania, in 1838, cruelly disfranchised her free colored people, and in 1843, she became bankrupt. Men who look deeper than the surface of things will perceive in the former act a moral obliquity, to which the latter was a necessary sequence.[19]

I now, respectfully, submit the case. Let the public judge whether it be made out. If to have a right over his own person be better than to be deprived of that right, if to possess his own wife be better than to hold her at another's will, if to enjoy common school privileges be better than the doom of brutal ignorance, if to sit under his own gospel vine be better than to listen to alien adjurations to passive obedience,[20] if to live long in the land be better than to be cut off in life's early prime, then the free blacks of the North are *not* worse off than the slaves of the South. The evidence is altogether in favor of emancipation.

Much has been said about the free black population of the North filling the almshouses. Some inquiry enables me to state that most of them to be found in these almshouses are those who have escaped, maimed, halt, or blind, from the slavery of the South, or remain from the slavery of our now free States. In 183[6] the free colored people of Philadelphia paid into the poor fund of that city $500 more than was required to support colored paupers living at the public expense. In the city of New York, the colored population is to the white as 1 to 18.1; of 3,089 persons in the almshouse department on Saturday, January 20, 1844, there were 198 colored persons, about 1 colored to 15.5 white. In the lunatic asylum, December 23, 1843, there were 278 white and 17 colored patients, or 1 colored to 17 white; taking into account the number of whites in private institutions, it would seem that there is less insanity among the colored than the white population.

I cannot conclude without pointing out two sources of the errors which many commit in judging of the free black population. One is that men, ignorant of our actual condition, and hindered by their prejudices, from inquiring thereinto, gather their opinions of us from specimens visible in the Five Points—they seem satisfied by a single glance at the "deformed leg."[21] Again, men of narrow views and limited information are apt to conceive that society and refinement are confined to the little heaven in which they are privileged to "thunder," regarding all as outcasts—*barbaroi*[22]—who are not embraced within their charmed environ; such men cannot perceive that there is around every intelligent "home" all the elements of refined manners and dignified deportment. There are, thank heaven, a thousand such homes among the free blacks of the free States—homes in which the sounds of "my wife, my child, my mother, my father, *my Bible*," and their thousand clustering joys, weave the sweet harmonies of content and happiness. We toil hard for these, but we toil willingly, with stout and hopeful hearts. And if, occasionally, one from "wandering to and fro over the face of the earth" be sent among us, to try us with the affliction of a Parthian warfare,[23] we shall be found at our post, ready and willing to give an account of the faith that is in us—a faith which holds first to the Bible, and secondly to American institutions, which have made us free, which will free our brethren in bonds, and which will be triumphant in pulling down the strongholds of tyranny throughout our globe.

I sincerely thank you, Mr. Editor, for your kind liberality in publishing these letters without money or price, but with perfect typographical accuracy. With your clear head and sound heart, long may you preside over the *Tribune* of the people. Very gratefully yours,

JAMES McCUNE SMITH

Erratum—In my last letter, instead of 13.28, I should have said 75 per cent improvement in the ratio of mortality of the colored people, in this city, in 15 years.

National Anti-Slavery Standard (New York, N.Y.), 8 February, 18 April 1844.

1. Horace Greeley (1811–1872) founded the *New York Tribune* in 1841. Under his editorial guidance, it became the most influential American newspaper of the mid-nineteenth century, reflecting his Whig politics and opposition to slavery. Greeley's support of westward expansion, as embodied in his famous exhortation, "Go West, young man," and the publication of numerous articles on agriculture attracted a wide following in the Midwest, in addition to the concentrated readership in the Northeast. In 1872 Greeley ran unsuccessfully against Ulysses S. Grant for the presidency. *DAB*, 7:528–34; Mott, *American Journalism*, 267–78.

2. Smith refers to a phenomenon known as passing. Light-skinned mulattoes often dropped out of sight, moved to a new city or neighborhood, and allowed their new neighbors to assume that they were white. Because of its secretive nature, it is difficult to determine how often passing occurred, but it was a frequent theme in black literature of the time, most notably Frank J. Webb's *The Garies and Their Friends* (1857). Williamson, *New People*, 100–103.

3. New York City's first African Free School was opened by the New York Manumission Society in 1787 as part of its effort to encourage gradual emancipation. Charles Andrews, an English pedagogue, operated the school from 1809 to 1832, instructing Smith and dozens of other future black abolitionists. A second facility opened in 1820 to accommodate expanding enrollments. The two schools initially enjoyed the support of the local black community, but blacks repudiated the school in 1830 after Andrews voiced support for the American Colonization Society. Growing protest eventually forced his retirement and the hiring of black teachers. Five other African Free Schools were opened in the city during the early 1830s. In 1853 they all became part of New York City's public school system. John L. Rury, "The New York African Free School, 1827–1836: Conflict over Community Control of Black Education," *Phy* 44:187–98 (September 1983); Walker, "Afro-American in New York City," 65–77.

4. The white population of antebellum America consisted largely of individuals who traced their ancestry to the British Isles and the German-speaking areas of northern Europe. Smith uses the term *Berserkir* to refer to people of German background. The term, derived from an Old Norse word meaning "bear shirt," was frequently used by Ralph Waldo Emerson to describe the Germanic tribes

that invaded England in the fifth century. German, British, and Irish immigrants poured into the northern United States in increasing numbers during the antebellum period. As Smith indicates, the rate of immigration had reached 23,322 a year at the time of the 1830 census, but it turned into a flood in the 1840s. Compared to free blacks, these newcomers were quickly integrated into the political and economic spheres of American life. William H. Gilman, Alfred R. Ferguson, Merrell R. Davis, et al., eds., *The Journals and Miscellaneous Notebooks of Ralph Waldo Emerson*, 11 vols. (Cambridge, Mass., 1960–75), 5:100, 109, 153, 217, 10:184, 11:157.

5. Texas independence in 1836, and the resulting campaign for annexation by the United States, dramatically increased the volume of the Texas slave trade. There were only 5,000 slaves in Texas in 1836, but the number jumped to 30,000 by 1845 and 58,000 five years later. Although some slaves were illegally imported into Texas from foreign sources, the majority came from other parts of the South and were shipped to the eastern third of the state. Texas was the fastest-growing slave state by the Civil War. *DAAS*, 724–31.

6. The rate of black migration to Canada grew quickly after the 1820s, motivated in large part by racial violence and the declining status of blacks in the United States. The vast majority settled in Canada West (now Ontario). An 1843 estimate placed the total black population of Canada West at twenty thousand, most of whom were former slaves and their families. John K. A. Farrell, "Schemes for the Transplanting of Refugee American Negroes from Upper Canada in the 1840s," *OntH* 52:245 (1960); Ripley et al., *Black Abolitionist Papers*, 2:9.

7. George Tucker's *Progress of the United States in Population and Wealth in Fifty Years* (1843) was published in New York City by Hunt's Magazine Press. The volume employed data from the 1790 through 1840 censuses in a provocative examination of society in the early American nation. Tucker (1775–1861), a Virginia politician and social theorist, paid particular attention to statistics on blacks, and two of his conclusions contributed to the debate over slavery. First, he contended that America's burgeoning population would decrease the value of labor and naturally "extinguish" slavery by the twentieth century. Second, he noted more cases of incarceration for insanity per capita among northern than southern blacks. Although Tucker urged others to employ the data with caution, proslavery theorists quickly used the latter finding to support their argument that slavery was a positive good. *DAB*, 19:28–30.

8. Hezekiah Niles (1777–1839) reached a national audience through *Niles' Weekly Register*, which he edited and published in Baltimore from 1811 until his death. Although he was an outspoken advocate of gradual abolition, union, and economic nationalism, the paper achieved a reputation for consistently publishing facts, statistics, speeches, and documents on both sides of political and economic questions. *DAB*, 13:521–22; Mott, *American Journalism*, 188.

9. The *Southern Literary Messenger*, a monthly journal published in Richmond from 1834 to 1864, was a leading defender of the South, slavery, and southern beliefs about black inability to cope with freedom. "Reflections on the Census of 1840," a lengthy unsigned article in the June 1843 issue of the *Messenger*, used census figures to argue that free blacks were given to insanity, vice, and

crime. The author predicted that emancipation would lead to the most destructive consequences. Mott, *History of American Magazines,* 629–57.

10. The sixth federal decennial census of the United States was compiled in 1840. The first census to enumerate the mentally ill and mentally retarded, it reported the proportion of "insane and idiots" to be nearly eleven times higher among free blacks than among slaves. These figures provided southern proslavery congressmen with documentary "proof" of the benefits of black slavery and gave official credence to popular pseudoscientific notions of black unsuitability for freedom. Critics of the census discovered substantial errors, including figures for many northern towns in which the number of reported insane blacks exceeded the total black population. In 1844 the American Statistical Association submitted to Congress an enumeration of the errors found in the insanity tables, urging that they be corrected. But proslavery apologists (led by John C. Calhoun) successfully resisted these attempts, and the 1840 census remained unaltered. Litwack, *North of Slavery,* 40–46; Gerald N. Grob, "Edward Jarvis and the Federal Census: A Chapter in the History of Nineteenth-Century American Medicine," *BHM* 50:9–10 (Spring 1976).

11. Edward Jarvis (1803–1884), a Dorchester, Massachusetts, physician and statistician, was a founder and longtime president of the American Statistical Association. Between 1842 and 1850, he campaigned to correct errors and contradictions in the census of 1840. Jarvis's findings reached a large audience when he published an article entitled "Insanity among the Coloured Population of the Free States" in the January 1844 issue of the *American Journal of the Medical Sciences.* By comparing the original tally sheets with the official report, he exposed the statistical fallacy underlying southern charges that free blacks were much more likely to suffer from insanity than slaves. He continued to fight for the reform of federal census procedures until his retirement in 1870. Grob, "Edward Jarvis and the Federal Census," 4–27.

12. Blacks had limited access to higher education in antebellum America. Smith identifies five colleges, all with ties to the Presbyterians, which admitted black students in the early 1840s. Abolitionist institutions like Oberlin College in Ohio and the Oneida Institute at Whitesboro, New York, regularly accepted blacks. Nearly three hundred attended Oberlin between 1835 and the Civil War. Some fourteen blacks studied at Oneida between 1834 and the closing of the school in 1844. Lafayette College in Easton, Pennsylvania, trained African blacks for foreign missionary work during the early 1840s. The Western Theological Seminary at Allegheny, Pennsylvania, admitted several black candidates for the ministry. One of them, William Walker, claimed that "no difference [was] made there on account of color." Although Dartmouth College began admitting black students in 1824, those few who attended faced frequent racial hostility. But several blacks, most notably Thomas Paul, Jr., graduated from the school by the 1840s, and it enjoyed a favorable reputation among northern blacks. Oberlin College Catalog & Record of Colored Students, 1835–62, Cowles Papers, OO [1:0541–47]; Sernett, *Abolition's Axe,* 50–62; *AR,* August 1842; *WAA,* 7 October 1859 [12:0014]; Leon Burr Richardson, *History of Dartmouth College* (Hanover, N.H., 1932), 381; *Lib,* 17 September 1841; *CA,* 22 April 1837.

13. At least five black journals appeared in early 1844: the *Palladium of Lib-*

erty, published in Columbus, Ohio, by David Jenkins; the *Mystery*, published in Pittsburgh by Martin R. Delany; the *Clarksonian*, published in Hartford by J. W. C. Pennington; and George Hogarth's New York City–based monthly, the *African Methodist Episcopal Church Magazine*. During the spring of 1844, Smith apparently assumed editorial duties with a fifth journal, Stephen Myers's *Northern Star and Freeman's Advocate*, which was published in Albany, New York. *PL*, 27 December 1843, 21 February, 27 March 1844 [4:0712, 0761, 0771]; *AP*, 29 May 1844; Alexander Crummell to John Jay, 29 December 1843, Jay Family Papers, NNC [4:0715].

14. Smith compiled his figures on the number of black churches from two sources—Philadelphia's *United States Gazette*, a Whig paper published under various names from 1789 to 1847, and *A Short Account of the Rise and Progress of the African Methodist Episcopal Church in America* (1843), a history of the AMEZ denomination written by Christopher Rush (1777–1873) of New York City, an AMEZ bishop active in the antislavery and black convention movements. Mott, *American Journalism*, 122–23, 188, 260; Walls, *African Methodist Episcopal Zion Church*, 45, 144–45, 566.

15. Smith quotes from Mark 14:58. He indicates that many of the black churches are not large, impressive structures like those churches found on Broadway in New York City.

16. Smith quotes from book 2, line 221, of Virgil's *Aeneid*, which translates from the Latin as "priestly headbands drenched with gore and venom."

17. Obedience to masters was a major theme in the sermons and writings of antebellum southern clergymen. Southern theologians drew heavily from the letters of St. Paul—particularly Ephesians 6:5–8, Colossians 3:22, and Philemon—to provide a biblical justification for slave obedience. Methodist, Baptist, and Presbyterian missionaries carried this message to the plantation, simultaneously soothing the concerns of slaveholders and promoting docility, honesty, and loyalty among slaves. Sernett, *Black Religion and American Evangelicalism*, 73–78.

18. Smith charged that racial discrimination in antebellum churches ("the church militant") mocked the spiritual unity believed to exist in heaven ("the church triumphant"). The relative racial tolerance found in northern Catholic parishes led him to mistakenly assume that Catholics everywhere welcomed blacks on equal terms. But southern Catholic churches generally conformed to local attitudes about slavery and race. Separate "Negro pews" and galleries, a segregated Eucharist, and other discriminatory practices were common in southern Protestant and Catholic congregations alike. And unlike the Baptists and Methodists, there was no place in Catholicism for slave preachers or exhorters and no possibility of organizing separate black Catholic congregations. Litwack, *North of Slavery*, 204; John B. Boles, ed., *Masters and Slaves in the House of the Lord: Race and Religion in the American South, 1740–1870* (Lexington, Ky., 1988), 10–18, 127–52.

19. Using New York, Massachusetts, and Rhode Island as examples, Smith argues that those northern states which granted free blacks a substantial measure of civil and political equality had prospered. In New York state, merchant John Murray, Jr., jurist John Jay, and politician Daniel D. Tompkins had fostered more humane treatment of blacks through the New York Manumission Society during

the post-Revolutionary decades. Their descendants continued to promote anti-slavery, black education, and various black philanthropic causes throughout the antebellum years. In Massachusetts, after Paul Cuffe and other blacks filed a 1780 petition protesting taxation without representation, voters approved a state constitution removing racial restrictions on suffrage. When working-class whites led by Thomas Dorr attempted to overthrow the elected government of Rhode Island in 1841, blacks rallied behind the administration in power and were awarded the franchise. Smith suggests that Pennsylvania, which had disfran-chised blacks in 1838, was punished for that action with a subsequent financial crisis. Economic depression, pyramiding public debt, and the cost of internal improvements brought the state government to the brink of bankruptcy and debt repudiation in the early 1840s. By 1843 Pennsylvania was temporarily required to suspend payment of interest on public debts. *DAB*, 10:10–12, 13:356–67, 18:583–84; Merrill and Ruchames, *Letters of William Lloyd Garrison*, 2:99–100; *CA*, 18 April 1838 [2:0460]; Litwack, *North of Slavery*, 16, 79–80, 84–86; Lamont D. Thomas, *Rise to Be a People: A Biography of Paul Cuffe* (Urbana, Ill., 1986), 9–11; Philip S. Klein and Ari Hoogenboom, *A History of Pennsylvania* (New York, N.Y., 1973), 135–38.

20. Smith suggests that free blacks are better served by attending their own separate churches than by listening to the proslavery sermons of many white clergymen. The "gospel vine" reference is a paraphrase of Micah 4:4, "They shall sit every man under his vine and under his fig tree," a verse frequently used to defend the existence of separate black churches.

21. Five Points, the most notorious slum in antebellum New York City, was named for the peculiar intersection of five streets that formed a star-shaped neighborhood. Located between Broadway and the Bowery, the area became known for its high crime rate, poverty, overcrowding, unsanitary conditions, prostitution, saloons, dance and gaming halls, and gang violence. It was pri-marily peopled by free blacks, Irish immigrants, and unskilled native whites. Smith's "deformed leg" reference is to the odd shape of Mulberry Bend, a one-block section of Mulberry Street in Five Points. The neighborhood became a central focus of Protestant mission efforts in New York City during the 1850s. Carroll Smith Rosenberg, *Religion and the Rise of the American City: The New York City Mission Movement, 1812–1870* (Ithaca, N.Y., 1971), 34–36, 99, 109, 207, 225–44; Maxwell F. Marcuse, *This Was New York!: A Nostalgic Picture of Gotham in the Gaslight Era* (New York, N.Y., 1969), 60.

22. *Barbaroi* is a Greek term meaning barbarians.

23. Smith refers to the mode of fighting on horseback employed by warriors in the ancient Kingdom of Parthia (modern Iran). When retreating, Parthian war-riors discharged their arrows at their enemies. Smith uses this term to character-ize the continuing published attacks on the free black community in the North.

66.
Speech by Charles Lenox Remond
Delivered at Marlboro Chapel
Boston, Massachusetts
29 May 1844

By the early 1840s, Garrisonian abolitionists had concluded that the
Constitution was a proslavery document—"a covenant with death and
an agreement with hell." They reasoned that by dissolving the political
union between North and South, they would separate themselves from
the sin of slavery, and that slavery, once isolated, would eventually
wither and die. The American Anti-Slavery Society formally adopted the
principal of disunion at its anniversary meeting on 7 May 1844. "No
Union With Slaveholders" became the society's official motto. At the
New England Anti-Slavery Convention in Boston's Marlboro Chapel
three weeks later, the question of disunion dominated the proceedings.
Francis Jackson chaired the convention, and several delegates—including Charles L. Remond, Frederick Douglass, and Abby Kelley—spoke
on the subject. Remond responded to Dr. Walter Channing who defended the Constitution as a "sacred instrument." Remond justified disunion not on moral grounds, but rather as the proper response to a political order that denied black Americans their rights. By a vote of 252
to 24, the convention adopted the resolutions favoring disunion. *Lib*,
31 May, 7 June 1844; Kraditor, *Means and Ends in American Abolitionism*, 196–217.

I do not intend, Sir, even to attempt an answer to the respected friend
who has just taken his seat. My point of view is too distant from his to
leave me the vantage-ground for doing so. But I feel a deep interest in the
question, and the present moment is perhaps the most fitting one for the
expression of my humble views. I cannot expect them to make much
impression upon the many—upon the body of this nation, for whose
benefit the Constitution was made; but they will meet a response from
the few whom it entirely overlooks, or sees but to trample upon, and the
fewer still, who identify themselves with the outcast, by occupying this
position, of a dissolution of their union with Slaveholders.

It does very well for nine-tenths of the people of the United States, to
speak of the awe and reverence they feel as they contemplate the Constitution, but there are those who look upon it with a very different feeling,
for they are in a very different position. What is it to *them* that it talks
about peace—tranquillity—domestic enjoyments—civil rights? To them
it is no such union; and resting, as it does, upon all their dearest and
holiest rights, I cannot but express surprise that there are so many to

wonder that they, and those who feel with them, should look upon this Union as one that ought to be dissolved. Oh, Sir! look at them as they are falling, generation after generation, beneath the sway of the Union, sinking into their ignominious graves unwept, uncared for, unprayed for, enslaved, and say what has the Union been to them that they should look upon it with filial reverence! There was McIntosh, of St. Louis.[1] He raised his dark, fettered hand, in defence of the chastity of his wife, as it is claimed that a *white* man ought to do, and he was burned in a slow fire! What was the Union to him? What was it to Turner of Southampton, than whom a nobler soul has never risen upon the human race in all the long line of its prophets and its heroes! The Union does not even preserve his name. *He* had no place in life under its protecting aegis—in history he is only Nat Turner, the miserable negro. Sir, *I* will never contemptuously call him *Nat* Turner, for had he been a white man, Massachusetts and Virginia would have united to glorify his name and to build his monument; and is it strange, seeing all these things, that I should feel them too, and act upon the feeling? Yet, when such thoughts as these get such imperfect utterance as I am able to give them, men say to me, "Remond! you're wild! Remond! you're mad! Remond! you're a revolutionist!" Sir, in view of all these things, ought not this whole assembly—this whole nation to be revolutionists too?

I belong to that class of persons called women's rights men; and I look upon this matter in the light of my principles on that subject. Do you not all recollect the case of the woman in Maryland, which went the round of the papers not long since? She was endeavoring to make her escape to the land of Victoria—she was pursued and overtaken, and was about to be returned to her home of whips, and chains, and fetters, and of the American Constitution. She sprang into the Potomac, and sank from the clutch of her pursuers. As her condition was, then, stands that of one million of American women today! And when she was seized, I well remember that it was pleaded in favor of her savage pursuers, that, by the provisions of the American Constitution, she must be returned!—that all their proceedings were legal!

What if the word "slave" is not in it? It does not matter to me nor mine. Slavery was in the understanding that framed it—Slavery is in the will that administers it. If there were nothing but Liberty in it, would there be two and a half millions ground to the dust beneath it this day?

If any authority besides this fact were needed, I might cite the words of John Quincy Adams to the people of color, when we applied to him in the case of Latimer.[2] He said his opinion should be forthcoming, *subject to the provisions of the American Constitution.*

With all my knowledge of the origin and the progress, and my experience of the present practical workings of the American Constitution, shall I be found here advocating it as a glorious means to a glorious end!

No! my fellow countrymen, I am here to register my testimony against it! Not because I do not feel how valuable it might be, were its provisions secured to the few as they are to the many—not because I wish to claim anything more for the few than an equality of privileges—not because I am not ready to "yield everything to the Union *but* Truth—Honor—Liberty" [*pointing to a banner inscribed with those words of Dr. Channing*][3]—but because (and I regret to say it) we have, as a people, yielded even these; and with such a people, I feel that I must not, as an individual, be numbered.

I have spoken of particular instances in illustration of the nullity of the Union. How is it with every colored man and woman in Boston? Can one of you plead its provisions at the South? No! It will be with you there even as it was with Nat Turner, and the Fugitive of the Potomac. If I am wronged, I may appeal, and I may go on appealing and appealing till I am grey-headed—in vain! Go the rounds of the Union, and tell me at what tribunal the man of color can have justice? Court, Judge, Jury—all are against him; and to what is it owing? Why, as an honest Buckeye (for he was fond of calling himself so) told me in Cincinnati,[4] "it is this everlasting yielding to Slavery," which always must take place, when Freedom yields the first step, by coming into union with it. If the Union had been formed upon the supposition that the colored man was a *man*, a man he would have been considered, whether in New Hampshire or Kentucky. But under the Union as it was, and as it is, he is kicked, stoned, insulted, enslaved, and the public sentiment that does it, falls back upon the Constitution for support, and will turn its back upon you, wherever you may be, if you deny that instrument to be obligatory as the paramount law.

I need not say how greatly I am troubled whenever a difference of opinion exists in the minds of those who love the cause of Freedom. I have tried in my own mind to make out a case for those who do not see eye to eye with us in this matter. But the more I have labored at it, the stronger becomes my conviction of duty in calling for a dissolution of the union between Freedom and Slavery. I speak after long thought, free and full discussion, and the clearest view of all the consequences and all the obstacles. I have taken all things into consideration; and in view of each and of all, I say here, as I did in New York, that if I can only sustain the Constitution, by sustaining Slavery, then—"live or die—sink or swim—survive or perish," I give my voice for the dissolution of the Union.

National Anti-Slavery Standard (New York, N.Y.), 18 July 1844.

1. Francis J. McIntosh, a free black steamboat cook, was arrested in St. Louis on the evening of 28 April 1836, when he attempted to prevent the arrest of two other boatmen for fighting. On the way to jail, he broke free and drew a knife, killing a deputy sheriff and wounding a constable. After being rearrested, a mob

dragged him from the jail and burned him to death, mutilating and decapitating his body in the search for souvenirs. No one was indicted in the affair. Abolitionist editor Elijah Lovejoy immediately protested the barbaric action in his St. Louis *Observer*, provoking antiabolitionists and prompting his move to Alton, Illinois. Merton L. Dillon, *Elijah P. Lovejoy: Abolitionist Editor* (Urbana, Ill., 1961), 81–83, 87.

2. George Latimer (ca. 1820–?), the slave of Norfolk merchant James B. Gray, escaped with his wife and child in October 1842. Gray followed him to Boston and had him arrested on larceny charges. After an unsuccessful attempt to "rescue" Latimer from police custody, local blacks joined with white abolitionists to mount a legal defense and to organize a massive petition and fund-raising campaign. A committee of Boston blacks appealed to former president John Quincy Adams to act as Latimer's attorney before the U.S. Circuit Court. Adams, then a member of the U.S. House of Representatives, had previously served as a defense attorney in the *Amistad* case. He responded to the committee's request by indicating that his sympathy for the slave did not extend to challenging constitutional law. He declined to serve as counsel but offered to provide legal advice to Latimer's attorneys, "subject to [his] bounden duty of fidelity to the Constitution of the United States." Latimer eventually won his freedom through the intervention of Nathaniel Colver, a local Baptist clergyman, who purchased his freedom for $400. Public outcry over the Latimer incident led to the passage of the 1843 Personal Liberty Act, which prohibited Massachusetts officials from participating in the recapture of fugitive slaves. After his release, Latimer made an antislavery lecture tour with Frederick Douglass, then settled near Boston and worked as a paperhanger. During the 1851 rescue of the fugitive slave Shadrach, the Boston Vigilance Committee employed him to do surveillance work. Latimer disappeared in 1858. *Lib*, 28 October 1842, 3 March 1843; *DANB*, 385–86; Horton and Horton, *Black Bostonians*, 99, 105; Blassingame, *Frederick Douglass Papers*, 1:230n.

3. The words on the banner borrow from a line in William Ellery Channing's *Slavery* (1836): "Language cannot easily do justice to our attachment to the Union. We will yield every thing to it but truth, honor, and liberty. These we can never yield." *The Works of William E. Channing, D.D.* (Boston, Mass., 1882), 739.

4. Ohio residents are nicknamed "Buckeyes" due to the preponderance of buckeye trees in the state. The "honest Buckeye" to whom Remond refers may be Gamaliel Bailey, the abolitionist editor of the Cincinnati *Philanthropist*, whom he met in October 1843 during the "One Hundred Conventions" campaign. Mathews, *Dictionary of Americanisms*, 202; *P*, 18 October 1843.

67.
Resolutions by a Meeting of Boston Blacks
Convened at the First Independent
Baptist Church, Boston, Massachusetts
18 June 1844

The campaign against separate schools exemplified the black struggle
for equality. Black abolitionists insisted that segregated schools were in-
herently unequal, perpetuated racial stereotypes, and crushed black aspirations. Beginning in 1840, William C. Nell, John T. Hilton, and
Henry L. W. Thacker began a fifteen-year campaign against Boston's
segregated educational facilities, concentrating their first efforts on the
Smith School. Persistent accusations of sexual misconduct, racism, and
brutal treatment of students by headmaster Abner Forbes and his staff
led to demands that Forbes be dismissed and the school be closed. On
12 June 1844, the Boston school committee rejected those demands. Six
days later blacks submitted the following petition to the commission. It
too was rejected. Boston blacks withdrew their children from all the
city's separate schools and continued their protests. When the petition
strategy failed to change city policy, blacks turned to organized boycotts, protest meetings, and legal action. They achieved victory in 1855
when the Massachusetts legislature desegregated the state's schools. Jacobs, "Nineteenth-Century Struggle," 76–85; Horton and Horton,
Black Bostonians, 73–76; *Lib*, 28 June 1844.

At a meeting of the colored citizens of the city of Boston, held in the
First Independent Baptist Church,[1] on Monday Evening, June 18, 1844,
the following resolutions were unanimously adopted:

> Whereas, we, the Colored Citizens of the City of Boston have
> recently sent a petition to the School Committee respectfully pray-
> ing for the abolition of the separate schools for colored children, &
> asking for the rights & privileges extended to other citizens in
> respect to the Common School System, viz: the right to send our
> children to the schools established in the respective Districts in
> which we reside, and
> Whereas, the School Committee at their last meeting passed a
> vote, stating, in substance, that the prayer of our petition would
> not be granted, & that the separate schools for colored children be
> continued, and
> Whereas we believe, & have the opinion of eminent counsel,[2]
> that the institution & support of separate schools at the public
> charge for any one class of the inhabitants in exclusion of any other

class is contrary to the laws of this Commonwealth, therefore,

Resolved, that we consider the late action of the School Committee in regard to our petition asking for the entire abolition of separate schools for colored children as erroneous & unsatisfactory.

Resolved, that while we would not turn aside from our main object, the abolition of the separate colored schools, we cannot allow this occasion to pass without an expression of our suprize & regret at the recent acquittal by the School Committee of Abner Forbes, Principal of the Smith School,[3] & of our deep conviction that he is totally unworthy of his present responsible station; & that the colored parents of this City are recommended to withdraw their children from the exclusive schools established in contravention of that equality of priviliges which is the vital principal of the school system of Massachusetts.

Resolved, that a copy of the above preamble and resolutions be sent to the Chairman of the School Committee with a request that the petition heretofore presented may be reconsidered, & that we be allowed a hearing on said petition before them.

John T. Hilton, President
Henry L. W. Thacker[4] } Vice
Jonas W. Clark[5]   } Presidents
William C. Nell   }
Robert Morris Jr.[6] } Secretaries

1. Local antislavery gatherings and black community organizations frequently met at Boston's First Independent Baptist Church, which was sometimes known as the "Abolition Church." Founded by Rev. Thomas Paul in 1805 as the African Baptist Church, it was located on Smith Court near Belknap (later Joy) Street. The name was changed in 1837 "for the very good reason that the name African is ill applied to a church composed of American citizens." Many of the pastors of the congregation—Paul, John T. Raymond, and J. Sella Martin—were prominent abolitionists; the New England Anti-Slavery Society was organized in 1832 in the church's basement. Horton and Horton, *Black Bostonians*, 28, 40–43, 91, 101; Smith, *Climbing Jacob's Ladder*, 51–53.

2. The petitioners probably refer to Judge Richard Fletcher of Boston, a member of the Massachusetts Supreme Court, who encouraged Boston blacks by his 1844 opinion on Salem's segregated school system. Fletcher argued that racially exclusive schools disadvantaged black students and asserted that public schools "must be open equally to all classes of the community." Other jurists involved in the legal effort to integrate Boston schools were John C. Park, Charles Sumner, Wendell Phillips, and black lawyer Robert Morris. *Lib*, 28 June, 12 July 1844.

3. The resolution refers to the refusal of the Boston School Committee to

remove Abner Forbes from his post as headmaster of the black Smith School, which was built in 1835 in the heart of Boston's black community. Forbes, a white teacher and an officer of the Massachusetts Anti-Slavery Society, had earlier served as headmaster of the Boston African School in 1834. At first Forbes and the Smith School won plaudits from local blacks. But by the early 1840s, the school symbolized the failings of segregated education. Blacks accused Forbes and his all-white teaching staff of racism, brutality, and immoral conduct. These charges, and complaints about the school's poor physical state, energized a movement to end segregated education in Boston. Blacks boycotted the Smith School, lowering attendance from 263 pupils in 1840 to 51 by the end of the decade. The school committee replaced Forbes with Thomas Paul, Jr., a black graduate of Dartmouth College, in 1849, but despite staff changes, the school continued to decline. It closed soon after the passage in 1855 of a state law mandating integrated education. Horton and Horton, *Black Bostonians*, 70–75; Stanley Schultz, *The Culture Factory: Boston Public Schools, 1789–1860* (New York, N.Y., 1973), 157–206; *Lib*, 2 August 1844 [4:0888–90].

4. Henry L. W. Thacker, a loyal Garrisonian, first worked as a bootblack in Boston before establishing a successful catering business in the late 1850s. In the 1840s, he played a major role in the struggle to end segregated schools in the city. During the following decade, he supported efforts to organize the Massasoit Guards, a black militia. He also sheltered fugitive slaves escaping through Boston. *Lib*, 5 November 1831, 13 April 1833, 7 September, 9 November 1849, 26 April 1850, 4 April 1851 [1:0131, 0272, 6:0132, 0213, 0455, 0871]; Horton and Horton, *Black Bostonians*, 16, 101, 120; *Boston City Directory*, 1822–28, 1830, 1859.

5. Jonas W. Clark (?–1870), a Boston clothier, was a prominent figure in the local black community. He joined public protests against the black seamen's acts, the Fugitive Slave Law, and the Dred Scott decision. Clark participated in the decade-long struggle to end school segregation in Boston, served on the Massachusetts State Council of the Colored People in the 1850s, and used his business to contribute to the antislavery effort. He provided the Boston Vigilance Committee with winter clothing and financial support, which aided fugitive slaves passing through the city. *Lib*, 28 June, 2 August 1844, 7 February 1845, 5 April, 29 November 1850, 4 April 1851, 24 February 1854, 5 September 1856, 16, 26 February 1858 [4:0834, 0888, 0987, 6:0435, 0673, 0871, 8:0663–65, 10:0286, 11:0149, 0160–61]; Horton and Horton, *Black Bostonians*, 71; Foner and Walker, *Proceedings of the Black State Conventions*, 2:94.

6. Robert Morris (1823–1882) was born in Salem, Massachusetts, the son of York Morris, a freed slave. After receiving some schooling, he became a servant in the household of Ellis Gray Loring, who generously provided Morris the opportunity to work as a clerk in his law office and to pursue legal studies. Morris passed the Suffolk County bar examination in 1847, becoming one of the first black Americans licensed to practice law. He used his legal practice to further antislavery goals and black civil rights. In 1849 he assisted Charles Sumner in *Roberts v. City of Boston*—an attempt by Boston blacks to integrate public schools. After the courts ruled against his case, Morris helped organize a black boycott of Boston's segregated schools. He also played a major role in legal proceedings to integrate public conveyances, restaurants, and other facilities.

Active in the Boston Vigilance Committee in the 1850s, he participated in the successful Shadrach rescue. Although arrested and tried for his part in the 1851 rescue, he won acquittal by a decisive eleven-to-one jury vote. Morris's reputation as an effective lawyer brought him white as well as black clients. In the 1850s, he was appointed a justice of the peace in Suffolk County and was admitted to practice in the U.S. district courts. As one of only a few black attorneys in the United States, he became a celebrity at antislavery meetings, black state and national conventions, and other public gatherings. A loyal Garrisonian, Morris was nonetheless attracted to political antislavery and won the Free Soil party nomination for a Boston mayoral election.

In addition to his legal work, Morris was active in local black civic life. He held membership in the Boston Lyceum. Although a member of the African Methodist Episcopal church, he conformed to his wife's religious background by converting to Catholicism during the 1850s. He promoted the formation of a black militia—the Massasoit Guards—and petitioned the state legislature for a memorial to Crispus Attucks. In the late 1850s, Morris became increasingly pessimistic about the prospects for a peaceful resolution to the slavery issue. When the Civil War erupted, he encouraged blacks to enlist as soldiers, but at the same time, he protested the mistreatment of black recruits and the exclusion of black officers from the Union army. *DANB*, 454–55; Horton and Horton, *Black Bostonians*, 55–60, 87, 120, 127; Daniels, *In Freedom's Birthplace*, 450–51; *Lib*, 14 March, 21 November 1851, 13 August, 24 September 1858, 18 February 1859 [7:0190, 11:0324, 0373, 0592]; *NSt*, 27 April 1849.

68.
Jehiel C. Beman to Joshua Leavitt
10 August 1844

Nothing in the northern black experience prepared black abolitionists who ventured South for the realities of slave life. In July 1844, Jehiel C. Beman, an African Methodist Episcopal Zion clergyman, traveled by train to Baltimore, Maryland, and the nation's capital. Beman had been an active abolitionist for over ten years by the time of his trip, but neither his antislavery work nor his encounters with racial prejudice had readied him for what he found. Beman's powerlessness "in a land of whips" and the sight of his "sisters toiling, pitchfork and rake in hand, under the scorching rays of the sun" left him with an acute sense of sorrow, which is evident in his letter to Joshua Leavitt.

Boston, [Massachusetts]
Aug[ust] 10, 1844

Mr. Editor:[1]

Should the following sketch of my recent tour to Baltimore, Md., and Washington, be thought worthy a place in your valuable paper, it is at your disposal.

I left Boston July 16th, via New York and Philadelphia, and on the 21st, left the latter place in the car for Baltimore, in company with the Rev. Wm. Miller,[2] of Philadelphia, one of the superintendants of our connection, and Br. Collins, the preacher in charge of the Wesley church in Philadelphia.[3] After paying our fare, we were pointed to the Jim Crow[4] or separate car. Nothing very particular transpired until we arrived at the ferry to cross to Havre de Grace, Md. While on the boat, which is fitted up with refreshment tables, Br. Collins proposed our taking some refreshments, to which I consented; and after buying and paying for what we wanted, we commenced eating. Instantly, the man in attendance says, "Here, here, you must not eat here"; and calling a boy (colored), says to him, "Open that door, and show the men where they may eat, and be quick." This door opened into the kitchen or pantry. "There," said he, sternly, "is the place for you." Resistance was useless in a land of whips.

As we proceeded on our way, it was painful to see the way passengers [were] coming into the car destined to neighboring plantations; and as the conductor came into the car to receive the fare, they would show each one a scrap of paper (pass), and he would read and nod the head and pass out.

Having arrived at Baltimore, I took my seat with my brethren in the

Conference, which I came to attend, as a delegate from the New York Conference.[5] On the 25th July, the Conference granting leave of absence for the day, in company with Br. Mars[6] we repaired to the depot to obtain tickets for Washington. On asking the clerk for tickets, the answer was, "Who is your bondsman? You can have no ticket unless a white man gives bonds for you." It was fortunate for me, that before I left the Old Bay State, I procured a protection from under the hand of the governor with the seal of the State.[7] Not only so, I took a line from under the hand of the clerk of the Philadelphia depot, when I arrived in Baltimore, stating that my name was on the way-bill from Philadelphia.

Thus I obtained my ticket, and took my seat in another JIMMY or separate car; and as we moved towards the capital, what scenes presented to my view—the plantations, the farmhouses, and log cabins. But in the fields, to see my sisters toiling, pitchfork and rake in hand, under the scorching rays of the sun, with no covering on the head, and but little on the body—as this was the first scene of the kind I ever saw, my feelings were such as I cannot describe. I tried to raise my cries to Heaven, but in this I was interrupted, for the flowing tear forced its way down my care-worn cheek, and with the brother that was with me, I remained in silence while the car rolled on, and I could but think of the words of the statesman, "I tremble for my country, when I know that God is just."[8]

We were soon in the great metropolis. We first visited the patent office; from thence to the school of the Rev. Mr. Cook[9] (colored), and here I was struck with the different shades of complexion; some very dark, and some almost white. I thought the *inseparable barrier* had been passed. From thence to the president's house. Viewing this in the interior, I thought, must this nation pay a man $25,000 per year, to enjoy all this splendor, and he holds my brother in bonds? From thence I found my way to the Capitol—viewed the paintings, the Senate chamber, the Representative hall, and from its splendid dome, viewed the District of Columbia; but notwithstanding all its greatness, I thought slavery was wafted on every breeze. I then dined at a Mr. Walker's eatinghouse,[10] and at four o'clock took the cars for Baltimore, sighing to think that my father faced the cannon's mouth for this country's liberty, and I and my brother still bound.[11]

During my stay in Baltimore, I attended what they call a bush meeting, in Anne Arundel Co., on the plantation of Mr. R. Cromwell, who has a large number of slaves that were in attendance.[12] There was powerful preaching by the brethren in attendance. Yet to see some two thousand people, all colored, and a large number of them in bonds, although they appeared to enjoy the meeting, and had plenty of food for the time being, yet slavery poisoned all its sweets to me, and I turn from the sickening picture, while the loss of reason alone can erase from my mind the scenes through which I have just passed.

J. C. BEMAN[13]

Morning Chronicle (Boston, Mass.), 15 August 1844.

1. Joshua Leavitt (1794–1873) edited the *Morning Chronicle*, a daily Liberty party paper published in Boston from March 1844 until September 1845. Although he was an early abolitionist and a key advocate of political antislavery during the 1840s, Leavitt is best known for his editorial work on several reform journals—the *New York Evangelist* (1832–37), the *Emancipator* (1837–48), and the New York *Independent* (1848–73). *DAB*, 6(1):84–85; Reinhard O. Johnson, "The Liberty Party in Massachusetts, 1840–1848: Antislavery Third Party Politics in the Bay State," *CWH* 28:244, 247 (September 1982); *E*, 1 October 1845.

2. William Miller (1775–1845), a free black, was born in Queen Annes County, Maryland. As a young man, he settled in New York City and practiced the cabinetmaking trade. Miller began preaching to black Methodists during the 1790s. Over the next three decades, he performed a major role in directing the withdrawal of these New York blacks from the larger Methodist body. He was ordained a deacon in 1808. But Miller's interests extended beyond religion. As early as 1810, his *Sermon on the Abolition of the Slave Trade* demonstrated a moderate antislavery view. He also helped found black Masonry in New York City, started and directed the New York African Bible Society (an American Bible Society affiliate), and attended the 1831 black national convention in Philadelphia. In 1814 Miller led disgruntled members out of New York City's black Zion African Methodist Church and formed the African Asbury Church. Despite his independent spirit, he was selected in 1820 to help draw up the discipline for an independent African Methodist Episcopal Zion denomination. Soon after, he began a flirtation with the rival African Methodist Episcopal church, which led to his ordination as an AME elder in 1823 and to his subsequent appointment to the pastorate of an AME congregation in Washington, D.C. Miller returned to the AMEZ church by the early 1830s and was given charge of the First Wesley AMEZ Church in Philadelphia, where he remained until his death in 1845. In 1840 he was elected bishop of the AMEZ's New York Conference, but he functioned more in the role of assistant superintendent of that body. Walls, *African Methodist Episcopal Zion Church*, 44, 47–48, 63, 68–82, 90–91, 121–24, 129, 148, 172–73, 183, 567; William Miller, *A Sermon on the Abolition of the Slave Trade* (New York, N.Y., 1810); *Minutes of the First Annual Convention* (1831), 3 [1:0077]; *Lib*, 7 July 1832; *CA*, 21 October 1837, 27 July 1839 [3:0151].

3. Leonard Collins (1806–?), a Pennsylvania native, served African Methodist Episcopal Zion congregations in Centre County in the late 1830s, then joined Rev. William Miller in the ministry of the First Wesley AMEZ Church in Philadelphia during the following decade. He was involved in a wide range of reform efforts. A committed temperance advocate, he used his ministry to encourage the growth of total abstinence societies. Collins helped organize Pennsylvania's 1841 black state convention, and in August 1845, he joined with four Philadelphia blacks to establish a national black organization—the short-lived Colored American National Society. Collins's pastoral duties later took him to New Bed-

ford, Massachusetts, then to Bridgeport, Connecticut. In both cities, he participated in local antislavery and anticolonization efforts. He represented Massachusetts at the 1847 black national convention and served on its national press committee. He later represented Bridgeport at Connecticut's 1849 black state convention. Collins's religious work drew criticism from the black press. In an attack on separate churches, Frederick Douglass singled him out as a "clerical sycophant" to slaveholders. Collins responded in a March 1848 letter to the *North Star*, which defended his personal conduct and presented a brief, well-argued justification of separate black churches. He eventually lost his standing in the AMEZ church "by yielding to the temptation of strong drink." U.S. Census, 1850; Walls, *African Methodist Episcopal Zion Church*, 127; *CA*, 29 June 1839, 27 February 1841 [3:0129, 0918]; Winch, *Philadelphia's Black Elite*, 202n; *NSt*, 3 December 1847, 14 January, 25 February, 3, 10, 24 March 1848 [5:0533, 0554, 0598]; *Lib*, 15 August 1851, 27 February 1852 [7:0062, 0441]; Foner and Walker, *Proceedings of the Black State Conventions*, 1:116 [4:0174]; *Convention of Colored People . . . in Troy* (1847), 3 [5:0486]; *Proceedings of the Connecticut State Convention of Colored Men* (New Haven, Conn., 1849), 2–12 [6:0142–47].

4. Jim Crow cars were railroad cars exclusively reserved for blacks. The term "Jim Crow" was used as early as 1832 by blackface performer Thomas D. Rice, who performed a song and dance by that name. By 1837 the term had become an adjective indicating discrimination based on race. It was used to describe separate railroad cars by the early 1840s. Mathews, *Dictionary of Americanisms*, 907; Robert C. Toll, *Blacking Up: The Minstrel Show in Nineteenth-Century America* (London, 1974), 28.

5. The recently organized Baltimore Conference of the African Methodist Episcopal Zion church met at Baltimore in July 1844. Beman attended as a delegate from the New York Conference. David H. Bradley, *A History of the AMEZ Church*, 2 vols. (Nashville, Tenn., 1970), 1:129–30.

6. John N. Mars (1804–1884), a black Methodist clergyman, was born in Connecticut. He joined the New York Conference of the African Methodist Episcopal Zion church in 1829 and served AMEZ congregations in Fishkill and Poughkeepsie, New York, and Newark, New Jersey, during the 1830s. Mars then resettled in Salem, Massachusetts, where he worked as an assistant to a white minister. After conducting missionary work in Canada West, he accepted an AMEZ pastorate in Springfield, Massachusetts, in 1850. The itinerant nature of his ministry there allowed Mars to bring his antislavery message to several New England communities. He participated in local antislavery meetings and used his pulpit to urge militant resistance to the Fugitive Slave Law. At the 1859 New England Colored Citizens Convention, he called on blacks to abandon their demeaning, urban existence and settle in the West.

In 1863, after serving as interim pastor at Boston's First Independent Baptist Church, Mars was commissioned as a chaplain in the Union army in General Edward Wild's North Carolina Colored Volunteers. He left the Union army in April 1864 to work for the American Missionary Association in Portsmouth, Virginia. Mars organized congregations and Sabbath schools and taught classes to local freedmen. His reports to AMA secretary George Whipple offer a poignant description of the condition of the freedmen in eastern Virginia. Although optimistic about the progress of his mission work, he complained of the insensitivity and racist behavior of white missionaries. These criticisms alienated his white colleagues and undermined efforts to continue his mission work under the auspices of the New England Conference of the Methodist Episcopal church, which he had recently joined. Mars resigned his AMA post in November 1864, having accepted an appointment as pastor of Sharp Street Methodist Episcopal Church in Baltimore. After the Civil War, he helped raise funds for a Lincoln monument. Mars returned to Massachusetts in 1869 and served for a decade as pastor of the Revere Street Methodist Church in Boston. Bradley, *History of the AMEZ Church*, 1:125; Walls, *African Methodist Episcopal Zion Church*, 127; Joseph Carvalho III, *Black Families in Hampden County, Massachusetts, 1650–1855* (West Springfield, Mass., 1984), 86–87; *Newark City Directory*, 1839–40; *Lib*, 19 April 1844, 26 August 1859 [4:0790, 11:0966]; *CA*, 1 June 1839, 12 September 1840, 2, 9 January 1841 [3:0077, 0615, 0808, 0822]; *IC*, 26 March 1850 [6:0433]; *ASB*, 12 October 1850; *WAA*, 14 February, 11 April 1863, 12 August, 3 September 1865 [16:0058, 0154]; *NASS*, 15 August 1863; John N. Mars to George Whipple, 1, 15 March, 6, 25 April, 27 May, 18 June, 29 July, 29 August, 3, 11, 29 November 1864, AMA-ARC [15:0264–66, 0283, 0300, 0319–20, 0358–59, 0404, 0467–69, 0512–14, 0589, 0598–600, 0609]; William Gravely, *Gilbert Haven: Methodist Abolitionist* (Nashville, Tenn., 1973), 128–32, 139, 199.

7. Like most southern states, Maryland required free blacks to carry certificates verifying their status. Before going South, Beman obtained such a document from George Nixon Briggs, the governor of Massachusetts. Berlin, *Slaves without Masters*, 93, 317; *BDGUS*, 702–3.

8. Beman quotes loosely from *Notes on the State of Virginia* (1785), query 18, by Thomas Jefferson. Although a slaveholder, Jefferson conceded the immorality of slavery: "Indeed I tremble for my country when I reflect that God is just, that his justice cannot sleep forever. Commerce between master and slave is despotism. Nothing is more certainly written in the book of fate than that these people are to be free."

9. John F. Cook (1810–1855), a Washington, D.C., minister and educator, was born a slave. Cook's aunt, Alethia Tanner, purchased his family's freedom in 1826. He repaid the cost of his manumission by working as a shoemaker's apprentice. From 1831 to 1833, he worked as a messenger and clerk in the U.S. Land Office, then quit government work to take charge of the Columbian Institute—a school for free blacks founded in the early 1820s. He renamed it the Union Seminary and—except for a brief period after it was destroyed in the 1835 race riots—supervised its affairs until his death. Cook had a variety of reform interests. He participated in the black national convention movement in the 1830s, was a founding member of the American Moral Reform Society, and lectured against the use of tobacco and other products of slave labor. He is best remembered for his preeminent position in the black religious life of Washington, D.C. He preached at the Israel African Methodist Episcopal Church in the 1830s, organized fund-raising tours in Pennsylvania on behalf of the Union Bethel Church, and founded the Fifteenth Street Presbyterian Church (1841). He became an ordained Presbyterian minister in 1843 and later presided at a session

of the Richmond Presbytery—a white assembly. His sons, John F. Cook, Jr., and George F. T. Cook, were both prominent public servants in Washington, D.C., during Reconstruction. *DANB*, 125–26; Delany, *Condition of the Colored People*, 114; "Biographical Sketches" and "Sources Making Reference to J. F. Cook," Cook Family Papers, DHU.

10. Henry Walker operated an eatery on 18 Avenue, between I and K streets, on Washington's west side during the 1840s. He later ran the National Eating House on Pennsylvania Avenue. *Washington City Directory*, 1843–53.

11. Beman's father, Cesar Beman (sometimes spelled Beamont) of Colchester, Connecticut, fought with the rebel forces during the latter years of the American Revolution. An invalid in later life, he died in 1821. Beman indicates that even though black men like his father "faced the cannon's mouth" for American independence, their children were denied the rights that the Revolution promised. David O. White, *Connecticut's Black Soldiers, 1775–1783* (Chester, Conn., 1973), 43–44, 57, 69n.

12. Bush meetings were outdoor religious gatherings of slaves. On some plantations, masters allowed slave preachers to conduct religious services on Sunday afternoons or at night. These assemblies usually consisted of enthusiastic preaching, shouting, and the singing of spirituals. When masters refused to allow such gatherings, slaves secretly worshiped in secluded places—woods, gullies, ravines, and thickets (called "hush harbors"). The size of the bush meeting that Beman attended indicates that it must have been held with the permission of Richard Cromwell (ca. 1807–?), a Maryland-born farmer who owned a plantation in Anne Arundel County on the northern arm of the Chesapeake Bay in Maryland. Mathews, *Dictionary of Americanisms*, 226; Albert J. Raboteau, *Slave Religion: The "Invisible Institution" in the Antebellum South* (Oxford, England, 1978), 212–24; U.S. Census, 1850.

13. Jehiel C. Beman (?–1858), a black shoemaker and African Methodist Episcopal Zion minister, was the father of black abolitionist Amos G. Beman. The elder Beman was born in Connecticut, the son of a former slave and a Revolutionary War veteran. During the 1830s, Beman was a central figure in religious, temperance, and antislavery activities in New England. He first appeared on the AMEZ rolls in 1831 as pastor of a church in Middletown, Connecticut. He denounced discriminatory practices in the Methodist Episcopal denomination and encouraged the formation of separate black congregations. Perhaps best known for his work in the black temperance movement, Beman organized and served as president of several local, state, and regional temperance societies in New England. He was no less active as an abolitionist. A founding member of the American Anti-Slavery Society, he organized AASS auxiliaries in Middletown and South Glastonburg, Connecticut, served as an agent for the *Liberator*, and joined the Garrisonian attack on colonization. He sought to strengthen the society's commitment to economic and civil rights issues affecting free blacks. Garrisonians criticized Beman when he became general agent of the rival Massachusetts Abolition Society in 1839. The *Liberator* attributed his defection to "selfish considerations." Beman openly admitted that financial need had led him to accept the position, but he denied any contradiction between his Garrisonian principles and his work with the new abolition society. By 1840 the split was irrevo-

cable. Beman joined the newly organized American and Foreign Anti-Slavery Society, demonstrated a growing interest in political abolition, and later supported the Liberty and Free Soil parties.

In 1838 Beman accepted the pastorate of an AMEZ church in Boston. He used his church as a base for antislavery and temperance activities. In 1842 he devoted Sunday services to raising funds for the legal defense of fugitive slave George Latimer. At the same time, his refusal to allow women a greater role in his church apparently created a schism in the congregation. Beman returned to Middletown in the late 1840s, where he continued his ministry and acted as a local agent for the underground railroad. During the 1850s, he was involved in several black conventions. He presided at two black state gatherings and attended the 1855 national convention at Philadelphia. Delegates to the 1853 black national convention in Rochester recognized his leadership by electing him to the National Council of the Colored People. *Lib*, 23 July 1831, 28 June, 22 July, 11 August 1832, 11 May 1833, 26 March, 29 October, 3 December 1836, 29 September 1837, 30 August 1839, 21, 28 February, 20 March 1840, 10 December 1852 [1:0092, 0198, 0212, 0283, 0651, 0722, 0751, 2:0201, 3:0185, 0347, 7:0854]; *CA*, 20 May, 23 September 1837, 27 January 1838, 28 September 1839 [2:0194, 0366, 3:0185, 0210]; *P*, 9 June 1837 [2:0068], *NSt*, 12 October 1849 [6:0184]; *FDP*, 15 July, 26 August 1853, 19 May, 1, 22 September, 13 October 1854 [8:0359, 0424, 0821, 9:0055, 0109, 0133]; Untitled petition, 27 October 1842, Latimer Papers, MHi [4:0485]; *Colored National Convention . . . at Rochester* (1853), 3–6 [8:0328–30]; William L. Andrews, ed., *Sisters of the Spirit: Three Black Women's Autobiographies of the Nineteenth Century* (Bloomington, Ind., 1986), 203–7, 243–44; Bradley, *History of the AMEZ Church*, 124; Quarles, *Black Abolitionists*, 20, 25–26, 44, 68, 94, 187; Barbara Brown and James M. Rose, *Black Roots in Southeastern Connecticut, 1650–1900* (Detroit, Mich., 1980), 26–27.

69.
William P. Powell to the Members of the
Massachusetts Anti-Slavery Society
21 January 1845

The emergence of disunionism and radical nonresistance in the 1840s made Garrisonian abolitionism increasingly unacceptable to many black abolitionists. In a 21 January 1845 letter to the Massachusetts Anti-Slavery Society, long-standing Garrisonian William P. Powell expressed his reservations about the antislavery movement's new direction. He directed his comments to the society's delegates on the eve of their annual meeting held 24–27 January at the Marlboro Chapel in Boston. Powell rejected some tenets of disunionism and called for a return to unity—to "first principles" and to an "anti-slavery platform broad enough to contain ALL"—sentiments that reflected the growing divergence between Garrisonian antislavery and black abolitionism. *Lib*, 24 May 1844, 31 January 1845.

NEW YORK, [New York]
Jan[uary] 21, 1845

DEAR BRETHREN:

Circumstances beyond my control constrain me to forego the pleasure of meeting with you at the thirteenth annual meeting of the Massachusetts Anti-Slavery Society. Though one of the least of those engaged in the glorious struggle for the peaceful overthrow of that iniquitous system, American slavery, I feel a deep interest in your deliberations. And every feasible plan emanating from your body for the immediate and unconditional emancipation of the enslaved—for the total abrogation of all the disabilities under which our people (the nominally free) labor—stripped of sects, creeds, or party predilections—shall have my unequivocal support.

Brethren, remember you occupy an important station in the eyes of the world. You have pledged your lives, your sacred honor, on the altar of freedom. You have proclaimed it on the housetop, that man cannot hold property in man. You now have a solemn and an important duty to perform—great principles to settle, but no particular views to establish.

The great question of human slavery must be decided NOW!—not prospectively, not gradually, but immediately. Shall this iniquitous system of enormities, towering up to the heavens, like your granite shaft on Bunker Hill,[1] filling the land with the groans and the cries of suffering millions of our countrymen, cease to exist—cease to pollute this soil—cease to make merchandize of God's image? Or shall it be handed down to our posterity forever?

Painful as it is to me, yet I feel it no less my duty to call upon you to ponder well before you adopt any new experiment, any new test, by which to regulate the right of opinion, or the right of speech. Is not the anti-slavery platform broad enough to contain ALL, without regard to sect, creed, or party? If "no union with slaveholders" means that abolitionists, as such, shall withdraw from pro-slavery parties—refrain from voting under a pro-slavery constitution—or refuse to do military or civil duty, state or national—or in any manner, directly or indirectly, under this slaveholding government (which, by the way, they have a perfect right to do)—then I must confess my inability to buckle on this new anti-slavery armor—it is too cumbersome.

To withdraw from a pro-slavery church and pro-slavery parties,[2] I have no objection. I go further. To stand aloof from the would-be Liberty party, and give it no countenance, is an inherent principle in my anti-slavery manual. But to avowedly declare that I owe no allegiance to the government I live under, whose protection I claim, under any circumstances, right or wrong, is to my mind perfectly inconsistent, and contrary to the genius and spirit of this governmental polity, as such, which declares that the power of redressing public grievances is vested in the people, the sovereign people. Now, whenever this mighty lever can be applied to the rotten system of American slavery—operated upon by anti-slavery truth, fresh from the artillery of heaven—it certainly must fall; for our cause is just, and must and will prevail.

But how, I ask, are we to abolish slavery by a resort to new weapons of defence? In reply, our friends say that "no union with slaveholders" will abolish the evil. Suppose, then, we dissolve the Union—will it abolish slavery? A case in point. The great body of the Methodist Episcopal Church, in 1844, dissolved the union between themselves, and now have a southern and northern Conference.[3] Have they abolished slavery in the Methodist connexion? Is not slavery in the church as rampant as ever?

Further—no man in his senses will advocate the rightfulness of legalized murder. For instance, war. "How shall we abolish war?" enquires the anxious reformer. Shall we abandon the use of the common flintlock muskets—the clumsy cannon, in the use of which we hazard the incalculable loss of lives—the slow process of terminating the bloody contest disastrous to both nations? Or shall we improve these messengers of death by new inventions—the percussion caps, instead of flintlocks—the Paixhan guns and mammoth PEACE-maker,[4] instead of the old common cannon? These are the means, say certain philanthropists (!) and statesmen, to remove the evils of war; because, inasmuch as they are sure and certain in the destruction of human life, these inventions would inevitably put an end to all wars.

Is this sound reasoning? Is it in accordance with that holy command,

"Thou shalt love thy neighbor as thyself"? So argue many of the slave's best and truest friends. What shall I say, my brethren?

Oh, I imploringly beseech of you to go back to first principles. Choose ye rather the simple pebbles of truth, out of the pure brook of wisdom, than the glittering, clumsy armor of SAUL.[5]

And may God, in his wisdom, guide and direct your deliberations in the spirit of kindness and love. And believe me to be, truly your brother in the bonds of American slavery,

WILLIAM P. POWELL

Liberator (Boston, Mass.), 7 February 1845.

1. Powell refers to the monument erected on Breed's Hill in 1843. The granite obelisk overlooking Boston commemorates the Revolutionary War engagement popularly known as the Battle of Bunker Hill, which occurred there on 17 June 1775.

2. Powell refers to the decision of many abolitionists to leave organizations—like mainline churches and major political parties—not firmly committed to antislavery principles. Many left major Protestant denominations during the 1840s and 1850s and founded small "comeouter" sects. These included the Wesleyan Methodists, the American Baptist Free Mission Society, the Free Presbyterian church, the Franckean Evangelical Lutheran Synod, and Gerrit Smith's Union churches in western New York state. McKivigan, *War against Proslavery Religion*, 81, 93–96.

3. The Methodist Episcopal church divided over the question of slavery at the General Conference held in New York City during May 1844. Growing antislavery sentiment among northern members, and intractable issues relating to itineracy, missions to the slaves, and a slaveholding bishop, split Methodists into separate northern and southern camps. The following year, southern members gathered at Louisville, Kentucky, and organized the Methodist Episcopal church, South. Donald G. Mathews, *Slavery and Methodism: A Chapter in American Morality, 1780–1845* (Princeton, N.J., 1965), 246–82.

4. Powell refers to two artillery developments that promised to revolutionize nineteenth-century warfare. Henri J. Paixhans, a French artillerist, introduced the shell gun in 1824. Twenty years later, the American navy built a ten-ton wrought-iron cannon, nicknamed the "Peace Maker," for use on one of its vessels. It was capable of firing a cannon ball more than five miles. Edward L. Beach, *The United States Navy: Two Hundred Years* (New York, N.Y., 1986), 202–22.

5. Powell refers to a well-known tale in 1 Samuel 17:31–49. When David, a young shepherd, battled the Philistine giant Goliath, King Saul of Israel clothed him in armor and offered him a sword. But David was barely able to move in the armor and instead fought the giant with only a slingshot and round stones from a nearby brook. He killed Goliath by striking him in the forehead with one of the stones. Powell employs this tale to call for a return to more focused antislavery objectives.

70.
Henry Bibb to James G. Birney
25 February 1845

The autobiographical lectures and writings of former slaves effectively challenged proslavery propaganda. Yet abolitionists recognized that a hint of dishonesty or fraud surrounding a fugitive slave's story damaged his effectiveness and threatened the credibility of the antislavery movement. Henry Bibb, who spent the early 1840s speaking throughout the North, gathered endorsements attesting to his honesty. A committee of white Detroit Liberty party men, who were concerned about Bibb's past, subjected him to a "rigorous examination." They contacted "slave owners, slave dealers, fugitives from slavery, political friends and political foes" to establish "the undoubted truth of Mr. Bibb's statements." When fugitives like Bibb published their life stories, the same exacting standards applied. Bibb's *Narrative* (1849) contained an introduction by Lucius C. Matlack, a New York minister, and testimonials from other whites confirming the accuracy of his account. In a February 1845 letter to James G. Birney, an abolitionist and former slaveholder, Bibb responded to Birney's concern about his narrative. William L. Andrews, *To Tell a Free Story: The First Century of Afro-American Autobiography, 1760–1865* (Urbana, Ill., 1986), 66–69, 77–81; Gilbert Osofsky, ed., *Puttin' on Ole Massa* (New York, N.Y., 1969), 12; John W. Blassingame, ed., *Slave Testimony* (Baton Rouge, La., 1977), xxii–xxvii, xxxv.

Detroit, [Michigan]
Feb[ruar]y 25th, 1845

Esteem Friend:

After my respects to you, Sir, I thank you very kindly for your remarks respecting my Narative. You suposed I was an imposter & was kind a neugh to tell me for my own good. I had better go home & go to work & that I must stop or you would expose me & I have offten wished that I could find a friend of high standing who would tell my very kindly & plain what he thought of my story after hearing my Lectures. But you are the only gentleman that have spoken so frankly on the subject. It is tru I have not been as carful in explaining dates and some other things as I should have been, which has led you & others to doubt my honesty. But I am now trying to colect some facts to prove the reality of my Narative & by so doing, I hope to be able to prove to the public that I am honest in pleeding the cause of a poor brokenhearted Wife & Child, who ware severd from my·imbrace by a professor of Religion & they are now clanking thir Chanes in slavery.[1] Oh when I think of it My heart birns with endegnation against slavery. Yeas, when I think of that Wife &

Child who was dearer than Life haveing to take the parting hand never to meet againe in this Life with bursting crys of sorrow floing from hert to hert & souding in my year & at the same time a profest Christen could put the lash on. These things help to make me a strong Abolitionist. Am I not Justifiable in exposeing such Christianity. Have I not a rite to pleed my own cause & the cause of the enslaved, being responsible. Sir nothing but for want of ability shall ever prevent me from a faithful discharge of my duty to my enslaved Cuntryman. I Close by saying I am a friend to my Cuntry & to all who are oppresst & all tho I may be denounced & calld an imposter, because I am of the dispised Race yet I hop I shall be able to prove to the world that I have told the truth & I will be herd for my people. Truly yours,

Henry Bibb[2] and Liberty forever

Birney Papers, William L. Clements Library, University of Michigan, Ann Arbor, Michigan. Published by permission.

1. Bibb, his wife Malinda, and their daughter Mary Frances were slaves of Francis E. Whitfield, a Louisiana planter and Baptist deacon. Whitfield eventually sold Bibb to two gamblers, keeping his wife and daughter for sale at a later date. They were never reunited. Henry Bibb, *Narrative of the Life and Adventures of Henry Bibb, An American Slave* (New York, N.Y., 1849; reprint, Miami, Fla., 1969), 108–49.

2. Henry Bibb (1815–1854) was the eldest of seven children born to the Kentucky slave Mildred Jackson. Bibb's father was a slaveholder named James Bibb. When he was "young and small," Bibb was separated from his mother and hired out for several years to a succession of cruel masters. During this service, Bibb acquired the rudiments of an education. Bibb met and married a slave named Malinda in 1834; they had one child, Mary Frances. In December 1837, Bibb fled slavery and briefly settled in Perrysburg, Ohio. Determined to rescue his family, he returned to Kentucky in June 1838. He was captured but managed to escape and make two more unsuccessful rescue attempts before being recaptured and shipped with his family to New Orleans. After another escape attempt, Bibb was separated from his family. He endured a journey that took him into Texas and Indian territory (where he was resold to a part-Indian owner) and culminated in 1841 with his final, successful flight to freedom. Bibb settled in Detroit in January 1842. He briefly attended a school for blacks run by Rev. William C. Munroe. He again attempted to locate his family, but when he discovered in 1845 that his wife had been sold and was the mistress of her new owner, he made no further rescue attempts.

Bibb returned to Detroit and increasingly involved himself in antislavery and Liberty party ventures. He became employed as an antislavery lecturer, joined Joshua Leavitt's Bibles-for-slaves crusade, and gained notoriety, along with Frederick Douglass, William Wells Brown, and J. W. C. Pennington, as one of the most dynamic former slave abolitionist speakers. Bibb married Boston abolitionist Mary Miles in January 1848. In October 1849, Bibb published the highly regarded *Narrative of the Life and Adventures of Henry Bibb, An American*

Slave. In the fall of 1850, passage of the Fugitive Slave Law forced Bibb to flee to Canada. He and his wife soon established the *Voice of the Fugitive* (January 1851)—an antislavery weekly with an emigrationist message—which was meant to serve the burgeoning black community of Canada West.

Working with black abolitionists James Theodore Holly and J. T. Fisher, Bibb organized a convention of North American blacks in Toronto during September 1851 that led to the founding of the North American League—an organization meant to serve as a central authority for blacks in the Americas as well as an agency for promoting immigration to Canada and aiding blacks once they arrived. The league was short-lived, but Bibb, in January 1852, again tried to institutionalize his emigrationist efforts by joining with Michigan philanthropists to form the joint-stock Refugee Home Society—an association whose purpose was to acquire thousands of acres of Canadian land for sale to black immigrants. Friction between Bibb and other black Canadian leaders doomed the society. Bibb died on Emancipation Day in 1854. Bibb, *Narrative*; *DANB*, 44; *NSt*, 29 March 1848; *E*, 19 April 1848.

71.
Jeremiah B. Sanderson to Amy Post
8 May 1845

The American Anti-Slavery Society held its eleventh anniversary meeting on 6–8 May 1845 in New York City. Among the black abolitionists in attendance were Frederick Douglass, Charles L. Remond, and Jeremiah B. Sanderson. Sanderson related his impressions of the opening session at the Broadway Tabernacle in a 8 May 1845 letter to friend and correspondent Amy Post. He noted with particular interest the participation of women in the proceedings and emphasized that their presence on the podium was no longer a point of controversy. Sanderson also mentioned Frederick Douglass, who created a sensation by revealing for the first time in public the details of his life as a slave. Sanderson's letter conveyed some of the ambience of an antislavery convention and the personal satisfaction he derived from being a part of such an auspicious reform gathering. *Lib*, 9, 16 May 1845.

New York City, [New York]
5th mo[nth], 8th day, 1845

My Dear Friend:

Today while I am seated in the Anti Slavery Convention, in Session in the Minerva Rooms, I will write you a few words hurriedly of necessity. This is the third, and perhaps, the last day of the Convention. I think it is not quite so large a Convention, as some of the preceding, yet the principles discussed are broad, thorough, as the times demand, and the Speeches made to give them lodgment and effect in the hearts of the people, are thrilling, for Philips,[1] Garrison, Clapp,[2] Douglass,[3] Remond,[4] Abby Kelly, Stephen Foster,[5] & Jane Hitchcock,[6] and many other speakers are in attendance.

I must say a word of the Anniversary Meeting. It was held Tuesday A.M. 10 O Clock, in the Broadway Tabernacle.[7] The Building was crowded, a large, and intelligent concourse. W. L. Garrison, was in the chair, sustained by several V. Prests, among them, the venerable I. T. Hopper, F. Jackson,[8] H. Grew[9] and others.

S. H. Gay, the Recording Sec'y read the Annual Report of the <u>Ex Com</u>.[10] Having been requested by W. Philips, I stepped forward, and said a few words, in favor of a motion to adopt it.

Mr. Philips, followed with a Resolve, which he sustained in one of his most happy and eloquent Speeches. He spoke about an hour. I wish you had been there. I know your interest in the cause of the downtrodden. I know you would have been delighted, I thought of you, and most heartily wished you, and all of those noble Anti Slavery Women of Rochester,[11] might have been there listening to the thunder and lightening [word illegible] of Philips. He possesses the greatest power of words, to stir up men's hearts, of any man to whom I've ever listened. I have felt the strength of words, and if I have ever been ambitious to possess some of that strength, it is to expend it for the good of my Race.

Miss E. J. Hitchcock made a most eloquent and logical speech, occupying nearly an hour. She was listened to with delight, and often applauded, how strange. What a change has come over the face of Society's character. A few years ago Men in this City hissed at the mere idea of Women's speaking in public in promiscuous assemblies. Now Men come to Anti Slavery Conventions, attracted by the announcement that Women are to take part in the deliberations, and they are often more desirous of hearing Women, than Men. The world is becoming habituated to it. It's heart seemed impenetrable at first, so with every Reformatory truth Principle, but does not, "Constant dropping wears a stone?"[12] Woman is rising up, becoming free, the progress, manifest at present of the idea of Woman's Rights in the public mind, is an earnest. Oh what a few years comparatively may effect. Man cannot be free, while the developer of his heart, soul, moral character, or the maker of Man, in the highest sense, Woman is enslaved to conventionalisms.

What an inspiring thought. The day approaches, the light breaks now only upon a few. Humanity will yet be free, in a truer Liberty than the World has yet been blessed with. Nay the World can't appreciate it. Blessed are those who can. It is the fruition of all true Christian hopes, a promised Land, full of truth & Love. It cant be seen from Sectarian Churches, or Meeting House Steeples. The highest of them reach only to the base of that Pisgah, from the summit of which only it can be seen.[13]

Fredk. Douglass made an excellent speech. Indeed one of the best I ever heard him make. He was exceedingly bold. As I never known him to do before he openly and boldly told the audience where He came from, and who his Master was. Said he, "I may be thought bold indiscreet, but if by such a course, I can do good to the cause of truth, and the Slave (and I believe it will), I glory in being bold, and indiscreet—I shall never again tamely submit to being captured and dragged back to be mancled, and scourged. No! While I hope never to be obliged to resist any such an attempt, yet if it is made, I shall not be, will not be made a Slave tamely. I have known what Slavery is, and I now know what Liberty is, and I love it so dearly that I will not part with it, but with Life." These sentiments and many more in character, were received with bursts of applause. Oh! It was grand.[14] You will doubtless get a better, fuller account of the Anniversary Meeting, and the succeeding meetings from Newspapers than I can give here. The Minerva Rooms is the place where have been held the discussion Meetings since the Anniversary Meetings.[15]

The discussions have been exceedingly interesting and many excellent and noble words have been spoken, some startling [tru]ths have been uttered. Of course there has been some opposition. The Enemies of the Anti Slavery cause though large in number, are weak morally. I thought to say a word of myself, how I got along to this city, &c. I met with some little difficulty on the Canal Packet of which I hav'nt time to speak now. I sent to Isaac begging him for aid at a time when I needed it, very much, very much indeed or I should not most certainly have sent. I abhor begging especially for myself. I am sorry not, because I received it not, but, I'm sure I was not understood nor the peculiar circumstances under which I wrote. If you had known, I think you would have aided me. But it is a matter of small importance now. I hope to be Home soon in New England. You know the New England Convention[16] is soon to come off. Whos coming from Western N.Y.? I shall ~~happy~~ be happy to see you, Sarah, Mary, Isaac, L. & Sarah Burtis, Elias & Rhoda Degarmo,[17] to whom remember me with much Love.

Believe me yours indebtedly truly,

J. B. Sanderson

Isaac and Amy Post Family Papers, Department of Rare Books and Special Collections, Rush-Rhees Library, University of Rochester, Rochester, New York. Published by permission.

1. Wendell Phillips.

2. Henry Clapp (1814–1875) operated a mercantile business in Boston prior to becoming an abolitionist and popular temperance speaker. During the 1840s, he edited the Lynn, Massachusetts, *Pioneer* and used the paper to criticize the Garrisonians. Clapp eventually moved to New York City, where he edited several short-lived papers and gained renown as a humorist. Merrill and Ruchames, *Letters of William Lloyd Garrison*, 3:270, 414, 473; *NCAB*, 9:121.

3. Frederick Douglass.

4. Charles Lenox Remond.

5. Abigail (Abby) Kelley and Stephen Symonds Foster were prominent Garrisonian abolitionists. Abby (1810–1887) served as secretary of the Lynn, Massachusetts, Female Anti-Slavery Society (1835–37) and helped found the New England Non-Resistance Society in 1838. One of the most important female Garrisonian lecturers, her elevation to the executive committee of the American Anti-Slavery Society in 1840 sparked the schism within the organization. She lectured throughout the North during the 1840s, advocating disunionism, non-resistance, temperance, and feminism. Her volatile husband, Stephen (1809–1881), abandoned plans for the ministry to devote his life to abolitionism, black rights, feminism, and pacifism. He repeatedly ran afoul of religious and civil authorities because of his confrontational style. His major work, *Brotherhood of Thieves* (1843), epitomized abolitionist anticlericalism. Stephen met Abby in 1841, and they married in 1845. Although Abby Kelley Foster reduced her activ-

ism after 1845 to raise a family, both Fosters continued to promote universal reform and black rights into the Reconstruction era. *NAW*, 1:647–50; Pease and Pease, *Bound with Them in Chains*, 191–217.

6. Jane E. Hitchcock Jones (1813–1896) was born in Oneida County, New York. She served on the executive committee of the Western Anti-Slavery Society and authored a children's text, *The Young Abolitionists* (1848). Jones, an active feminist, championed married women's property rights and custodial rights over their children before the Ohio legislature. In the early 1840s, Abby Kelley Foster persuaded Jones to join her antislavery lecture tour of New England and western Pennsylvania. During the Pennsylvania tour, Hitchcock met the Quaker abolitionist Benjamin Smith Jones (1812–1862), whom she married in 1846; she helped him edit the *Anti-Slavery Bugle* until June 1849. *NAW*, 2:285–86.

7. The Broadway Tabernacle, a Congregational church located at the corner of Broadway and Anthony Street in New York City, was a frequent gathering place for local and national reform societies. Constructed in 1836 to accommodate the preaching style of noted revivalist Charles Finney, it comfortably seated twenty-five hundred persons. Blacks were segregated in the sanctuary during Finney's pastorate, but from 1836 to 1839, the black Phoenix Society met regularly at the church and conducted an Evening School for Colored People in its basement. Keith J. Hardeman, *Charles Grandison Finney, 1792–1875: Revivalist and Reformer* (Syracuse, N.Y., 1987), 257, 262, 274, 301–3, 311–14, 337–38, 407, 426; Perlman, "Organizations of the Free Negro," 191–93.

8. Francis Jackson (1789–1861), a lifelong friend and financial supporter of William Lloyd Garrison, held various offices in the Massachusetts Anti-Slavery Society, the annual New England Anti-Slavery Convention, and the American Anti-Slavery Society. Jackson's acceptance of basic Garrisonian tenets led him to refuse to take an oath to support the U.S. Constitution and to publicly declare that he would not obey any law or document that sanctioned the return of fugitive slaves. At his death, he bequeathed $10,000 for "Negro freedmen," $5,000 for the women's rights movement, and a small amount to Garrison. *NCAB*, 2:318.

9. Henry Grew (1781–1862), the father of the feminist-abolitionist Mary Grew, was born in Birmingham, England, and ministered to Baptist congregations in Hartford and Philadelphia. Grew became a moderate Garrisonian abolitionist, serving as a manager of the Philadelphia Anti-Slavery Society and helping to found the Pennsylvania Anti-Slavery Society. He attended the 1840 World's Anti-Slavery Convention and sided with conservatives who refused to seat female delegates. Despite Garrison's and his own daughter's feminism, he opposed the women's rights movement. *Lib*, 30 July 1836, 7 December 1838, 2 November 1849, 4 January 1850, 3 January 1851; *NECAUL*, 29 October 1836 [1:0724–25]; *NAW*, 2:91; Merrill and Ruchames, *Letters of William Lloyd Garrison*, 3:637; Maynard, "World's Anti-Slavery Convention," 460.

10. Sydney Howard Gay read the annual report of the executive committee of the American Anti-Slavery Society before an afternoon session of the annual meeting on 6 May 1845. The delegates then voted to refer the report to the AASS business committee for further consideration. *Lib*, 23 May 1845.

11. Beginning in the 1840s, Rochester became a center of women's antislavery activism. Garrisonian women dominated the Western New York Anti-Slavery

Society, which was founded in 1843 and led by Amy Post, Sarah Burtis, and Sarah Hallowell. Elizabeth Cady Stanton and Susan B. Anthony joined the WNYASS during the 1850s. The women formed a series of related organizations, such as the Working Women's Protective Union, and for a time they worked closely with Frederick Douglass and other western New York blacks. The WNYASS competed with the more conservative Rochester Ladies Anti-Slavery Society. The latter society remained active until 1867 and regularly sent supplies to the freedmen in Alexandria, Virginia, during the Civil War. Hewitt, *Women's Activism and Social Change*, 116–22, 136–76, 191–99.

12. Sanderson paraphrases line 314 from book 1 of *On the Order of Things* by the Roman poet and philosopher Lucretius (99–55 B.C.): "The fall of dripping water hollows the stone." Variants of this proverb appear in other classical writings, including those of Ovid and Plutarch. Sanderson employs the phrase to indicate that persistent protest inevitably leads to social change.

13. Mount Pisgah is the elevation in ancient Moab (now part of Jordan) from which Moses is said to have viewed the "Promised Land" of Canaan. Deut. 3:27, 34:1.

14. On 6 May 1845, Frederick Douglass spoke before a large and excited audience at the annual meeting of the American Anti-Slavery Society. According to the *Liberator*, his thirty-minute address was filled "with much warmth and manly energy." Douglass's remarks, which previewed his forthcoming *Narrative*, disclosed for the first time the specific facts surrounding his slave experiences. He revealed the location of the Maryland plantation from which he had escaped and gave the names of his former owner and overseer, using the brutality of the latter to symbolize the evil of slavery. Blassingame, *Frederick Douglass Papers*, 1:27–34; *Lib*, 16 May 1845.

15. Sanderson refers to the business meetings of the American Anti-Slavery Society, which were held in the Minerva Rooms of the Broadway Tabernacle following the opening ceremonies of the AASS annual meeting and the reading of the society's annual report. *NASS*, 15 May 1844.

16. Sanderson refers to the New England Anti-Slavery Convention, which met on 27 May 1845 at Marlboro Chapel in Boston. The Massachusetts Anti-Slavery Society sponsored the annual meeting of New England abolitionists and other Garrisonians. The 1845 gathering was one of the largest ever held. *Lib*, 9 May, 6 June 1845.

17. Sanderson refers to Sarah Hallowell Willis, Mary Post Hallowell, Isaac Post, Lewis and Sarah Burtis, and Elias (1787–1876) and Rhoda DeGarmo (1798–1873). The DeGarmos were leading members of the Western New York Anti-Slavery Society. The Quaker Genesee Yearly Meeting expelled the DeGarmos in 1849 for their abolitionist and integrationist activities. A neighbor of Susan B. Anthony, Rhoda DeGarmo became an active feminist, joining the National Woman Suffrage Association and voting with Anthony in the 1872 presidential election. The DeGarmos worked with Lewis and Sarah Burtis in the WNYASS. Hewitt, *Women's Activism and Social Change*, 61, 130, 143, 169, 209, 211, 230; List of Burials in Mt. Hope Cemetery, Rochester, New York, NRU.

72.

Ransom F. Wake, John Peterson, Alexander Crummell, Henry Williams, Daniel J. Elston, George Montgomery, Benjamin Stanly, and John J. Zuille to Gerrit Smith
13 June 1845

Antislavery politics required black abolitionists once again to seek influence and power within white-dominated organizations. New York black leaders were drawn to the Liberty party. Theodore S. Wright, John J. Zuille, and Charles B. Ray served on the party's central nominating committee. The June 1846 state constitutional convention offered an opportunity to revise the suffrage requirements and expand the black electorate, then limited to about a thousand voters. Black abolitionists hoped to cooperate with the Liberty party in electing delegates to the convention who would support black interests, particularly the franchise. When party leader Gerrit Smith questioned the wisdom of increasing black suffrage because most blacks voted Whig, New York's black leaders sought a clarification of the party's stand on the issue. They wrote to Smith on 13 June 1845, several months before the selection of delegates to the constitutional convention. John L. Stanley, "Majority Tyranny in Tocqueville's America: The Failure of Negro Suffrage in 1846," *PSQ* 84:414–15 (September 1969); *CA*, 21 November 1840 [3:0714]; *NASS*, 27 March 1851 [6:0864–65].

New York, [New York]
June 13, 1845

Dear Sir:

The undersigned colored citizens of the city and County of New York, and deeply interested in regard to their own enfranchisement and the freedom of their brethren, observe with the liveliest emotions the indications of public opinion in reference to the proposed alterations to our State Constitution by a Convention for that purpose.[1]

It is clear that the alterations which are popular with the parties, do not include the removal of the property qualification now required of colored citizens to enable them to vote. It is also clear that no very considerable portion of the dominant party have declared themselves in favor of such change, and that its leading men are cautious not to declare their opinions in regard to that important matter. It may also be regarded as a certainty that a portion of the Whig party will go against that measure.

If the convention should be sanctioned by the people (in regard of which there does not seem to be any reasonable doubt), and if, as may be the case, any considerable portion of the Democratic and Whig parties are opposed to the measure herein contemplated, the whole matter will rest in our humble judgement with the Liberty party, and the decision for or against the measure refers itself to the action of that party.

Under the circumstances above enumerated, the undersigned have thought it important to inquire, and as far as possible ascertain, what is likely to be the course of action by leading minds in the Liberty party in regard to a measure dear to them as a matter of right and due to us from the people of the State as a matter of justice.

Without generalizing further, the undersigned would respectfully inquire, whether, in your opinion, leading minds in the Liberty party would consent to vote for such men as delegates to the proposed convention, without distinction of party, as may be in favor of an extension of the suffrage right to colored citizens, without the requirement of property as a qualification.

With the commanding vote which the Liberty party has in the Counties of Allegany, Cattaraugus, Cayuga, Clinton, Cortland, Franklin, Fulton and Hamilton, Jefferson, Onandaga, Oswego, Tompkins, Wayne, Yates, of Madison and Oneida, the nomination of such men as the Liberty party will vote for can be secured, and then they can be elected.[2]

For example: in Oneida Co. there is a difference between the Democratic and Whig votes of 734 in favor of the Democratic party, and the Liberty vote (by the election returns for President &c. 1844) is 1144. So that if the Democratic candidates are not in favor of enfranchisement and the Whig candidates are, the Liberty vote thrown in favor of the Whig candidates would elect them; and so in Cortland Co. there is a difference of 20 votes in favor of the Whig party, and the Liberty vote is 543, and if the Whig candidates should not favor extension, and the Democratic should, the liberty vote could elect the favorable candidates.

The undersigned are firmly of the opinion that if a direct use of the Liberty vote in this State in the manner herein proposed can be secured, that most of the opposition to an extension of the suffrage will be broken down, and in so far as the above Counties can do it, good men and true will be elected as delegates to the convention.

Your opinion in regard to the matter is respectfully solicited. Very respectfully yours &c.,

Ransom F. Wake[3]
John Peterson[4]
Alex. Crummell[5]
Henry Williams[6]
[Daniel] J. Elston[7]

Geo. Montgomery

Benjn. Stanly[8]

John J. Zuille

P.S. This correspondence will be regarded as strictly confidential.

An answer at your earliest convenience may be directed to John J. Zuille, 48 Watts St., N.Y. City.

Gerrit Smith Papers, George Arents Research Library, Syracuse University, Syracuse, New York. Published by permission.

1. Between 1837 and 1846, an alliance of blacks, white abolitionists, and Liberty party supporters worked to overturn the property requirement for black suffrage in the 1821 New York state constitution. Whig leaders, in an effort to steal Liberty party votes and take advantage of popular discontent with the constitution, called for a constitutional convention to consider equal suffrage. The convention, which began its deliberations on 1 June 1846, was dominated by Democrats, who prevented approval of unqualified black suffrage but agreed to a referendum on the issue in the fall elections. Voters overwhelmingly rejected an expansion of the black electorate in the state. New York blacks could not vote on an equal basis with whites until after passage of the Fifteenth Amendment (1870). Phyllis F. Field, *The Politics of Race: The Struggle for Black Suffrage in the Civil War Era* (Ithaca, N.Y., 1982), 43–53.

2. Based on the 1844 election returns, Liberty party strength was concentrated in seventeen of the fifty-nine counties in New York state. Twelve of these lay in the western part of the state, with Liberty party support being greatest in Gerrit Smith's home county of Madison and in and near the cities of Syracuse, Rochester, and Utica. In almost all cases, between 1840 and 1844, Liberty party support grew at Whig expense. Walter Dean Burnham, comp., *Presidential Ballots, 1836–1892* (Baltimore, Md., 1955), 632–46; Kraut, *Crusaders and Compromisers*, 120–27.

3. Ransom F. Wake, a black educator, taught at New York City's Colored Public School No. 2 in the 1830s and 1840s and eventually became the school's principal. His commitment to education extended beyond the classroom. He was a member of the Philomathean Society, and for more than thirty years, he helped organize many of the cultural events in the city's black community. His wife, Mary Blake, whom he married in 1827, was involved with charitable concerns including the Colored Orphan Asylum. Wake contributed to antislavery reform through a variety of activities. During the 1830s, he aided the local vigilance committee. Opposed to black settlement outside the United States, he protested against colonization and later criticized the emigration program of the African Civilization Society. He represented New York blacks at the 1833 national convention at Philadelphia and the 1841 state convention at Troy. An advocate of the black press, he served on a supervisory committee for the *Colored American*. He also corresponded in the 1840s with Stephen Myers's *Northern Star and Freeman's Advocate*. Wake's interest in political abolition was underscored by his role as vice-president of the New York Political Association and his support for the Liberty party. *FJ*, 9 November 1827; *Lib*, 10 December 1831, 16 February

1833, 24 May 1844, 23 May 1862 [1:0136, 0243, 4:0812]; *CA*, 13 January, 16 June, 25 August, 15 December 1838, 26 January, 17 August 1839, 24 October, 21 November 1840, 10 July, 14 August 1841 [2:0345, 0494, 0561, 0680, 0984, 3:0173, 0677, 4:0103, 0158]; *NASS*, 3 May 1849 [5:1072]; *WAA*, 24 March, 21 April, 29 December 1860, 12 August 1865 [12:0593].

4. John Peterson (1805–ca. 1886), a prominent black educator, was born to poor, free black parents in New York City. He graduated from Charles C. Andrews's African Free School, then, after two years of tutoring by Andrews, he taught at the school (1826–32). Peterson later served as master of Colored Public School No. 1 (1832–78) in New York City. During his tenure there, he helped organize a society to operate local black charity schools and directed the Saturday Colored Normal School, which trained black teachers. A popular spokesman in the black community, Peterson cofounded several black literary and benevolent societies in the early 1830s and actively supported black temperance organizations. During the latter part of the decade, he was a local leader (through the New York Political Association) in the movement to enfranchise New York blacks.

Although initially opposed to colonization schemes, Peterson supported black emigration in the late 1850s. He served as treasurer and recording secretary of the African Civilization Society and in 1863 joined other black leaders in petitioning for federal funding of its emigration schemes. When the society began to promote freedmen's education, he labored for that cause. In 1865 he agitated for creation of a black college in Washington, D.C. Peterson was a devoutly religious man and devoted much of his energy to Episcopal church affairs, particularly at the black St. Philip's Episcopal Church in New York City. After being ordained an Episcopal deacon in 1865, he frequently served St. Philip's as assistant or interim pastor. Late in life, he established the Conference of Church Workers among Colored People (1883). Peterson was married to Elizabeth G. Glasgow from the 1840s until her death in 1874. Alexander Crummell, "Sermon on John Peterson," 2 May 1886, Alexander Crummell Papers, NN-Sc; Mabee, *Black Education in New York State*, 39, 63–64, 105–7, 126–27, 170; *Lib*, 19 April 1834 [1:0411]; *ESF*, 12 June 1868; *E*, 25 March 1834 [1:0406]; *WAA*, 22 October 1859, 5 May 1860 [12:0686], 8 March 1862, 12 August 1865; *CA*, 28 October 1837, 16 January, 26 June 1841 [2:0242, 3:0836, 4:0078]; George W. Levere, Henry [Highland] Garnet, Junius C. Morel et. al. to Abraham Lincoln, 25 November 1863, Records of the Secretary of the Interior Relating to the Suppression of the African Slave Trade and Negro Colonization, DNA [15:0062–71]; *CR*, 18 June 1864 [15:0405]; *NSt*, 25 May 1849; George F. Bragg, *History of the Afro-American Group of the Episcopal Church* (Baltimore, Md., 1922; reprint, New York, N.Y., 1968), 86.

5. Alexander Crummell (1819–1898) was born free in Brooklyn, New York. His father, Boston Crummell, was a modestly prosperous small businessman, who was active in New York's black community and helped found the reformist black newspaper *Freedom's Journal*. Crummell attended the African Free School (1826) and the Canal Street High School (1831), which had been established to teach black students classical studies. Along with friends Henry Highland Garnet and Thomas Sidney, Crummell enrolled at William Scales's Noyes Academy (1835) in Canaan, New Hampshire, but was forced to leave the school by an

antiintegrationist mob. Crummell graduated from Beriah Green's Oneida Institute in 1839. The same year, he was refused admission to the General Theological Seminary of New York City because of his race. With the help of William and John Jay, Crummell secured a tutorial with Rev. Alexander Vinton of Providence, Rhode Island, and was ordained to the diaconate in 1842. He moved to Philadelphia and was ordained an Episcopal priest in 1844 but was refused permission by Philadelphia Bishop Henry Onderdonk to apply for a seat in the local Episcopal convention. Crummell became pastor to the Church of the Messiah in New York City and, four years later (1848), journeyed to Britain to raise funds for construction of a new chapel. In the spring of 1849, Crummell entered Queens College at Cambridge University. He graduated four years later with a bachelor of arts degree. During Crummell's enrollment at Cambridge, he was active in British antislavery circles and promoted the use of free labor products.

Since Crummell's father had been an abolitionist, Crummell was raised on the fringes of antislavery reform, but his formal participation in the movement began during his tutorial with Vinton. It continued throughout the 1840s when he attended numerous black national and state conventions and supported New York black efforts for suffrage. In 1847 he attended the black national convention held in Troy and spoke in favor of a vigorous black press and the establishment of a national college for blacks; he also discussed the possibility of settling in Liberia. When he finished his education in Britain in 1853, he accepted an appointment from the Domestic and Foreign Missionary Society as an Episcopal missionary to Liberia. Crummell remained there for twenty years, first serving as pastor to the Trinity Church in Monrovia and, after 1866, as pastor of St. Peter's Church in Caldwell. Crummell was also appointed principal of Mount Vaughan High School and taught at Liberia College in the early 1860s. Crummell had immigrated to Liberia partially because of his interest in his African heritage, but mostly to inculcate Western standards of morality and culture. He left Liberia discouraged by the lack of response to his mission, disappointed by the failure of Liberian elites to support the "civilization" of the remaining populace, and disheartened by the country's internal political dissension. In 1873 Crummell was appointed pastor of St. Luke's Episcopal Church in Washington, D.C., where he directed the congregation until his death in 1898. During this period, Crummell played an active role in the community's cultural life, pressed for black civil rights, and continued to stress the importance of black self-help, education, and moral improvement. *DANB*, 145–47; Wilson J. Moses, *Alexander Crummell: A Study in Civilization and Discontent* (Oxford, England, 1988).

6. Henry Williams, a member of St. Philip's Episcopal Church in New York City, was involved in several black community activities. Through the New York Political Association and other local organizations, he participated in the campaign for black voting rights. Williams also took part in First of August celebrations and public protests against the Fugitive Slave Law. *Lib*, 30 August 1834 [1:0507]; *CA*, 20 October 1838, 12 September, 21 November, 12 December 1840, 25 September, 30 October, 20 November 1841 [2:0622, 3:0615, 0711, 0748, 4:0219, 0273–75, 0308]; *NASS*, 29 May 1845, 10 October 1850 [5:0039, 6:0606].

7. Daniel J. Elston, a black New York City shoemaker, belonged to the Phoenix Society and the New York Political Association. A prominent local leader, he

supported the petition campaign for black voting rights in the late 1830s, attended the 1841 black state convention at Troy, and joined the public protest against the Fugitive Slave Law during the early 1850s. *CA*, 19 August, 2 September 1837, 15 March, 16 June, 25 August, 20 October, 10 November 1838, 17 August 1839, 6 June, 21 November, 5 December 1840, 3 July, 14 August, 11 September 1841 [2:0167, 0152, 0436, 0494, 0556, 0622, 0644, 3:0173, 0449, 0711, 0732, 4:0091, 0158, 0191]; *NSt*, 5 April 1850 [6:0438–39].

8. Benjamin Stanly, a black Philadelphia hairdresser, was a North Carolina native and reputedly a relative of Congressman Edward Stanly. He had settled in Philadelphia by the early 1830s. His interest in education and moral reform drew him to several black organizations, including the Young Men's Union Literary Association, the Demosthenian Institute, the American Moral Reform Society, and its rival group, the Association for Mental and Moral Improvement. Stanly was also active in the black state convention movement and in the allied protest against black disfranchisement. By 1845 Stanly had resettled in New York City, where he continued his efforts to protect and expand black voting rights. A member of St. Philip's Episcopal Church, he joined with other black Episcopalians to protest discrimination by white church officials against black ministers. The Fugitive Slave Law of 1850 provoked his antislavery militancy. He called on free blacks and fugitive slaves to arm themselves in order to resist the slave catchers. During the Civil War, Stanly served on a committee that aided the Colored Orphan Asylum. *PF*, 24 January, 20 June 1839, 14 May 1840 [2:0983, 3:0118]; *CA*, 30 January, 24 April, 8 May, 25 September 1841 [3:0858, 1001, 1024, 4:0215]; *E*, 4 August 1842 [4:0457–58]; *NASS*, 29 May 1845, 10 October 1850 [5:0039, 6:0610–11]; *WAA*, 5 April 1862; Foner and Walker, *Proceedings of the Black State Conventions*, 1:117; John J. Zuille et al. to Gerrit Smith, 13 June 1845, Gerrit Smith Papers, NSyU [5:0052–53]; Winch, "Leaders of Philadelphia's Black Community," 66, 107, 429.

73.
J. W. C. Pennington to J. P. Williston
20 February 1846

Black leaders pointed to the British West Indies as proof that blacks could live in freedom as industrious citizens, deserving of full civil rights. J. W. C. Pennington, a Congregational clergyman and former slave, spent six months touring Jamaica and the West Indies as a representative of the Union Missionary Society. For Pennington and the UMS, Jamaica served as an important antislavery symbol that repudiated proslavery mythology. Pennington's 20 February 1846 letter to J. P. Williston, a Massachusetts abolitionist and member of the Committee for West Indian Missions, was written from Annotto Bay, a town on the northern coast of Jamaica. It was widely reprinted by the reform press as evidence of the slaves' ability to adapt to freedom. Upon his return to the states in April 1846, Pennington began organizing a Jamaican immigration movement. Although an opponent of other colonization and emigration schemes, he was convinced that the island offered blacks the freedom and equality denied them in the United States. R. J. M. Blackett, *Beating against the Barriers: Biographical Essays in Nineteenth-Century Afro-American History* (Baton Rouge, La., 1986), 3–4, 33–36; Johnson, "American Missionary Association," 61–64, 102–3, 315, 321–26; De Boer, "Afro-Americans in American Missionary Association," 170; *MCJ*, October 1847 [5:0484].

ANNOTTO BAY, J[amaic]a
Feb[ruary] 20th, 1846

MY DEAR SIR:[1]

As a wise Providence has cast my lot on this beautiful island for a few months, I have supposed from what I know of you, that you will be pleased to hear some facts. I have spent much of my time since the 17th of December, about Kingston and Spanish Town, now and then going into the country to the stations of the American Missionaries. From two full months' observation, I am fully satisfied that on all the great points with which we are concerned, things are working well. I speak without hesitation—*they are working well.* As I understand it, the questions with us are these—"Are the colored people peaceable? Are they willing to work for fair wages? Are they as good citizens as other classes of people? Are they as a people doing better than when they were slaves? Is there any reason why the government or the abolitionists in Great Britain should be ashamed of what they have done to free this people? Is there anything in the condition and conduct of the colored people that can be

16. J. W. C. Pennington

From Wilson Armistead, *A Tribute for the Negro* (Manchester, England, 1848)

seized upon by the American slaveholder as an argument to justify him in
continuing his oppression?"

The above, I believe, are the great questions involved; and I have made
my observations with a view to settle these points in my own mind. I
have seen these people on the cane field—men, women, and children; I
have seen them on the road going to market; I have seen them working
on their own little estates; I have gone into the cane field, and into the
sugar works; and I am quite prepared to say, that they are by no means a
lazy people. The women and children do more work than any class of
men in America. I do not except the Irish laborers on the public works.
I have also visited the colored people in their own cottages, in their
schools and in their chapels, on Sunday, at even, and on work days. The
people are very happy and cheerful, and withal, very peaceable.

In all this I do not mean to say, that every vestige of the Slave System
has been destroyed. No sensible man would credit me, if I should say so.
But, those which remain are not to be charged to the people who have
been freed, but to the author's and supporters of Slavery. I have been
dissatisfied with the accounts that have been circulated among us from
this place, because on the one hand they have been too bright, and on the
other too dark. I think, when I reach home I shall be able to show the
truth.

I have been engaged a few days in visiting Messrs. Renshaw, Beardsley,
Evarts and Thompson, at the American Missionary stations.[2] These
brethren are doing great good. The cause of Temperance in the Island
rests upon their shoulders, and so with education in a great degree. These
brethren are much respected, even by many who would rather not see
them here. I am now in compliance with an invitation of the Governor,[3]
making a tour through the principal places on the island, to lecture, and
awaken the people more on the subject of education.

In closing this letter, I will just say that, I will, if time and matter suit,
write you from some other point as I proceed. Yours, &c.

J. W. C. PENNINGTON[4]

Albany Patriot (Albany, N.Y.), 6 May 1846.

1. J. Payson Williston (1803–1872), a Northampton, Massachusetts, ink manufacturer and philanthropist, was an active abolitionist, temperance advocate, and
vice-president of the American Missionary Association. His home was a station
on the underground railroad, and he provided financial support for the *Mirror of
Liberty* and the *Colored American*. After the Civil War, Williston donated money
for the establishment of freedmen's schools. Merrill and Ruchames, *Letters of
William Lloyd Garrison*, 3:587; *ML*, January 1839; *Lib*, 26 October 1838; W.
B. Gay, *Gazetteer of Hampshire County, Massachusetts, 1654–1887* (Syracuse,
N.Y., 1888), 374.

2. In 1839 American Congregationalists founded five missionary stations

within twenty-six miles of Kingston, Jamaica, as bases for evangelical work among the freedmen of the island. These stations were supervised by C. Stewart Renshaw, Julius O. Beardslee, William H. Evarts, Loren Thompson, and Seth T. Wolcott—Congregational clergymen who had graduated from Oberlin College. The Boston-based Committee for West Indian Missions was established in 1844 to finance their efforts, but within three years, the American Missionary Association assumed responsibility for the Jamaican missions. Johnson, "American Missionary Association," 61–64, 309; *AM*, November 1846.

3. Pennington refers to James Bruce (1811–1863), the eighth earl of Elgin and the twelfth earl of Kincardine. After sitting in Parliament, he served as governor of Jamaica from 1842 to 1846, modernizing the island's agriculture and improving educational opportunities for blacks. Because of his successes in Jamaica, Bruce was appointed governor-general of Canada, where he remained, despite difficulties, until 1854. *DNB*, 3:104–6.

4. J. W. C. Pennington (1807–1870) was born to slave parents and was raised on a farm along Maryland's eastern shore. He remained there until November 1827, when a series of confrontations with his master prompted him to seek his freedom. Pennington—whose slave name was James Pembroke—settled in Brooklyn, New York, by 1829, taking a job as a coachman and acquiring a basic education, before being hired to teach at a black school on Long Island. He attended the black national conventions of the early 1830s and became a skilled antislavery speaker. After moving to Connecticut in 1835, he continued his antislavery work and first displayed his considerable organizational abilities, helping to found the Connecticut State Temperance Society for Colored People. At the same time, he pursued theological studies, attending lectures at Yale Divinity School, despite being barred from regular admission because of his race. In 1840, two years after being ordained, he became pastor of the Talcott Street Congregational Church in Hartford. The following year, he organized the Union Missionary Society to support and encourage the diverse goals of black churchmen. A vigorous advocate of black self-help and education, Pennington wrote a series of articles for the *Colored American* to inform blacks how to create effective schools. He also penned one of the earliest volumes on Afro-American history, *A Textbook of the Origin and History of the Colored People* (1841).

In 1843 Pennington made the first of four trips to Britain as a delegate to the World's Anti-Slavery Convention. After returning to the United States, he renewed earlier efforts in support of the Liberty party in Connecticut and edited the *Clarksonian*, a short-lived reform newspaper. He went to Jamaica in 1845 to visit American missionary stations and to investigate possibilities for black American immigration. About this time, he began to solicit funds to purchase his family members out of bondage—a lengthy effort that proved only partially successful when he bought his brother Stephen's freedom in 1854. Pennington left Hartford in 1848 to become pastor of the First Colored Presbyterian Church in New York City. Within a year, he returned to England and sought funds to build a school adjacent to his congregation. While abroad, he published his narrative (*The Fugitive Blacksmith*), visited France and Germany, and received an honorary doctor of divinity degree from the University of Heidelberg. Passage of the Fugitive Slave Law forced him to remain in Britain longer than planned and to raise the funds to purchase his freedom.

On returning to New York, Pennington joined other prominent black New Yorkers to form the Committee of Thirteen—an anticolonization association. A staunch integrationist, he accepted election as moderator of New York's largely white Third Presbytery in the face of some criticism from black community leaders and founded the Legal Rights Association to challenge streetcar segregation through the courts. Pennington went to Britain a third time in 1853 and helped organize the Glasgow New Association for the Abolition of Slavery, enlisting its women's auxiliary to provide funds for the New York State Vigilance Committee. In 1861 he made a fourth trip abroad. During the Civil War, Pennington urged black enlistment in the Union army, continued to advocate black suffrage, and became an outspoken opponent of West African and Haitian immigration schemes. After the war, he ministered to an African Methodist Episcopal congregation in Natchez, Mississippi, before returning North in 1867 to serve the Newbury Congregational Church in Portland, Maine, for two years. Pennington died in Jacksonville, Florida, while doing missionary work among the freedmen. Blackett, *Beating against the Barriers*, 1–84; J. W. C. Pennington, *The Fugitive Blacksmith; or, Events in the History of James W. C. Pennington*, 3d ed. (London, 1850; reprint, Westport, Conn., 1971); *CA*, 1 September 1838, 14 November 1840, 17 July 1841; *WAA*, 5 November 1859, 5 May 1860, 19 October 1861, 15 March 1862, 12 June 1863.

74.
James McCune Smith to Gerrit Smith
28 December 1846

The lack of progress in antislavery and civil rights reform in the 1840s discouraged many black leaders. The irreparable antislavery schism, the federal government's proslavery policies, and the westward expansion of slavery all suggested a waning of the antislavery movement. In a 28 December 1846 letter to Gerrit Smith, James McCune Smith conveyed the pessimism and uncertainty of black abolitionists. Although committed to political antislavery, he seemed to doubt the possibility of a political solution. Smith described the intractable quality of racial prejudice—"a hate deeper than I had imagined"—and concluded that any improvement in race relations was contingent upon a profound transformation of white attitudes. Smith's gloomy assessment of the prospects for black Americans serves as a prelude to the development of more radical and militant black abolitionist strategies in the 1850s. Blight, "Learning, Liberty, and Self-Definition," 7–25.

> New York, [New York]
> Dec[ember] 28th, 1846

Gerrit Smith Esq.

Dear Friend:

Please accept for yourself and your lady[1] the compliments of the season, together with my most earnest wish that you now enjoy that decided improvement in your ailment, which, in your letter of 21th you hoped for in a few days.

Messrs. Ray and Wright[2] join me in congratulating you for having effected the emancipation of the slaves of John Thompson Mason Esq.[3] If money should ever be coveted, it might in view of accomplishing such glorious objects. If neighbors should ever be envied, they might, when making themselves happy by such good deeds.

In relation to an address to the colored men of this State, I have not heart to write it. Each succeeding day, that terrible majority falls sadder, heavier, more crushingly on my soul. At times I am so weaned from hope, that I could lay me down and die, with the prayer, that the very memory of this existence should be blotted from my soul. There is in that majority a hate deeper than I had imagined. Caste, the creature of condition, I supposed to be feebler than any strong <u>necessity</u>. Yet here came a necessity, the strongest this people knows, a political necessity, and lo! it is weaker than caste! Money is weaker than caste. Political necessity is weaker than caste—to what else will this stiff-necked people yeild? Labouring under these views, I cannot write a cheering word & will not write a discouraging one. I must strive humbly to draw near unto God, for renewed faith and hope and encouragement. He Reigneth over the "raging of the waves and the madness of the people." At first, when I looked at the election of November, I felt strong, now when looking into it, I am alarmed & humbled.[4]

The direction in which our people must labour, is a point on which I am not certain. The heart of the whites must be changed, thoroughly, entirely, permanently changed. It is well, perhaps, that a temporary political necessity did not produce the outward sign of what is not yet an inward and spirit-owned conviction—the absence of this conviction now stands bared to the gaze, and men, colored men must go to work to produce that conviction of the eternal equality of the Human Race— which is the first principle of Good Government—of Bible Politics. This must be done, but how?

Of course it is mind-work. Physical force has no place in it. The possession of votes, on the property Qualification simply states the question.[5] My personal influence, manhood—presence at the ballot box is utterly destroyed when the earth-owning oath is thrust at me. The negro Man is merged into the negro Land-owner. The point of the moral is dipped into poison. It is established by the solemnity of an oath, that the vile earth has rights superior to Manhood! That "the dust of the earth" is the greater, without "the breath of life."[6] What horrible mockery! Is it right to be a party in such Blasphemy?

Dec. 30th Evening. This mornings post brought a copy of the Patriot, on which I was gladdened to find your cheirograph,[7] to me a happy proof of your returning health.

Dec. 31st. You will perceive in the piecemeal character of this note some evidence of an active medical life. On Wednesday of last week, we visited New Rochelle, & had an interesting delivery of Deeds to the Westchester Grantees. On Monday next, a portion of the Committee will visit & deliver Deeds in Ulster & Orange Counties.[8] At New Rochelle several signed the tee-total Pledge.[9] It is a sad fact, in regard to that county, that of the first seventeen Deeds delivered, but one grantee could sign his name, and he a runaway slave! He had learned to write at the South. There is no colored school in the County, except a small one at Sing sing, perhaps.[10]

This fact brings me to the question of our affranchisement and elevation. I am glad to see some symptoms of reaction in colored (?) ~~mind~~ men, in this State. Mr. Vanransellaer & Hodges have got up a paper with a quaint title,[11] but it is like the flame, pointing upward. The mere possession of land by our people, even if cultivated by them, must be associated with equal educational privileges, or they will fall into the sad night which darkens Westchester County. Next to owning land, if not equal to it in importance, is the school privilege for our people. I am convinced that if the next ten years finds them as badly provided with schools, in the Country, as they now are, but little advancement will have been made by them. If five thousand souls advance from five to fifteen years old, without learning to read & write, they will indeed form a lower grade, in the Classes of mind which make up our state. Along with the effort to make voters, therefore, we must labour to spread intelligence in the State. If I mistake not, there is a law in this state, providing for separate colored schools in any town containing a sufficient number of colored children to warrant such a school.[12]

Of course, the colored People alone, are, Politically too weak to demand the enforcement of this law. But might not their friends aid them by forming County Associations to attend to this matter? You would be appalled if you knew how badly provided we are in the Country, with school privileges. This matter, I confess weighs much on my mind, I feel a most urgent desire to do something to mend it.

With this letter, I mail some pamphlets mentioned in my former letter.[13] My reason for troubling you with their perusal, is, that one or two of them contain sentiments such as I heard you utter (when in New York) more fully & eloquently.

The veil of night is gradually closing over the old year, sad memories of crushed hope, of national shame, of ensanguined fields, will ever crowd around it, yet amid all, there are one or two generous Deeds about which it will be pleasant to linger, and they will be swept from the earth, before the Colored People of this State & Country will forget how you remembered them in their bonds. Sincerely & gratefully yours,

James McCune Smith

Gerrit Smith Papers, George Arents Research Library, Syracuse University, Syracuse, New York. Published by permission.

1. Gerrit Smith married Ann Carol Fitzhugh of Rochester, New York, in 1821. They had four children. Harlow, *Gerrit Smith*, 16–17, 40–41.

2. Charles B. Ray and Theodore S. Wright.

3. John Thomson Mason (1815–1873) practiced law in Hagerstown, Maryland. After brief periods in the Maryland legislature and the U.S. Congress, he sat on the U.S. Court of Appeals and was collector of customs at Baltimore. In 1836 Gerrit Smith paid him $1,000 to manumit some of his slaves. Ten years later, he paid him another $1,000 to free his ten remaining slaves. As a condition of their manumission, they agreed to remain with Mason for two additional years. *BDAC*, 1347; Harlow, *Gerrit Smith*, 269–74.

4. The Democratic party defeated equal suffrage in the fall 1846 New York state referendum by exploiting race hatred among the foreign born and the working classes and by mobilizing antievangelical voters. It discredited Whigs, many

of whom supported black enfranchisement, as fanatical and dangerous allies of blacks. The Democratic strategy led to an almost three-to-one victory, leaving intact the 1821 state constitution's property ownership qualifications for black suffrage. Field, *Politics of Race*, 60–63.

5. In order to exercise the franchise, black men in antebellum New York state were required to own real property worth at least $250. Litwack, *North of Slavery*, 83.

6. Genesis 2:7 claims that God "formed man of dust from the ground, and breathed into his nostrils the breath of life." Drawing upon this verse, Smith argues that the property requirement for black suffrage in New York state places greater value on land than on black men, into whom God has breathed "the breath of life."

7. Smith refers to an issue of the *Albany Weekly Patriot*, which was published from 1843 to 1848 in Albany, New York. It was an organ of the Liberty party in New York state. This particular copy bore Gerrit Smith's chirograph, something written in his own hand. Alan M. Kraut, "The Liberty Men of New York: Political Abolitionism in New York State, 1840–1848" (Ph.D. diss., Cornell University, 1975), 99.

8. Smith refers to those blacks in New York's Westchester, Ulster, and Orange counties who were deeded parcels of land by Gerrit Smith. On 1 August 1846, the philanthropist announced that he would donate 120,000 acres of his own land to blacks throughout New York state. Grants were limited to those between twenty-one and sixty years of age, who practiced temperance and owned no other land. Four committees were appointed to select the grantees in different regions of the state. The New York County committee consisted of James McCune Smith, Charles B. Ray, and Theodore S. Wright. Three thousand deeds were eventually granted for forty- to sixty-acre parcels of land in eight counties of upstate New York. Gerrit Smith hoped to promote the economic, moral, and political elevation of free blacks by encouraging them to leave cities and become independent, landowning farmers. But his dream was never fulfilled. The poor soil, harsh climate, and inexperience of the black settlers hindered development and kept many grantees from taking possession of the land. Walker, "Afro-American in New York City," 59–64; William Edward Farrison, *William Wells Brown: Author and Reformer* (Chicago, Ill., 1969), 98; Gerrit Smith to James McCune Smith et al., 10 September 1846, Gerrit Smith Papers, NSyU [5:0265–66].

9. The "teetotal pledge" was a tactic employed by temperance reformers to gain adherents and popularize opposition to alcohol in all forms. In ritual fashion, converts publicly signed a document pledging themselves to total abstinence.

10. By 1846 three black schools existed in Westchester County, New York, none of them at Sing Sing. A black private school opened in Harrison in 1839, while public schools were soon established for blacks in New Rochelle (1842) and White Plains (1845). Although the school at White Plains closed shortly before the Civil War, the other two remained active for several more decades. Mabee, *Black Education in New York State*, 149–50, 287–91.

11. Thomas Van Rensellaer and Willis Augustus Hodges began publishing the *Ram's Horn* in New York City in January 1847. Hodges (1815–1890), a free black grocer who had left his native Virginia for Brooklyn in 1836, started the

paper in reaction to the racial hostility of the local white press during the 1846 campaign to expand black suffrage. Hodges hoped that the paper, like the ram's horns in the biblical tale of the siege of Jericho (Joshua 6:1–22), would bring down the "walls of slavery and racial prejudice." The *Ram's Horn* sounded a militant tone, calling on at least one occasion for slave insurrection. It attracted the attention of John Brown, who befriended Hodges and provided financial support. In turn the paper published essays by Brown, including "Sambo's Mistakes," a scathing piece on the passivity of free blacks. Frederick Douglass also contributed frequent editorials. Hodges sold his interest in the paper in the spring of 1848, but Van Rensellaer proved unable to sustain it on his own. Regular publication of the *Ram's Horn* ended in July 1848, although issues appeared sporadically for another year.

After leaving the *Ram's Horn*, Hodges turned his attention to black agrarian ventures. He coauthored the report on agriculture at the 1847 black national convention, then settled in Franklin County, New York, on land set aside by Gerrit Smith for a black farming community. In 1853 he returned to Brooklyn, where he had earlier been active in a host of reform efforts—black education, moral reform, temperance, black state conventions, the Liberty party, and the campaign for equal suffrage. He again assumed a prominent role in local black affairs, participating in First of August celebrations and continuing to work for black voting rights.

While living in Franklin County, Hodges renewed his friendship with John Brown, who lived nearby. The two men shared a similar militant abolitionism. Hodges wrote in 1849 that he "truly believe[d] that blood is the only thing that can wash the stain of slavery from this land." Ten years later, in the spring of 1859, he met with Brown to discuss plans for the Harpers Ferry raid, but believing that the outbreak of civil war was imminent, he counseled against immediate action. Because he destroyed most of his correspondence from Brown, his role in the raid remains unclear. Hodges served as a scout for Union forces in Virginia during the Civil War. By 1864 he was in Norfolk, representing northern black groups concerned about the condition of the freedmen. But local authorities forced him to leave when he raised protests against Union profiteering. Hodges returned to Virginia after the war and became active in Republican politics. As a reward for his party work, he received appointments as customs inspector and justice of the peace. Forced out of politics by the end of Reconstruction, Hodges went back to Brooklyn in 1881, only to return four years later to Virginia, where he spent the remainder of his life. Willard B. Gatewood, Jr., ed., *Free Man of Color: The Autobiography of Willis Augustus Hodges* (Knoxville, Tenn., 1982), xxii–lxxiii, 56, 76–80; *CA*, 27 June 1840, 3 July 1841; *RHN*, 5 November 1847; *WAA*, 28 April 1860, 10 August 1861.

12. Antebellum education laws in New York state did not expressly bar black children from public schools, but many were denied access through local practice. In 1841 the state enacted legislation guaranteeing all children of school age access to public education. That same year, the state school superintendent also affirmed black rights to education. Mabee, *Black Education in New York State*, 69–72.

13. Smith probably refers to two pamphlets that he had recently published—*A Dissertation on the Influence of Climate on Longevity* (1846) and *An Address to*

the Three Thousand Colored Citizens of New York Who are the Owners of Land Given Them by Gerrit Smith (1846). The first, which was reprinted from the April and May 1846 issues of *Hunt's Merchant Magazine*, was written in response to assertions about black inferiority by John C. Calhoun. The second, which was coauthored with Charles B. Ray and Theodore S. Wright, dealt with an ill-fated attempt to resettle blacks on large tracts of land owned by Gerrit Smith in upstate New York. He had mentioned these pamphlets in a 17 December letter to Gerrit Smith. James McCune Smith to Gerrit Smith, 17 December 1846, Gerrit Smith Papers, NSyU [5:0328].

Index

Page numbers in boldface indicate the main discussion of the subject.